AF577297

nützlich, süß und museal / useful, cute and collected

Dank **Acknowledgments**

Für die finanzielle Unterstützung von Ausstellung und Publikation danken wir den folgenden Institutionen und Stiftungen / The exhibition and its accompanying publication were supported by:

The J. Paul Getty Museum, Los Angeles
Erna och Viktor Hasselblads Stiftelse, Göteborg
Kunststiftung NRW, Düsseldorf
Stiftung Presse-Haus NRZ, Essen
Wüstenrot Stiftung, Ludwigsburg
Folkwang Museumsverein, Essen

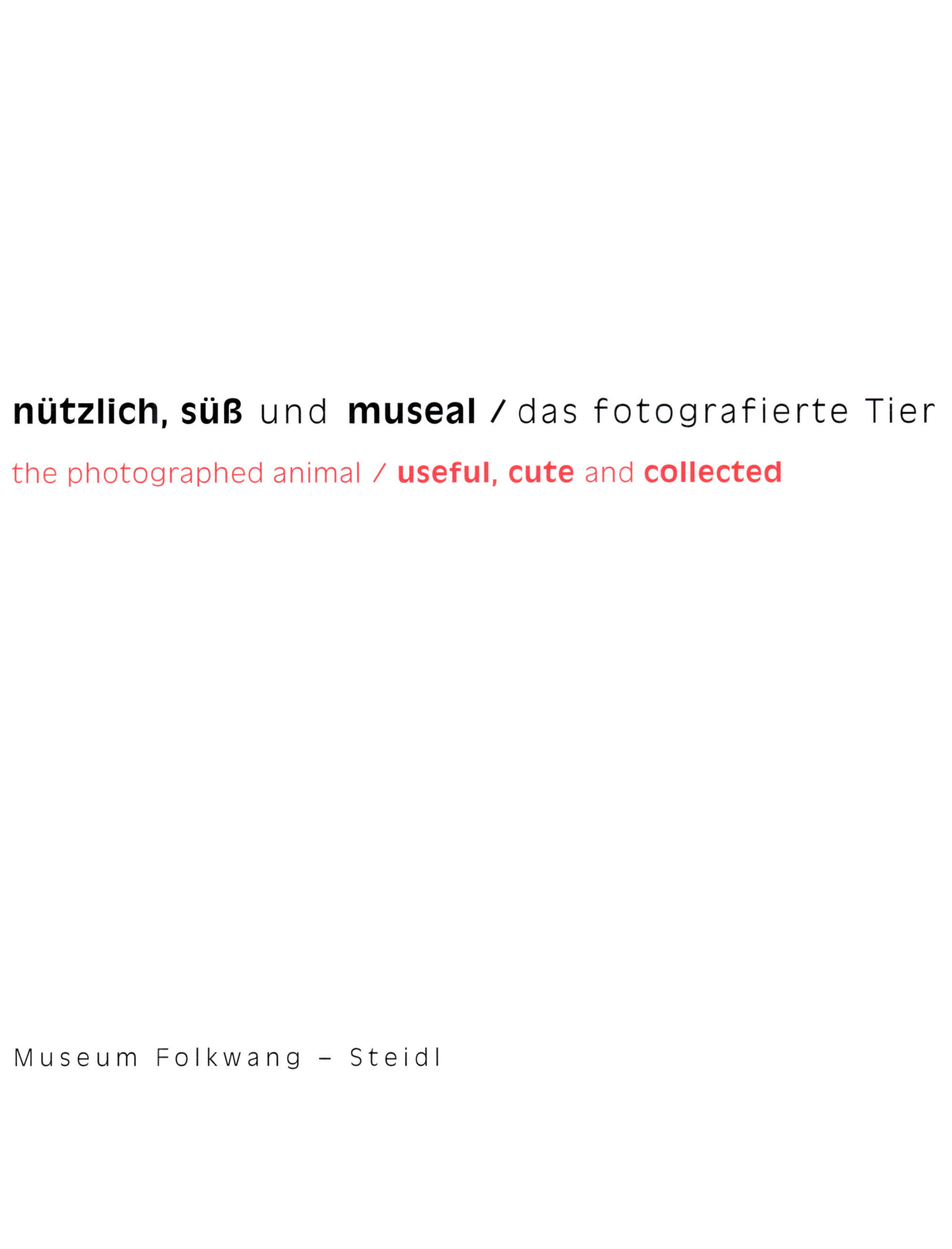

nützlich, süß und **museal** / das fotografierte Tier

the photographed animal / **useful, cute** and **collected**

Museum Folkwang – Steidl

Die Schirmherrschaft über die Ausstellung hat die Primatenforscherin Jane Goodall übernommen.
Die dokumentarische Fotografie besaß für ihre Karriere einen großen Stellenwert, "da ich keinen Universitätsabschluss hatte, war es sehr wichtig für mich, den fotografischen Beweis für das von mir beobachtete Verhalten zu liefern … die meisten Wissenschaftler hätten mir das ohne die Fotos als Beweis nicht geglaubt."

The exhibition is held under the patronage of the behavioural scientist Jane Goodall. Documentary photography played a significant role in her career: "From very early in my study, as I had no university degree, it was very important to provide photographic evidence for some of the behaviours I observed. Most scientists would not have believed me had I not had photographs to prove it."

Jane Goodall, August 2005

Inhalt Contents

Einführung Introduction

In den vergangenen zwei Jahrzehnten sind nur wenige Themen so häufig von Journalismus, Werbung und bildender Kunst aufgegriffen worden wie das Sujet Tier: Unübersehbar ist Natur zu einem Phänomen der Kultur geworden. Für die Fotografie im Besonderen ist zudem festzustellen, dass ihre Erfindung und Verbreitung in einem Zeitraum stattgefunden hat, in dem das Verhältnis des Menschen zur Natur eine fortschreitende Dynamisierung erlebte, die in krisenhaften Ereignissen kulminierte. Das umfangreiche Repertoire fotografischer Tierbilder ist in hervorragender Weise geeignet, den Verlauf dieses kulturellen Prozesses und seine medialen Formulierungen zu veranschaulichen: Die Fotografien dokumentieren sowohl die individuellen und gesellschaftlichen Bedingungen tierischer Existenz als auch die verschiedenen, häufig ambivalenten Beziehungen zwischen Mensch und Tier.

Die Beschäftigung mit der Darstellungsgeschichte des Tieres erhielt durch John Bergers 1980 erschienenen Essay *Why Look at Animals?* einen wichtigen und einflussreichen Impuls. Seiner Inter- pretation des Zoologischen Gartens als eine Demonstration kolonialer Macht („Das Fangen der Tiere stellte symbolisch die Eroberung all der entfernten und exotischen Länder dar.") folgte u.a. Harriet Ritvo, die in ihrer umfangreichen Studie *The Animal Estate. The English and other Creatures in the Victorian Age* an diese These anknüpfte und auf weitere Gebiete des menschlichen Umgangs mit Tieren ausdehnte. Ebenfalls in England erschien 1993 Steve Bakers *Picturing the Beast*, in dem der Autor die visuelle Repräsentation von Tieren im Kontext ihrer publizistischen Verwendungen untersuchte. Ungeachtet ihrer unterschiedlichen Perspektiven sind sich die erwähnten Autoren darin einig, dass die Kategorie Tier langsam verschwindet.[1]

Unser Interesse an dem motivgeschichtlichen Projekt *nützlich, süß und museal. Das fotografierte Tier* wurde durch Arbeiten zeitgenössischer Künstler angeregt, in denen die Mensch-Tier-Beziehung und unsere Wahrnehmung des Tieres problematisiert wird. Die parallel geführte interdisziplinäre und öffentliche Debatte über das Tier in der westlichen Kultur reaktivierte alte Fragestellungen und verknüpfte diese mit neu gesammelten empirischen Daten der biologischen Wissenschaften. Wir gingen von der Annahme aus, dass das vermeintlich exakte Bildmedium Fotografie und sein Potential der Reproduzierbarkeit die verschiedenen Interessen am Tier in eine Popularisierung des Motivs ‚Tier' überführt hat und damit wesentlichen Anteil sowohl an den historischen als auch an den aktuellen Formulierungen des menschlichen Naturverständnisses besitzt.

Der gesellschaftlichen Debatte der 1980er und 1990er Jahre waren internationale Aktivitäten der Umweltschutzbewegung vorausgegangen, die sich in den 1970er Jahren formiert hatte und den Ende des 19. Jahrhunderts begonnenen Naturschutzgedanken fortsetzte und radikalisierte. „In der Zwischenzeit findet etwas anderes statt: eine Rückkehr der Tiere im Denken der Menschen, ein intellektueller Aufstand im Namen der Tierheit. Ausstellungshäuser und Autoren liefern ihm die Waffen."[2] Allerdings ist das Tier, wie der gerade erschienene Aufsatzband *Der Geist der Tiere* deutlich macht, auch weiterhin ein ungelöstes Rätsel.[3]

Der vorliegende Bildband, der zusammen mit einem nur in deutscher Sprache erhältlichen Textband die Ausstellung *nützlich, süß und museal. Das fotografierte Tier* begleitet, verfolgt die Bildgeschichte dieses Sujets seit der Erfindung des Mediums Fotografie. Er versammelt Fotografien aus unterschiedlichen historischen Zeiträumen und Produktionszusammenhängen – er ist also keine Publikation über spezialisierte Tierfotografen. Wir knüpfen vielmehr an die von Alexandra Noble kuratierte Ausstellung *The Animal in Photography 1843–1985* an, deren Bildauswahl sich vornehmlich auf Werke namhafter Fotografen stützte.[4] Im Unterschied dazu resultiert die hier vorgestellte Bildauswahl aus der Frage nach den Bedingungen für die Darstellung des Tieres in einem Bildmedium, das ebenso wie das Sujet selbst einen direkten Bezug zur Industrialisierung aufweist. Deshalb wurden zahlreiche Anwendungsbereiche der Fotografie und auch anonyme Fotografien berücksichtigt.

Es ist ersichtlich, dass die Intention, Tiere zu fotografieren, nicht nur ein Reflex auf jeweils aktuelle Bedingungen tierischer Existenz und Mensch-Tier-Beziehungen ist, sondern dass Fotografien von Tieren Modelle des Menschen vorführen, ein Bildmittel der Kompensation sind und Erinnerungen an vergangene Möglichkeiten der Naturerfahrung bereitstellen. Tatsächlich bildet der Artenreichtum der Tiere und ihre verschiedenen Ausdrucks- und Bewegungsmöglichkeiten ein umfangreiches Angebot für die Herstellung dokumentarischer, werbewirksamer und künstlerischer Bilder dar; nicht zuletzt ist das Tier auch ein Sujet der experimentellen Wissenschaften.

In dem Maße, wie sich Fotografen und Amateure von etwaigen Vorbildern anderer Bildkünste und traditionellen Aufzeichnungsverfahren der Wissenschaft lösten und ein neues, aus den spezifischen technischen Möglichkeiten der Fotografie generiertes Tier-Bild zur Verfügung stellten, veränderte sich auch die Wahrnehmung des Tieres und seiner Wirklichkeit.

Wilde Tiere werben für Autos, Haustiere für Designerwaren; das Privatfernsehen und lokale Zeitungen vermitteln „Tiere in Not". Safari- und Abenteuerreisen werden mit ‚netten' Löwen beworben, und lebende Tiere sind Bestandteil künstlerischer Praxis.

Während Trickfilmfiguren, in denen menschliche und tierische Eigenschaften miteinander verschmelzen, im Kino Erfolge feiern, verkünden Zeitungen und Nachrichtenmagazine den „Abschied von der Tierwelt"![5] Kritische Reportagen über Pelz-, Elfenbein- und Hornjäger oder die Verwendung von exotischen Tieren als Nahrungsmittel haben die unbeantwortete alte Frage „Können Tiere fühlen?" in die aktuelle Fragestellung „Haben Tiere Rechte?" überführt.

Die Bandbreite der Produktion heutiger Tierbilder ist immens. Sie ist im Wesentlichen das Ergebnis des reproduzierbaren Bildmediums Fotografie, dem mit den ständig fortschreitenden drucktechnischen Möglichkeiten ein weit gefächerter Bildkonsum folgte. Seit der Erfindung der Fotografie wurde das Tier kontinuierlich beobachtet und abgebildet: als repräsentativer Besitz und preisgekrönte Züchtung, als Trophäe erfolgreicher Expeditionen und Jagden, als ‚treuer Freund' und ‚Arbeitsgerät' des Menschen, als Objekt naturwissenschaftlicher Forschung und kommerzieller Fotografie sowie als künstlerisches Sujet.

Das in dieser Publikation vorgestellte Bildmaterial stammt aus sehr unterschiedlichen Quellen: aus Bibliotheken und Archiven, Völkerkunde- und Kunstmuseen, naturhistorischen Sammlungen, Bildagenturen und fotografischen Sammlungen. Die historische Entstehung dieser Fotografien kann in diesem Zusammenhang nicht rekonstruiert werden, jedoch geben die Bilder und ihre Herkunft sowie die im Textband dokumentierten Recherchen und Thesen hoffentlich Anregungen für weiterführende Forschungen.

Der Bildband ist wie die Ausstellung thematisch nach Funktionen und Sujets in Kapitel gegliedert, in denen sowohl historische Brüche als auch Kontinuitäten nachvollzogen werden (die einleitenden Zitate stammen aus den Aufsätzen und Interviews des Textbandes). Sie veranschaulichen die zeitlich unterschiedlichen Erscheinungsformen der Mensch-Tier-Beziehungen und die damit verbundenen ökonomischen, politischen und sozialen Interessen und künstlerischen Vorstellungen. Erkennbar werden Darstellungsabsichten und Bildstrategien, die den Umgang mit Tieren und die Erinnerung an Tiere in einem historischen Kontext verorten.

Die Bildauswahl umfasst Daguerreotypien und andere frühe fototechnische Verfahren, Alben, Zeitschriften, Aufnahmen von Großwildjagden und Fotosafaris, Amateurfotografien und zu wissenschaftlichen oder Zuchtzwecken hergestellte Bilder; gezeigt werden dokumentarische, journalistische und künstlerisch intendierte Einzelbilder und Serien.

Vorgestellt werden bekannte und unbekannte Fotografen, darunter Ottomar Anschütz, George Barker, Bisson Frères, Steve Bloom, Adolphe Braun, Balthasar Burkhard, Lewis Carroll, Chien-Chi Chang, Archibald Cochrane, Madame d'Ora, Jean Louis Delton, Thomas James Dixon, A. Radclyffe Dugmore, Thomas Eakins, William Eggleston, Elliot Erwitt, Walker Evans, Paul Faulstich, Joan Fontcuberta, Robert Frank, Paul Geniaux, Hein Gorny, Candida Höfer, Willoughby Wallace Hooper, André Kertész, Philipp Kester, Josef Koudelka, Adolf Kull, Franz Lazi, Jo Longhurst, Aleksandras Macijauskas, Per Maning, Etienne-Jules Marey, Lisette Model, Louis Adolphe Humbert de Molard, Comte de Montizon, Eadweard Muybridge, Michael Nichols, Cas Oorthuys, Eric Poitevin, Archille Quinet, Albert Renger-Patzsch, Olivier Richon, Humberto Rivas, Horatio Ross, Walter Schels, Carl Georg Schillings, Friedrich Seidenstücker, Frederick Sommer, William Strode, Juha Suonpää, Henk Tas, Richard Tepe, Waldemar Titzenthaler, Adrien Tournachon, Rosemarie Trockel, William Wegman, Garry Winogrand, Wols, Walmsley Brothers, Ylla und Fritz Zielesch.

Neben Fotografien aus dem Bestand der Fotografischen Sammlung im Museum Folkwang versammelt das Projekt zahlreiche Leihgaben von Fotomuseen, öffentlichen und privaten Sammlungen, naturhistorischen Museen, Universitätsbeständen sowie aus den Archiven von Zoologischen Gärten und Privatsammlungen. Unser Dank gilt den zahlreichen nationalen und internationalen Leihgebern, darunter das J. Paul Getty Museum, Los Angeles, das Deutsche Literaturarchiv, Marbach, Ullstein Bild, das Archiv der Universität der Künste und das Bildarchiv Preußischer Kulturbesitz, Berlin, die Sammlung Herzog, Basel, die Albertina, Wien, die Bibliothèque nationale de France und die Société Française de Photographie Paris, das National Museum of Photography, Film and Television, Bradford, und die Royal Collection, Windsor Castle.

Besonderer Dank gilt den Förderern, deren Unterstützung die Durchführung des Projektes ermöglichte: dem J. Paul Getty Museum, Los Angeles, der Hasselblad Stiftelse, Göteborg, der Kunststiftung NRW, Düsseldorf, der Stiftung Presse-Haus NRZ, Essen, der Wüstenrot Stiftung, Ludwigsburg, dem Folkwang Museumsverein e.V., Essen, und dem Steidl Verlag, Göttingen.

Ute Eskildsen und Hans-Jürgen Lechtreck

In the past two decades, few subjects have been as popular a motif with journalists, advertisers, and fine artists as have animals. Nature has clearly become a phenomenon of culture. For photography in particular, it is also evident that its invention and distribution took place in a period in which the relationship of human beings to nature underwent a progressive dynamic movement that culminated in crises. The extensive repertoire of animal photography is perfectly suited for illustrating this cultural process and the way it has been described by the media: the photographs document both the individual and social conditions of animal existence, as well as the varying, often ambivalent relationships between animals and humans.

John Berger's 1980 essay "Why Look at Animals?" had a significant, influential impact on the preoccupation with the history of the portrayal of animals. His interpretation of the zoo as a demonstration of colonial power ("Capturing the animals symbolically represented conquering all of the faraway, exotic countries.") was followed by, among others, Harriet Ritvo's continuation of this thesis in her comprehensive study *The Animal Estate. The English and other Creatures in the Victorian Age.* She expanded the notion into other areas of human interaction with animals. Steve Baker's *Picturing the Beast* was likewise published in England in 1993; the author examined the use of visual representations of animals in the print media. Regardless of their various perspectives, the aforementioned authors agree that the category "animal" is slowly disappearing.[1]

Our interest in creating the project *nützlich, süß und museal. Das fotografierte Tier* (Useful, Cute and Collected. The Photographed Animal) about the history of animals as motifs was prompted by the works of contemporary artists who were questioning the relationship between humans and animals and our perception of them. The simultaneous interdisciplinary public debate about animals in Western society reactivated earlier questions and connected these with the empirical data that had meanwhile been collected by the biological sciences. We assumed that the supposedly exact form of depiction, namely photography, and its potential to be reproduced had transferred the various interests in animals into making the "animal" popular as a motif, and therefore has a major influence both on the historical as well as the current formulations of the human understanding of nature.

The social debate of the 1980s and 90s was preceded by the international activities of the environmental movement that had formed in the 1970s. That movement had continued and radicalized the thoughts about nature conservation that were being expressed at the end of the 19th century. "Meanwhile, something else is happening: animals are resurfacing in the thoughts of human beings. It's an intellectual uprising in the name of animal existence. Exhibition spaces and authors are supplying it with weapons."[2] However, the animal—as the just published collection of essays entitled *Der Geist der Tiere* (The Spirit of Animals) makes clear—remains a mystery.[3]

This illustrated book, along with another book of texts published only in German, accompanies the exhibition *nützlich, süß und museal. Das fotografierte Tier* (Useful, Cute and Collected). It traces the photographic history of the animal as a subject since the invention of photography. It encompasses photographs from different historical periods and areas of production. In other words, it is not a publication about photographers specializing in animals. Instead, we are picking up where the exhibition "The Animal in Photography 1843–1985," curated by Alexandra Noble, left off. That exhibition's selection of photographs was made up primarily of works by well-known photographers.[4] However, in contrast to that project, decisions about the selection shown here have been based on the conditions necessary for portraying an animal in a picture which itself refers directly to industrialization, just as the subject does. That is why photographs from many different areas of use as well as anonymous photographs have been included.

It is clear that the intention to photograph animals is not only a reaction to the given, current conditions of animal existence and the relationships between humans and animals, but that photographs of animals demonstrate human models, are compensation in the form of an image, and provide recollections of past possibilities of experiencing nature. Indeed, the wide variety of animals and their various forms of expression and movement offer an extensive range for creating documentary photographs, powerful advertising, and artistic pictures. And lastly, animals are also the subjects of scientific experiments.

To the degree that photographers and amateurs detached themselves from any of the possible role models of other fine arts and traditional illustrative methods of science and created a new form of depicting animals based on the specific, technical possibilities generated by photography, so too has the perception of animals and their realities changed.

Wild animals advertise for cars, house pets for designer goods; private television and local papers discuss "animals in danger." "Cute" lions advertise for safari and adventure trips and living animals are a vital part of artistic practice. While cartoon figures in which human and animal characteristics merge are celebrated in cinema, newspapers and news magazines announce the "Farewell to the Animal World!".[5] Critical reports about fur, ivory, and horn hunters or eating exotic animals have transformed the age-old, unanswered question "can animals feel?" into the current question "do animals have rights?".

The spectrum of production of today's pictures of animals is immense. It is primarily the result of the reproducible image medium of photography, followed by the widespread consumption of images due to steady developments in printing means. Since the invention of photography, animals have been continually studied and photographed: as representative property and prize-winning breeds, as trophies of successful expeditions and hunts, as "loyal" friends and "equipment" of human beings, as objects of scientific research and commercial photography, and as artistic subjects.

The photographs published here come from very different sources: from libraries and archives, ethnology and art museums, natural history collections, photography agencies, and collections. The historical conditions in which they were created cannot be reconstructed within the bounds of this project. However, the pictures and their origins, as well as the research and theses documented in the collection of texts accompanying the exhibition, will hopefully prompt viewers and readers to pursue more research on their own.

This illustrated book, like the exhibition, is thematically organized in chapters according to subjects and functions; both interruptions and continuities in history are evident (the introductory quotations here have been excerpted from the essays and interviews found in the textbook). They reflect the various forms of illustrating the relationship between animals and humans in different periods, and the economic, political, and social interests and artistic notions associated with them. The intentions and strategies behind the depictions become clear and place the treatment and memories of animals within an historical context.

The selection of pictures includes daguerreotypes and other earlier forms of photographic techniques, as well as albums, newspapers, pictures of big game hunts and photographic safaris, amateur photographs, and pictures produced for scientific or breeding purposes. Documentary, journalistic, and artistically-motivated individual photographs as well as series are shown.

On display are works by both famous and unknown photographers, including Ottomar Anschütz, George Barker, Bisson Frères, Steve Bloom, Adolphe Braun, Balthasar Burkhard, Lewis Carroll, Chien-Chi Chang, Archibald Cochrane, Madame d'Ora, Jean Louis Delton, Thomas James Dixon, A. Radclyffe Dugmore, Thomas Eakins, William Eggleston, Elliot Erwitt, Walker Evans, Paul Faulstich, Joan Fontcuberta, Robert Frank, Paul Geniaux, Hein Gorny, Candida Höfer, Willoughby Wallace Hooper, André Kertész, Philipp Kester, Josef Koudelka, Adolf Kull, Franz Lazi, Jo Longhurst, Aleksandras Macijauskas, Per Maning, Etienne-Jules Marey, Lisette Model, Louis Adolphe Humbert de Molard, Comte de Montizon, Eadweard Muybridge, Michael Nichols, Cas Oorthuys, Eric Poitevin, Archille Quinet, Albert Renger-Patzsch, Olivier Richon, Humberto Rivas, Horatio Ross, Walter Schels, Carl Georg Schillings, Friedrich Seidenstücker, Frederick Sommer, William Strode, Juha Suonpää, Henk Tas, Richard Tepe, Waldemar Titzenthaler, Adrien Tournachon, Rosemarie Trockel, William Wegman, Garry Winogrand, Wols, the Walmsley Brothers, Ylla and Fritz Zielesch.

In addition to photographs from Museum Folkwang's Photography Collection, the project includes numerous works on loan from photography museums, public and private collections, natural history museums, university collections, and from zoo archives. We would like to thank the many national and international loaning institutions, including the J. Paul Getty Museum in Los Angeles, Deutsches Literaturarchiv in Marbach, Ullstein Bild, the Archiv der Universität der Künste and the Bildarchiv Preußischer Kulturbesitz in Berlin, Sammlung Herzog in Basle, Albertina in Vienna, Bibliothèque nationale de France and Société Française de Photographie in Paris, the National Museum of Photography, Film and Television in Bradford, and the Royal Collection in Windsor Castle.

We would particularly like to express our appreciation to the sponsors who made this project possible: the J. Paul Getty Museum, Los Angeles; Hasselblad Stiftelse, Göteborg; Kunststiftung NRW, Düsseldorf; Stiftung Presse-Haus NRZ, Essen; Wüstenrot Stiftung, Ludwigsburg; Folkwang Museumsverein e.V., Essen; and Steidl Verlag, Göttingen.

Ute Eskildsen and Hans-Jürgen Lechtreck

1 John Berger, "Why Look at Animals?", in: ders., *About Looking*, London, 1980, pp. 1-26; Harriet Ritvo: *The Animal Estate. The English and other Creatures in the Victorian Age*, Cambridge, Mass., 1987; Steve Baker, *Picturing the Beast. Animals, Identity, and Representation*, Manchester, 1993.

2 Ulrich Raulff, "Treblinka der Tiere. Die Unterscheidungen der Philosophie als Lizenz zum Töten? Derrida, Agamben, Coetzee und die unerwartete Rückkehr der Kreatur," in: *Süddeutsche Zeitung*, No. 248, October 26/27, 2002.

3 Dominik Perler/Markus Wild (Eds.), *Der Geist der Tiere. Philosophische Texte zu einer aktuellen Diskussion*, Frankfurt/M., 2005. See also: Tim Ingold (Ed.), *What is an Animal?*, London, 1988.

4 Alexandra Noble (Ed.), *The Animal in Photography 1843–1985*, exhibition catalogue, London, 1985.

5 *Der Spiegel*, No. 48, November 27, 1995 (Cover).

„Aber die Popularität, die Dürers *Feldhase* bis heute besitzt, verdankt sich dem Umstand seiner unzähligen fotografischen und fotomechanischen Reproduktionen im 19. und 20. Jahrhundert. Gemeinsam mit den *Betenden Händen* ist Dürers Tierstudie zum Paradebeispiel einer verklärenden Kunstbegeisterung geworden. Die Aufmerksamkeit, die dem *Feldhasen* dabei zukam, verdankt sich der vermeintlichen Niedlichkeit des Motivs und sicherlich auch der Begeisterung für die realistische Darstellung."

"But the popularity that Dürer's *Feldhase* still continues to enjoy has to do with his countless photographic and photo-mechanic reproductions during the 19th and 20th century. Along with *Betende Hände*, Dürer's animal study is a prime example of a glorifying enthusiasm for art. The attention that *Feldhase* received as a result is owed to the supposed cuteness of the motif and surely to a passion for a realistic portrayal."

Jürgen Müller

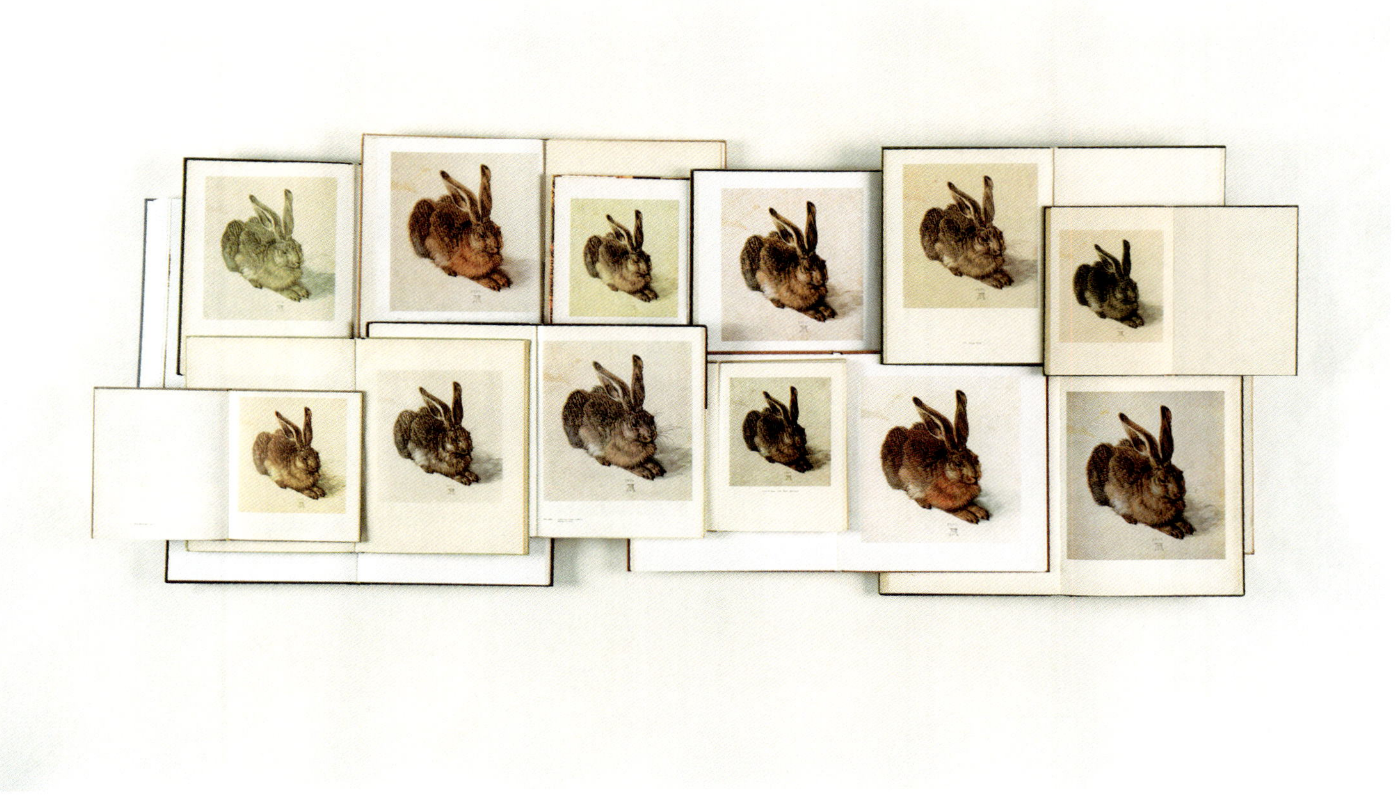

Claudia Angelmaier

Hase, 2004

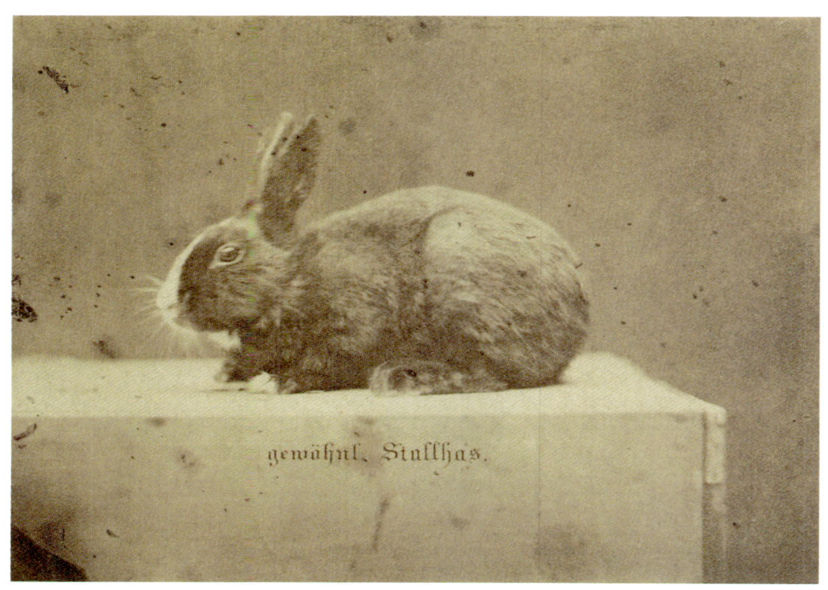

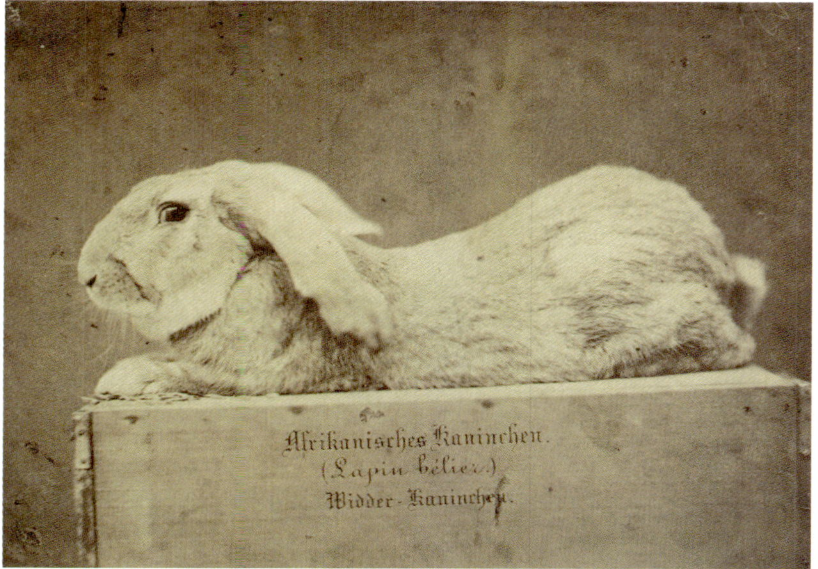

Anonym

Gewöhnlicher Stallhase, ca. 1895

Afrikanisches Kaninchen, ca. 1895

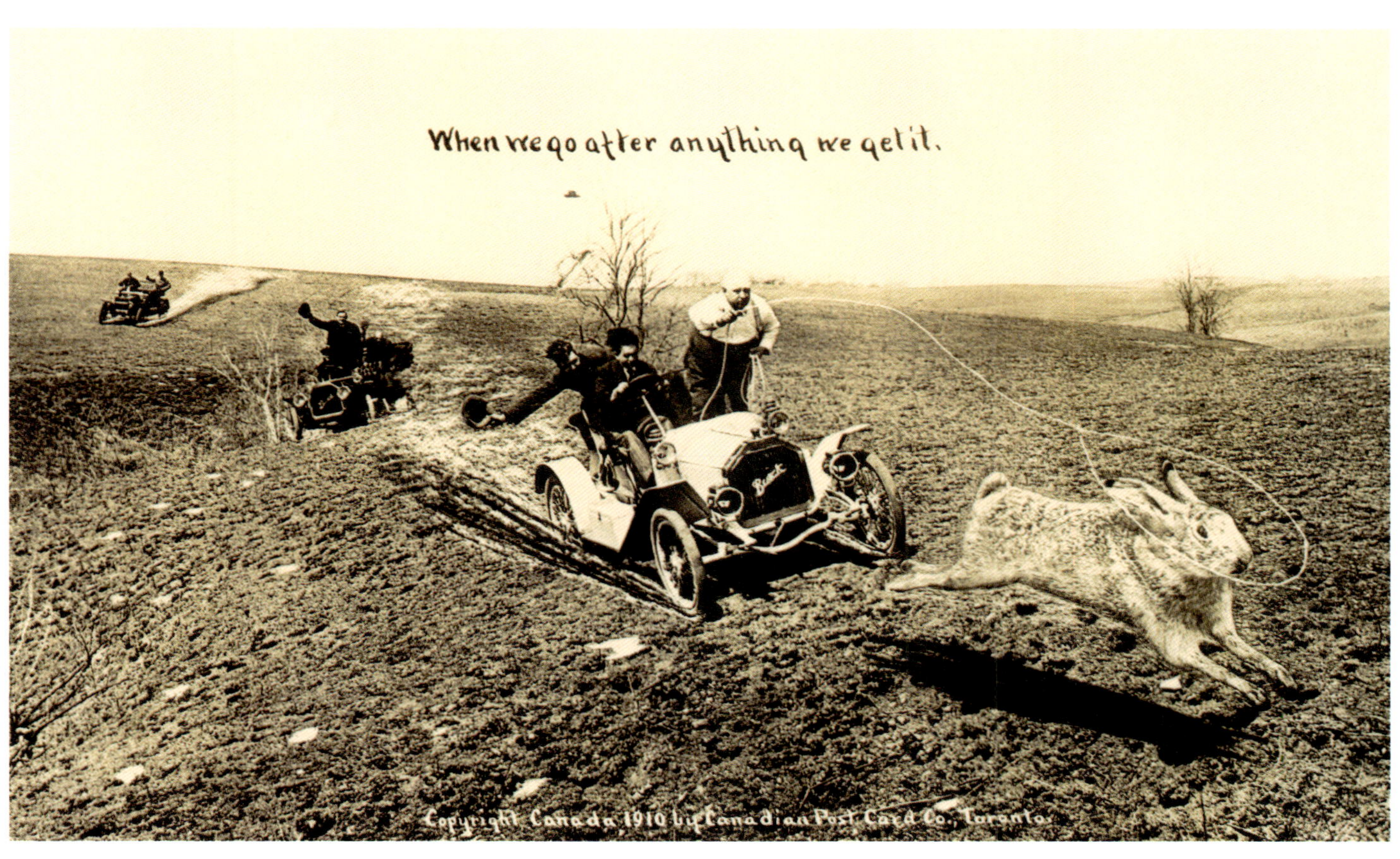

W. H. Martin

When we go after anything we get it, 1910

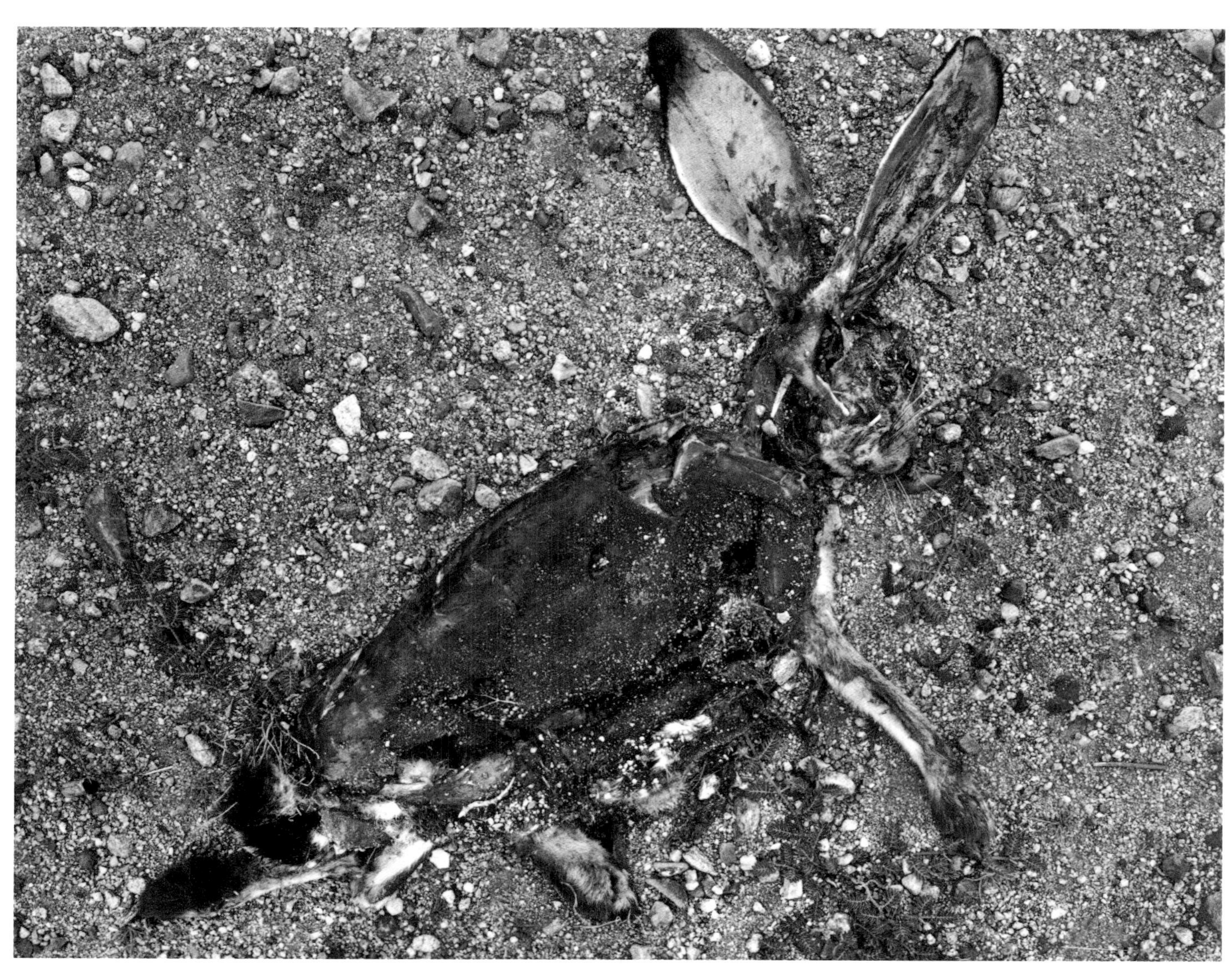

Frederick Sommer
Jack Rabbit, 1939

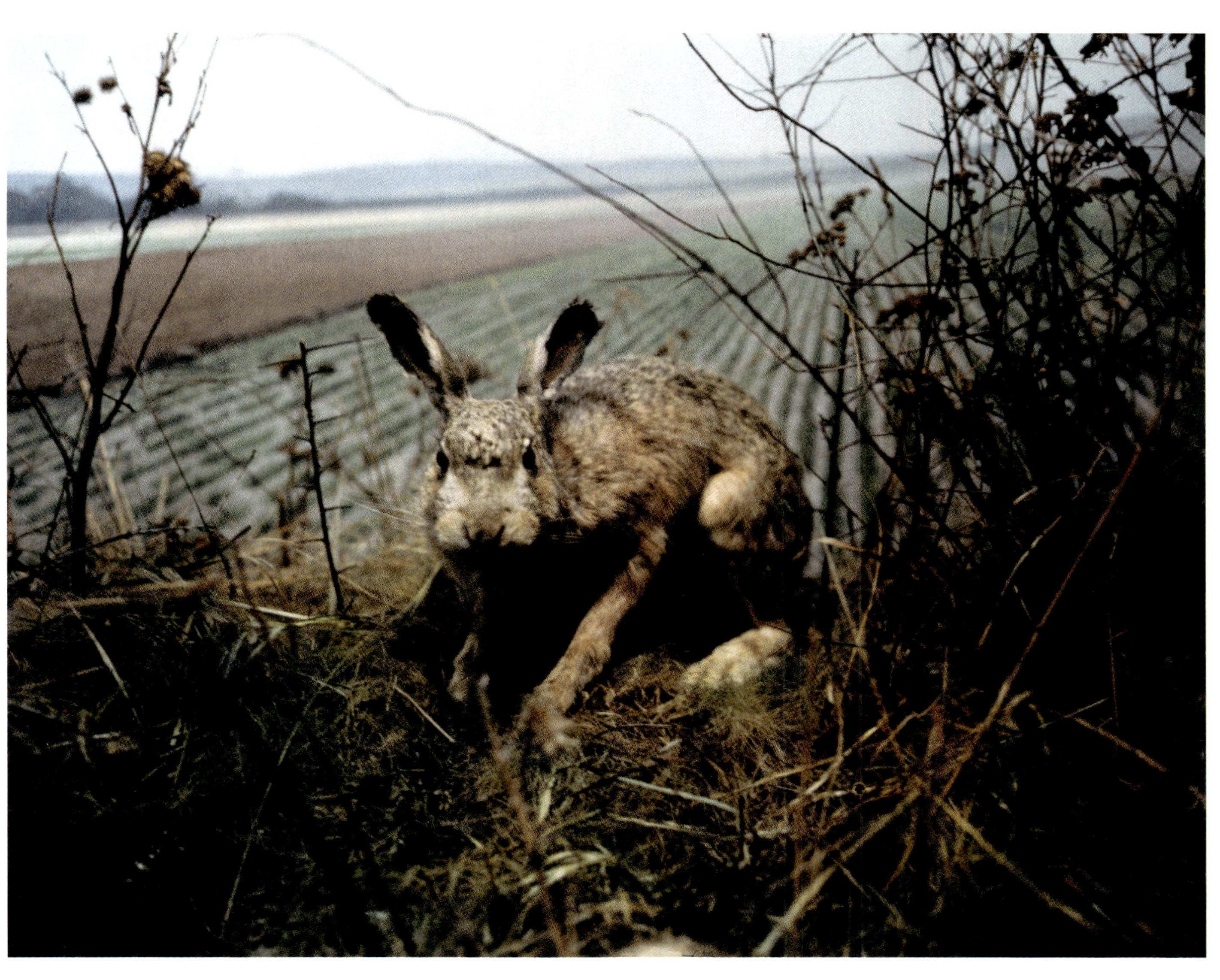

Wilmar Koenig

Hase auf dem Feld, 1992, a. d. Serie: *Le Bestiaire*

„Es bedurfte schon der Zuhilfenahme sämtlicher mechanischer Aufnahmetechniken wie Fotografie, Chronofotografie und Kino, um das Pferd für immer im Reich der Legenden und Mythen zu verankern."

"One would need the help of all forms of mechanical recording techniques such as photography, chronophotography, and cinema to anchor the horse once and for all in the realm of legends and myths."

André Gunthert

Pferd Horse

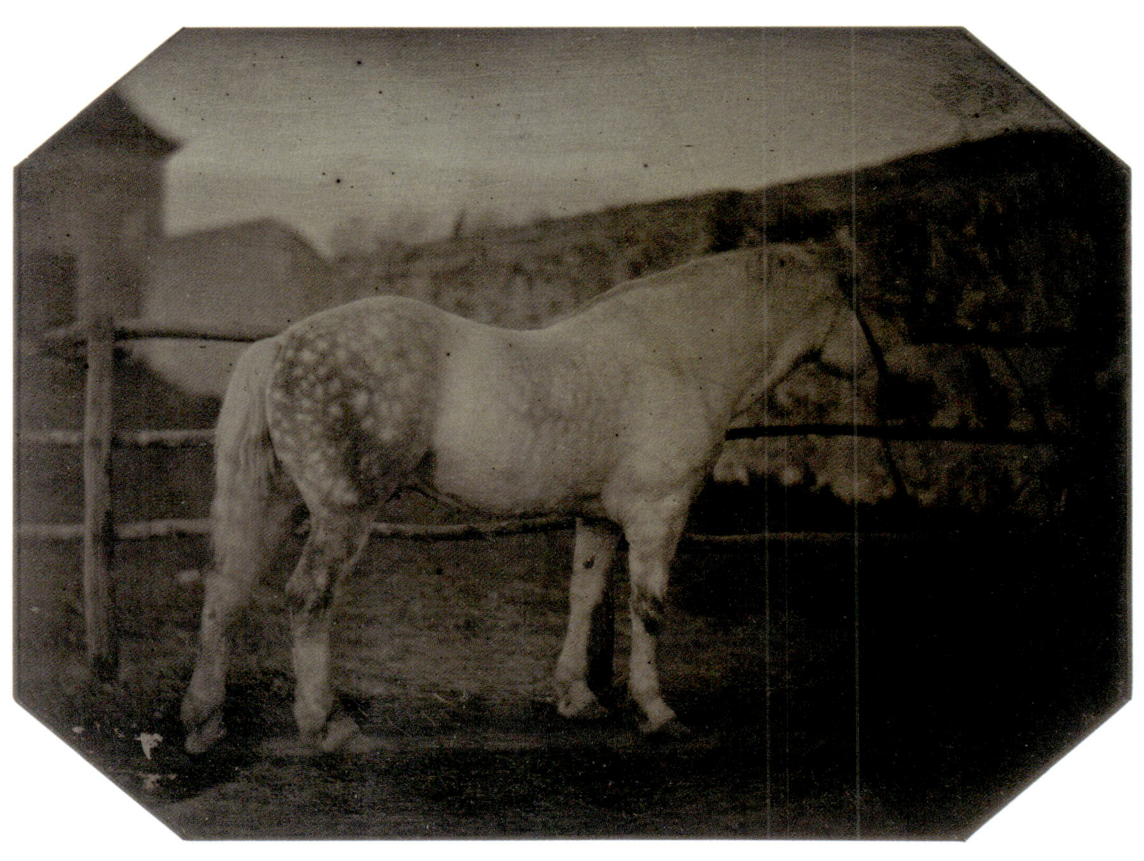

Bisson Frères
Das Pferd "Mouton" /
The horse "Mouton", 1844-1848

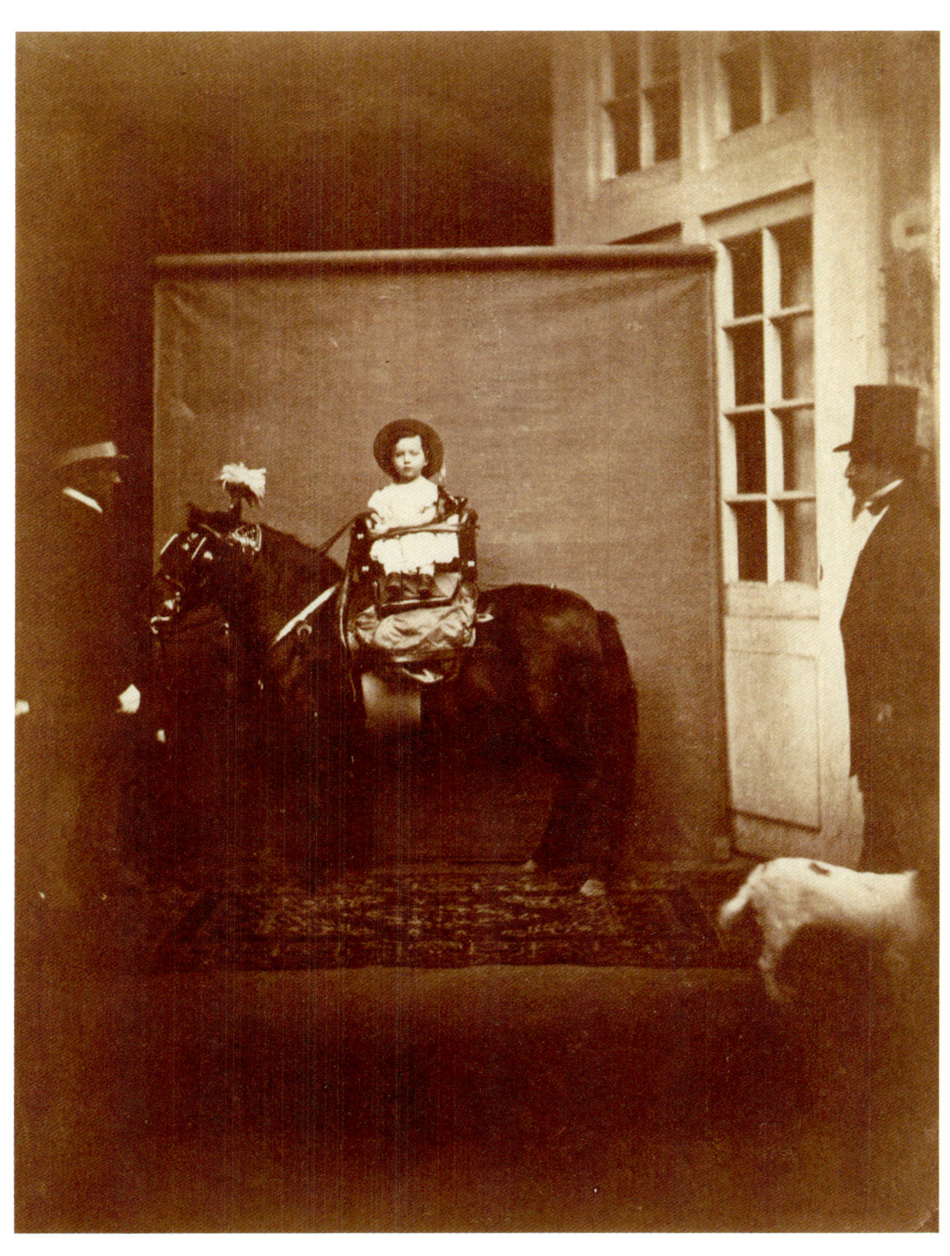

Pierre Louis Pierson

Napoleon III and the Prince Imperial, ca. 1859

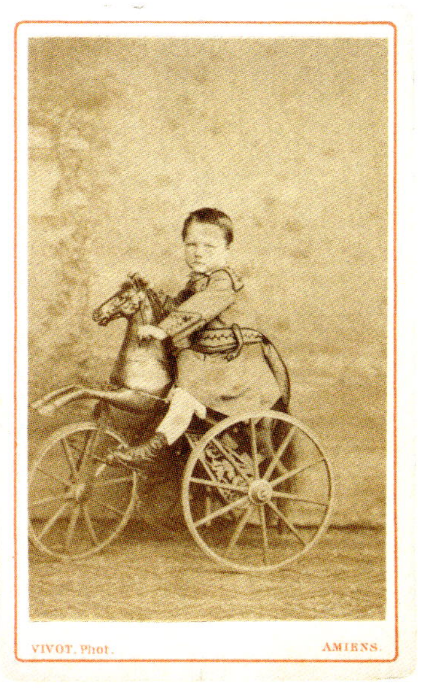

Vivot
Junge mit Spielzeugpferd /
Boy with toy horse, 1876

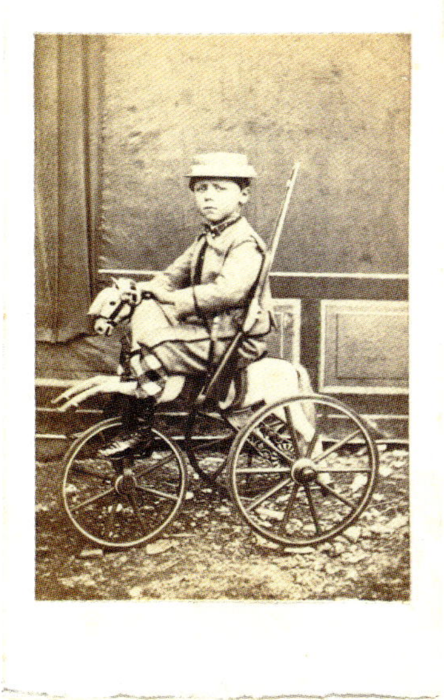

Anonym
Junge mit Spielzeugpferd /
Boy with toy horse, 1880er

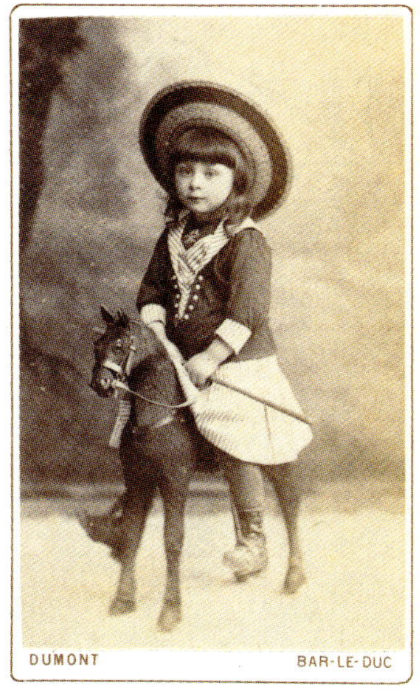

J. Adéodat Dumont
Mädchen mit Spielzeugpferd /
Girl with toy horse, ca. 1880

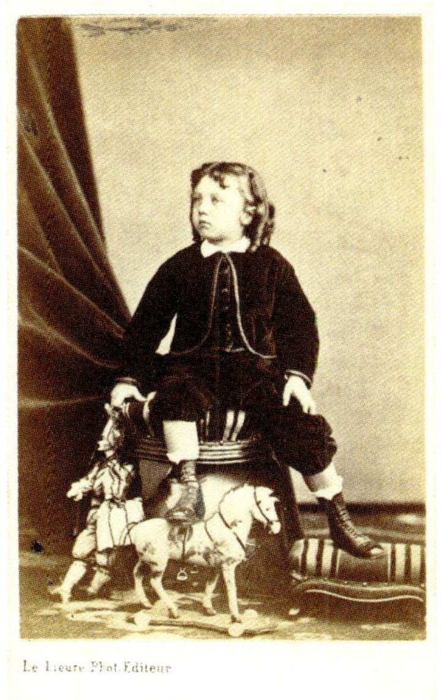

Henri Le Lieure
Junge mit Spielzeugpferden /
Boy with toy horses, ca. 1875

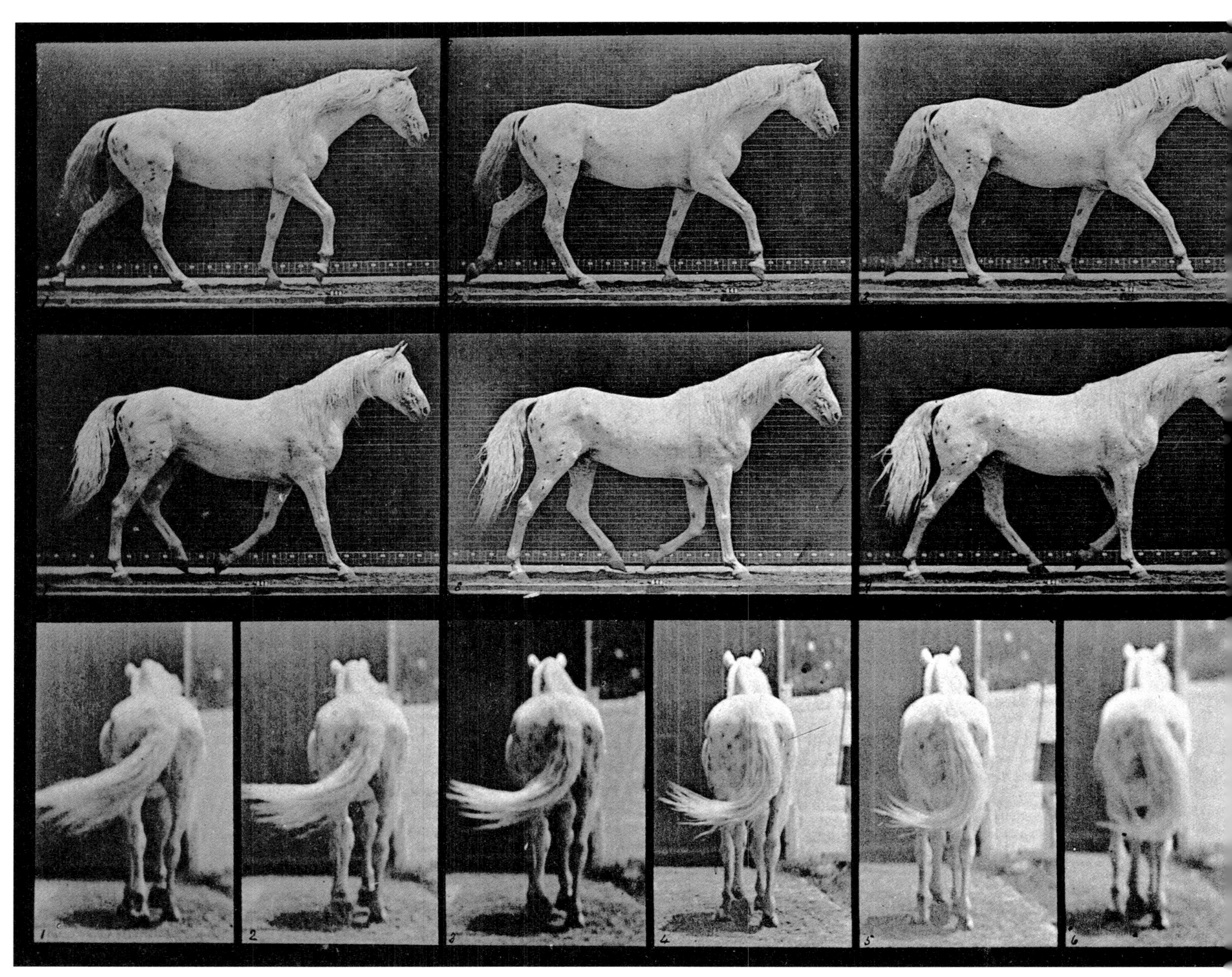

Eadweard Muybridge
Eagle walking, free, 1887

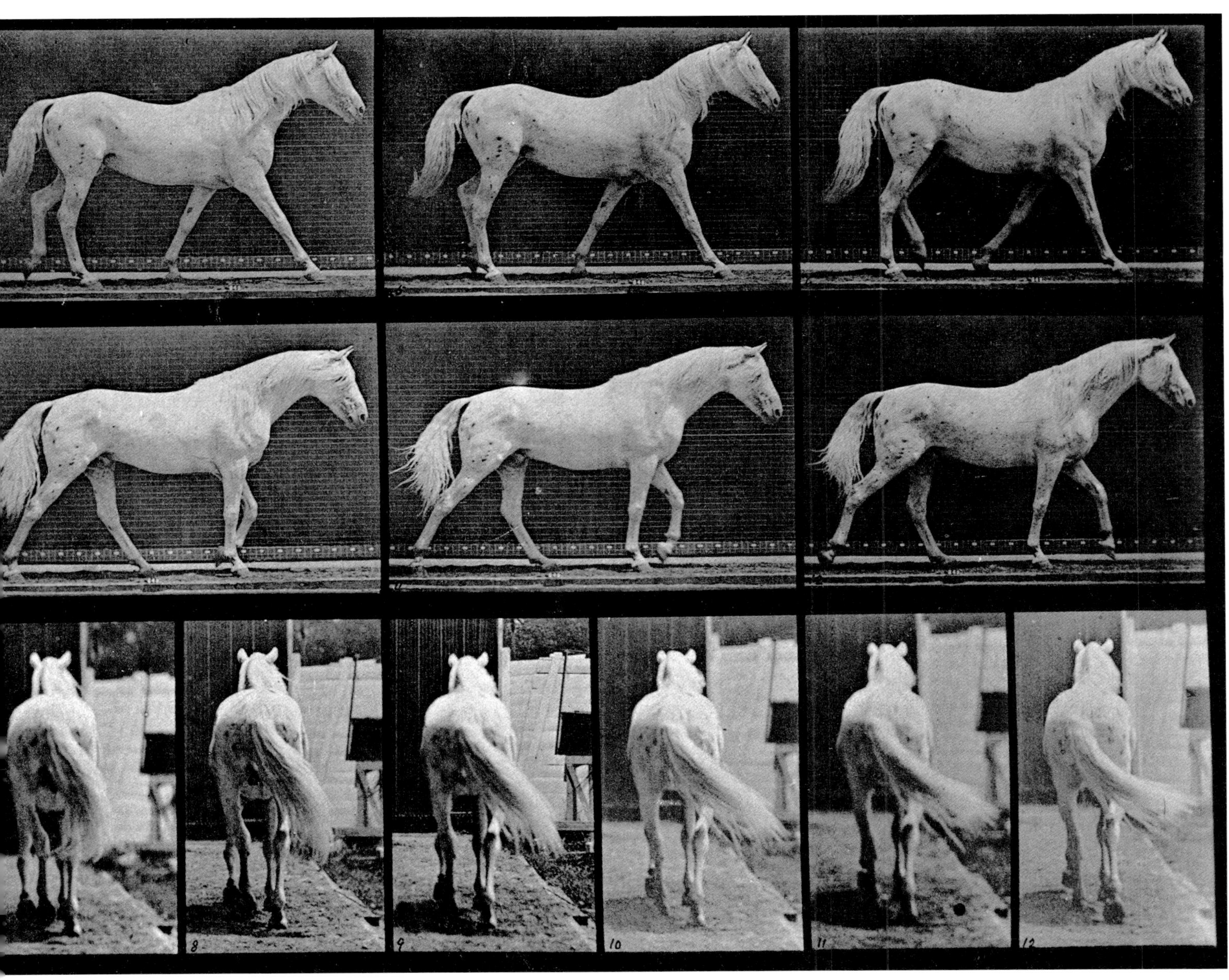

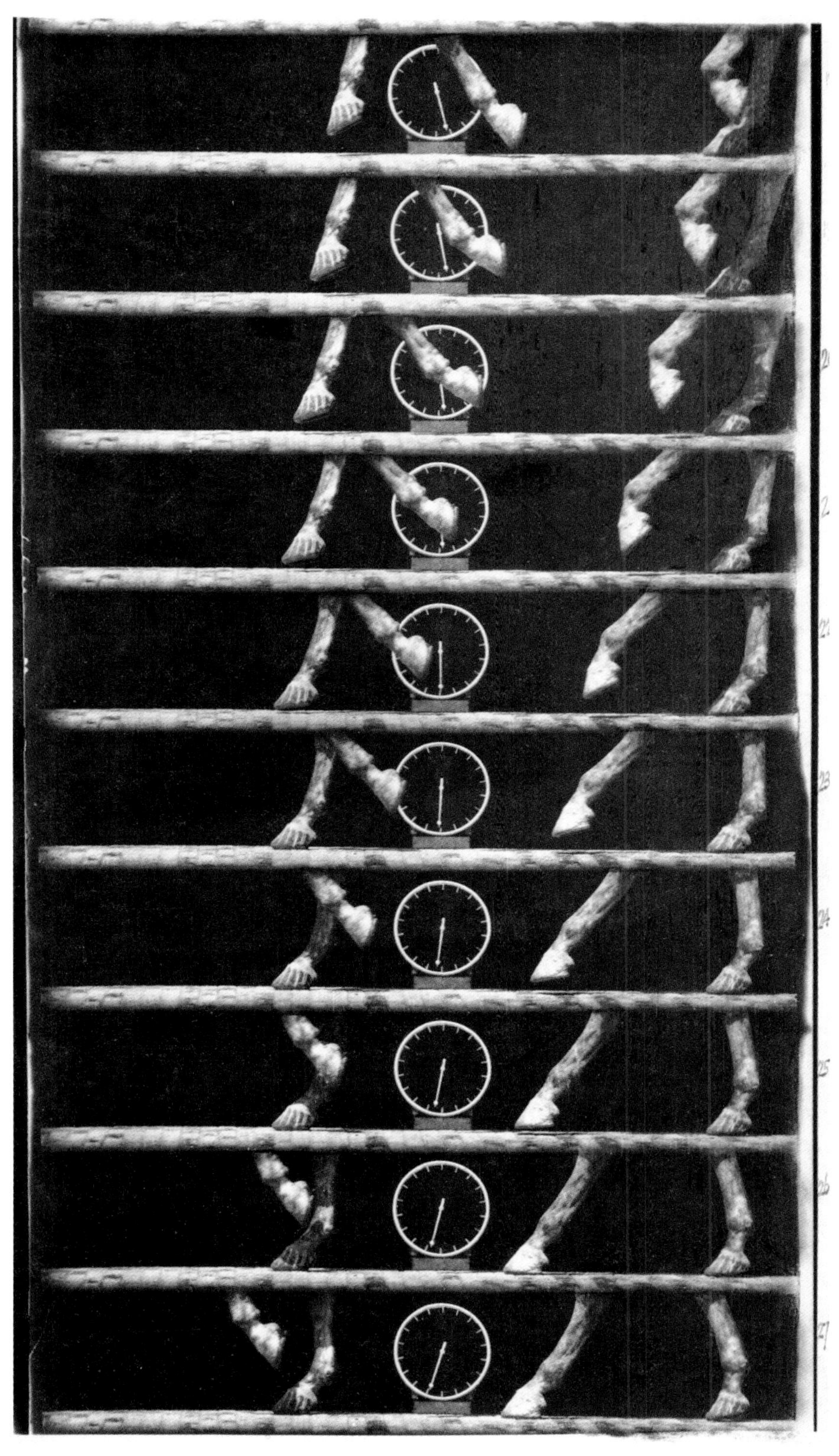

Etienne-Jules Marey
Horse's Hooves, ca. 1892

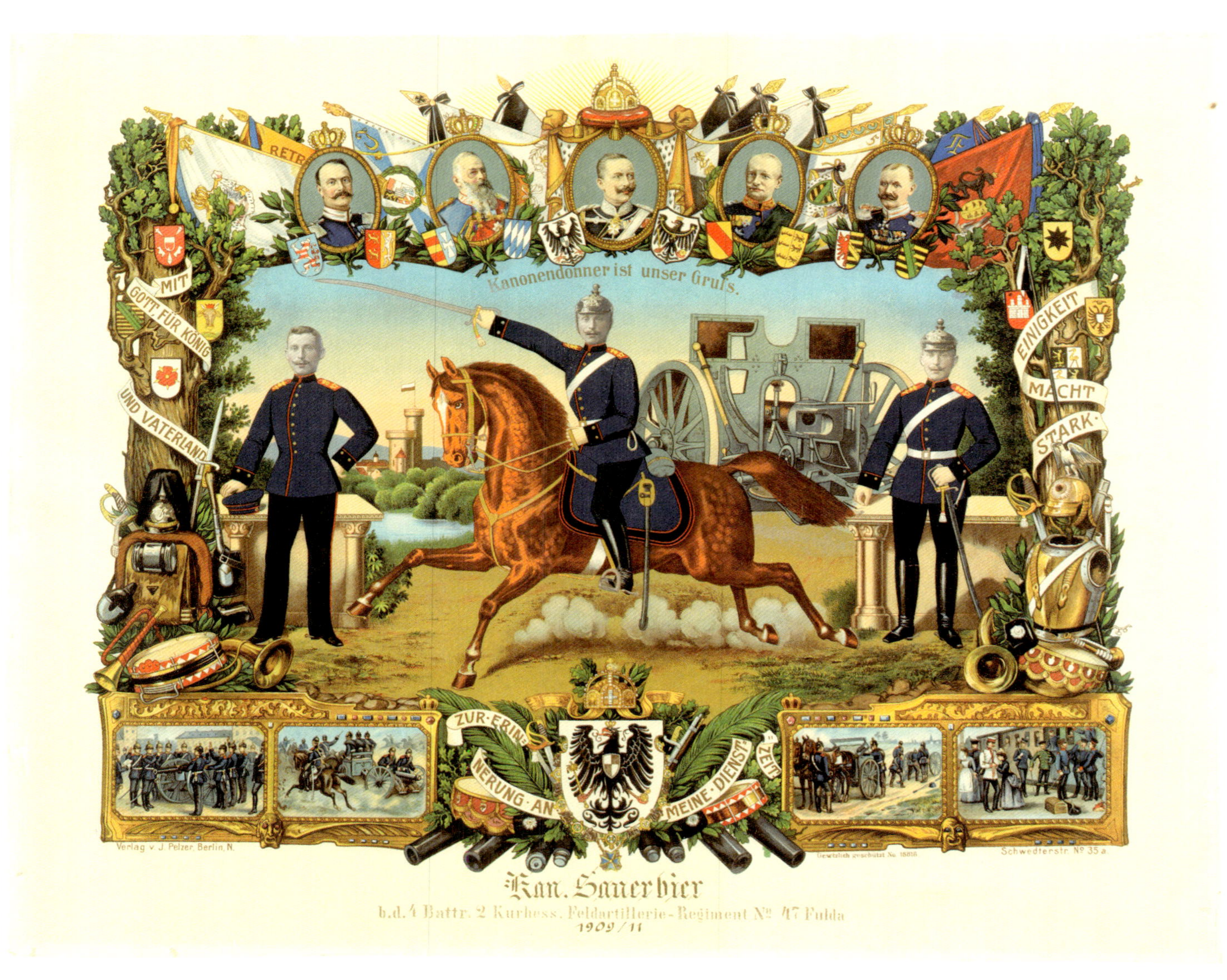

Anonym

Kanonier Sauerbier bei der 4. Batterie /

Gunner Sauerbier at the 4th battery, Fulda 1911

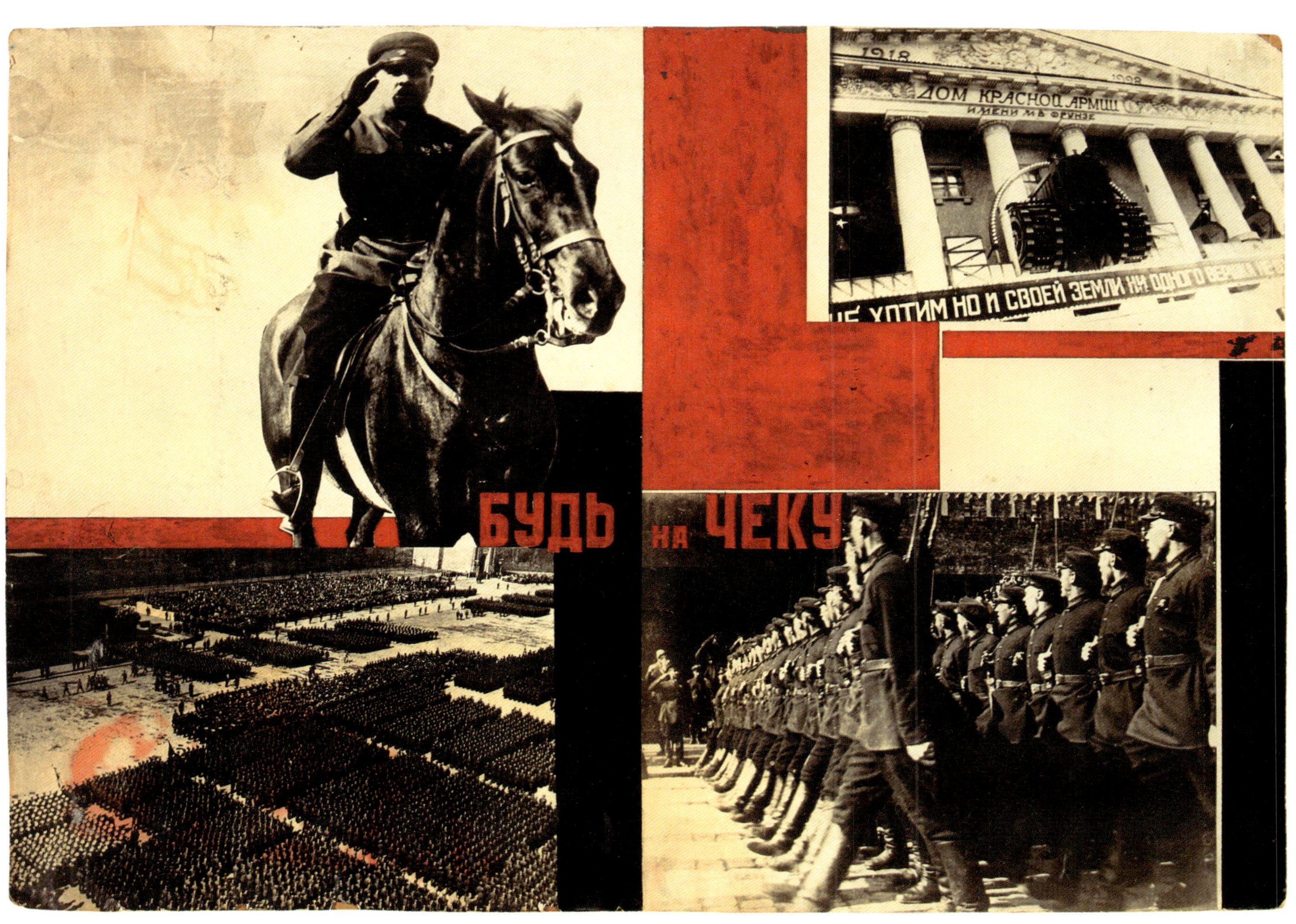

Warwara Stepanowa

Ergebnisse des 1. Fünfjahresplan, 1933

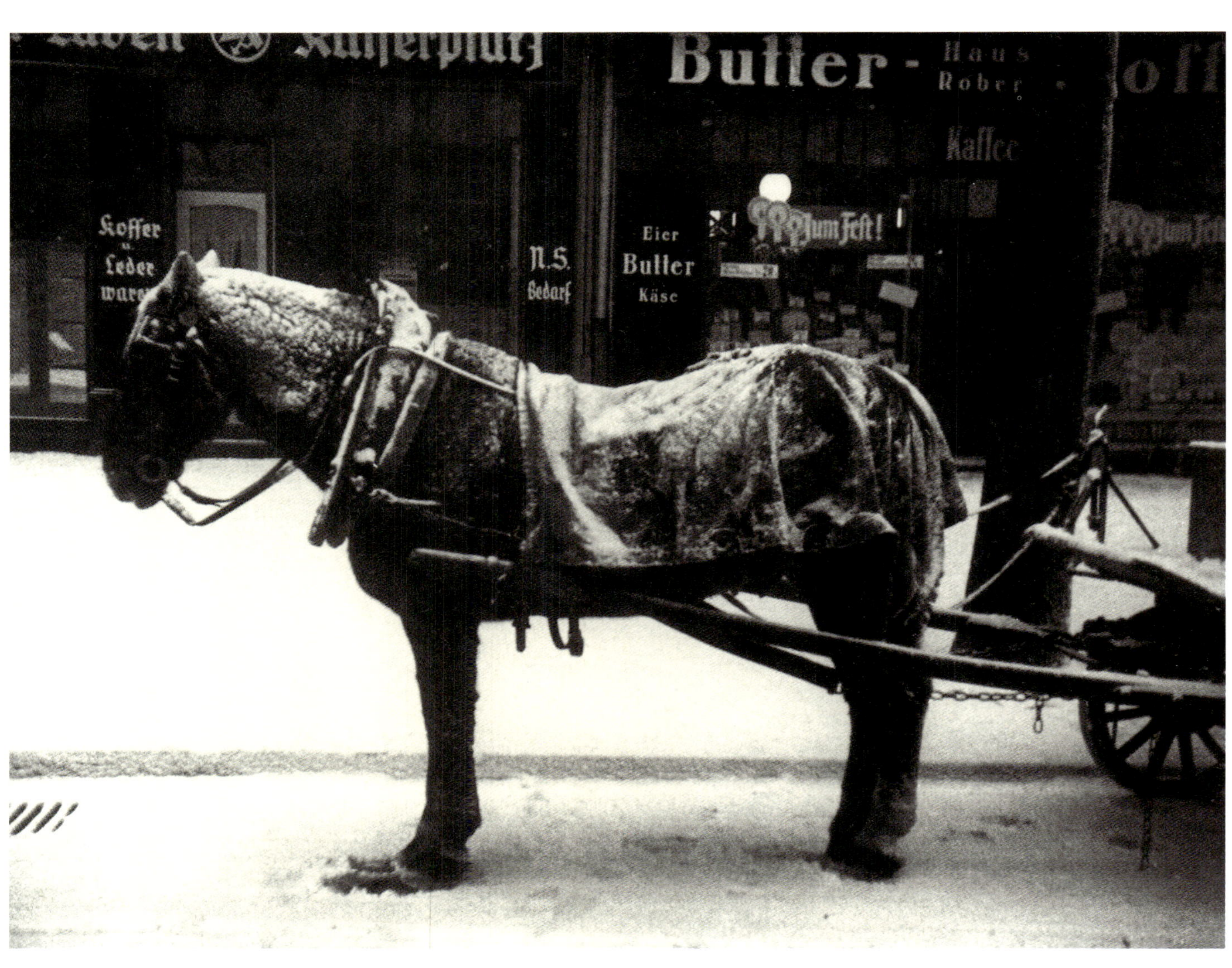

Friedrich Seidenstücker

Eingeschneites Pferd vor einer Kutsche am Kaiserplatz /

Horse carriage at Kaiserplatz, 1930er

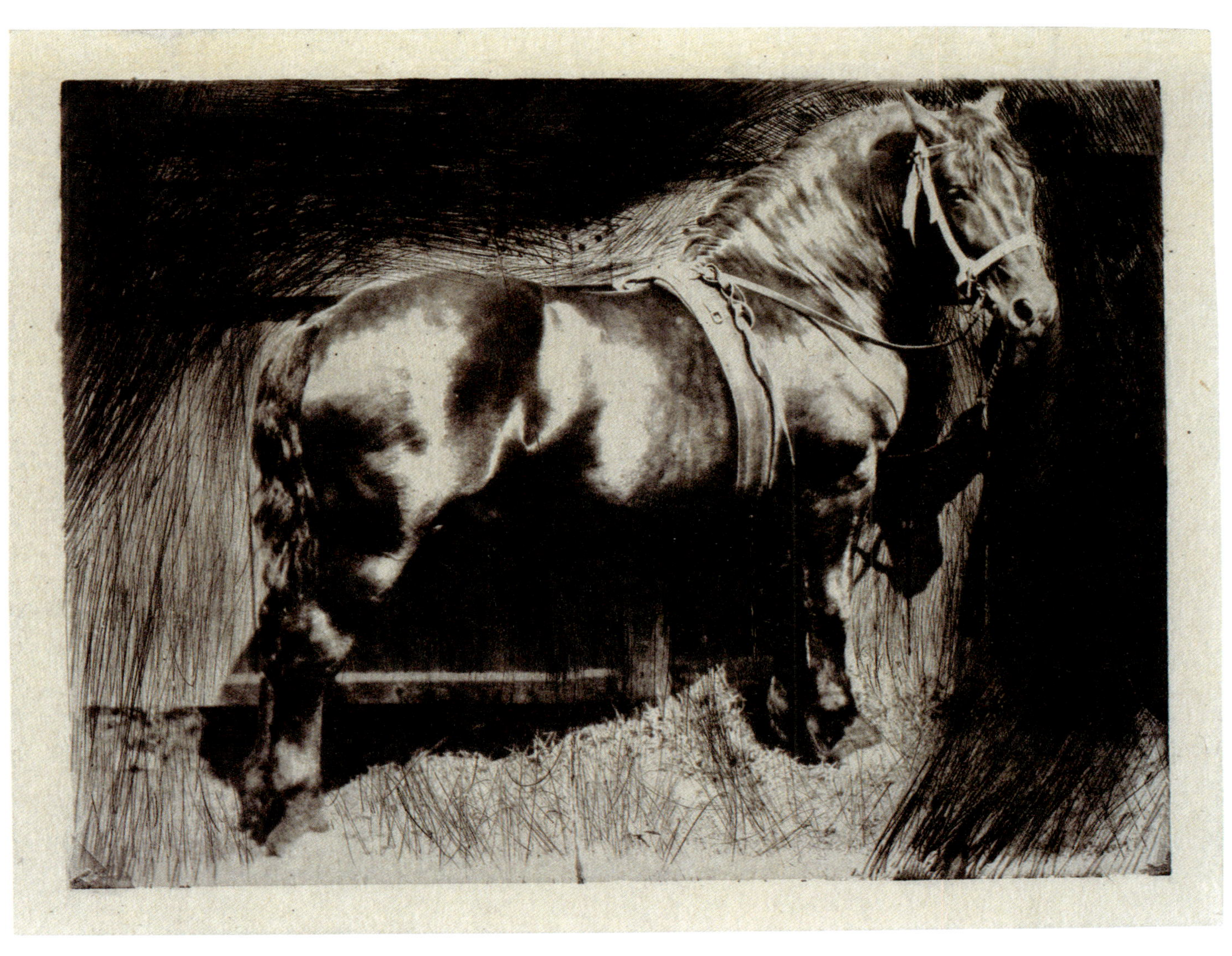

Frank Eugene
The Horse, 1898

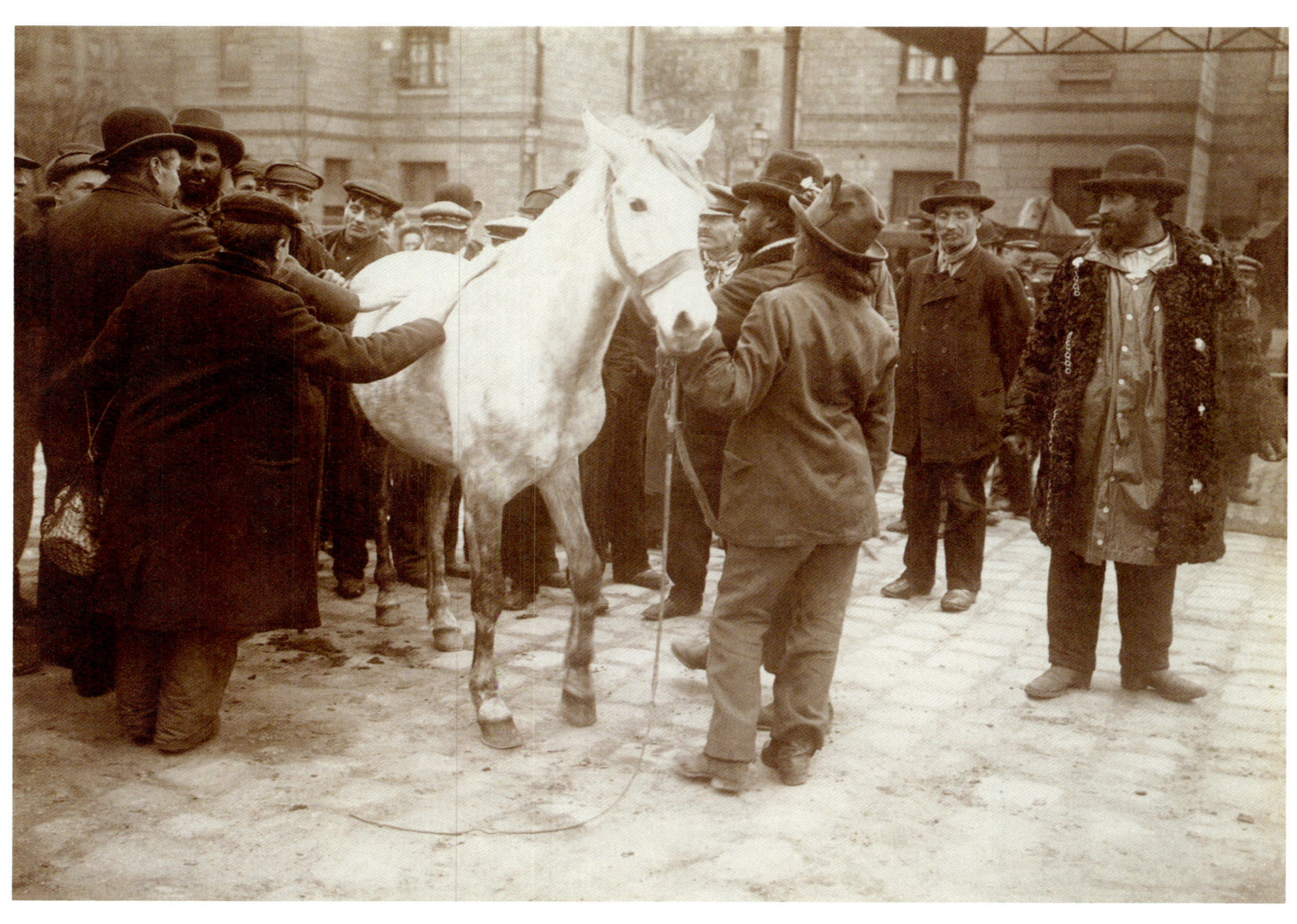

Paul Géniaux

Le marché aux chevaux, boulevard de l'Hôpital, ca. 1900

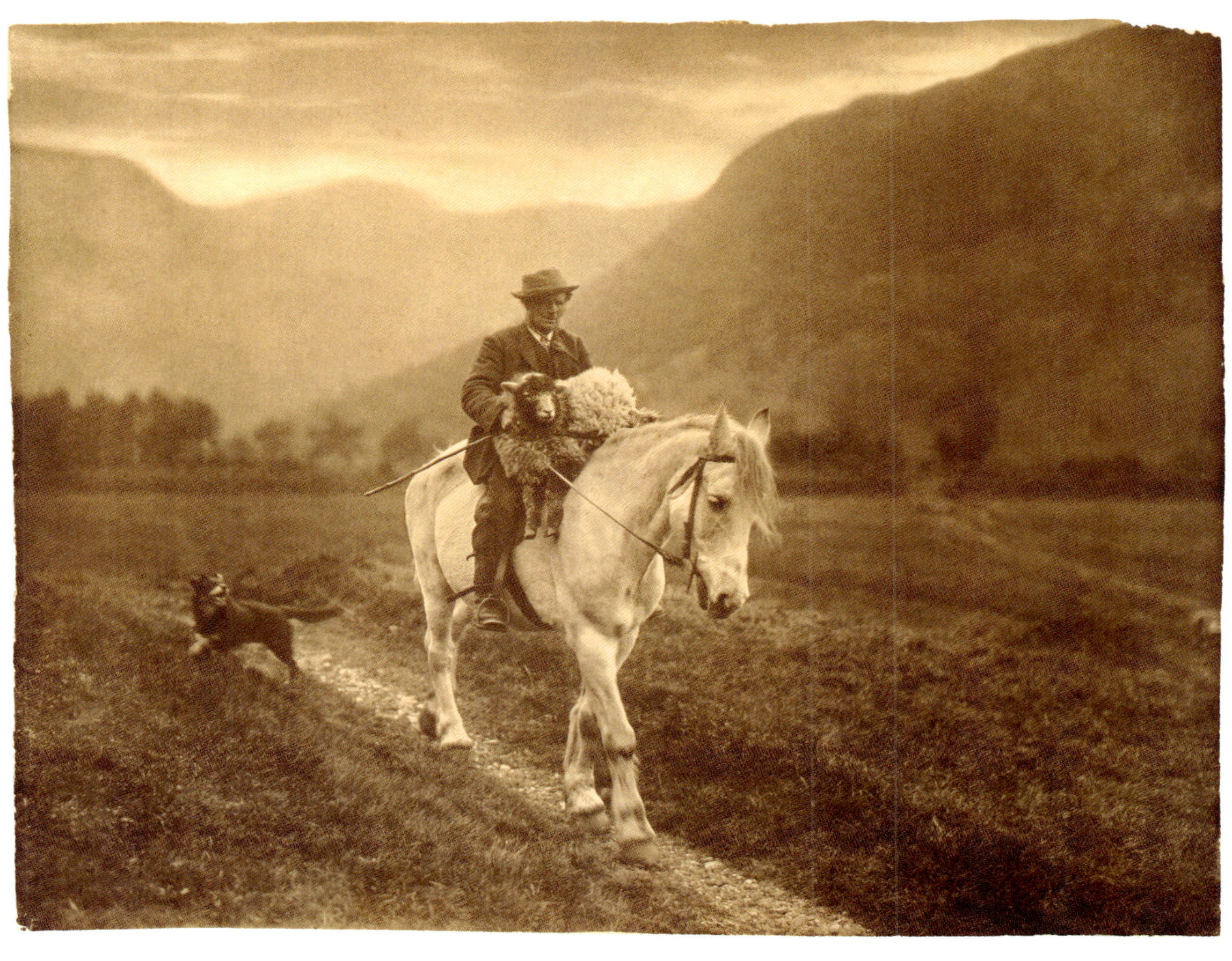

Walmsley Brothers

A Lonely Valley, ca. 1900

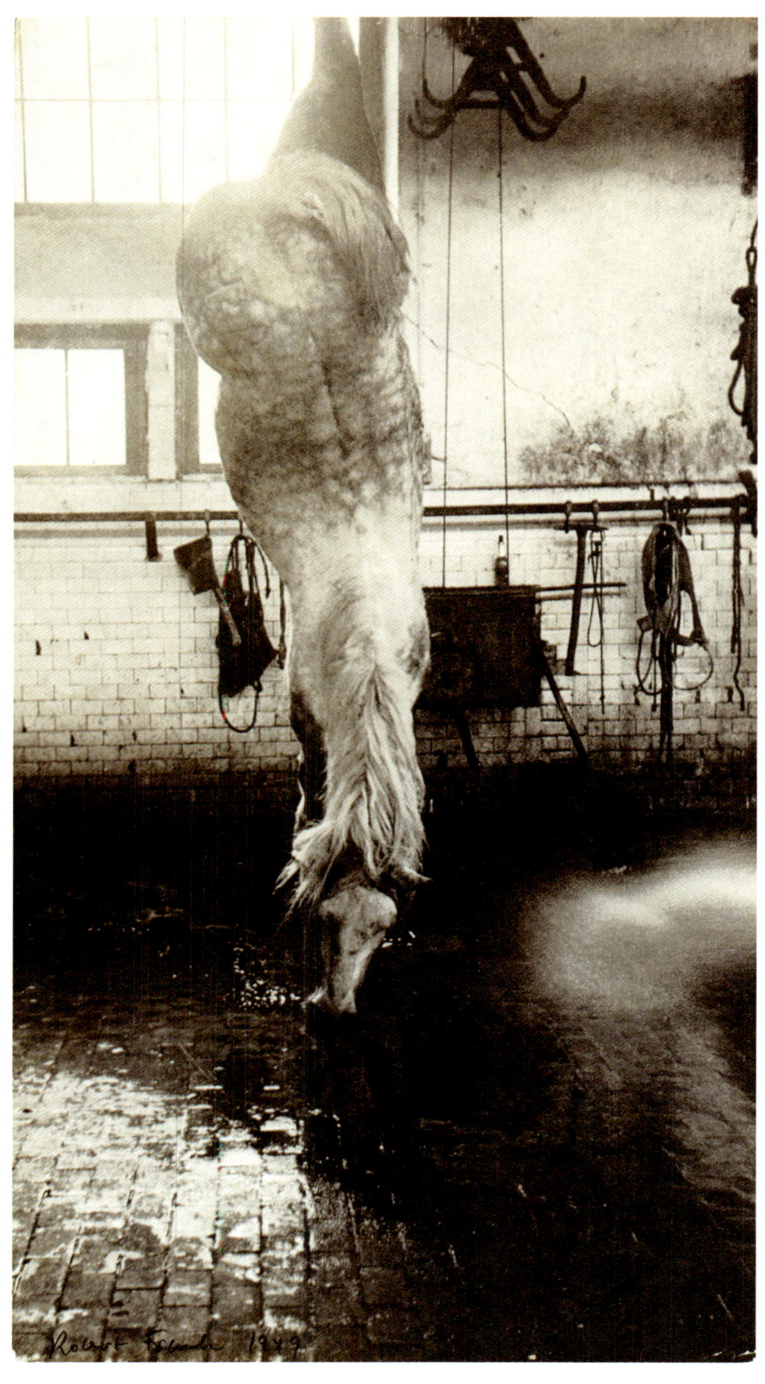

Robert Frank
Paris, 1949

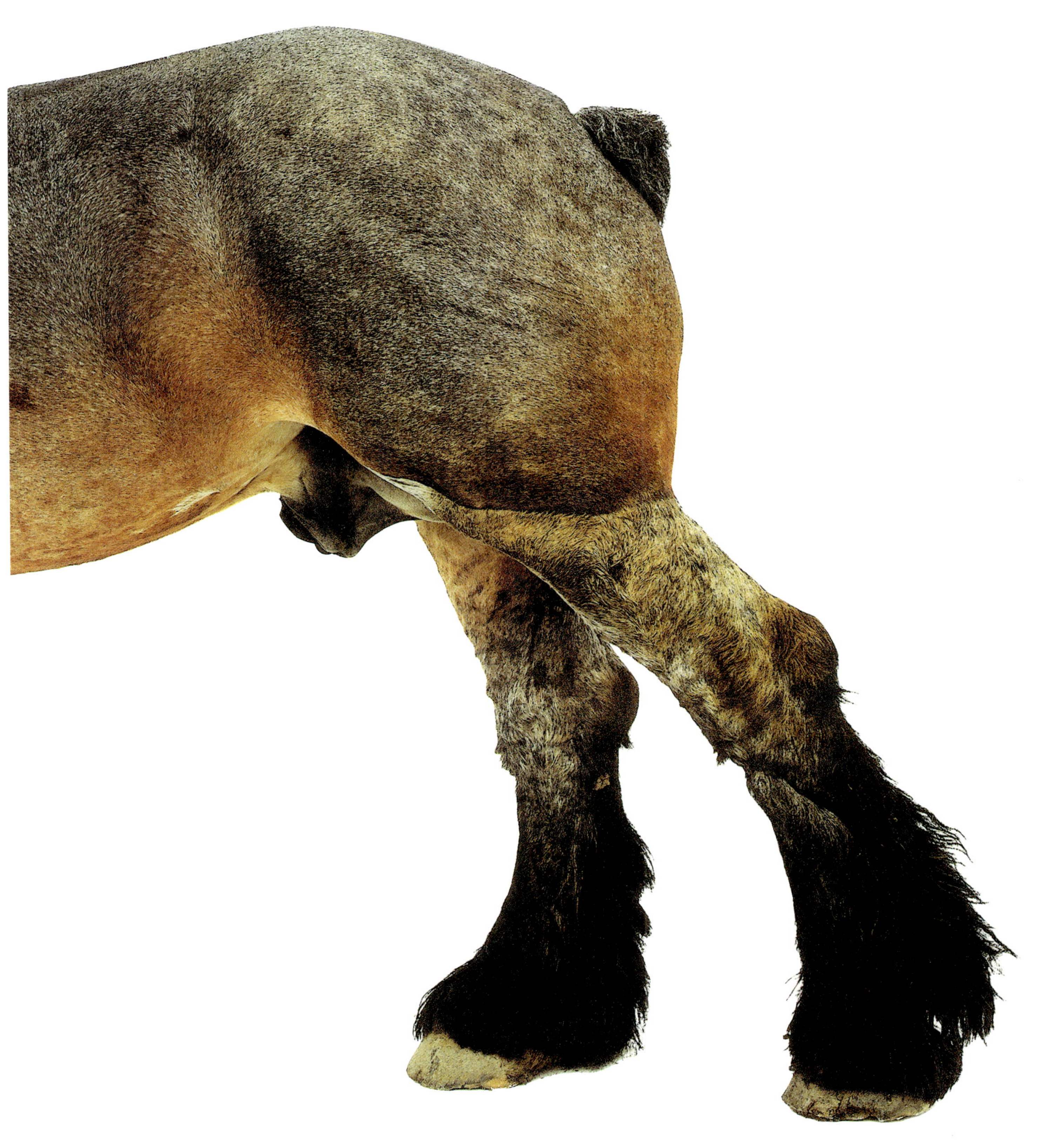

Eric Poitevin
Ohne Titel (No 8), 2000

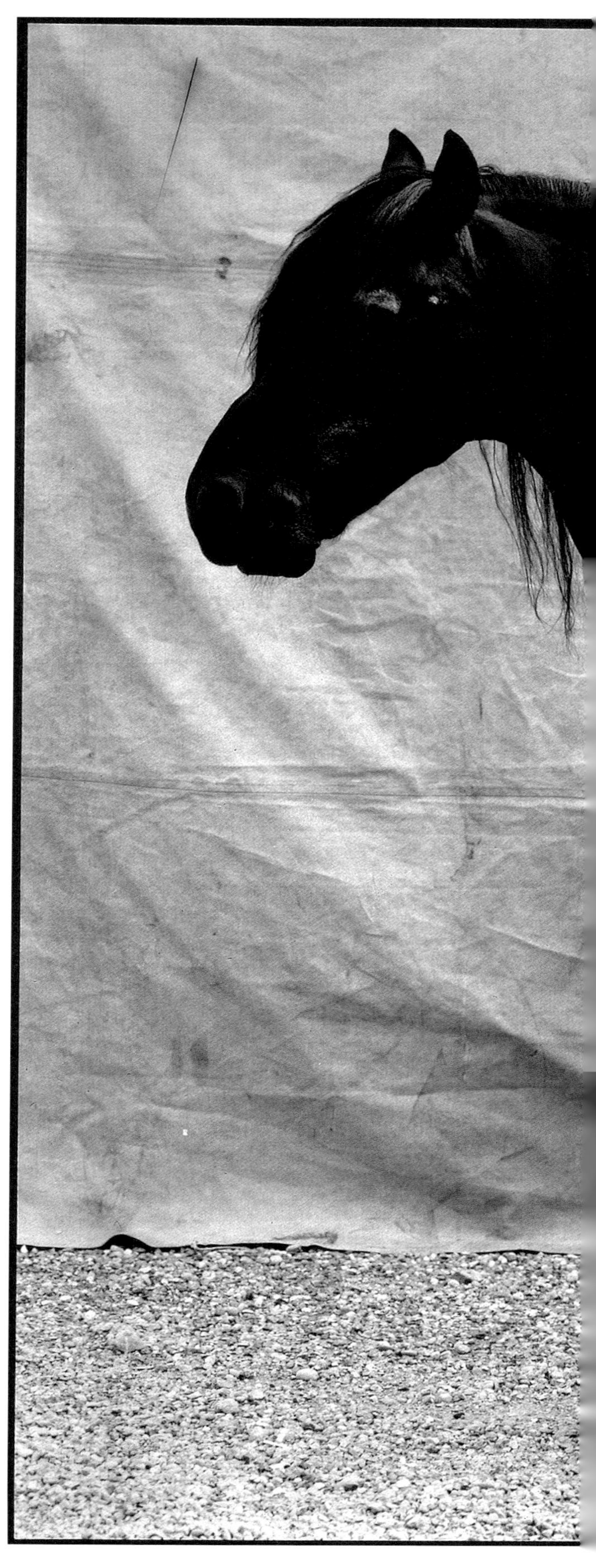

Balthasar Burkhard
Friesisches Pferd, 1995

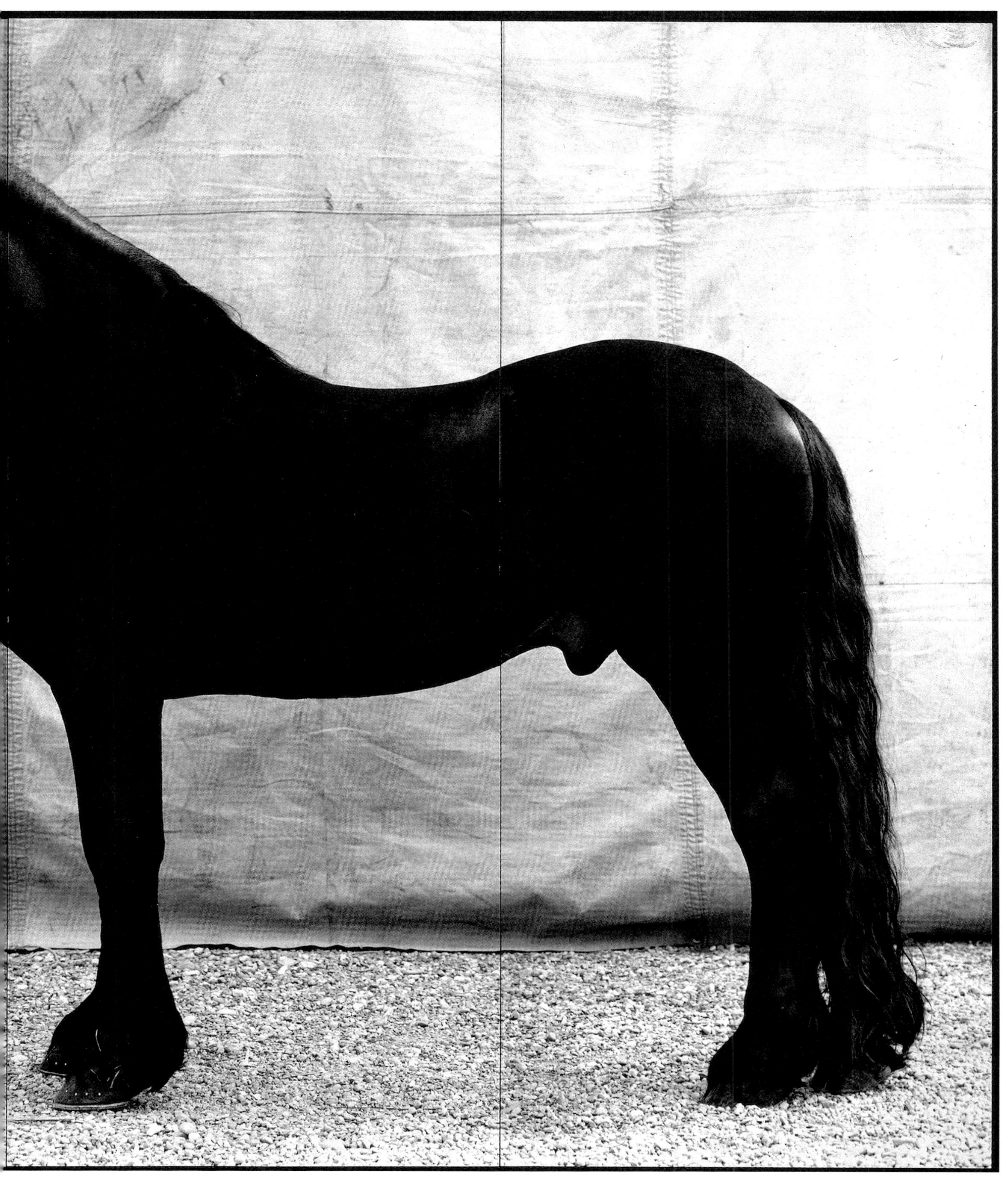

„Wenn die Tierfotografie Afrika als menschenleeren, nur von Tieren bewohnten Kontinent präsentierte, das männliche weiße Individuum als Bezwinger dieser Tierwelt zeigte und die Menschen des Kontinents dem Raum der Natur zuordnete, übernahm sie damit im kolonialen Kontext eine politische und herrschafts-stabilisierende Funktion.“

“When animal photography presented Africa as a continent inhabited only by animals and devoid of people, the white male individual as the conqueror of this animal world, and assigned the continent’s people to natural space, it assumed a political and dominance-stabilizing function within the context of colonialism.”

Bernhard Gissibl

Jagd Hunt

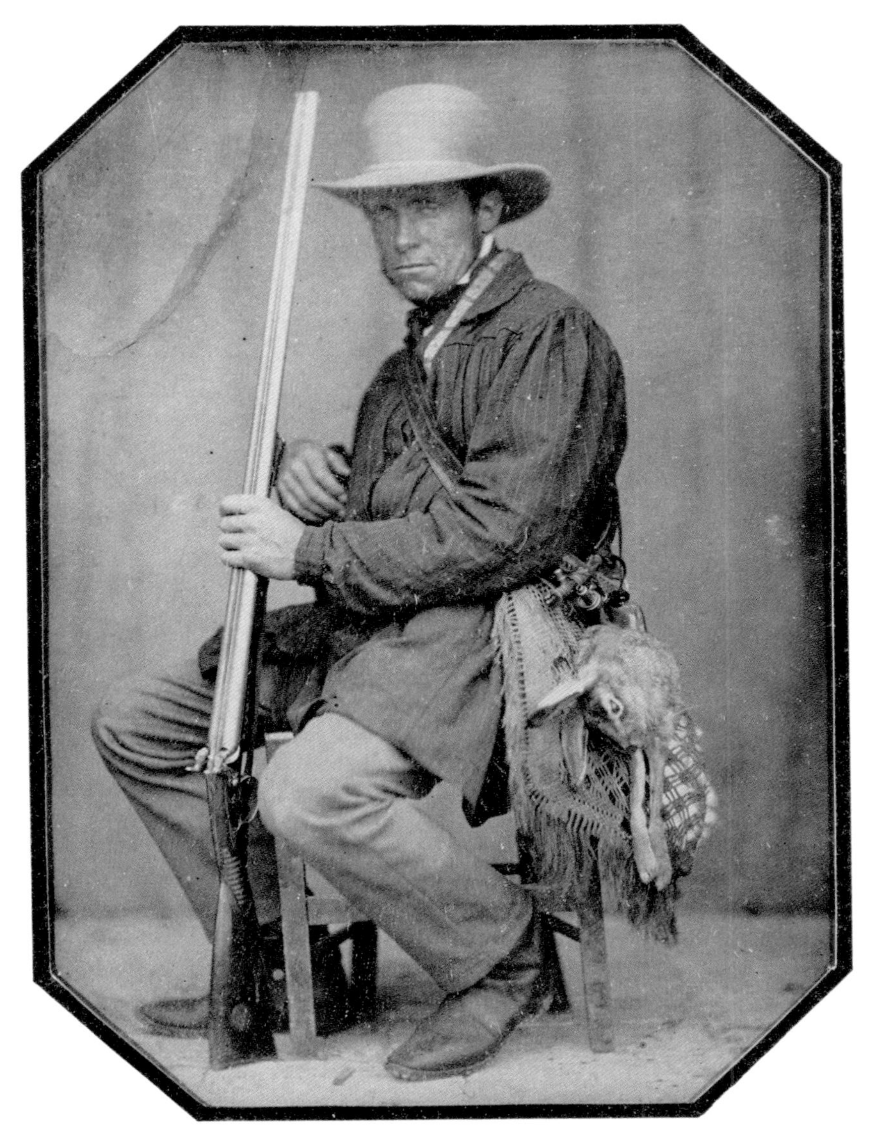

Louis-Adolphe-Humbert de Molard

Chasseur assis, 1840er

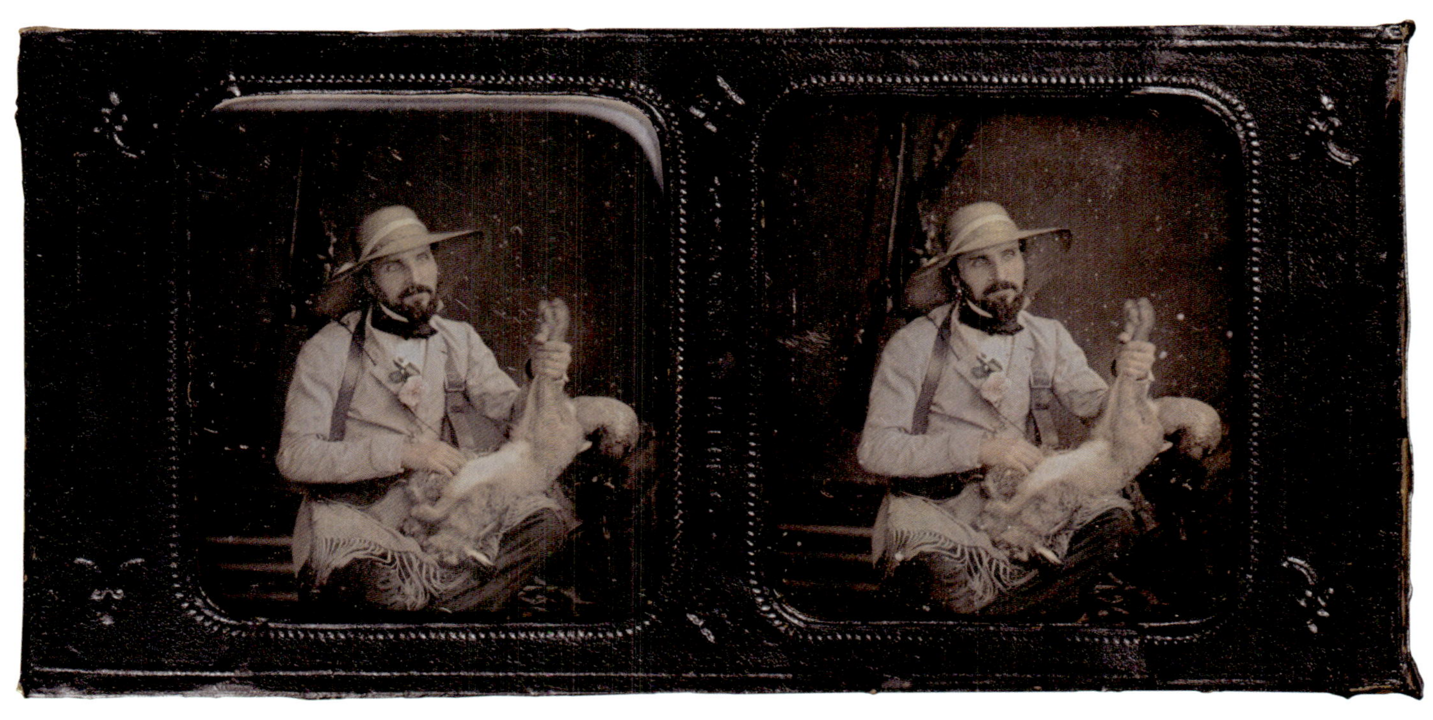

Warren T. Thompson
Selbstporträt als Jäger mit Hasen /
Self-portrait as hunter holding a hare, ca. 1855

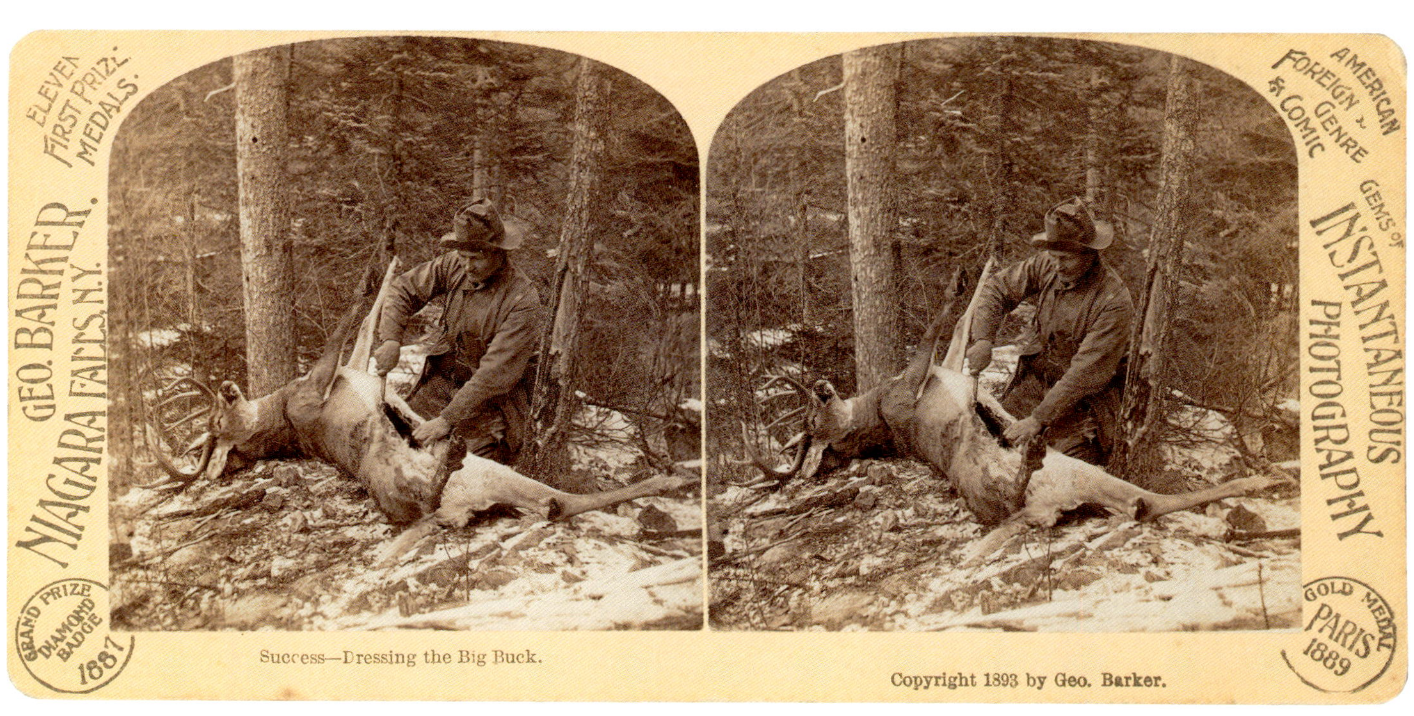

George Barker
Success – Dressing the Big Buck, 1893

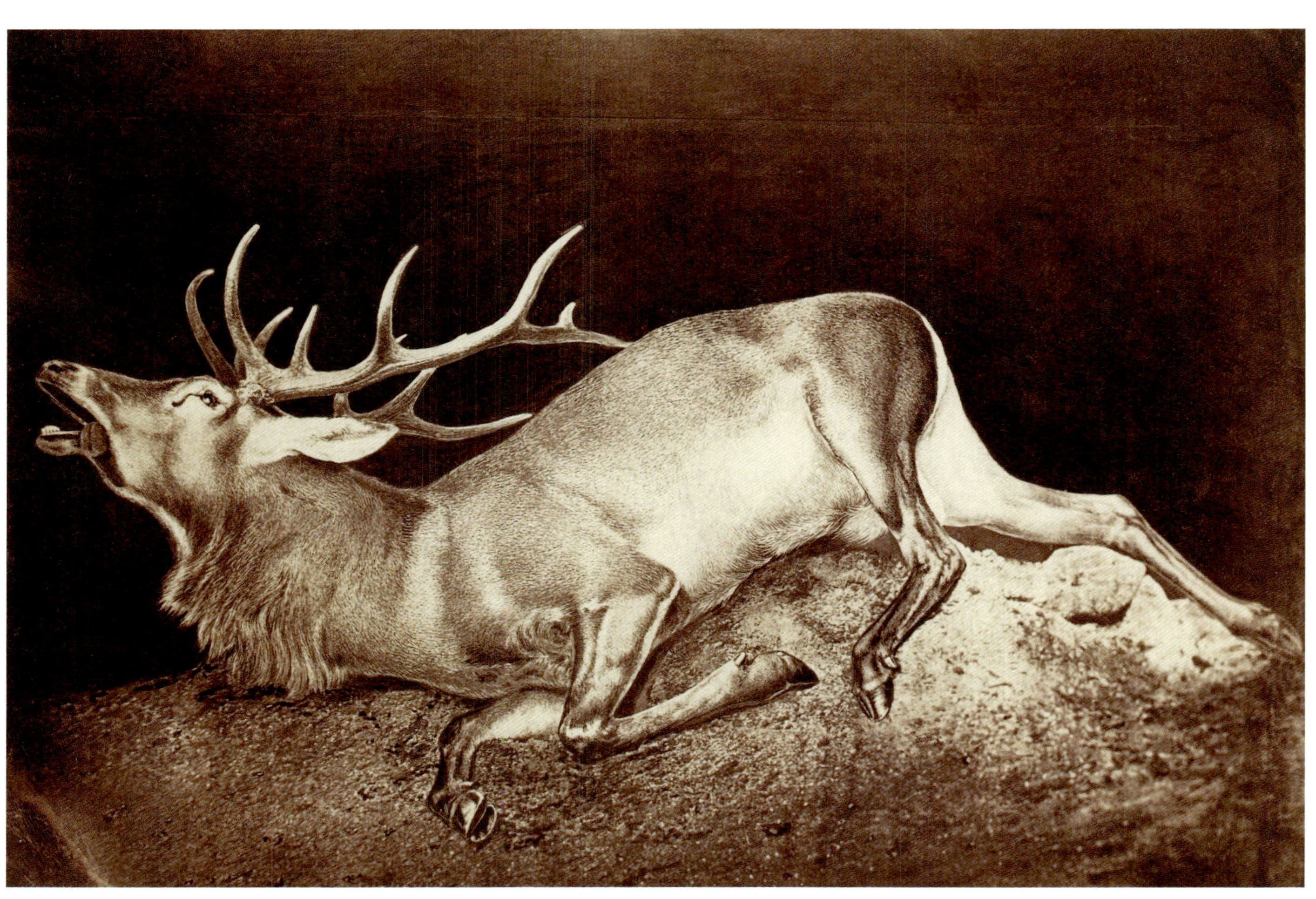

Anonym

Hirsch von 12 Enden, 470 pf. schwer, welcher am 18.9.1861 im Leonberger Stadtwald (Württemberg) durch einen Blattschuss erlegt und nach der Natur photographiert wurde /

Stag of twelve points, 470 pounds, shot through the shoulder to the heart on September 18, 1861 in the Leonberg municipal forest (Württemberg), photograph taken after nature

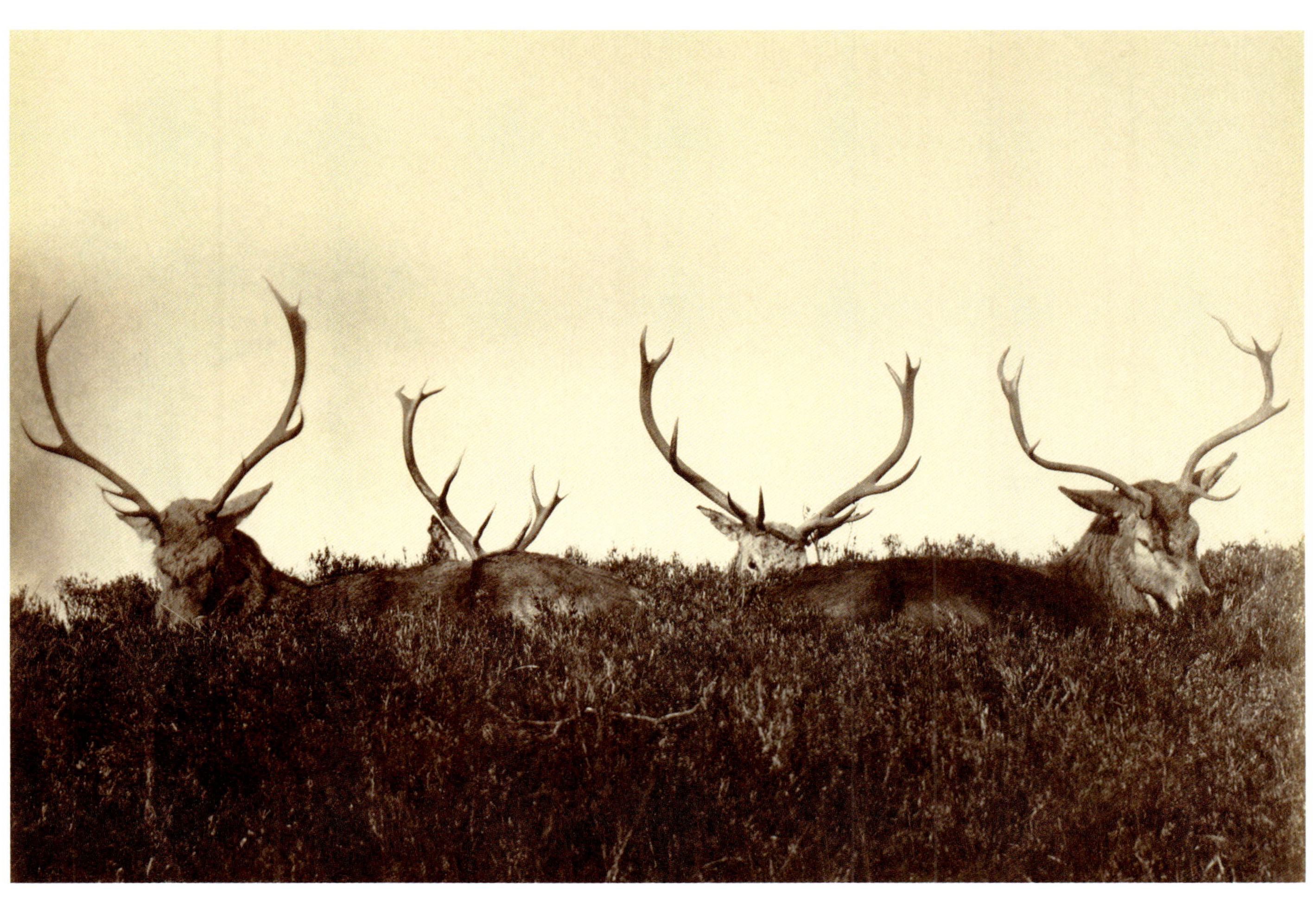

Horatio Ross

The Four Graces, ca. 1858

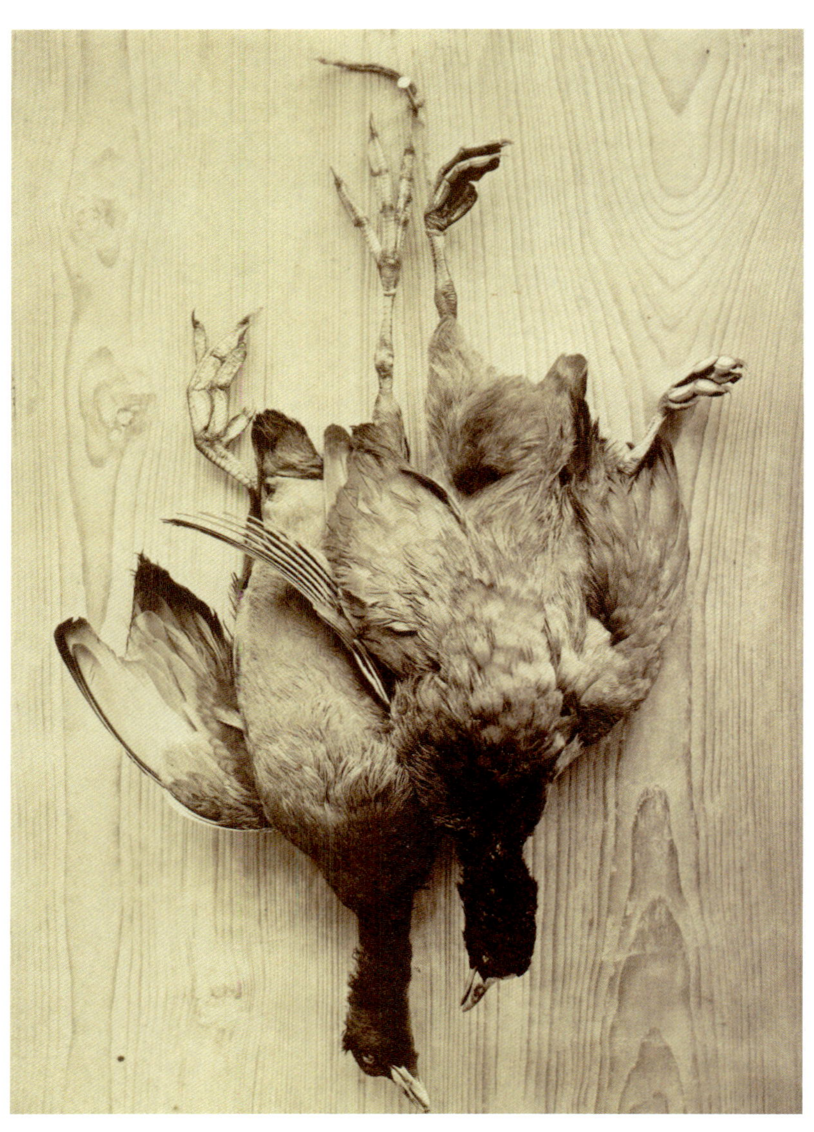

Julius Eduard Schindler

Graues Wasserhuhn – Taligula atra, 1867-1868

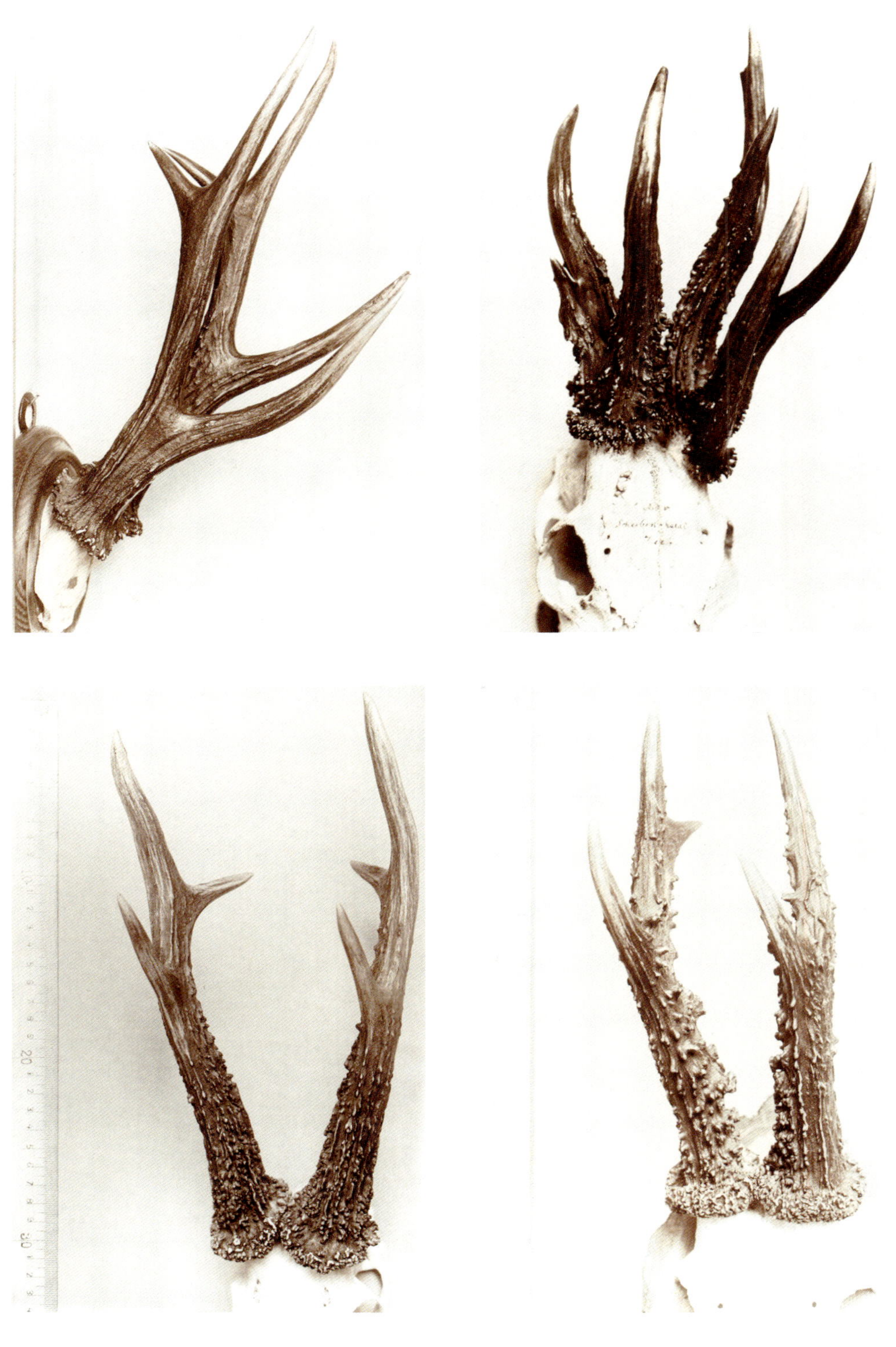

Karl Gerstner

Geweihe von *Capreolus capreolus*, vor 1920

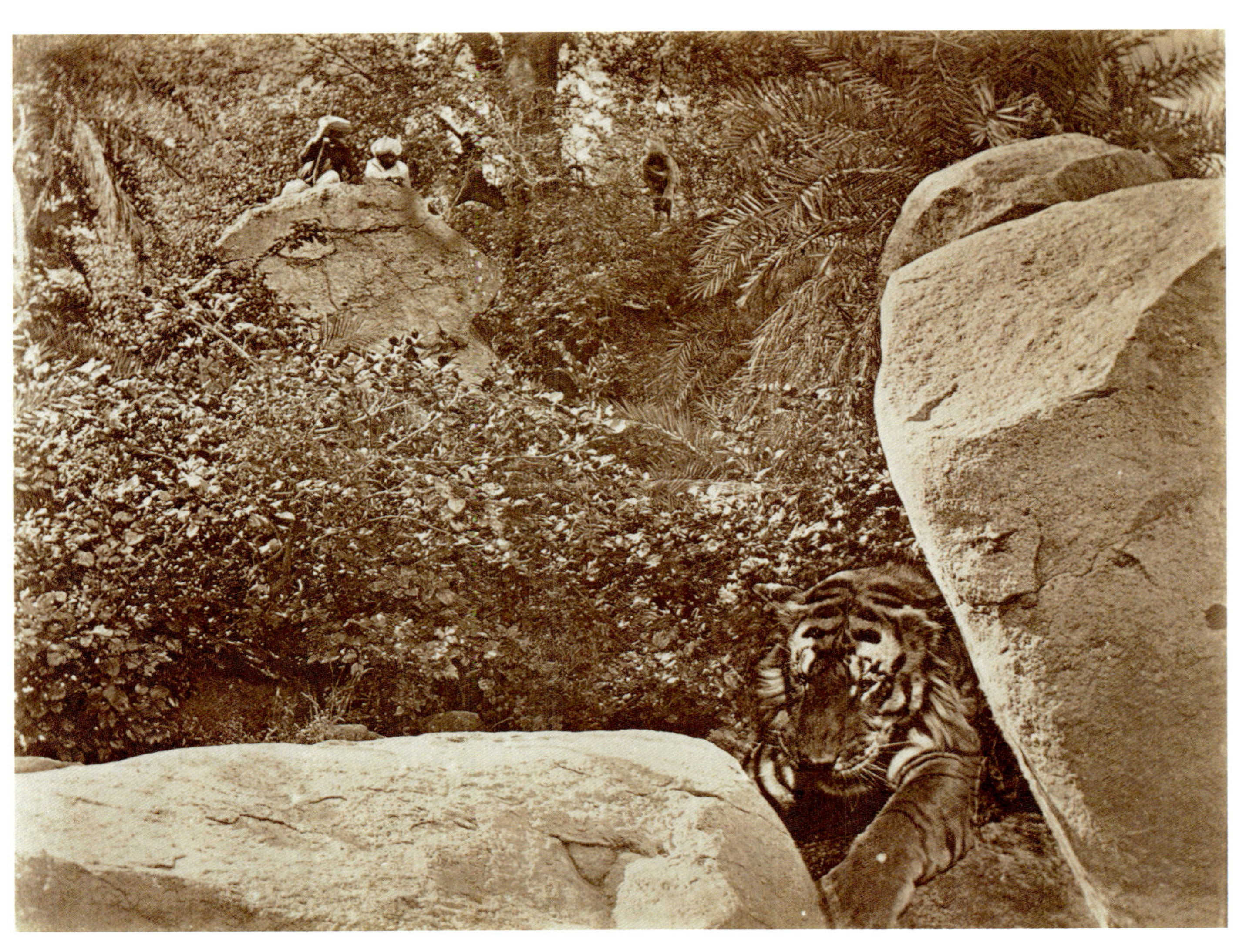

Willoughby Wallace Hooper

Tiger Hunt, Marked Down!, ca. 1872, a. d. Serie: *The Tiger Hunt*

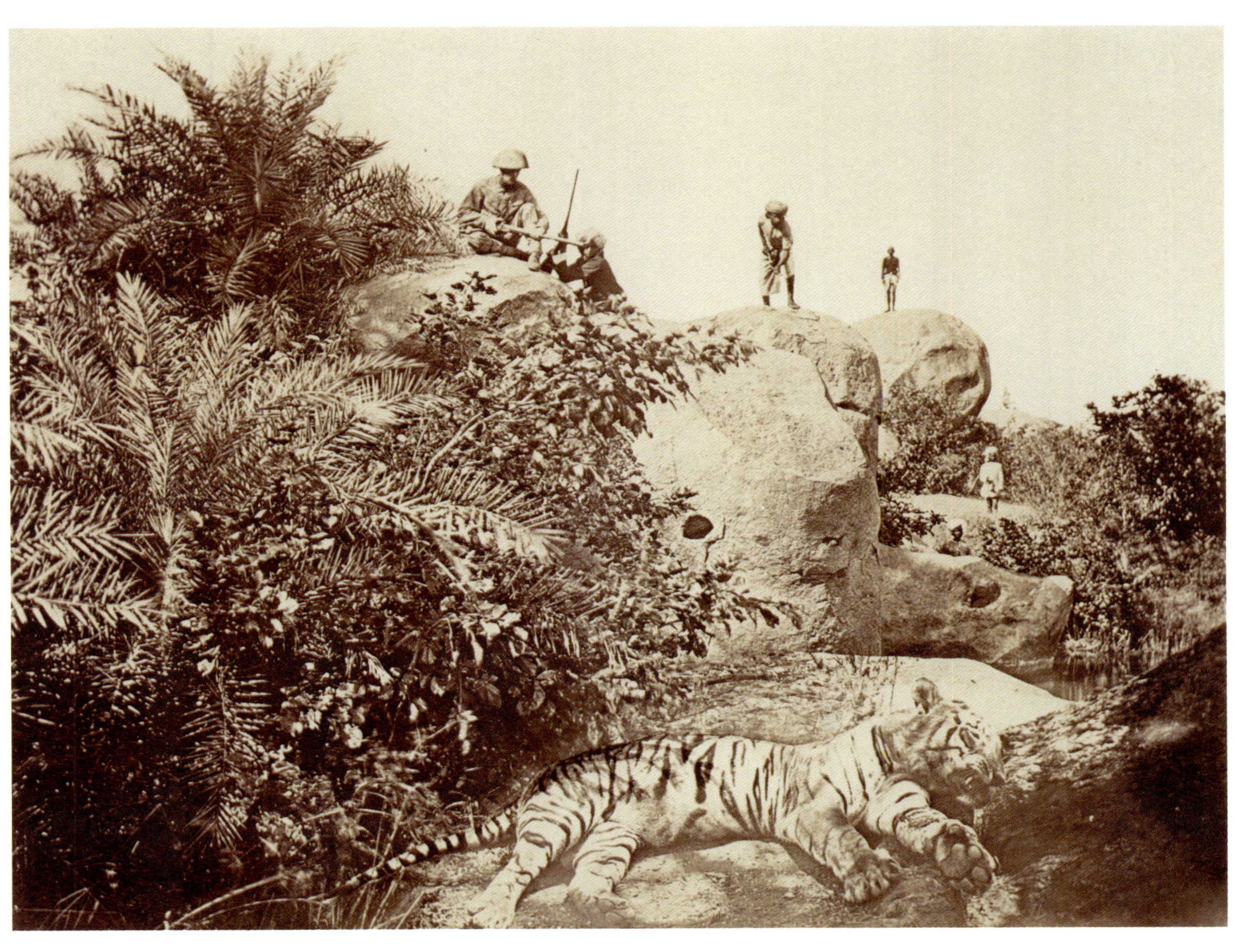

Tiger Hunt, Dead!

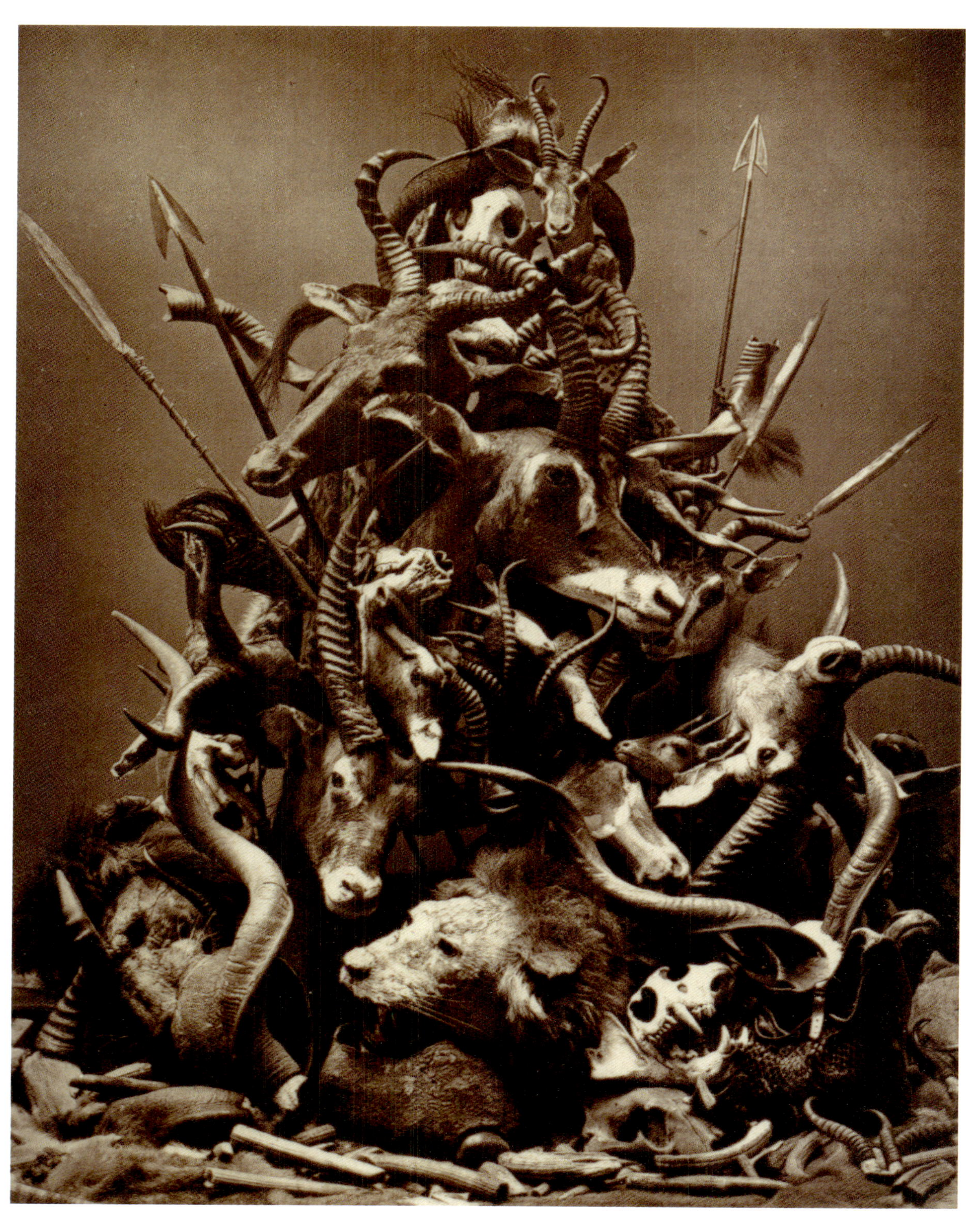

Arthur B. R. Myers

a. d. Buch: *Life with the Hamran Arabs*, London 1876

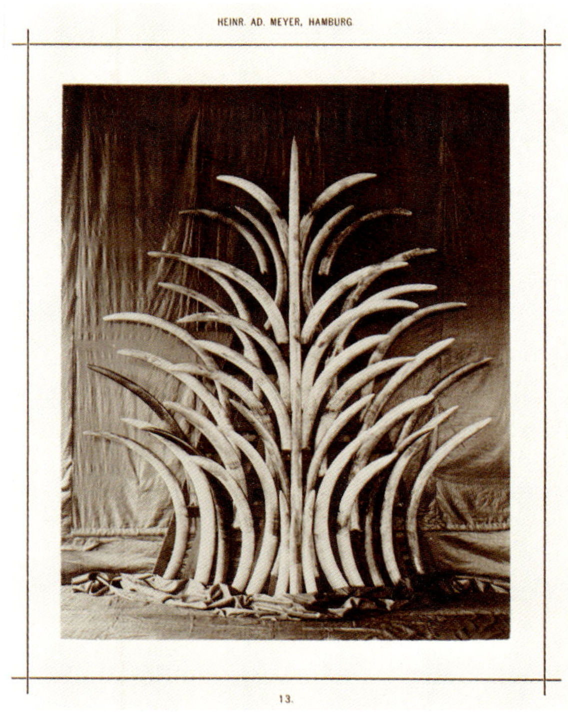

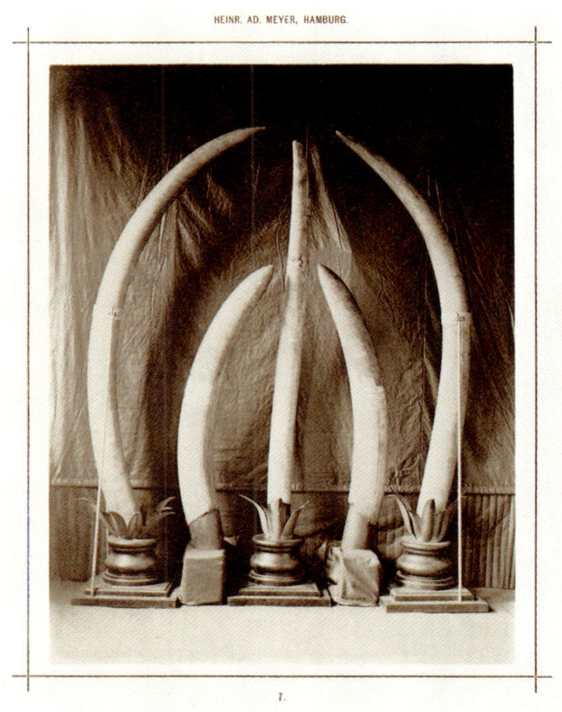

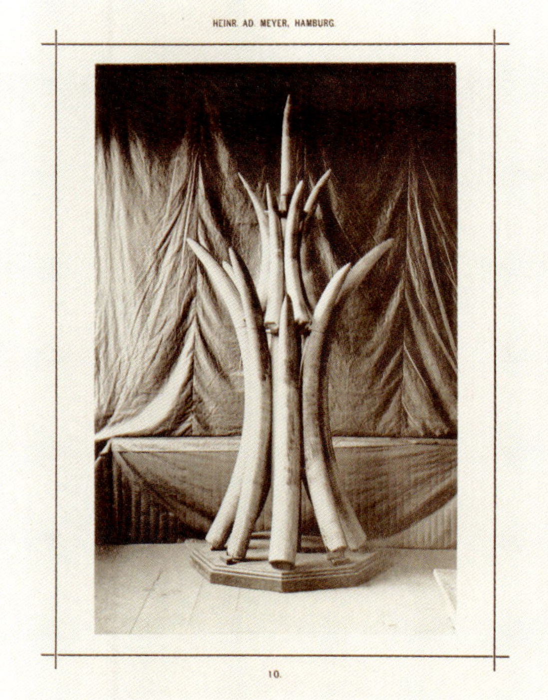

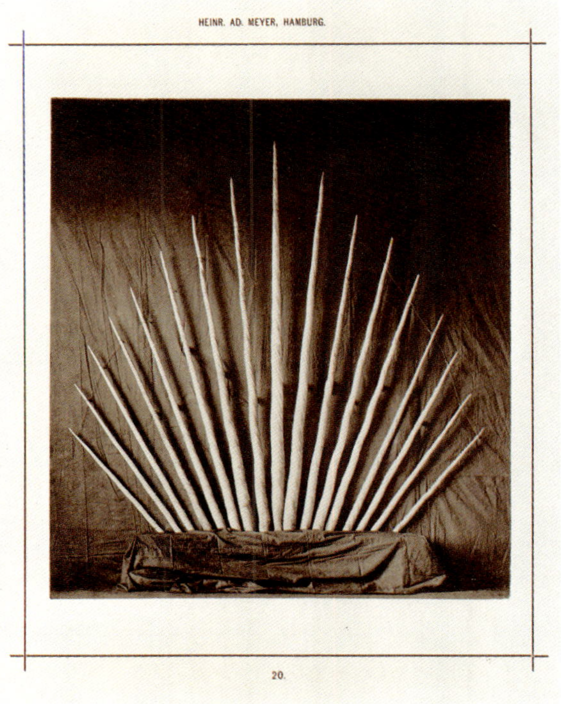

Strumper & Co.

a. d. Album der Firma Heinrich A. Meyer, ca. 1905

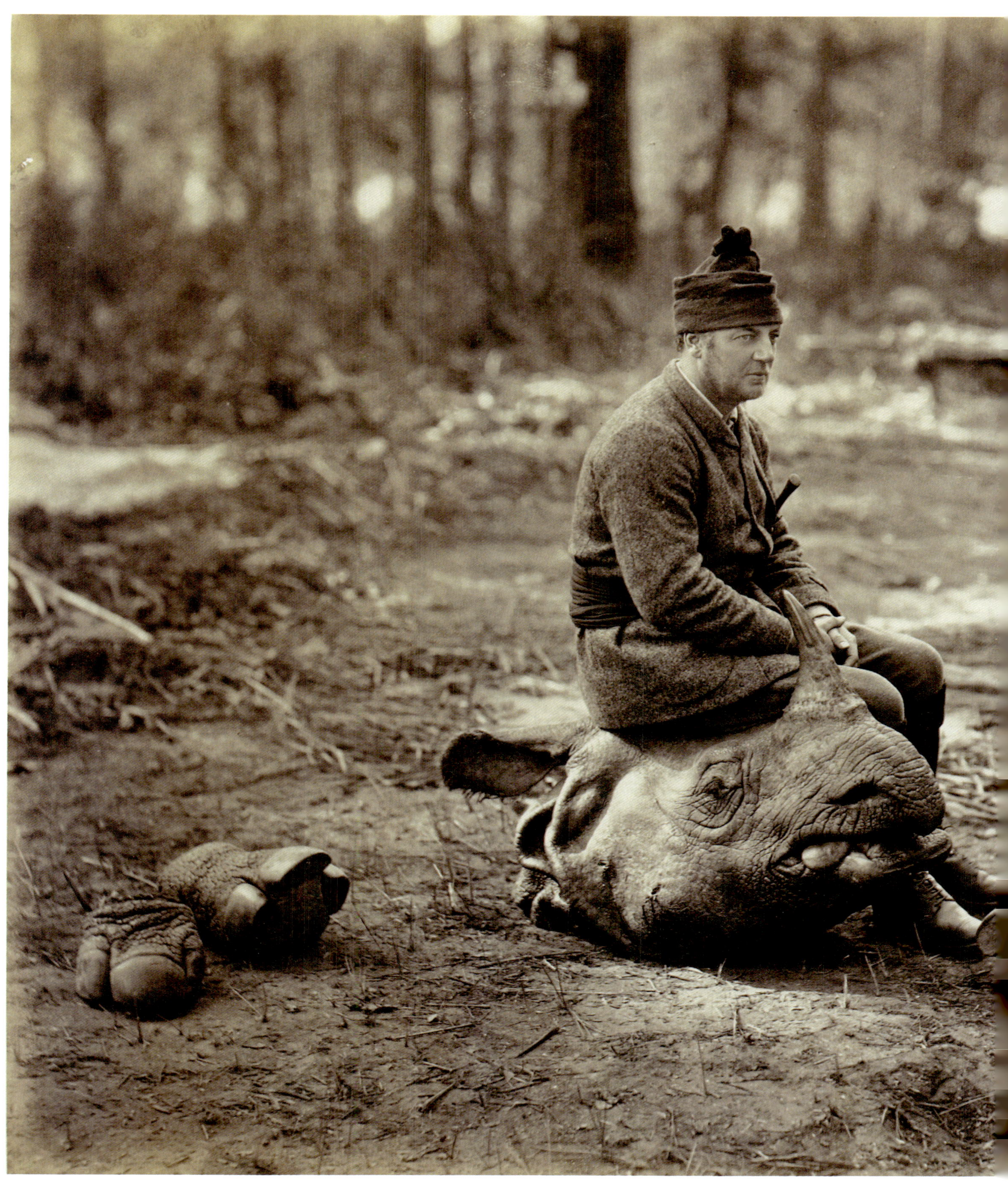

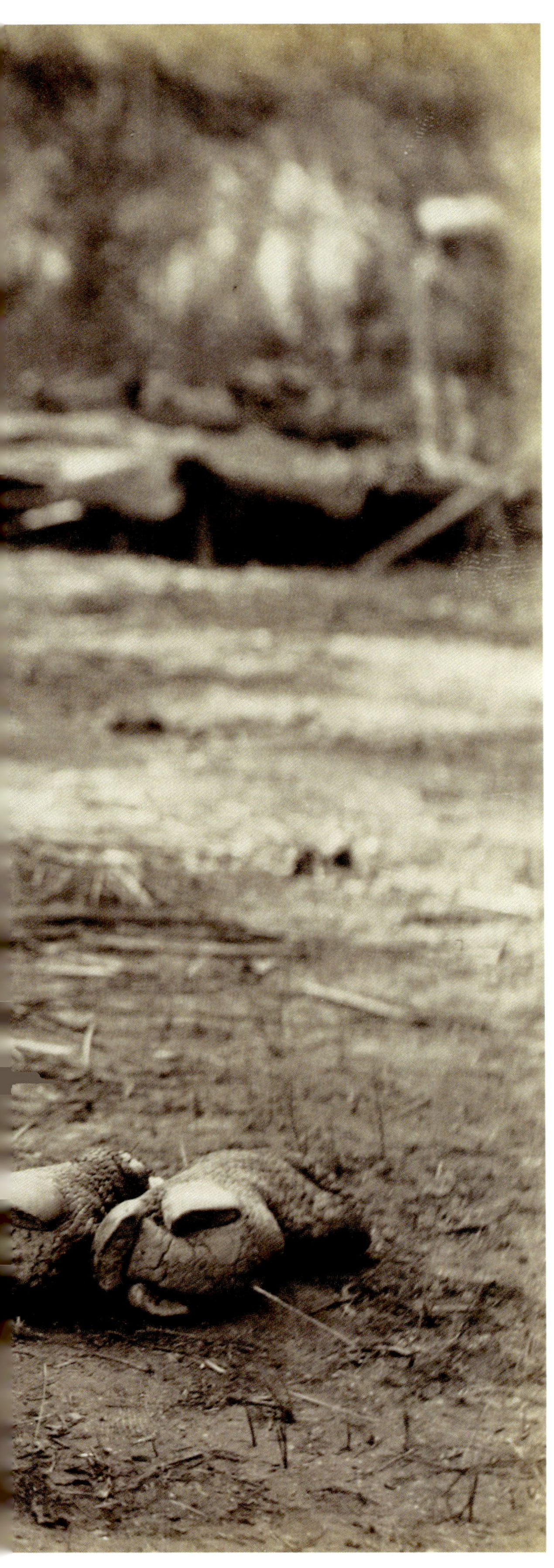

Anonym

Lord Charles Beresford, a. d. Album: *Nepaul*, 1883

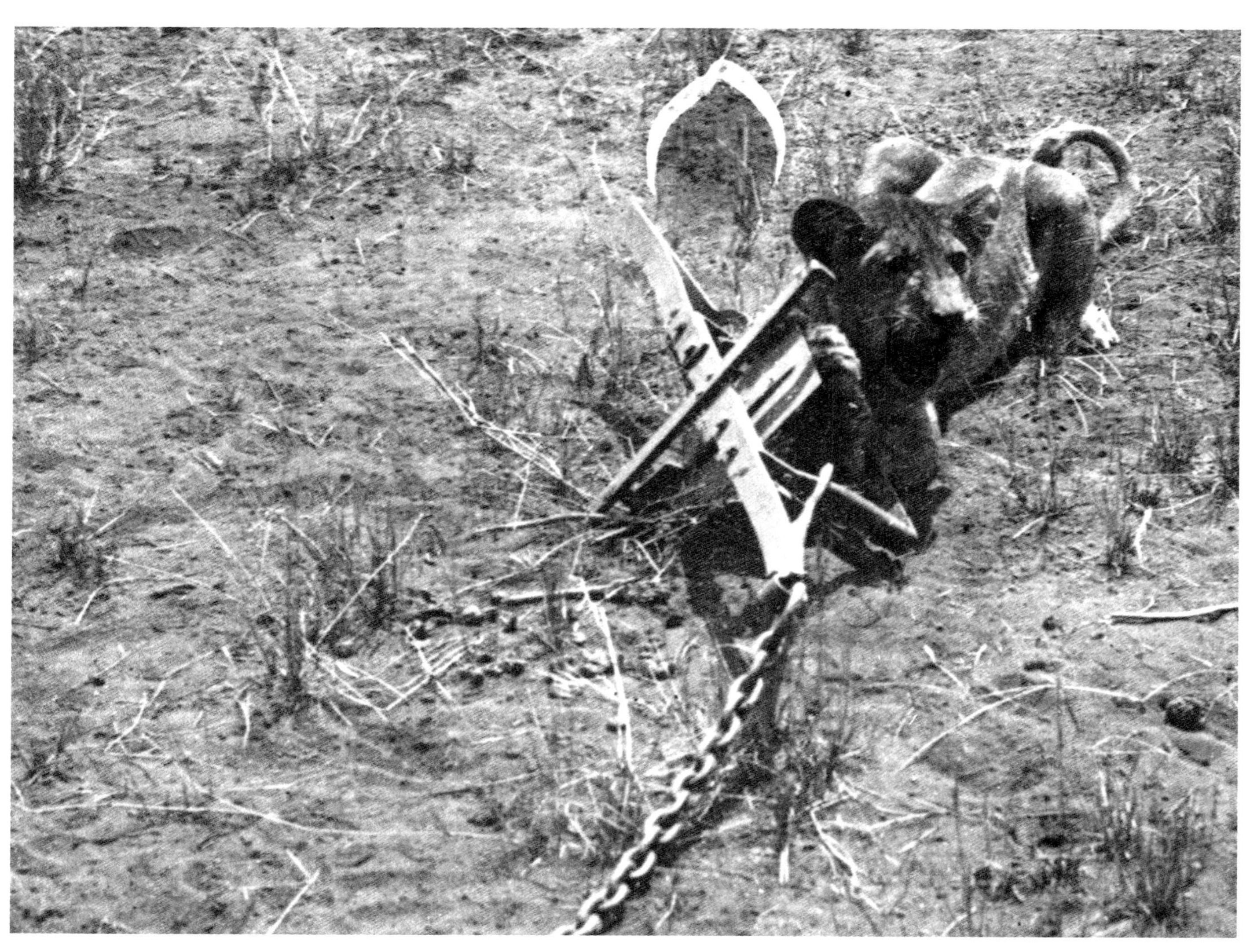

Carl Georg Schillings
Löwin in einer Falle /
lioness in a trap, ca. 1900

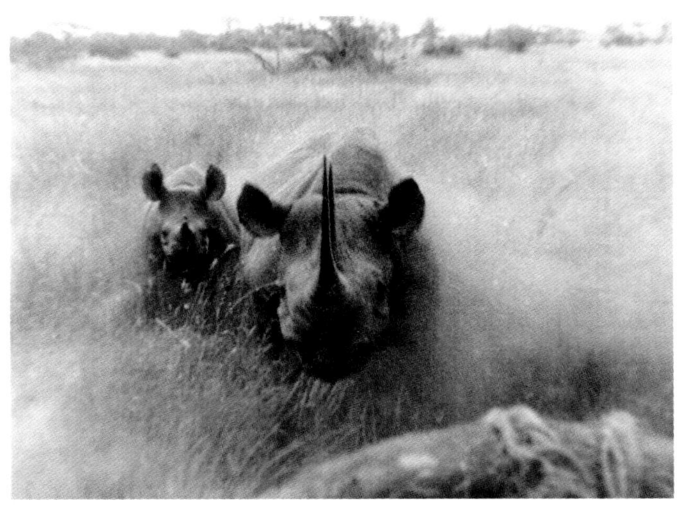

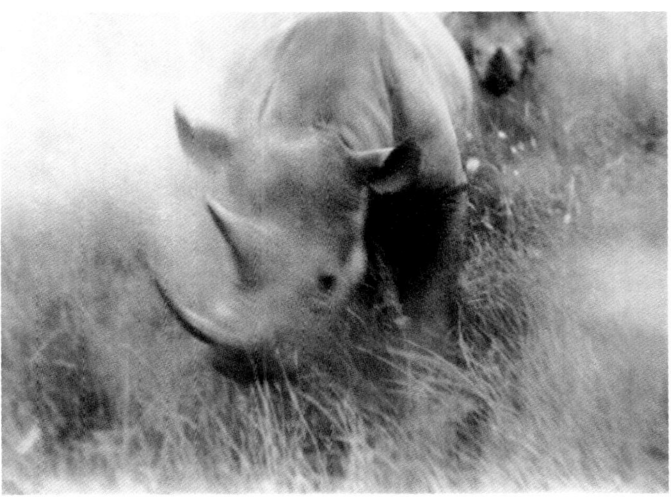

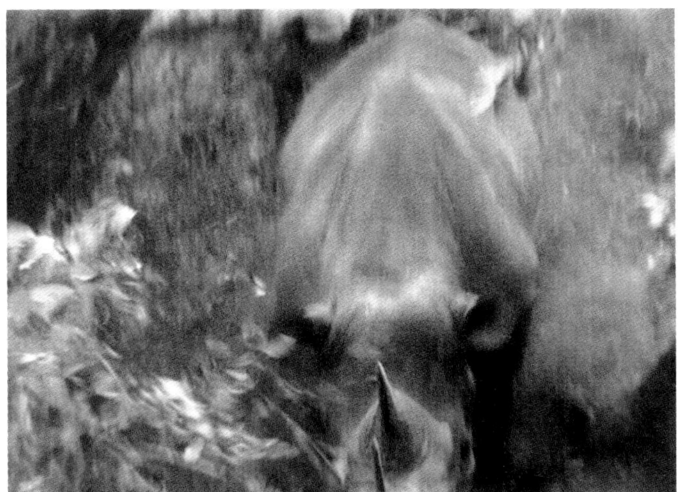

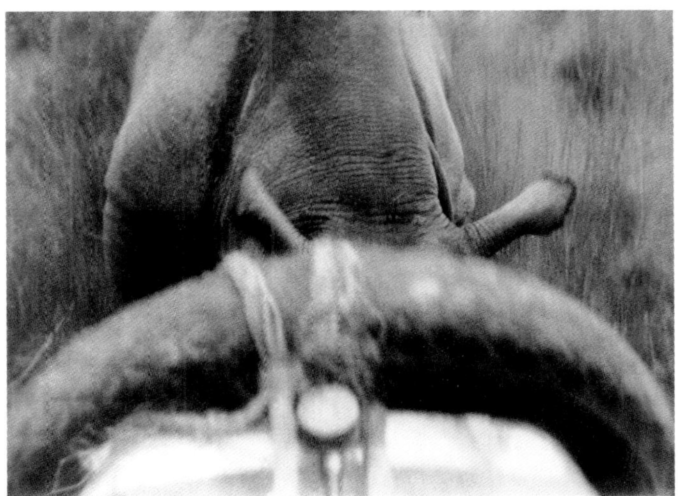

Wolfgang Weber

a. d. Reportage: *Ein Nashorn greift mein Auto an*, 1934

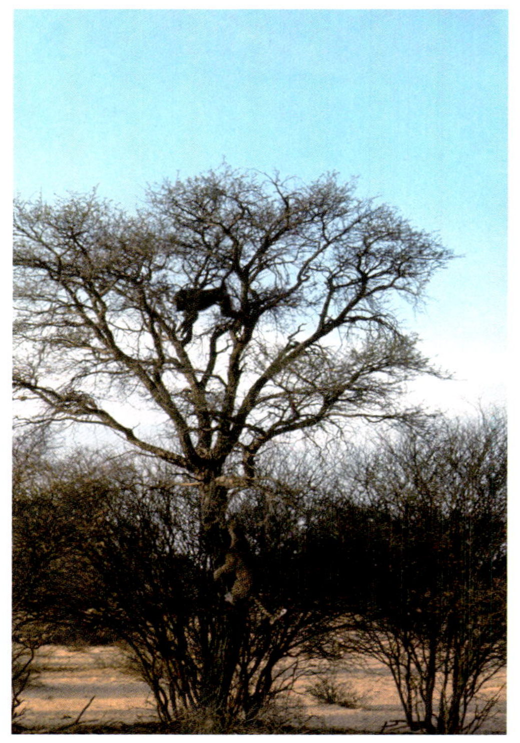
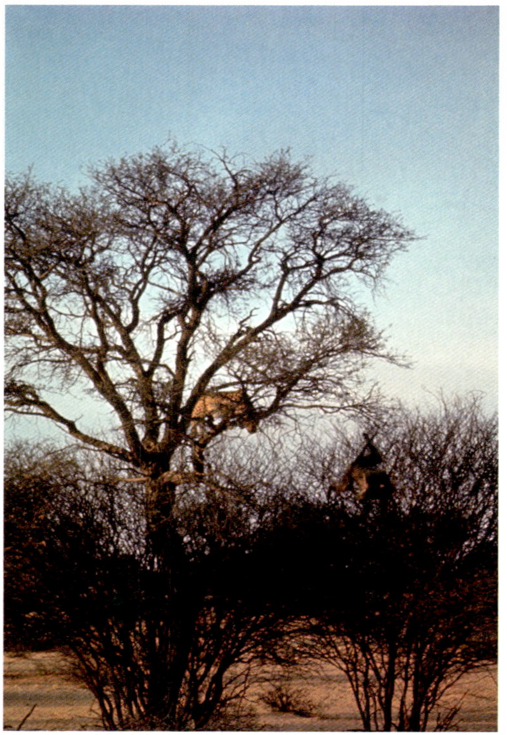
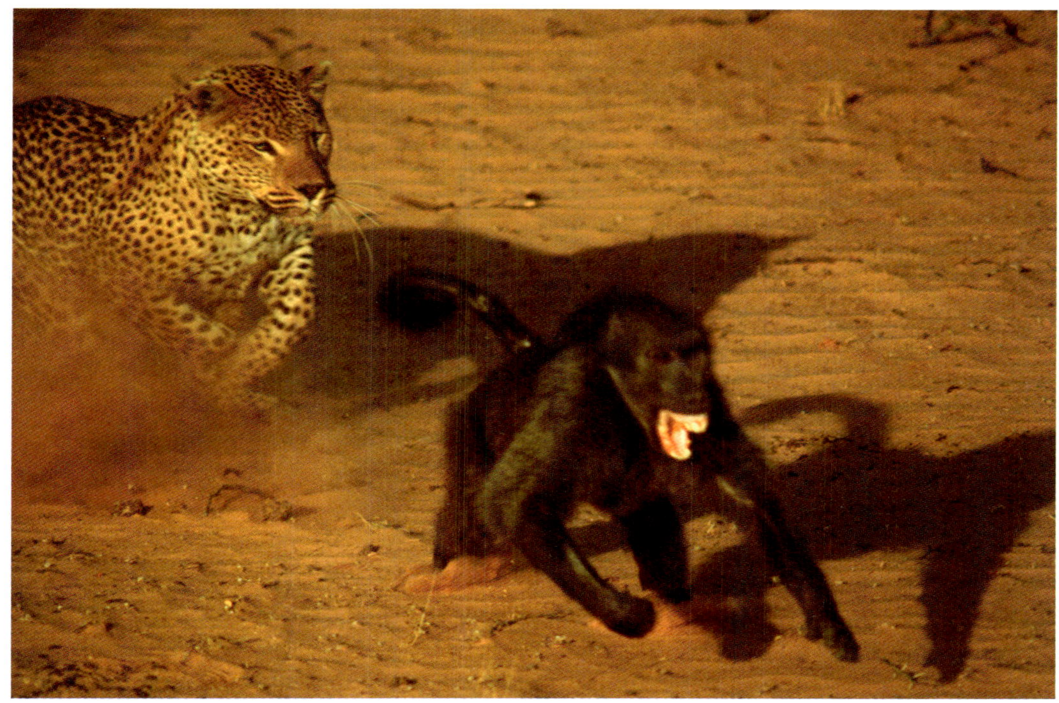

John Dominis

Leopard chasing a baboon, Botswana, Januar 1967

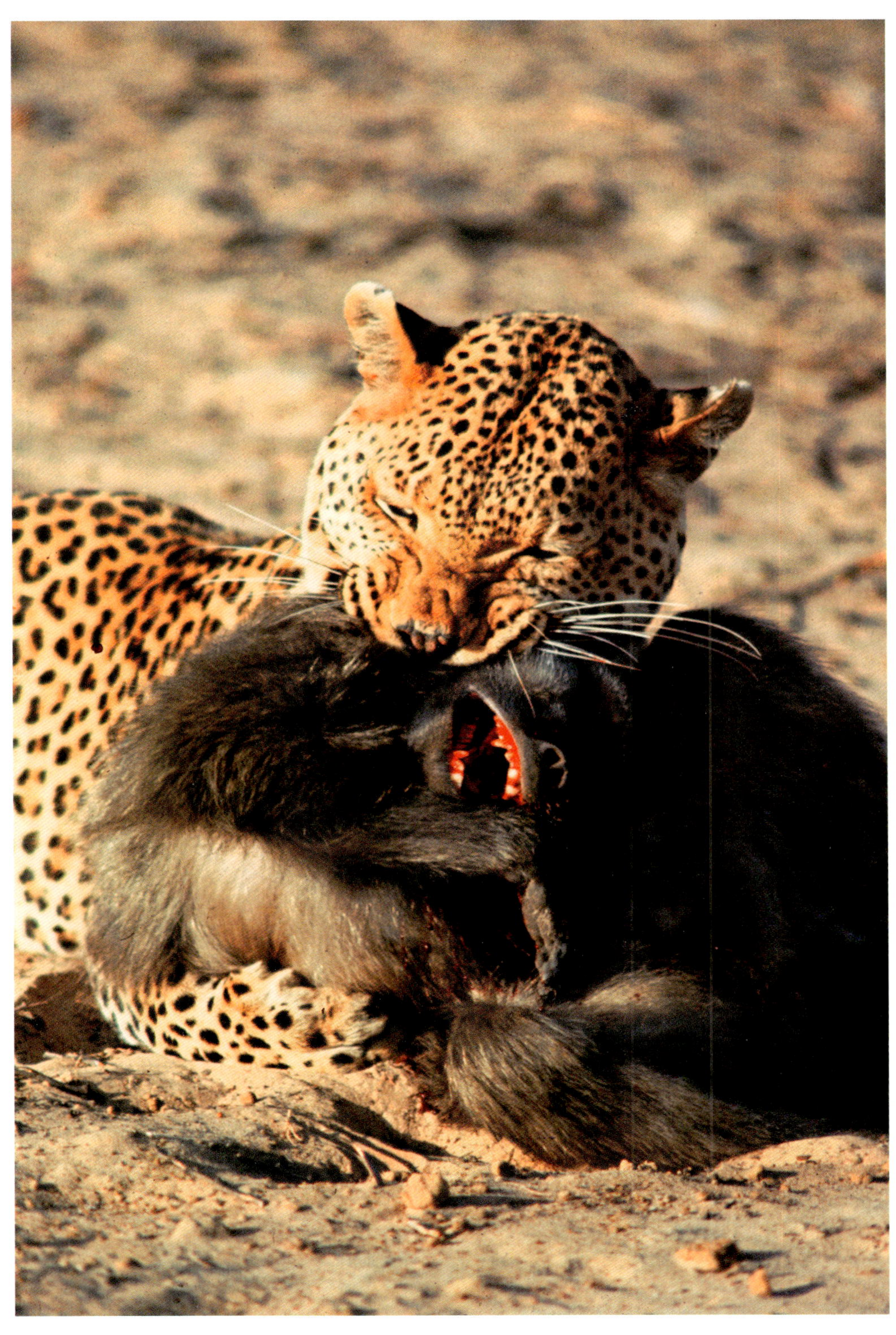

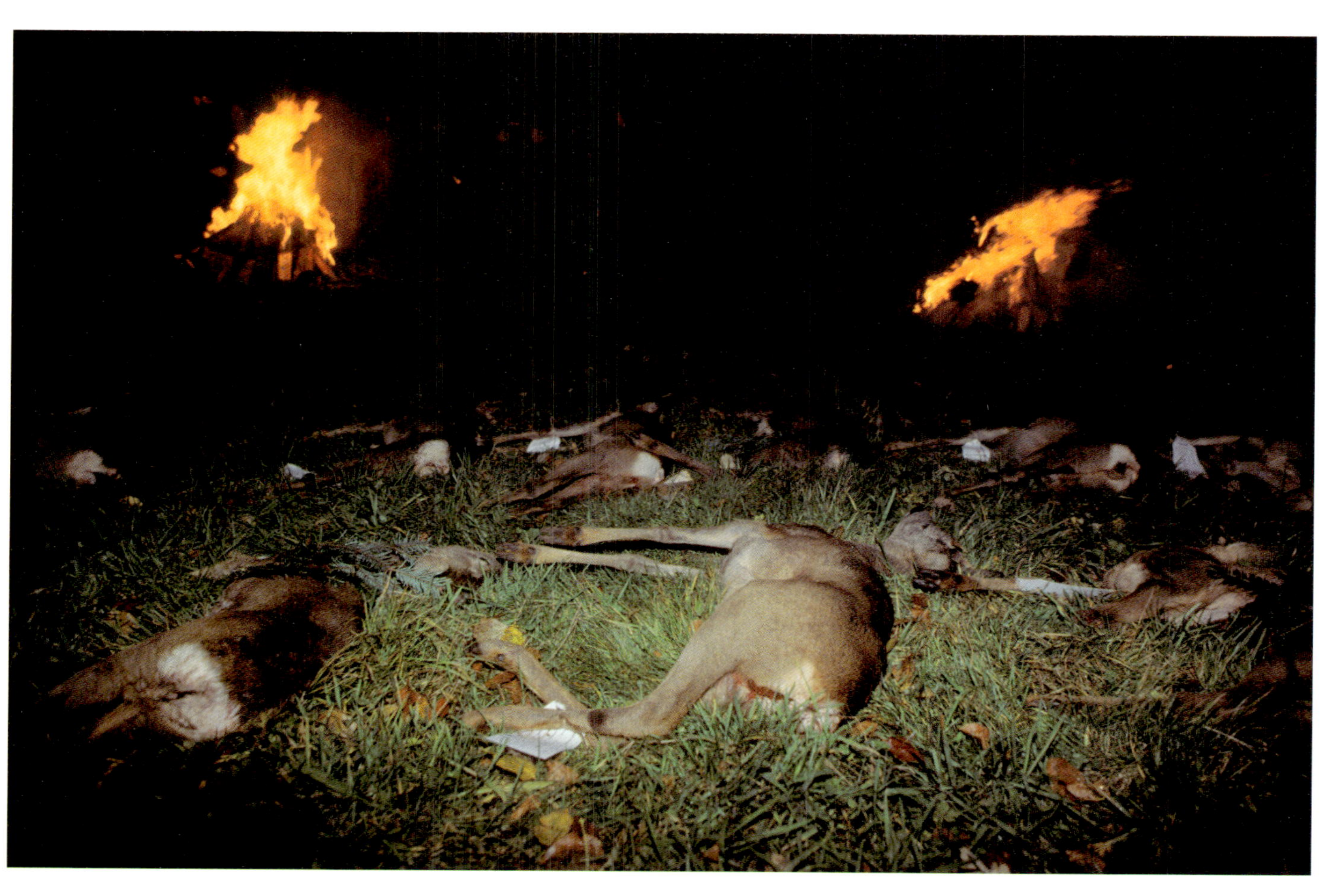

Walter Schmitz
Hunting, shot deers, 1992

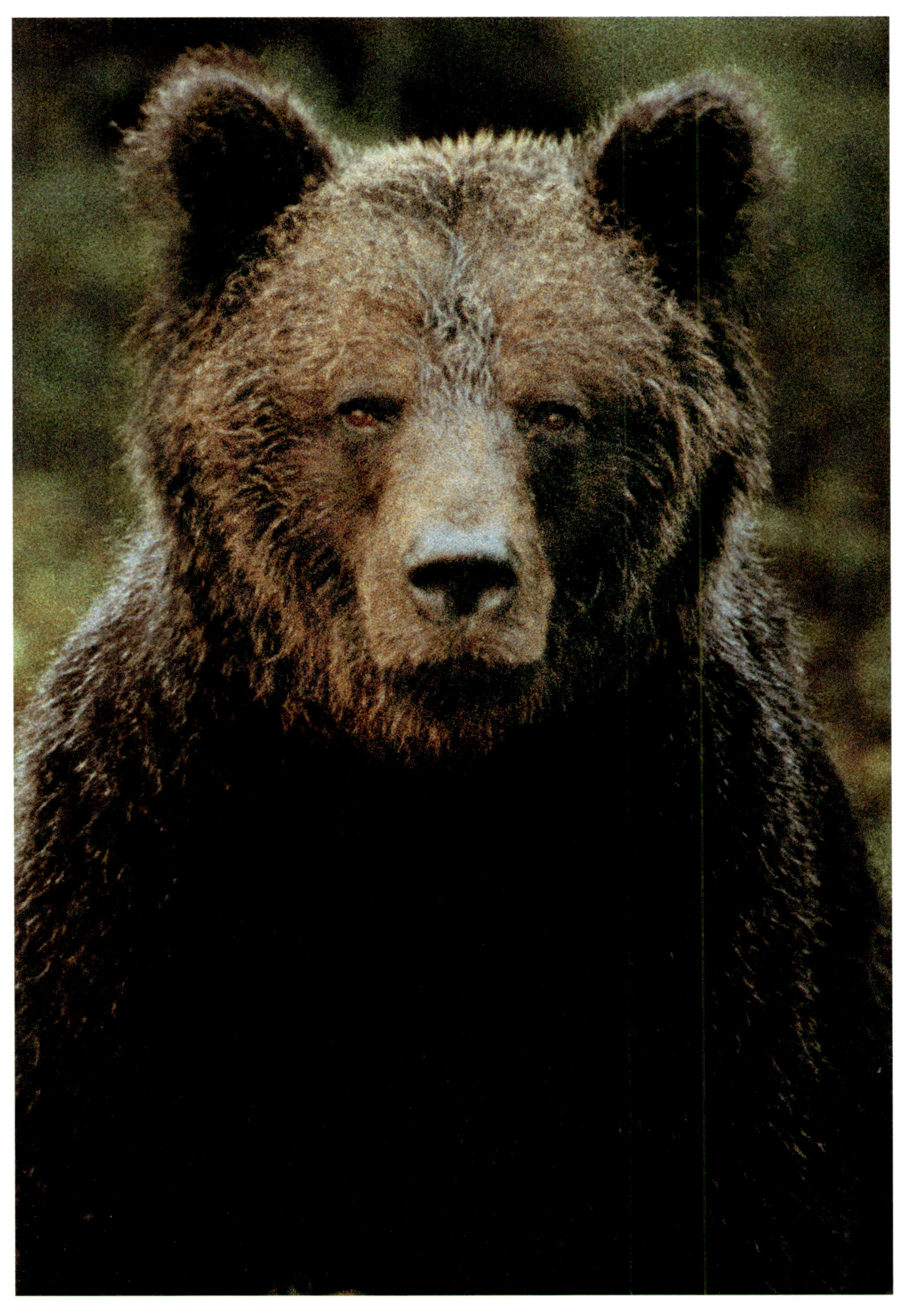

Juha Suonpää

Suomussalami, Finnland, 1991

„Die Fotografie eröffnete die Möglichkeit, die nur schwer zugänglichen visuellen Informationen vorhandener Präparate und Präparatsammlungen mit großer Genauigkeit einem größeren Publikum verfügbar zu machen.“

“Photography makes the rather inaccessible visual information provided by existing taxidermic specimens and specimen collections available to a larger audience and that with a great deal of precision.”

Hans-Jürgen Lechtreck

Studienobjekt Object of study

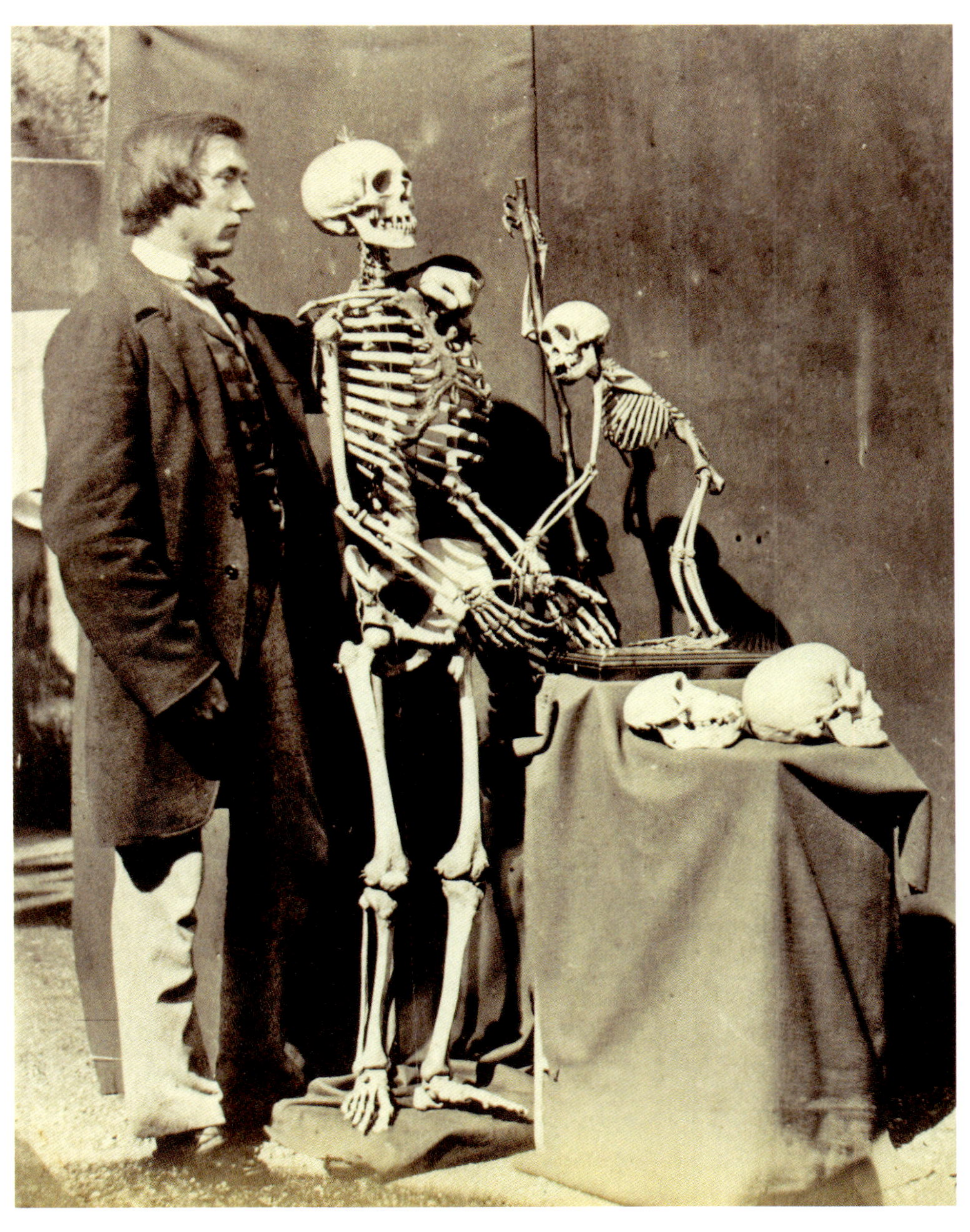

Lewis Carroll

Reginald Southey with Skeletons, 1857

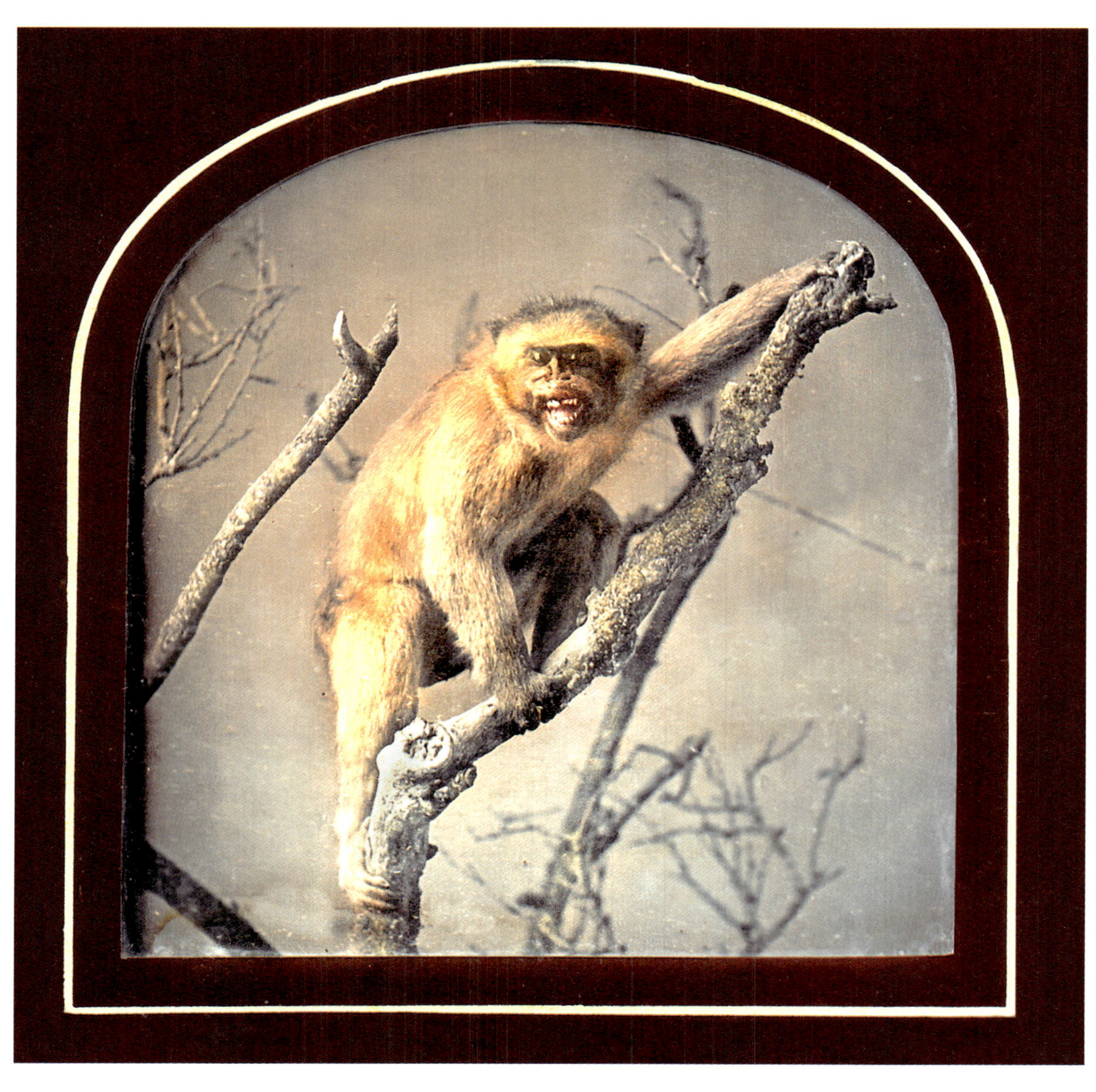

Warren T. Thompson
A Macaque in Aggressive Pose, 1853-1859

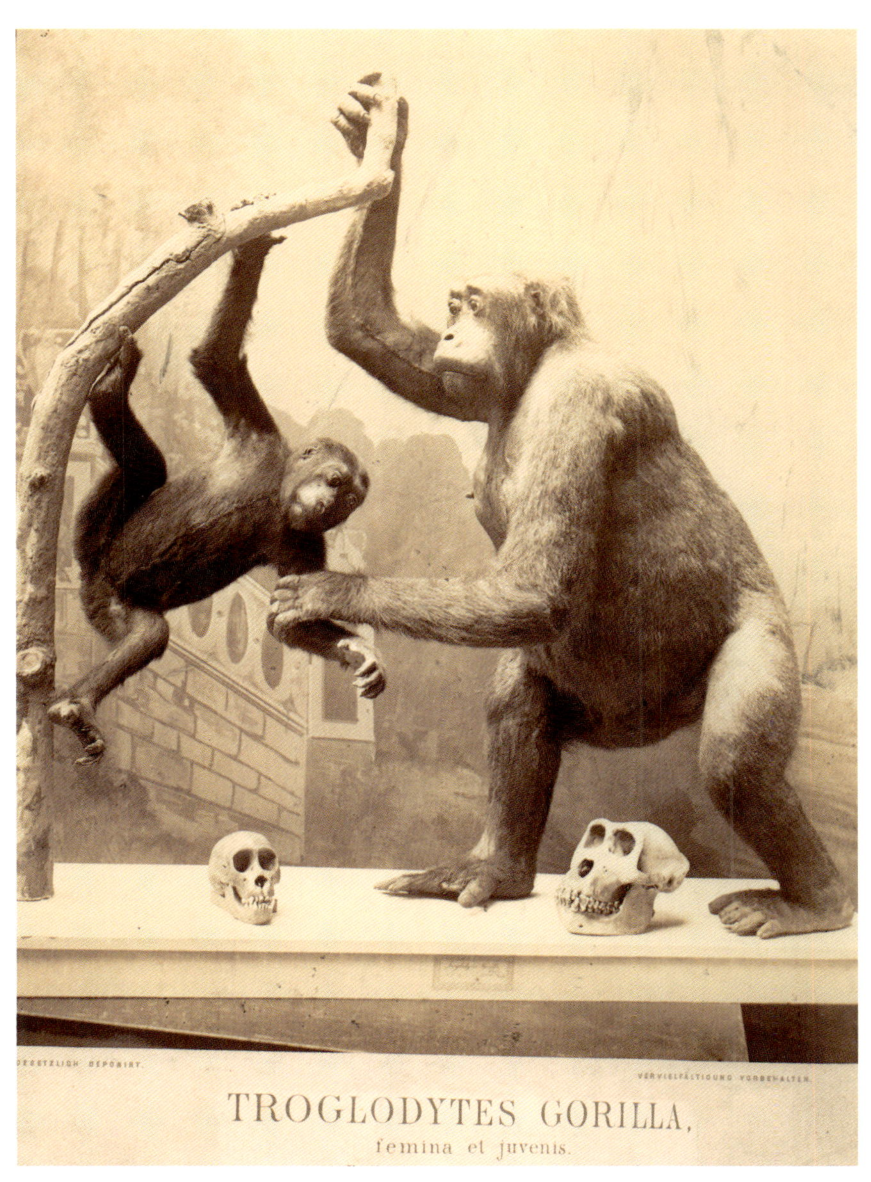

Johan Nöhring

Gorilla-Gruppe im Naturhistorischen Museum Lübeck, 1880er /

Group of gorillas in the Museum of Natural History, Lübeck, 1880s

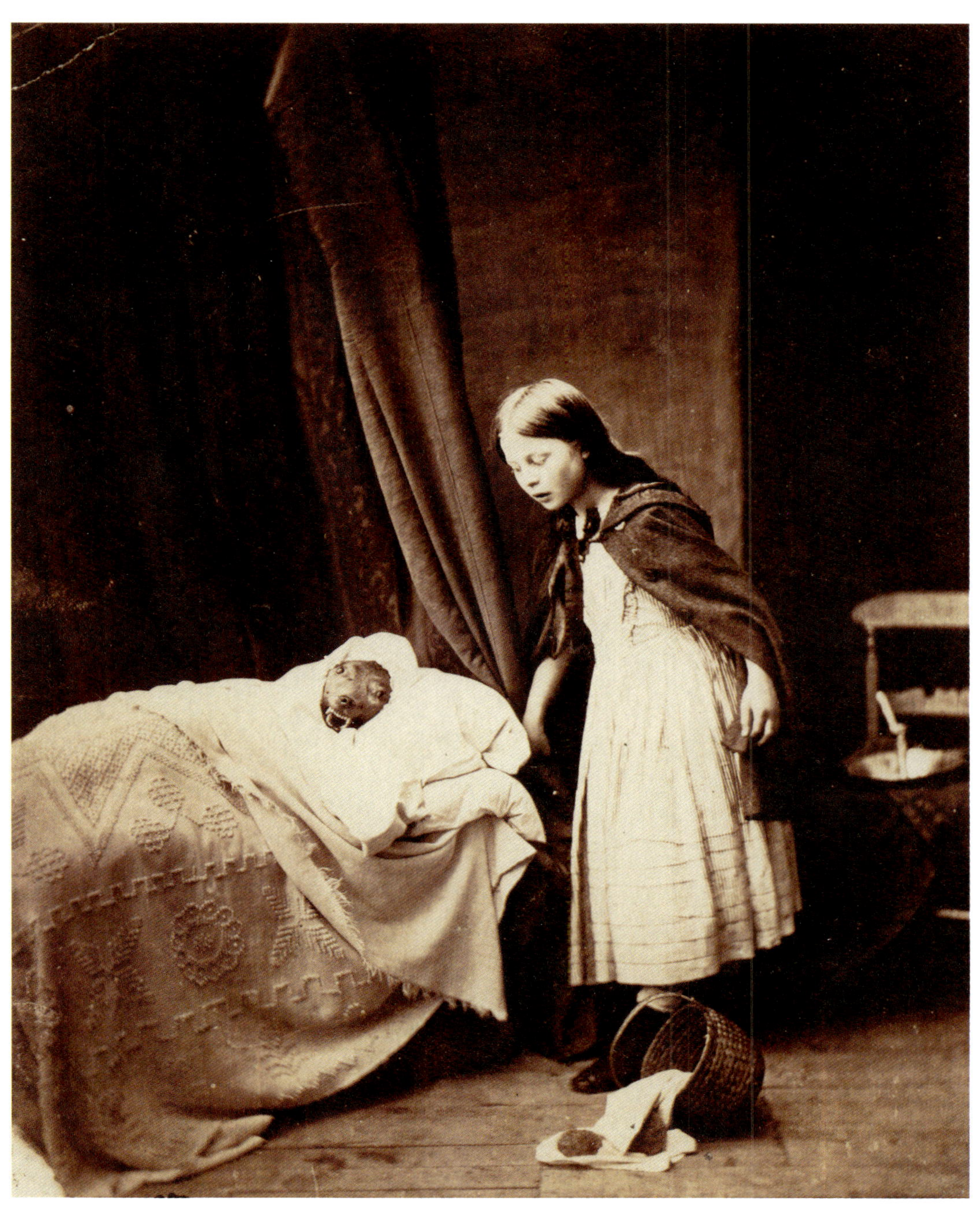

Henry Peach Robinson
Little Red Riding Hood, 1858

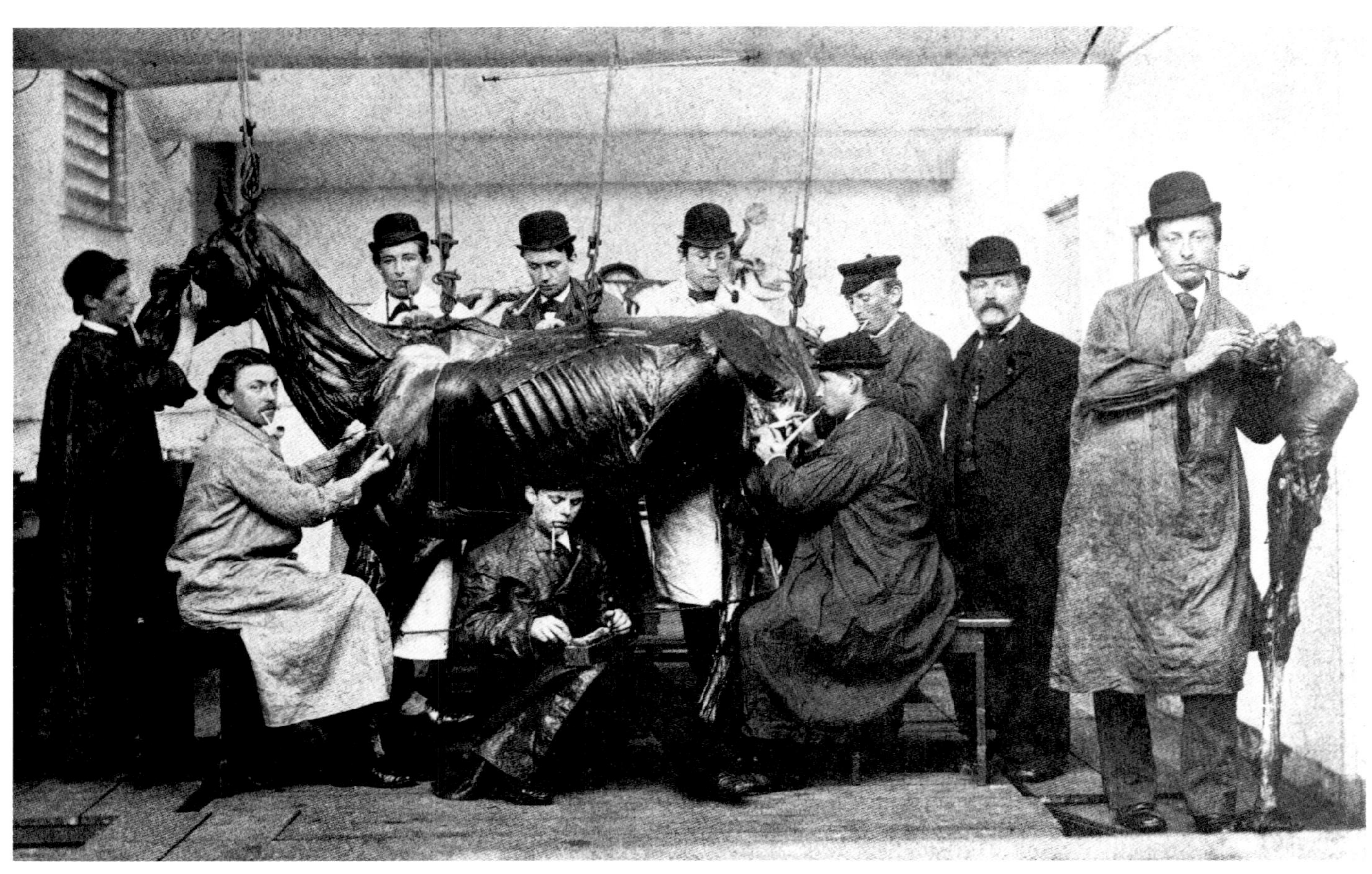

Anonym
Dozent A. F. Verhaar mit Studenten während einer Präparationsübung zur Anatomie des Pferdes an der Veterinärschule in Utrecht /
Lecturer A. F. Verhaar with students during a dissection lesson on the anatomy of the horse at the School of Veterinary Medicine in Utrecht, 1879

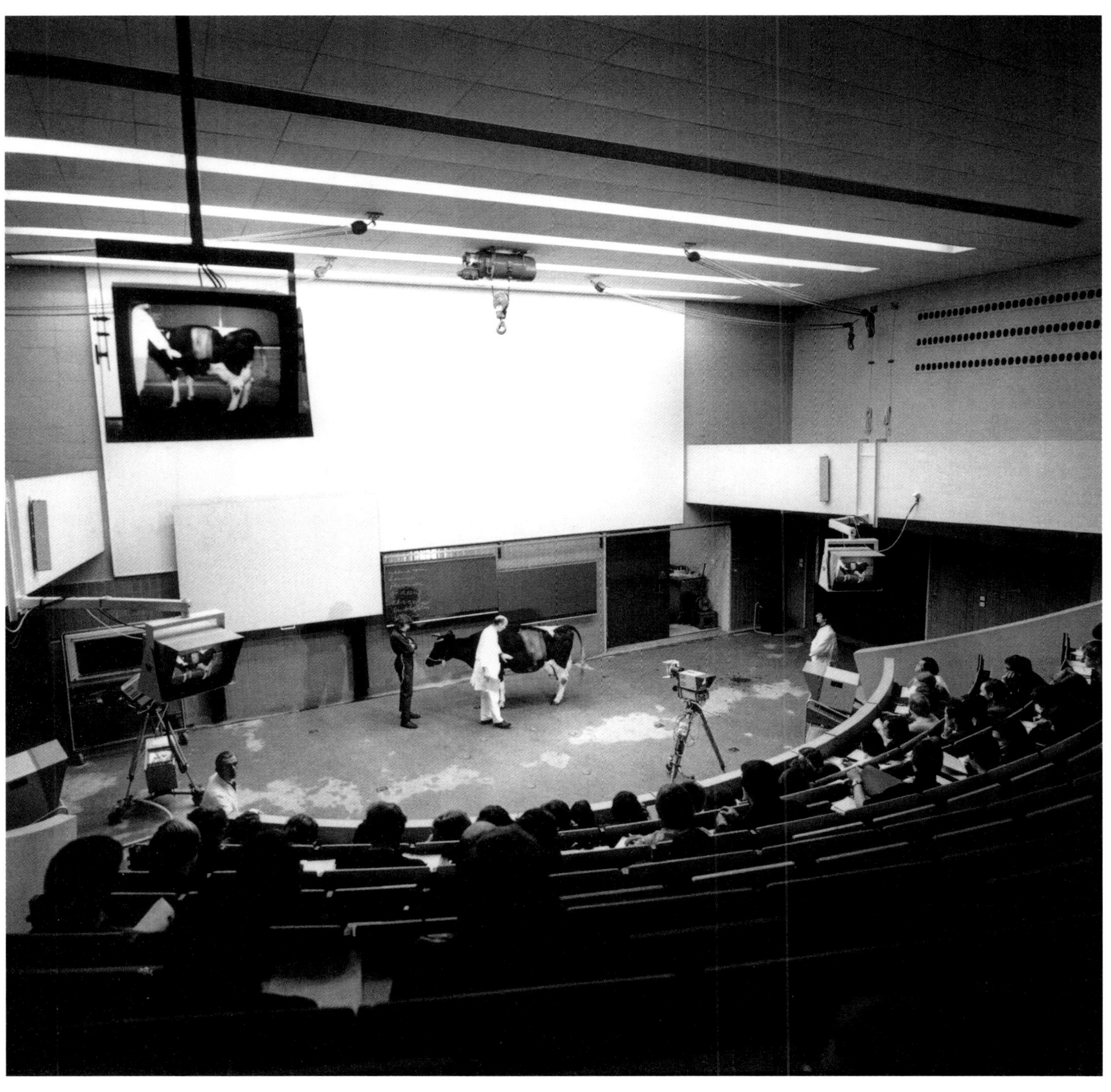

Cas Oorthuys
Faculty of veterinary science, University Utrecht, 1962

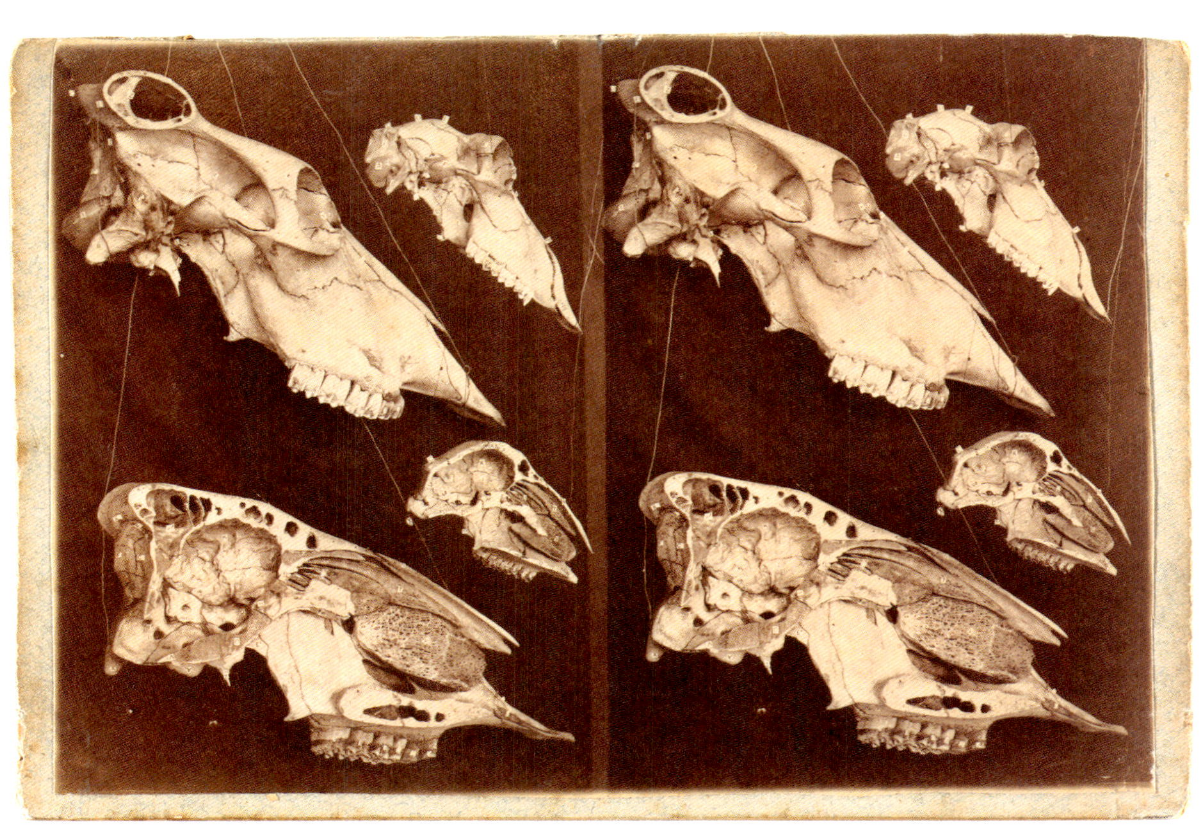

Anonym

Zoologisches Präparat, Pferd /

Zoological preparation, horse, ca. 1890

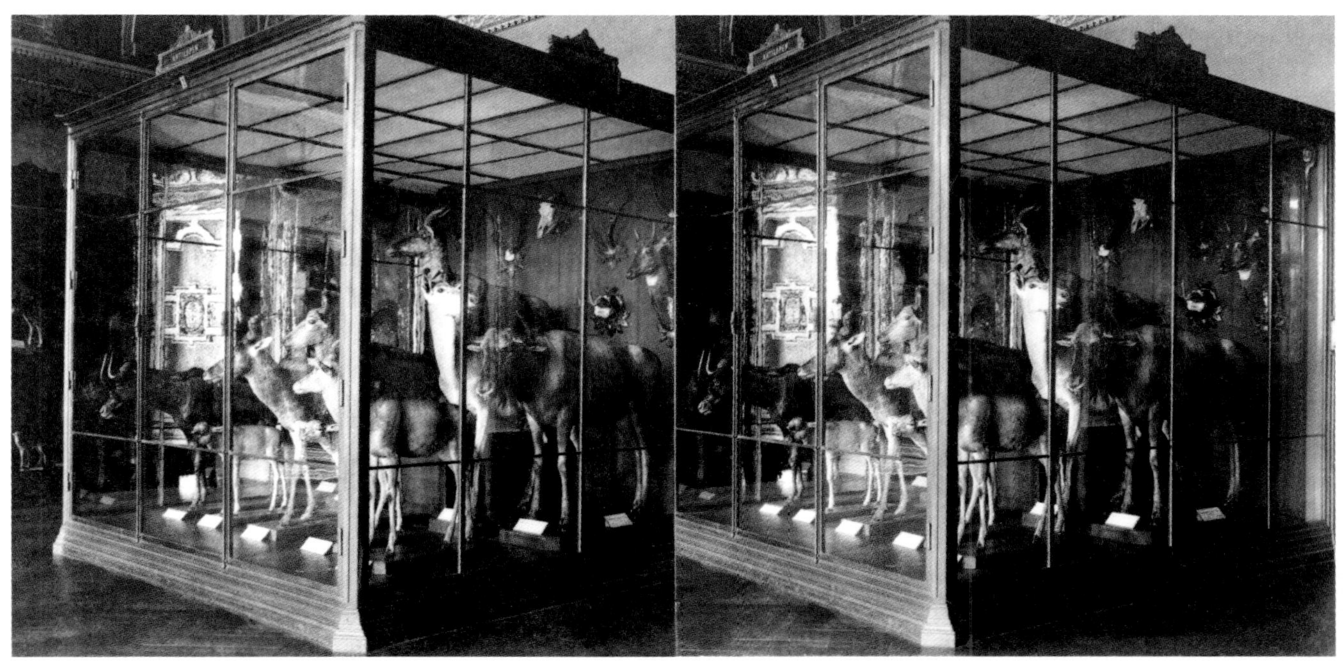

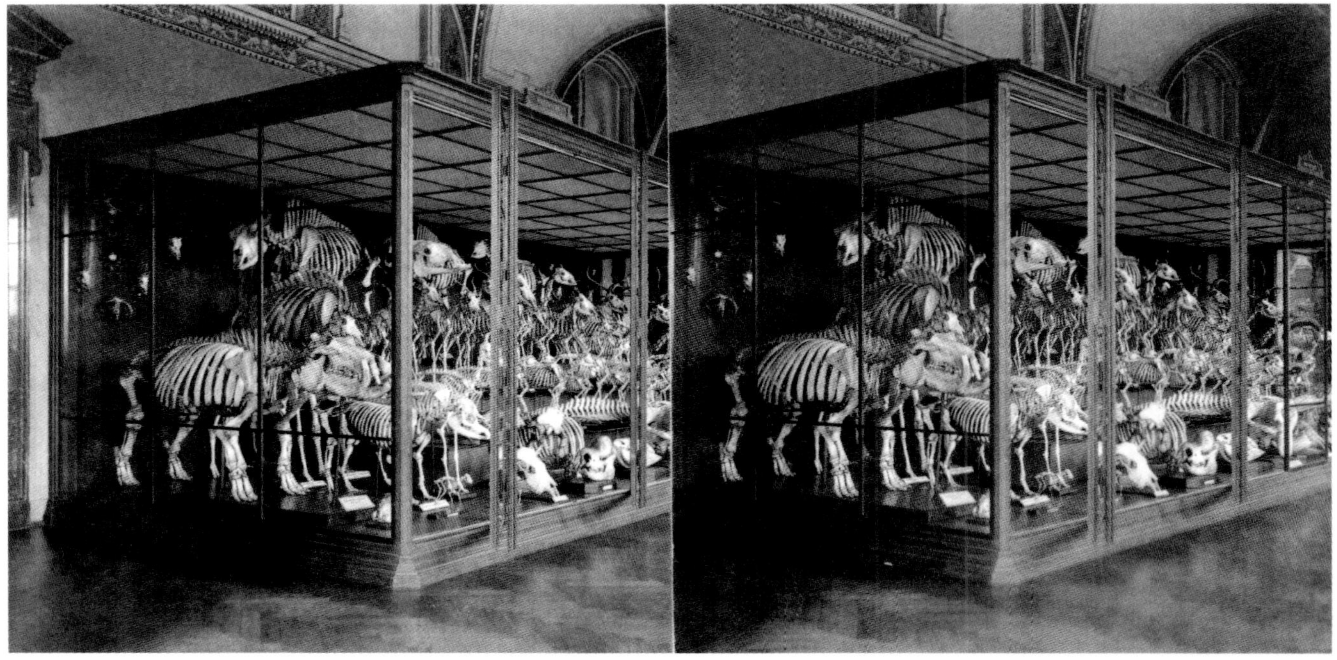

Ludwig Grillich

Naturhistorisches Hof-Museum Wien, Säugetiervitrinen / display cases for mammals, ca. 1890

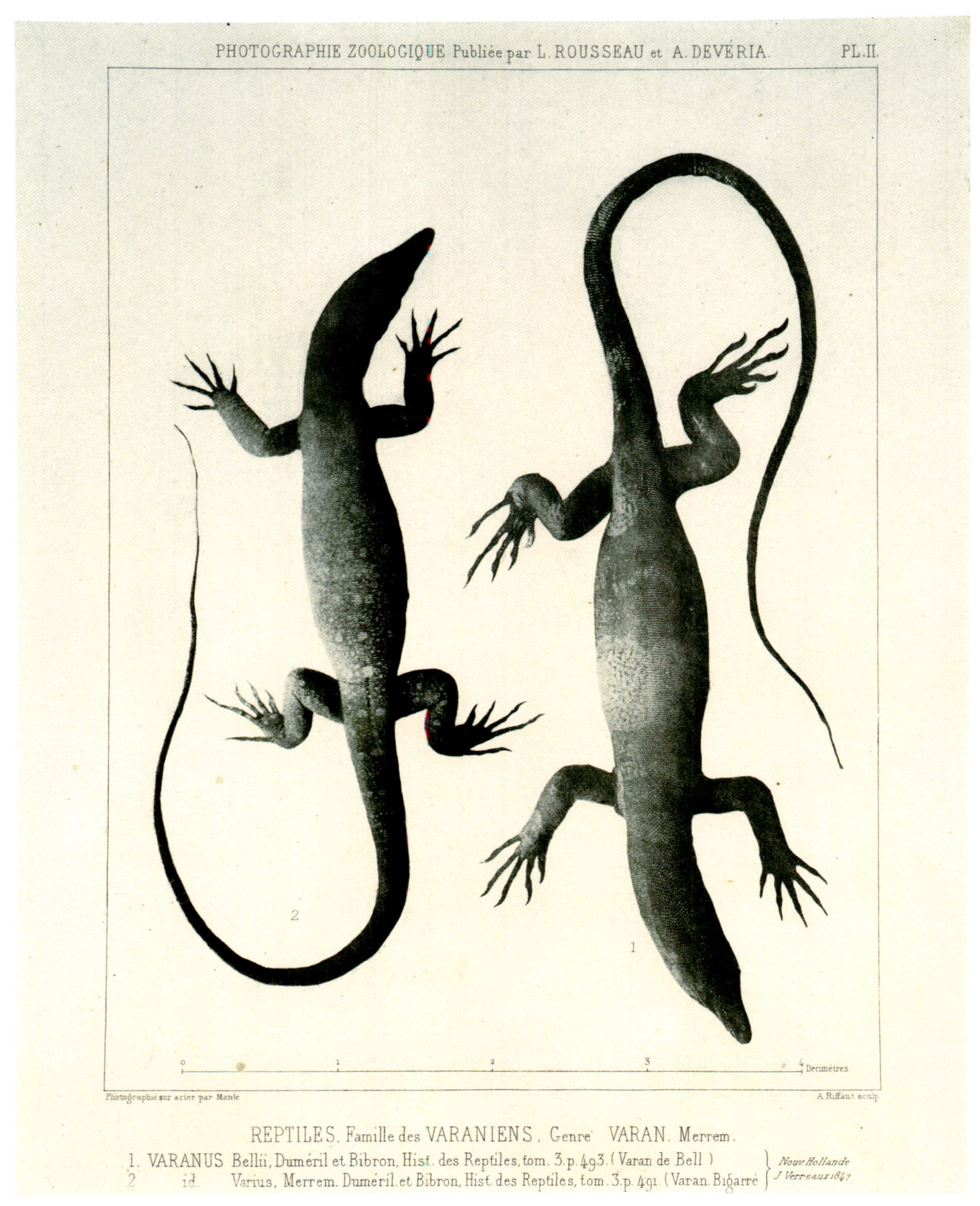

Louis-Auguste Bisson

Reptiles – Famille des Varaniens – Genre Varan. Merrem, 1853

Fortschritte a. d. Gebiete der Röntgenstr. XIX. Tafel II

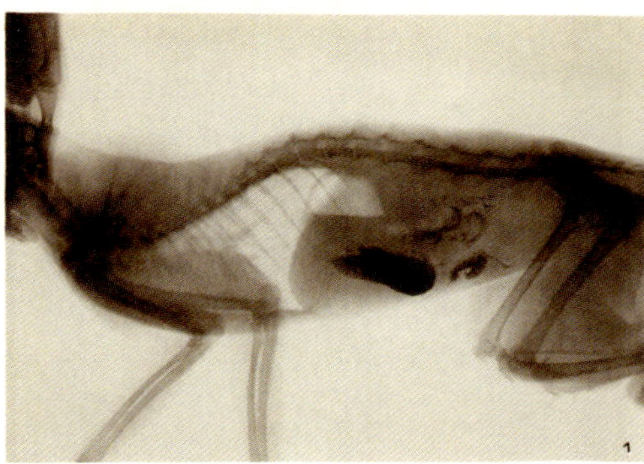

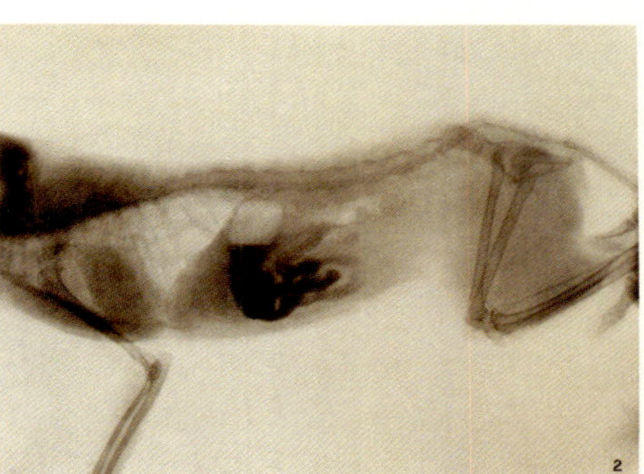

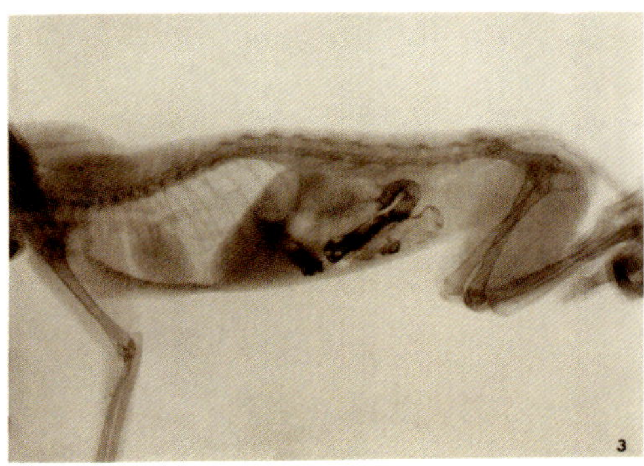

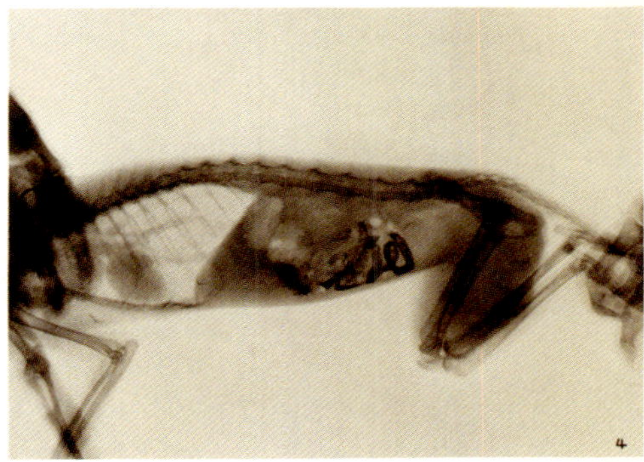

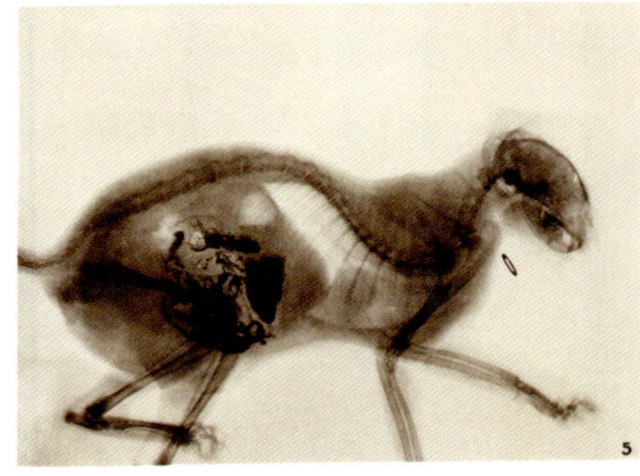

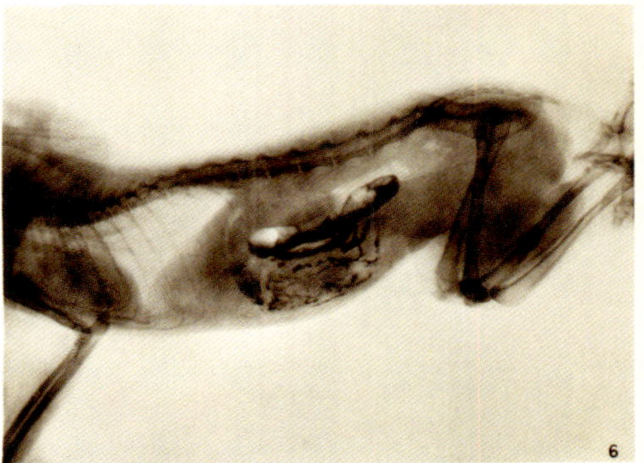

Neue Photographische Gesellschaft A.-G. Berlin-Steglitz. Verlag von Lucas Gräfe & Sillem in Hamburg.

Anonym (Neue Photographische Gesellschaft)
Verdauung des Hundes, a. d. Buch: *Fortschritte auf dem Gebiet der Röntgenstrahlung*, 1912/13

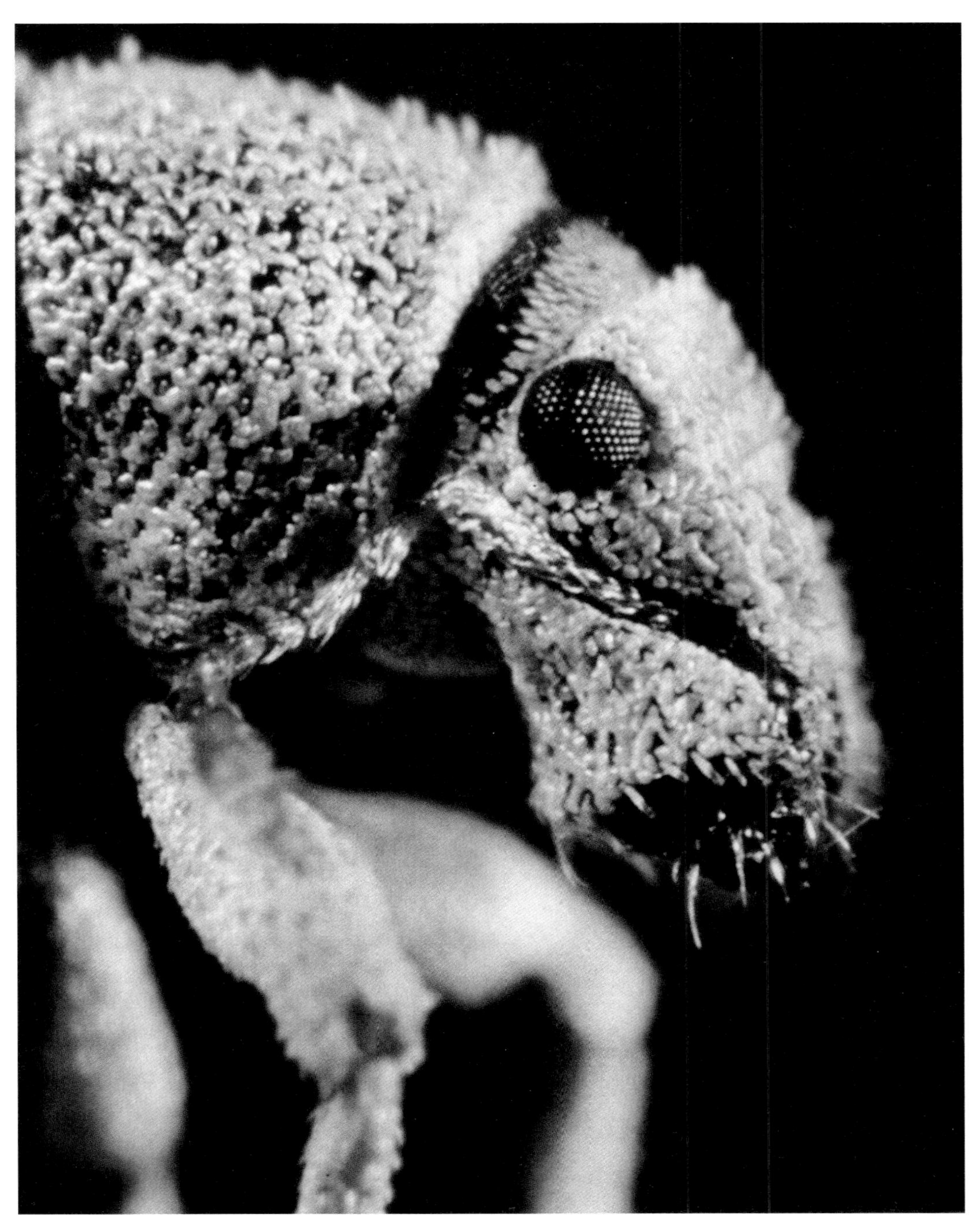

Otto Croy
Haselnußfüßler, 1930er

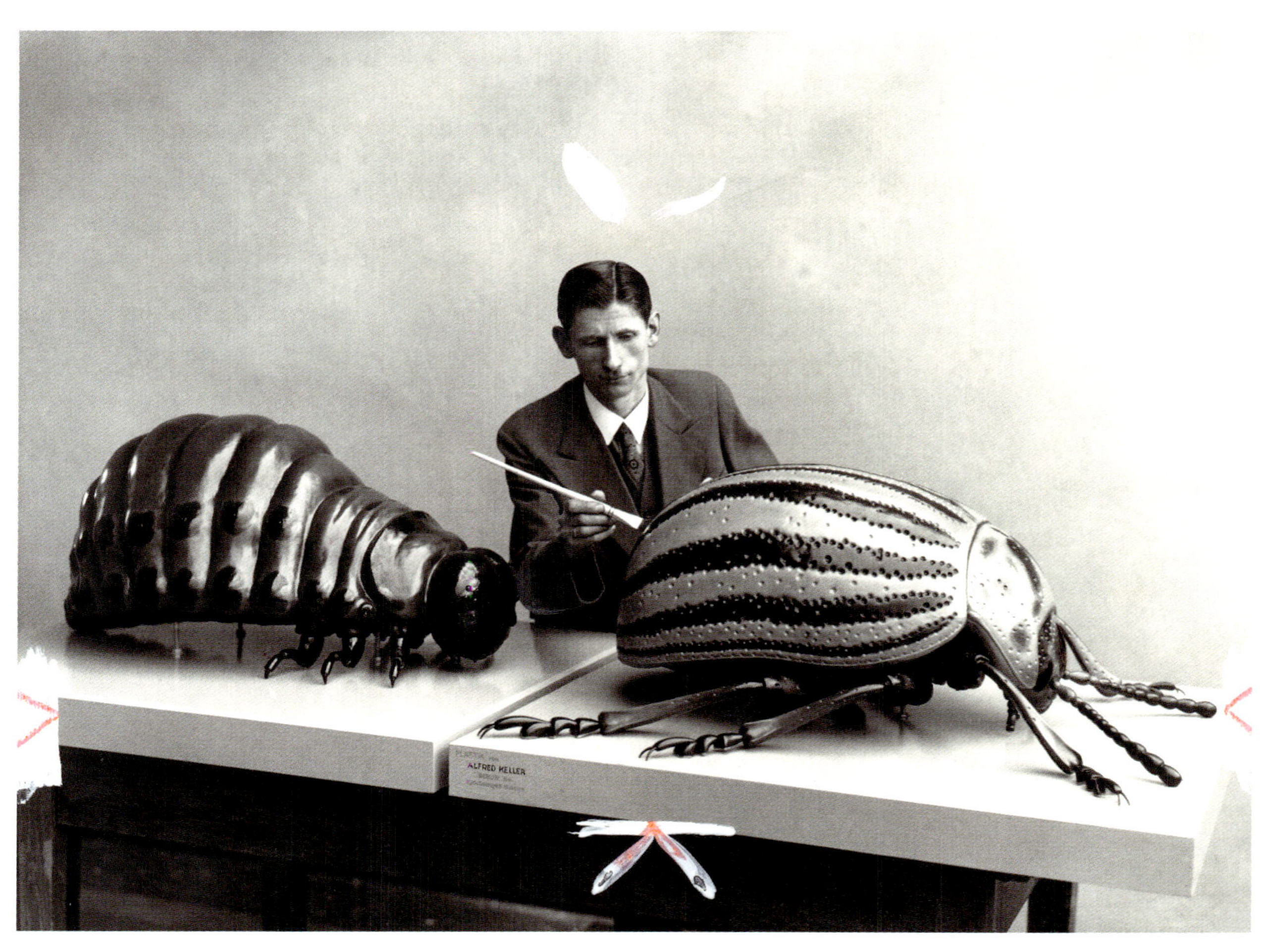

Agentur Scherl

Oberpräparator Keller, Zoologisches Museum /

Senior taxidermist Keller, Zoological Museum, Berlin, 1941

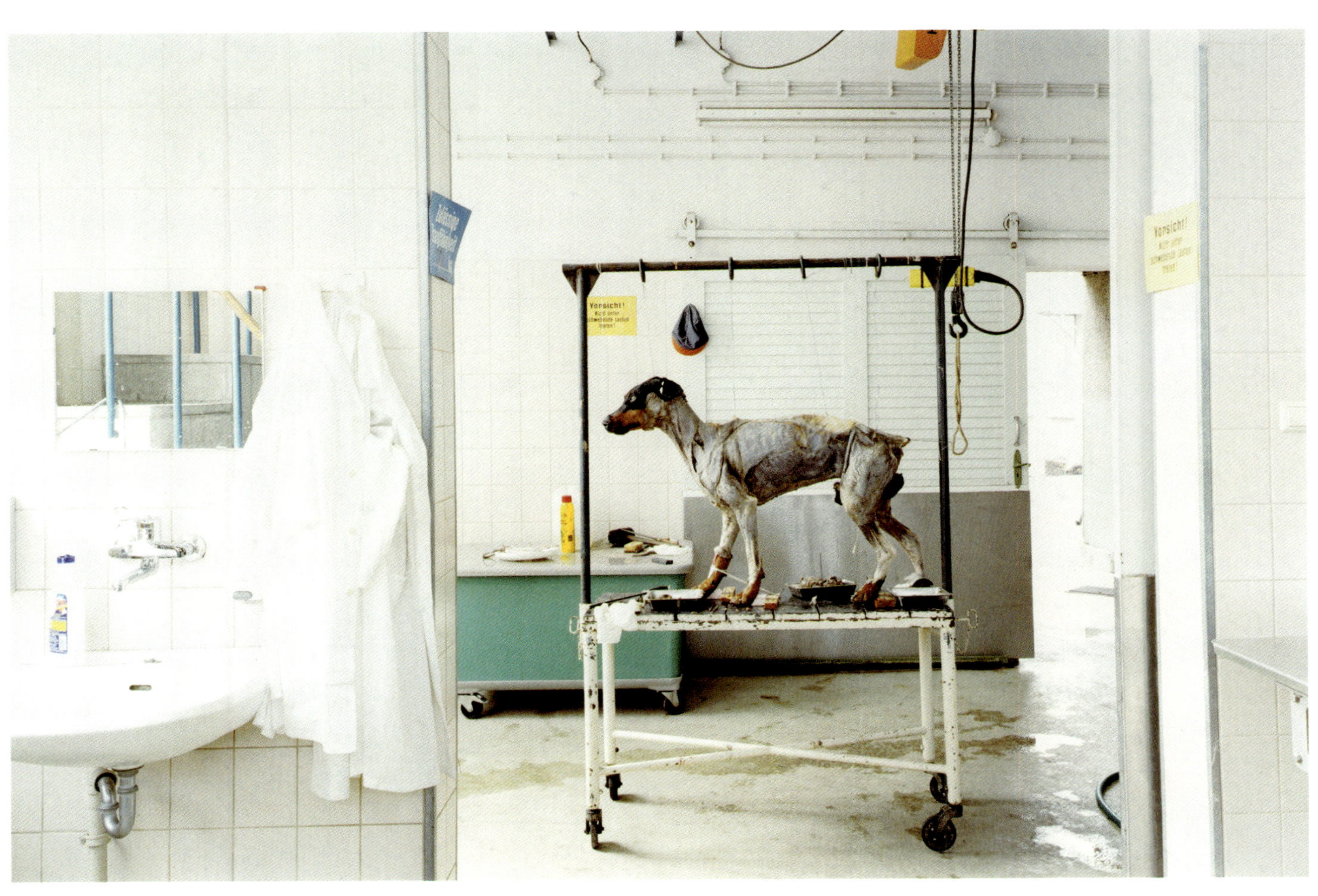

Steffen Junghans

a. d. Serie: *Einrichten*, 2000

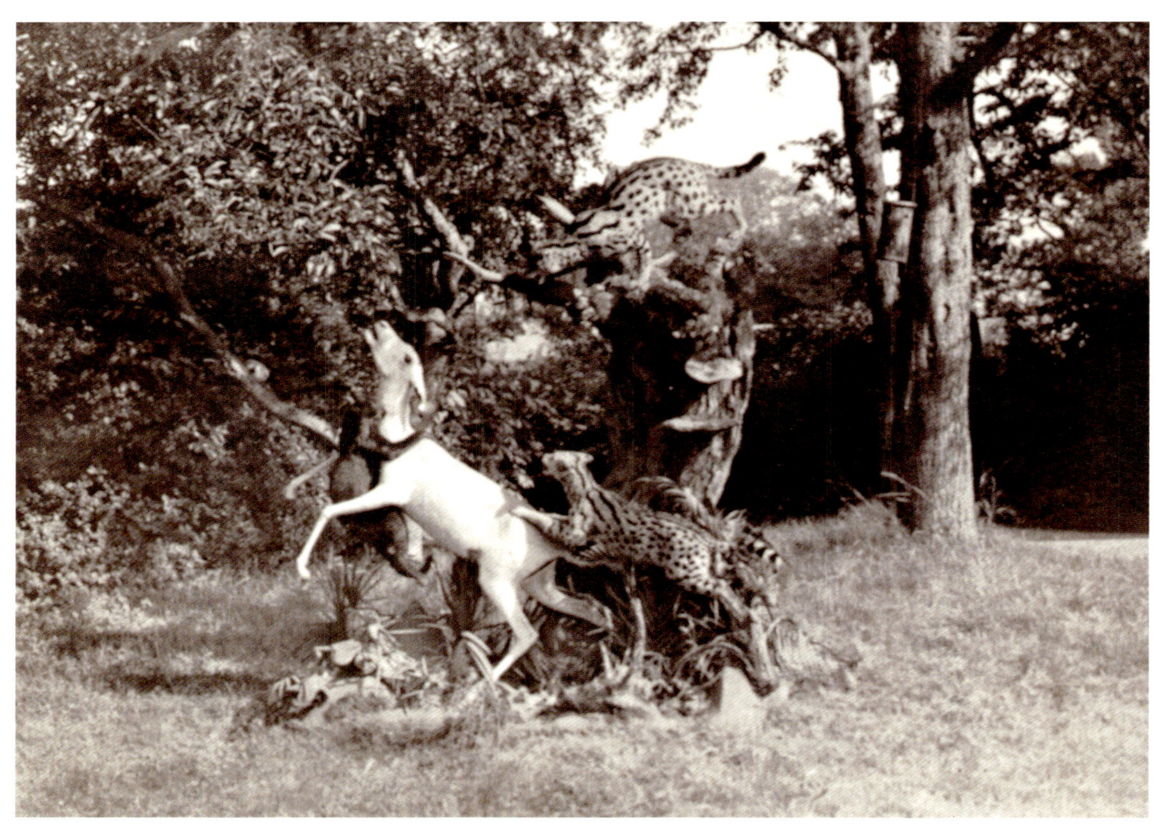

Carl Georg Schillings (?)

Trophäen-Pyramide, ca. 1900

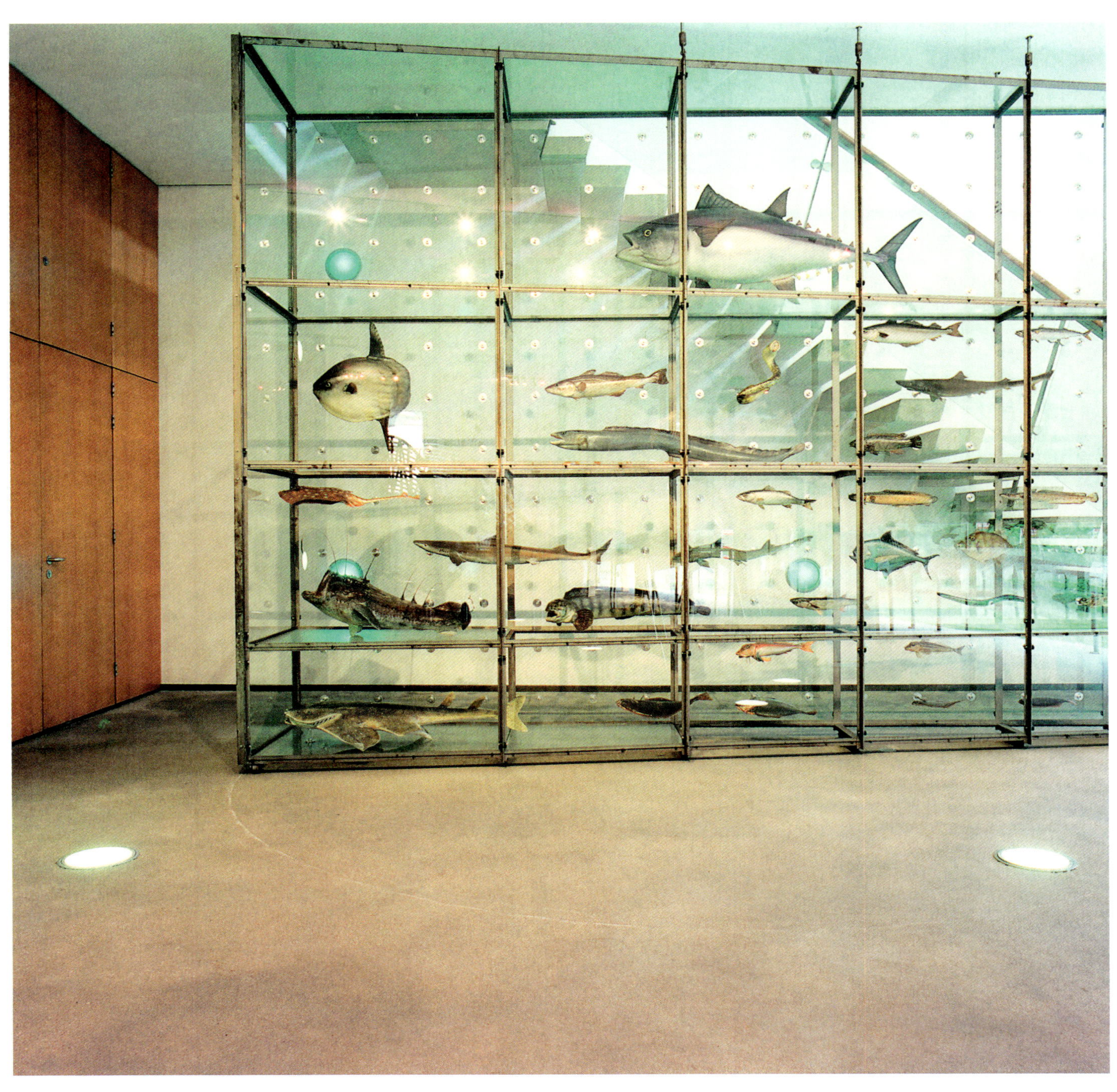

Candida Höfer

Naturkunde-Museum Rotterdam II 1999

„Das im 18. Jahrhundert entstandene Genre des Tierporträts ist noch immer die vorherrschende ‚Zuchtästhetik' und setzt sich fort in Form von Fotografien posierender Champions auf landwirtschaftlichen Ausstellungen, Viehkatalogen – und sogar in Amateur-Videos, aufgenommen auf den Viehmessen durch die Bauern selbst."

"The genre of animal portraiture established in the 18th century is still predominant as a 'breeding aesthetic,' and continues on in the form of photographs of posing champions at agricultural exhibitions, catalogues of livestock—and even video-recordings taken with amateur camcorders at cattle fairs by the farmers themselves."

Cristina Grasseni

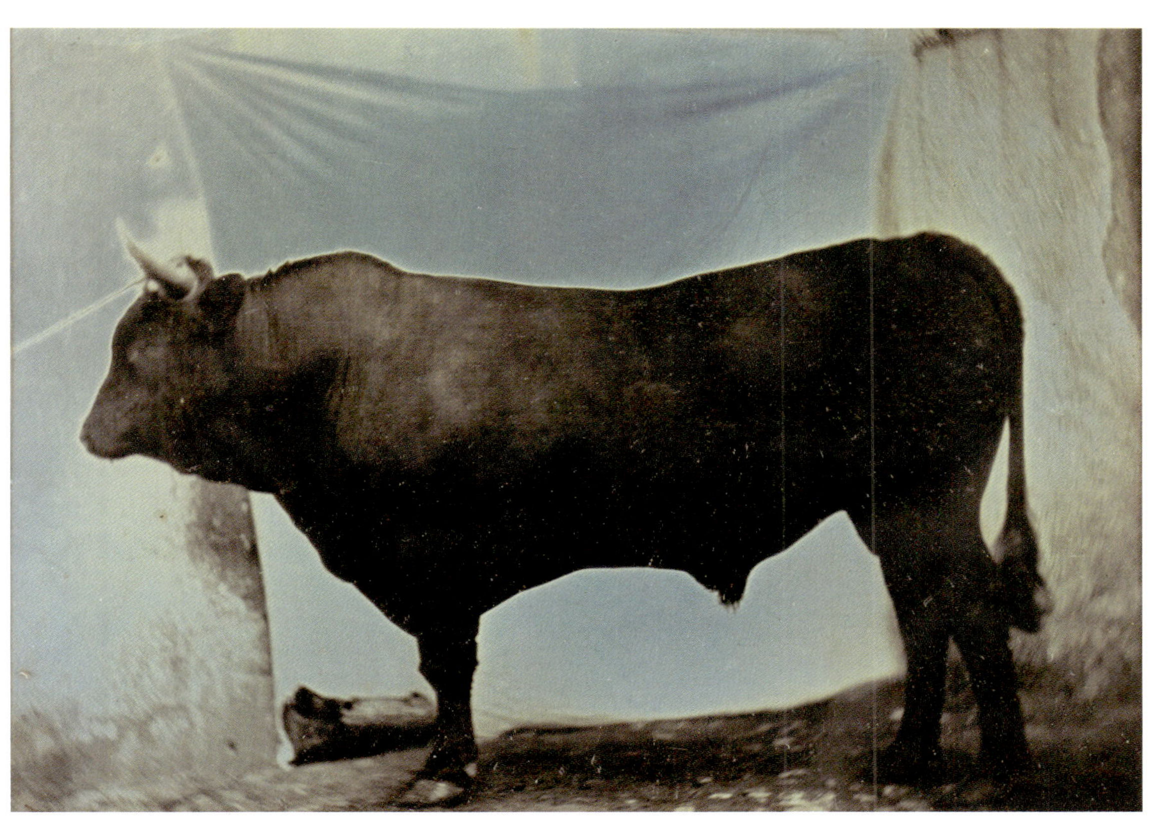

Louis-Auguste Bisson
Taureau, Aurillac, 1850

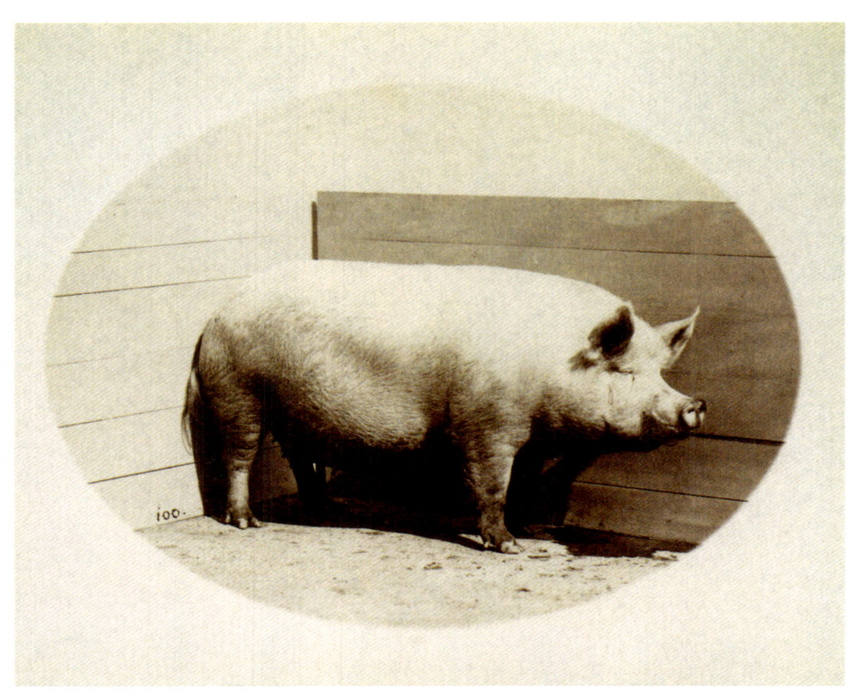

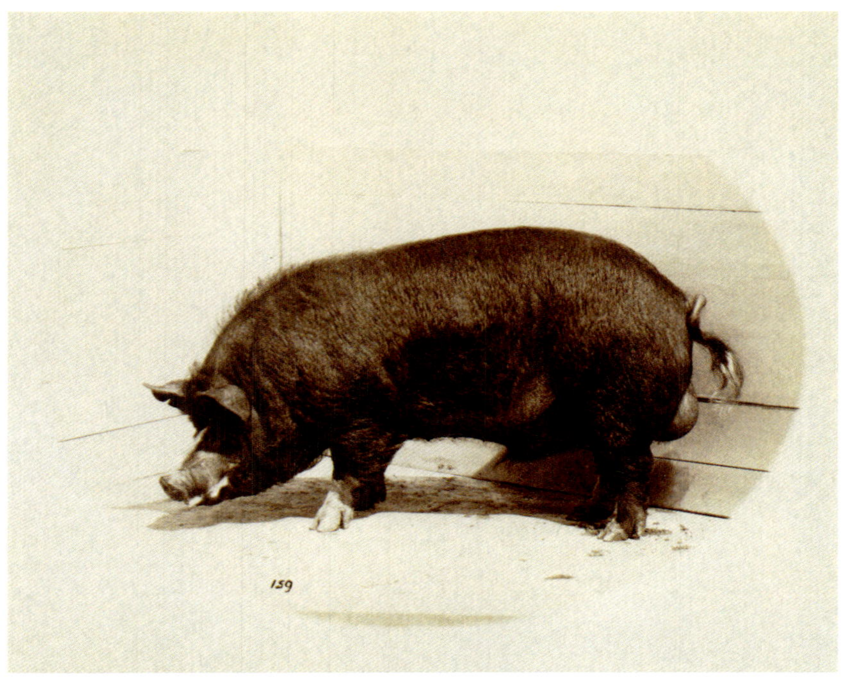

Ferdinand Albert Schwartz

Sau "Melodie" und *Eber "Prachtkerl"*, a. d. Album: *Deutsche Landwirtschaftsgesellschaft, Wanderausstellung Köln 6.-10. Juni 1895*

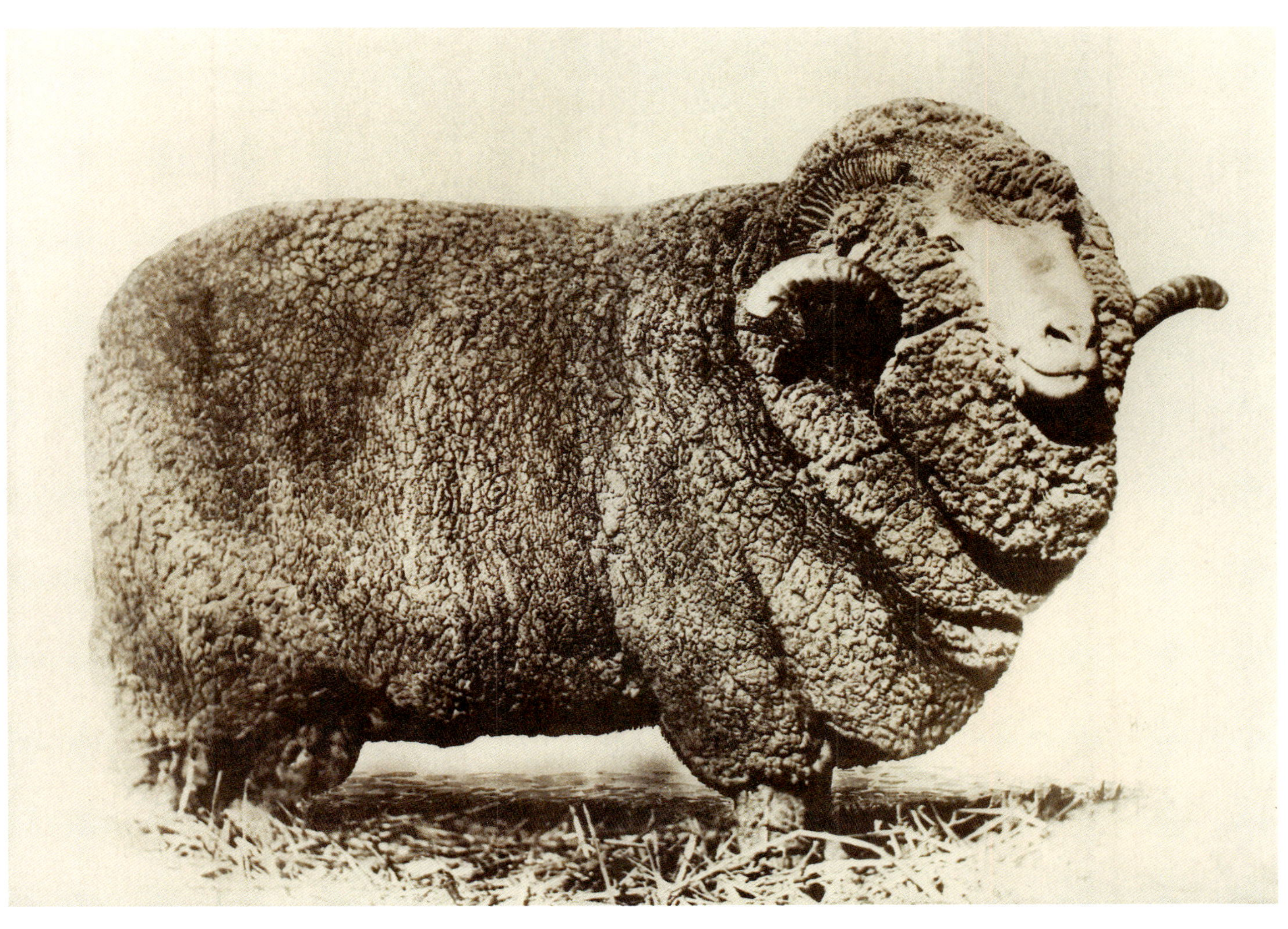

Anonym
Schaf / Sheep, 1910-1920

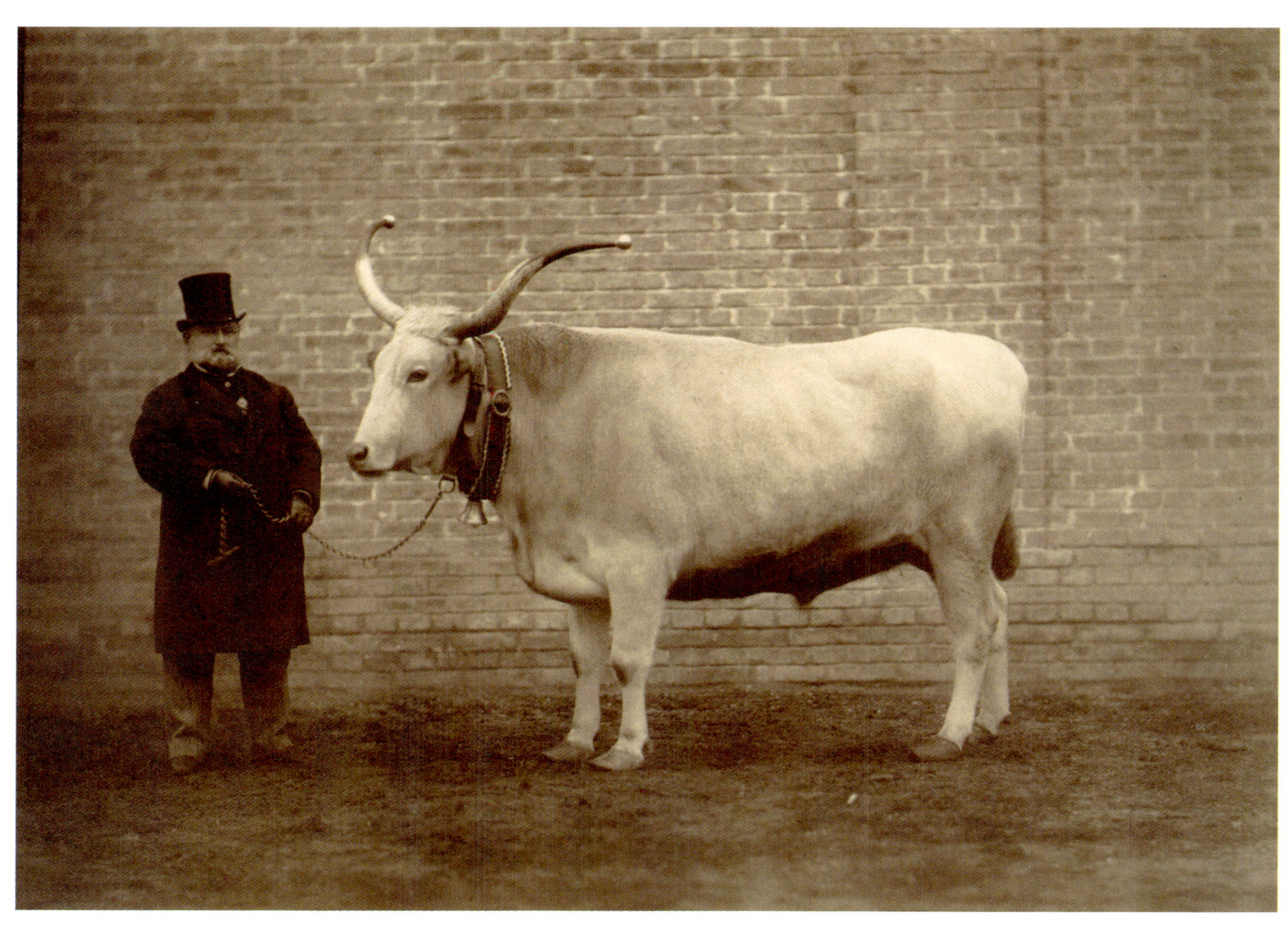

Hermann Heid
Viehauktion in Wien, ca. 1881

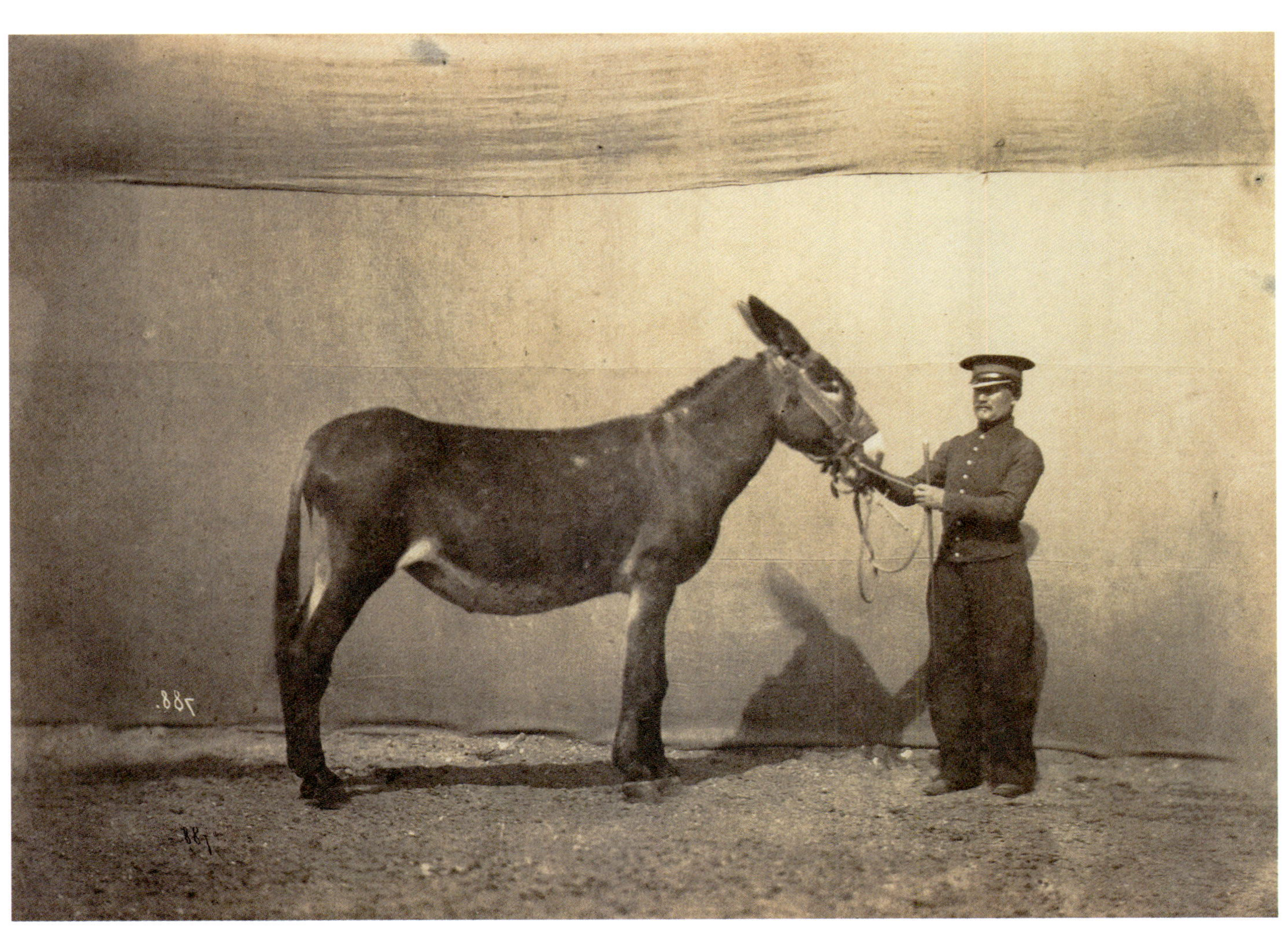

Adrien Alban Tournachon

Catharina, a. d. Album: *Race Chevaline. Concours de 1860*

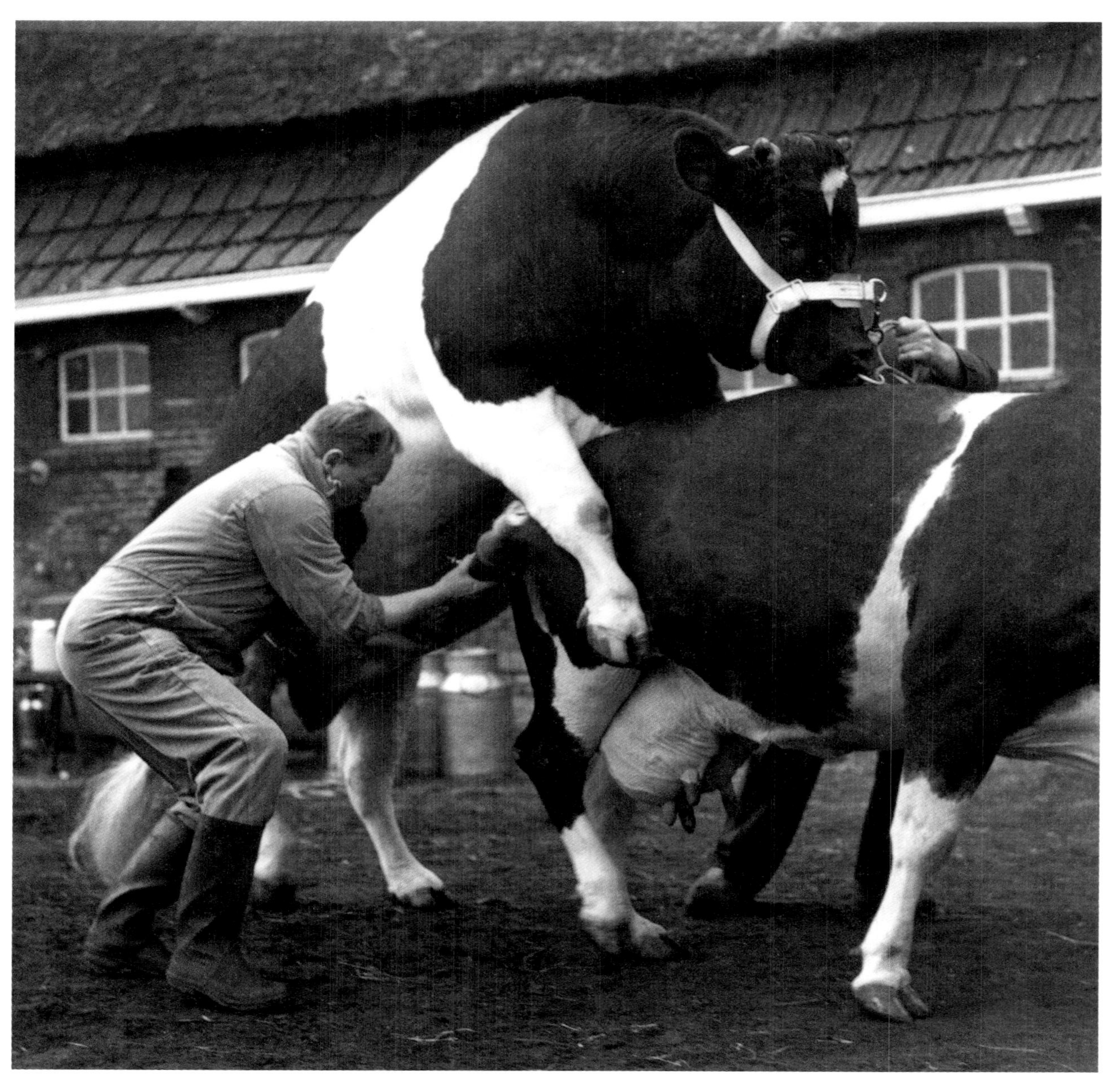

Cas Oorthuys

Faculty of veterinary science, University Utrecht, 1962

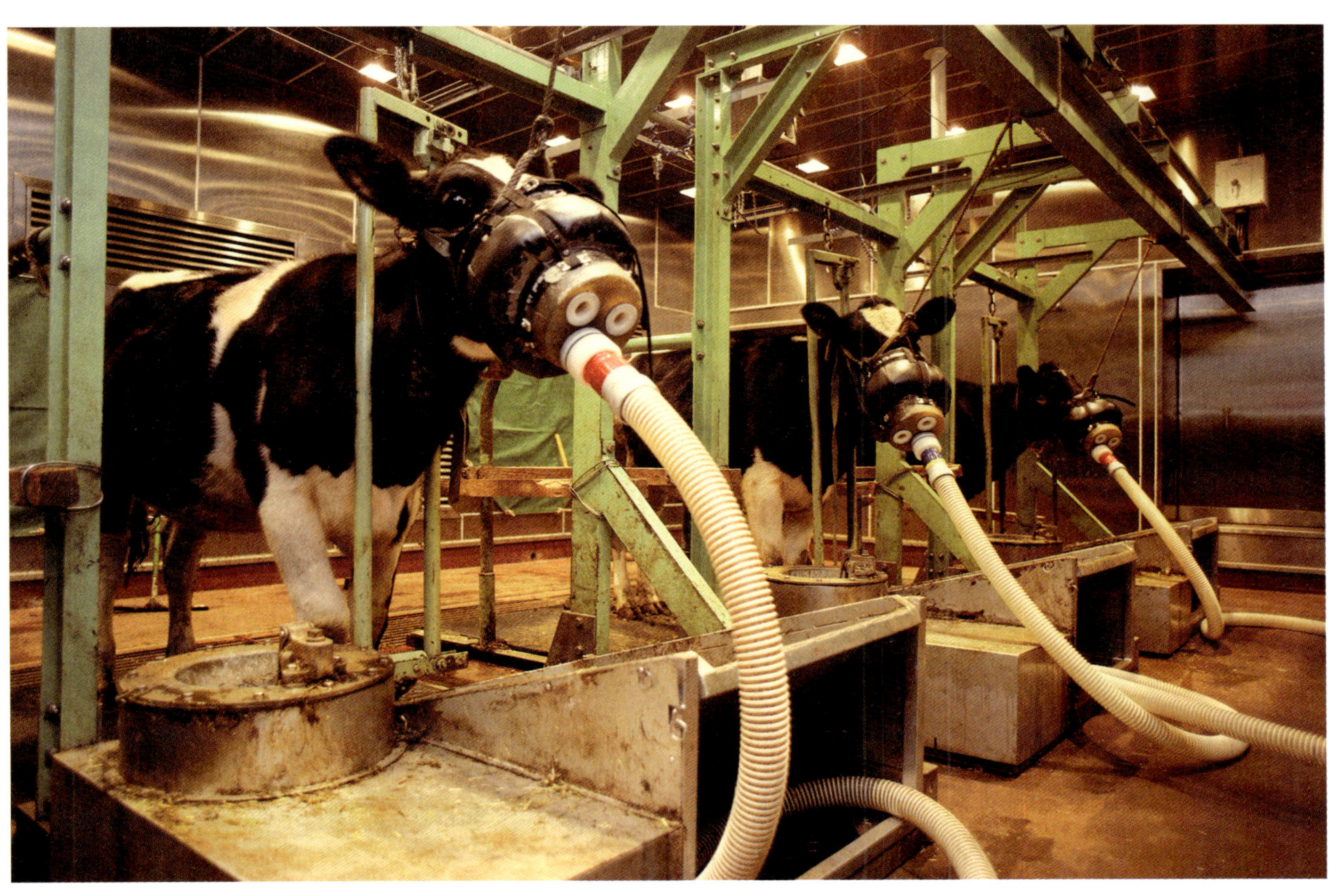

Georg Fischer

National Institute of Animal Industry, 1980.

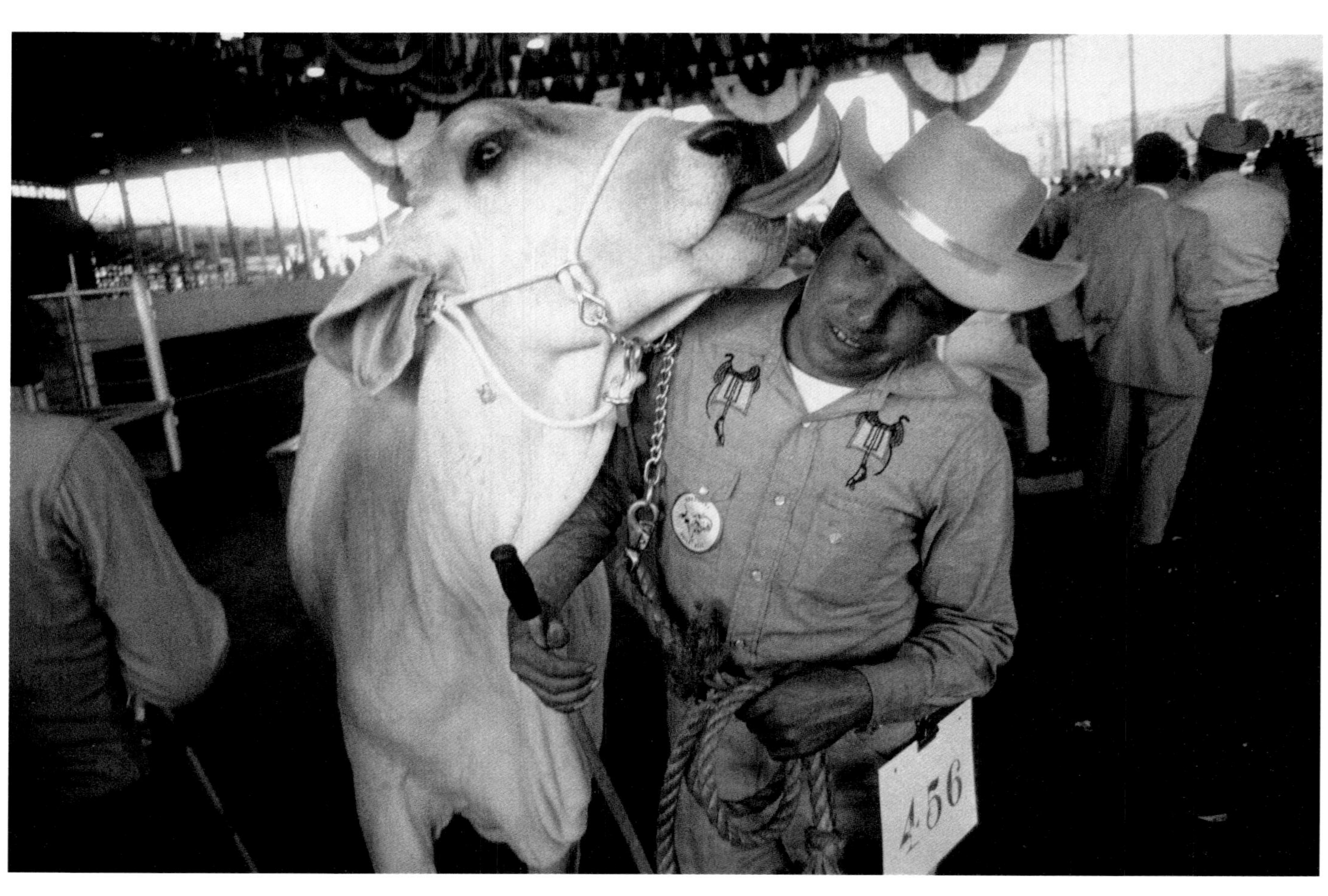

Garry Winogrand

Texas State Fair, Dallas, 1964

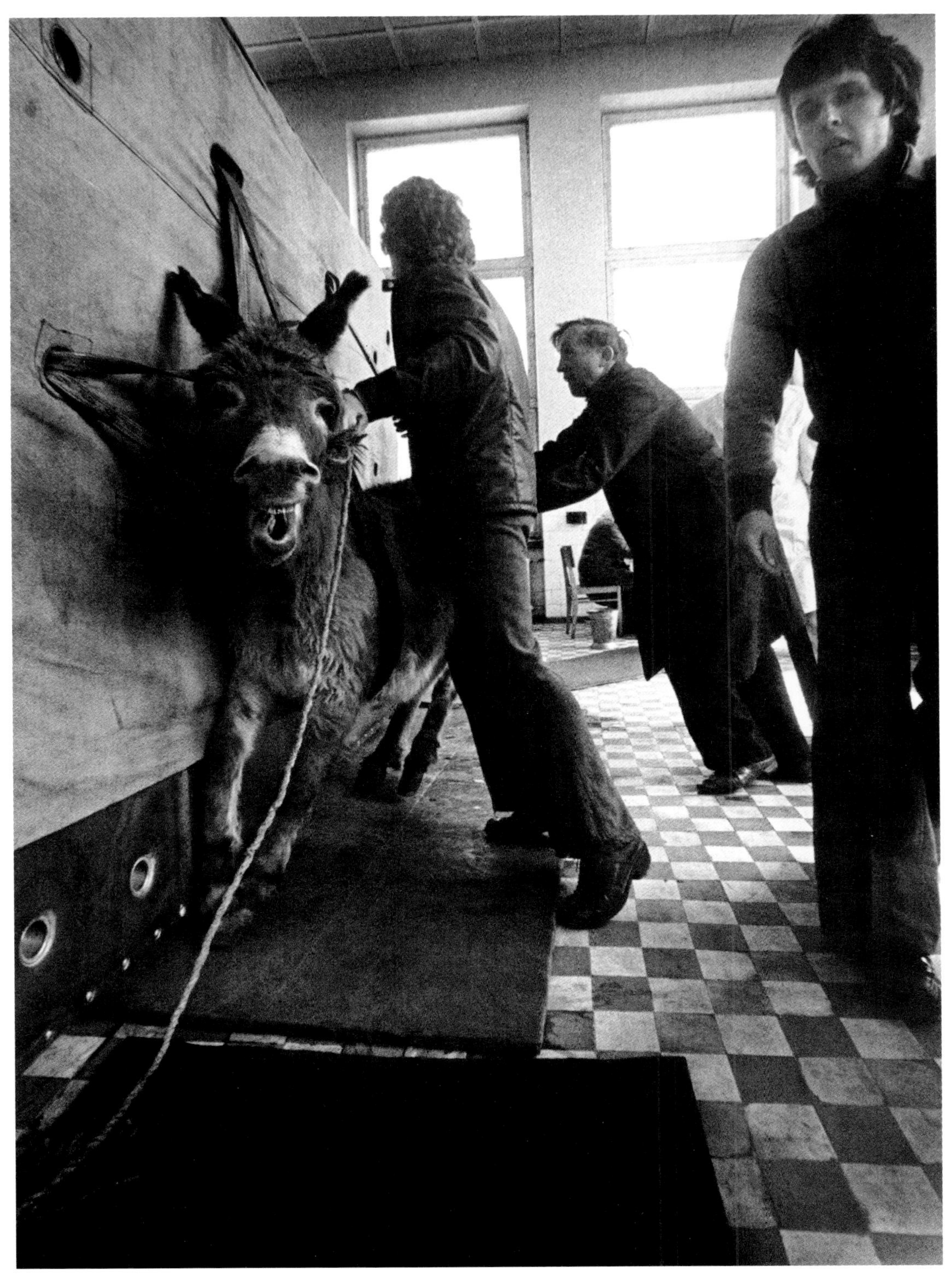

Aleksandras Macijauskas

a. d. Serie: *In the Veterinary Clinic in Kaunas,* 1978

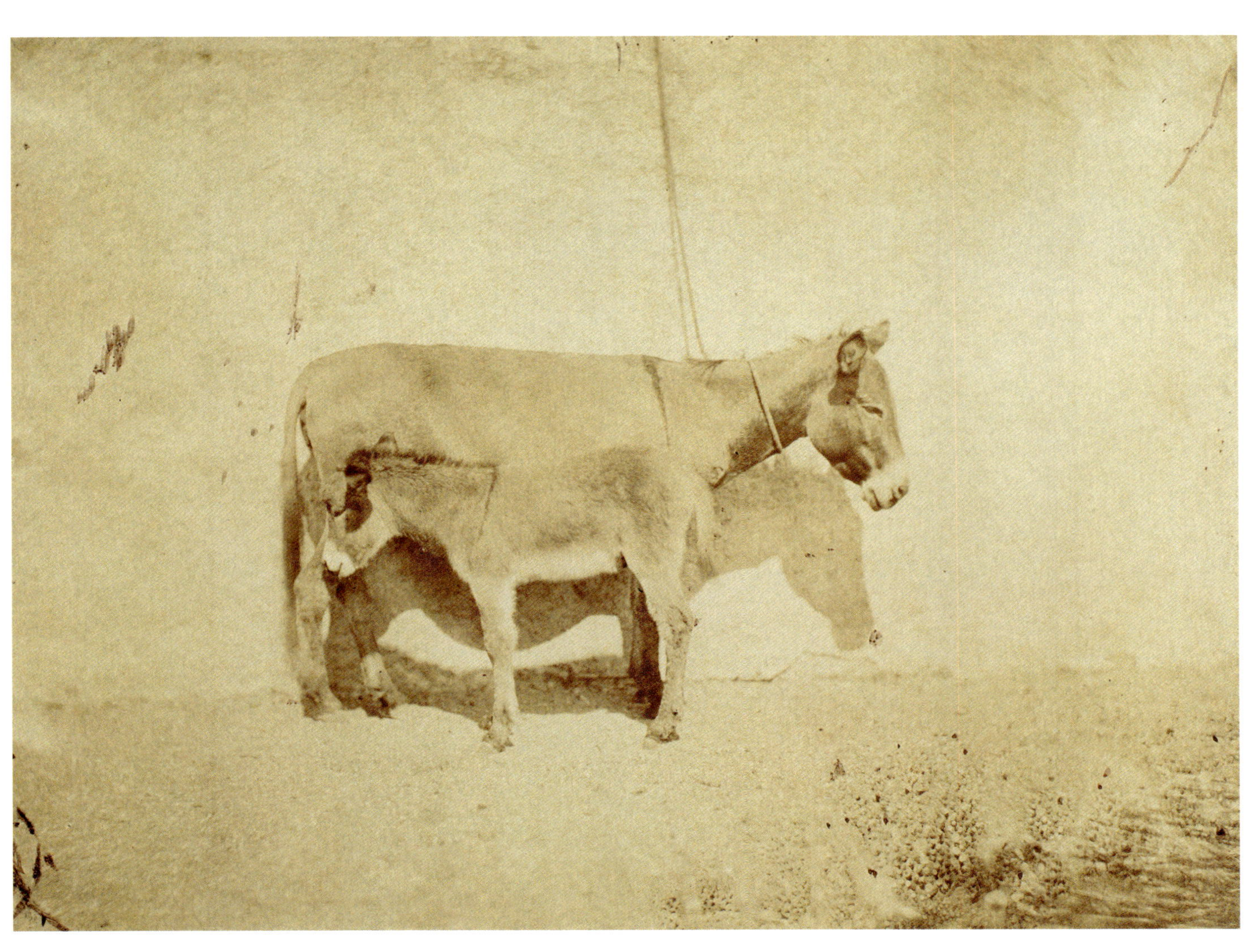

Comte Olympe Aguado
Deux ânes, 1857

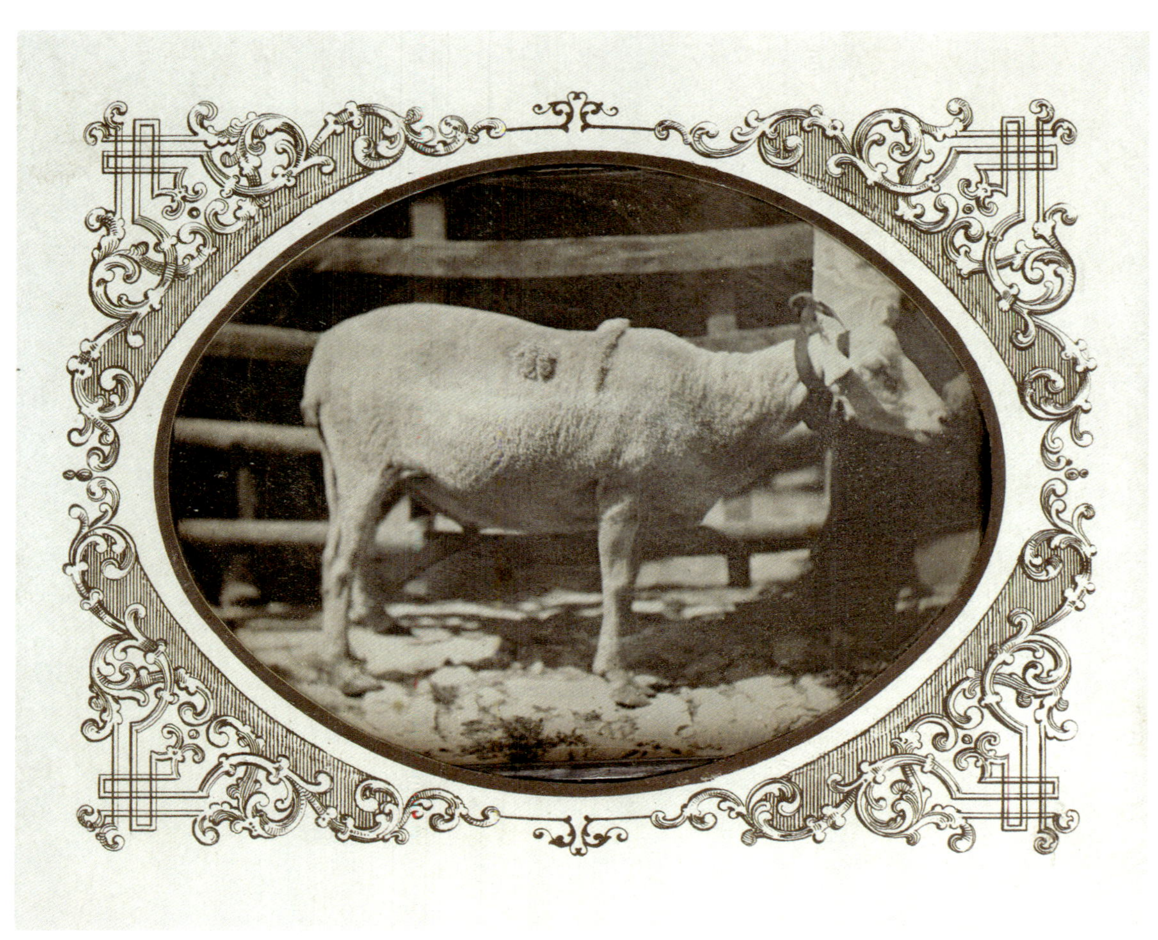

Louis-Auguste Bisson

Concours de Nismes, espèce ovine, race du Larzac, ca. 1845-1850

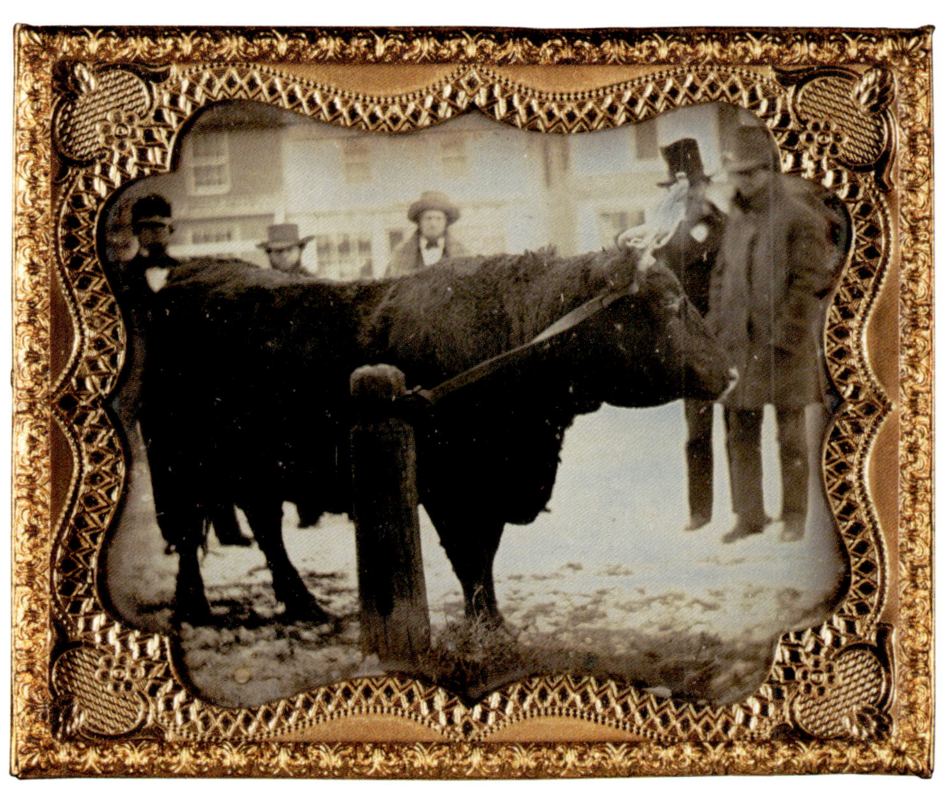

Anonym
Männer mit einem Bullen /
Men posing with a Bull, ca. 1850

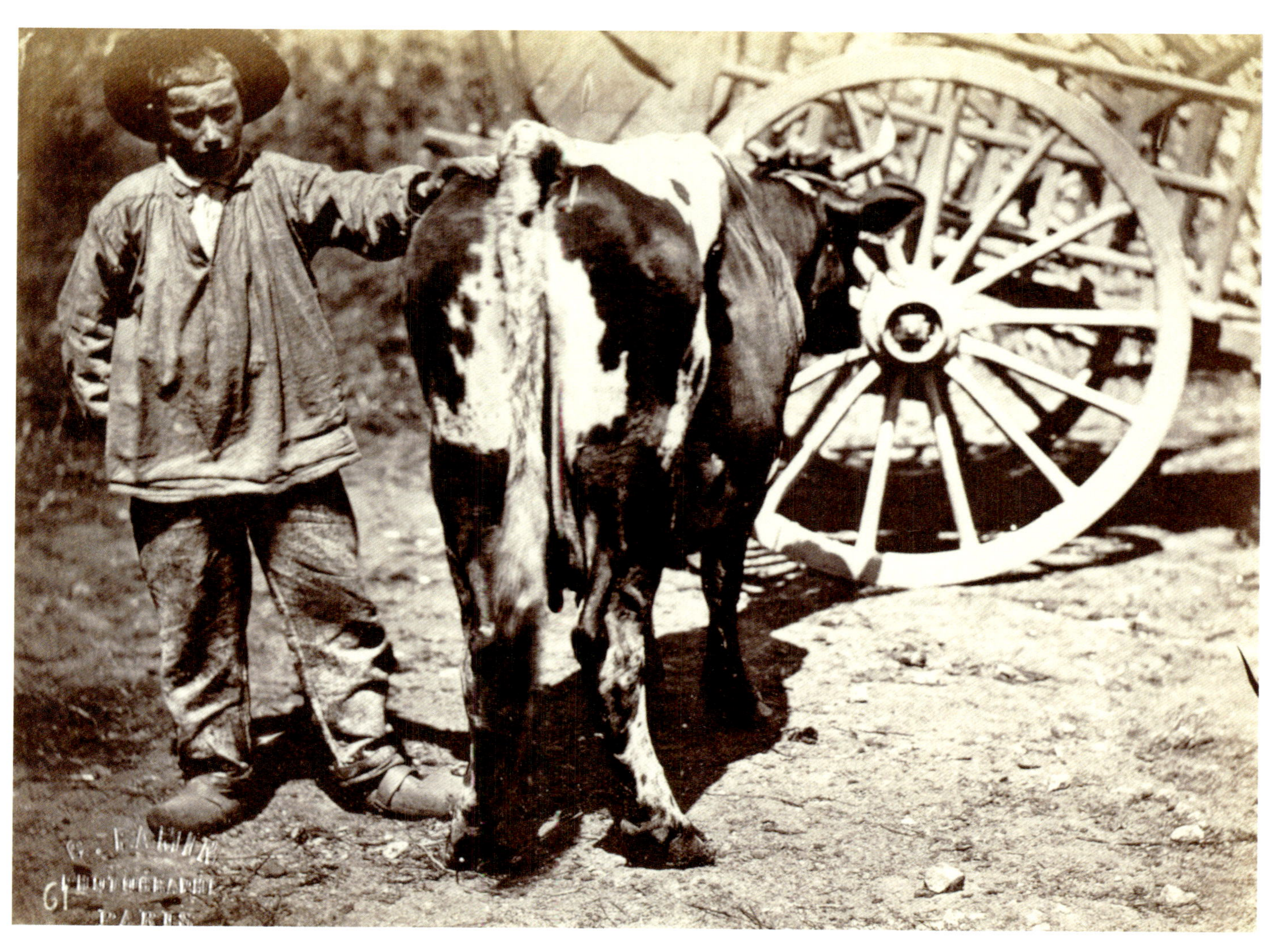

Constant Alexandre Famin

Pastorale, ca. 1870

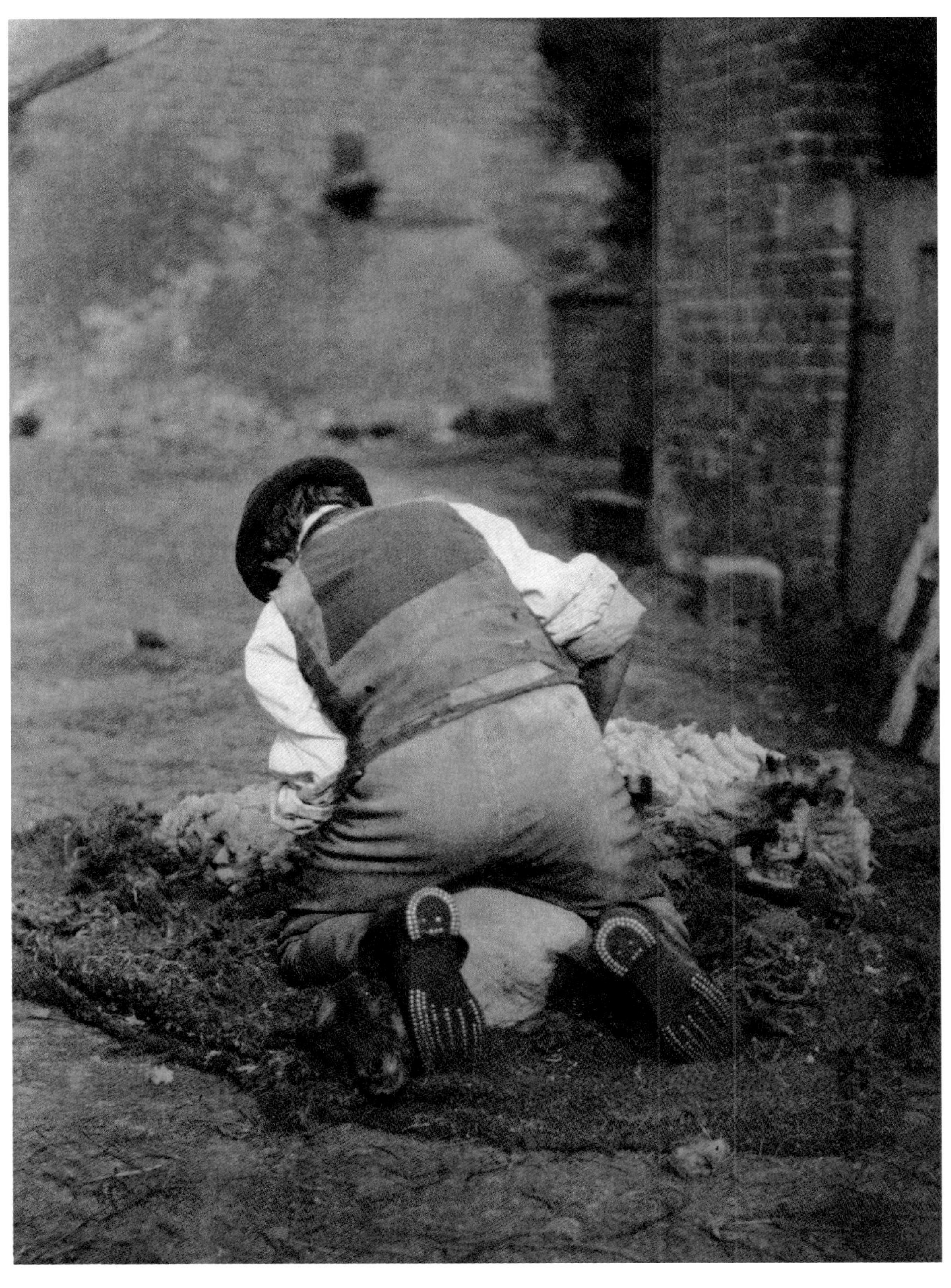

Frederick Hollyer
Schafschur, 1868

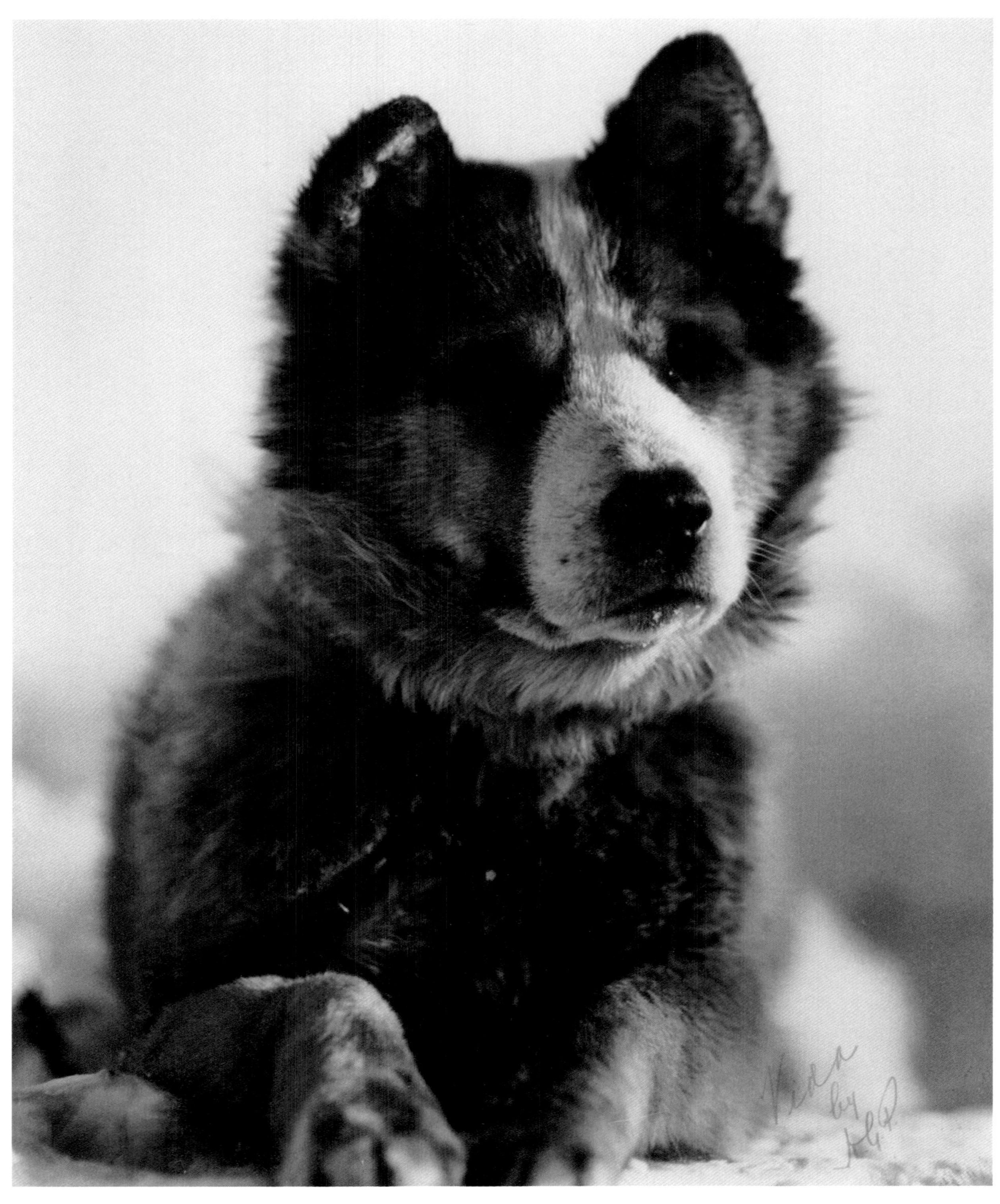

Herbert George Ponting

„Vida", one of the best of the dogs used by Capt. Smith on his South Pole Expedition (1910-13), ca. 1912

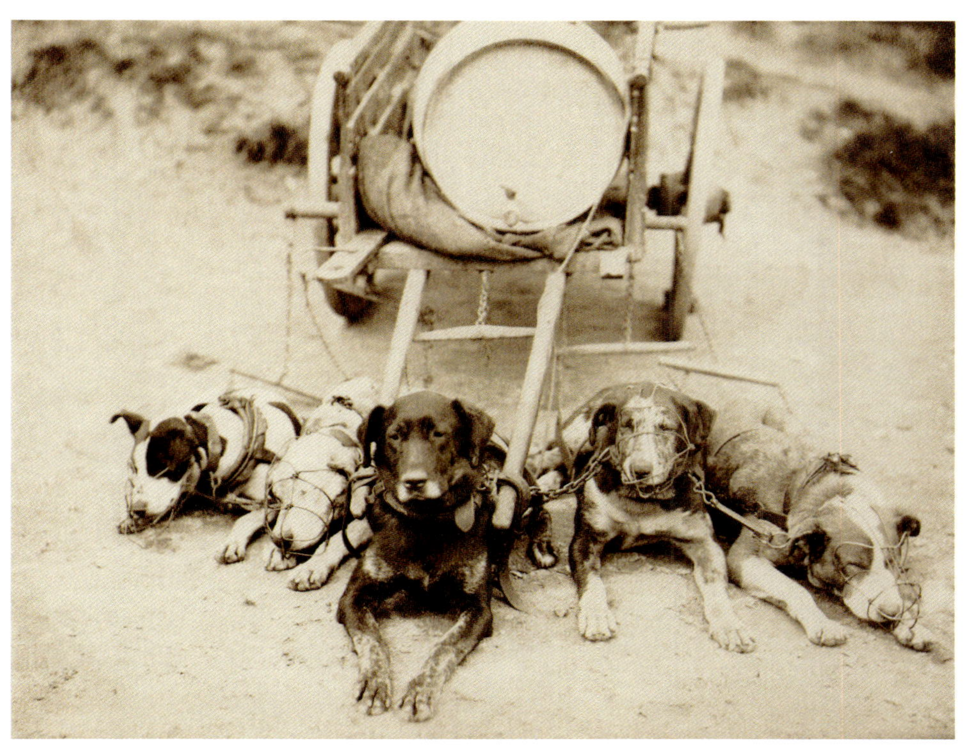

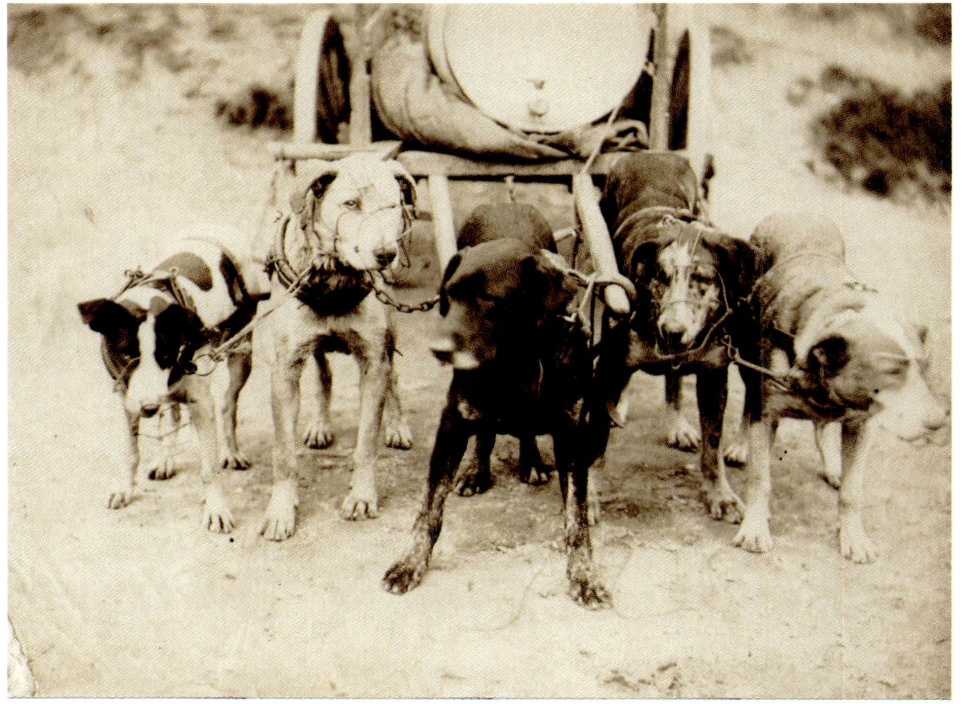

Anonym
Flämische Milchkarrenhunde /
Flemish milk cart dogs, ca. 1905

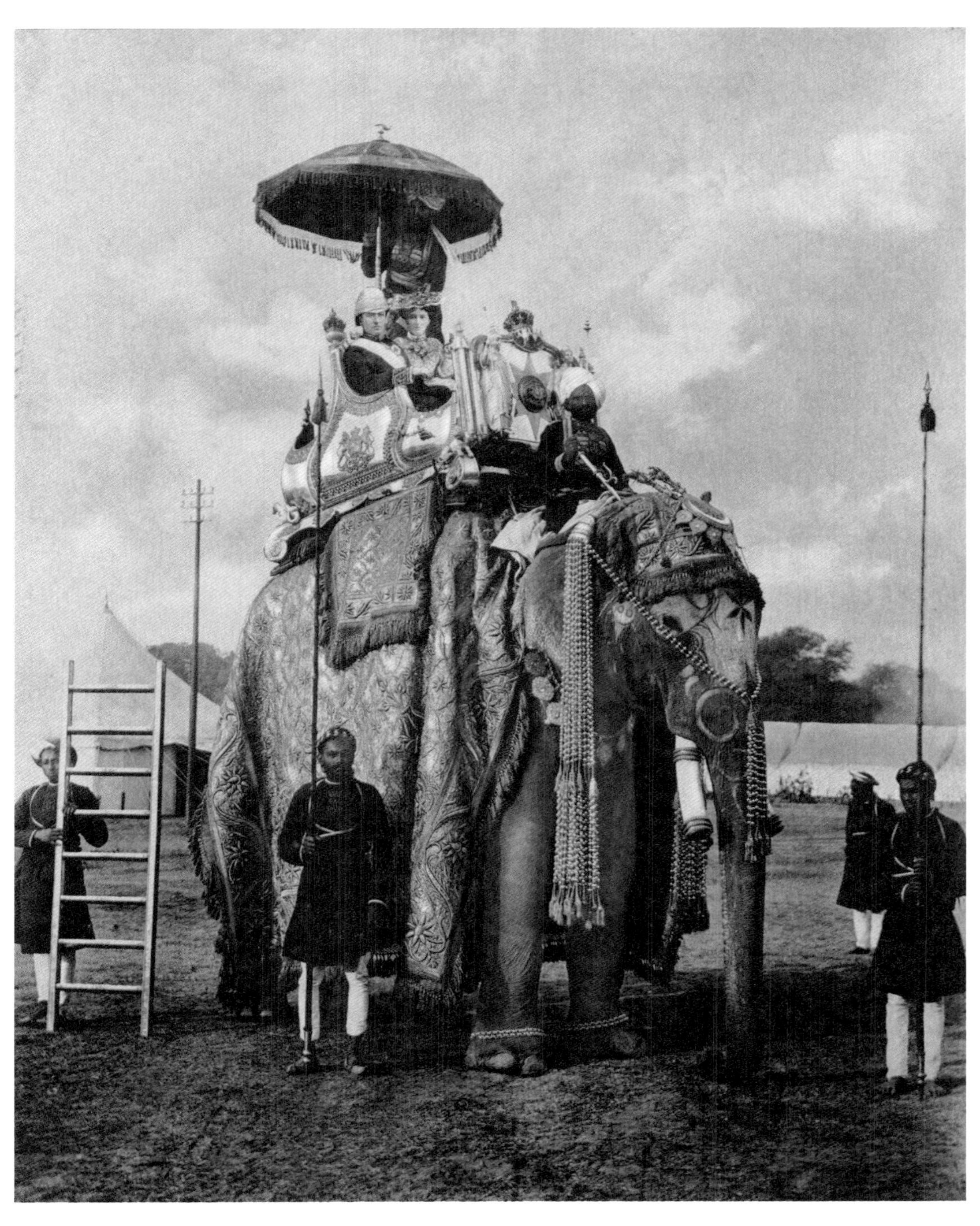

Anonym

Lord and Lady Curzon on an Elephant, 1903

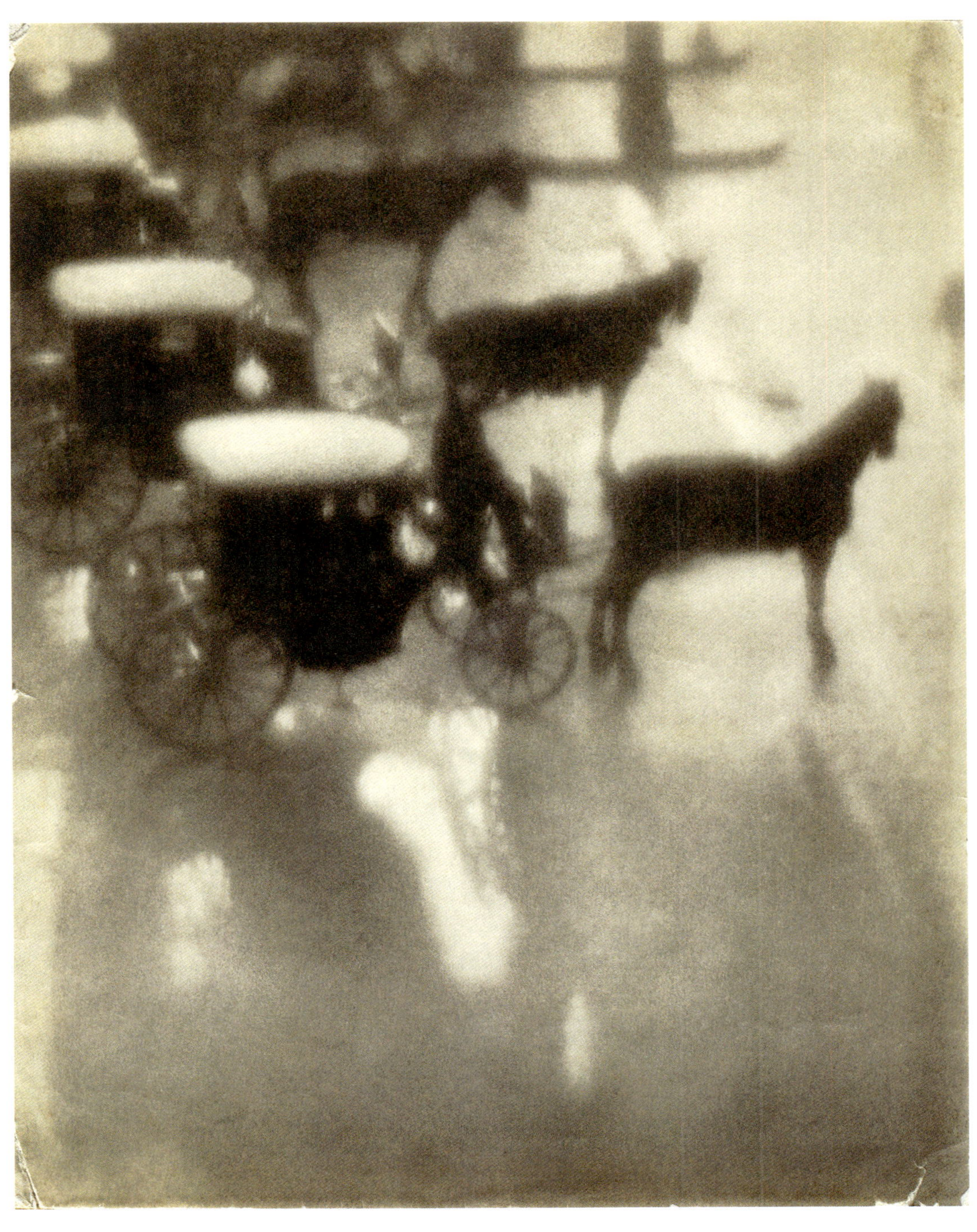

Pierre Dubreuil
Petite place de province, 1908

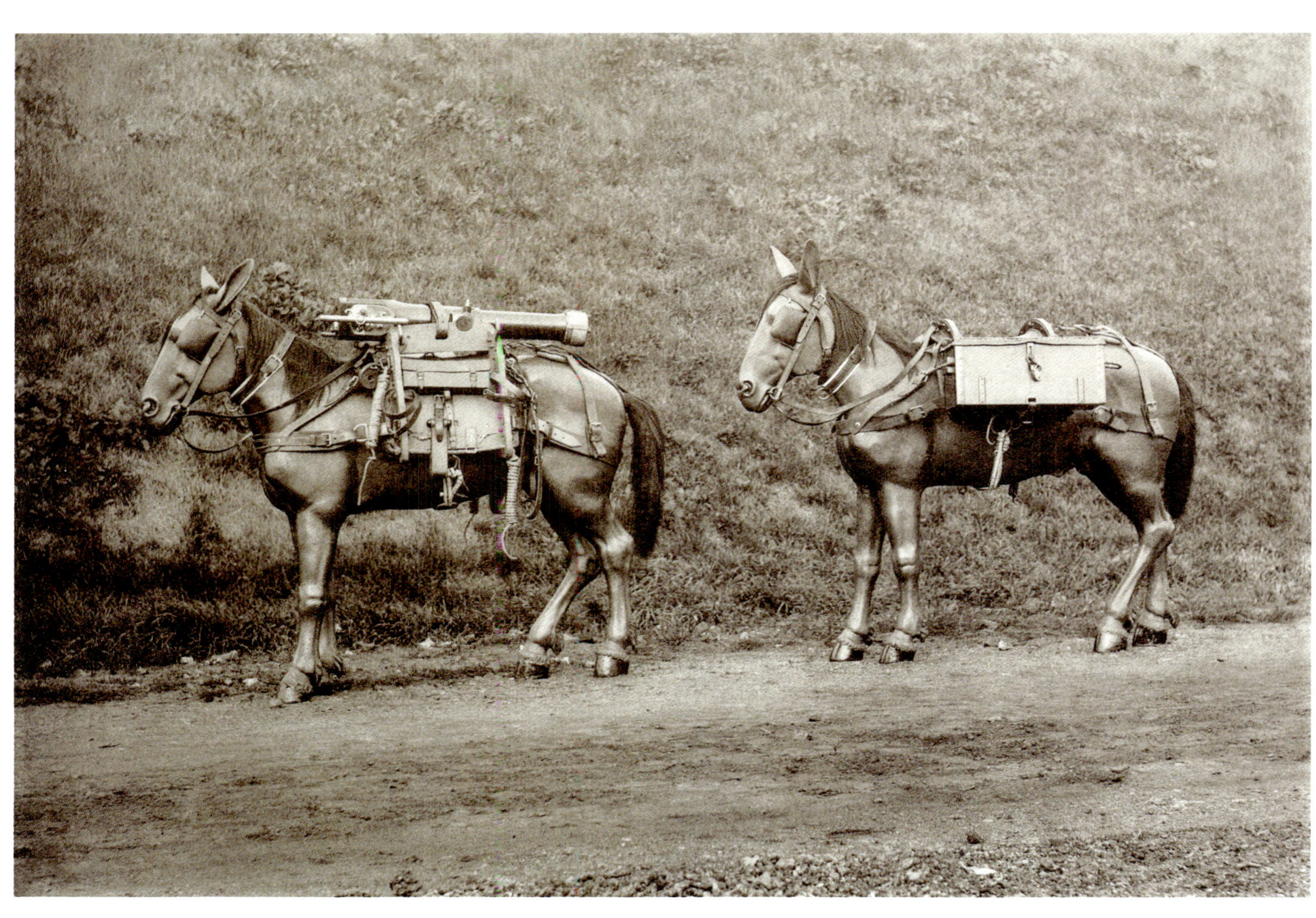

Photographisches Atelier der Gussstahlfabrik von Friedrich Krupp, Essen
Rohr-Tragethier, Munitions-Tragethier, 1883,
a. d. Album: *Artillerie-Material I. Essen*, 1892

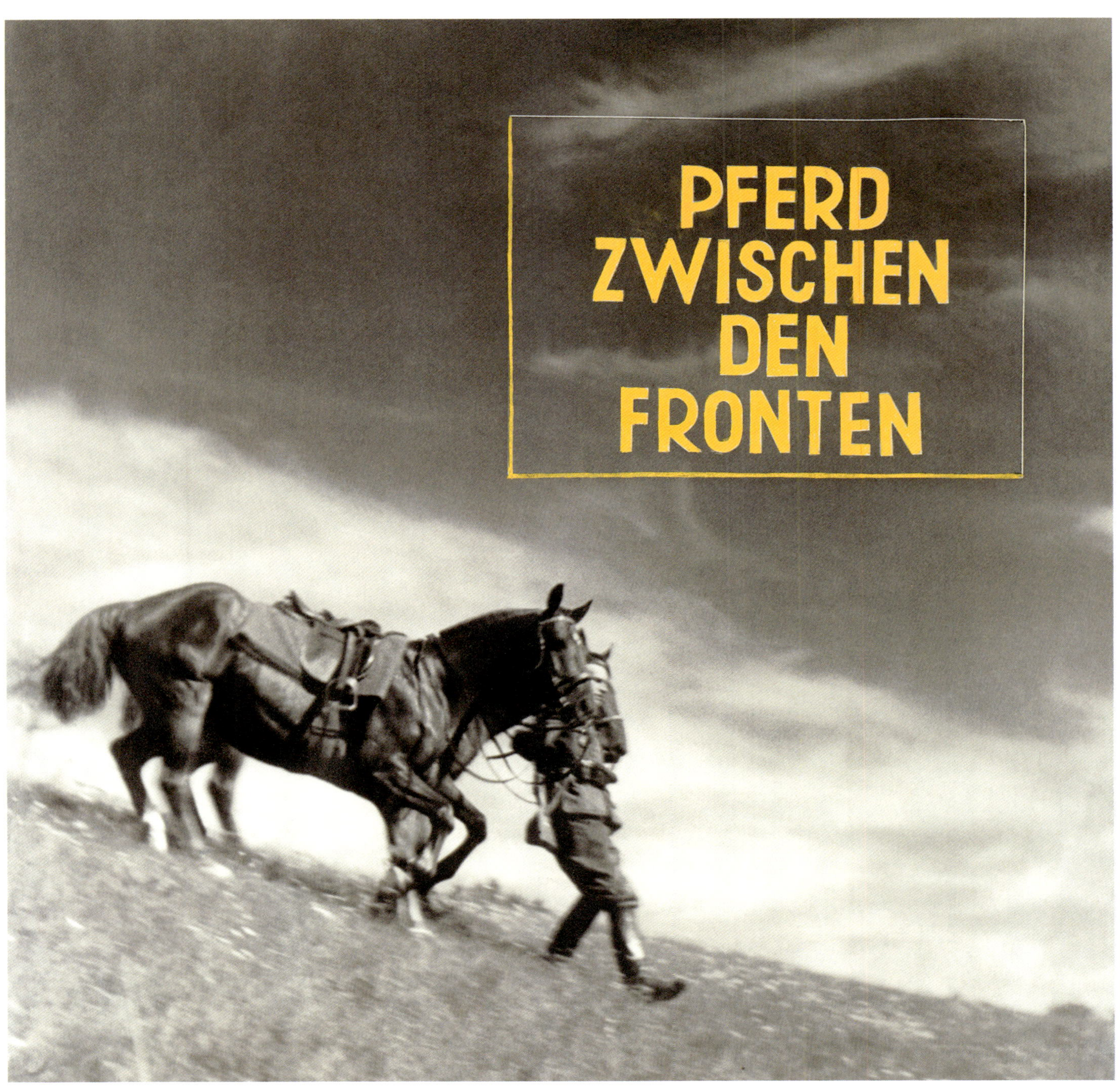

Gefreiter Ingenbrand

Album *Pferd zwischen den Fronten*, 1940-1945

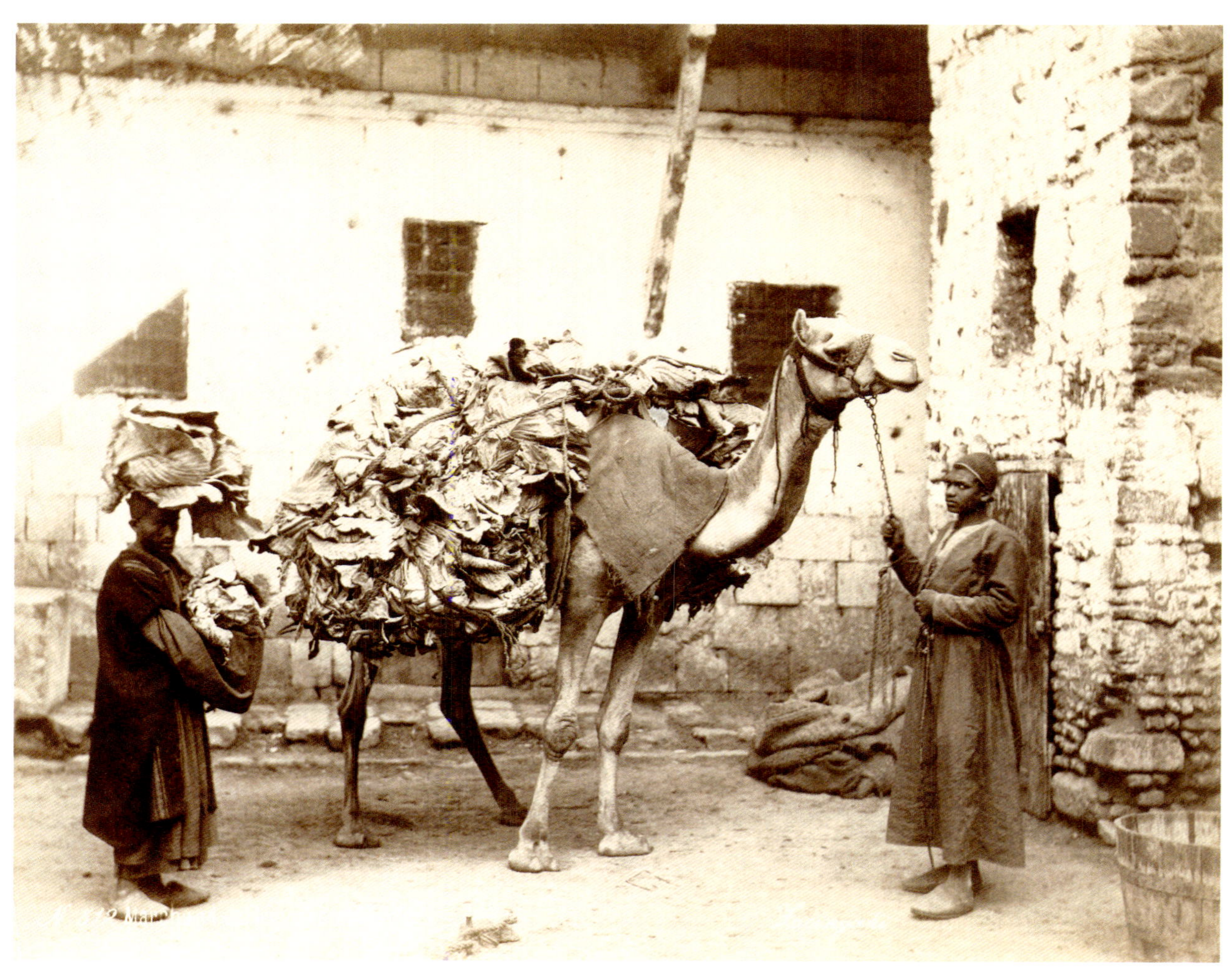

Atelier Adelphi und Constantine Zangaki
Gemüsehändler, *Aegypten*, ca. 1880

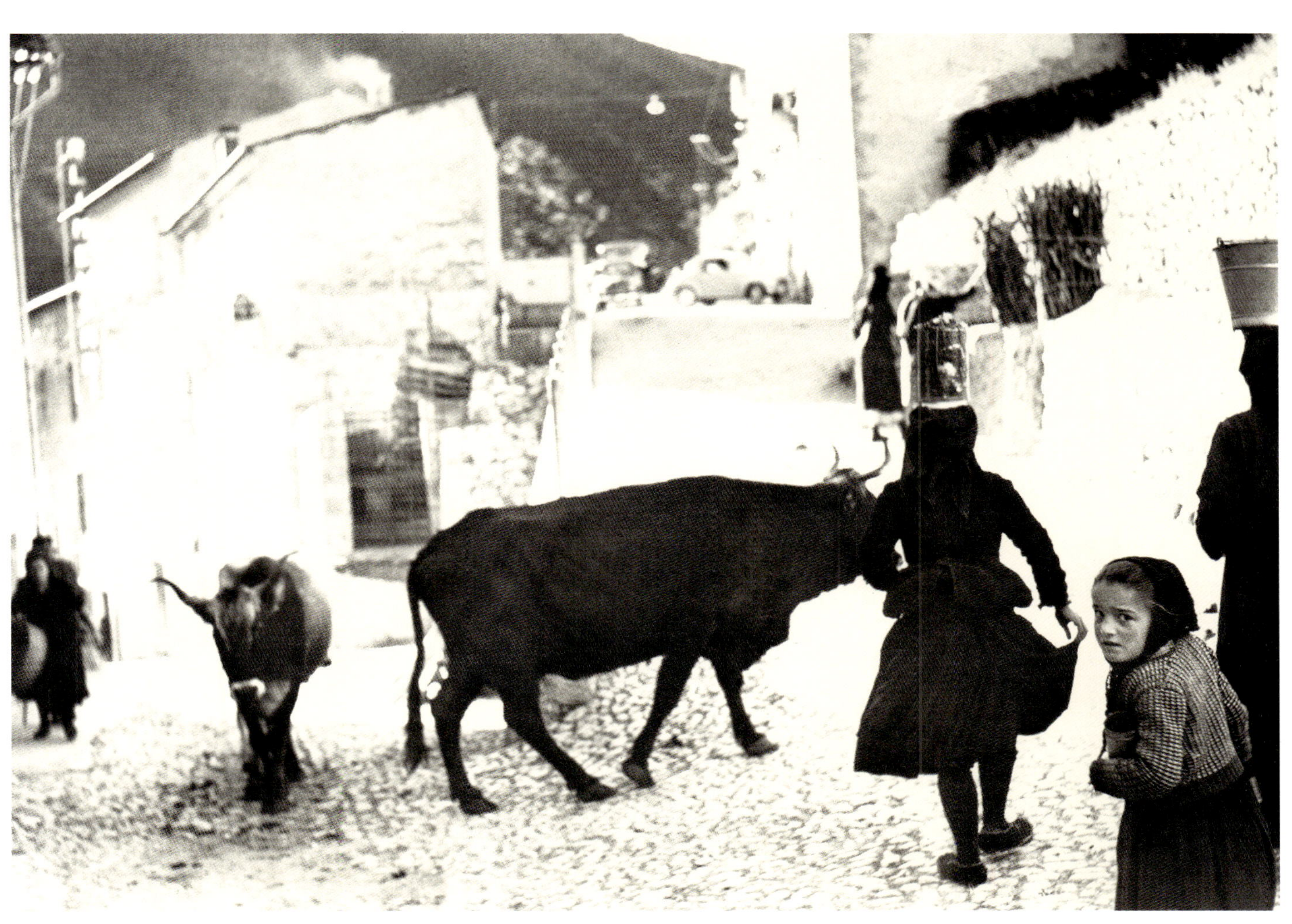

Mario Giacomelli

Via Mastai 6 – Senigallia (Ancona), Italia, 1957/58

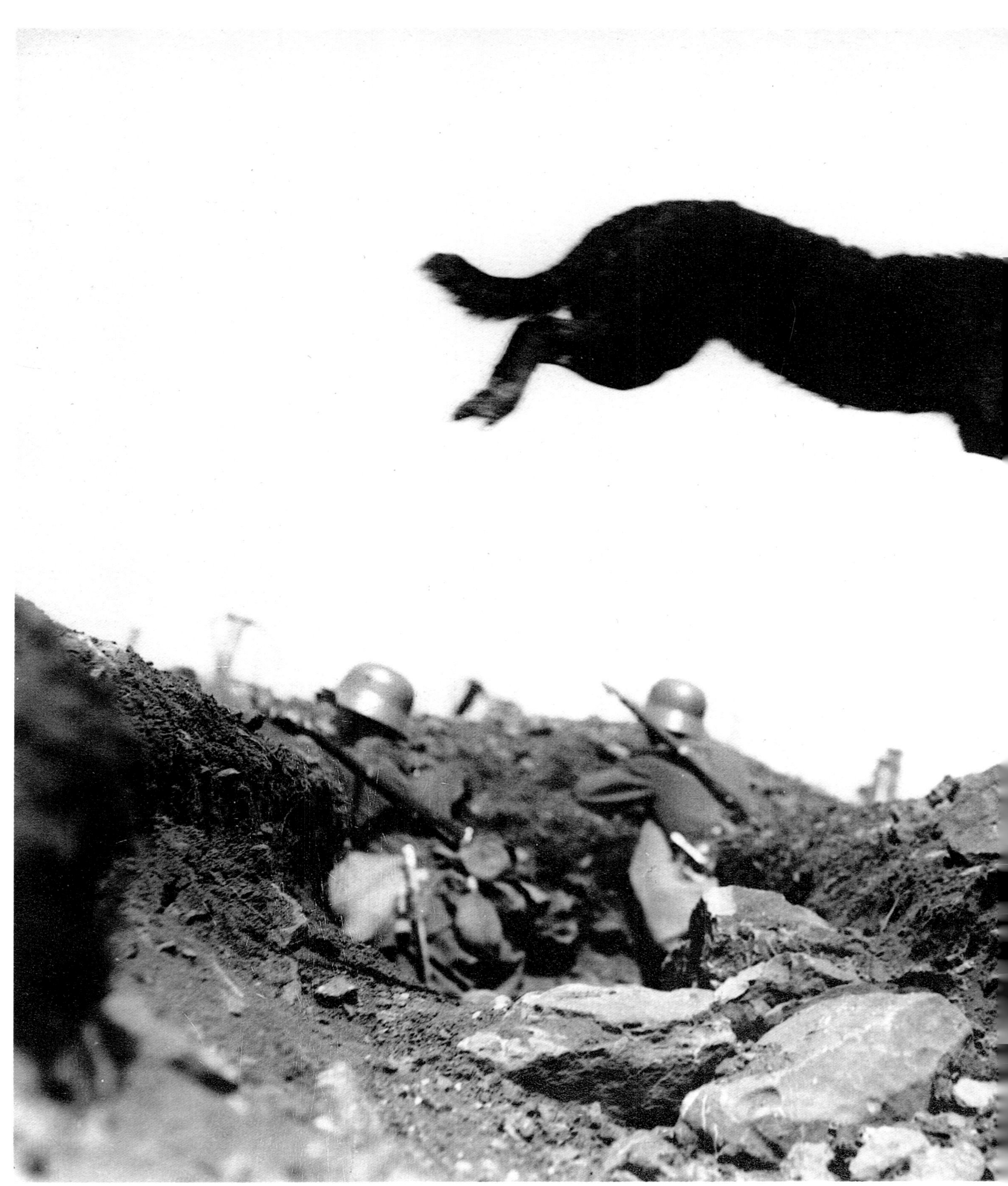

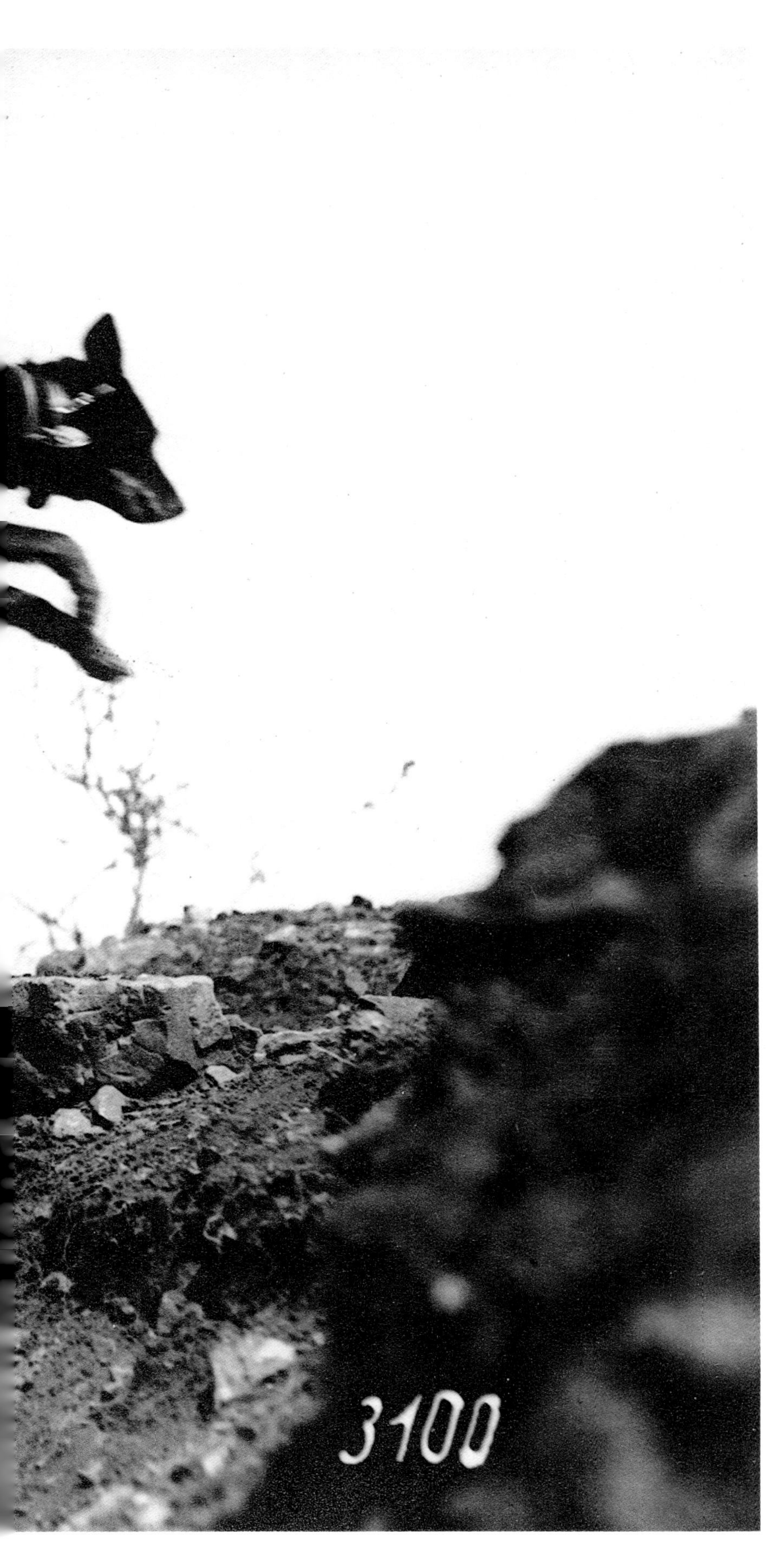

Anonym
Rapportierhund überbringt einen Bericht an die vorderste Stellung / Report dog brings a report to the frontline, 1916-1917

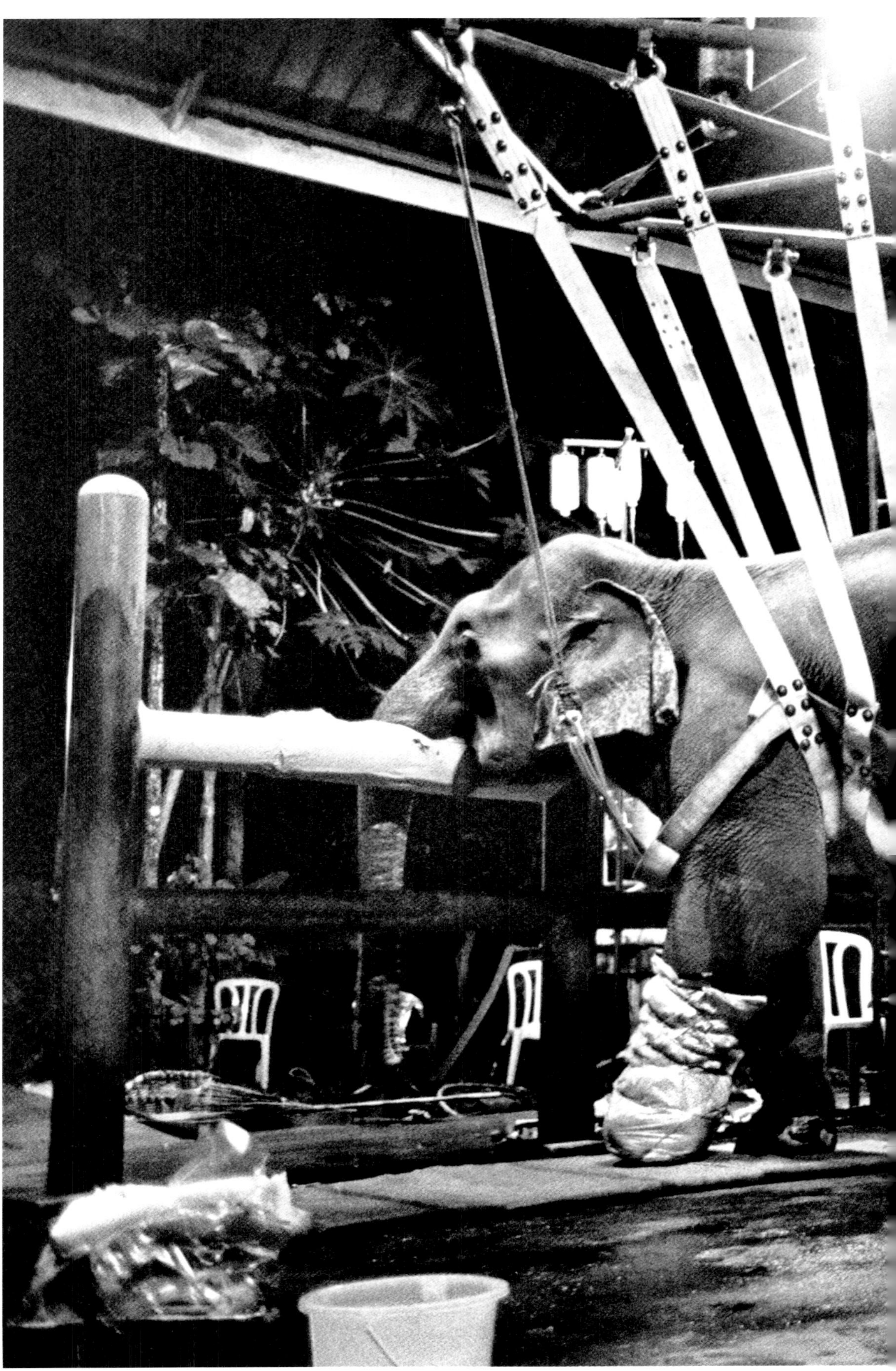

Chien-Chi Chang
Motala receives intensive care after her operation,
a. d. Serie: *Elephant Hospital,*
1999

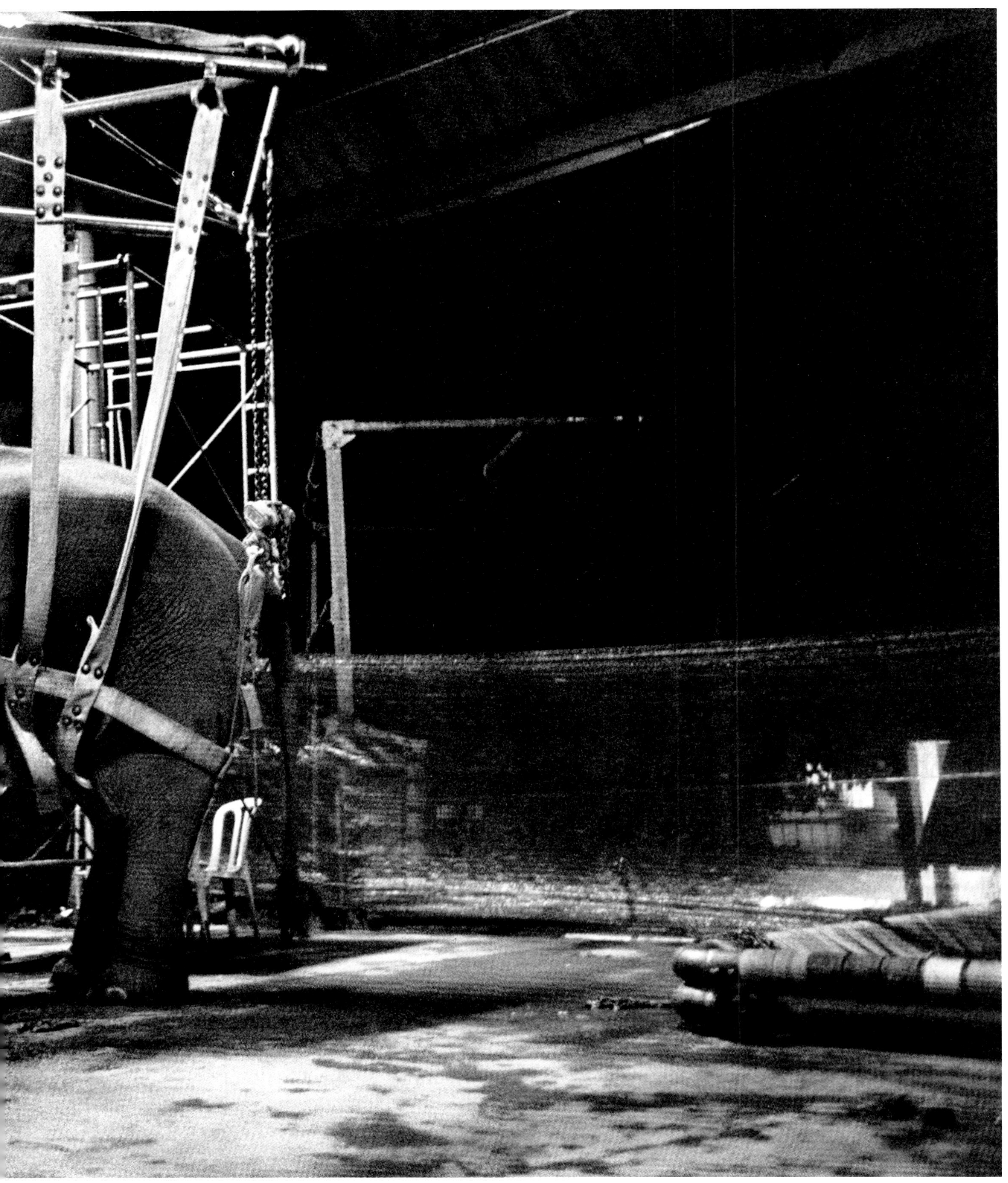

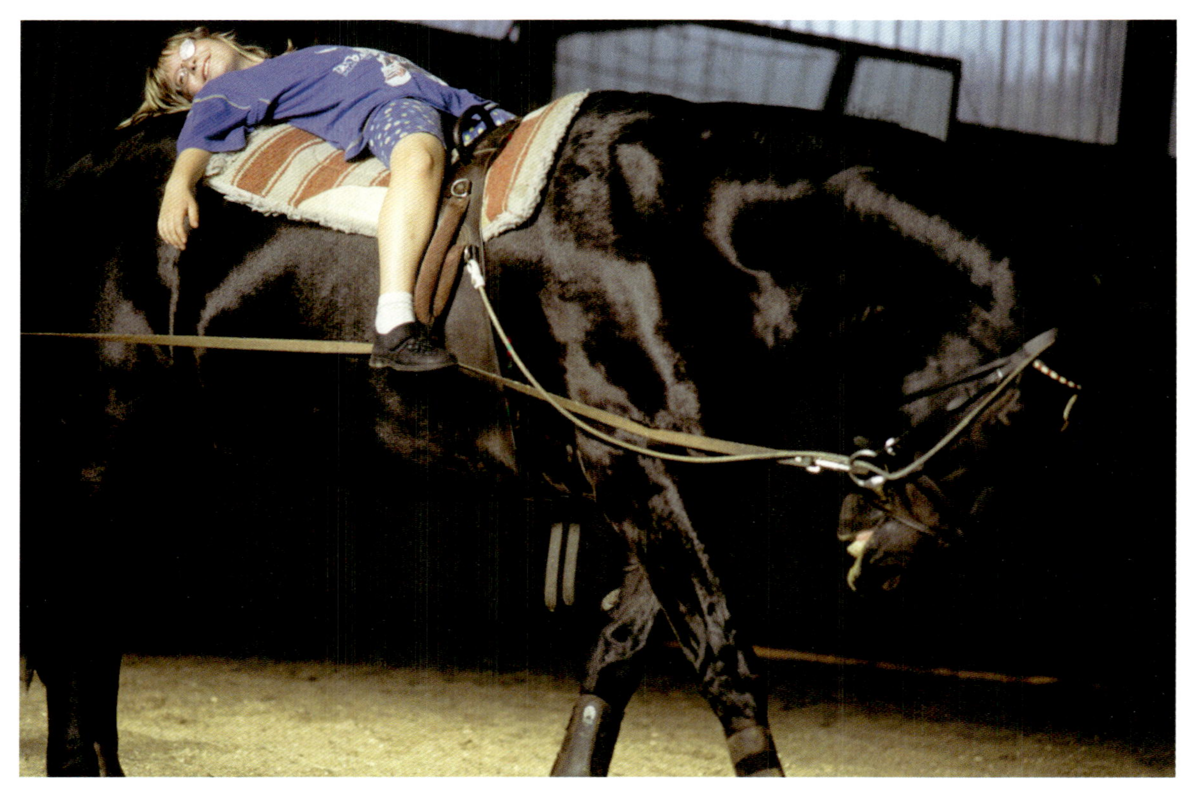

Walter Schmitz

a. d. Serie: *Tiere als Therapeuten*, 2001

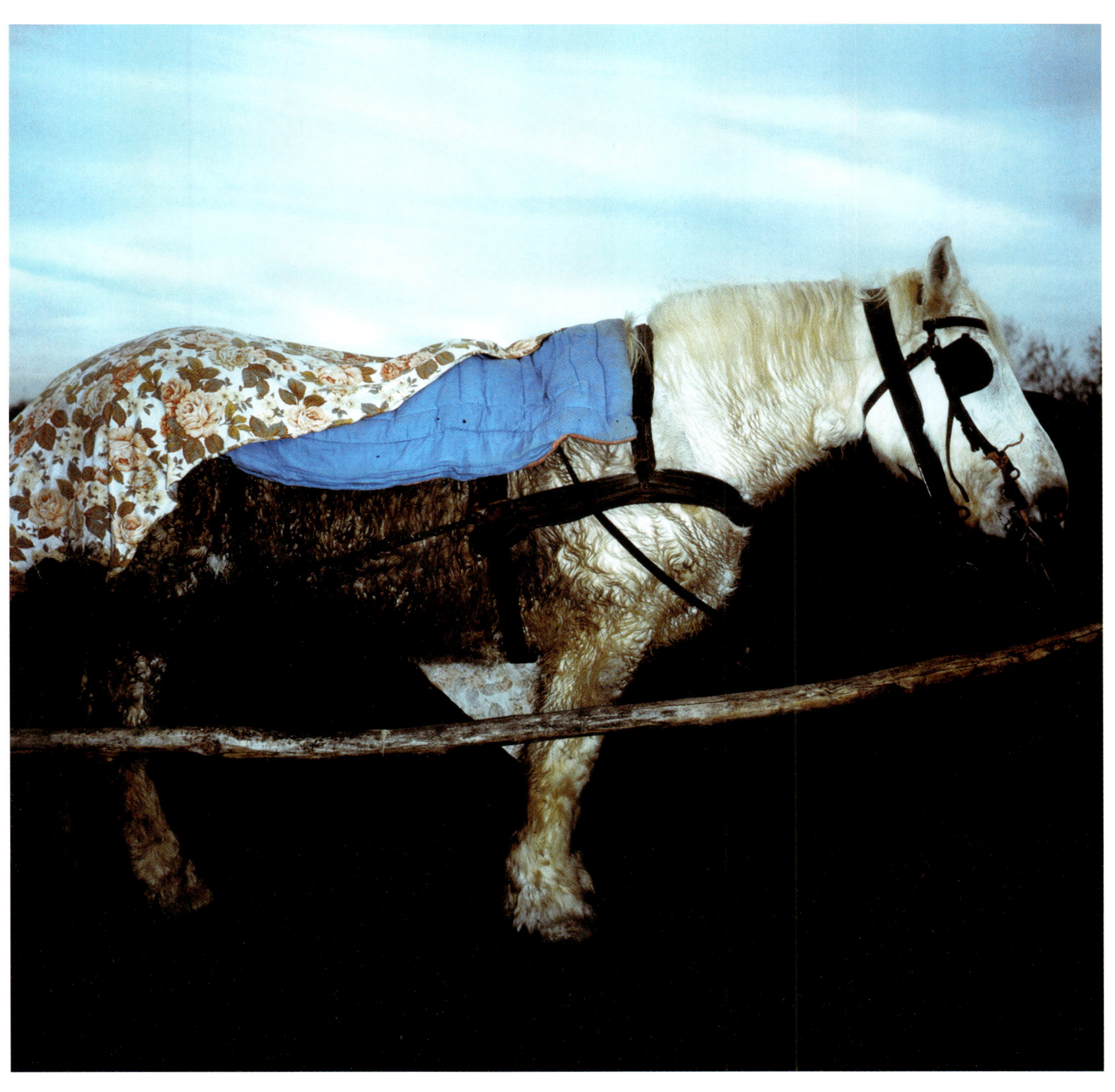

Manfred Willmann

Pferd, 1982, a. d. Serie: *Die Welt ist schön*, 1981-1983

„So kann man in den veröffentlichten Dokumentationen von physiologischen Tierexperimenten Fotos finden, die das betroffene Tier gezielt anonymisieren. Abgebildet werden dann nur die experimentell relevanten Körperpartien oder Organe, nicht aber das Tier als Ganzes. Diese hochselektive, fragmentierte Abbildung wird z. B. dann angewandt, wenn Blick und Körperhaltung des betroffenen Versuchstieres Unerwünschtes ausdrücken, wenn sie insbesondere Leiden und Schmerzen dokumentieren.“

“One can find photographs in the published documents of physiological experiments on animals that make the animal in question anonymous. Only parts or organs of the animal relevant to the experiment are shown, but not the animal as a whole. This highly selective, fragmented illustration is then used, for example, when the animal expresses something in its gaze or posture that is undesirable, in particular, when it documents pain and suffering.”

Rainer E. Wiedenmann

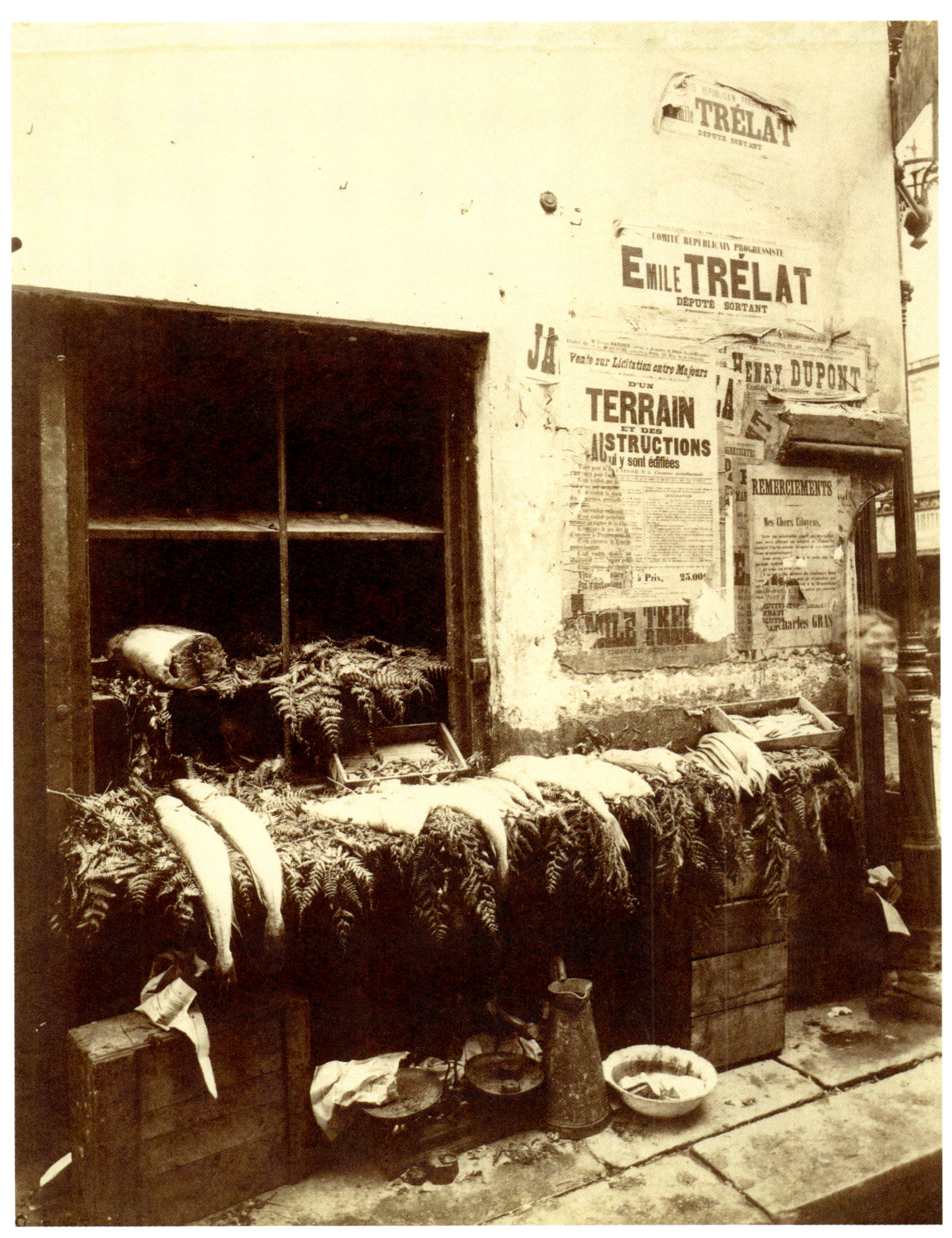

Eugène Atget

Marchande de poissons, rue Mouffetard, 1898

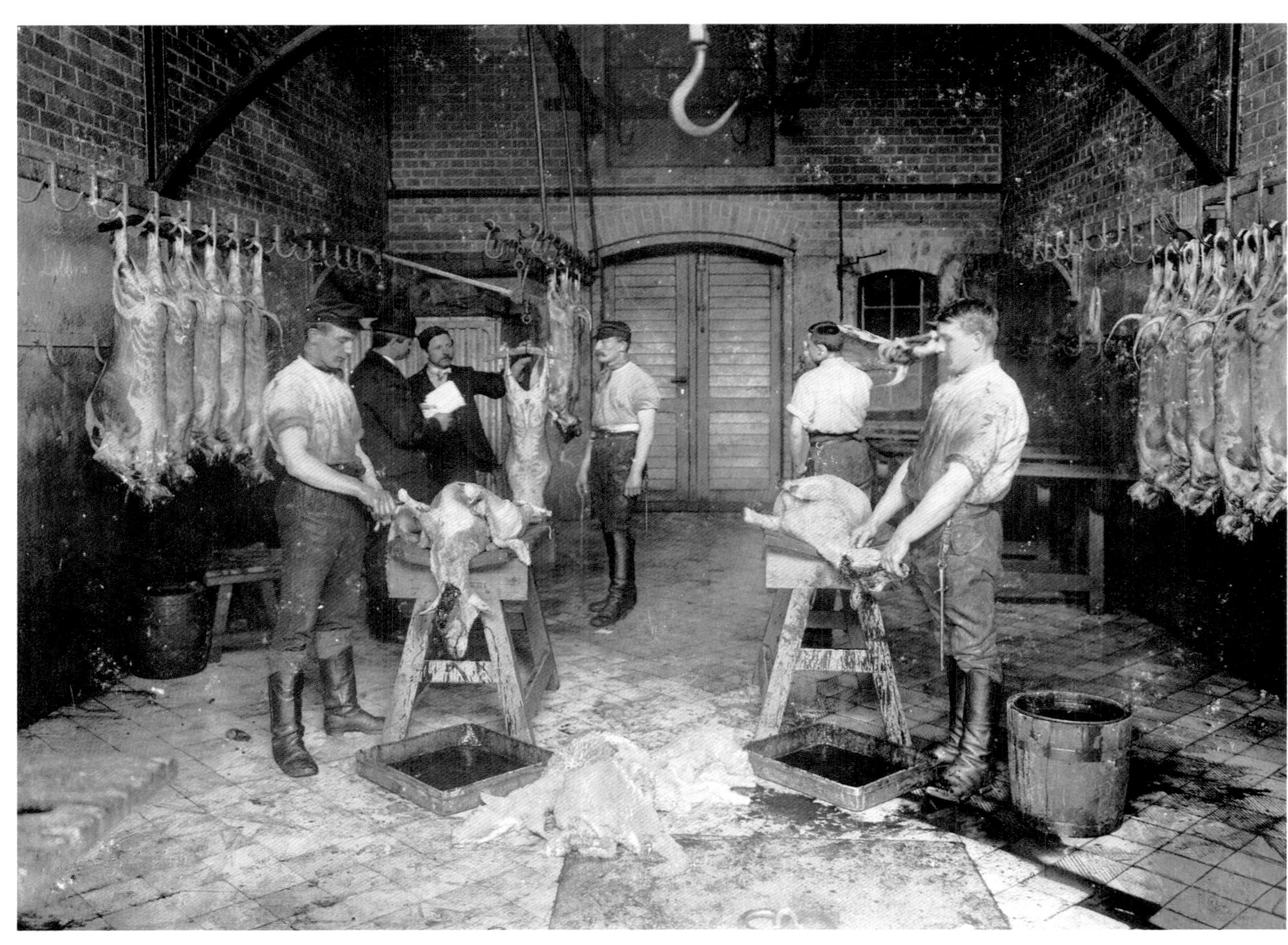

Waldemar Titzenthaler

Städtischer Schlachthof: Hammelschlachthaus Friedrichshain, 1897

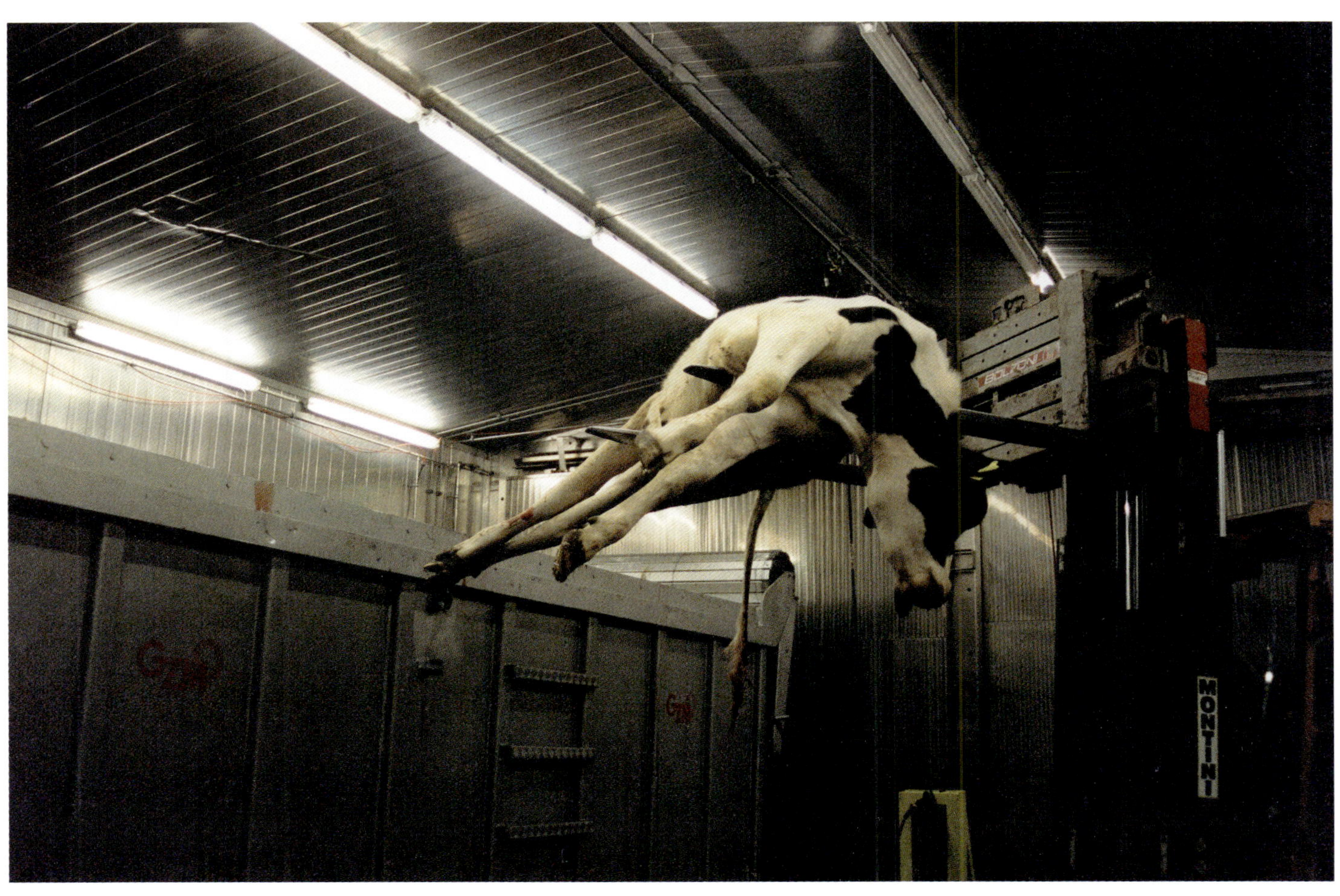

Nadin Maria Rüfenacht
a. d. Serie: *Vieh*, 2003

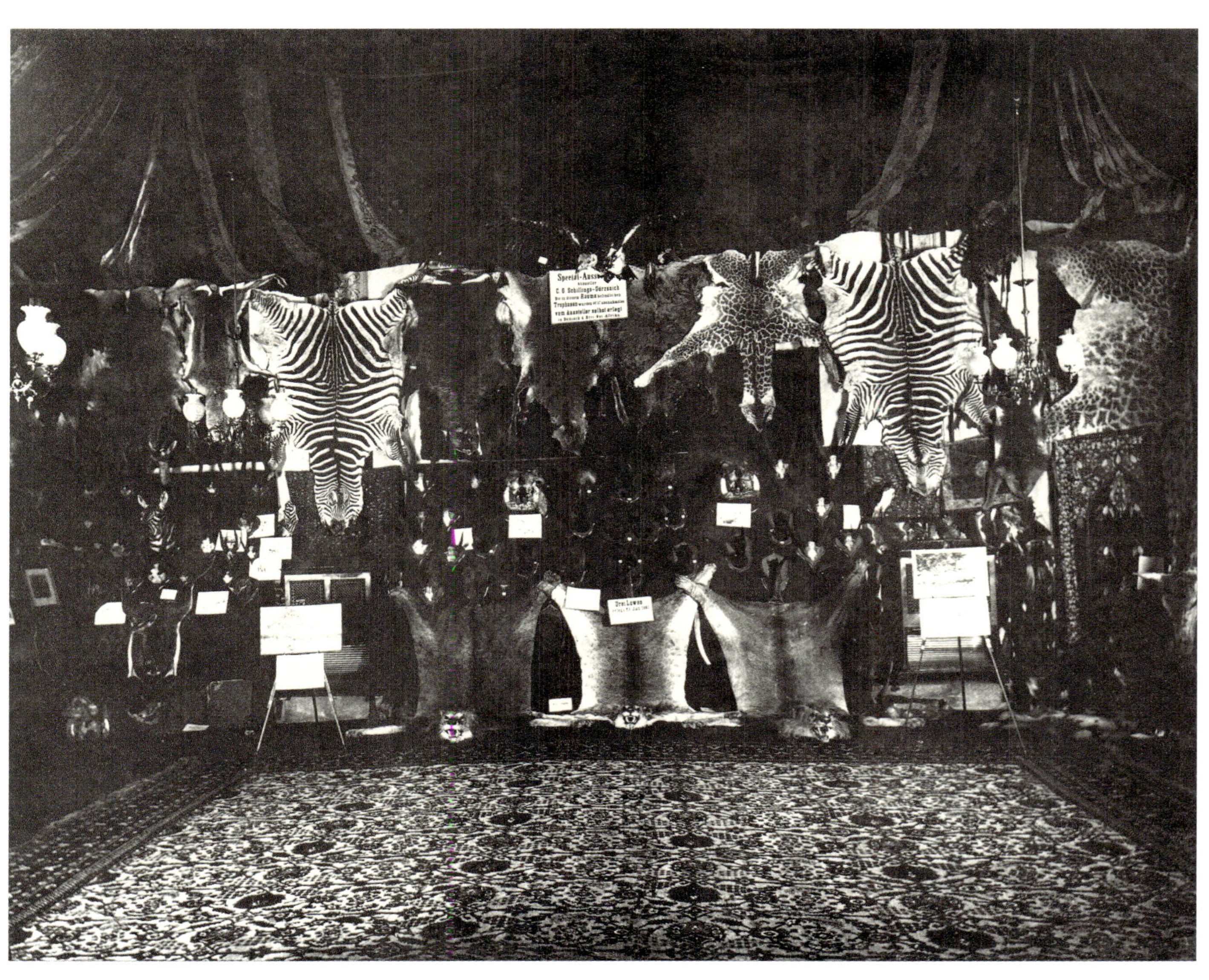

Carl Georg Schillings

Album *Specialausstellung von Jagdtrophäen ausgestellt gelegentlich der Deutschen Geweihausstellung* /

Special exhibition of hunting trophies, shown on the occasion of the German Antler Exhibition, 1889

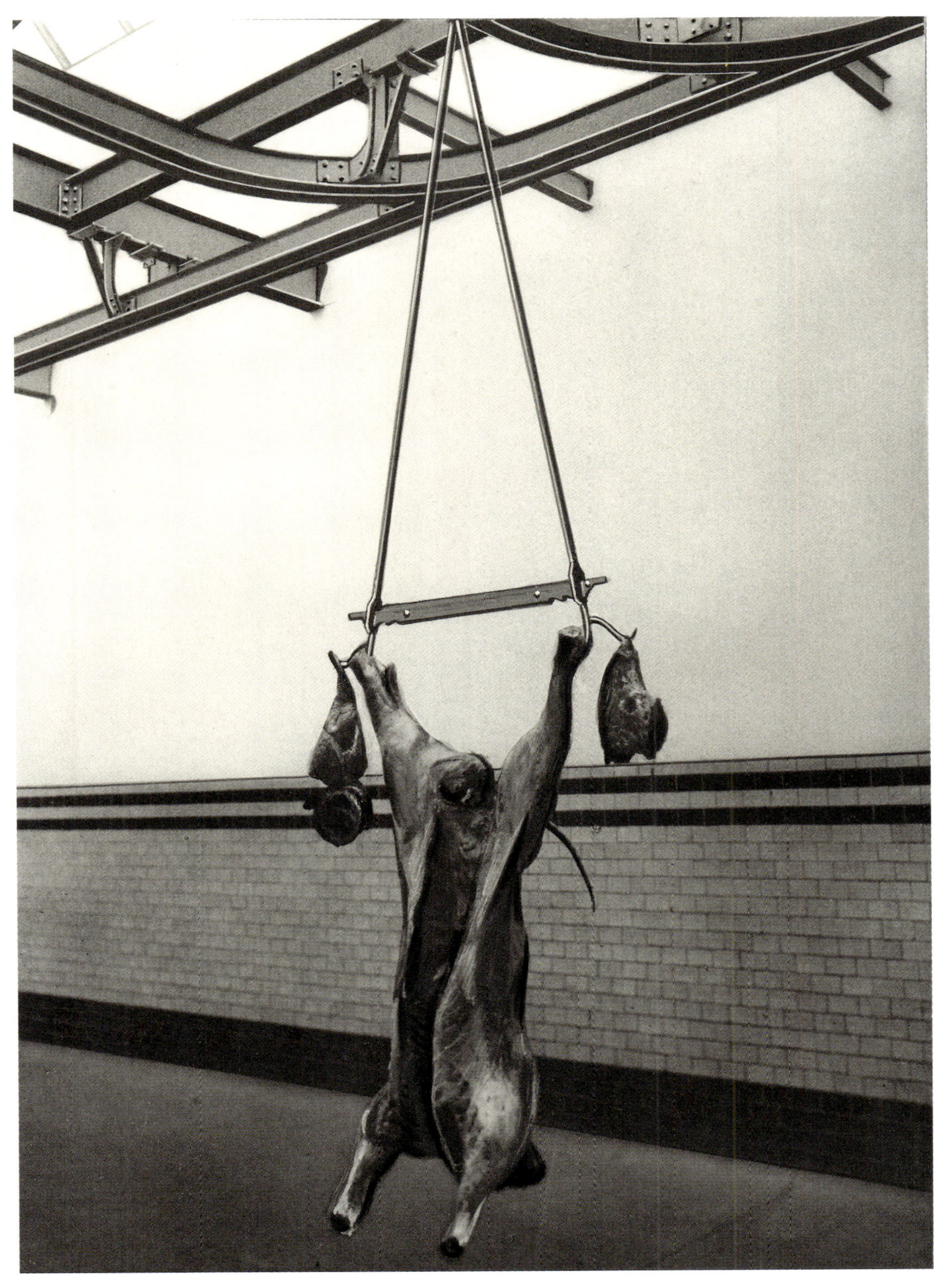

Atelier Köller
Schlachthof (Auftrag der Firma Presswerk Esser) /
Slaughterhouse (Commission by Presswerk Esser), ca. 1910

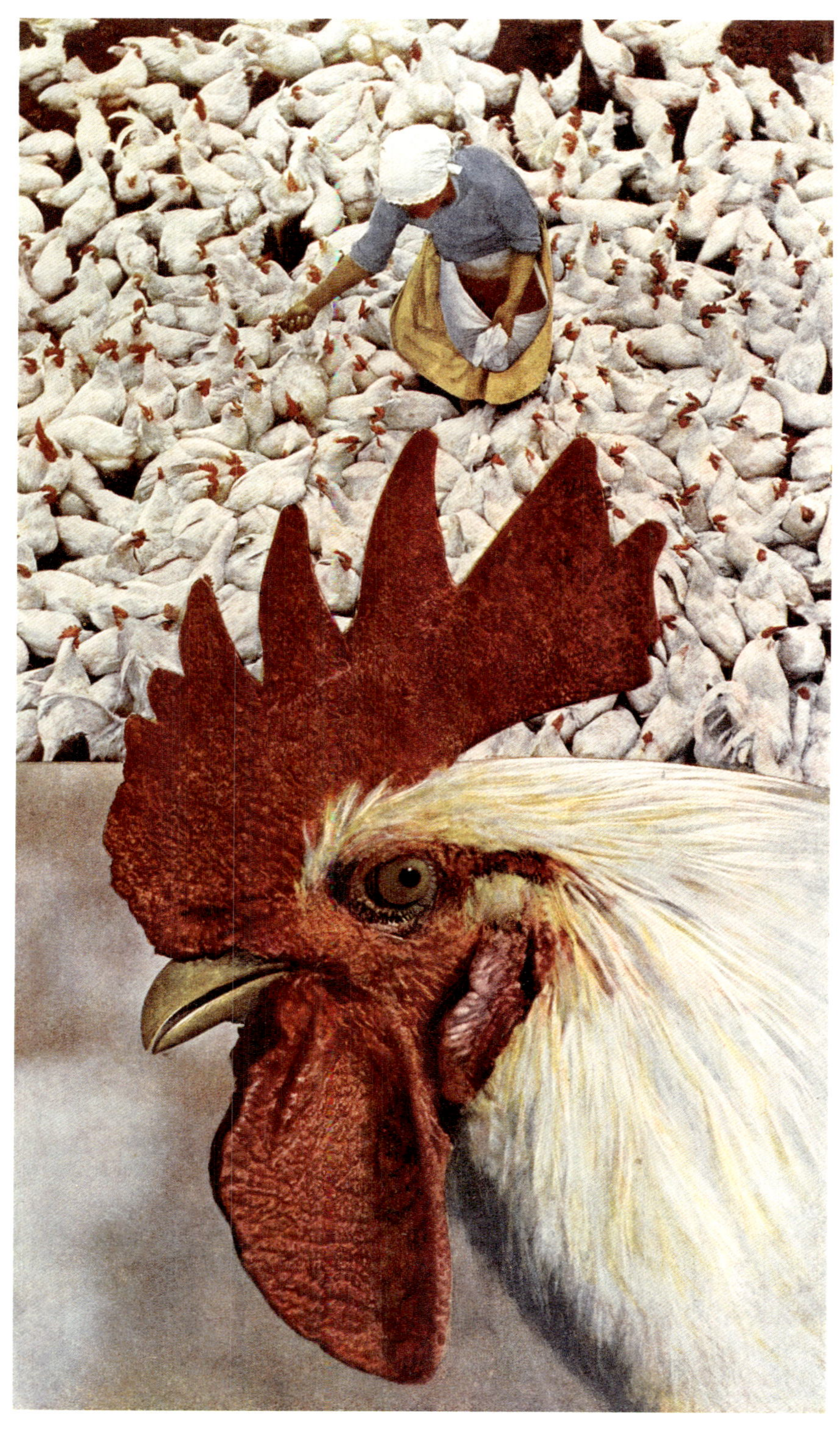

Anatolij Skurichin / Wladimir Grüntal
Hühnerkombinat, a. d. Portfolio: *Lebensmittelindustrie*, 1936 (Gestaltung El Lissitzky)

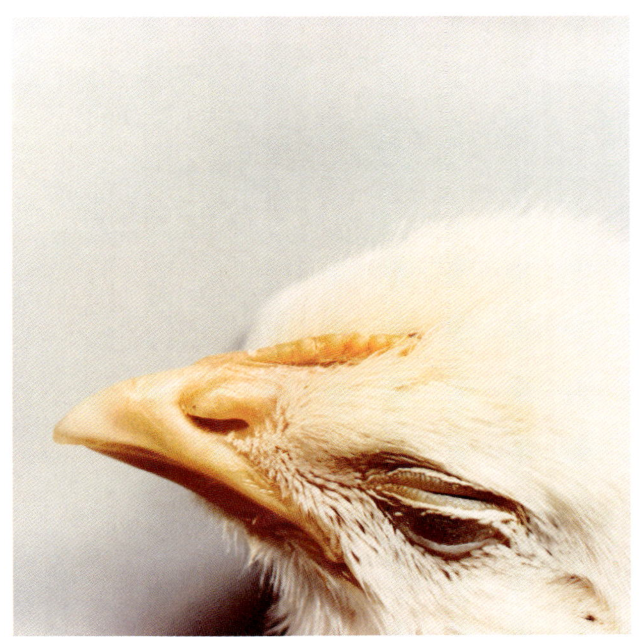

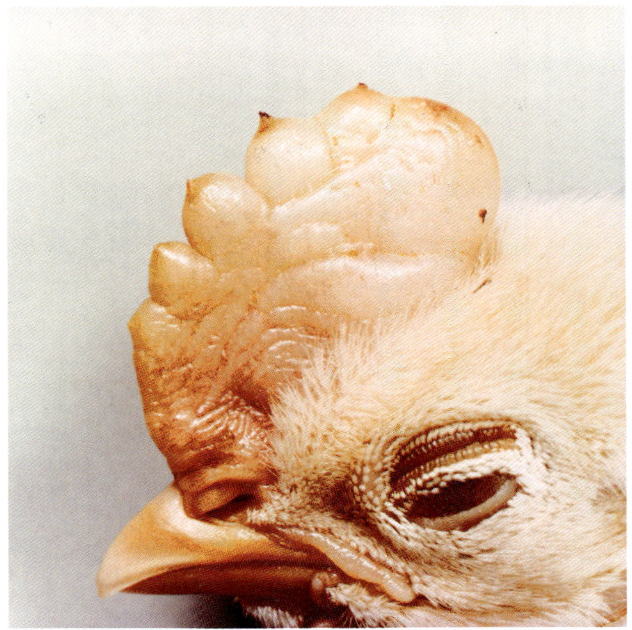

Anonym (Schering AG Berlin)
Hormonforschung, Kammbildung /
Hormone research, crest forming, 1971

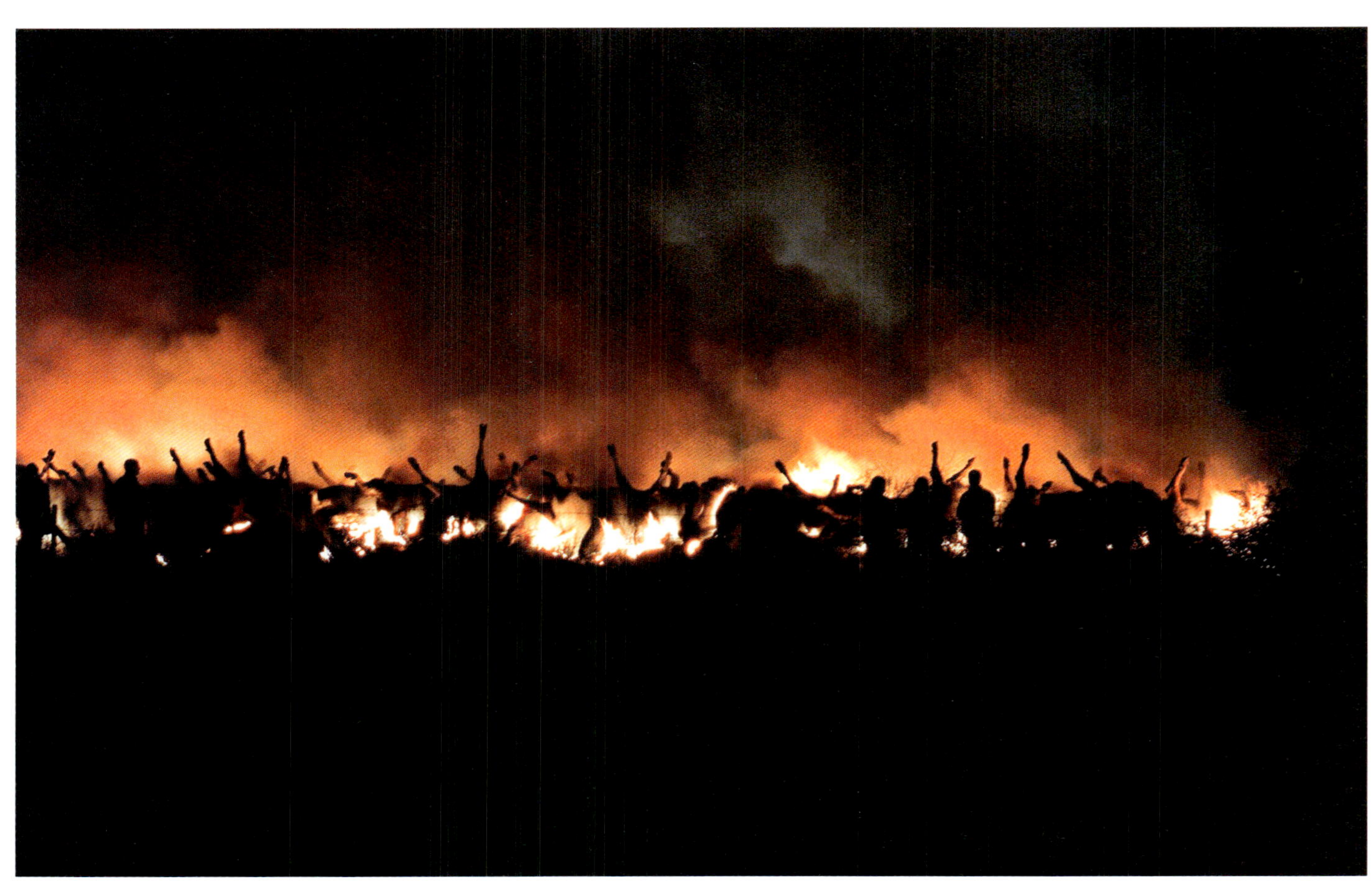

Anonym (action press)
Verbrennung BSE erkrankter Huftiere, Great Walley Farm, Großbritannien /
Burning of BSE infected hoofed animals, Great Walley Farm, Great Britain, 27.2.2001

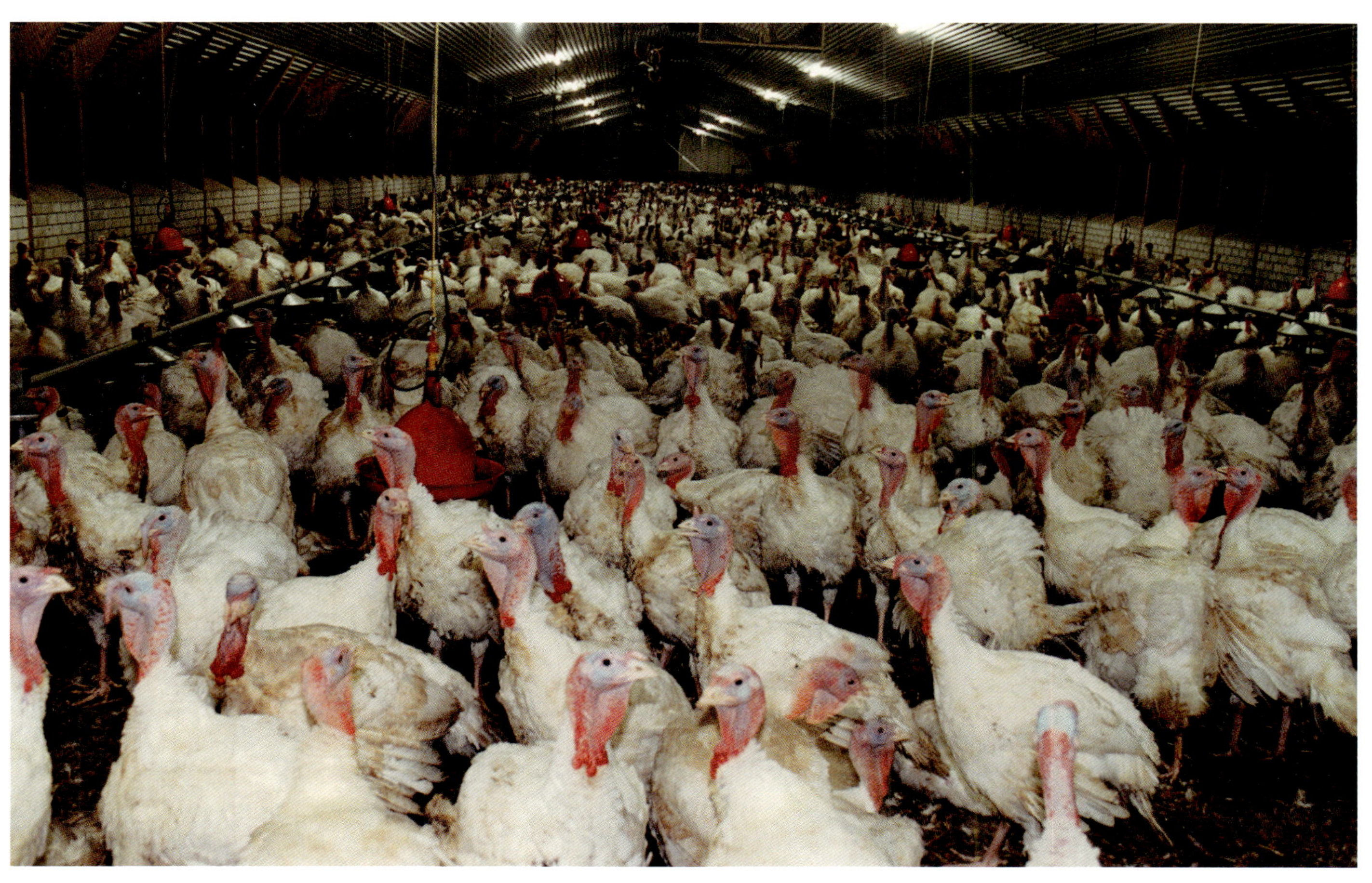

Greenpeace

Puten-Fabrik, 2001, *Masttierhaltung*

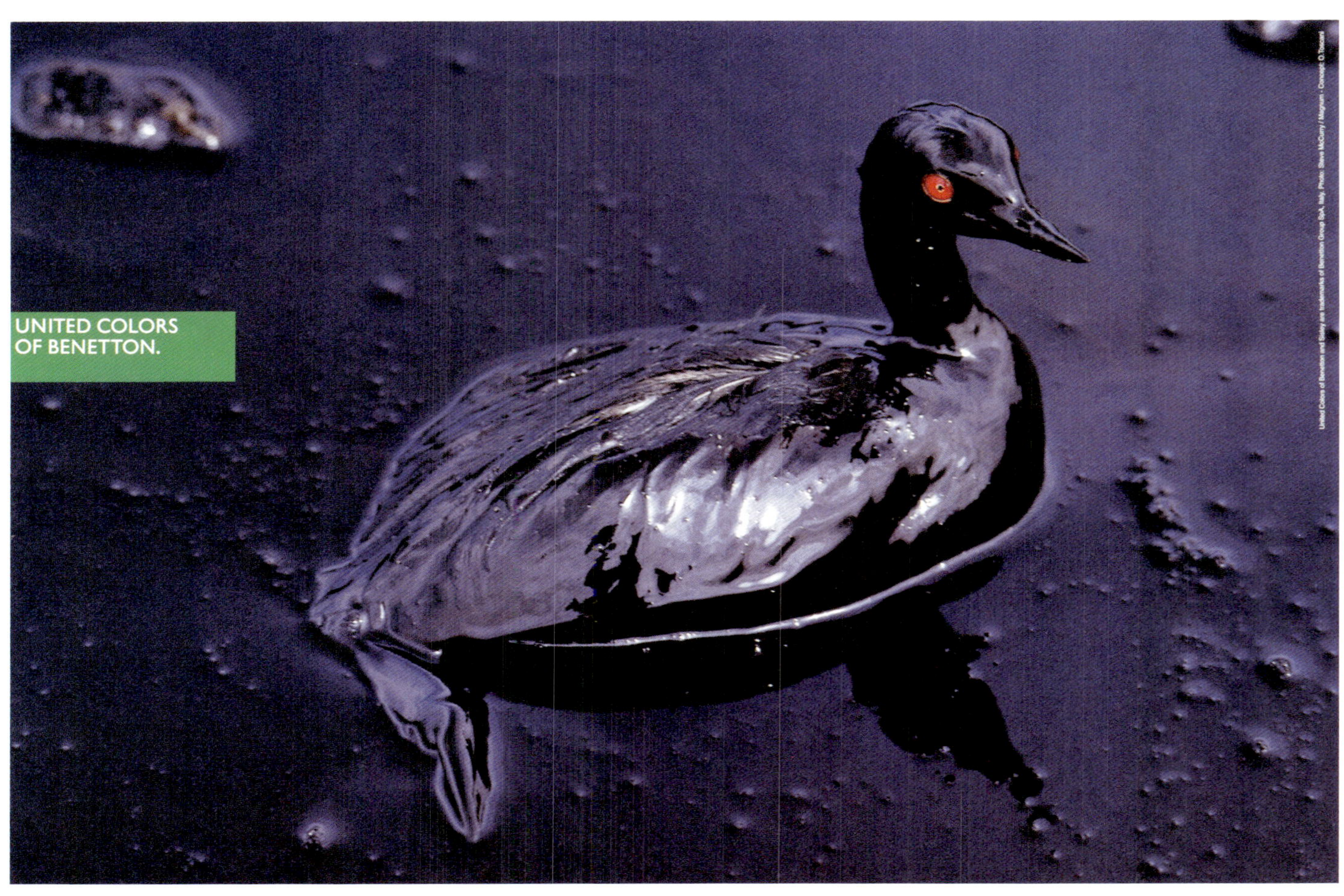

Ölverschmutzter Seevogel, Benetton-Werbung,
Konzept Olivier Toscani, Foto Steve McCurry /
Sea bird, badly soiled by oil, Benetton advertising,
concept Olivier Toscani, photo Steve Mc Curry, September 1992

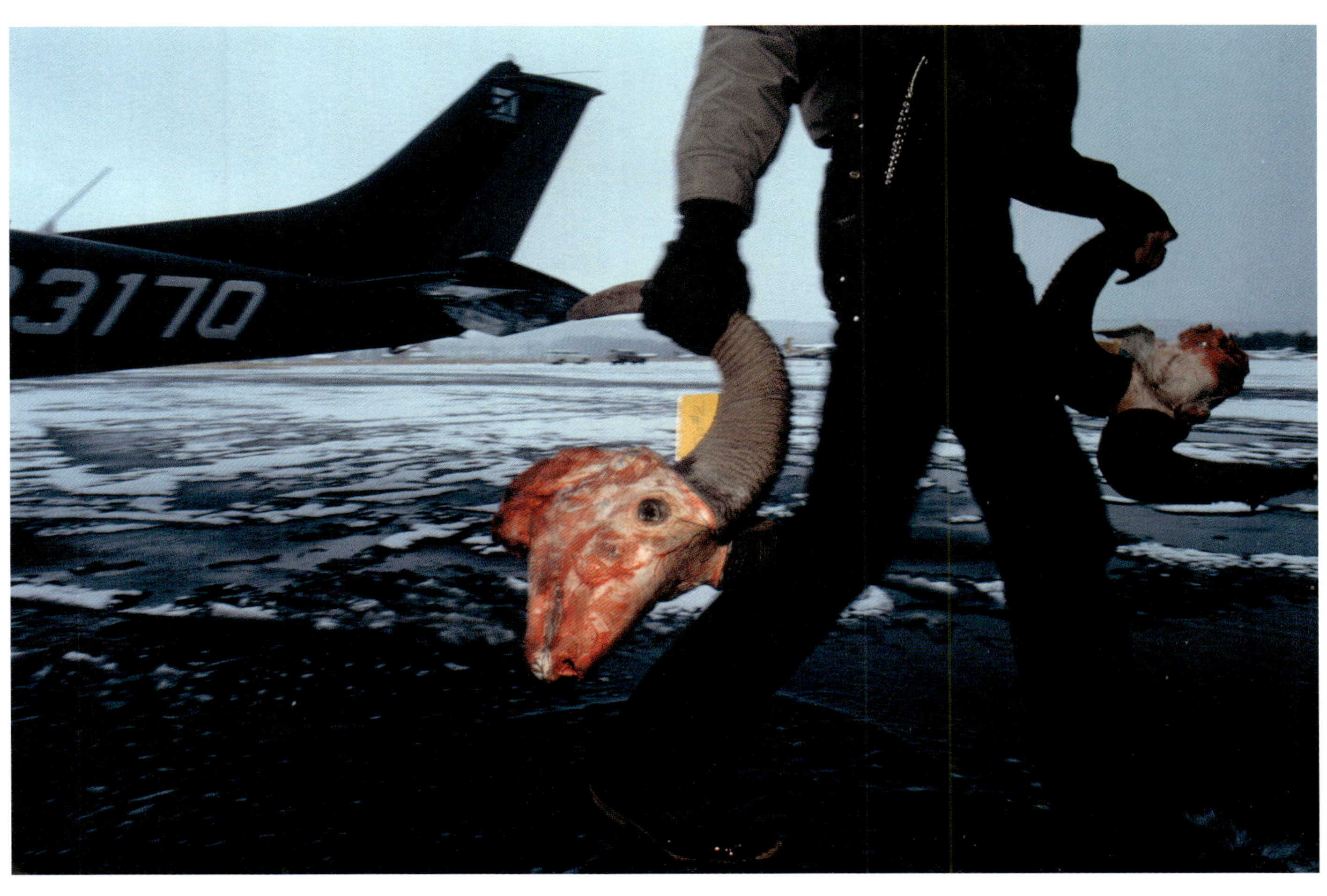

José Azel

Confiscated illegal Rocky Mountain Bighorn Sheep, 1996

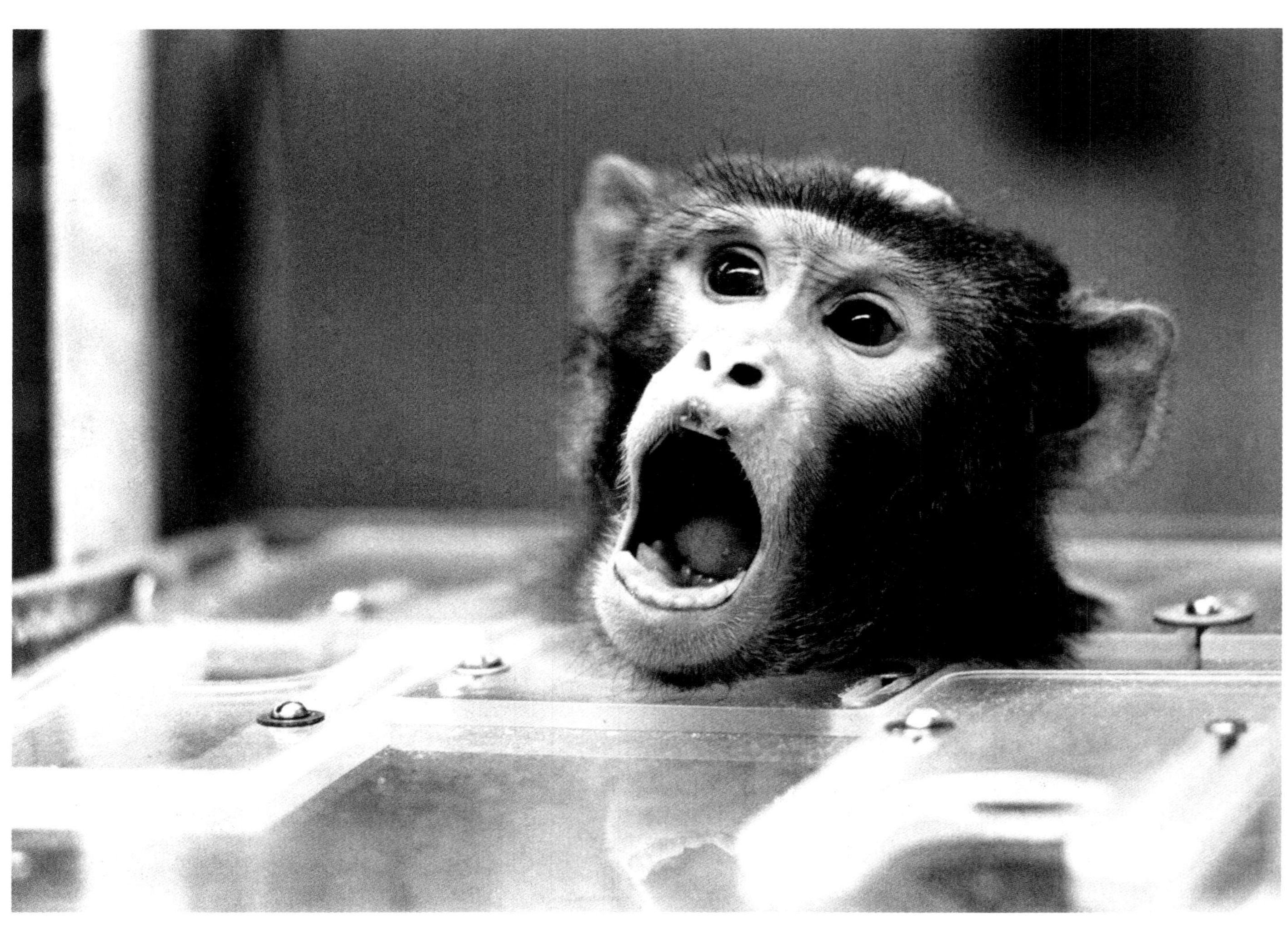

Eberhard Seeliger

Hirnforschung – Prof. Delgado, USA, April 1973

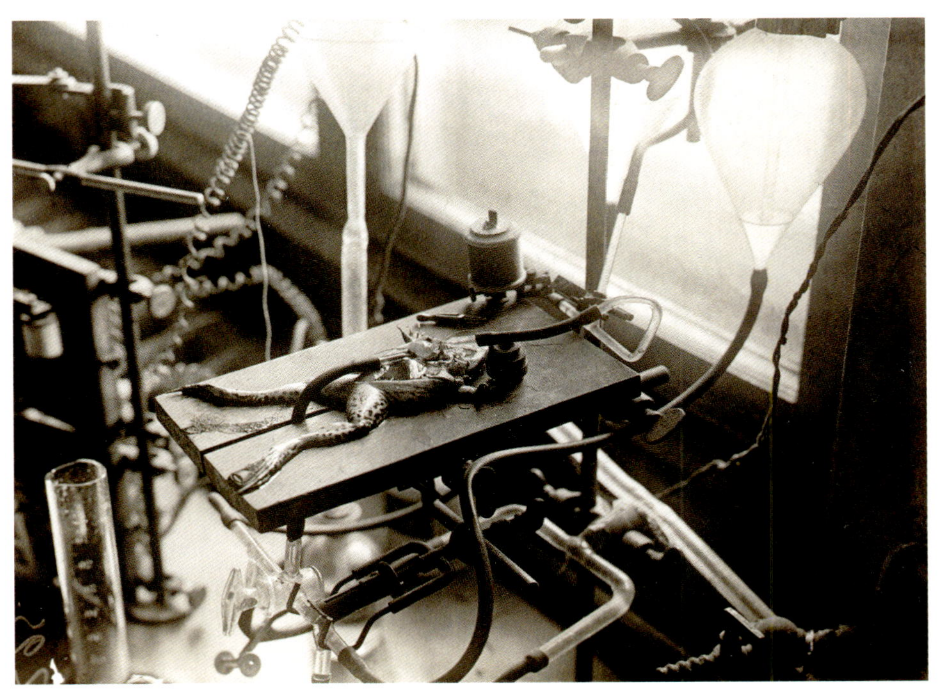

Fritz Zielesch
Tierversuche, Versuchsanordnung mit Frosch /
Animal experiments, experiment with frog, 1930

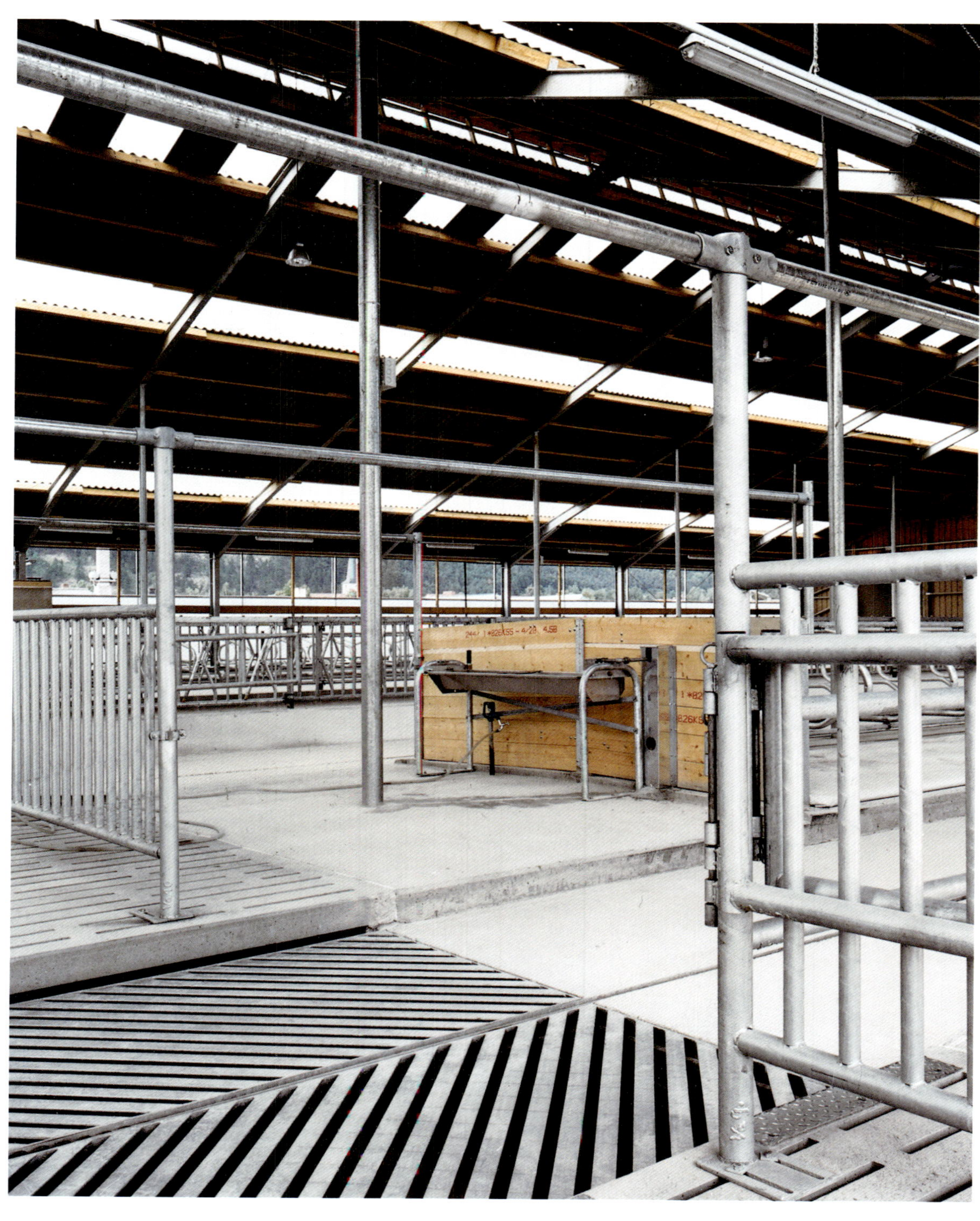

Martin Richter

a. d. Serie: *Moderne Ställe*, ca. 2001

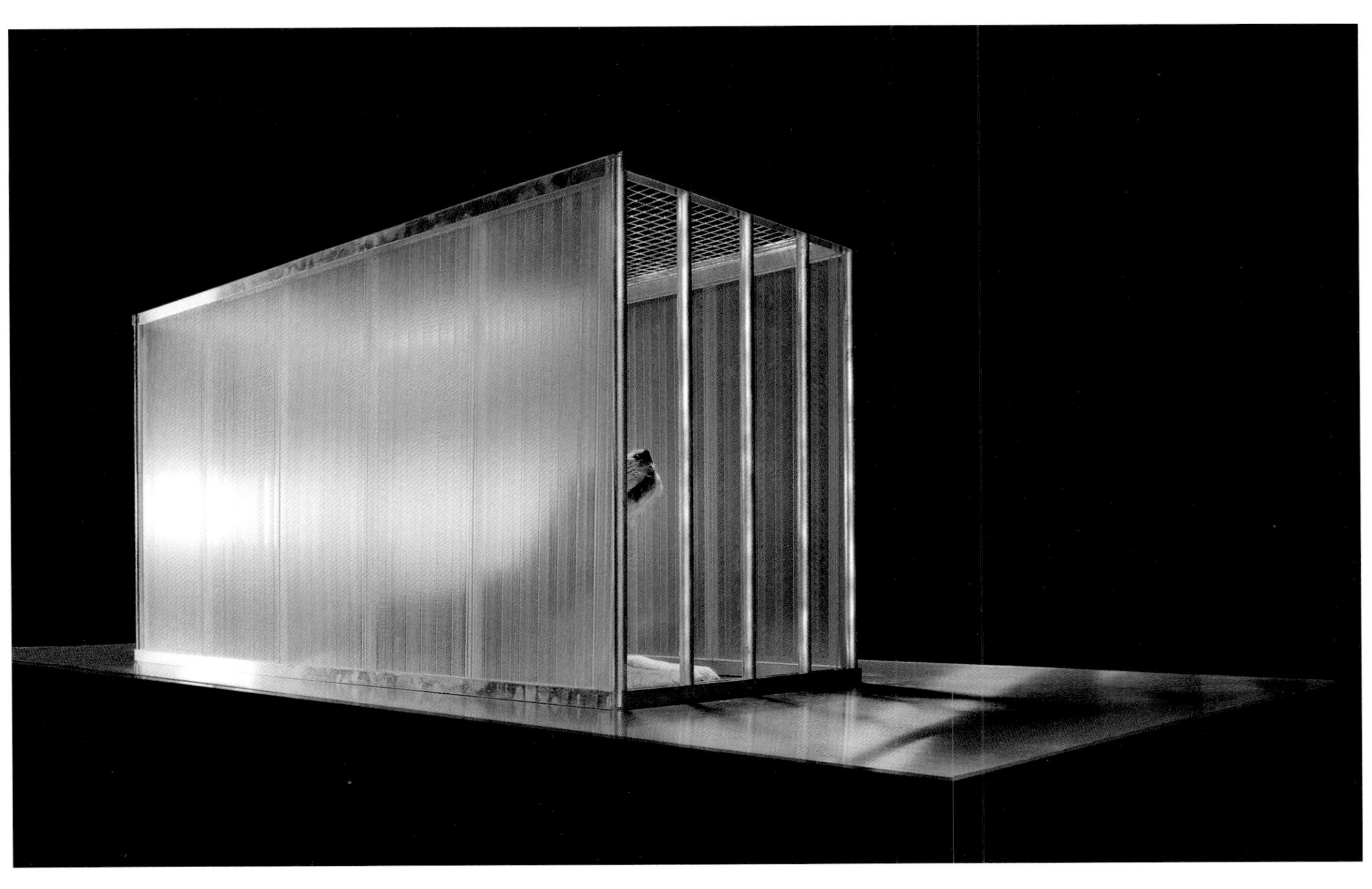

Jan Kornstaedt

Junger Beagle im Käfig, Hamburg, 2003

„Während Amateure ihre Tiere als einzigartig wahrnehmen, sind sie in der professionellen Fotografie weitgehend austauschbar. Ironischerweise werden letztere aus der Masse herausgehoben, während die anderen trotz des gegenteiligen Bemühens darin verschwinden."

"While amateurs perceive their animals as unique, in photographs by professionals, the animals are widely considered interchangeable. Ironically, it is often photographs of the second category that are selected out of the masses, while the others—despite their makers' opposing efforts—go unnoticed."

Bernhard Kathan

Zuhause At home

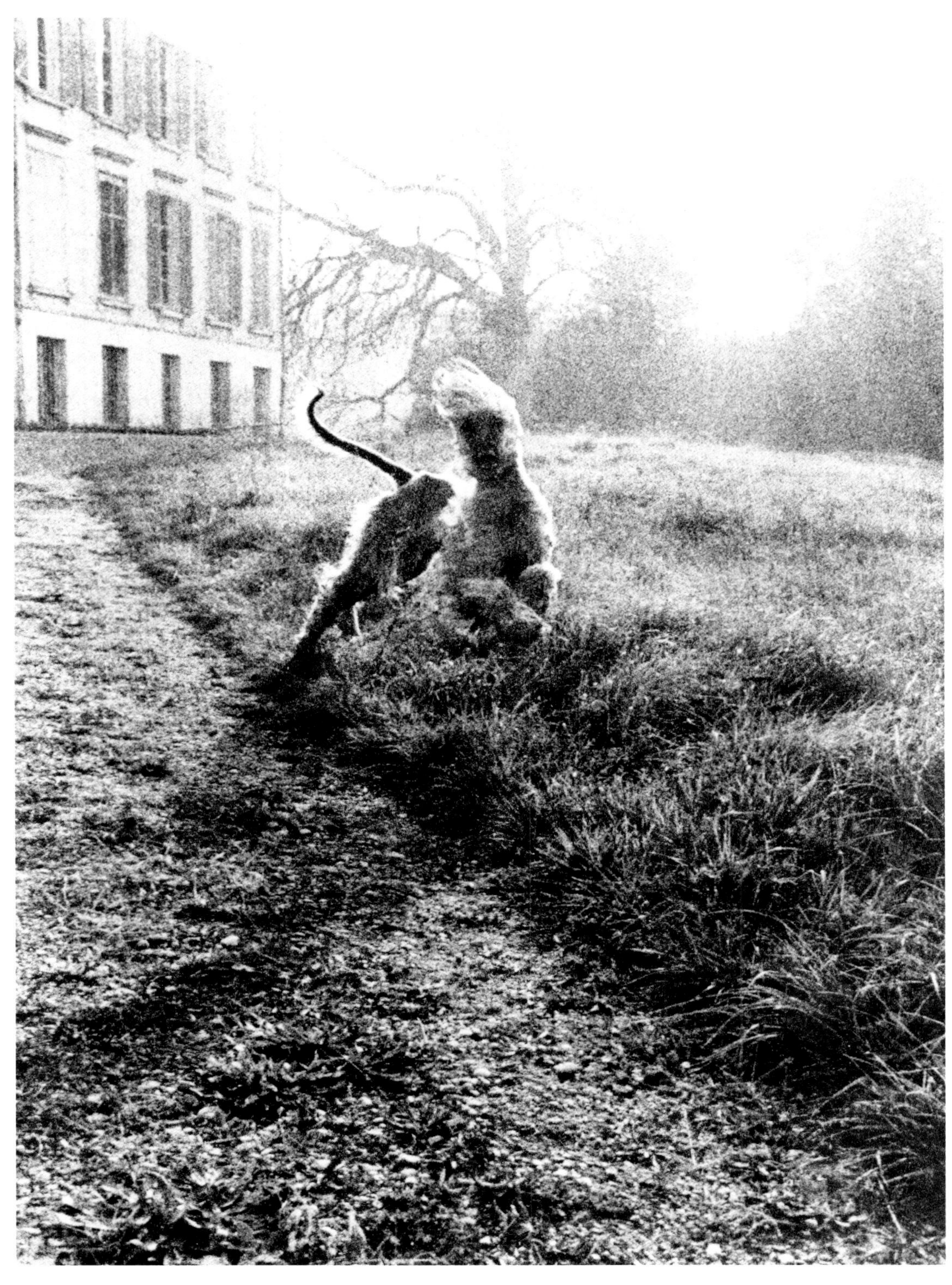

Jacques-Henri Lartigue

Dick, 1963

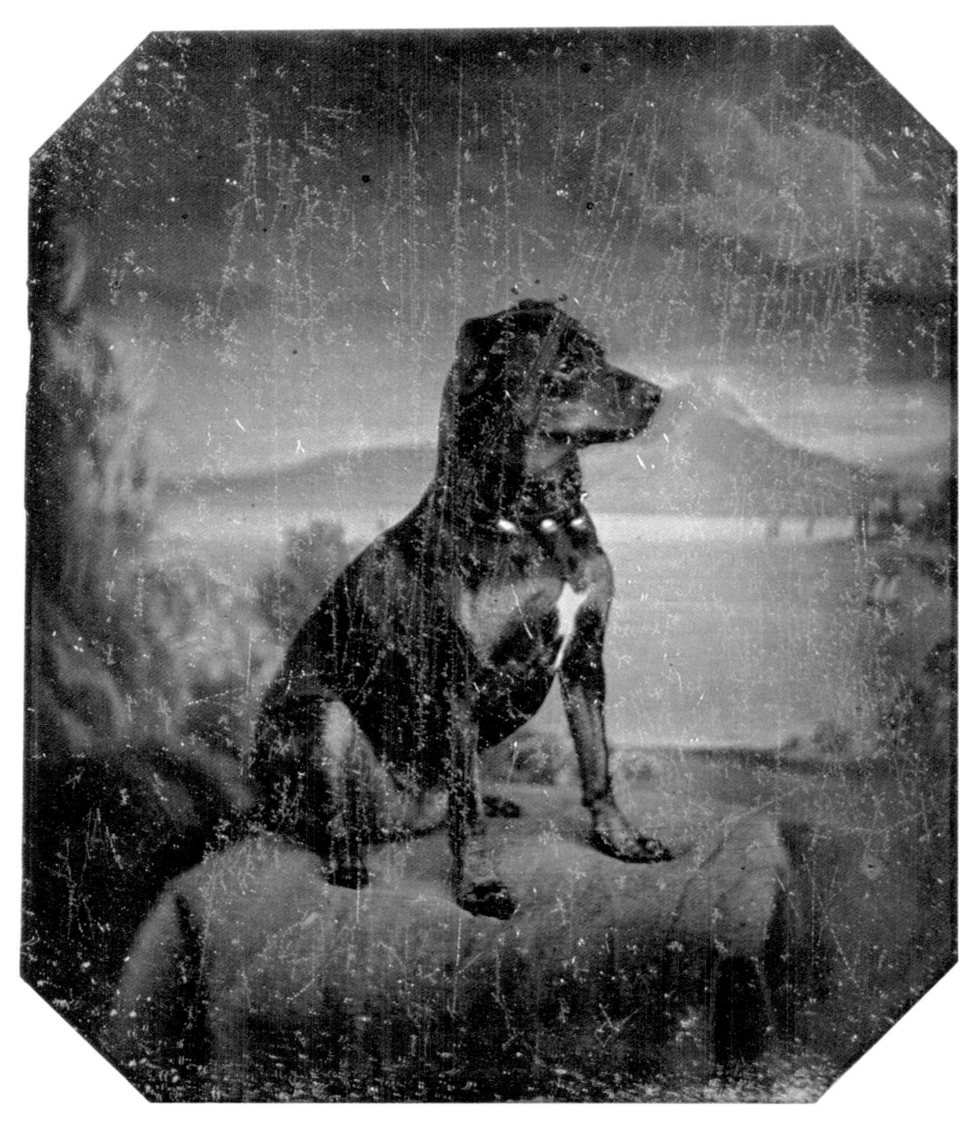

Carl Ferdinand Stelzner

"Ulla", der Hund im Hause Stelzner, o. D.

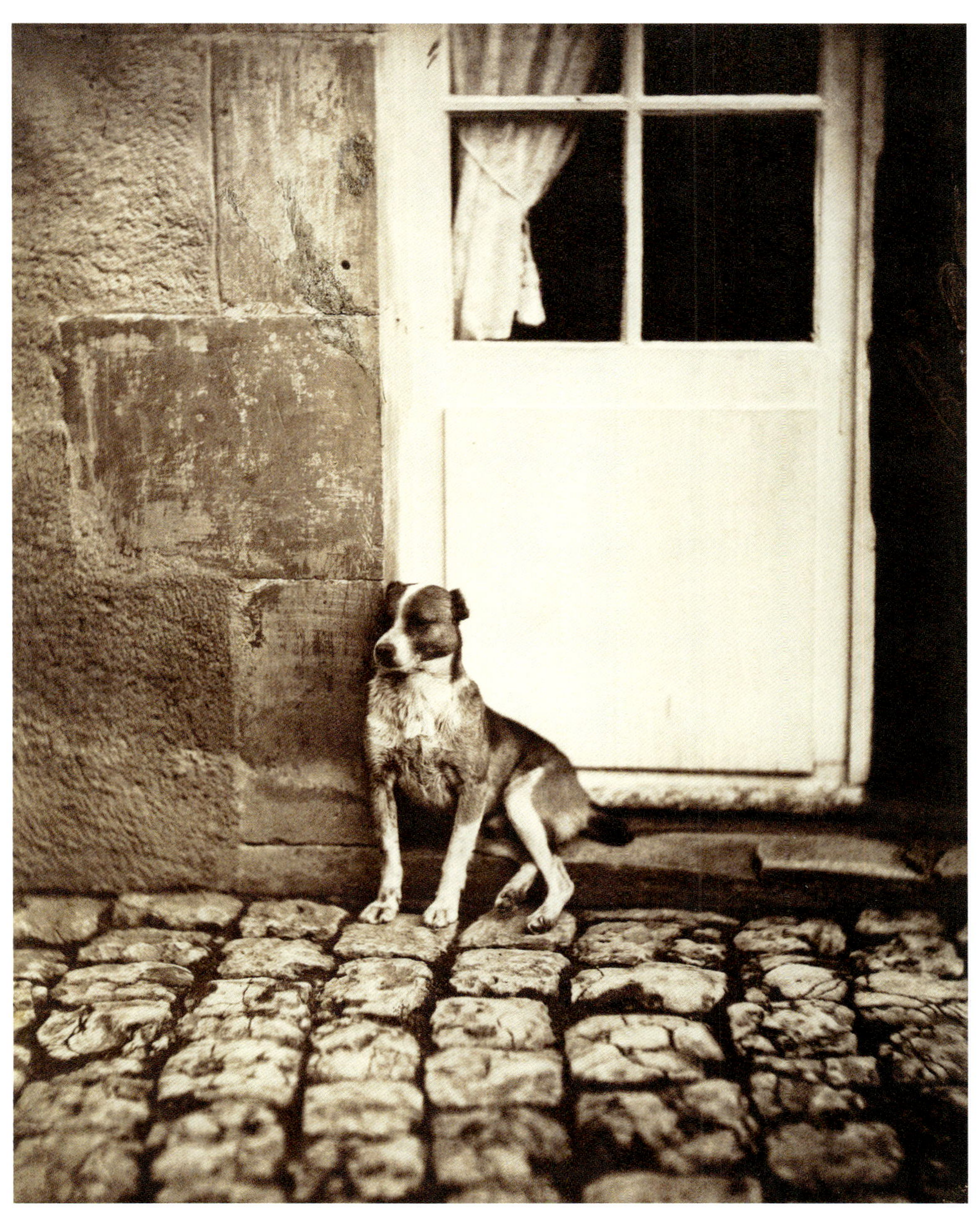

Comte Olympe Aguado

Chien assis devant une porte, 1857

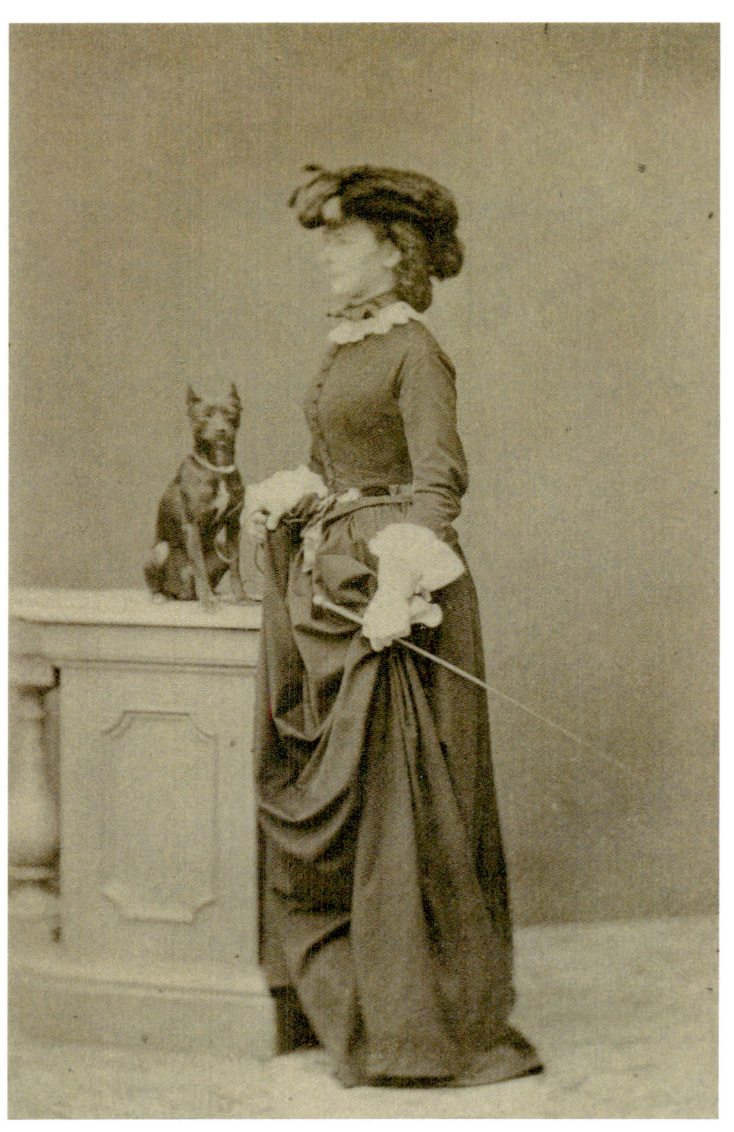

Ludwig Angerer
Portrait, ca. 1860

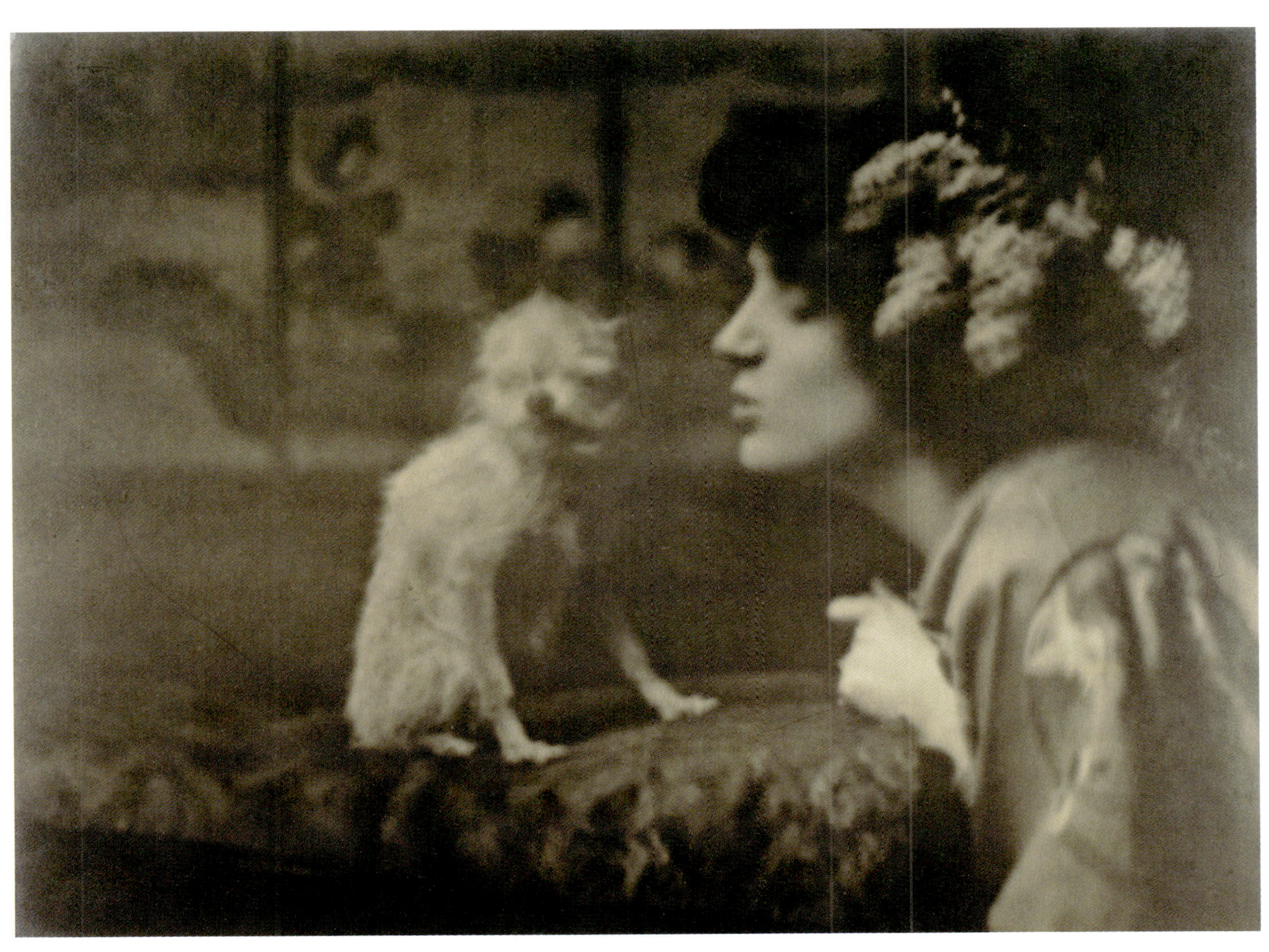

Arnold Genthe

Mrs Patrick Campbell, 1902

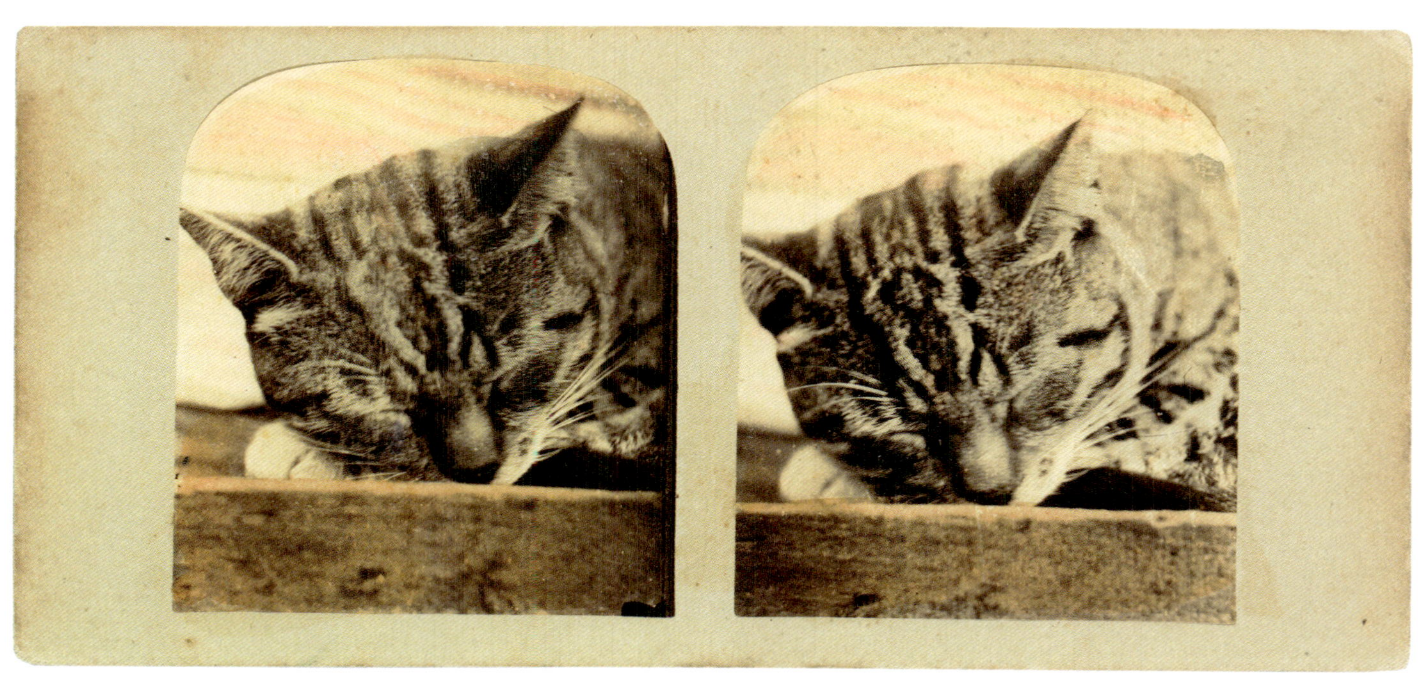

Anonym

A Member of a Maiden Lady's Family, ca. 1865

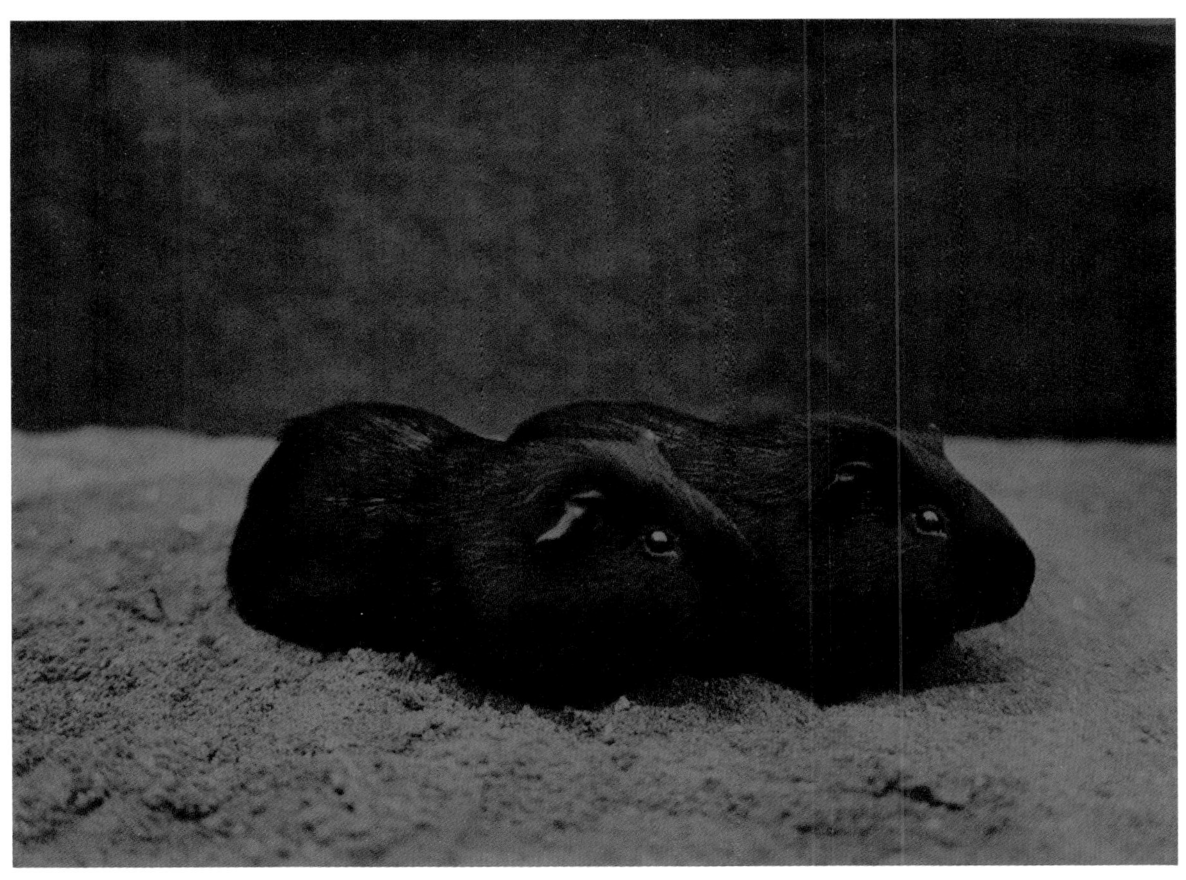

Richard Tepe
Cavias, ca. 1930

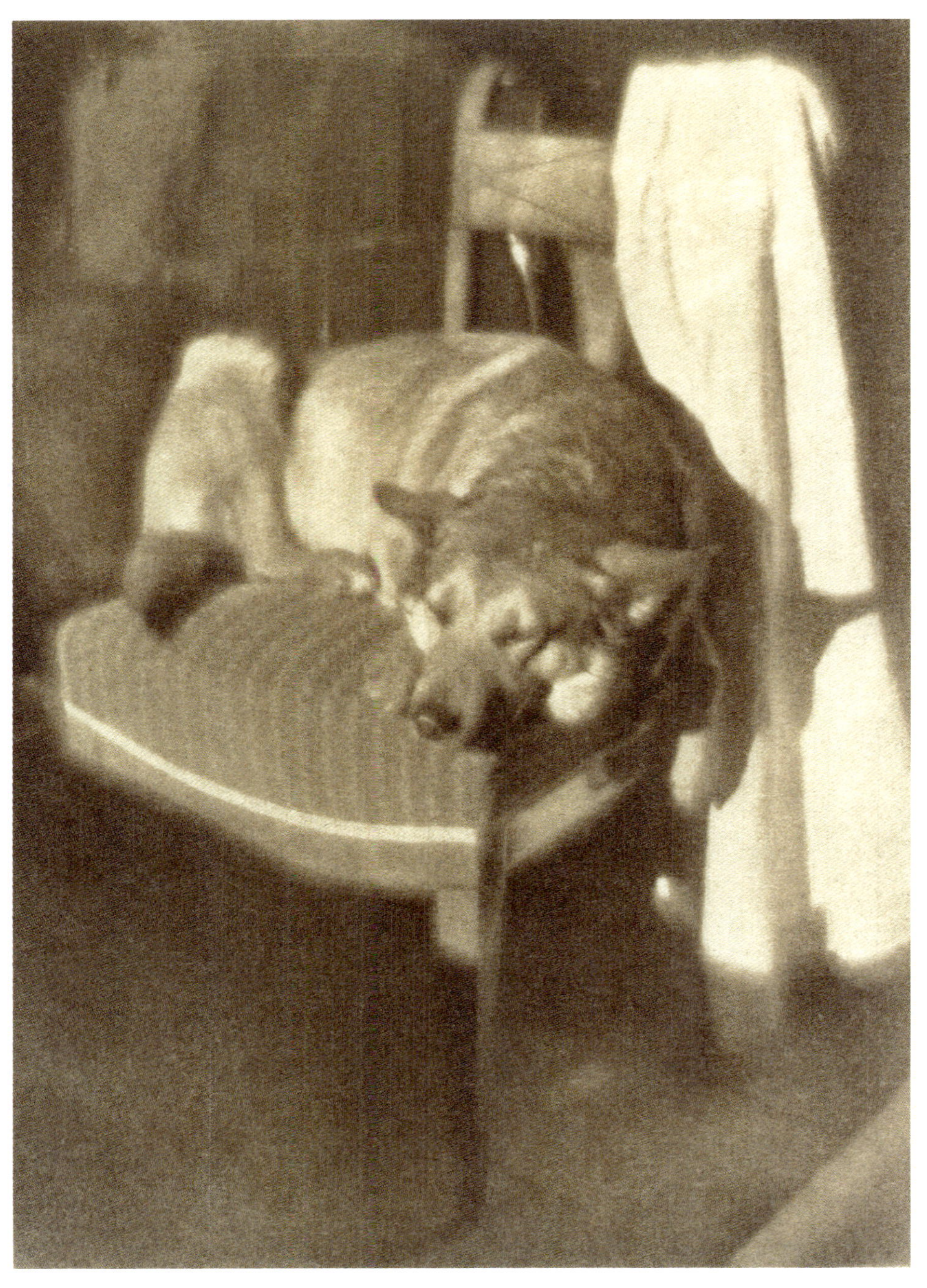

Heinrich Kühn
Schäferhund im Interieur /
Alsatian dog inside, ca. 1900

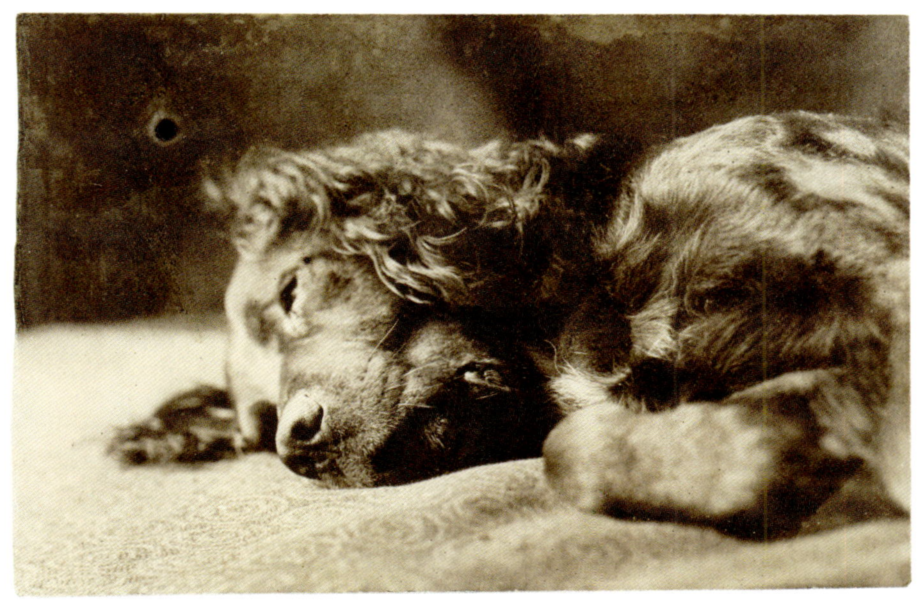

Thomas Eakins

Boyce, Portrait of a setter dog, 1880-1890

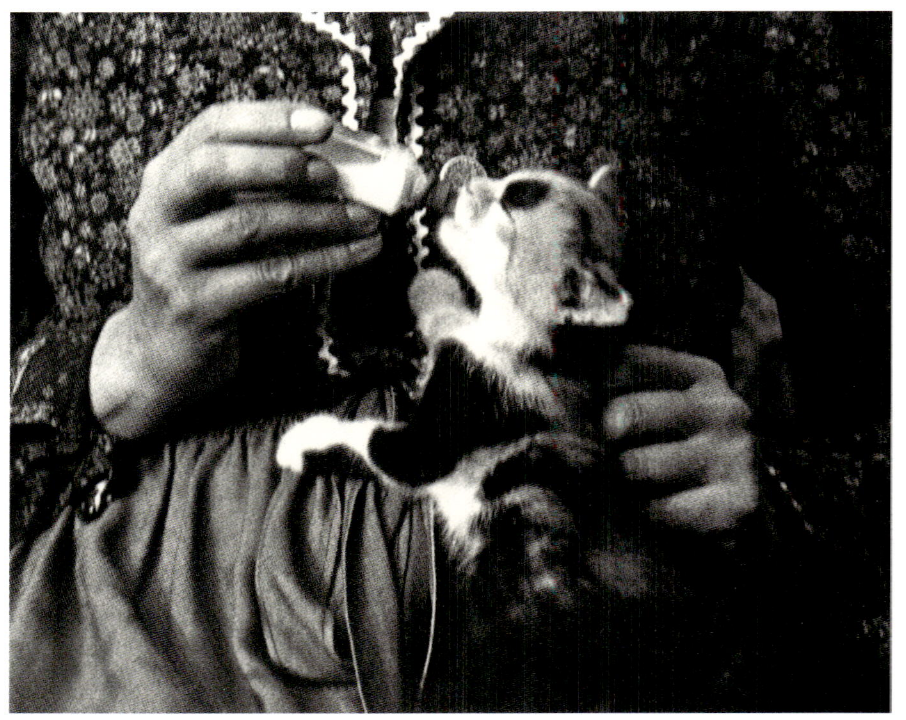

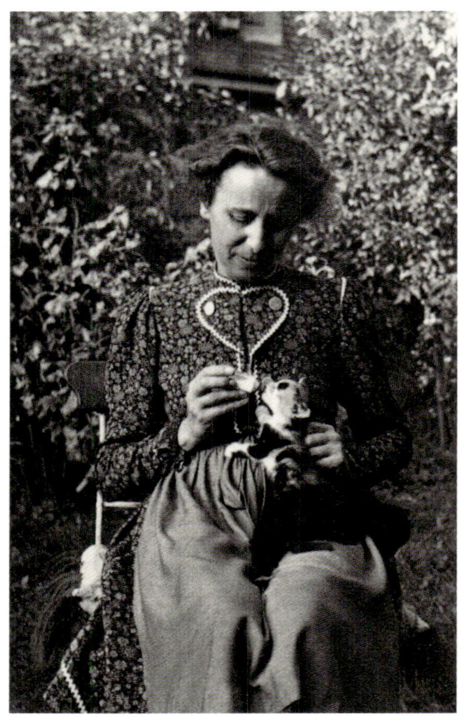

Anonym
Frau mit kleiner Katze, März 1954 /
Woman with little cat, March 1954

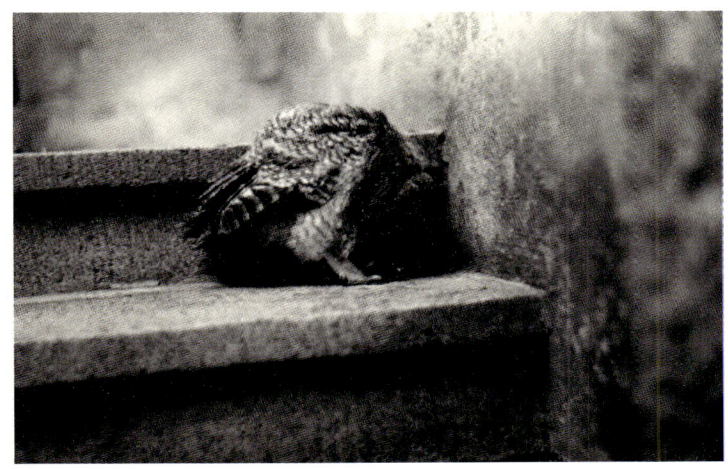

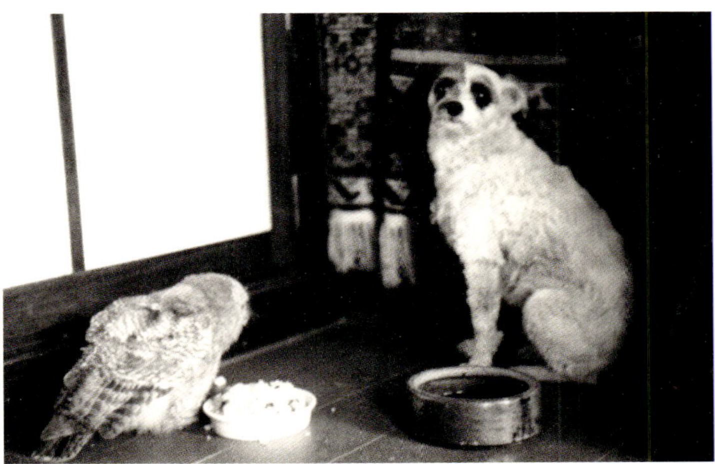

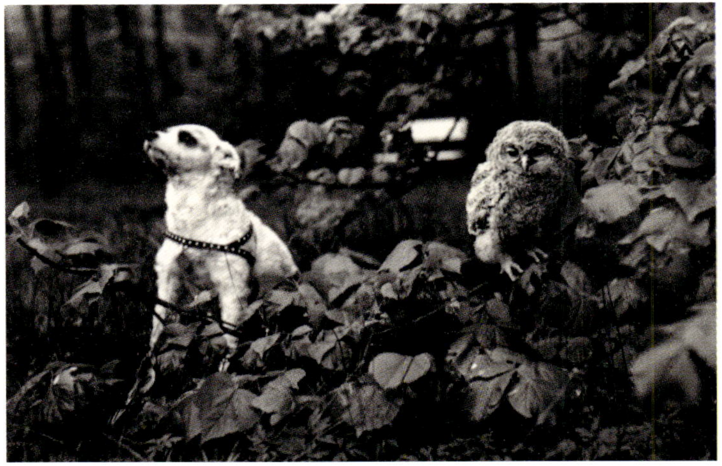

Anonym
Käuzchen und Hund /
Screech owl and dog, 1920er

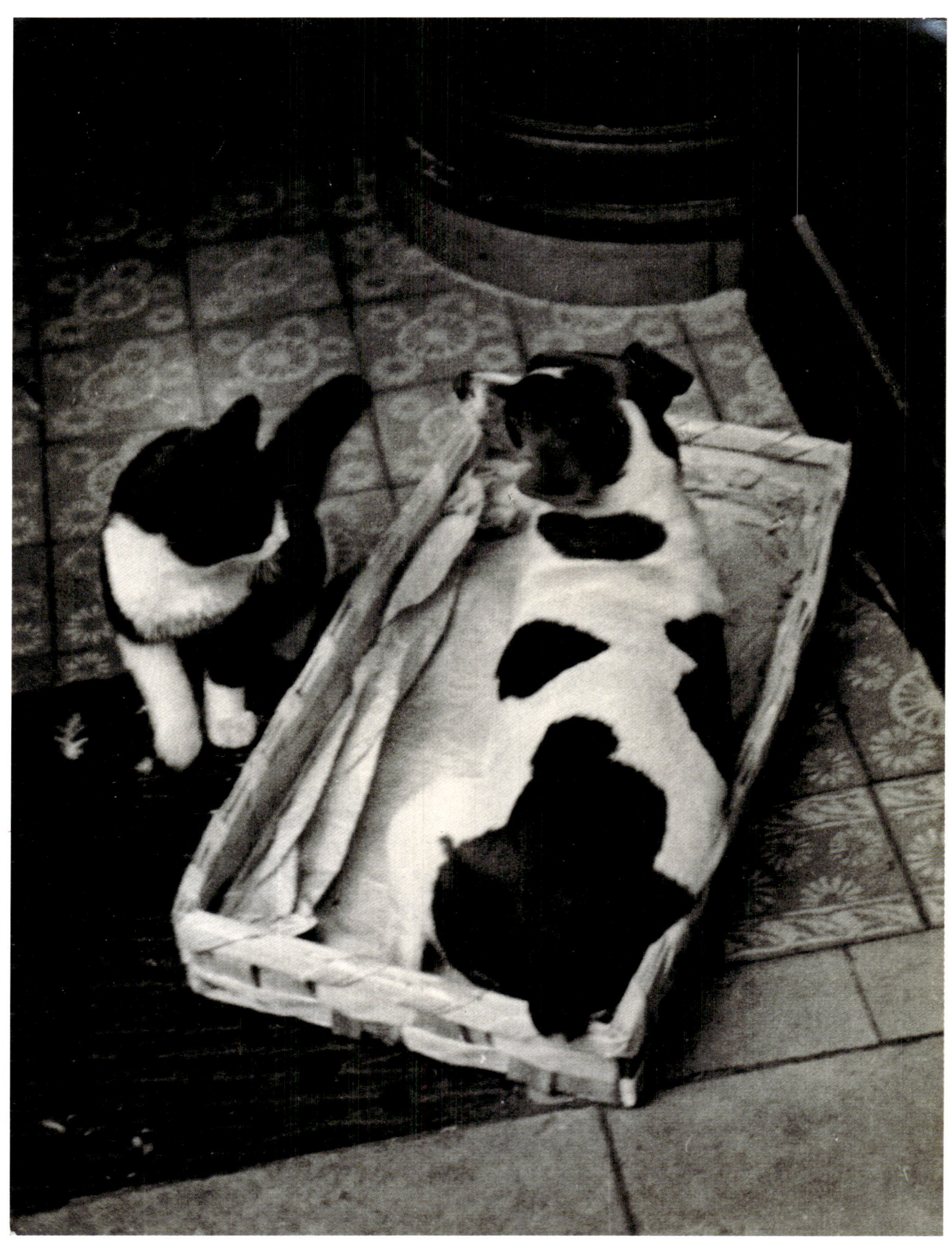

André Kertész
a. d. Serie: Hund und Katze /
Dog and Cat Series, no. 1, 5, 6, 7, 8, 1934

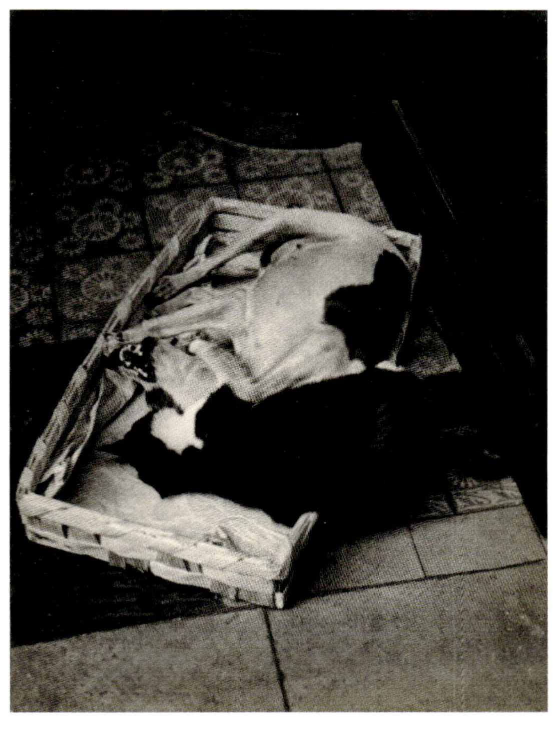

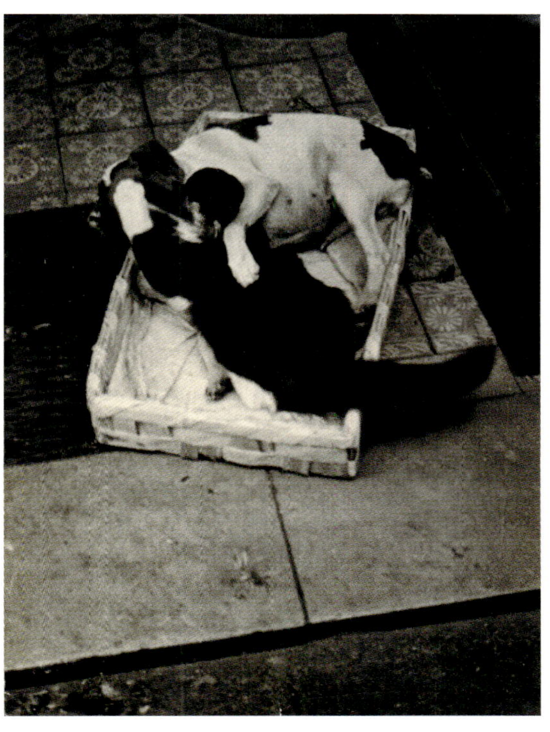

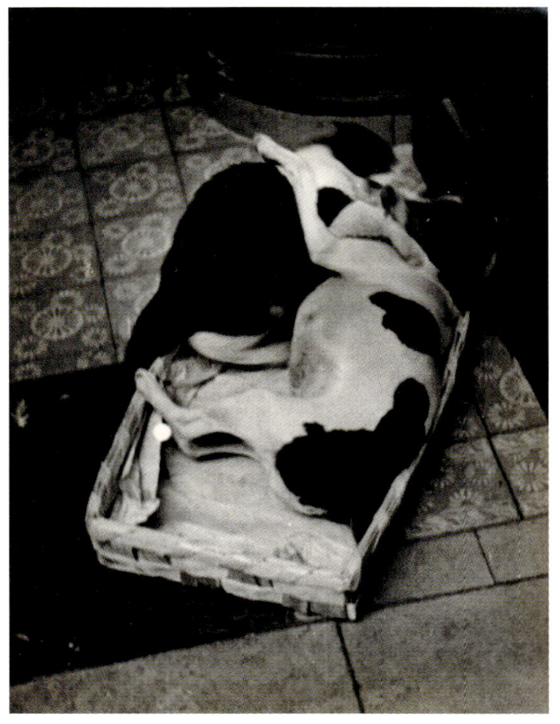

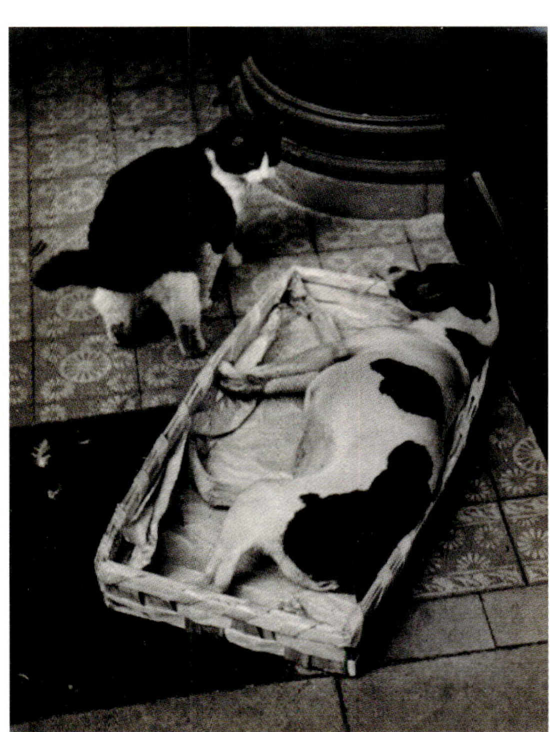

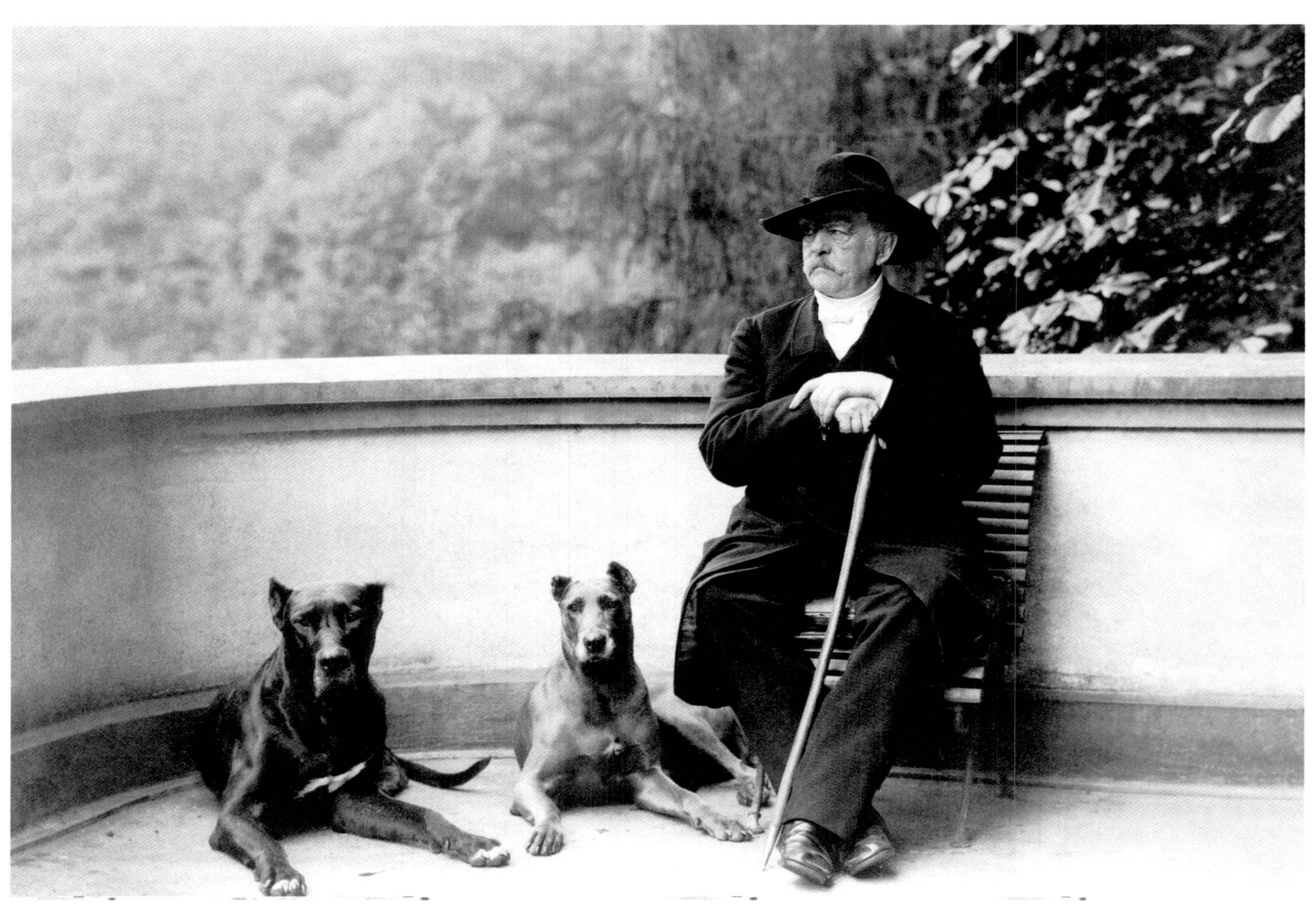

Strumper & Co.

Fürst Bismarck in Friedrichsruh am 6. Juli 1891

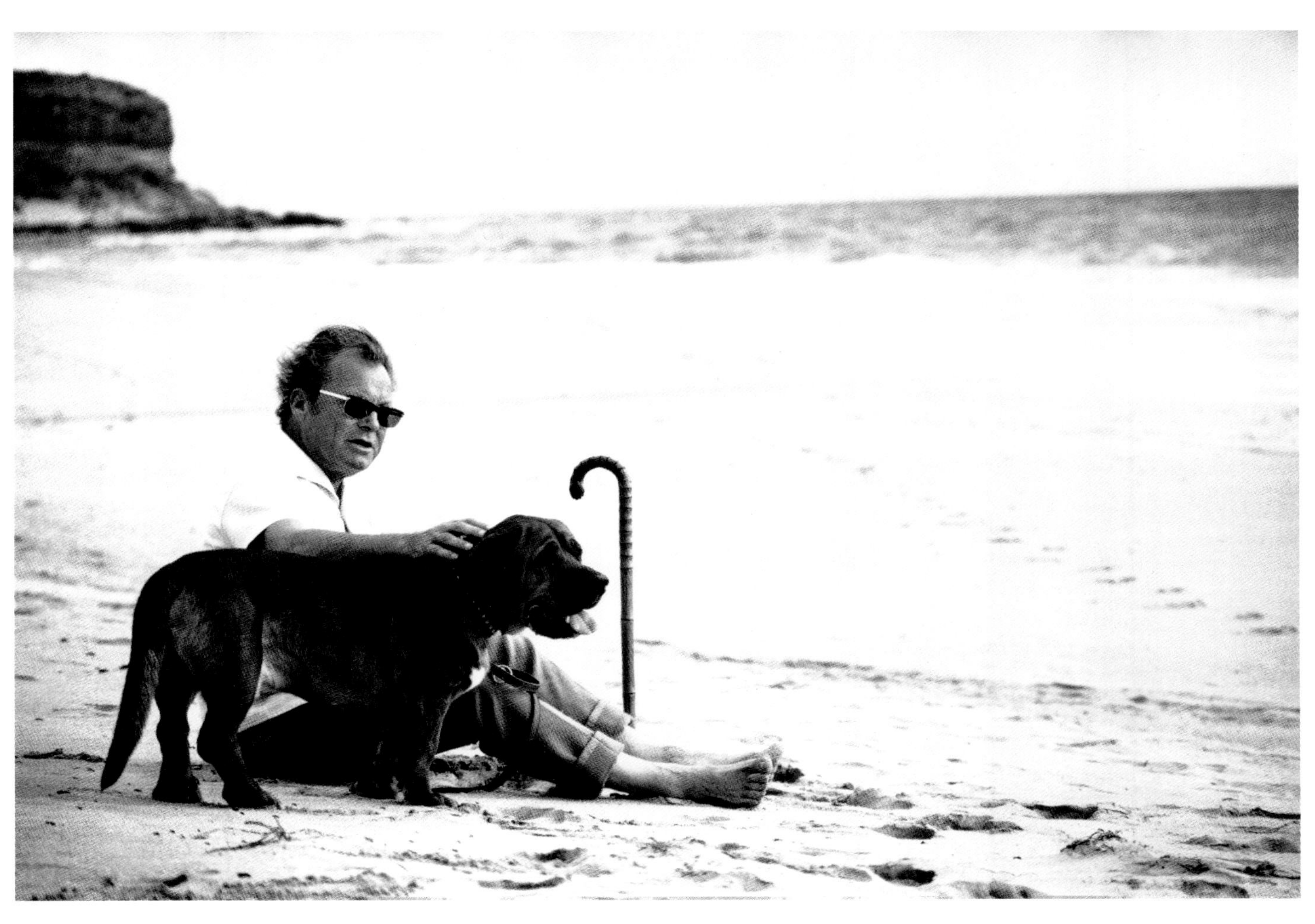

Robert Lebeck
Willy Brandt in Fuerteventura, 1972

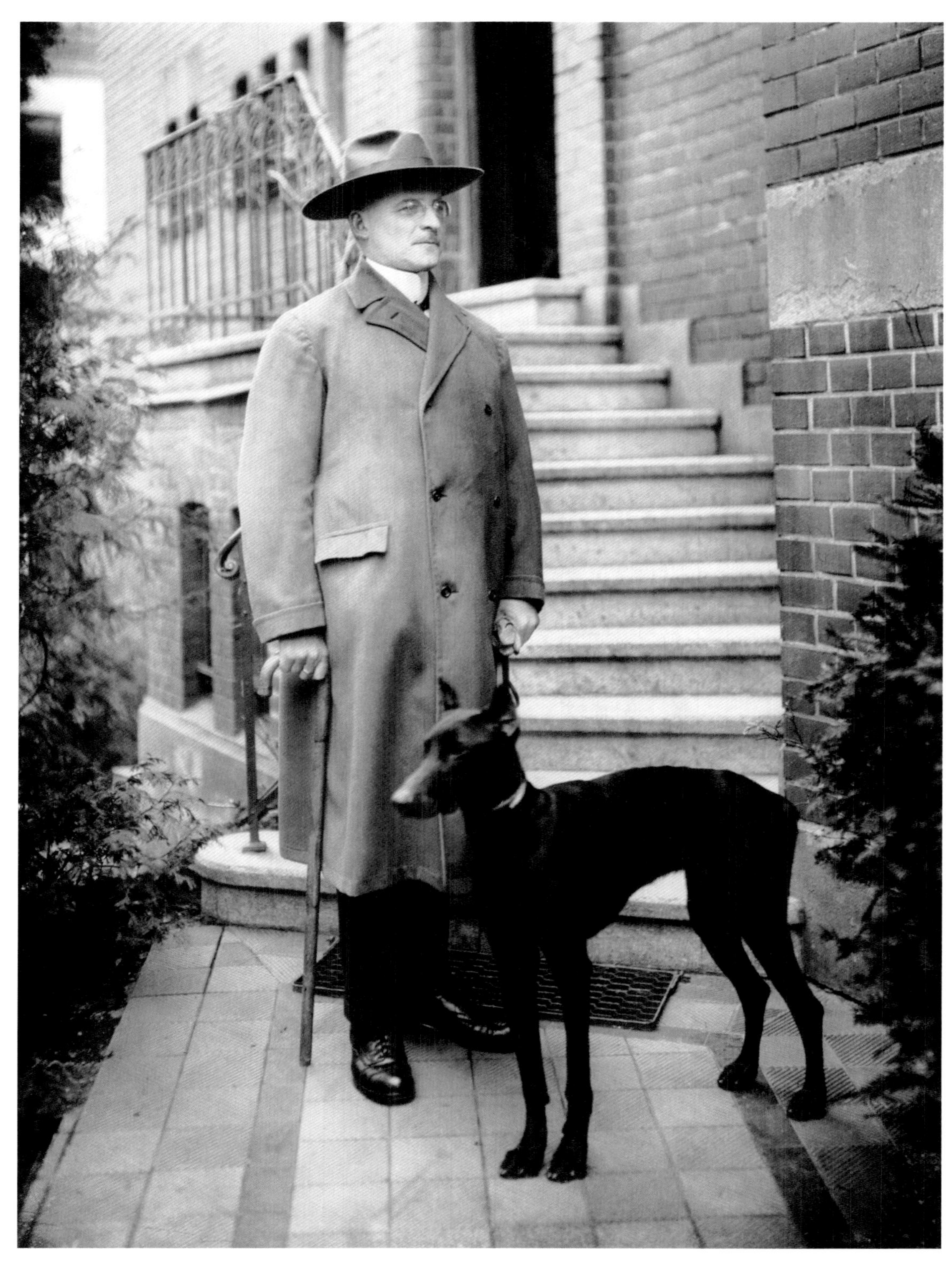

August Sander

Der Notar Dr. Quinke, Köln-Lindenthal, 1924

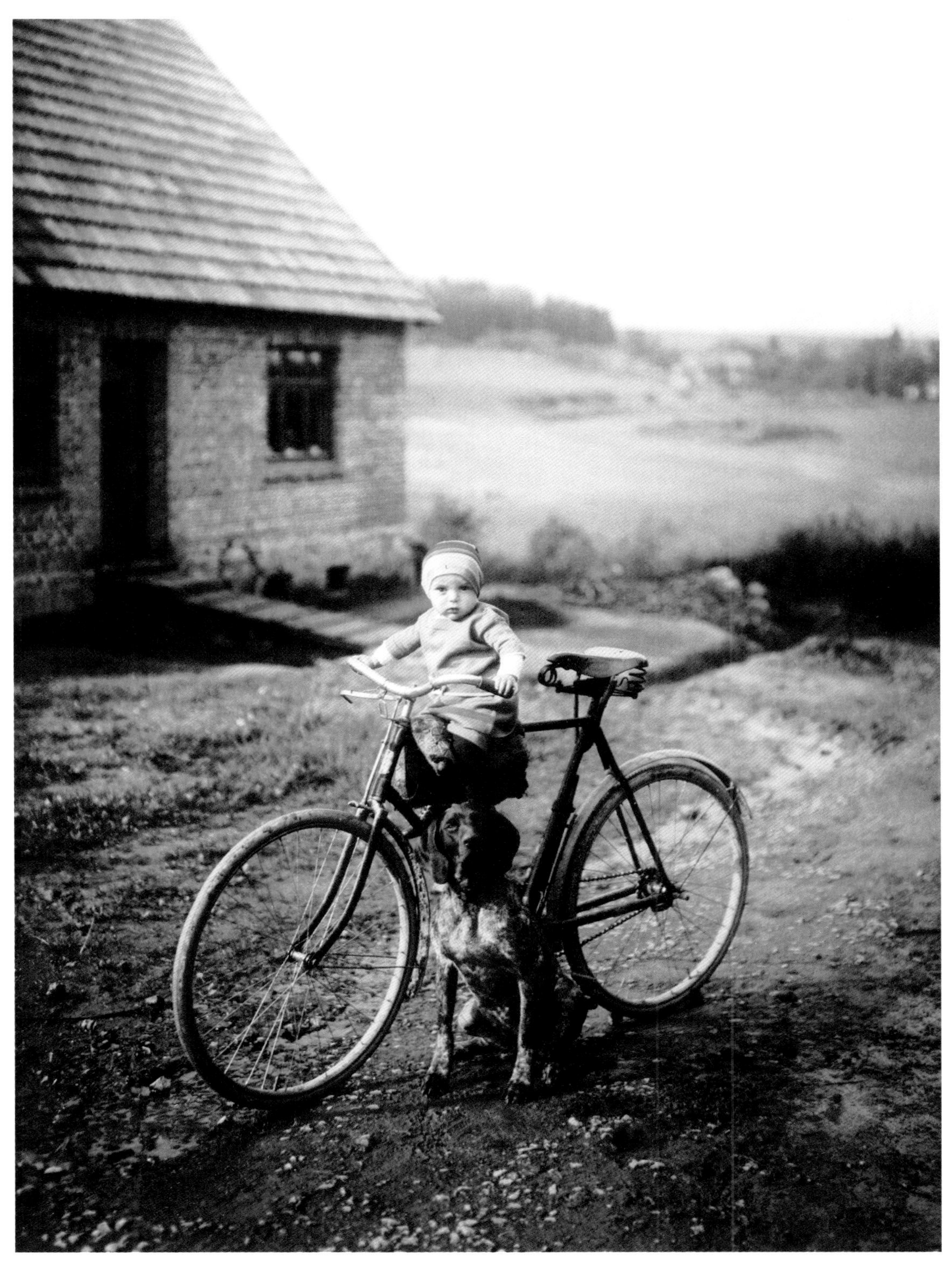

August Sander

Försterkind aus dem Westerwald, ca. 1925

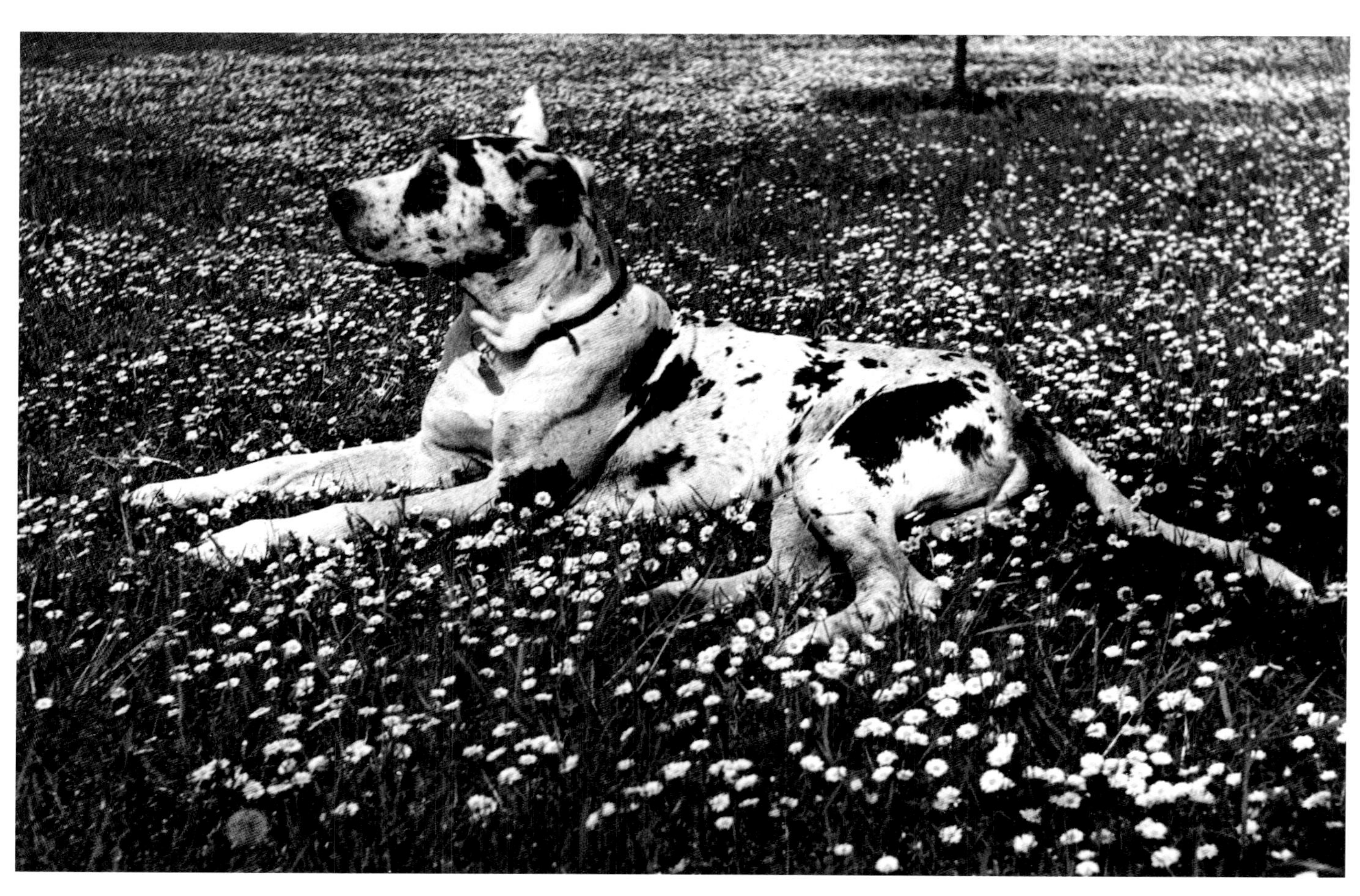

Friedrich Seidenstücker
Gefleckte Dogge, 1930er

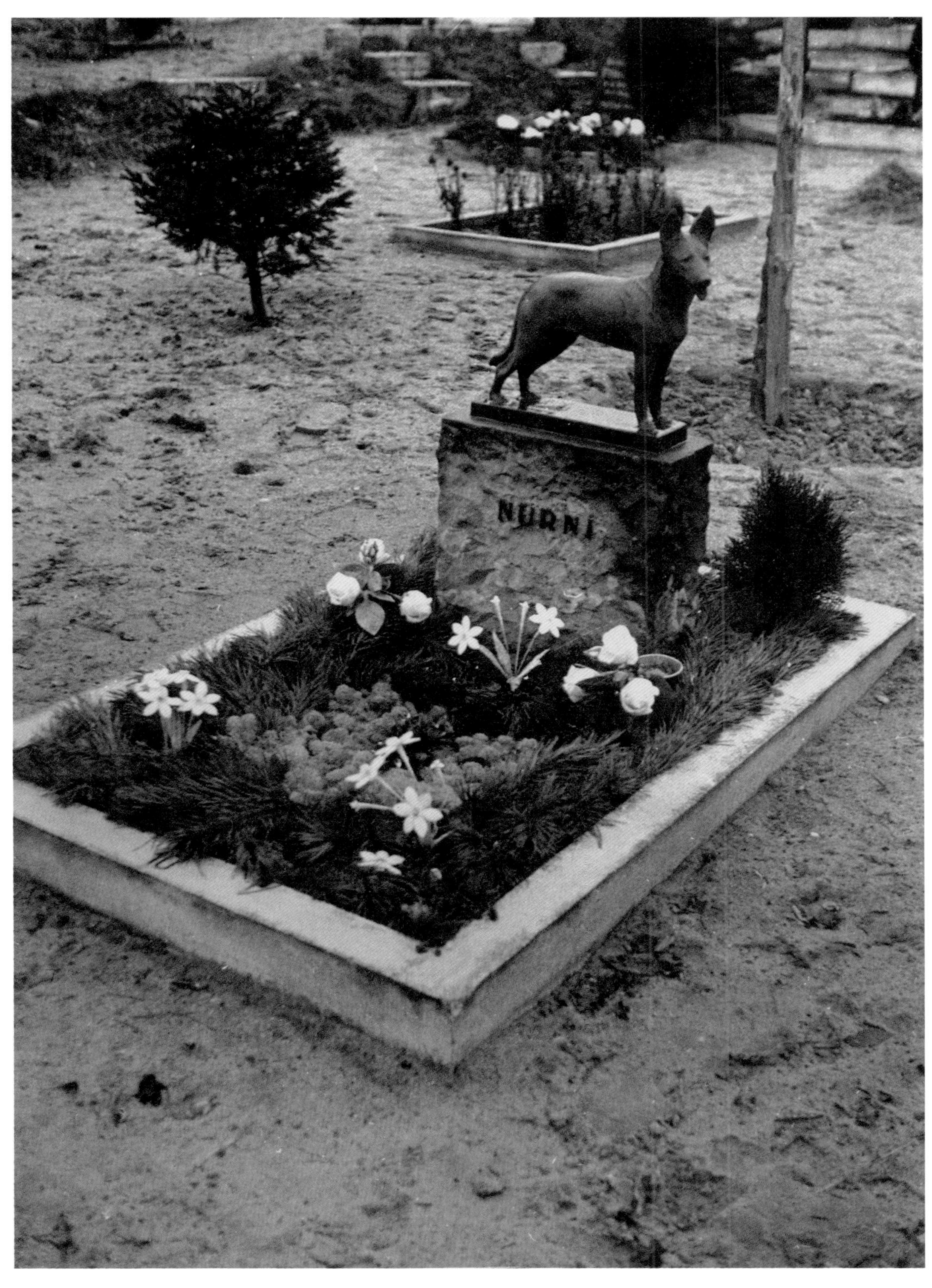

Friedrich Seidenstücker

Hundegrab, Berlin Stahnsdorf, 1920er

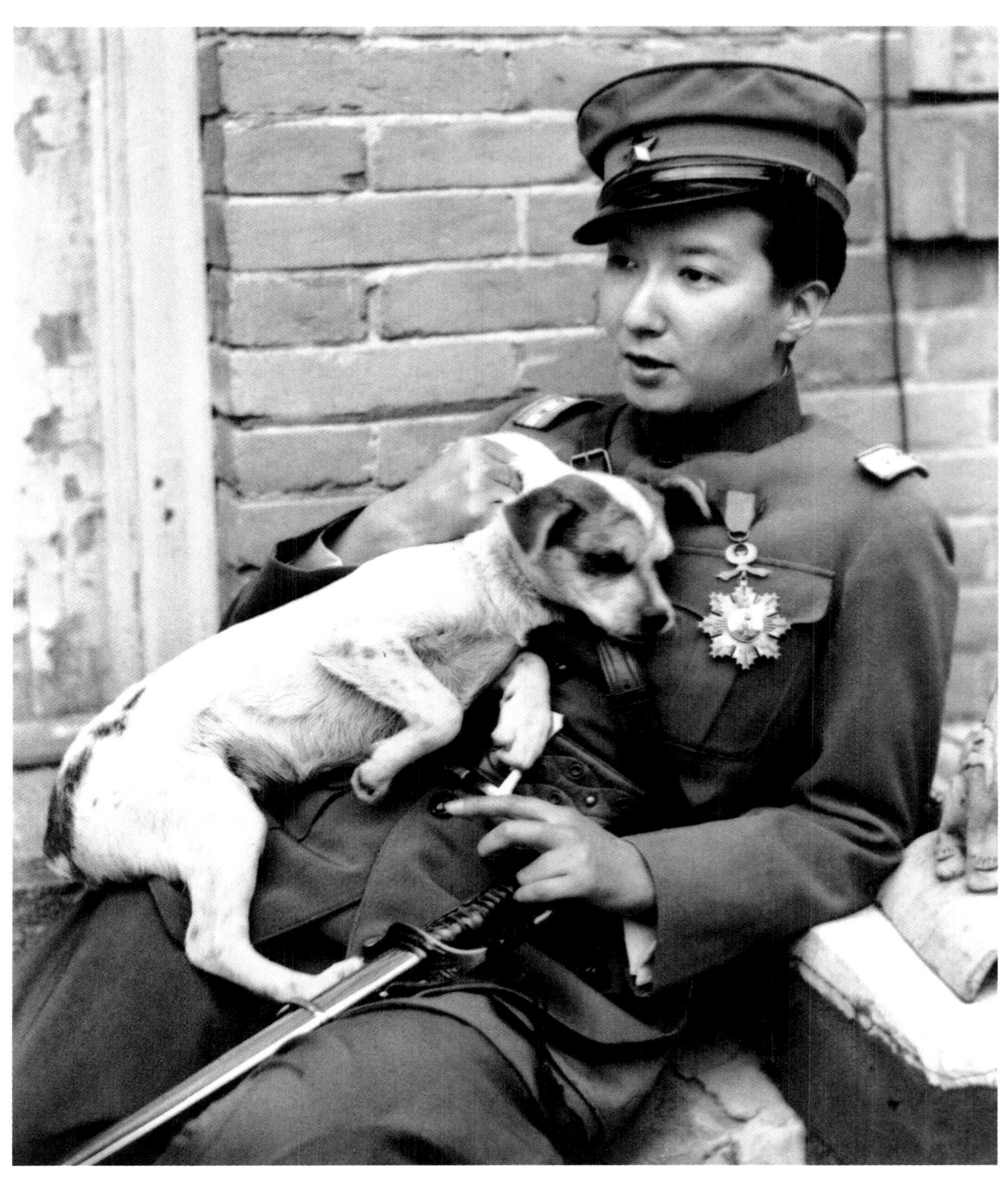

Lotte Errell

Nardine Yuan, China, 1931

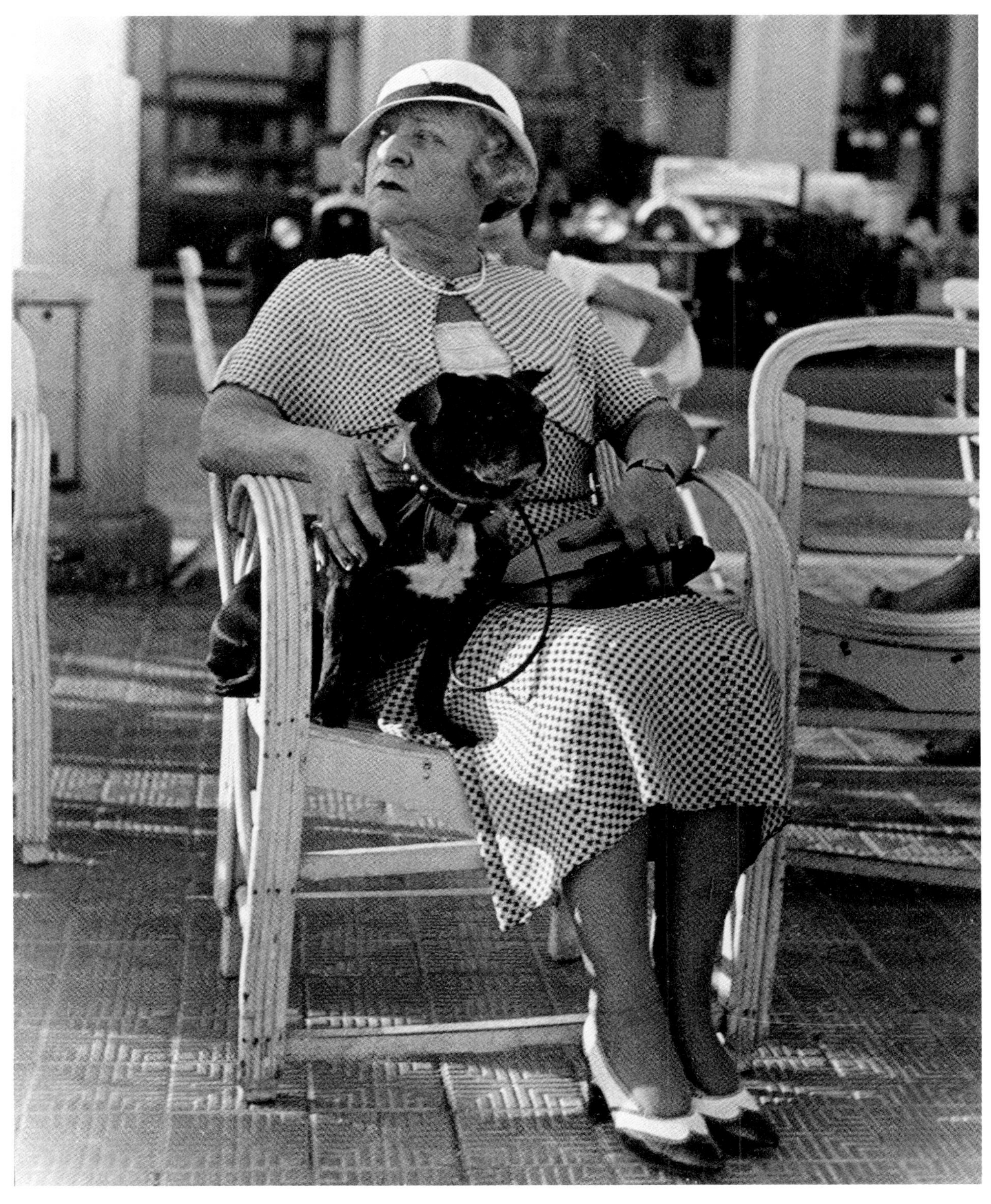

Lisette Model

Promenade des Anglais, Nice, ca. 1934

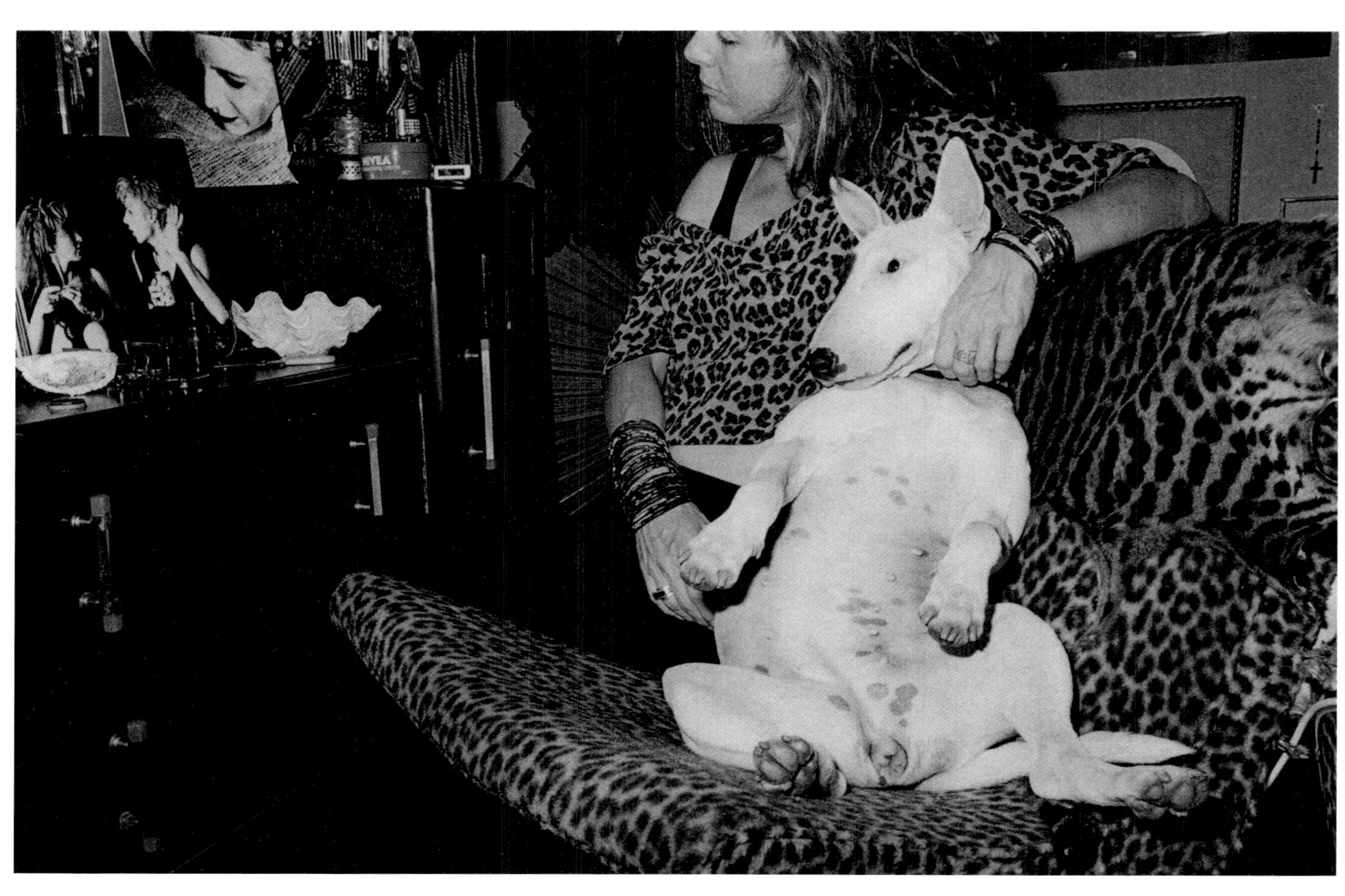

Robin Schwartz

Peedee and Missy, Hoboken, New Jersey, 1987

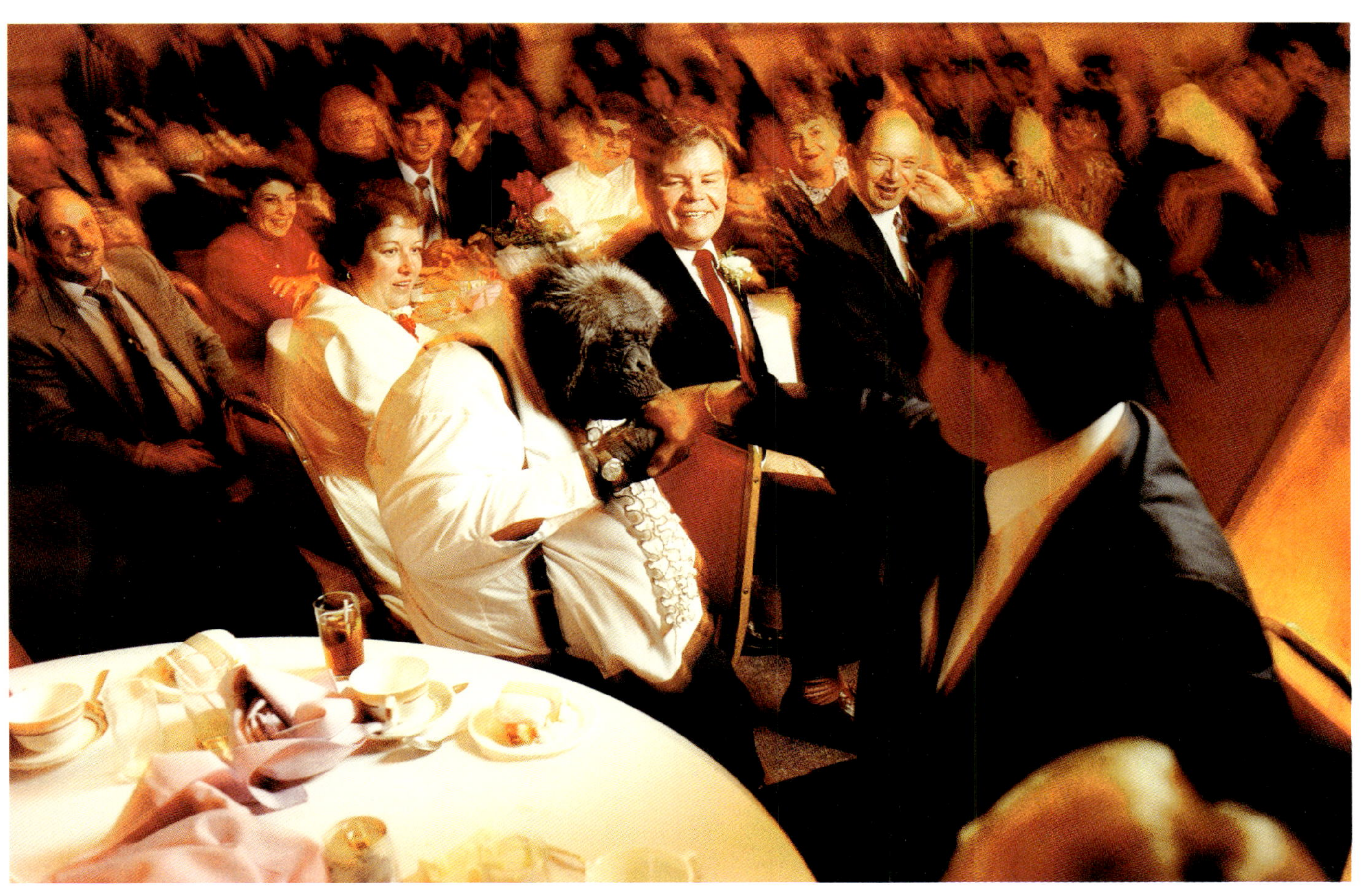

Michael Nichols

Mr. Jiggs, 1990

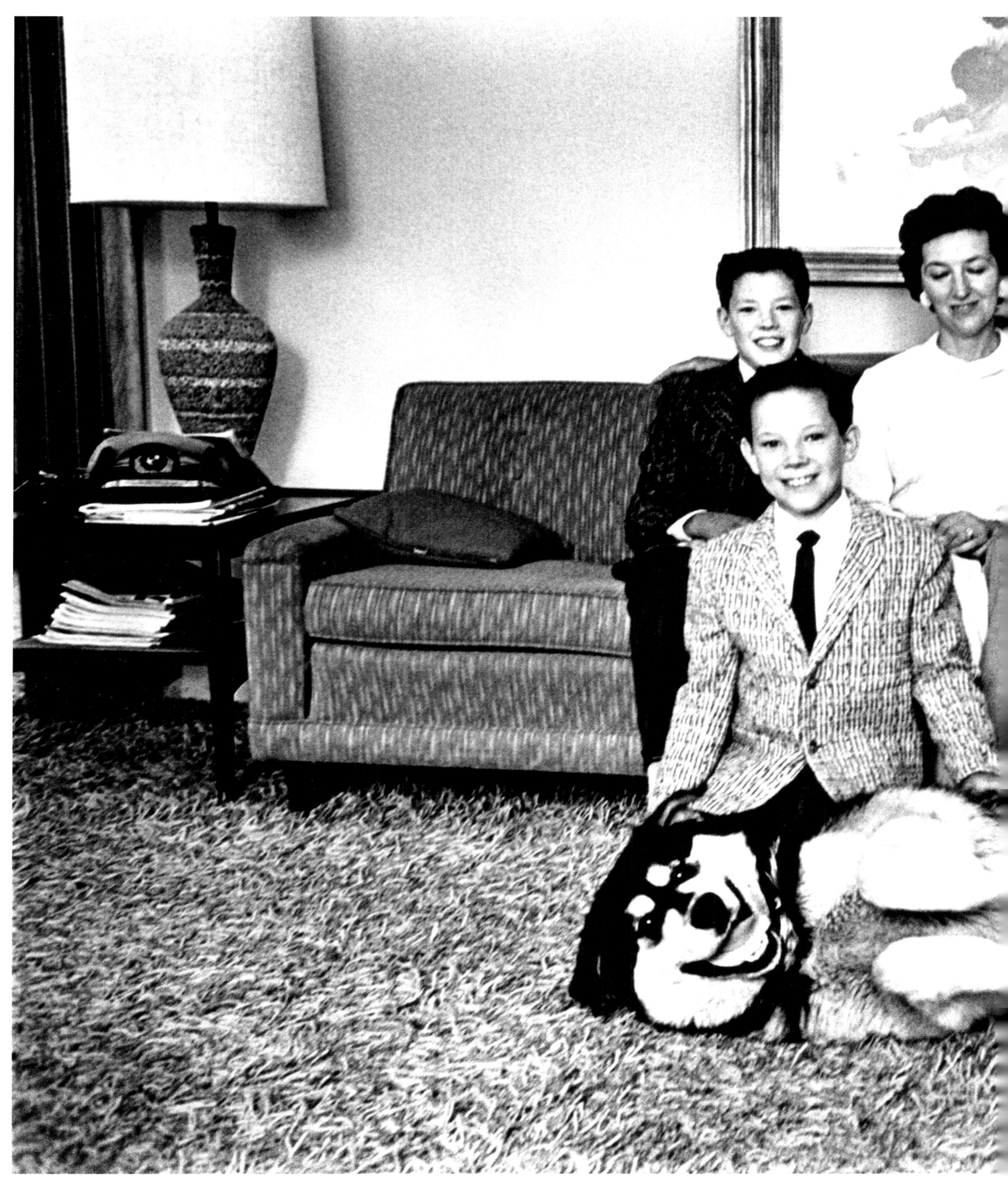

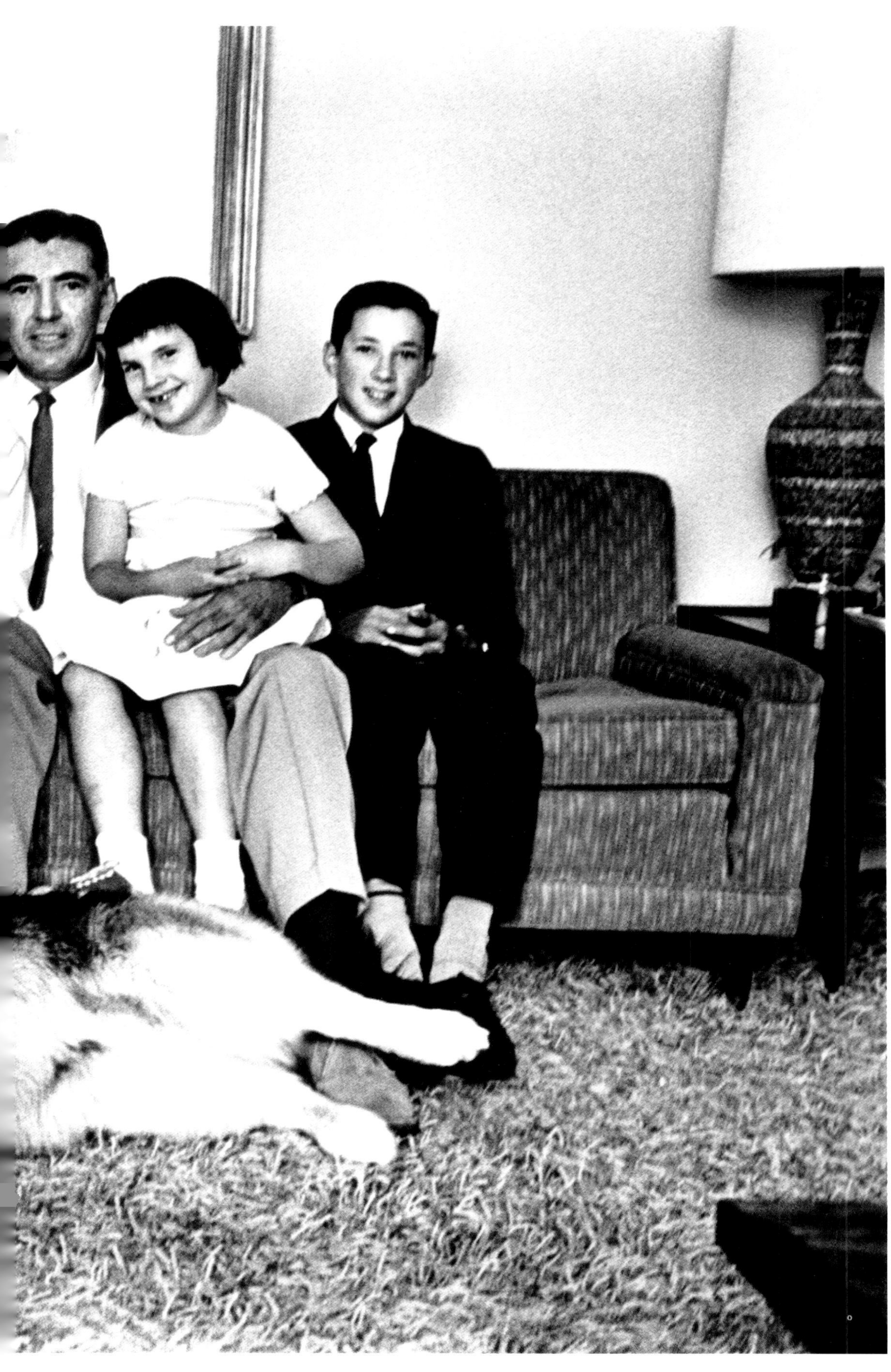

Elliott Erwitt
USA, Alaska,
The Fairbanks Family, 1964

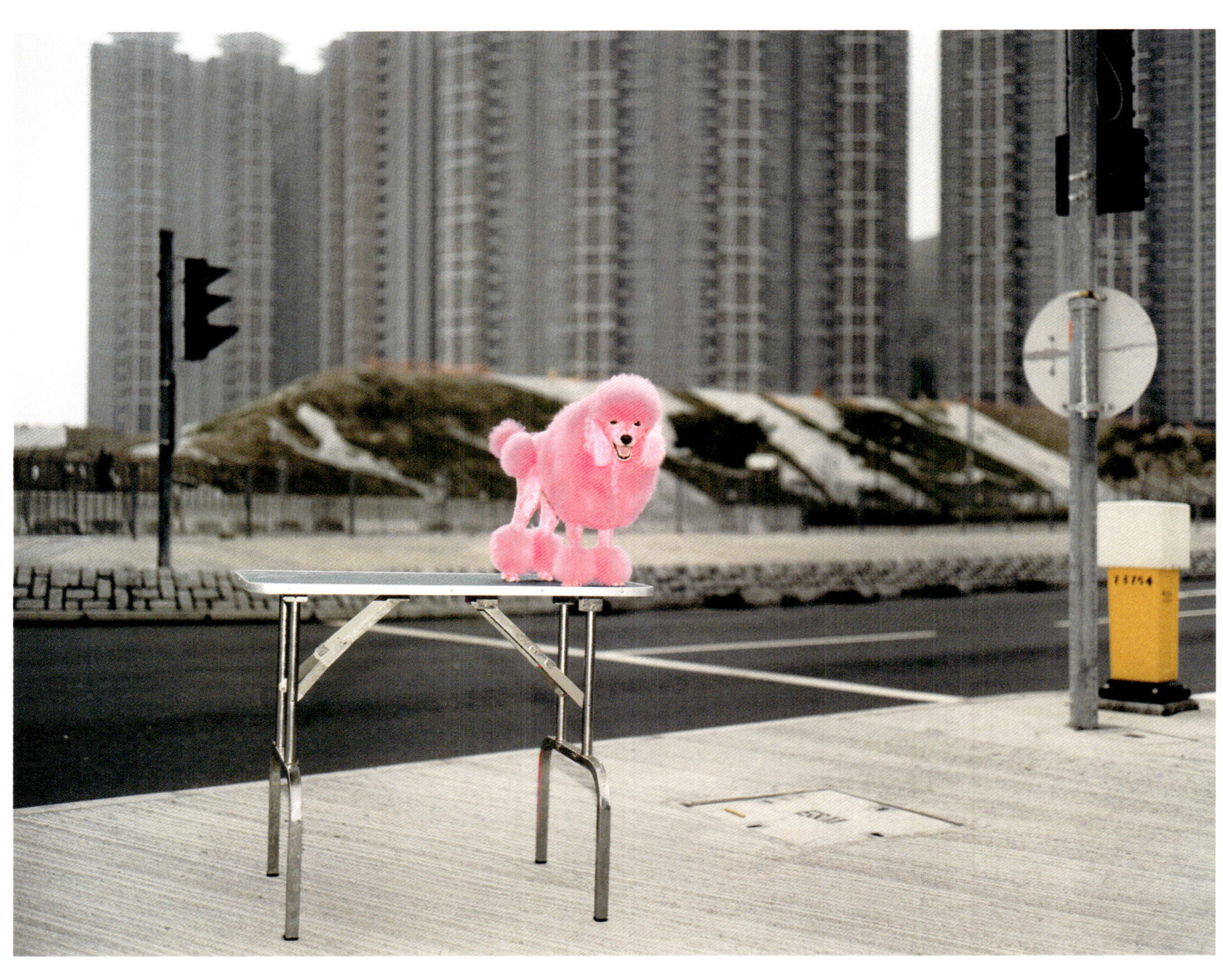

Michael Wolf
Pinker Pudel in Hongkong, 2004

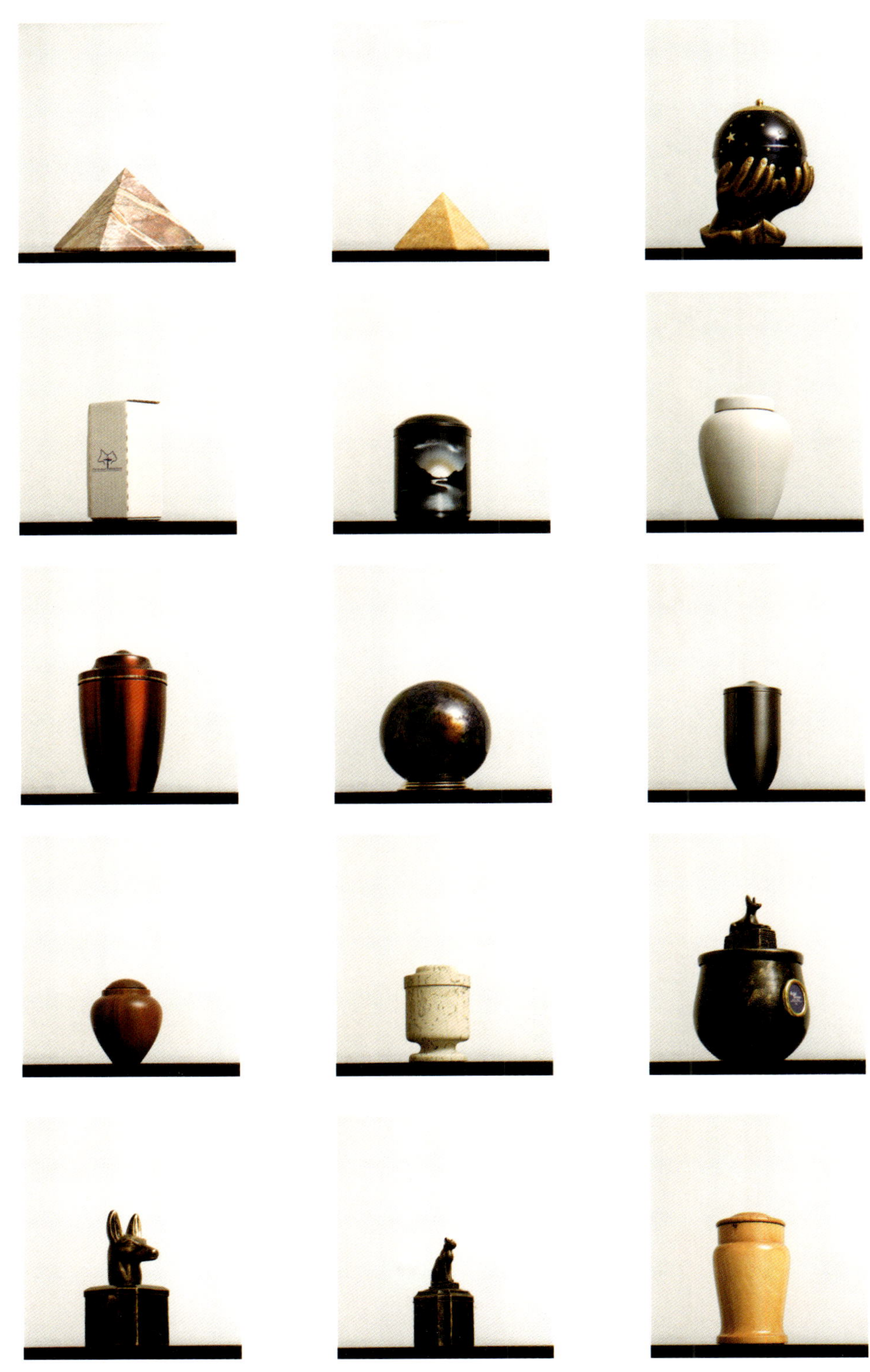

David Steets
Urnen für Haustiere /
Urns for pets, 2001/02

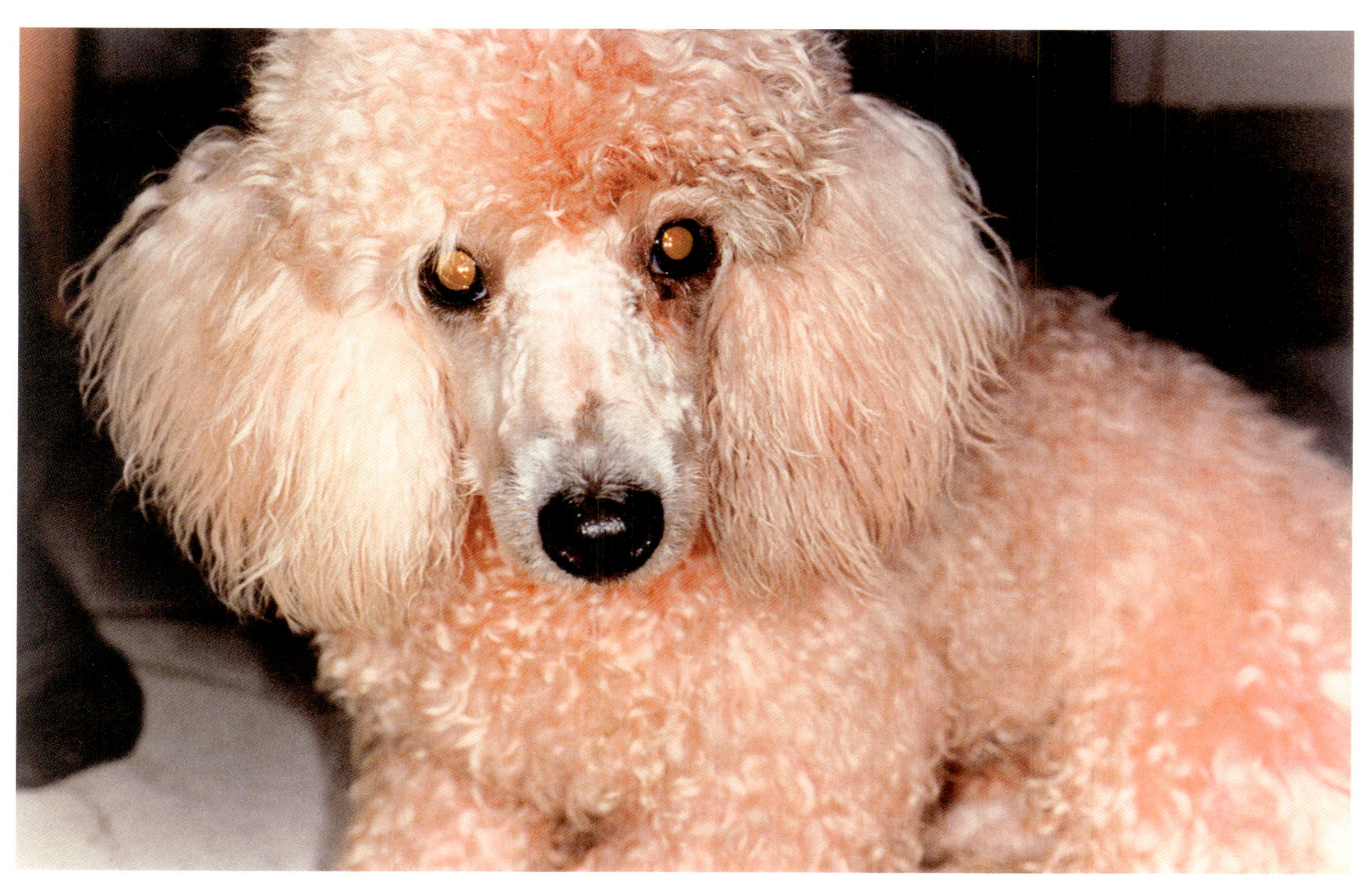

Martin Parr

Thailand, 1998, a. d. Serie: *Common Sense*

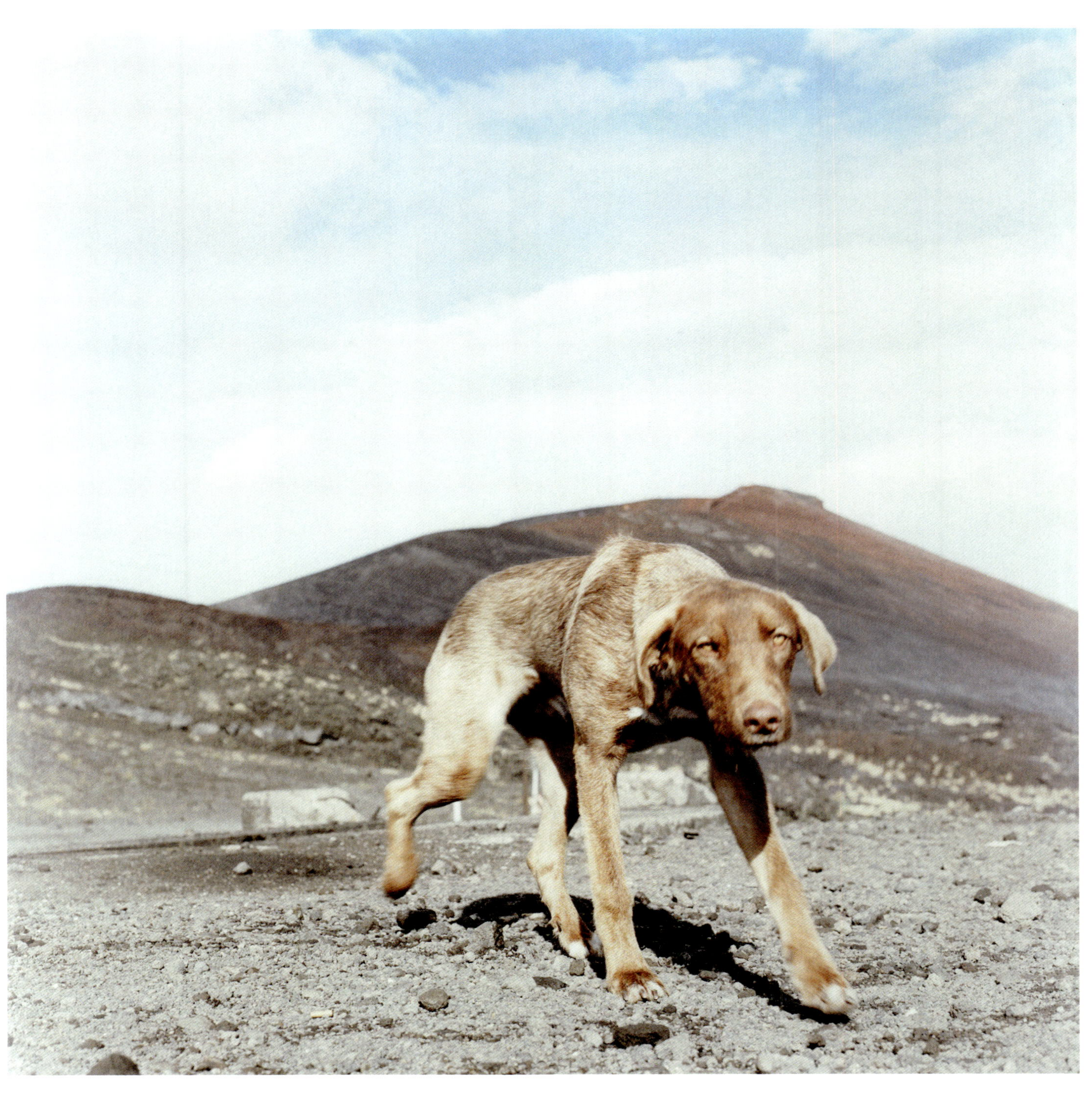

Florian Ebner

Etna, 1997, a. d. Serie: *Nomades*

„Angesichts einer gesteigerten Skepsis gegenüber einem Denken, das kein Bewusstsein für das zu entwickeln vermag, was in Klassifikationen, Taxonomien und Hierarchien ausgeschlossen bleibt oder ausgegrenzt wird, und das ‚Andere' des Tieres immer schon in den Kontext menschlicher Bedeutungszuweisungen zu rücken bereit ist, hat die zeitgenössische Zoofotografie ihre Bildsprache radikal verändert."

"Given the increased scepticism toward a form of thinking that has no sense for developing that which remains barred or excluded from classifications, taxonomies, and hierarchies, and that has always been ready to place the 'otherness' of an animal within the realm of human forms of interpretation, contemporary zoological photography has radically changed its language of images."

Eckhardt Köhn

Ausgestellt Exhibited

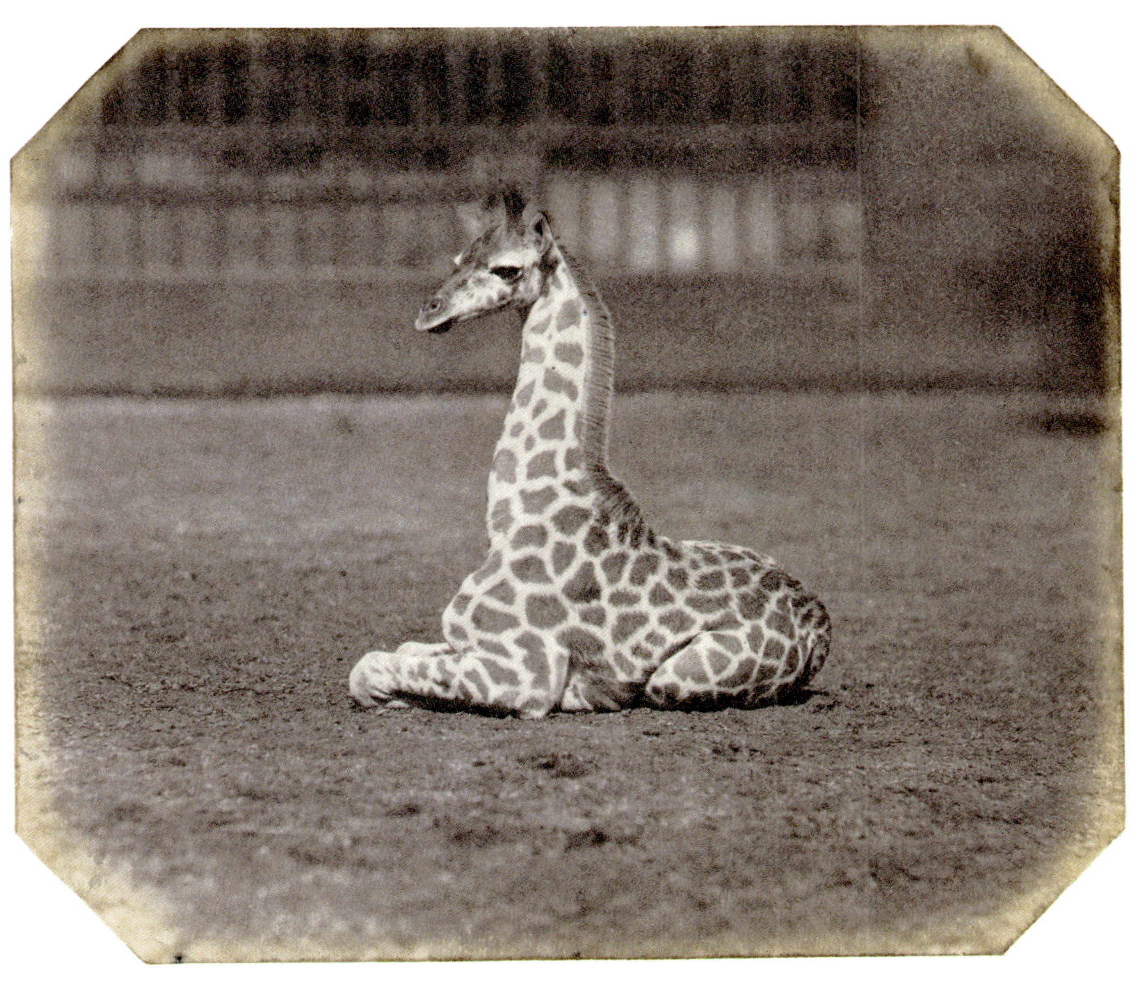

Comte de Montizon
Giraffe, London Zoo, 1852

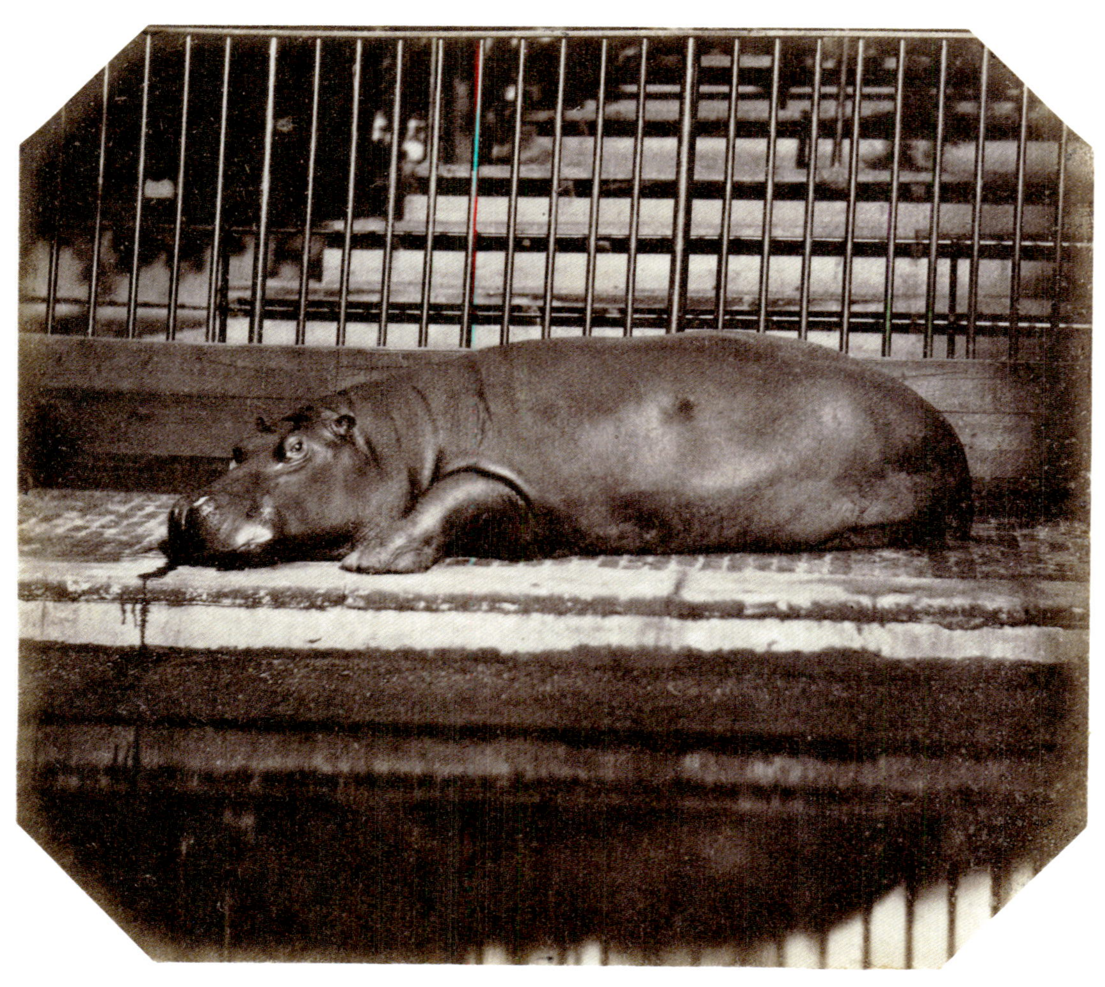

Comte de Montizon

Hippopotamus (without spectators), London Zoo, 1852

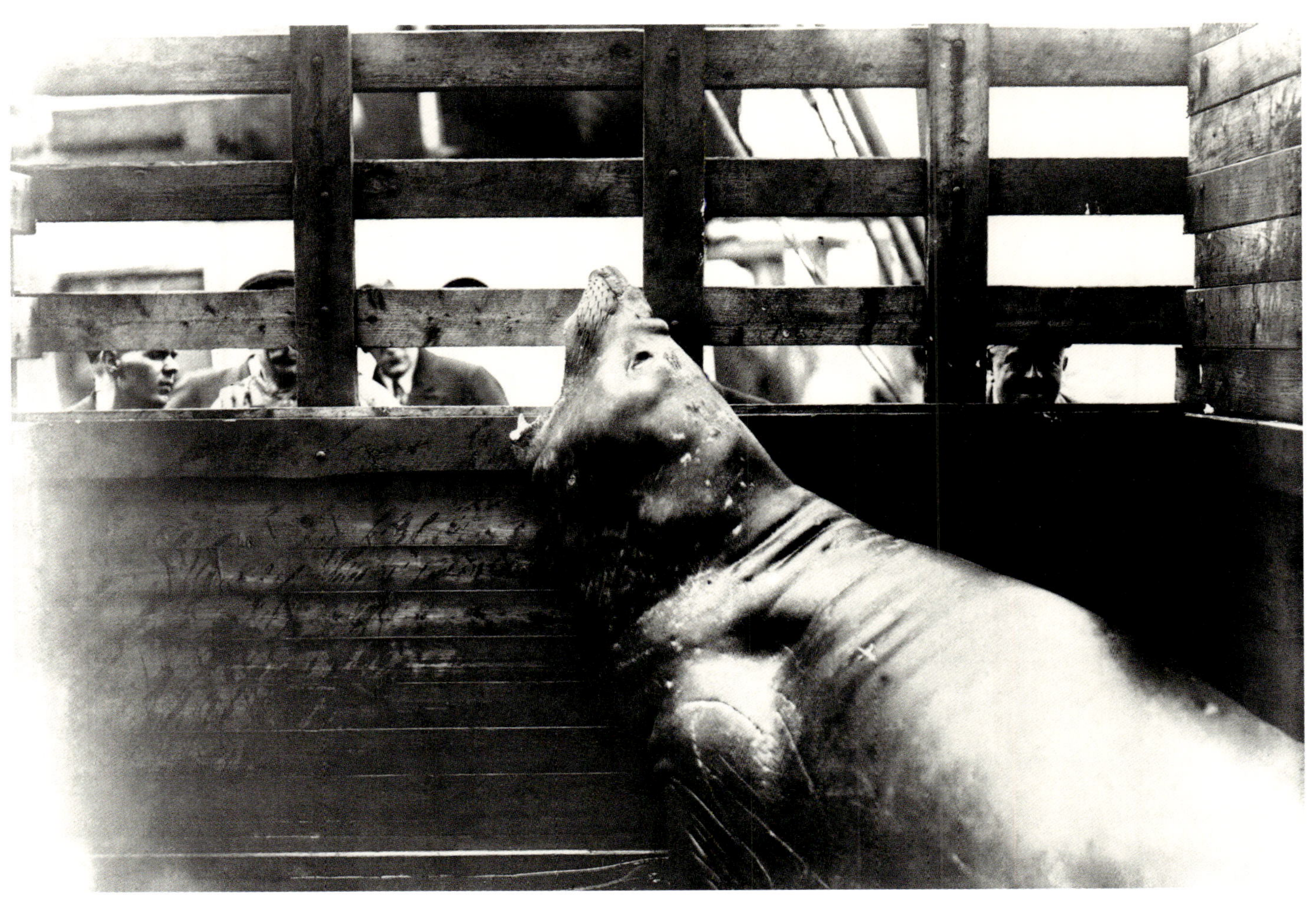

A. von Zhilinsky

Goliath in seiner Transportkiste beim Eintreffen im Tierpark, 1920er

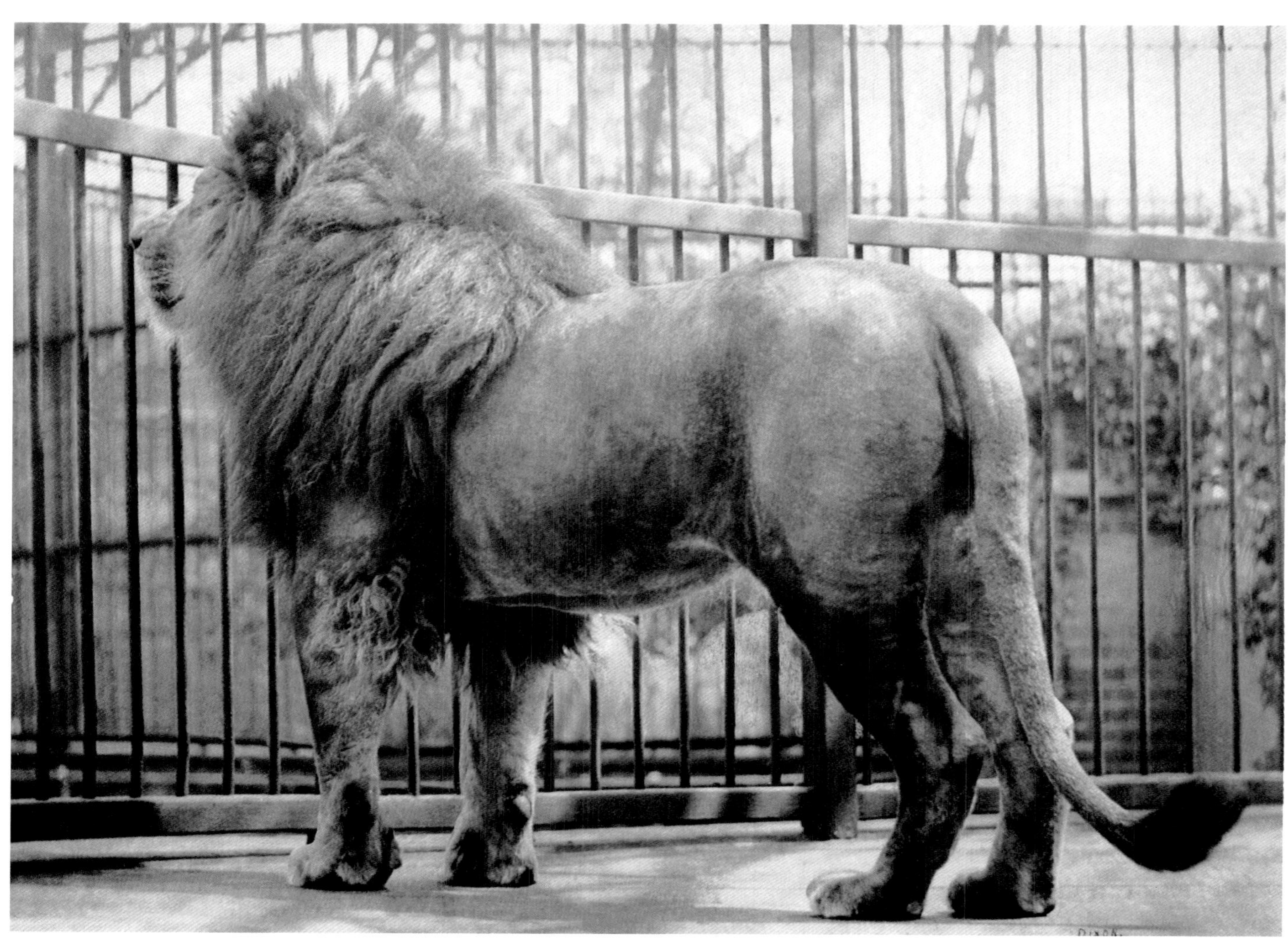

Henry Dixon
Löwe im Zoo /
Lion at Zoo, 1879-1884

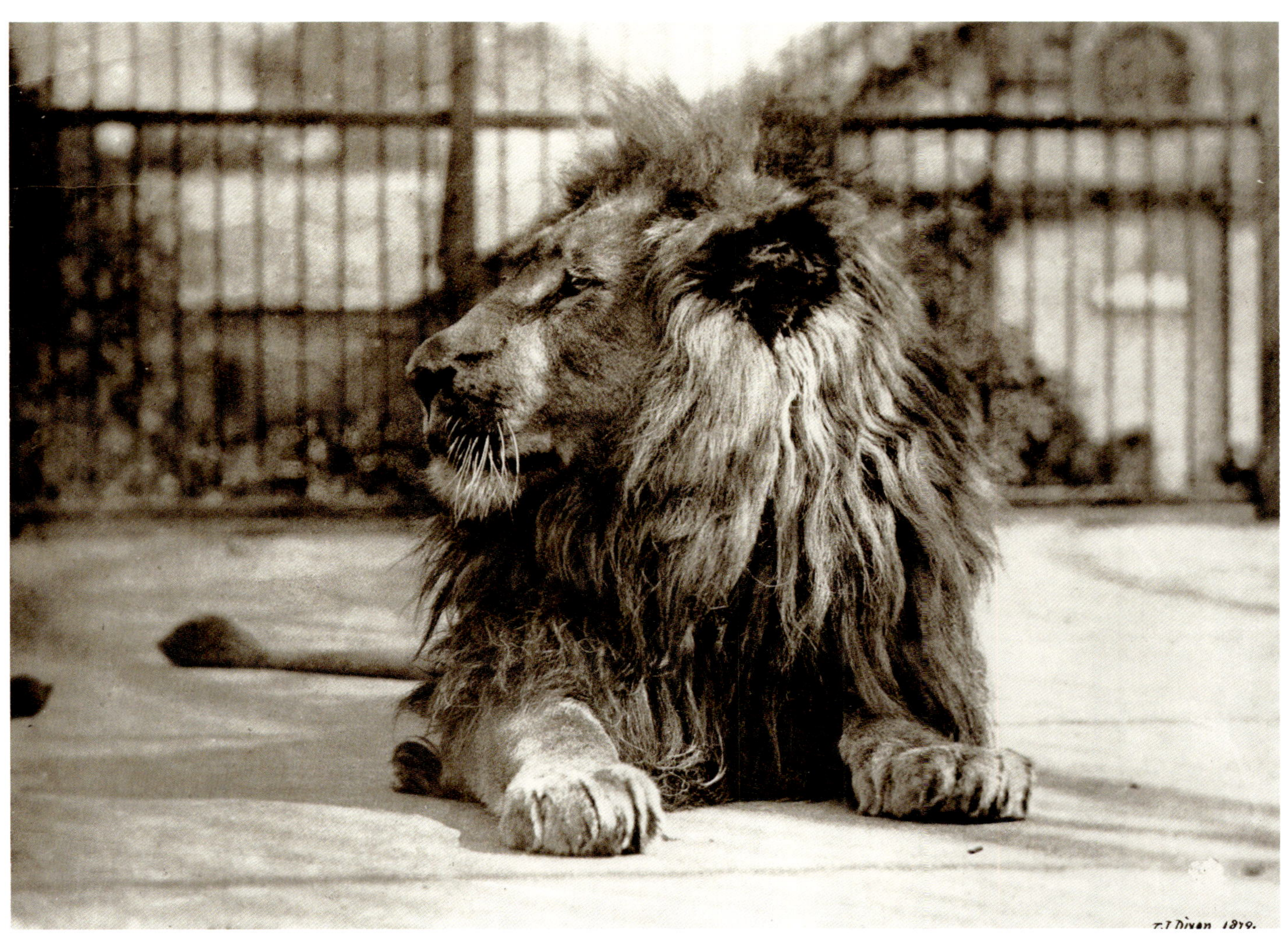

Thomas James Dixon
Löwe im Zoo /
Lion at Zoo, 1879

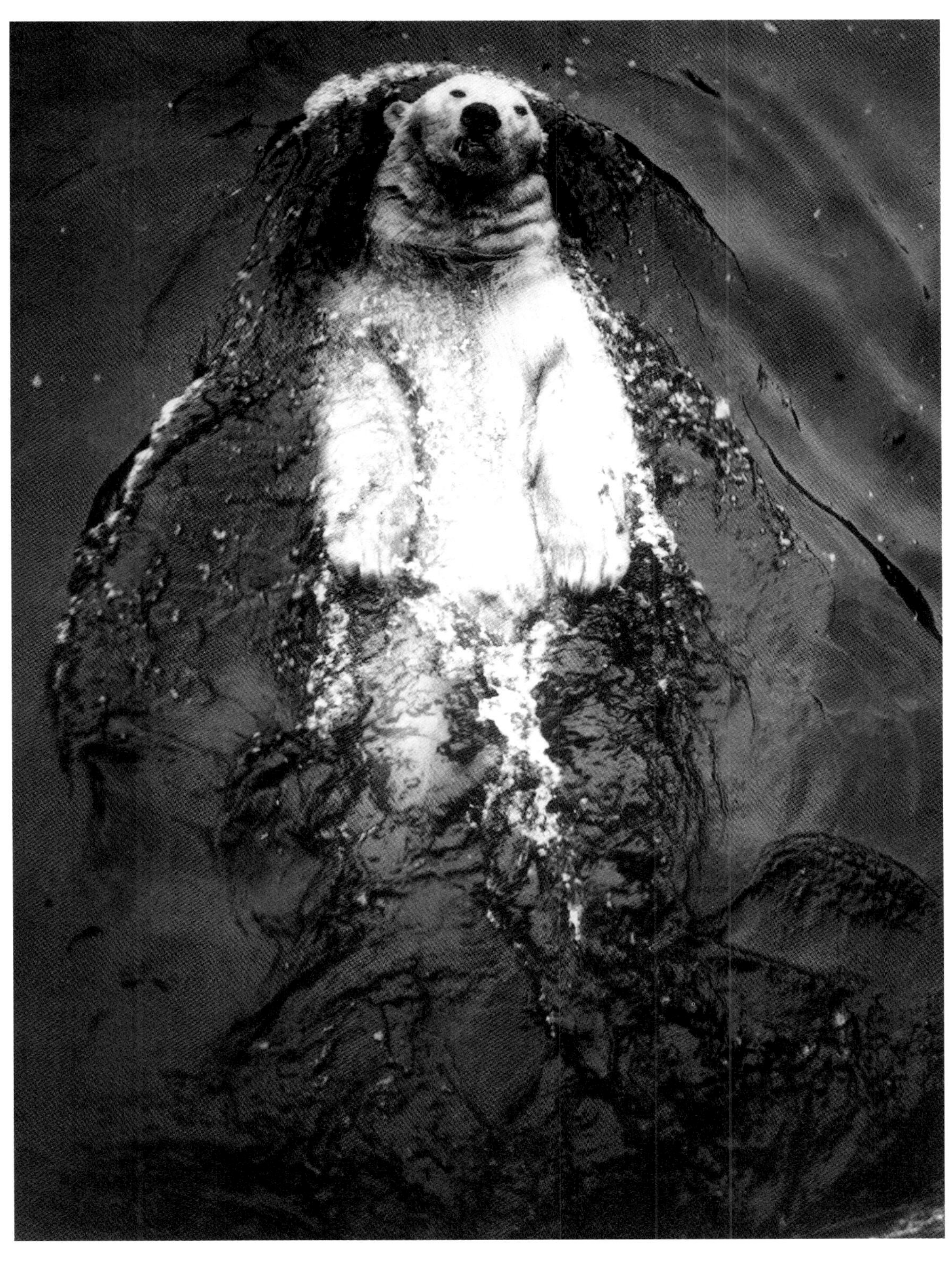

Friedrich Seidenstücker
Eisbär, vor 1933

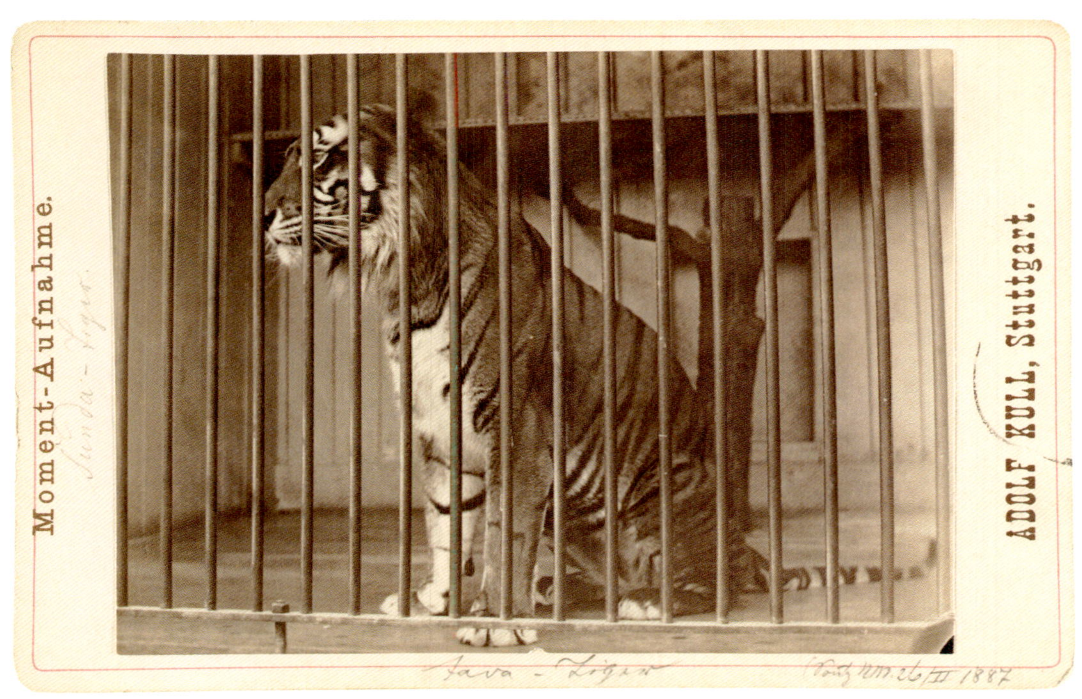

Adolf Kull

Java-Tiger, Oktober 1886

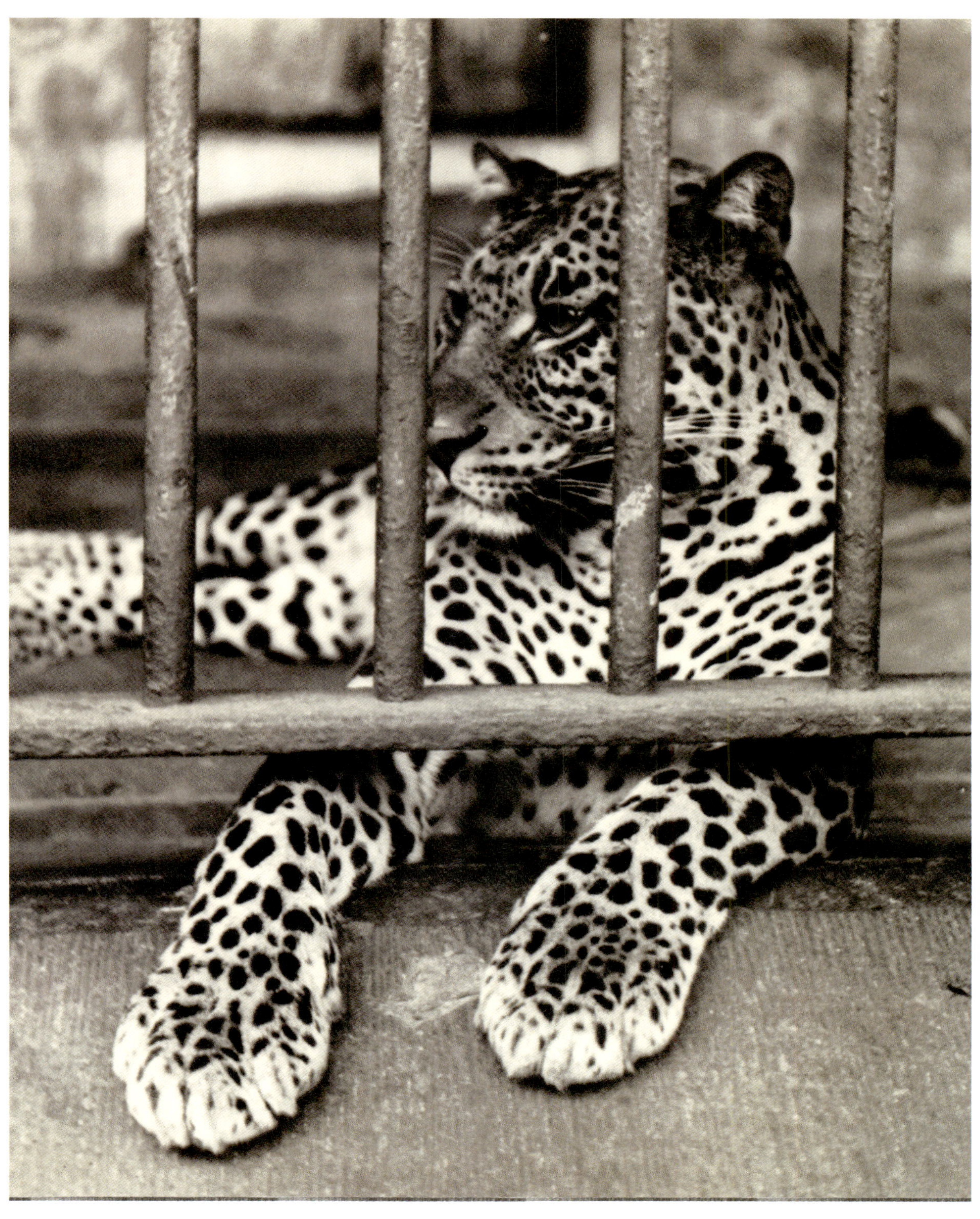

Elisabeth Hase
Leopard hinter Gittern /
Leopard behind bars, 1932

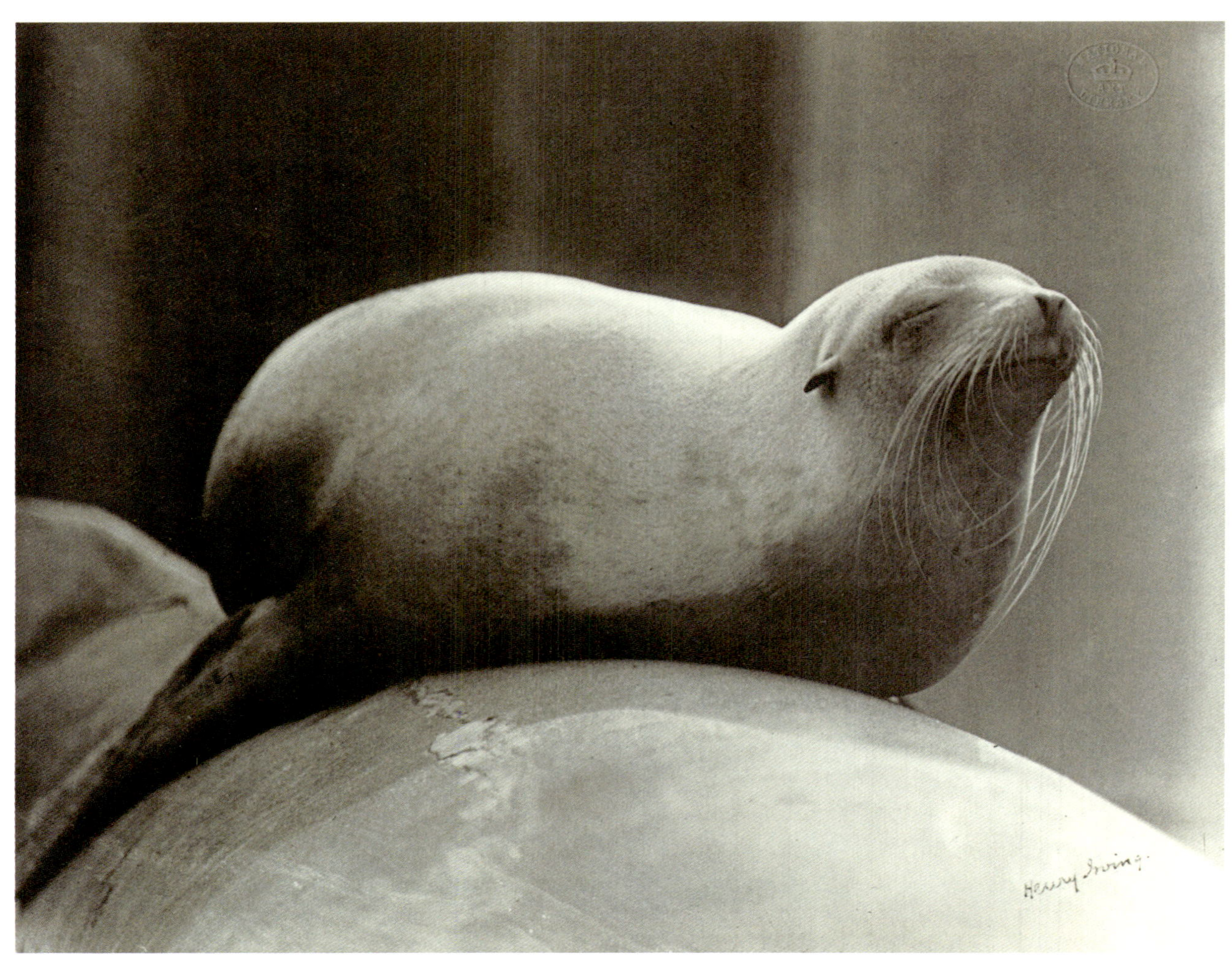

Henry Irving
Walross /
Walrus, ca. 1904

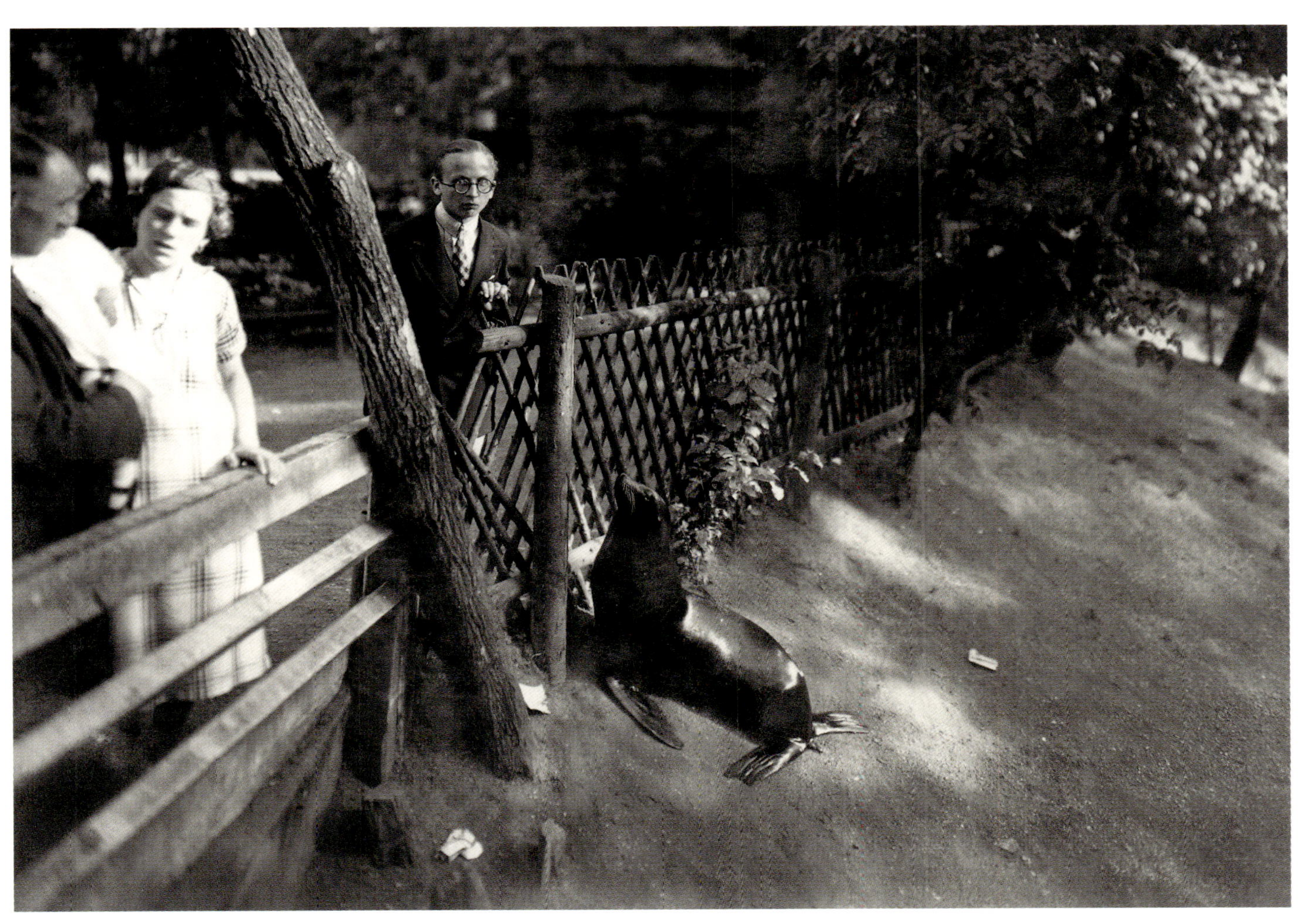

Paul Faulstich

Brillenträger am Seehundgehege /

Person wearing glasses standing at the seal compound, 1927

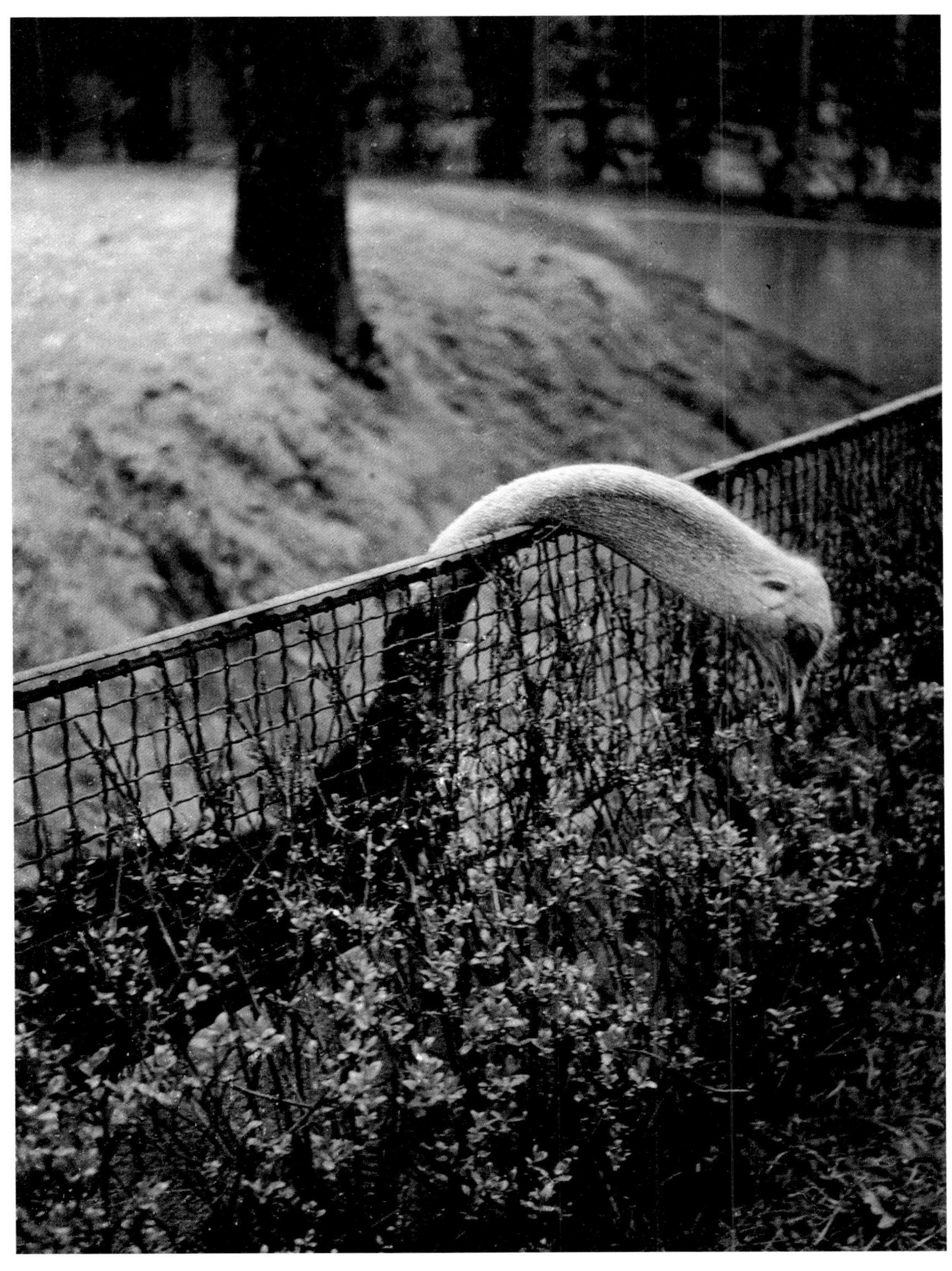

Friedrich Seidenstücker

Strauß rupft die Hecke ab /

Ostrich picking at a hedge, ca. 1930

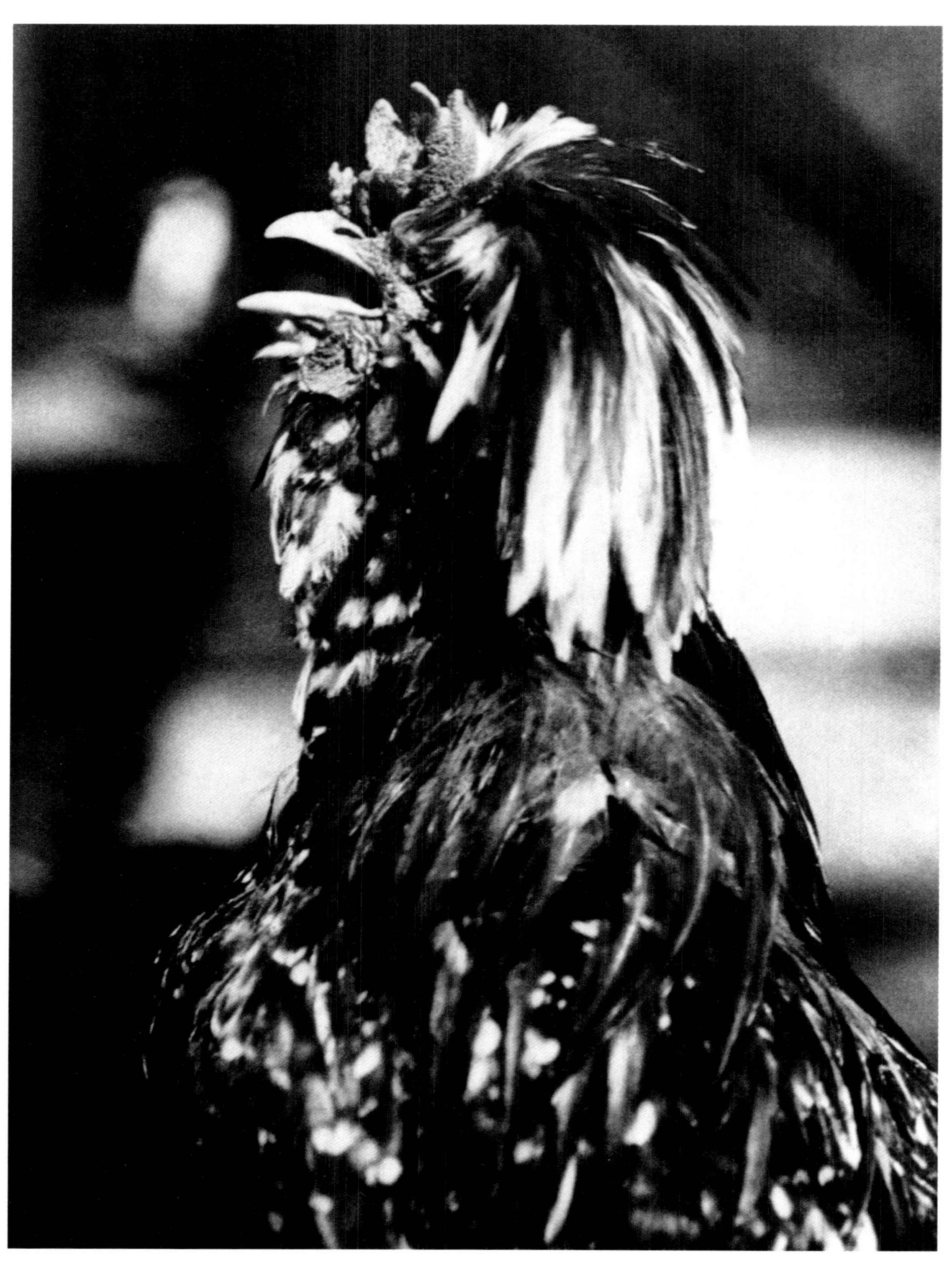

Hedda Walther
Hahn /
Rooster, 1927

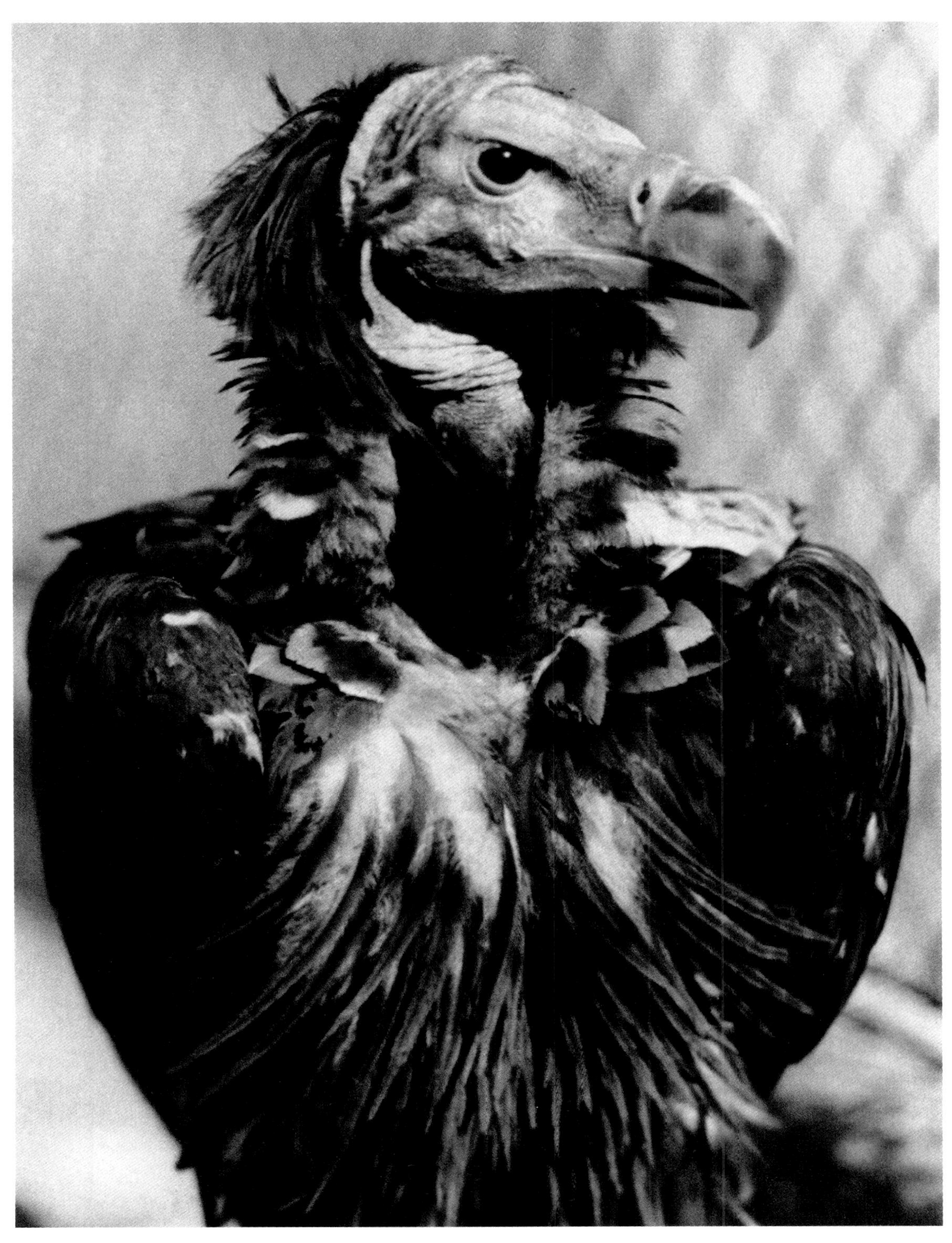

Hedda Walther
Sperbergeier, vor 1931 /
Sparrow hawk, before 1931

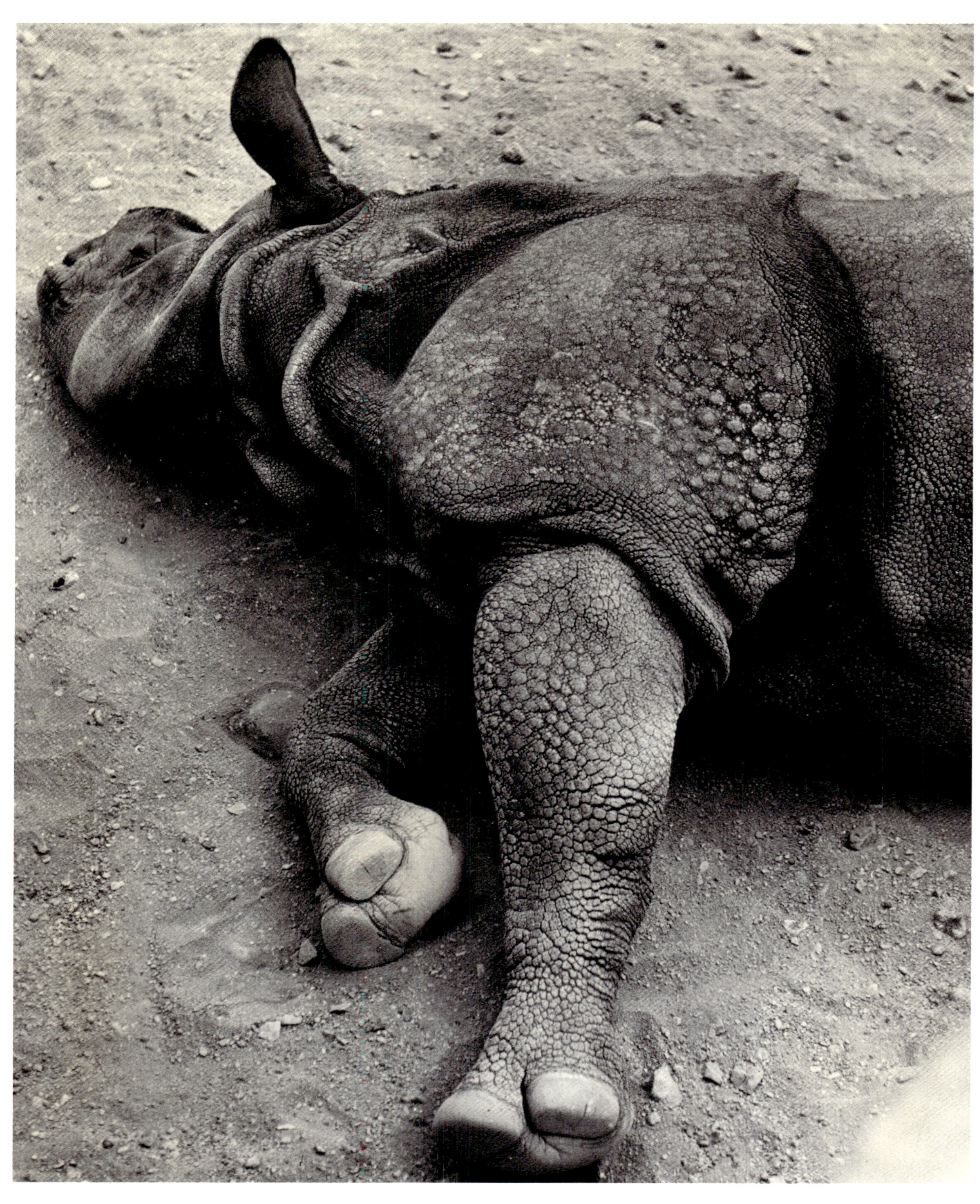

Lisette Model
Rhinoceros im Zoo von Vincennes /
Rhinoceros, Vincennes Zoo, Paris, 1933-1938

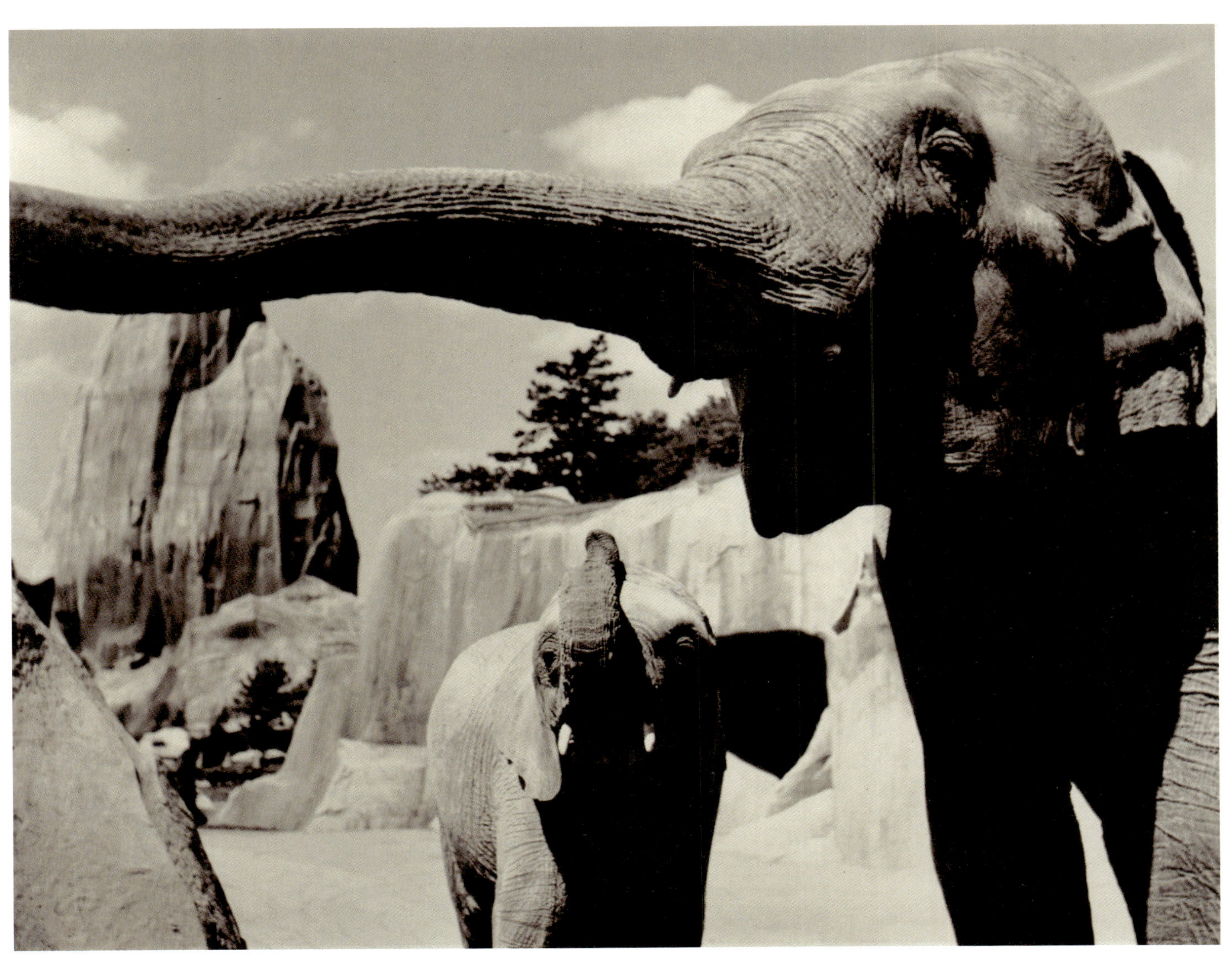

Lisette Model
Elefanten im Zoo von Vincennes /
Elephants, Vincennes Zoo, Paris, 1933-1938

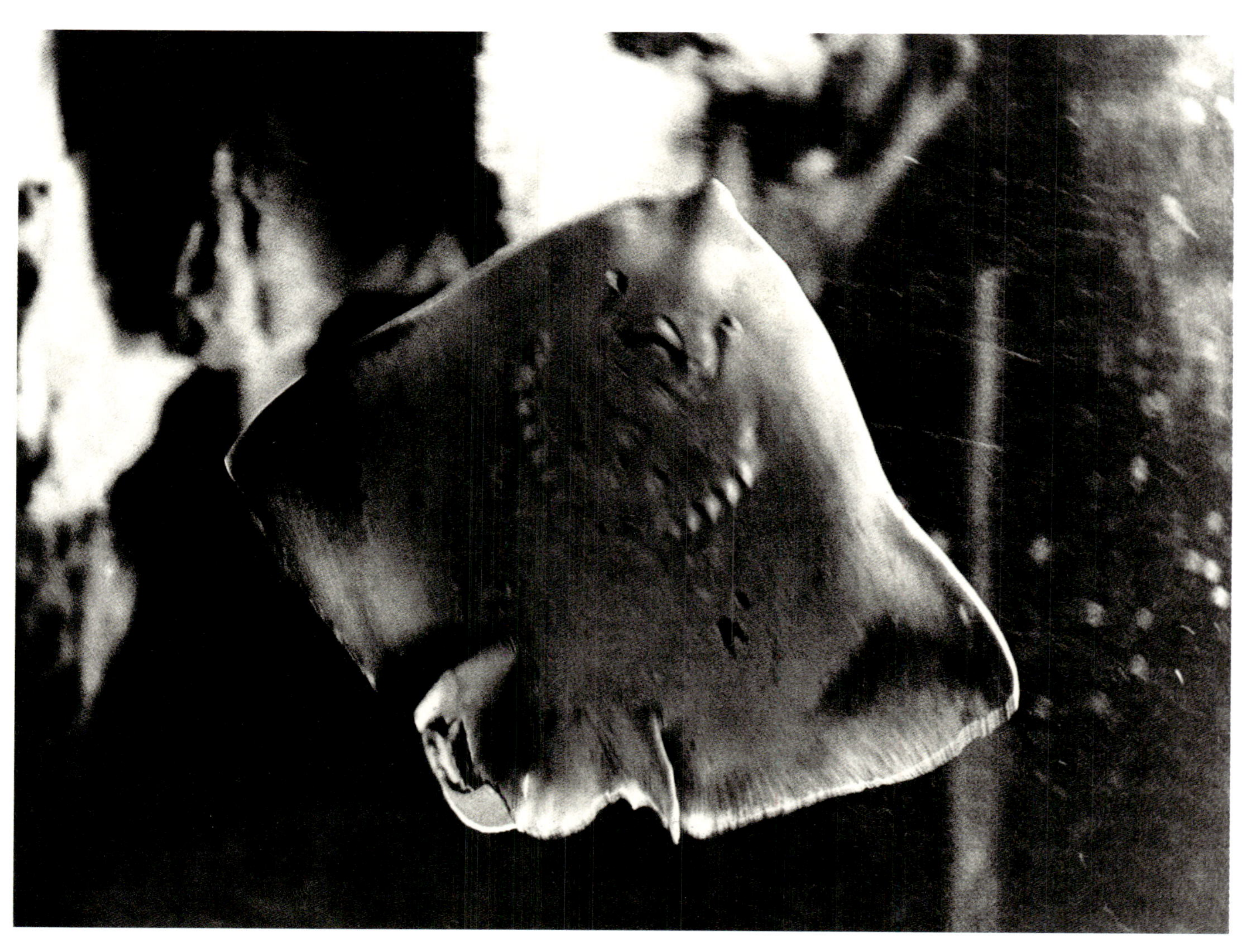

Hilmar Pabel

Dämonen unter Wasser, Zoo Berlin, 1930er

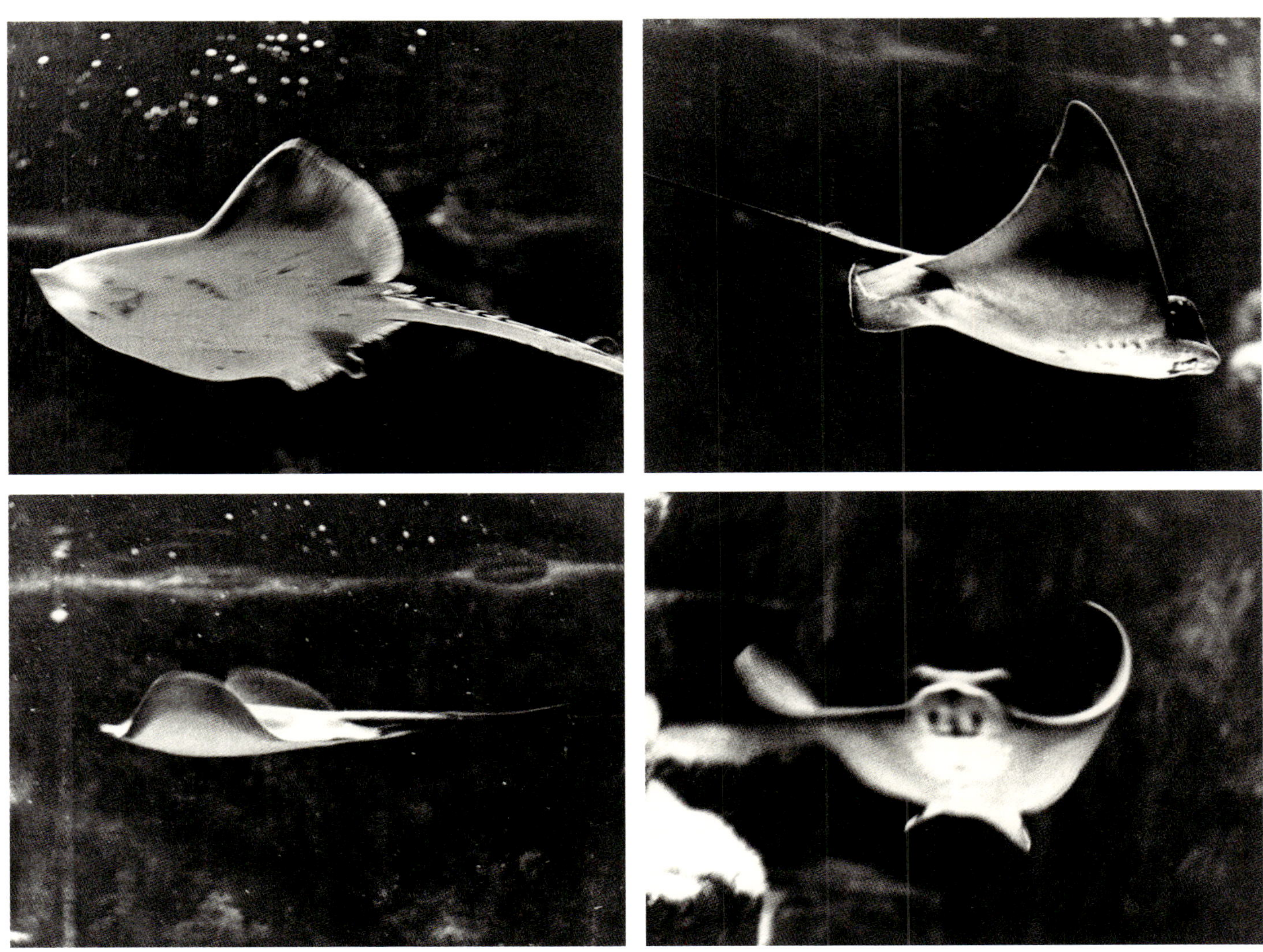

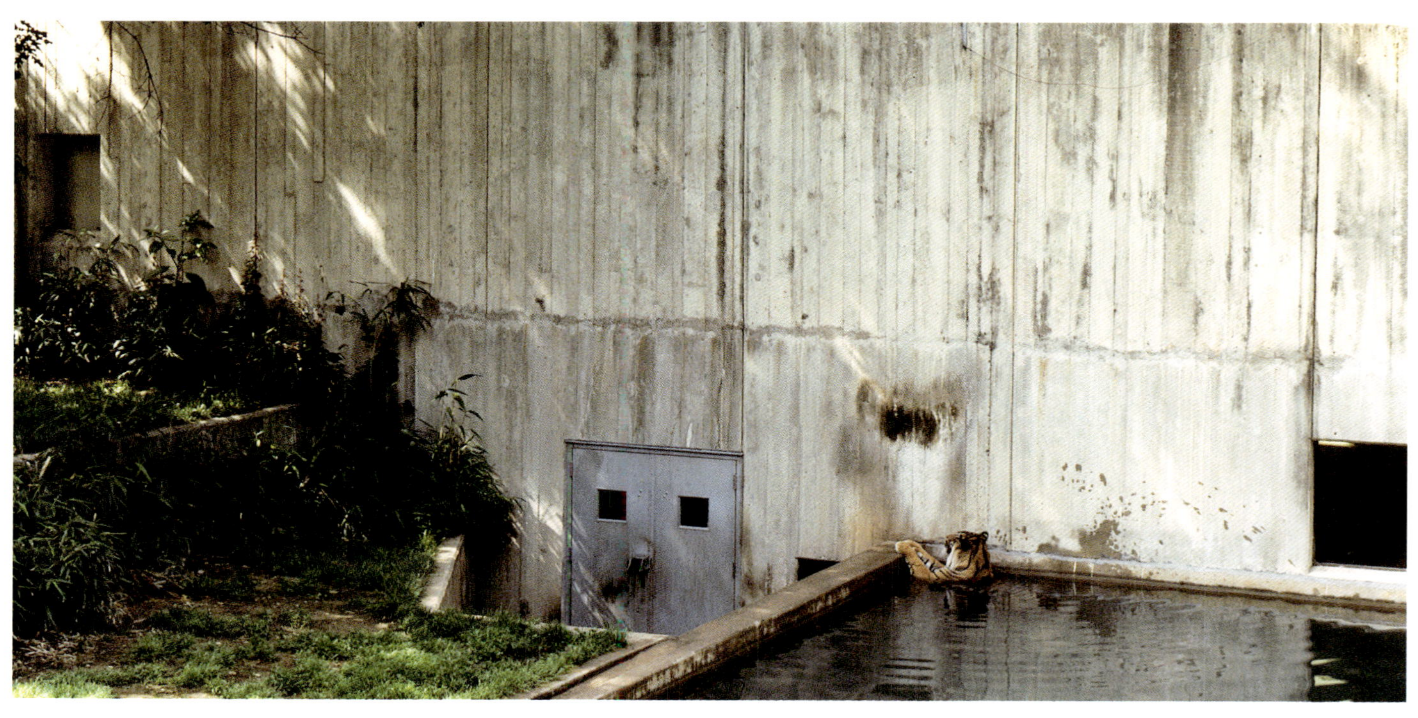

Candida Höfer

Zoologischer Garten Washington DC II 1992

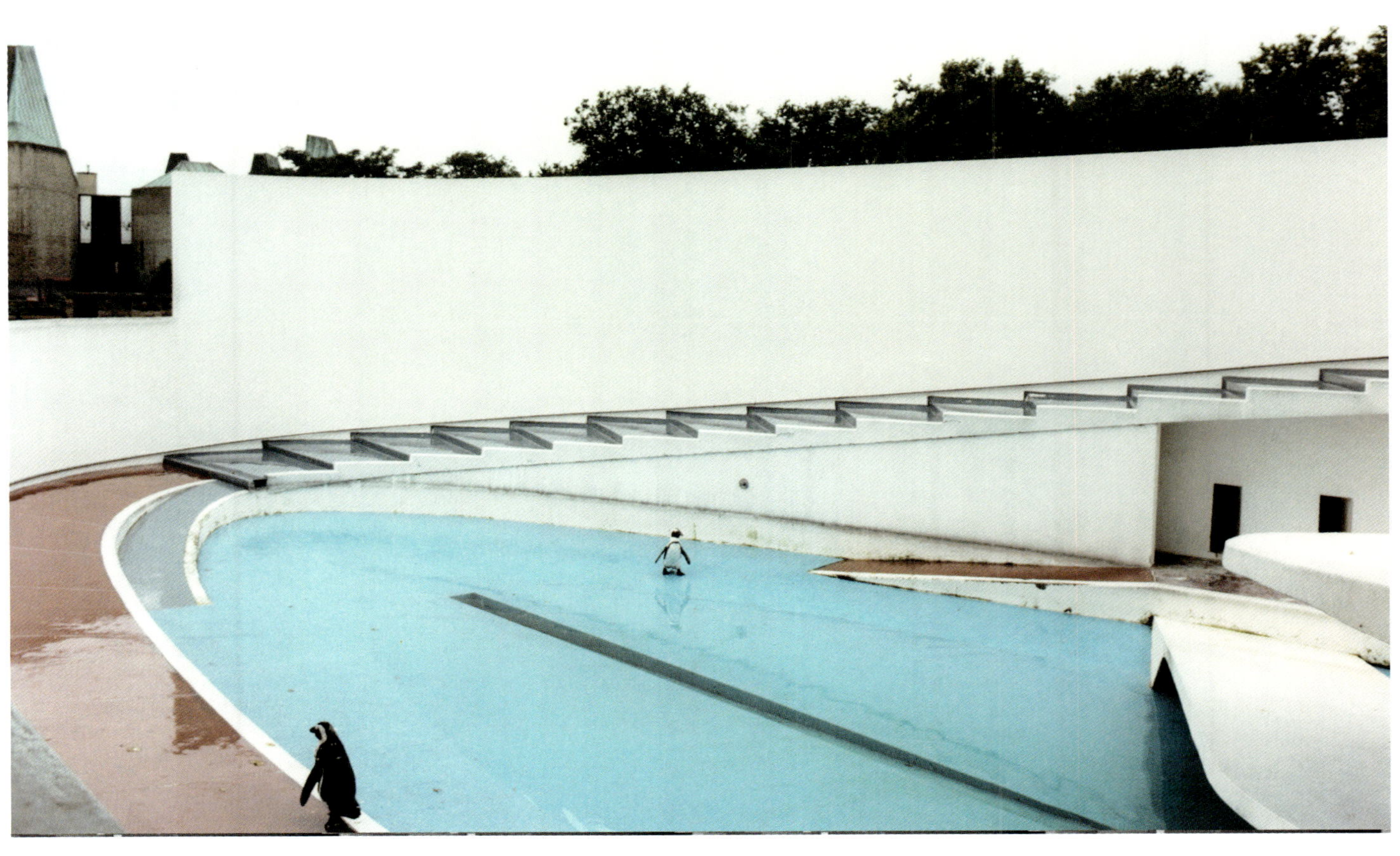

Candida Höfer

Zoologischer Garten London III 1992

„Es gibt eine Weigerung im philosophischen und theoretischen Denken, auch nur die Möglichkeit in Betracht zu ziehen, Tiere könnten auf die gleiche Art Individuen sein wie wir, die wir als Individuen die größere menschliche Gemeinschaft bilden."

"There is a refusal in philosophical and theoretical thinking to even fathom the notion that animals could be individuals in the same way that we are, that they live in the larger human community as individuals."

Jo Longhurst

Artisten Artistes

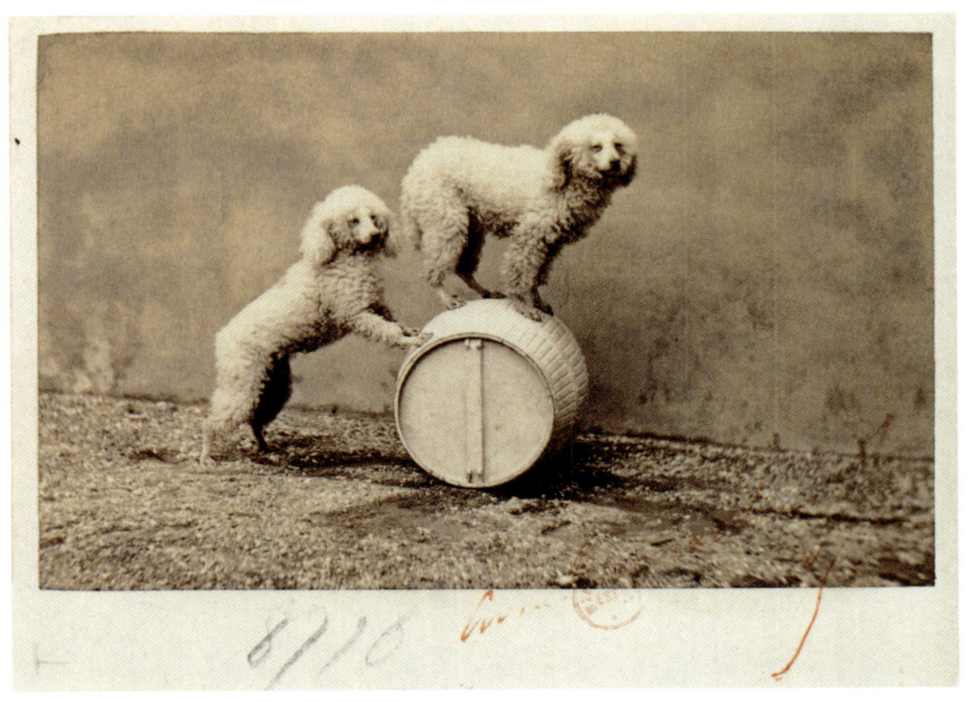

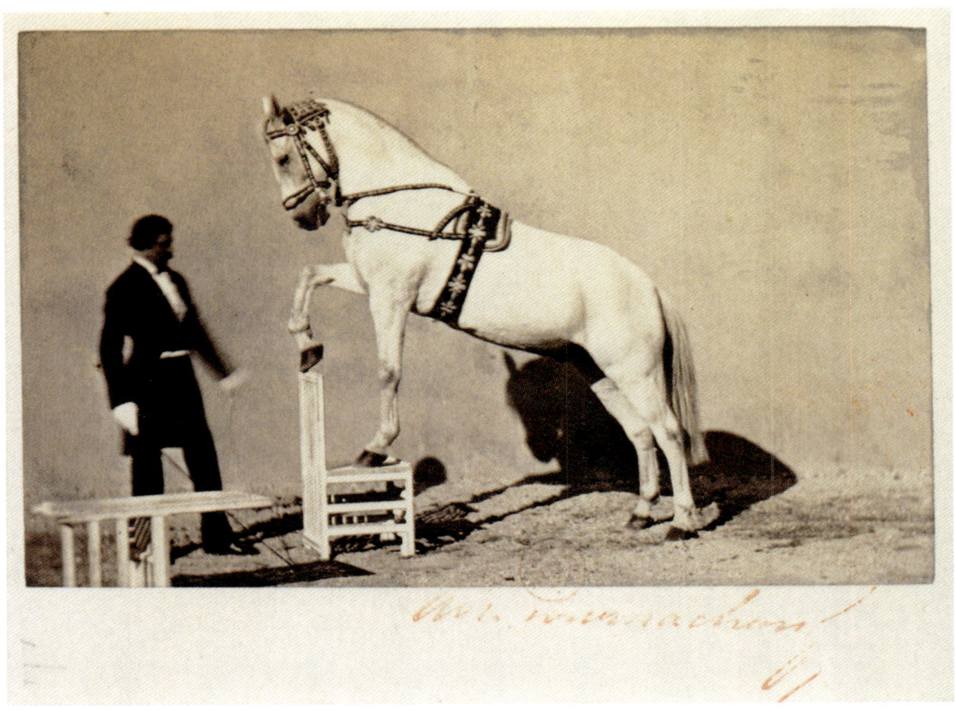

Adrien Alban Tournachon
Programmnummern aus dem Zirkus von Napoléon III und der Kaiserin /
Programme numbers from the circus of Napoléon III and the empress, 1861

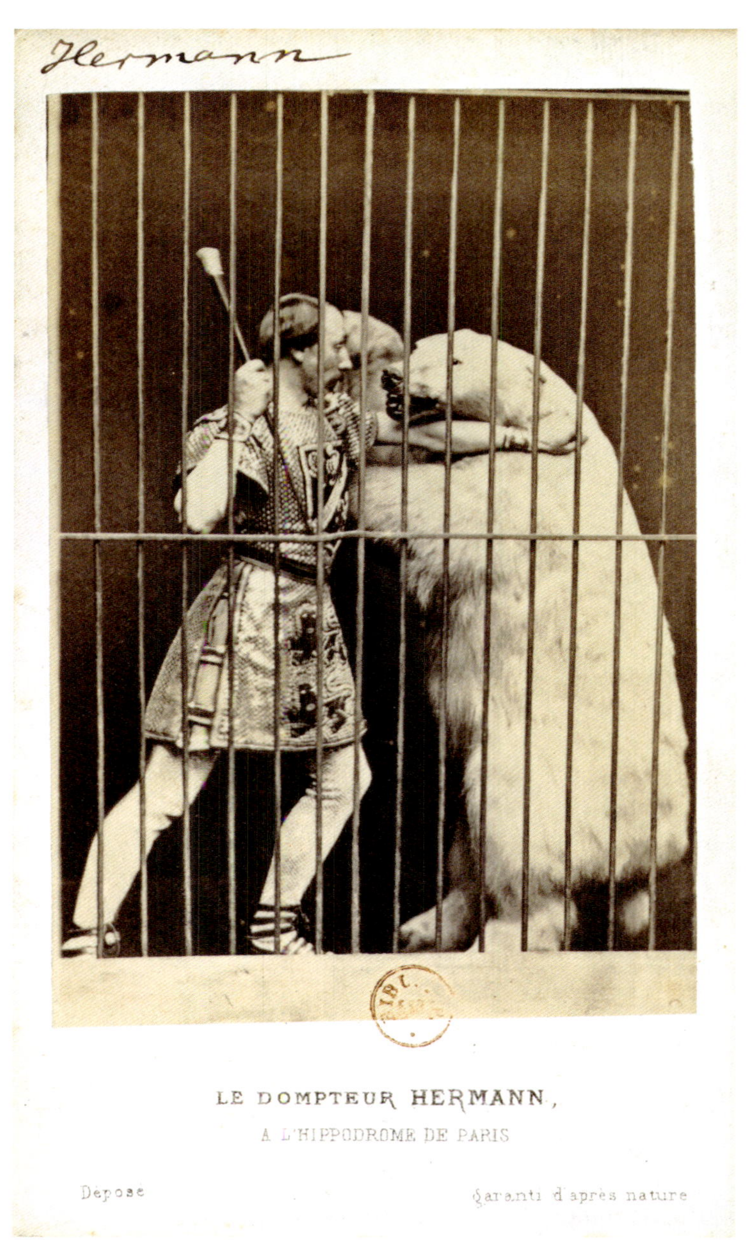

Mayer & Pierson
Le dompteur Hermann à l'hippodrome de Paris, garanti d'après nature, 1863

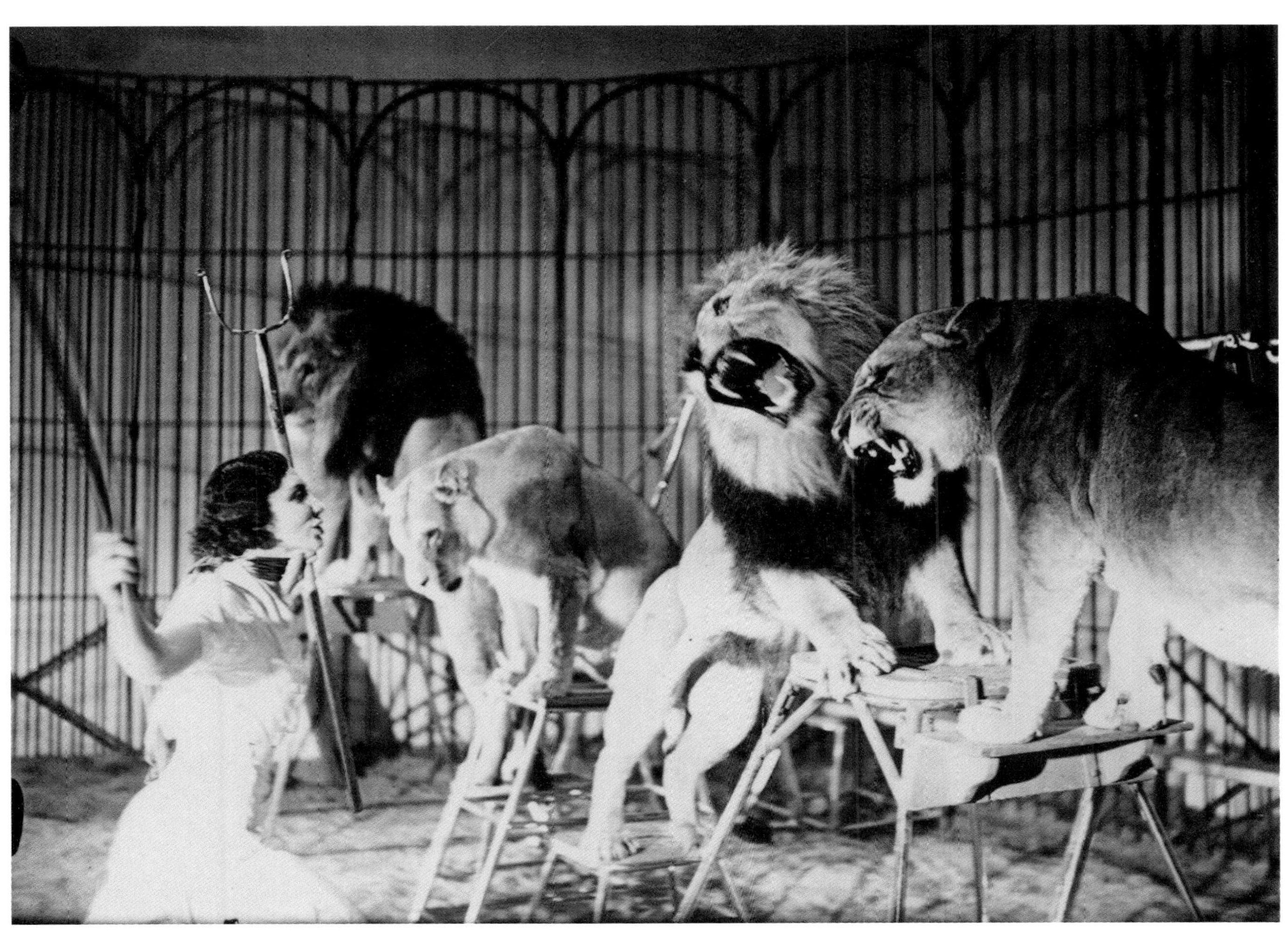

Edward Malindine

Bertram Mills Touring Circus in training at Ascot.

Miss Priscilla Kayes rehearsing her 6 lions, 1.4.1936

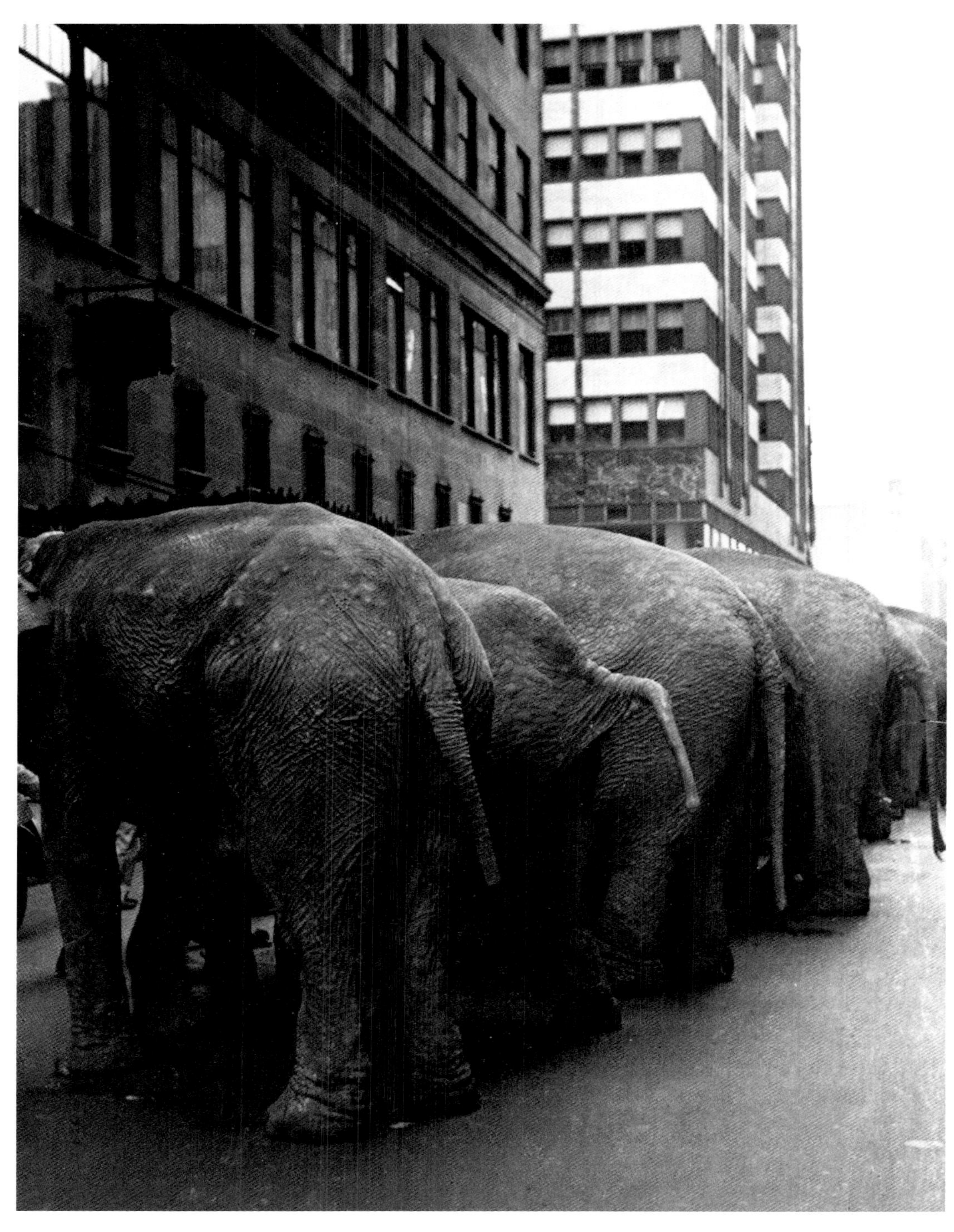

André Kertész
New York, 1936

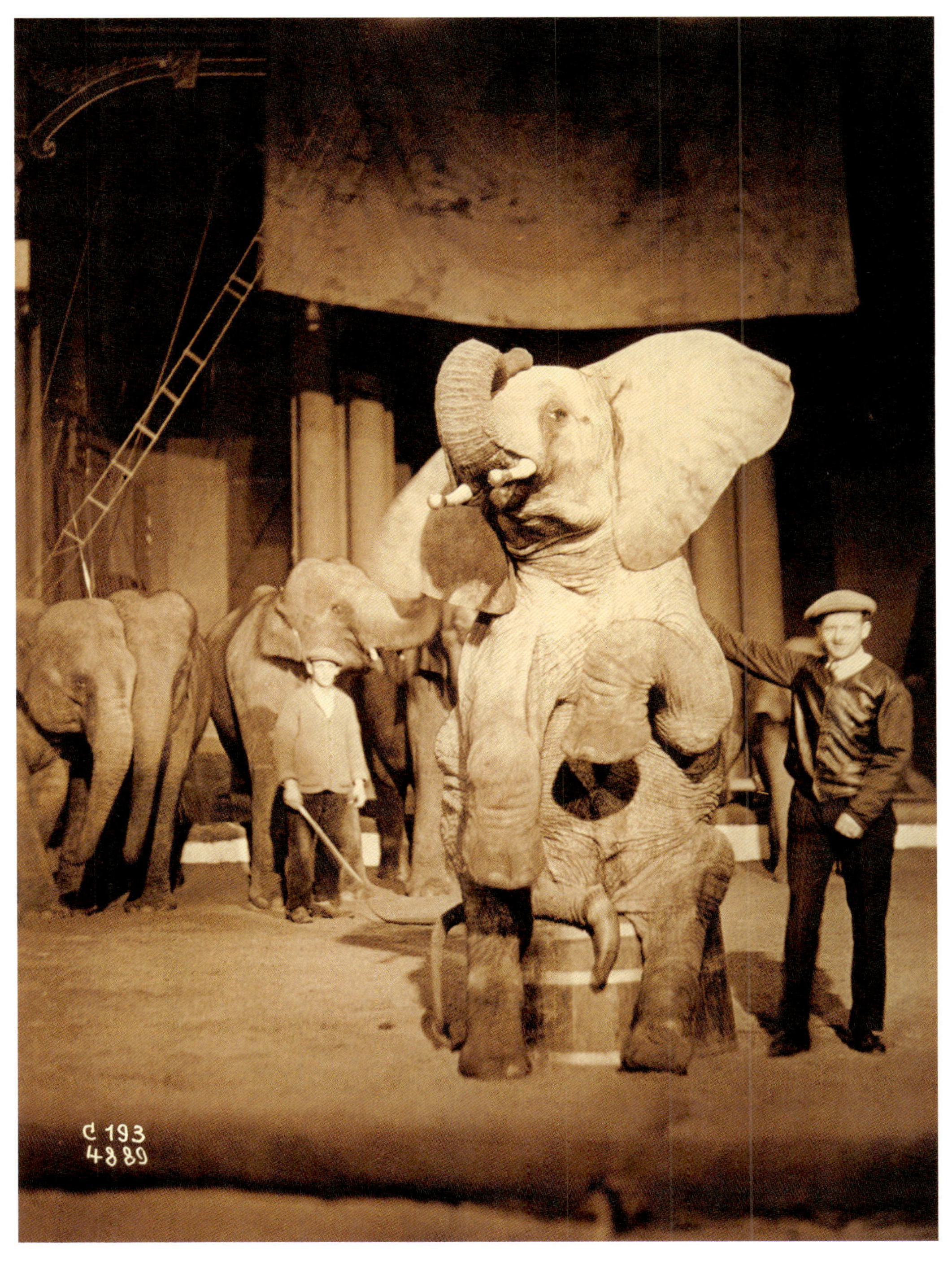

Sasha Stone

Circus Hagenbeck, Tierdressur, 1930

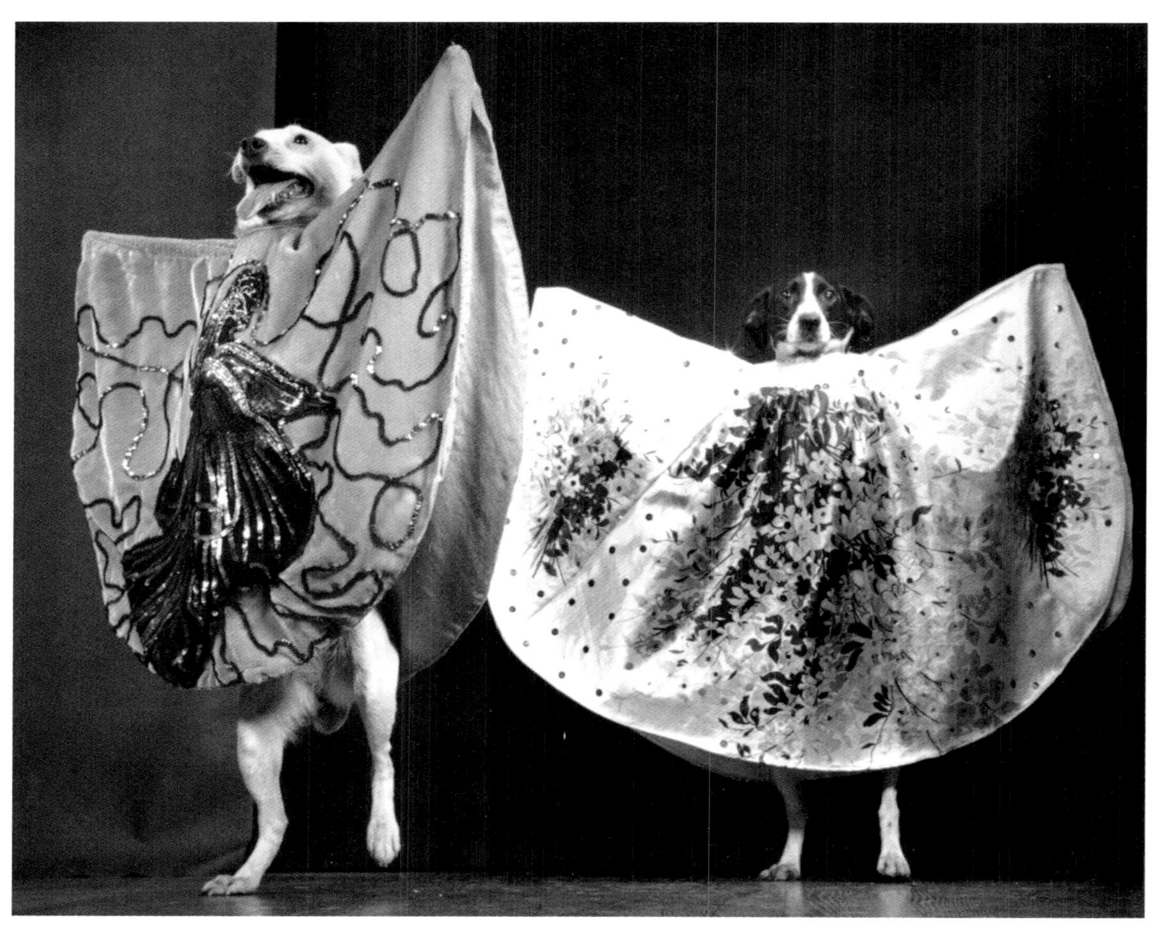

Ylla

Nellie and Judie, ca. 1950

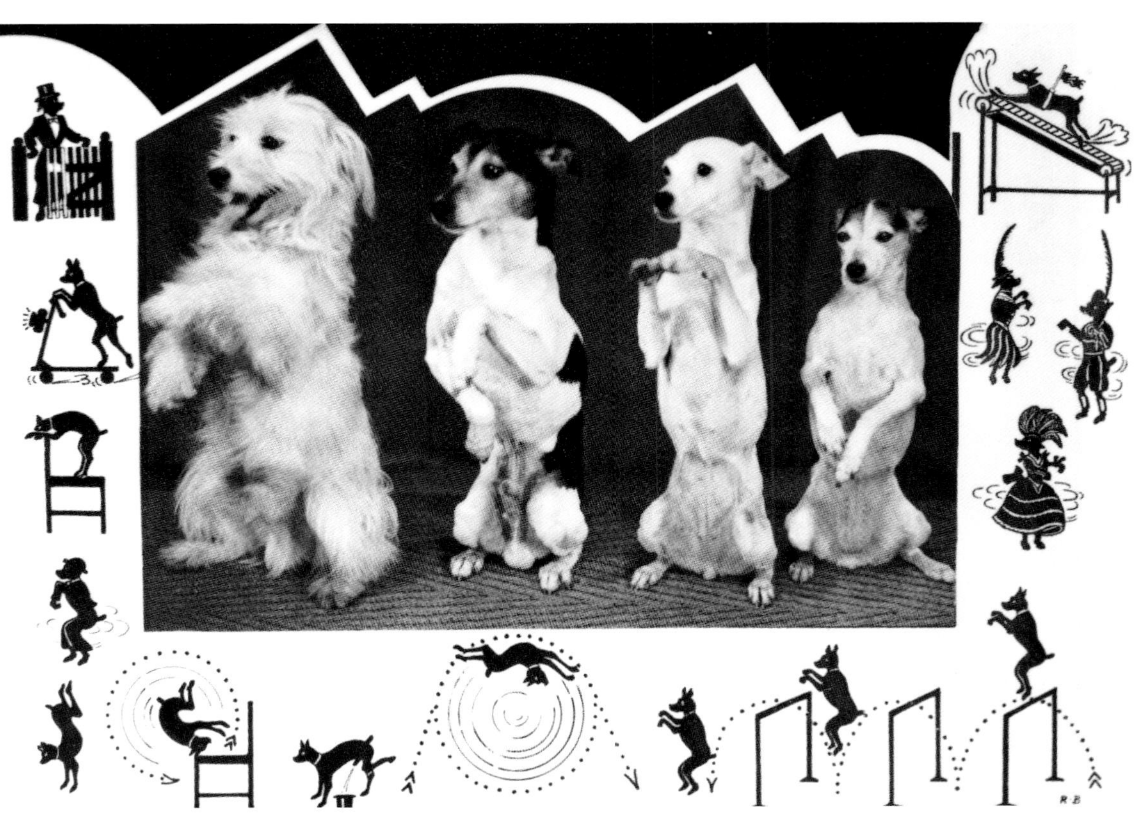

Anonym

Bell & Bell, Kopenhagen, 1949

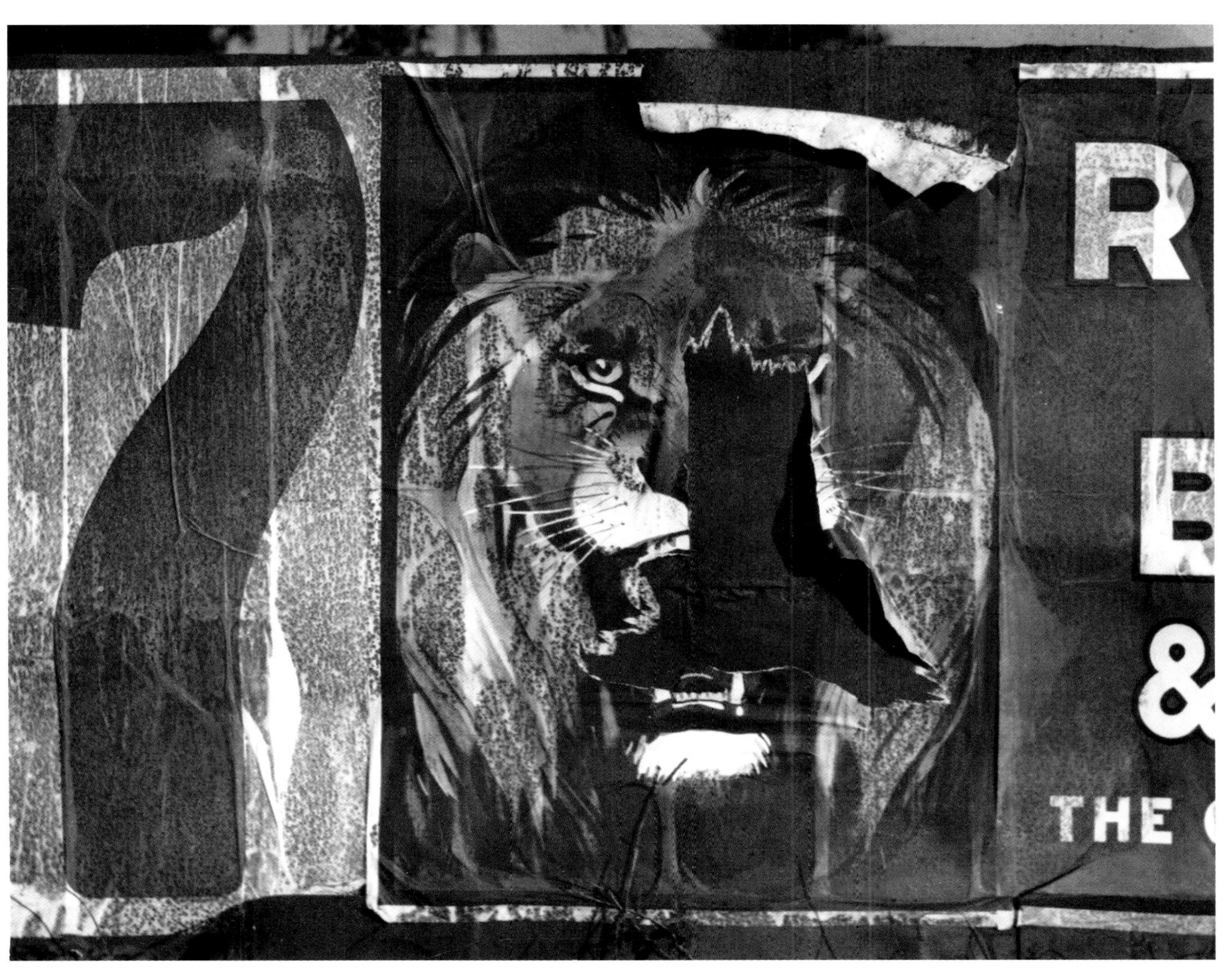

Walker Evans
Beschädigtes Ringling Brothers-Plakat /
Torn Ringling Brothers Poster, 1941

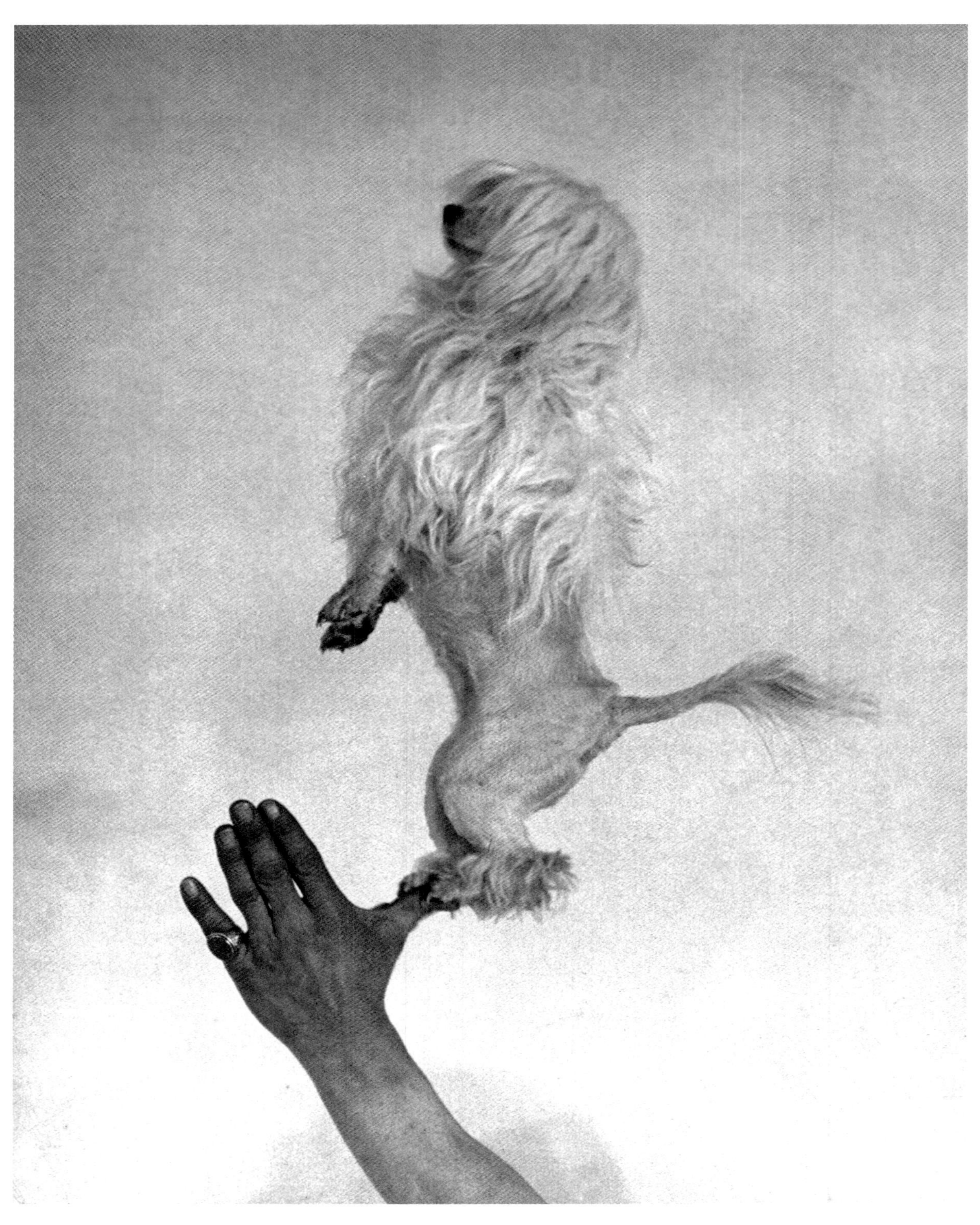

Martin Munkacsi
Balancierender Hund, ca. 1930

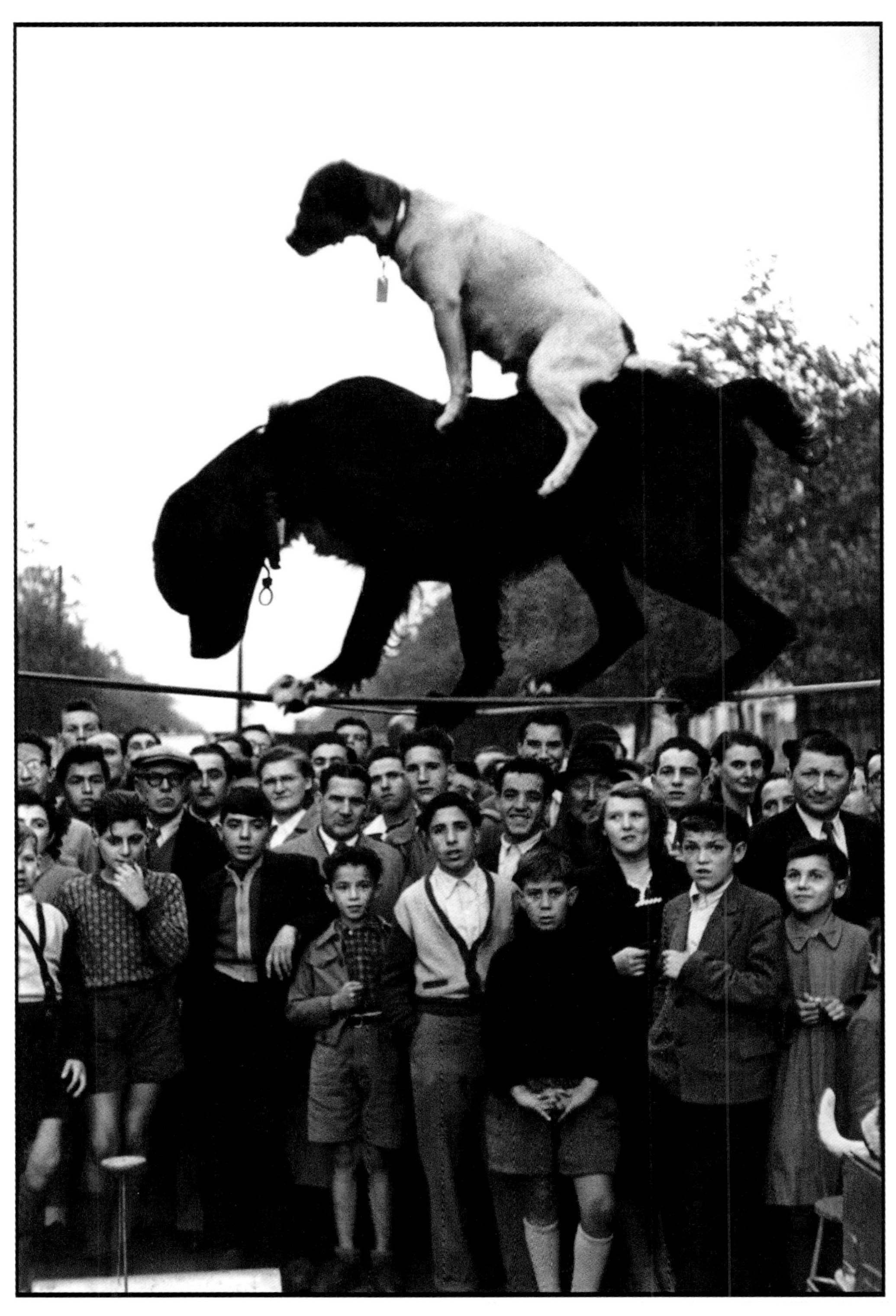

Henri Cartier-Bresson

Boulevard Richard Lenoir, 1952

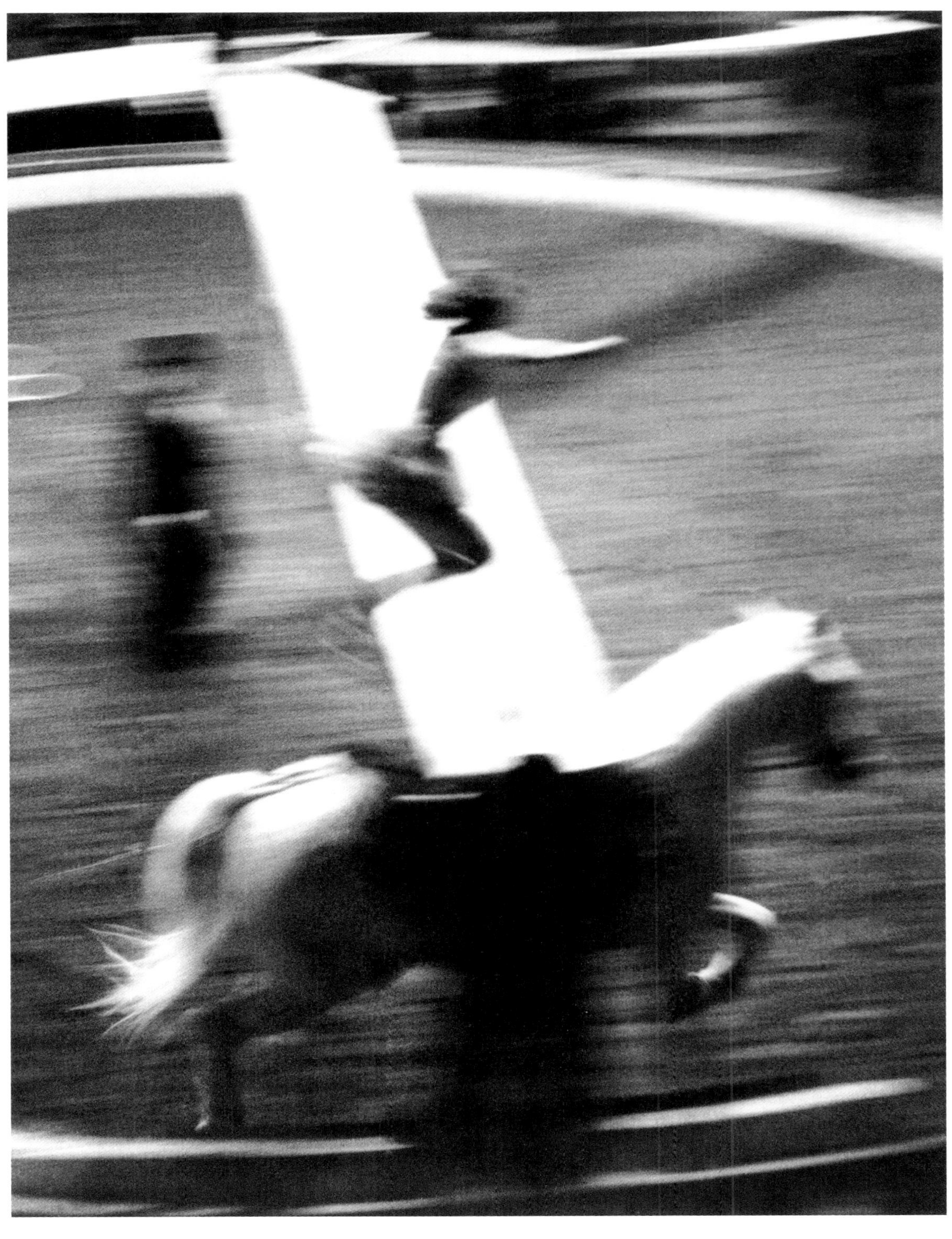

Aart Klein
Acrobat, 1954

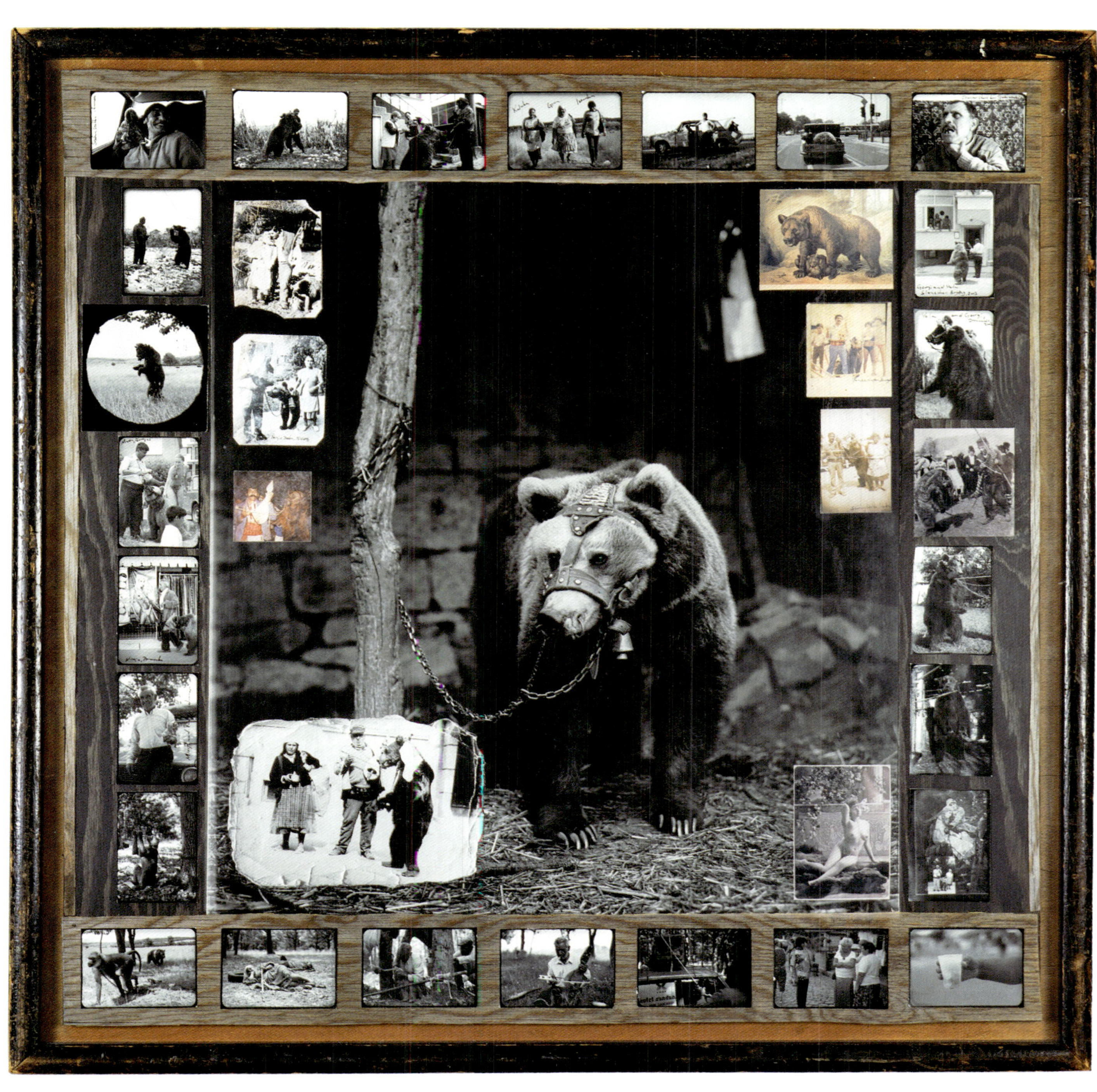

Albin Biblom

Mechkar, bulgaria's last dancing bears and their owner, 2004

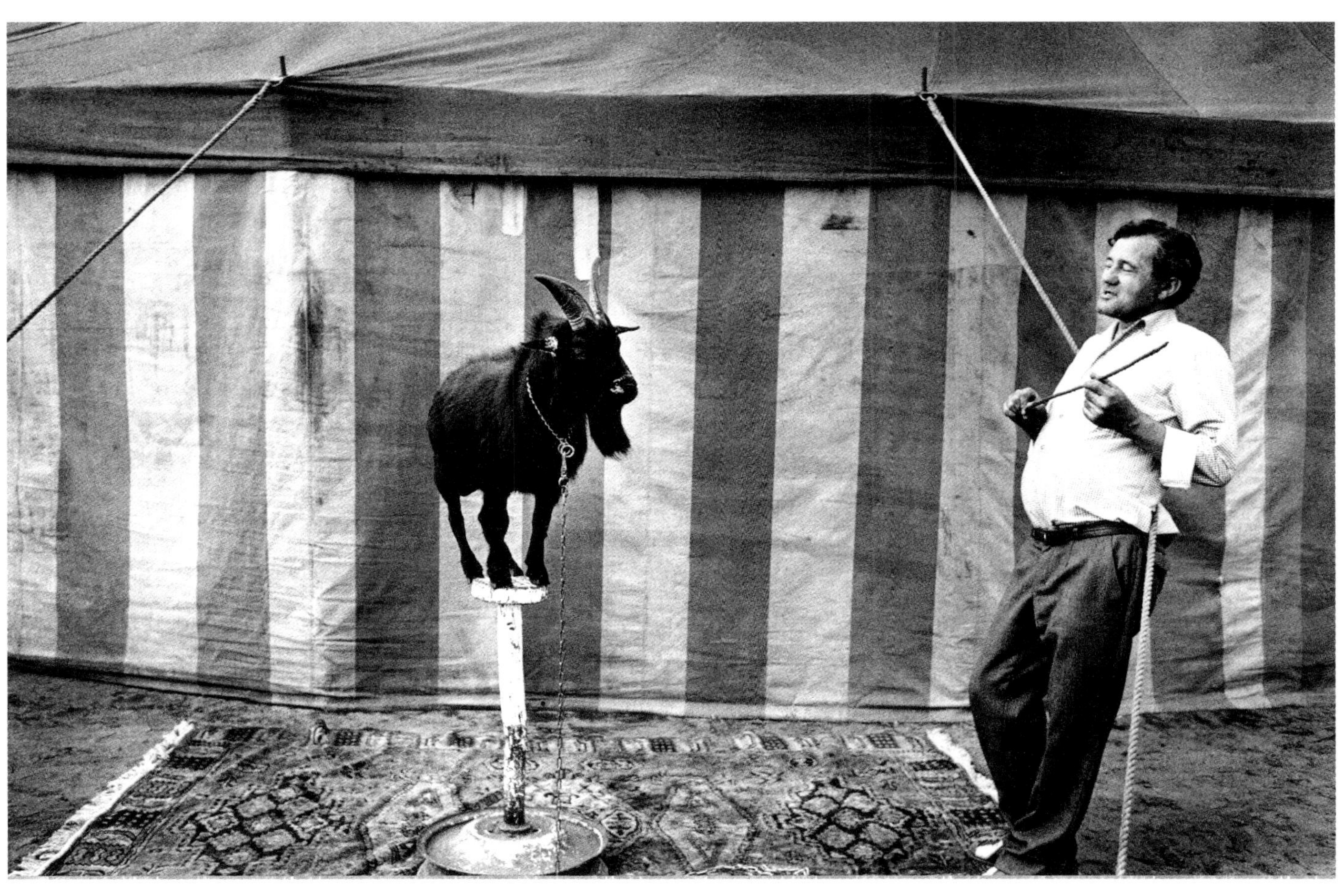

Heinrich Riebesehl
Dompteur mit Ziege /
Trainer with goat, 1974

„Sorgfältige Feldforschung, die Entdeckung der fossilen Dokumente, vergleichende Forschung – dies ist ein Teil der Information, auf dem die Evolutionstheorien basieren. Ein anderer Teil ist die sorgfältige Beobachtung lebender Tiere."

„Careful field work, discovery of fossil record, comparative research. This is one body of information from which theories of evolution are based. And another is the careful observations of the behavior of living animals."

Jane Goodall

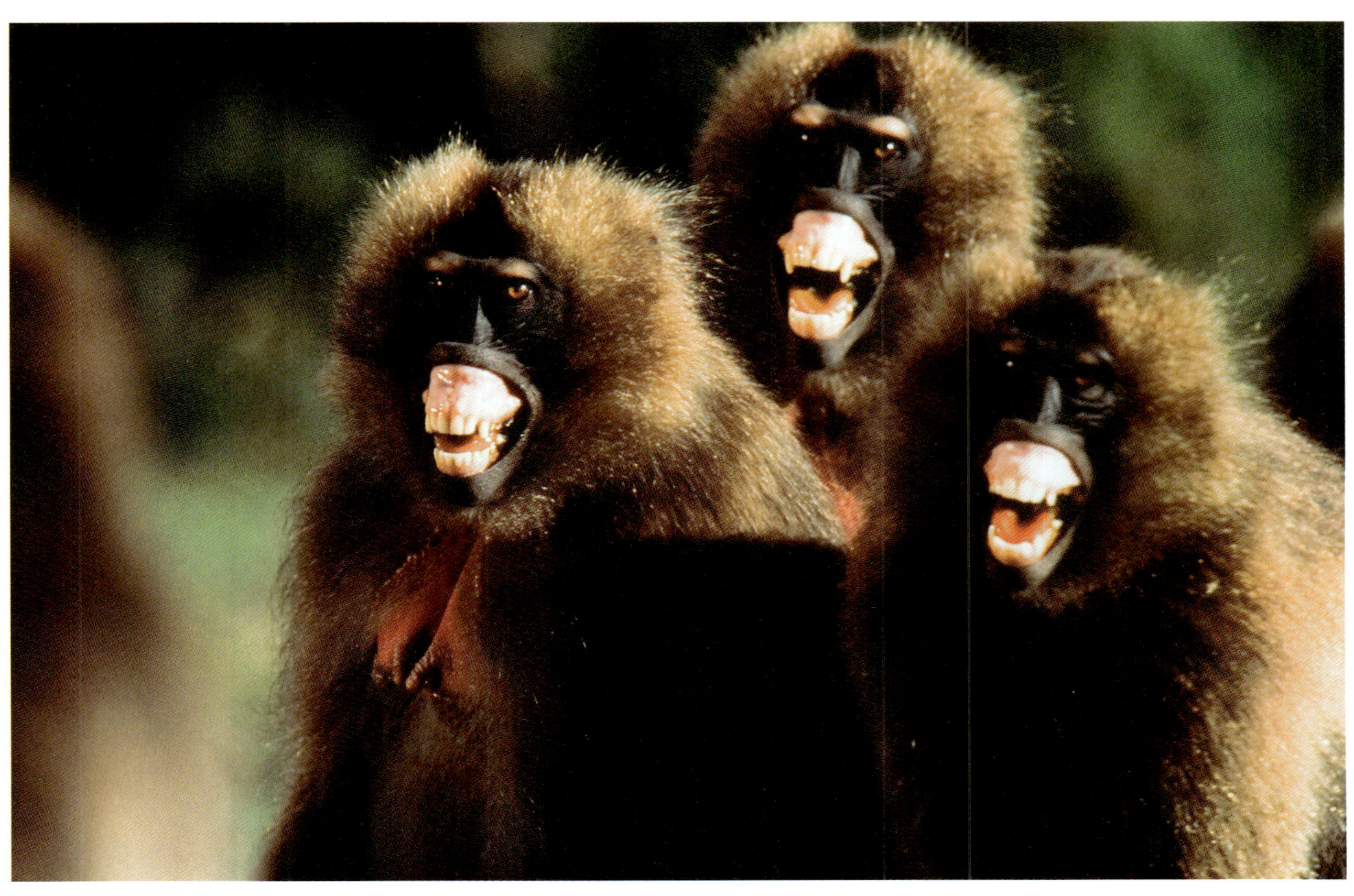

Michael Nichols
Babuinos de Gelada, Etiopía, 2002

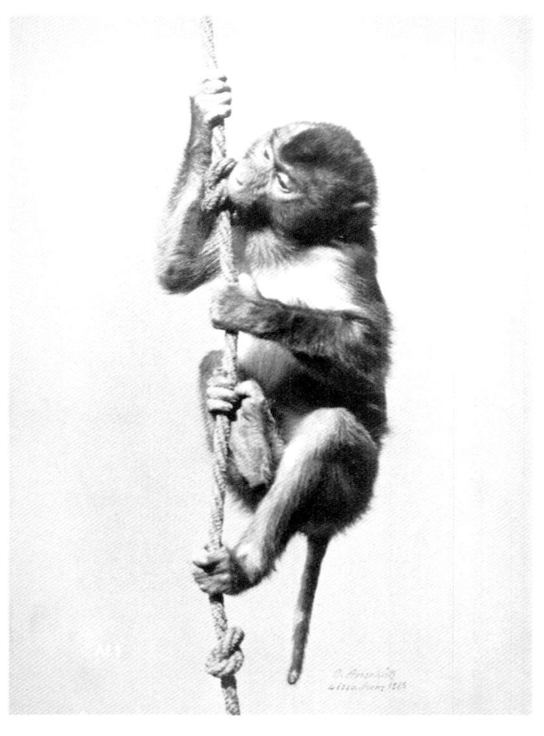

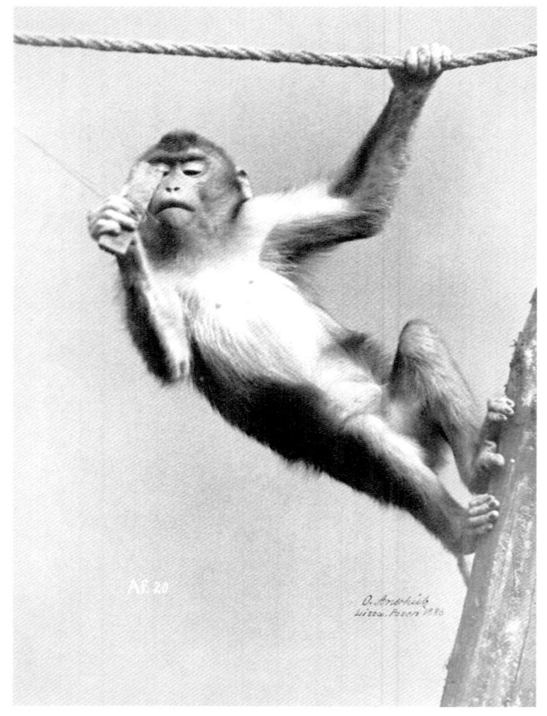

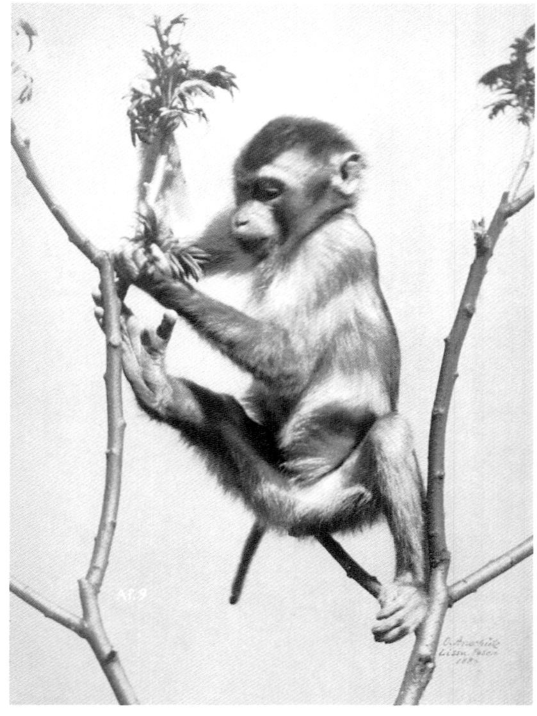

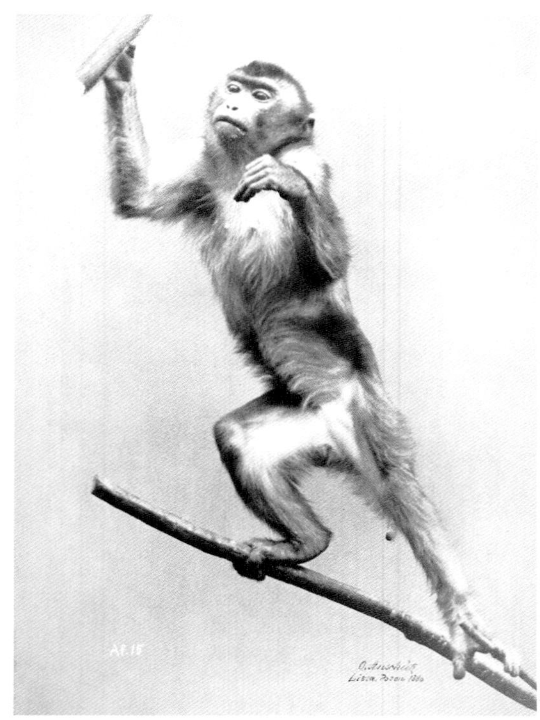

Ottomar Anschütz
Affen /
Apes, 1886

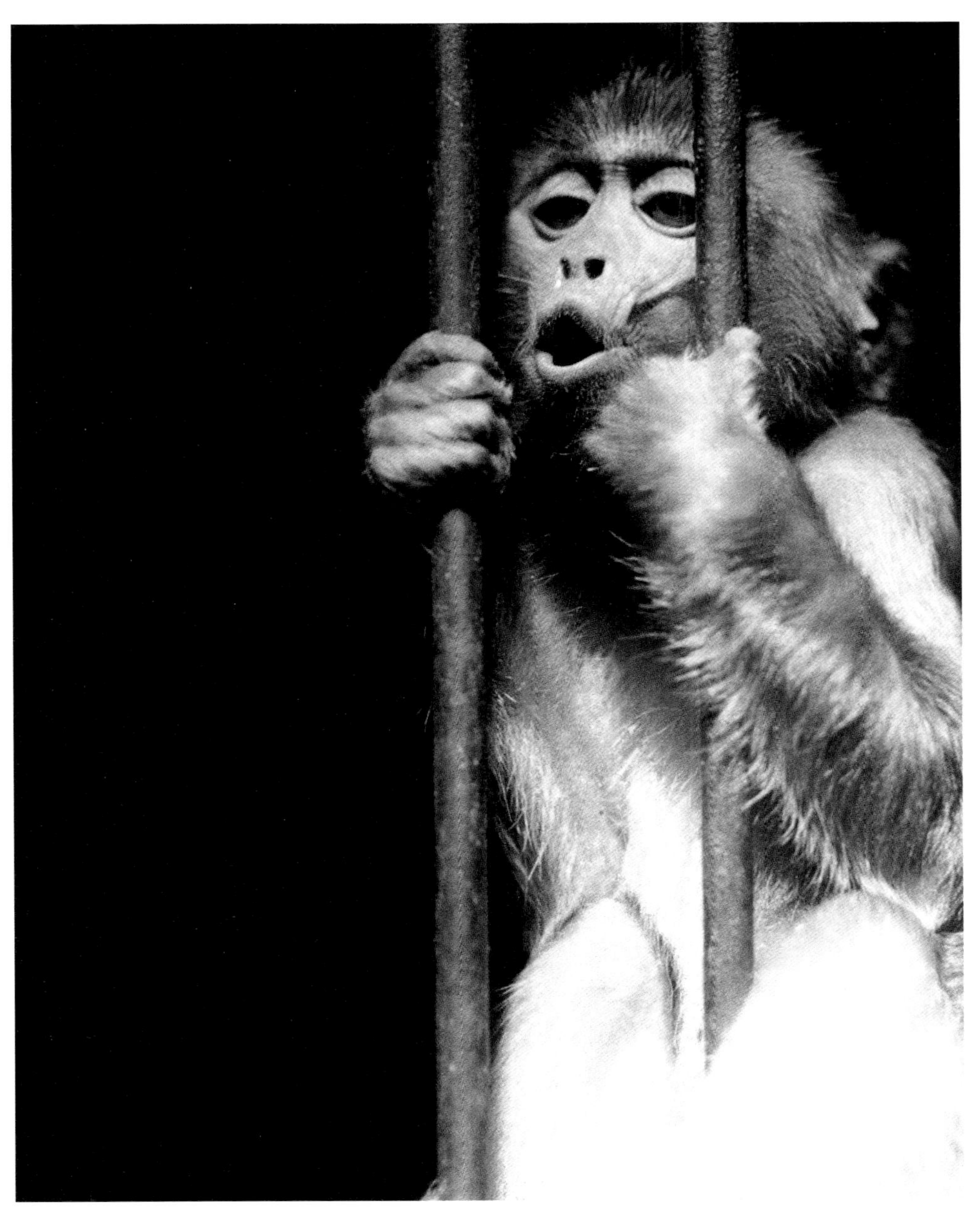

Hedda Walther
Junger Schimpanse /
Young chimp, 1920er

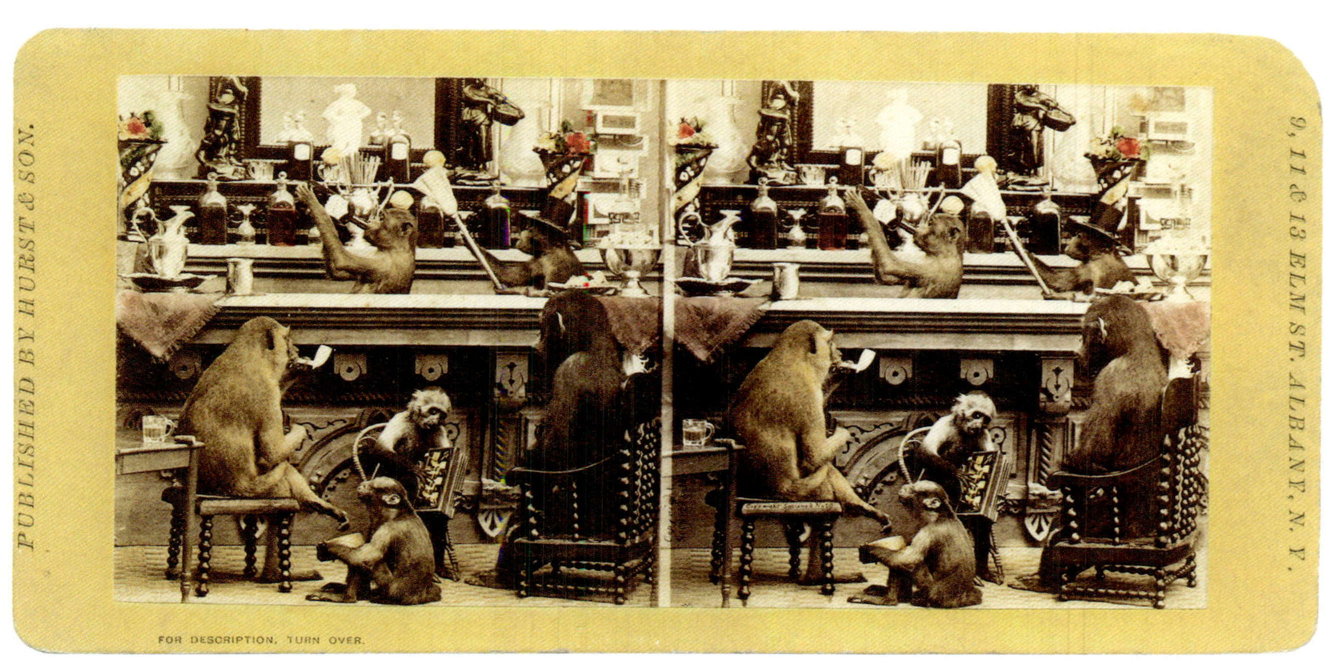

Eugene S. M. Haines

The Bar. – Where Justice is dispensed with, 1870

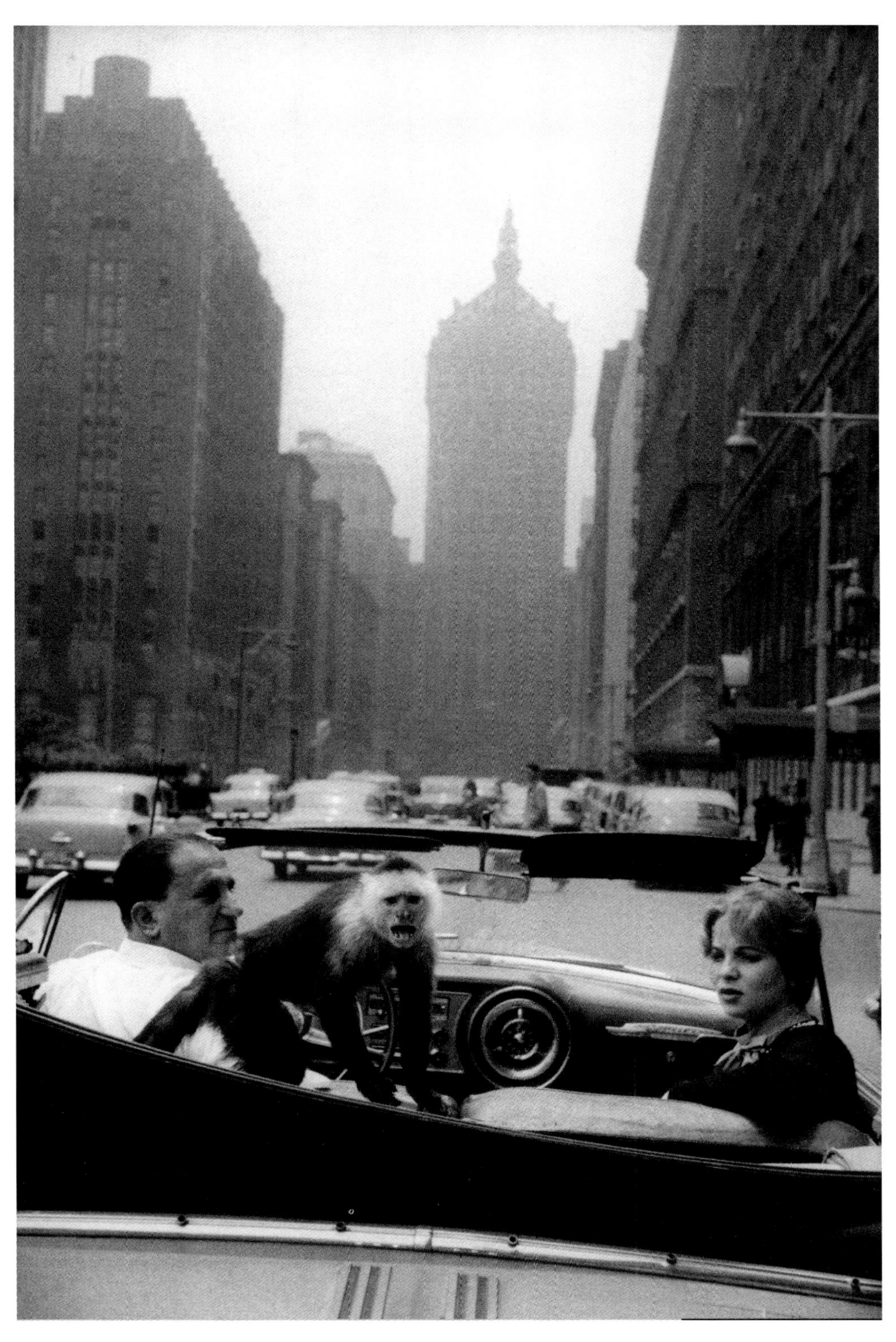

Garry Winogrand
Park Avenue, New York, 1959

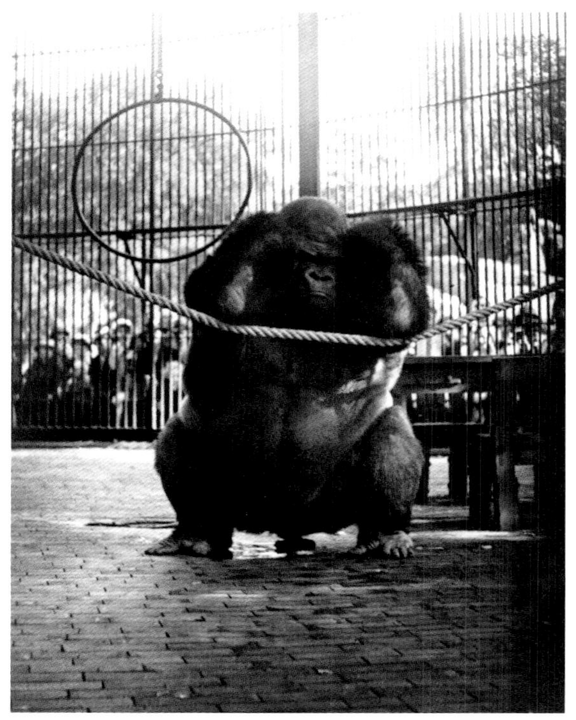

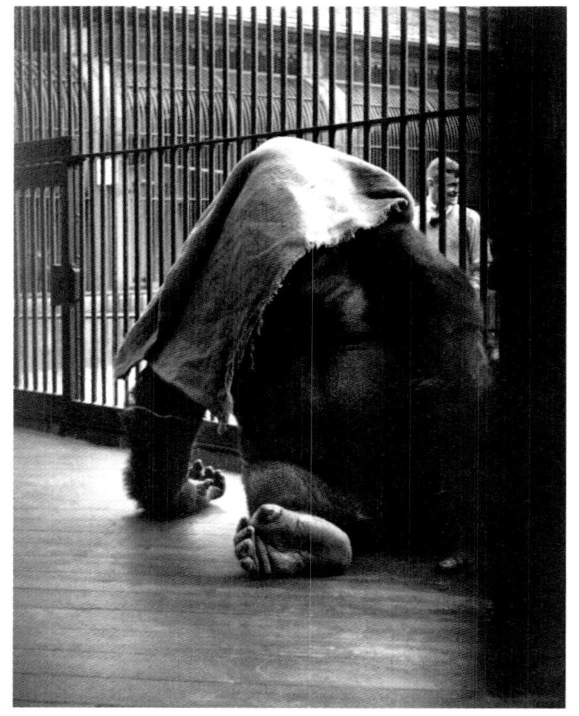

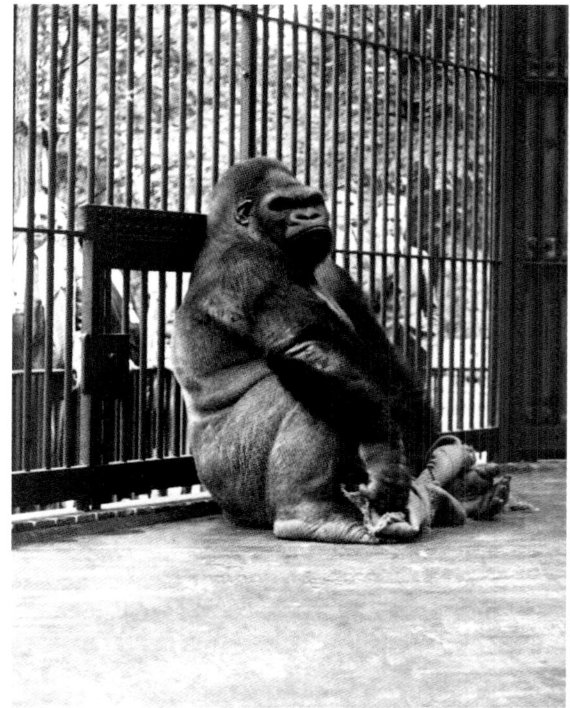

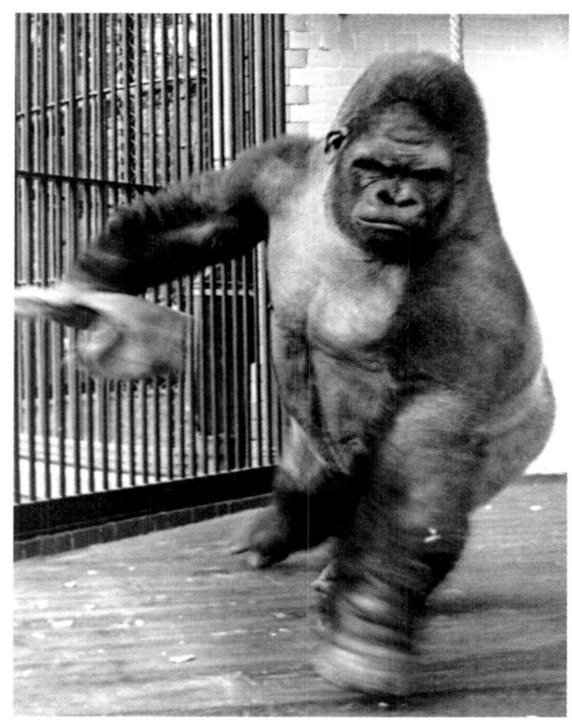

Hilmar Pabel

a. d. Reportage: *Bobby*, 20. Juli 1935

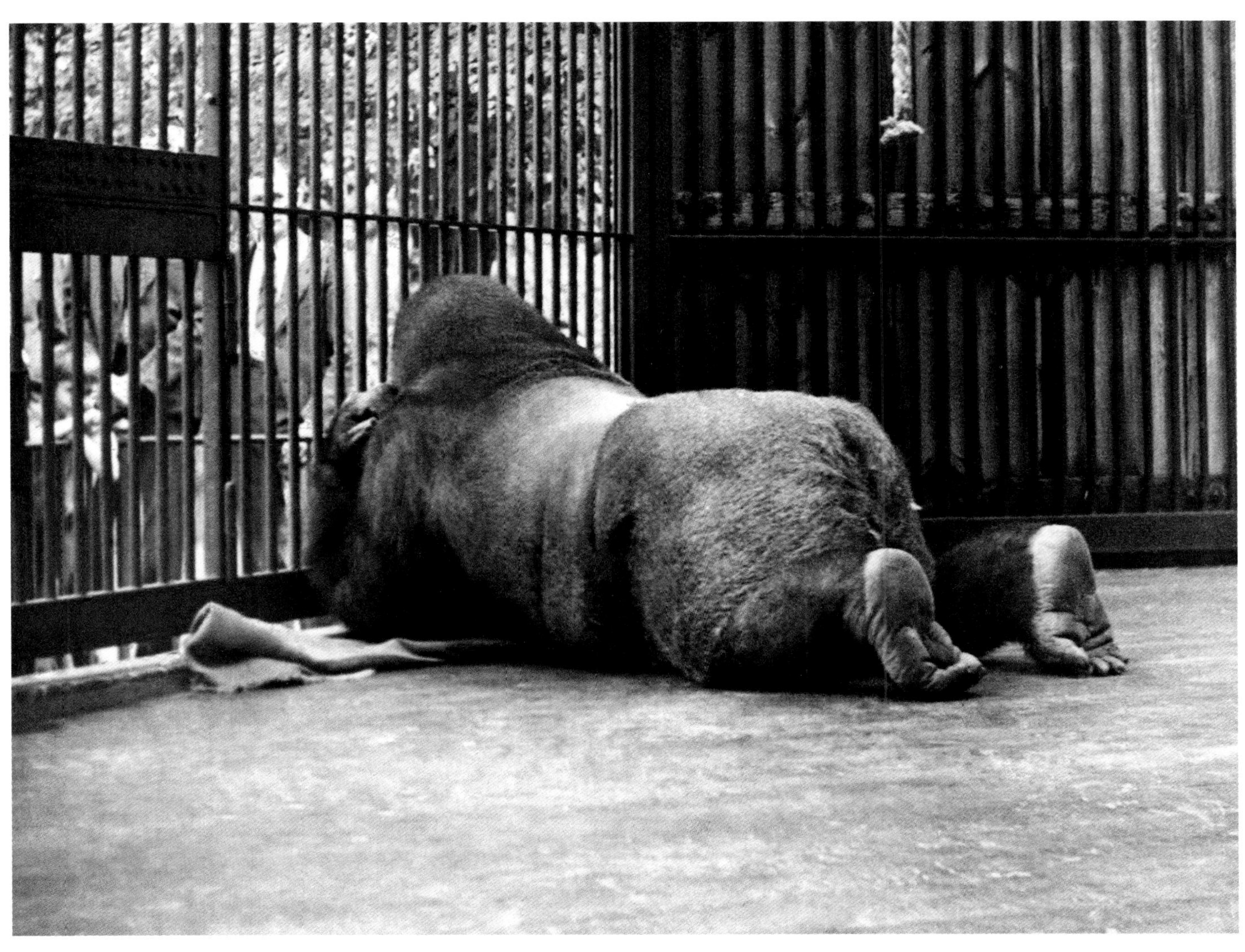

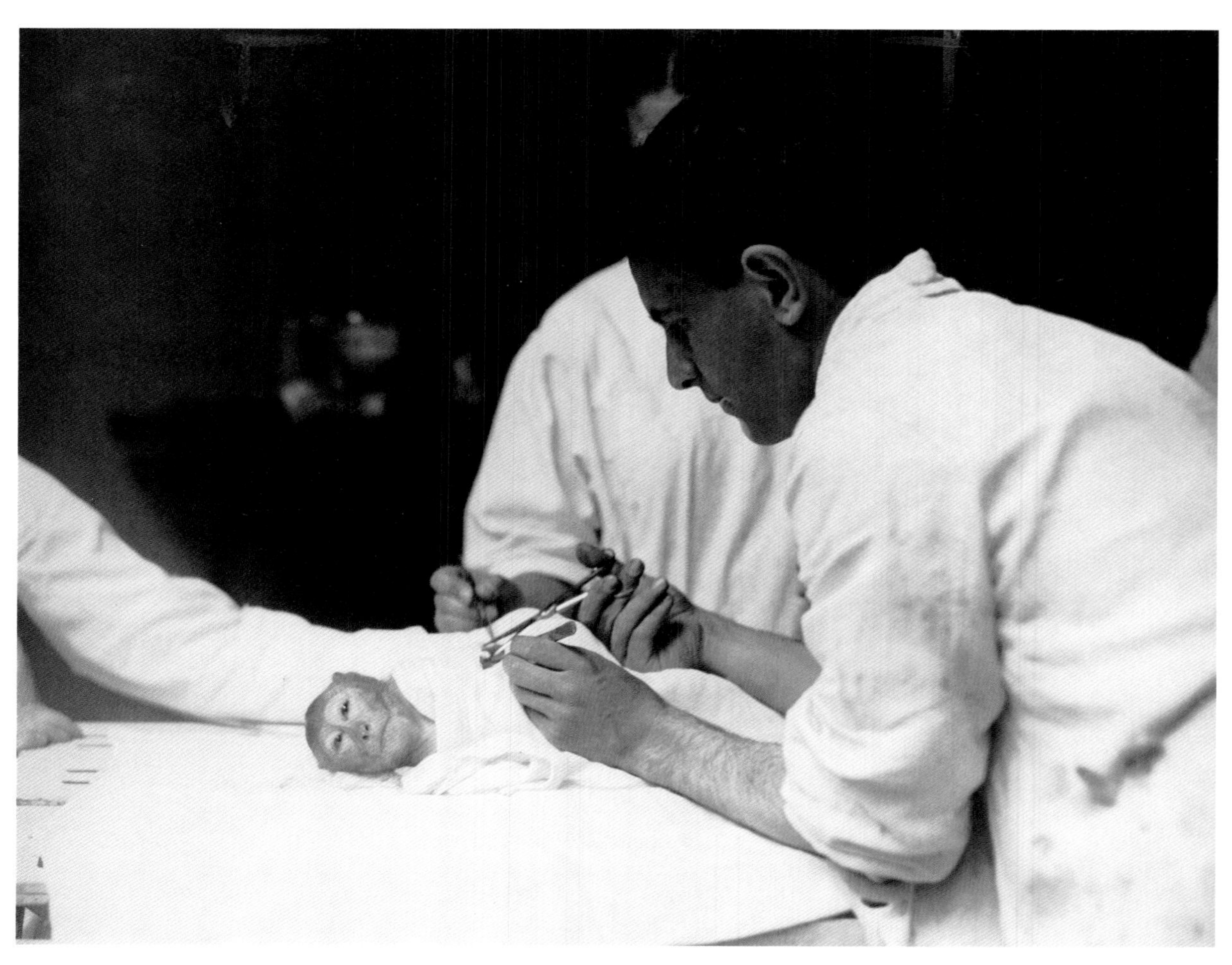

Alex Stöcker
Joko hält still, ca. 1926

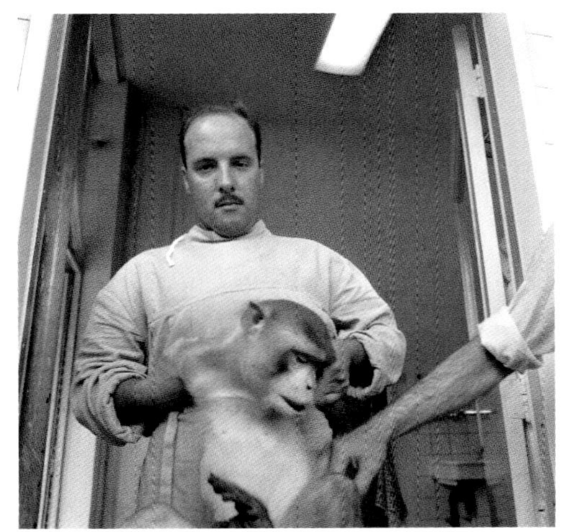

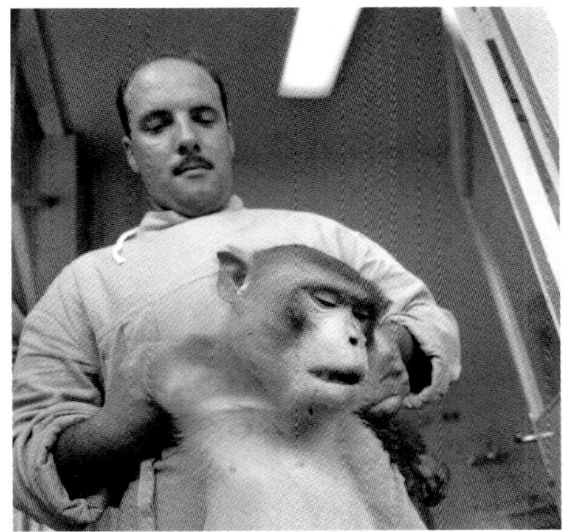

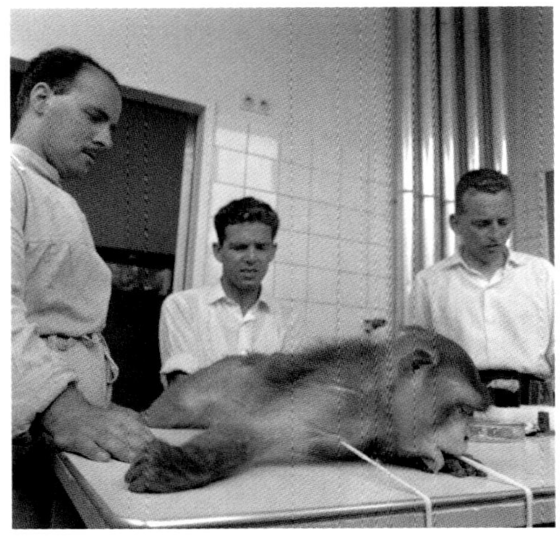

Cas Oorthuys
TNO Research Institute, 1960er

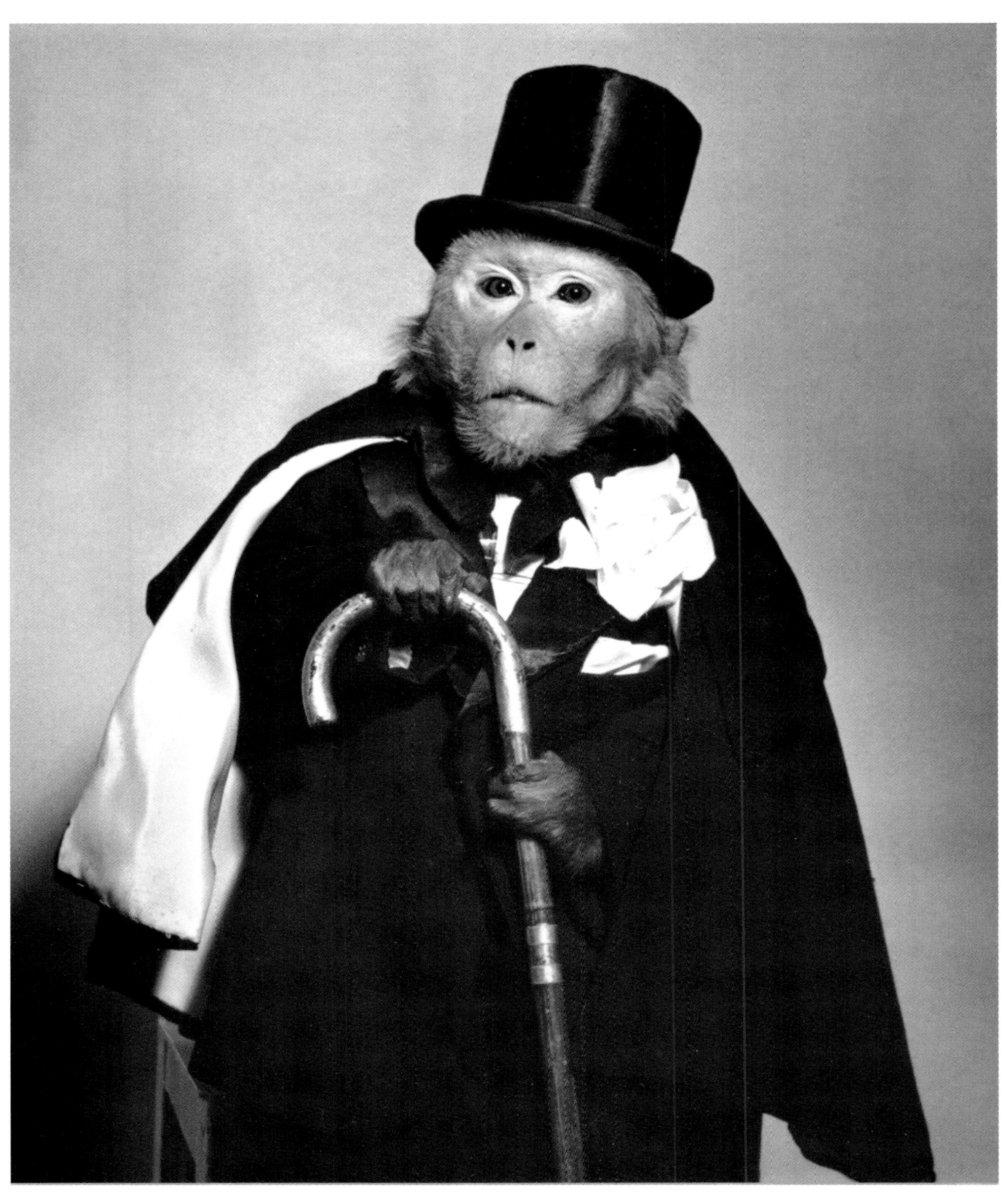

Ylla

Circus Chimpanzee, ca. 1950

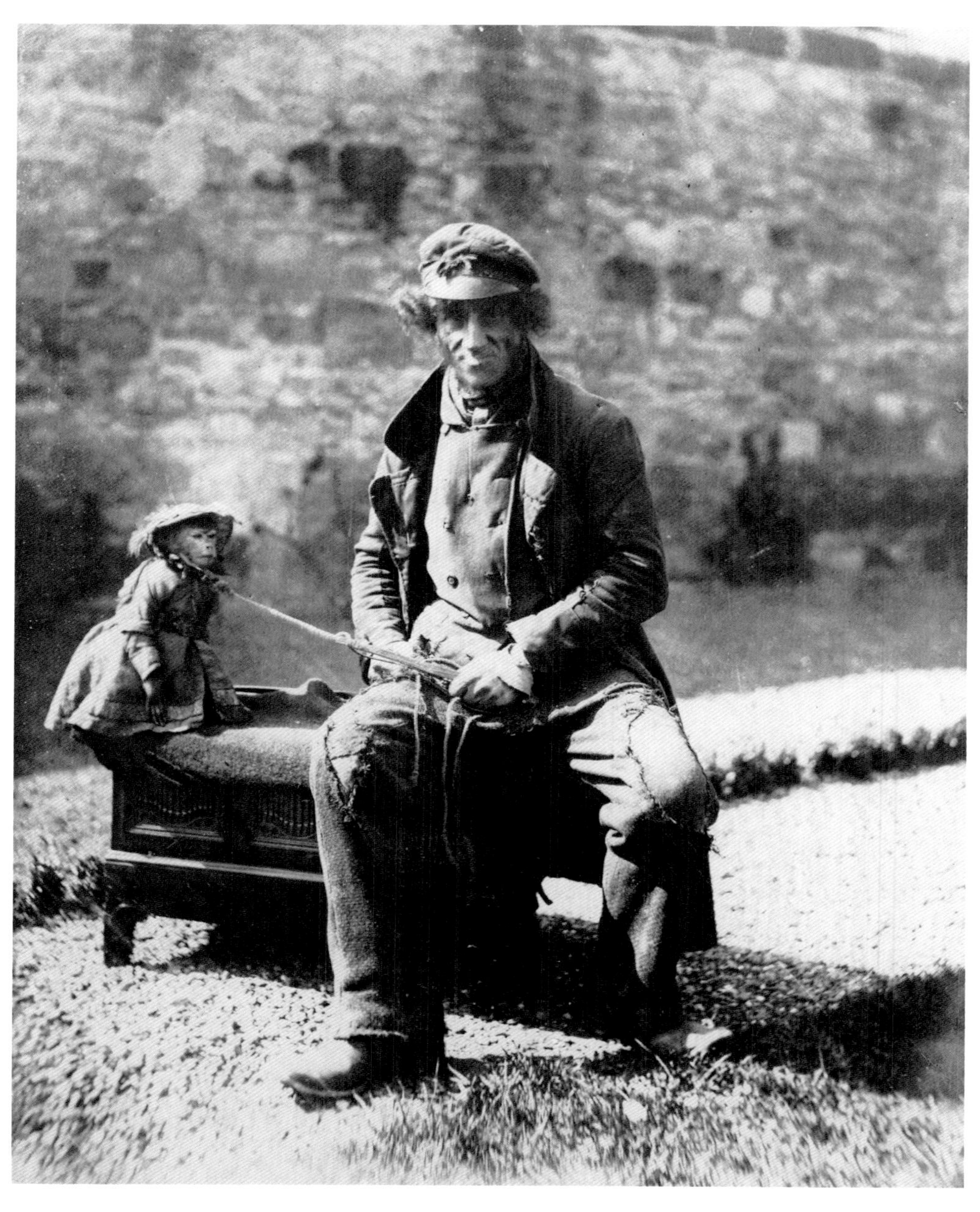

Horatio Ross
Italienischer Orgelmann und Affe /
Italian organ man and monkey, 1858

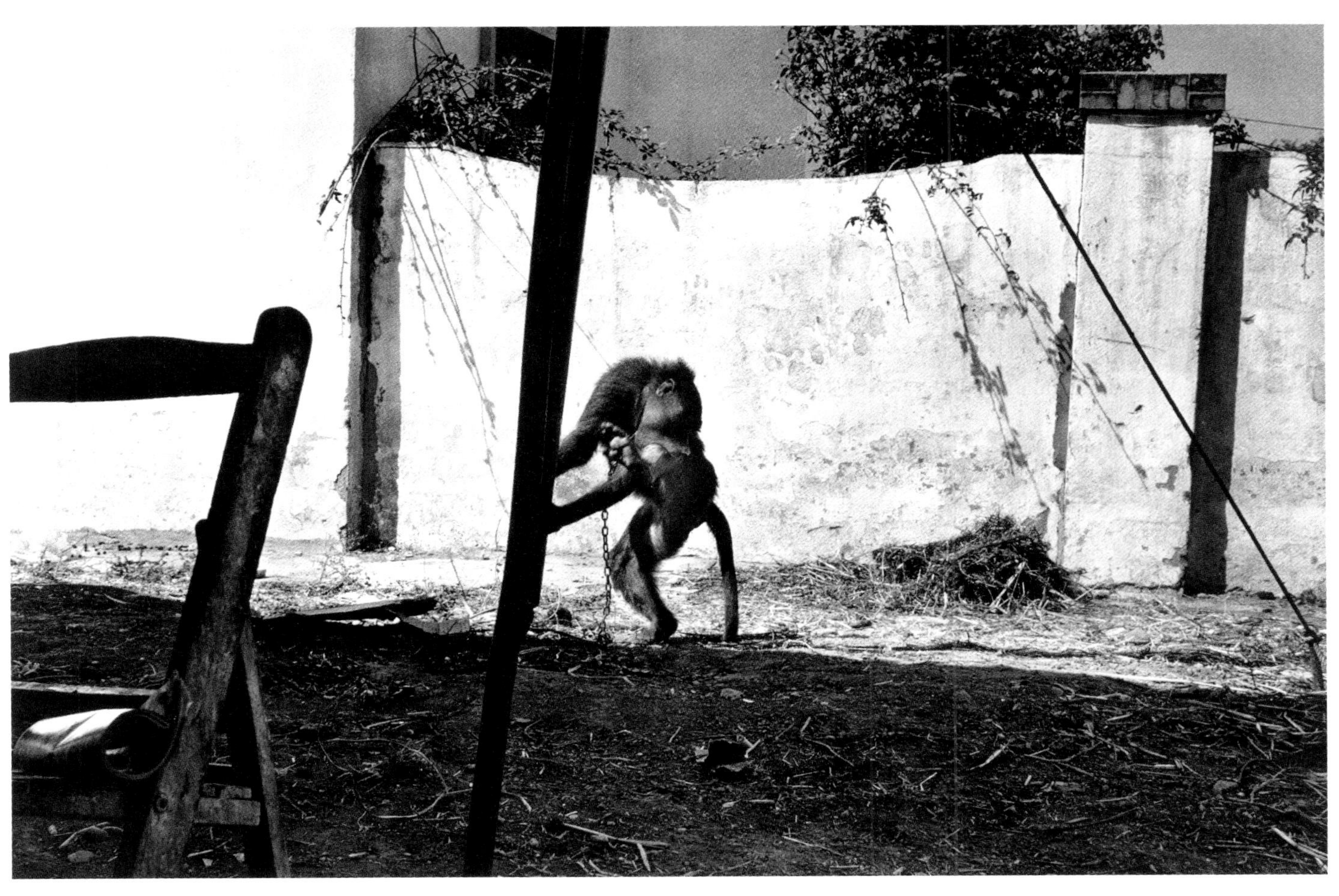

Josef Koudelka
Spanien, 1978

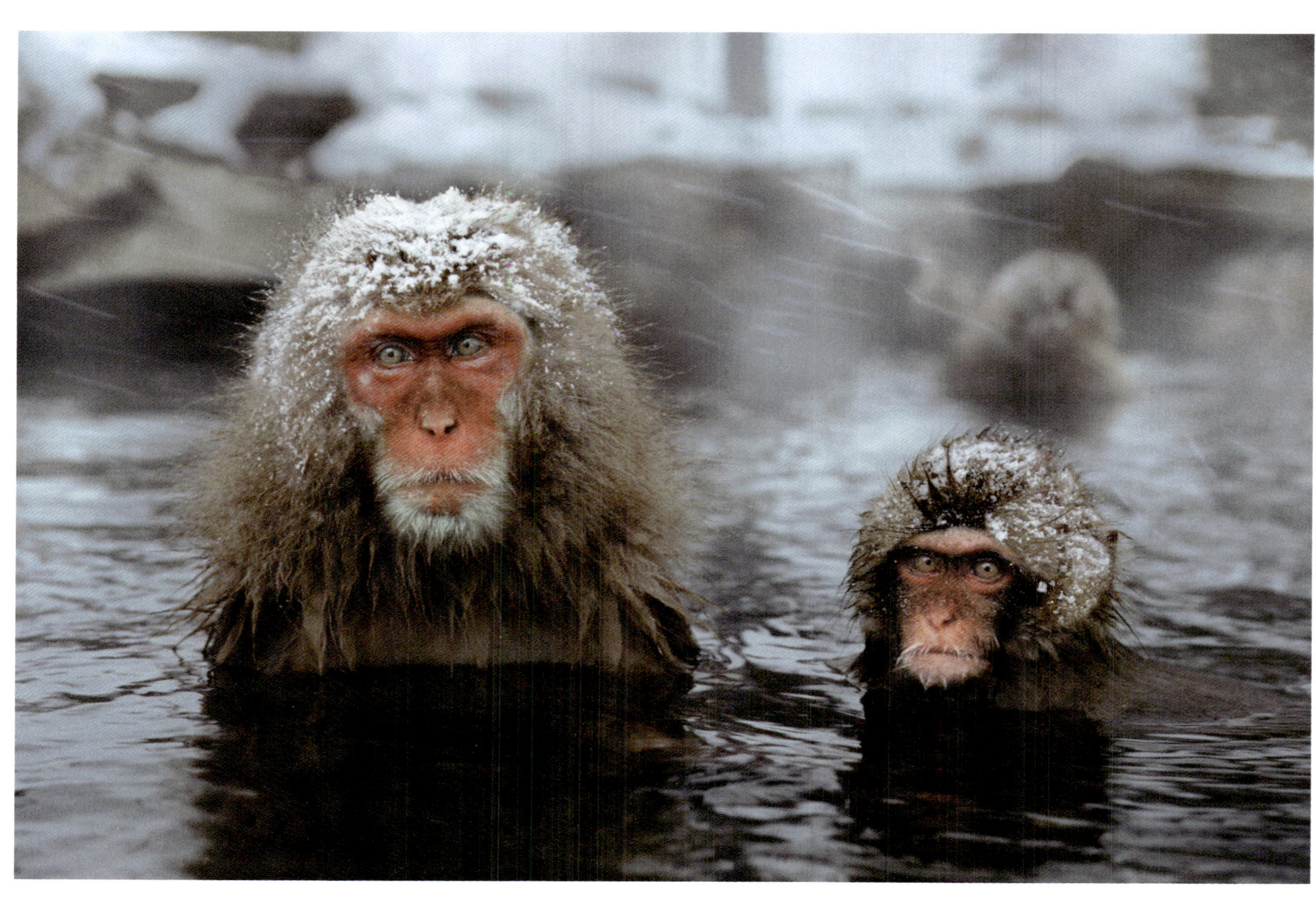

Steve Bloom
Snow monkeys (Japanese macaques) bathing in hot springs, Jigokudani National Park, Japan, Januar 1998

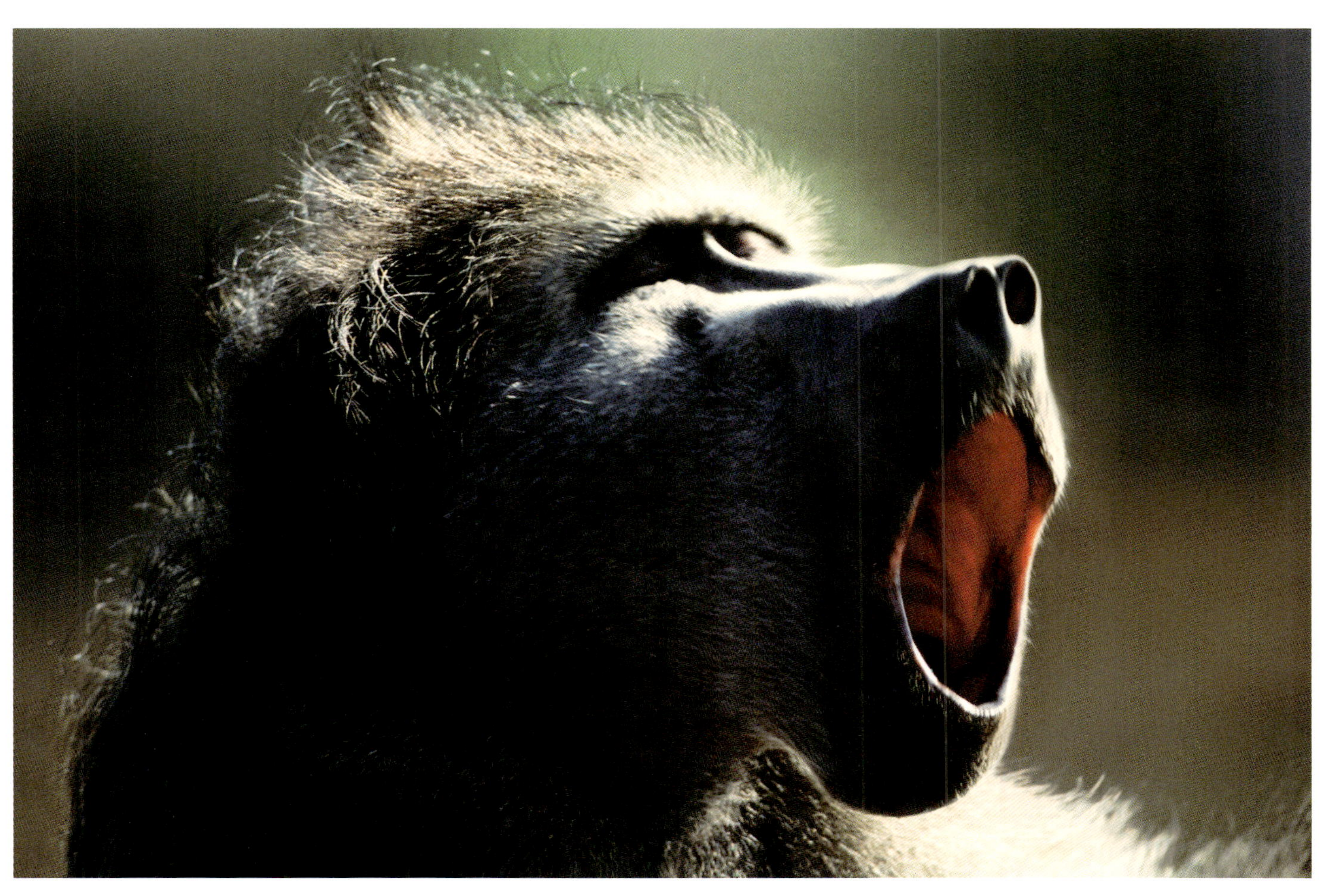

Steve Bloom
Chacma Baboon yawning, Kruger National Park, South Africa, August 1993

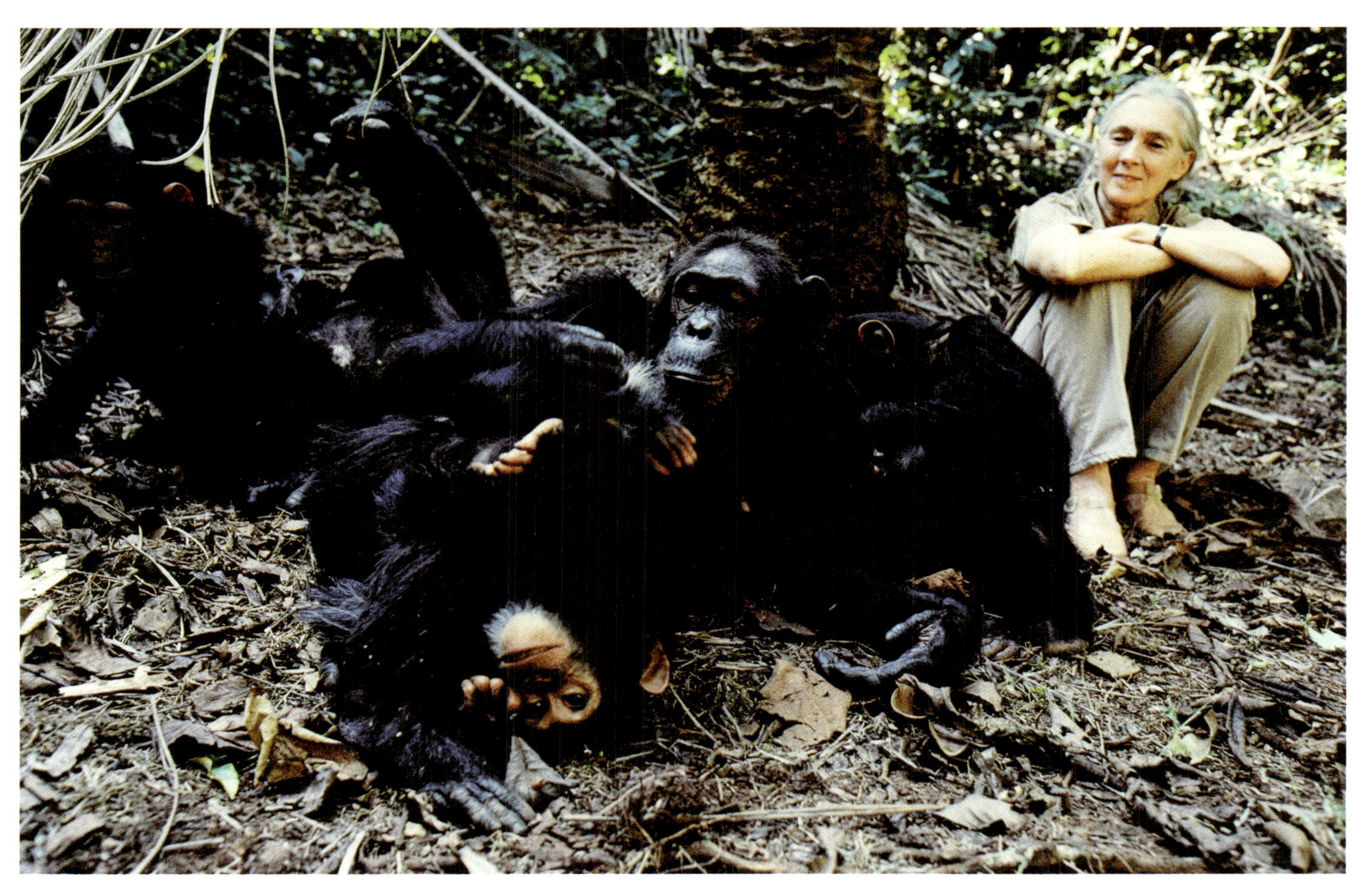

Michael Nichols
Jane with Gremlin, Gombe, Tanzania, 1995

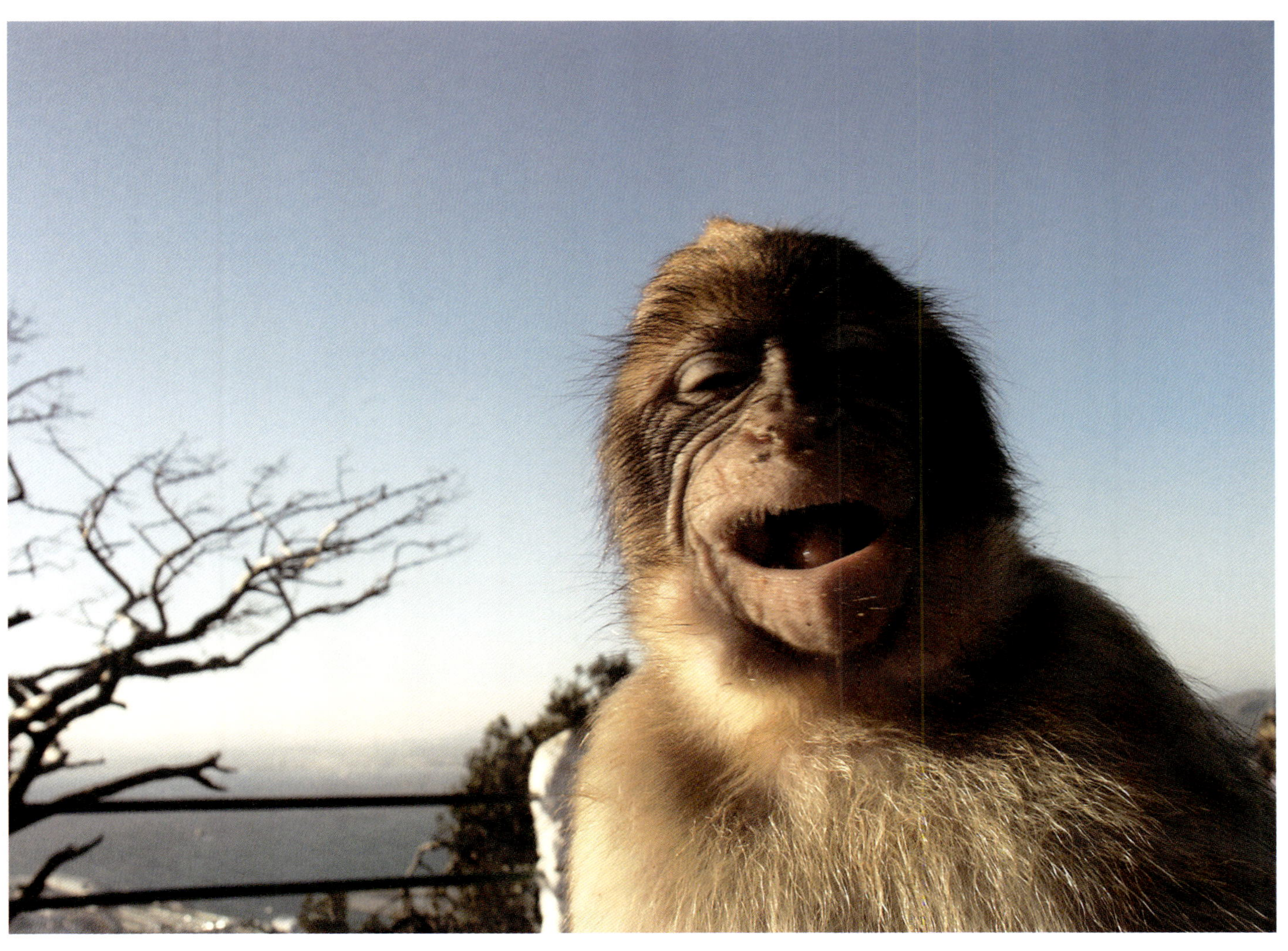

Peter Strong

The Laughing Monkey, 2002

„Alle diese Tiere repräsentieren in der Geschichte ihrer Darstellung Bedeutungen, d. h. ihnen werden Eigenschaften zugeschrieben, die sie als Bedeutungsträger in Analogie zu Eigenschaften des Menschen geeignet erscheinen lassen.“

“All these animals represent meanings in the history of their presentation, in other words, characteristics are assigned to them that make them—as bearers of meaning—appear analogous to human beings.”

Hermann Sturm

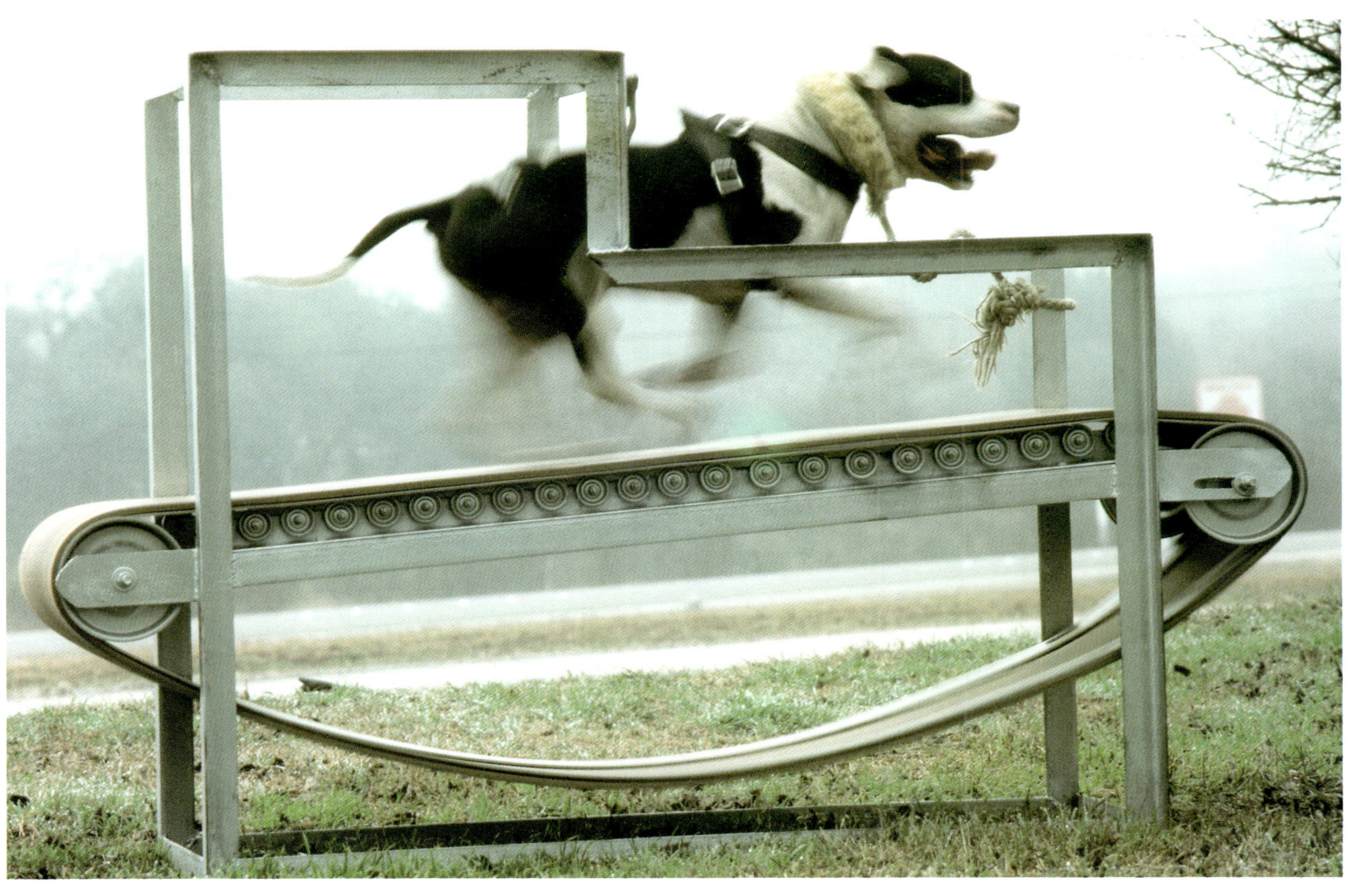

William Strode

a. d. Reportage: *Charlys treuer Killer*, 1979

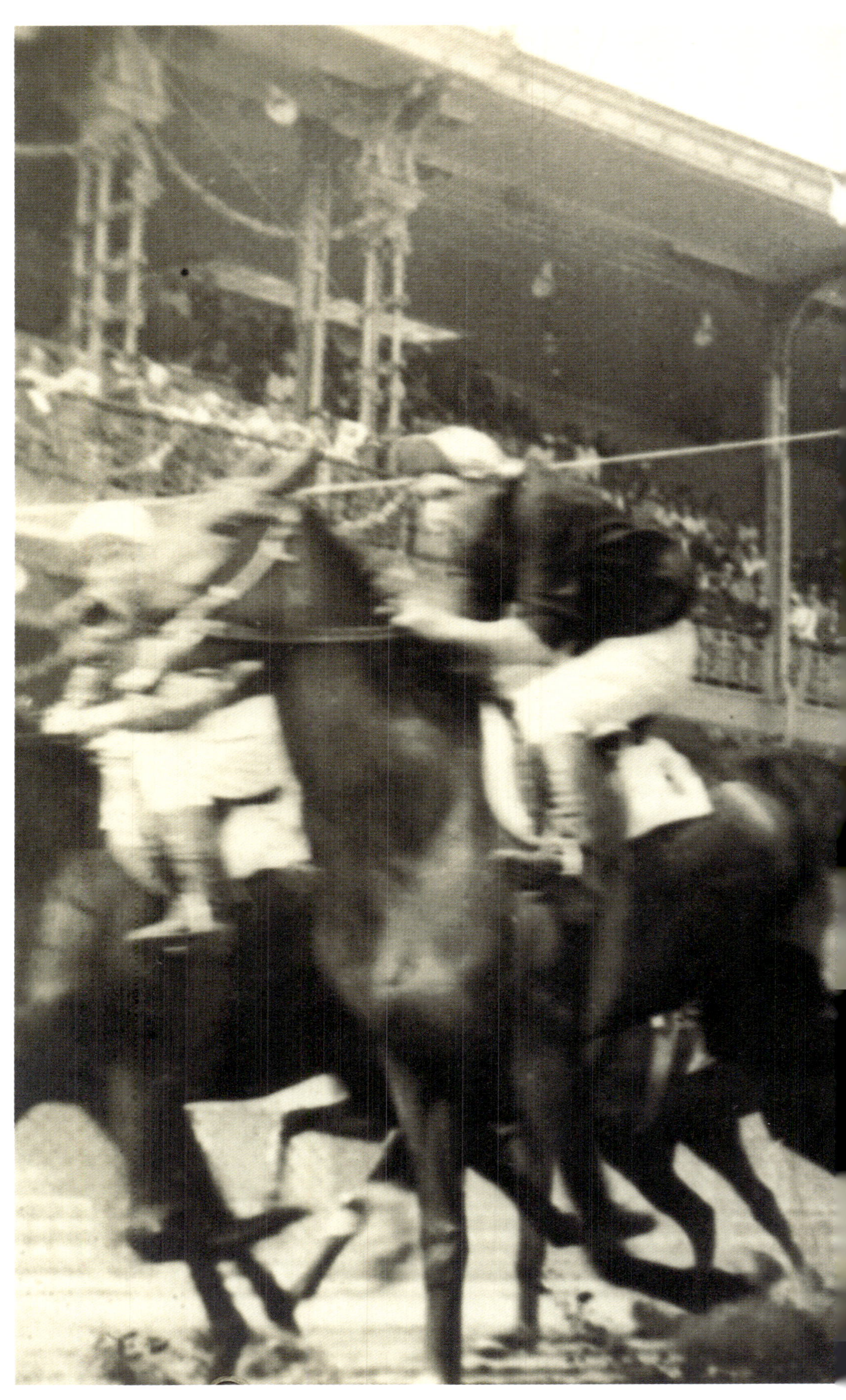

Alexander Rodtschenko
Pferderennen /
Horse race, 1935

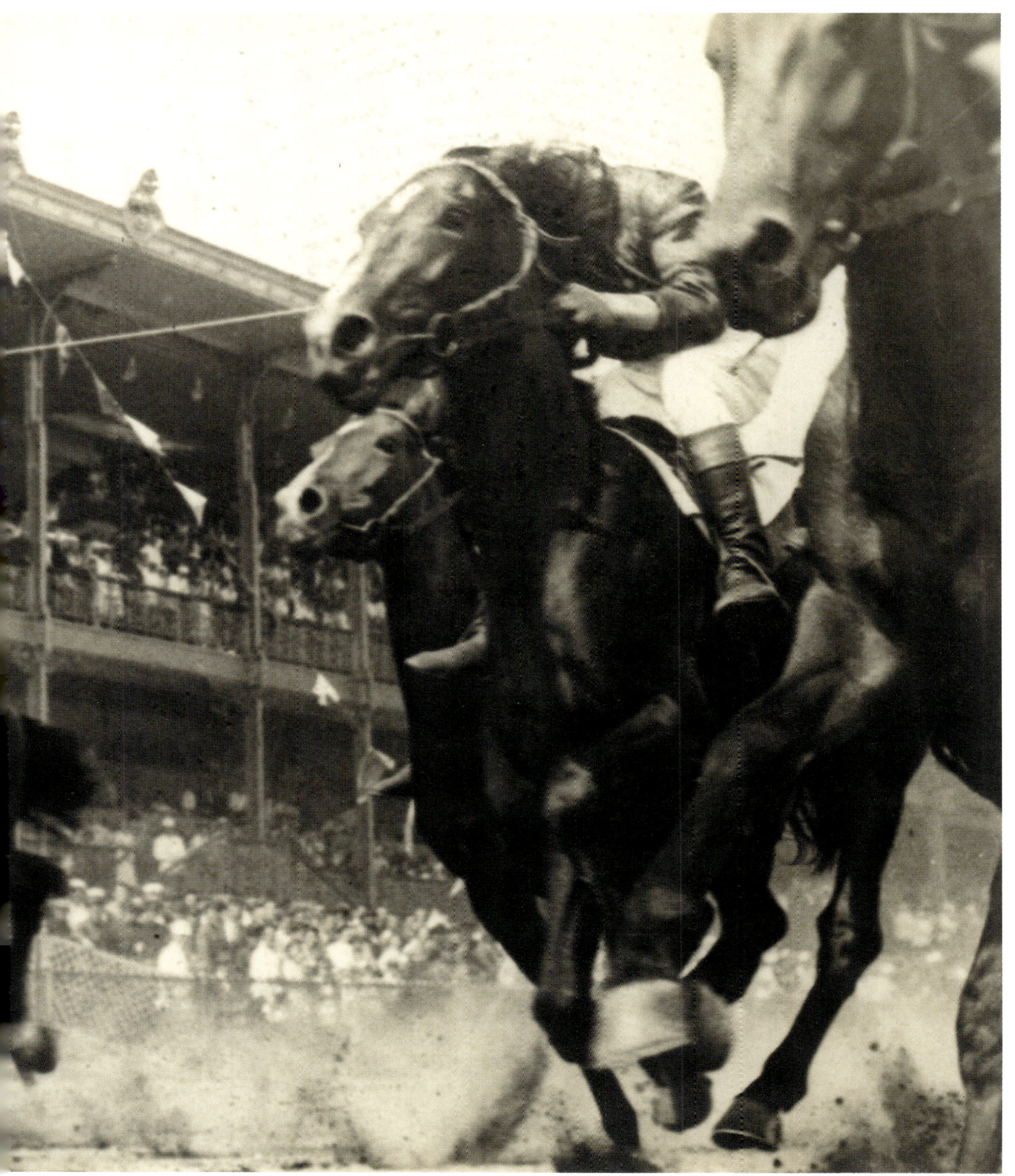

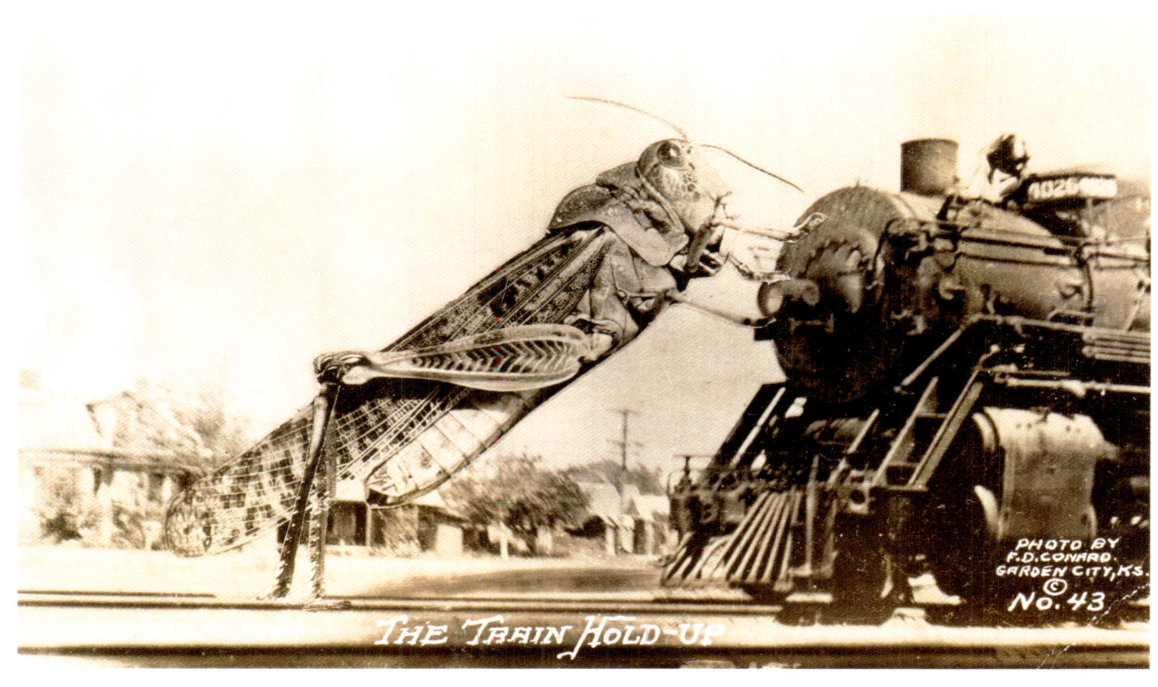

F. D. Conard
The Train Hold-Up, 1938

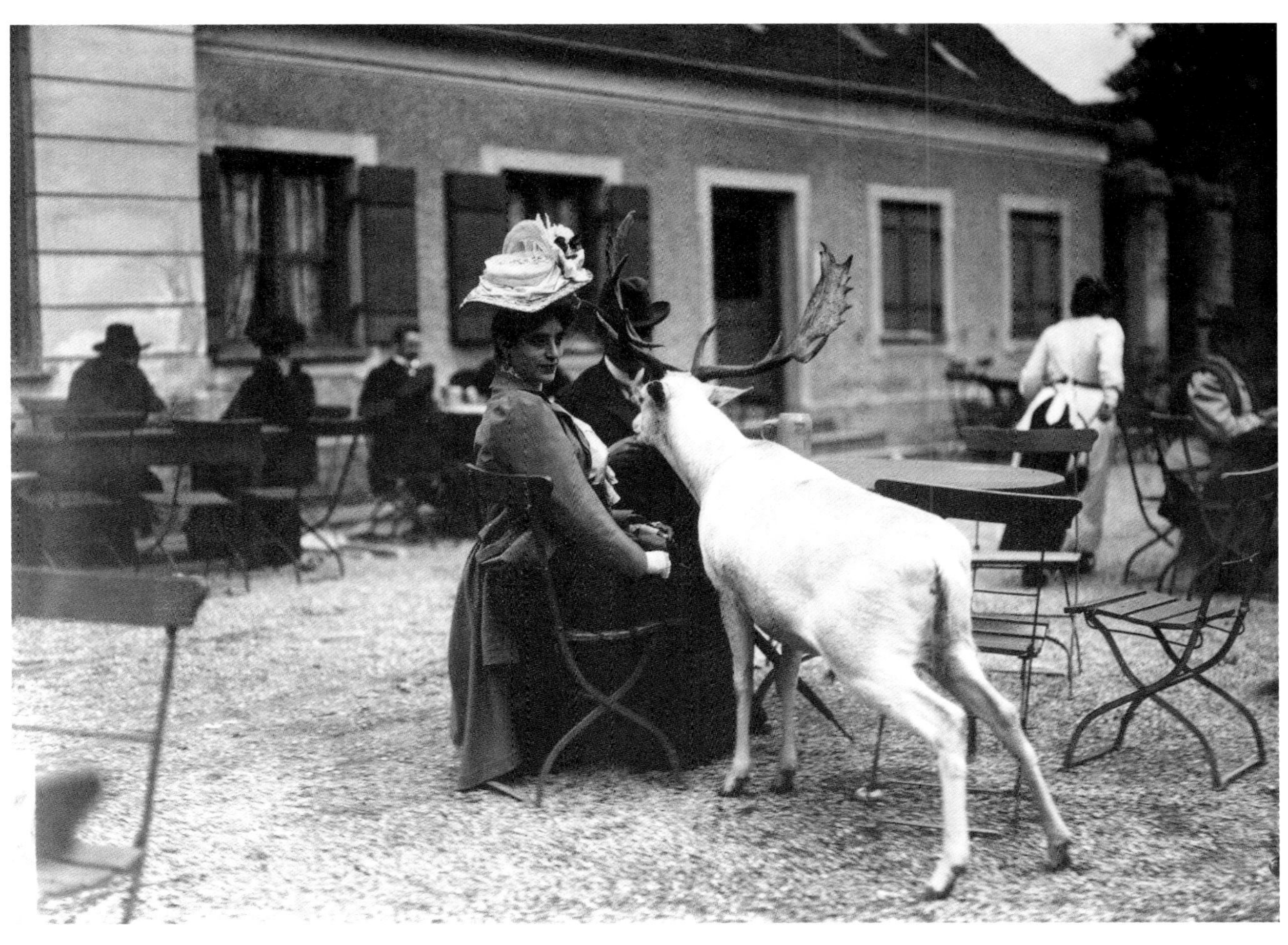

Philipp Kester

Zahmes Damwild im Nymphenburger Hirschgarten, München, 1909

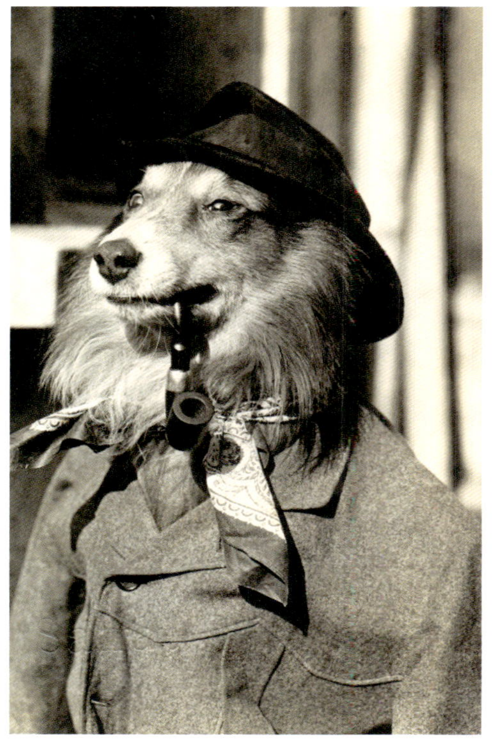

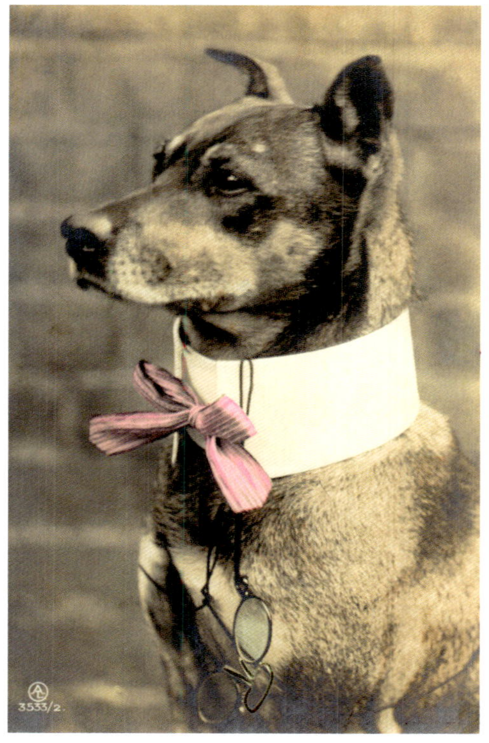

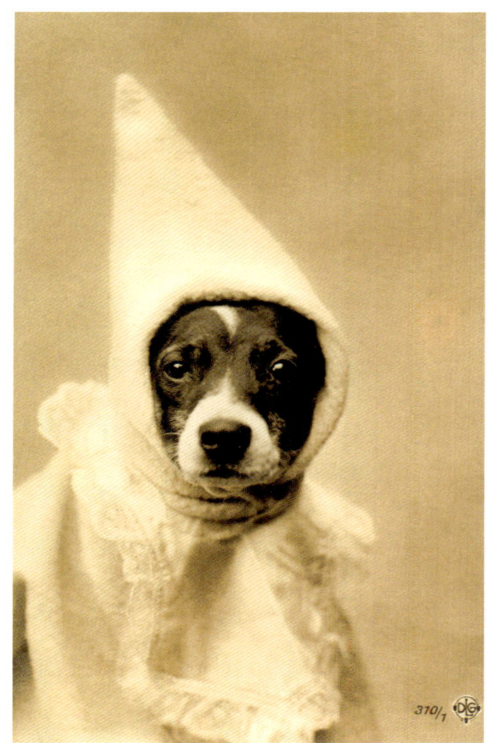

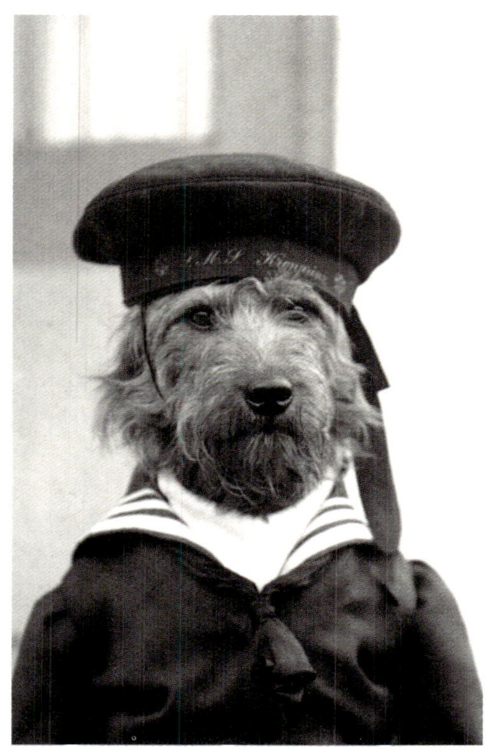

Anonym

Hund mit Pfeife / Dog with pipe, ca. 1910

Hund mit Haube / Dog with cap, 1908

Hund mit Fliege / Dog with bow tie, 1908

Hund in Matrosenanzug / Dog in sailor suit, ca. 1906

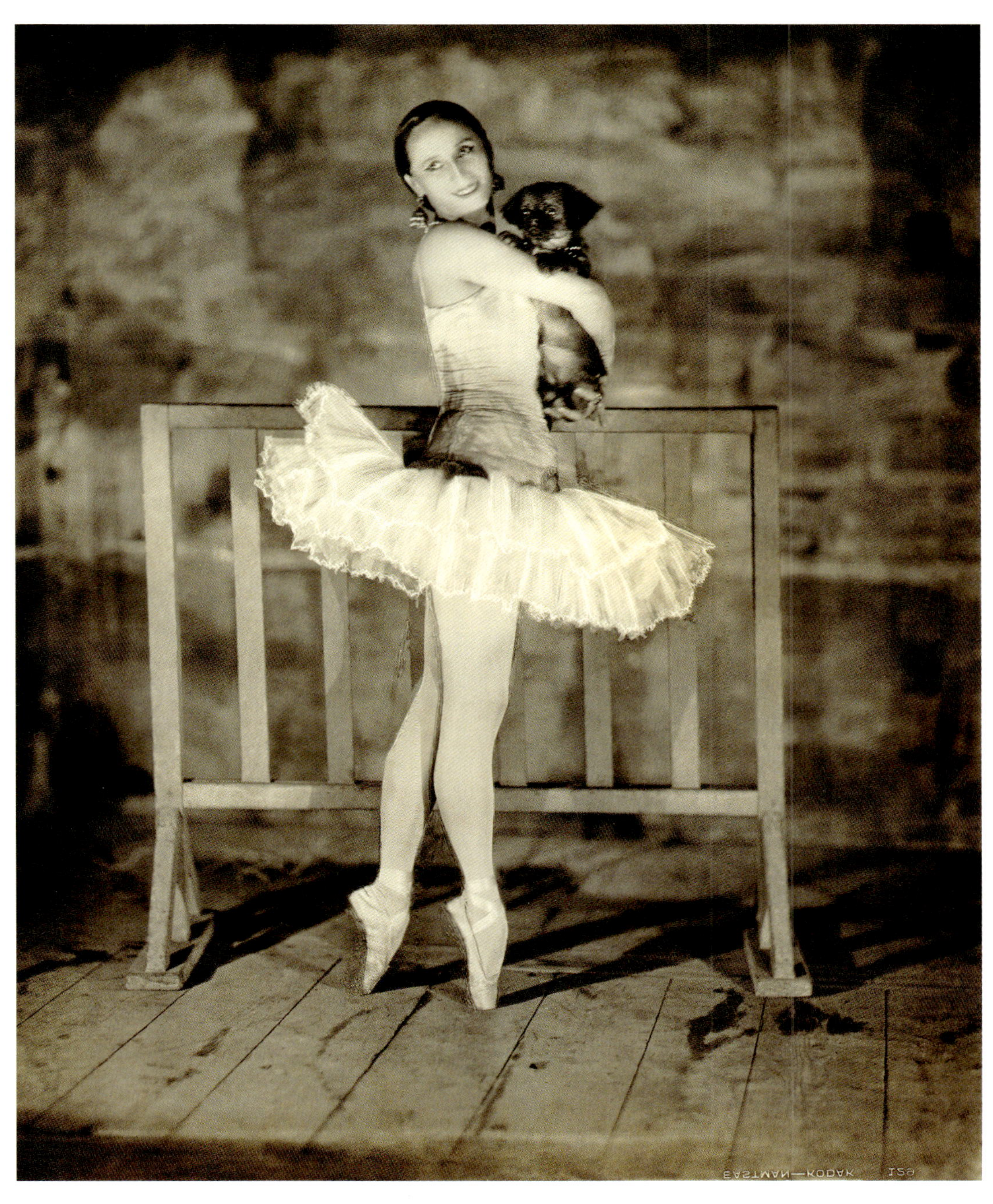

James Abbe
Anna Pavlova, 1927

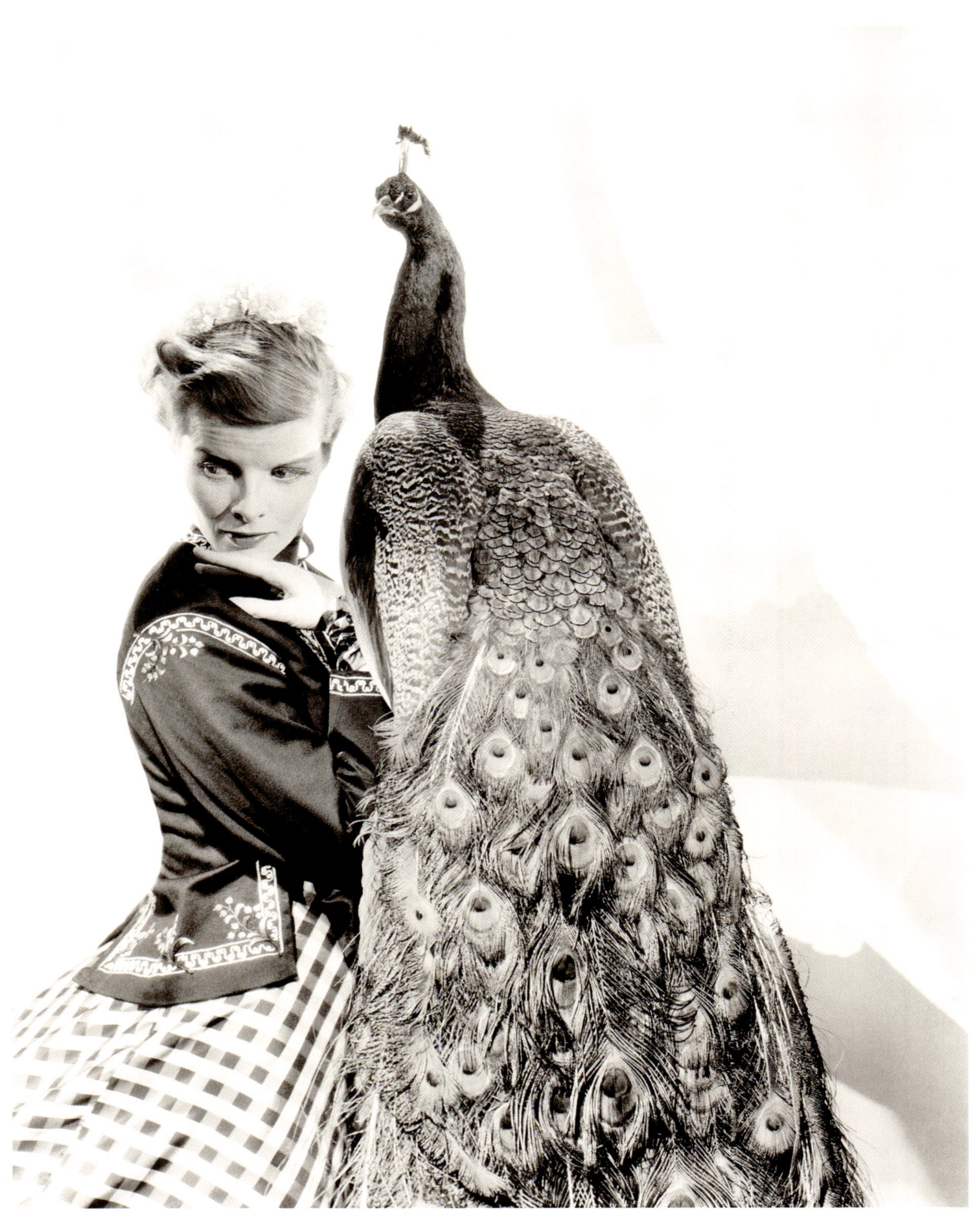

Cecil Beaton

Katharine Hepburn, 1935

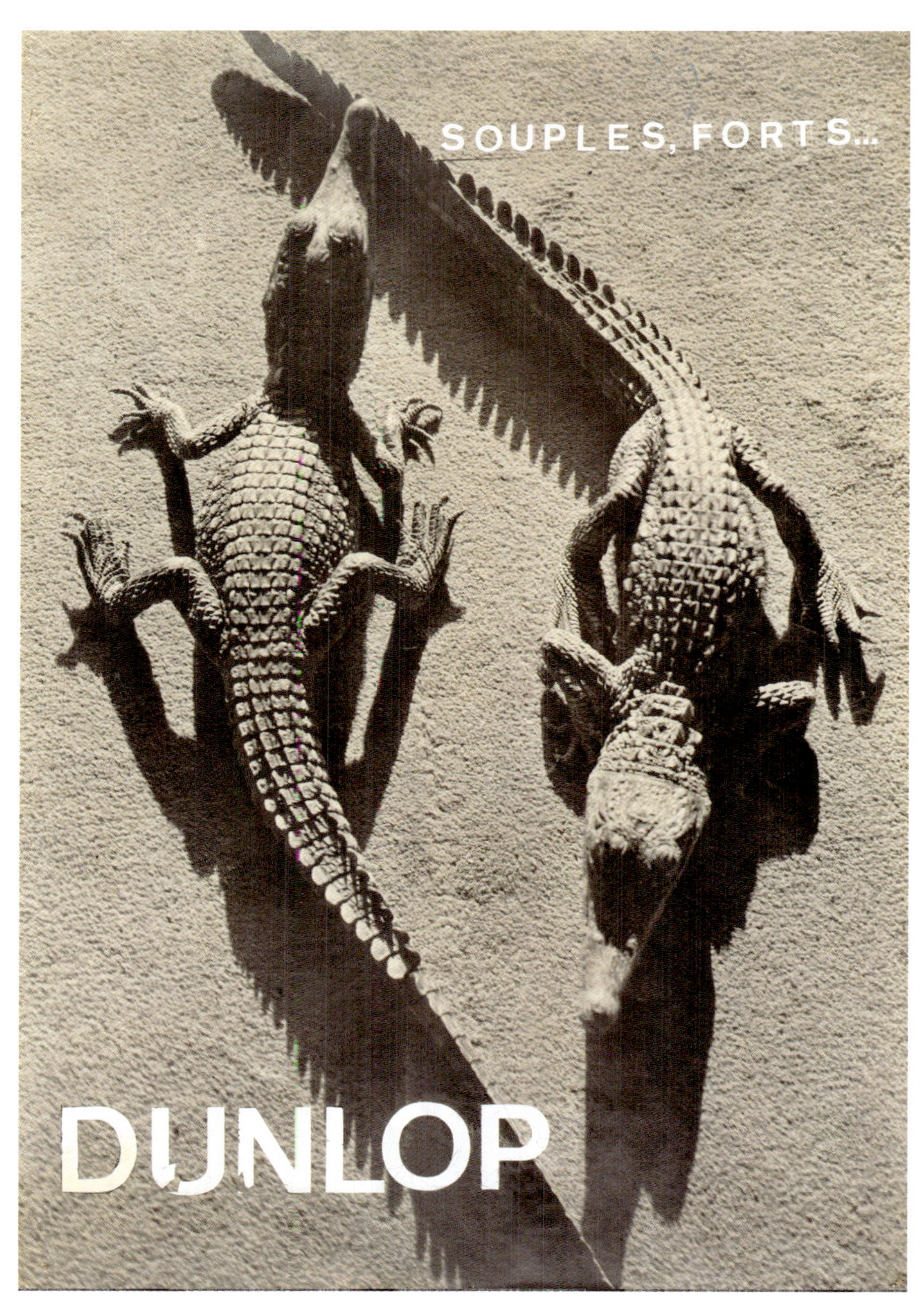

Errell
Dunlop-Werbung, vor 1930

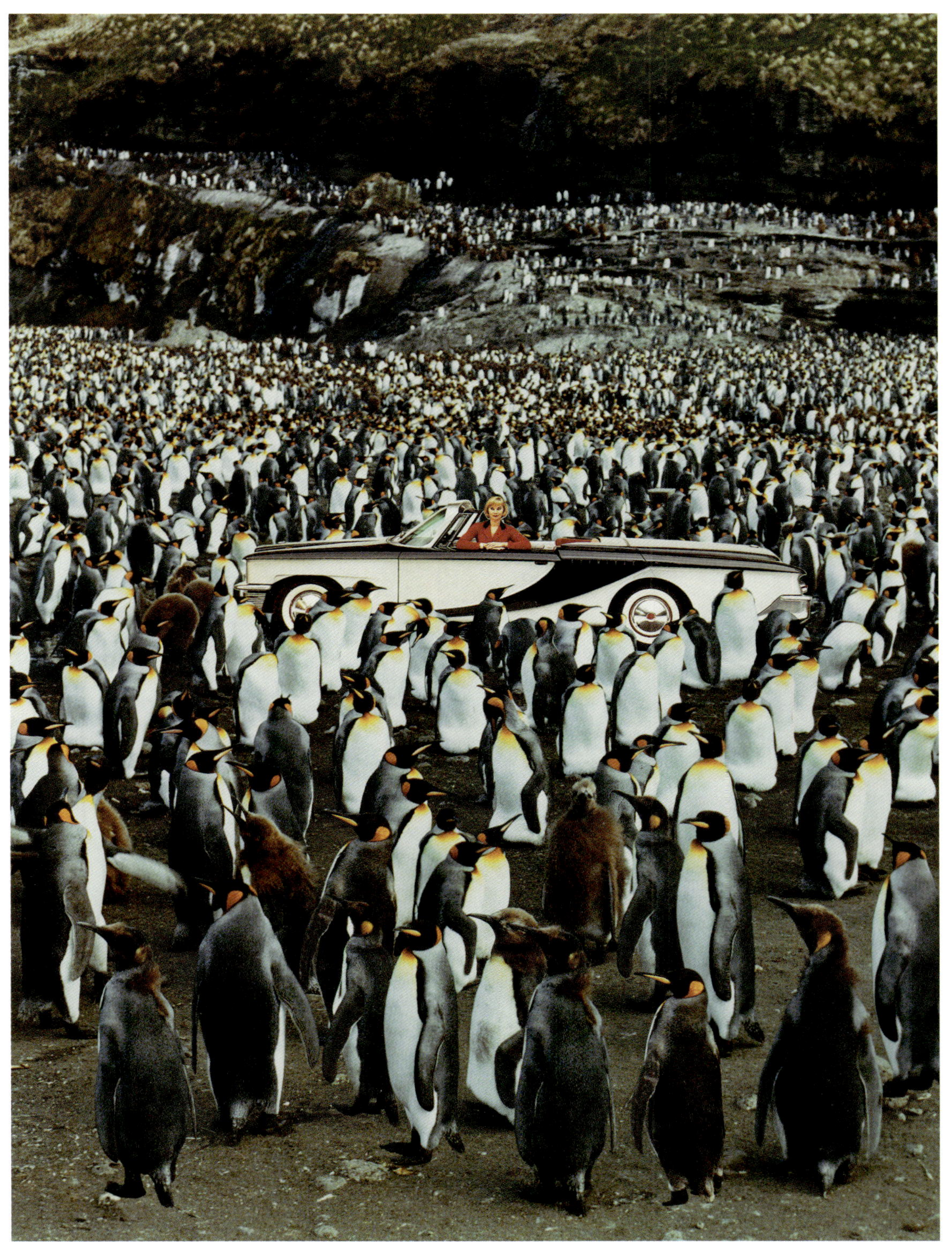

Franz Lazi

Königspinguine mit Auto, Persiflage, 1989

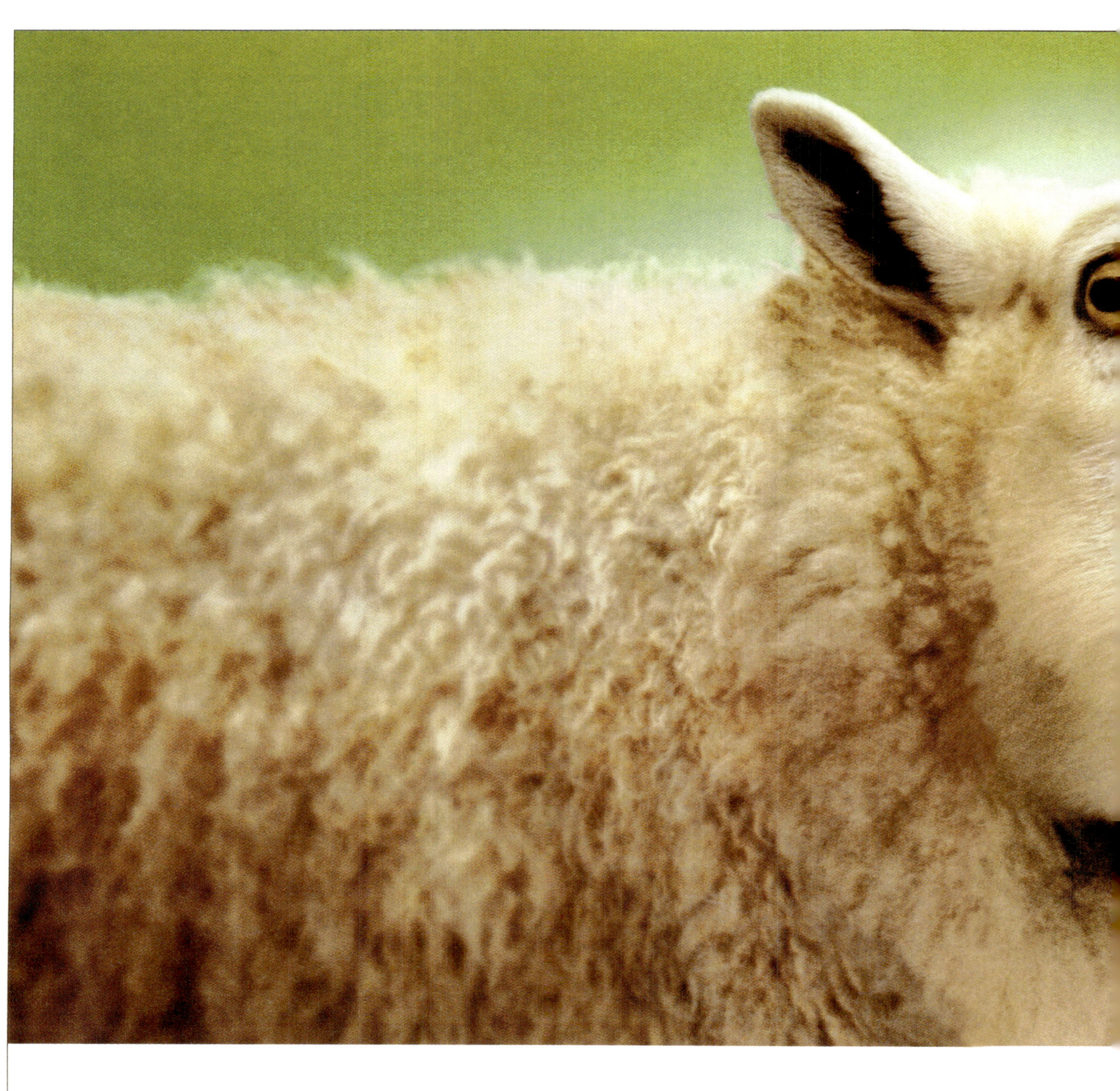

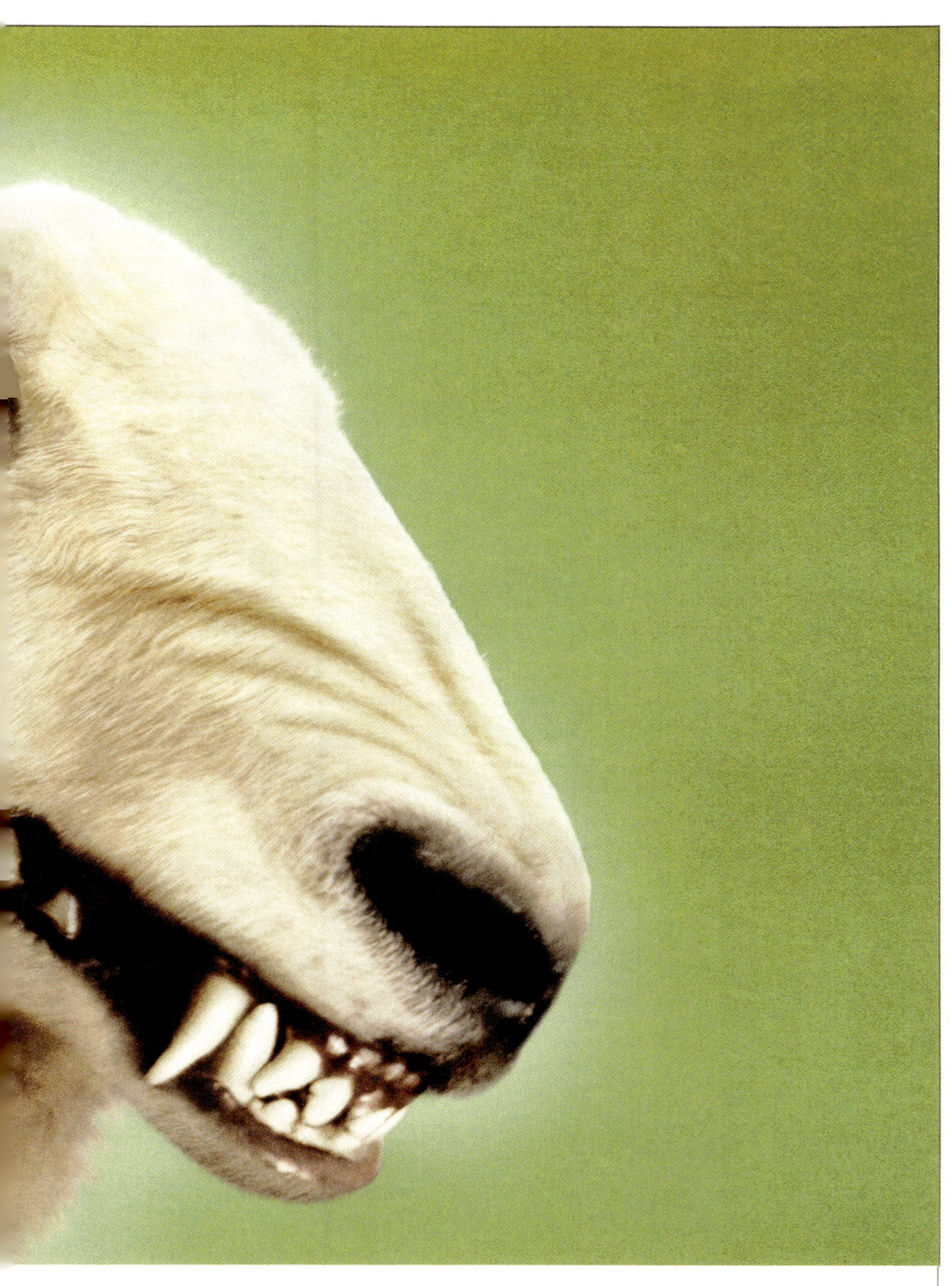

In 6,6 Sekunden von 0 auf 100 km/h, 2002
VW Kampagne
(Foto Bob Elsdale und Denis Felix)

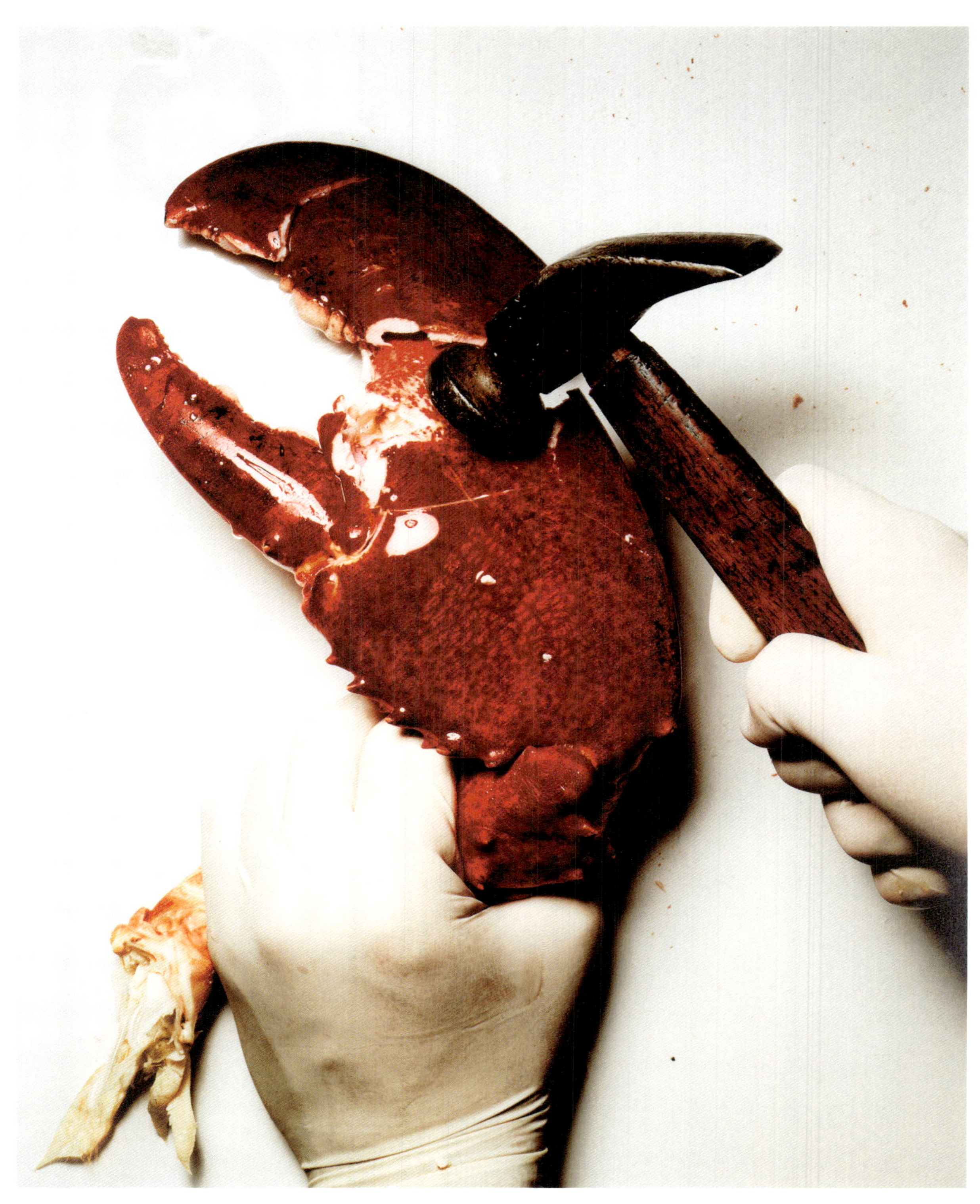

Irving Penn
Cracking a Lobster Claw, New York, 1999

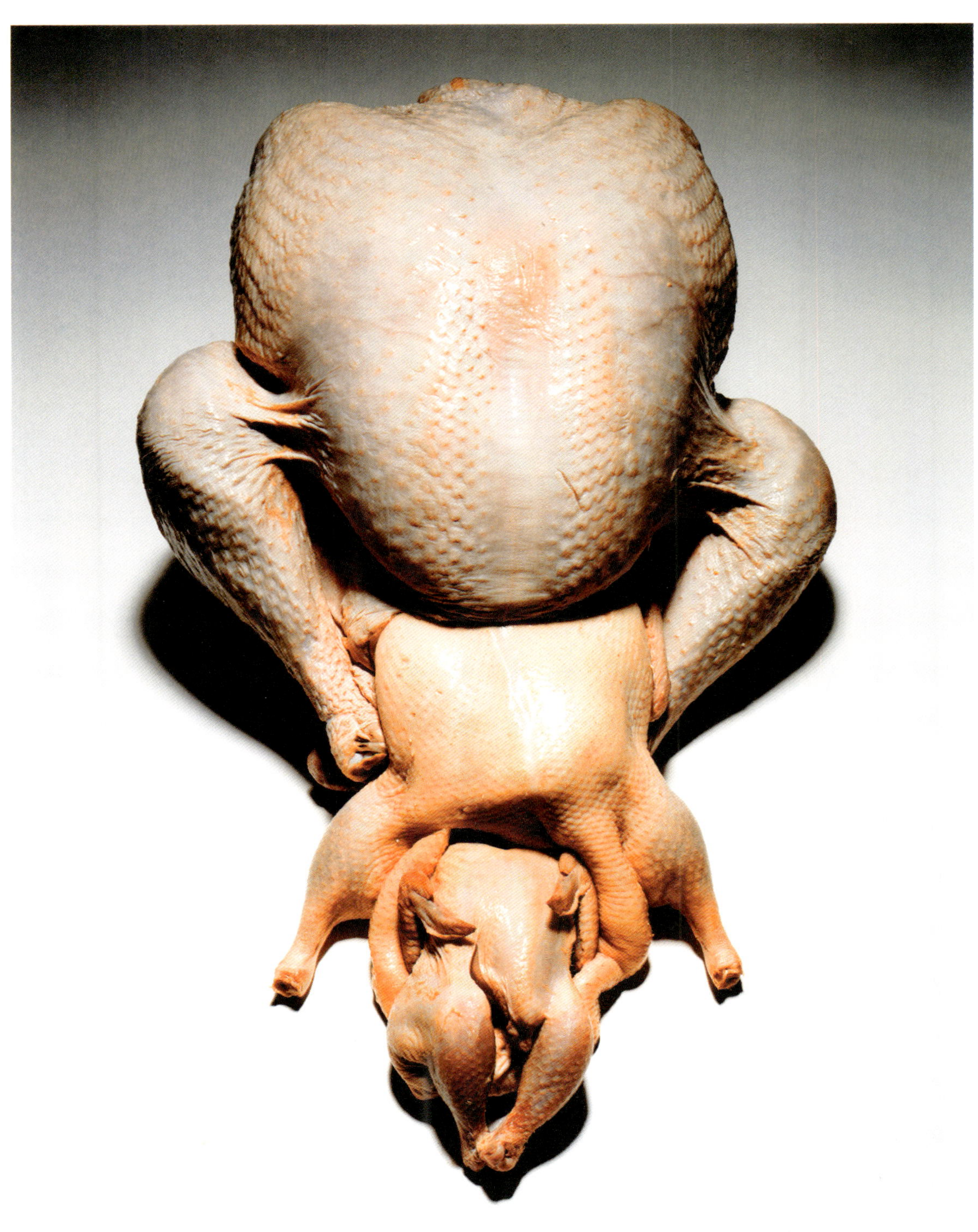

Irving Penn
Turducken, New York, 1999

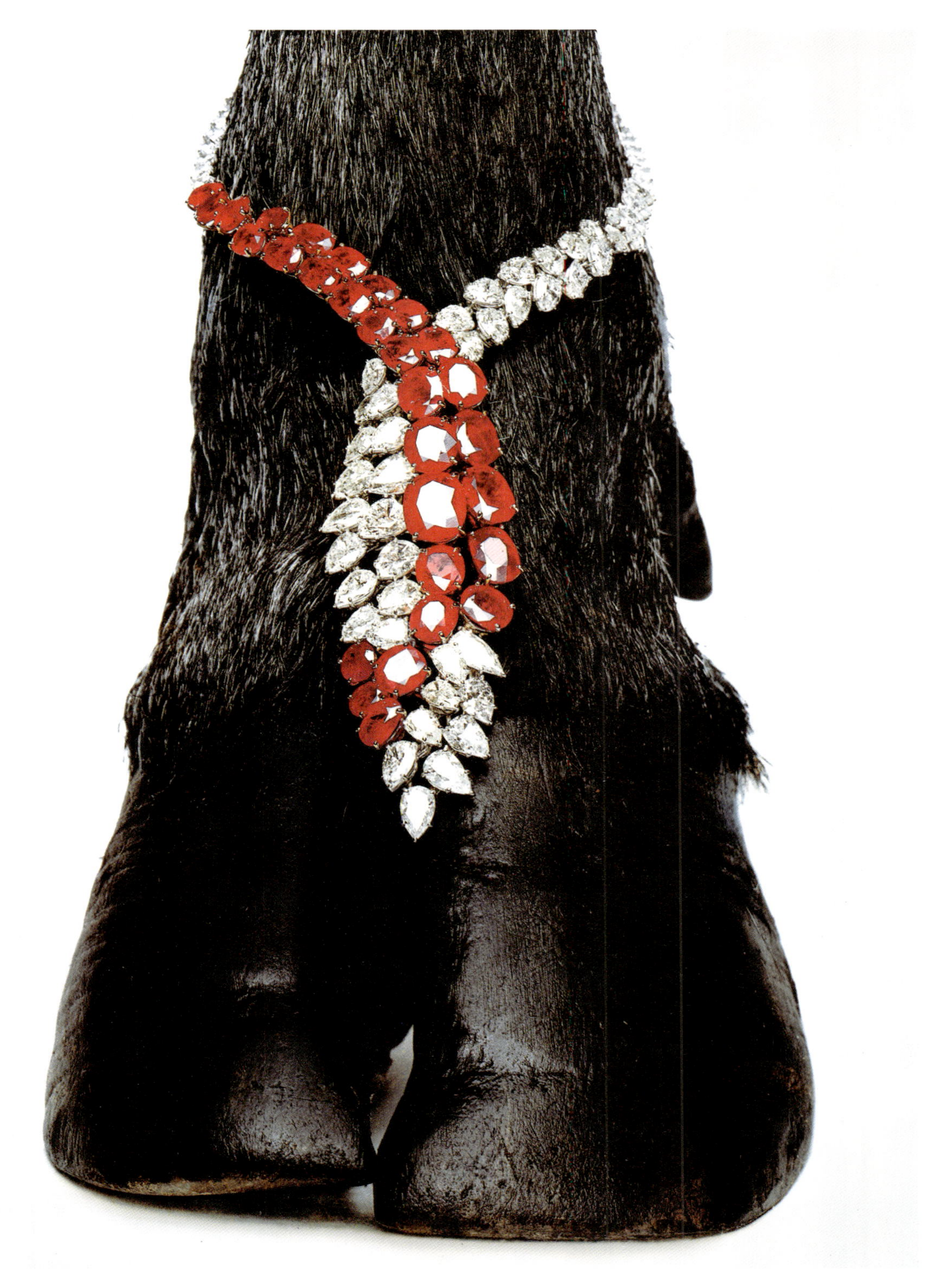

HIRO

Harry Winston Necklace, New York City, 1963

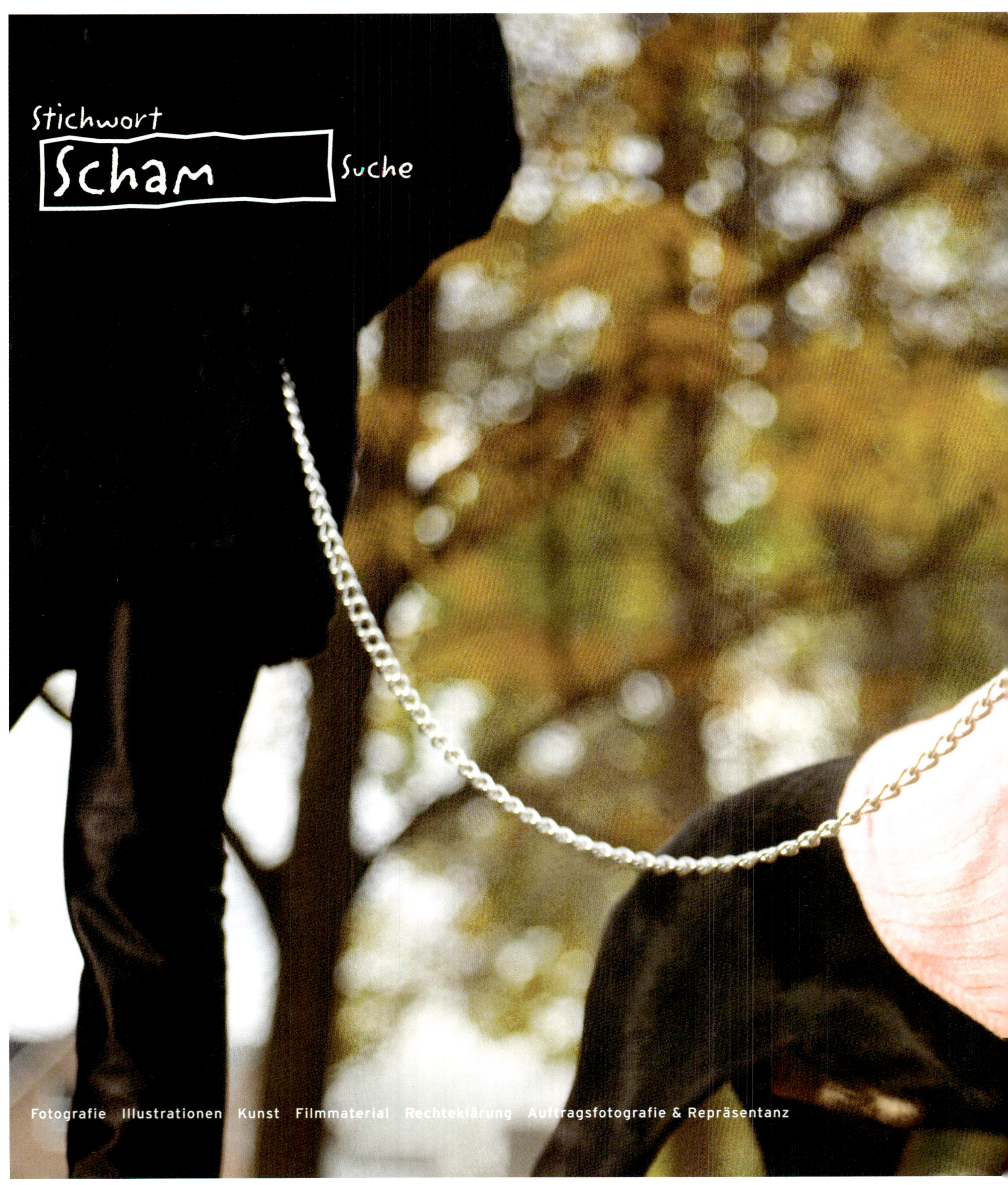
Stichwort
Scham
Suche
Fotografie Illustrationen Kunst Filmmaterial Rechteklärung Auftragsfotografie & Repräsentanz

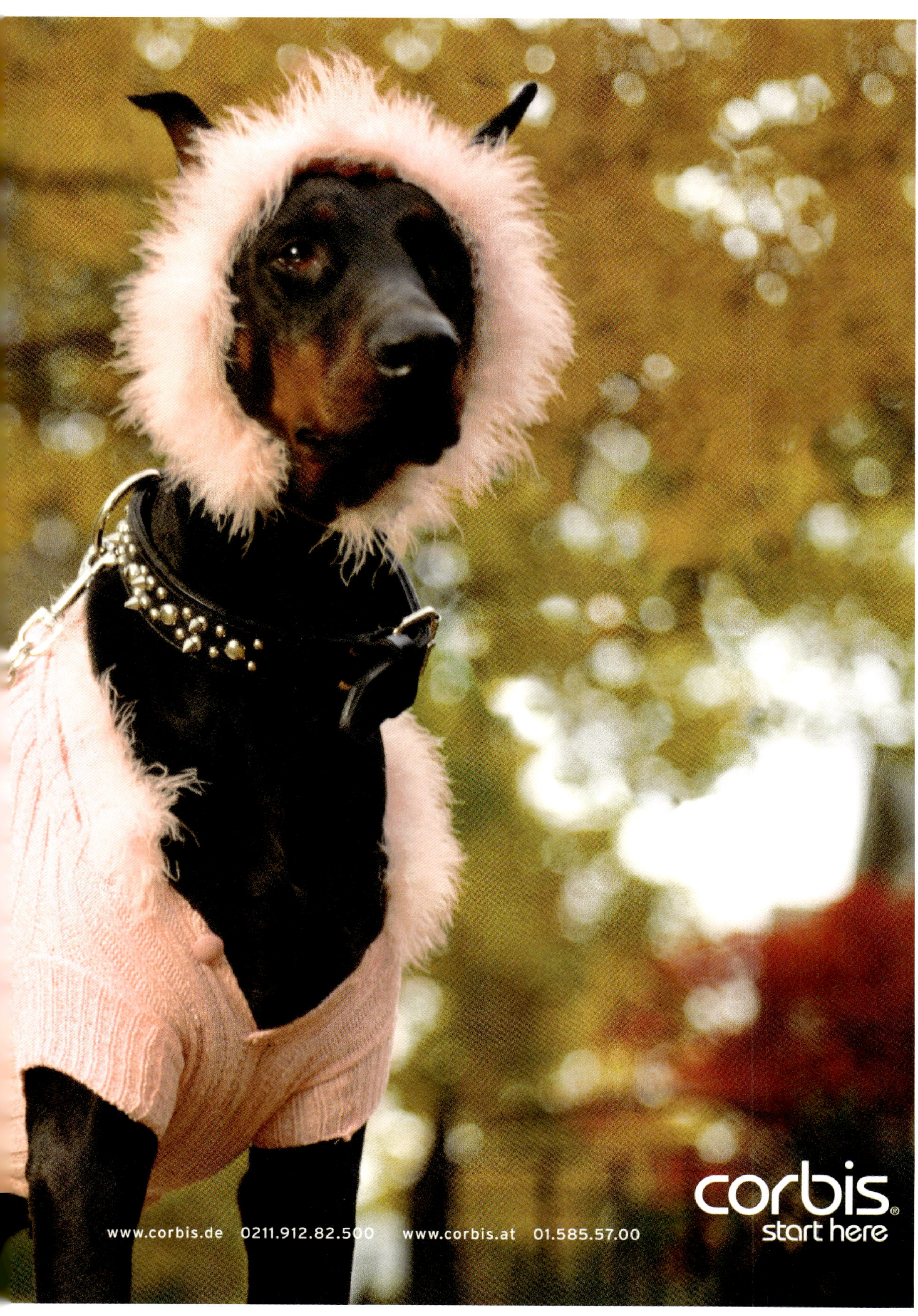

Scham, 2005
Corbis Werbung
(Foto Anthony Redpath 2001)

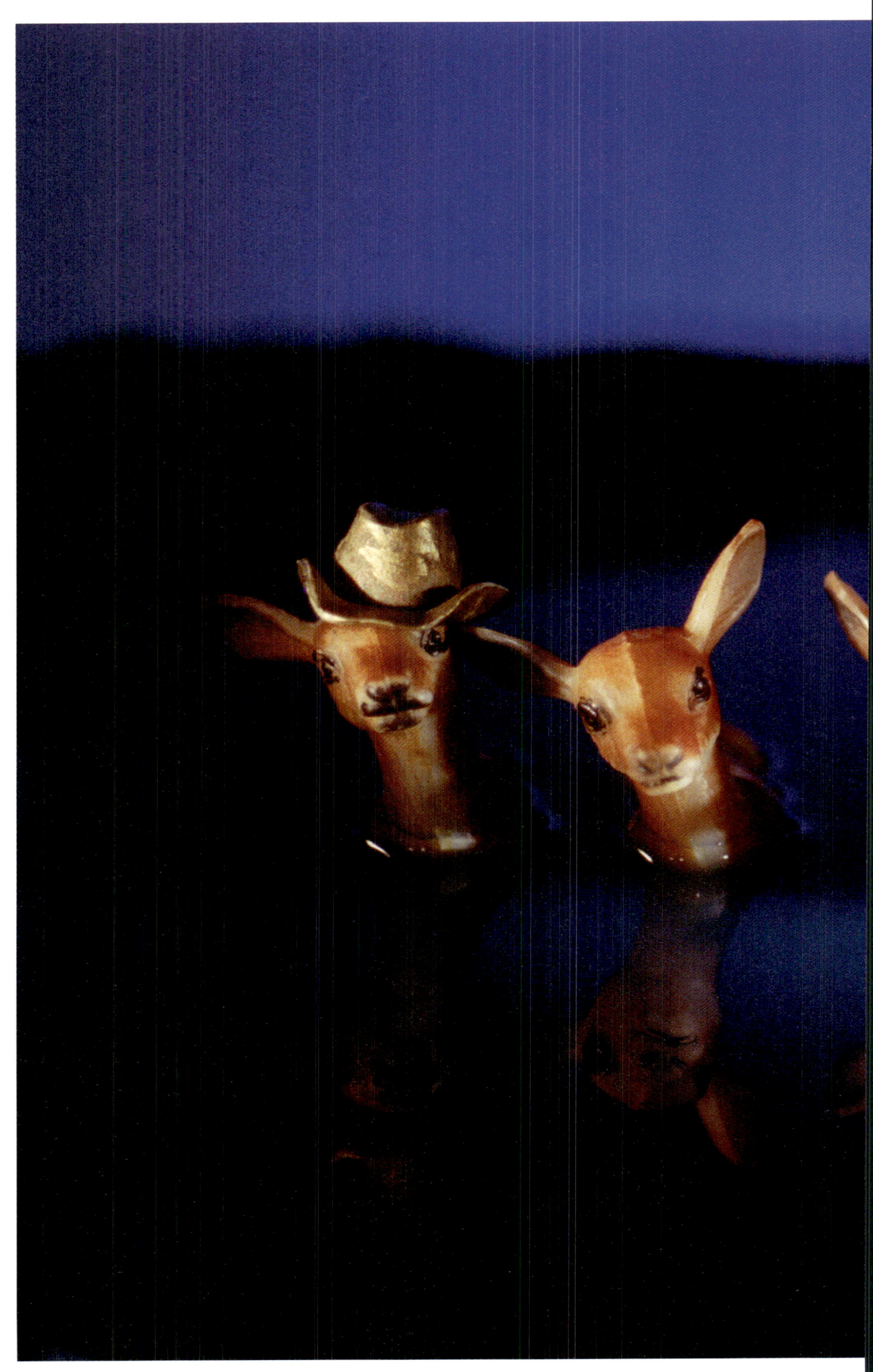

Henk Tas
Dreambrothers, 2000

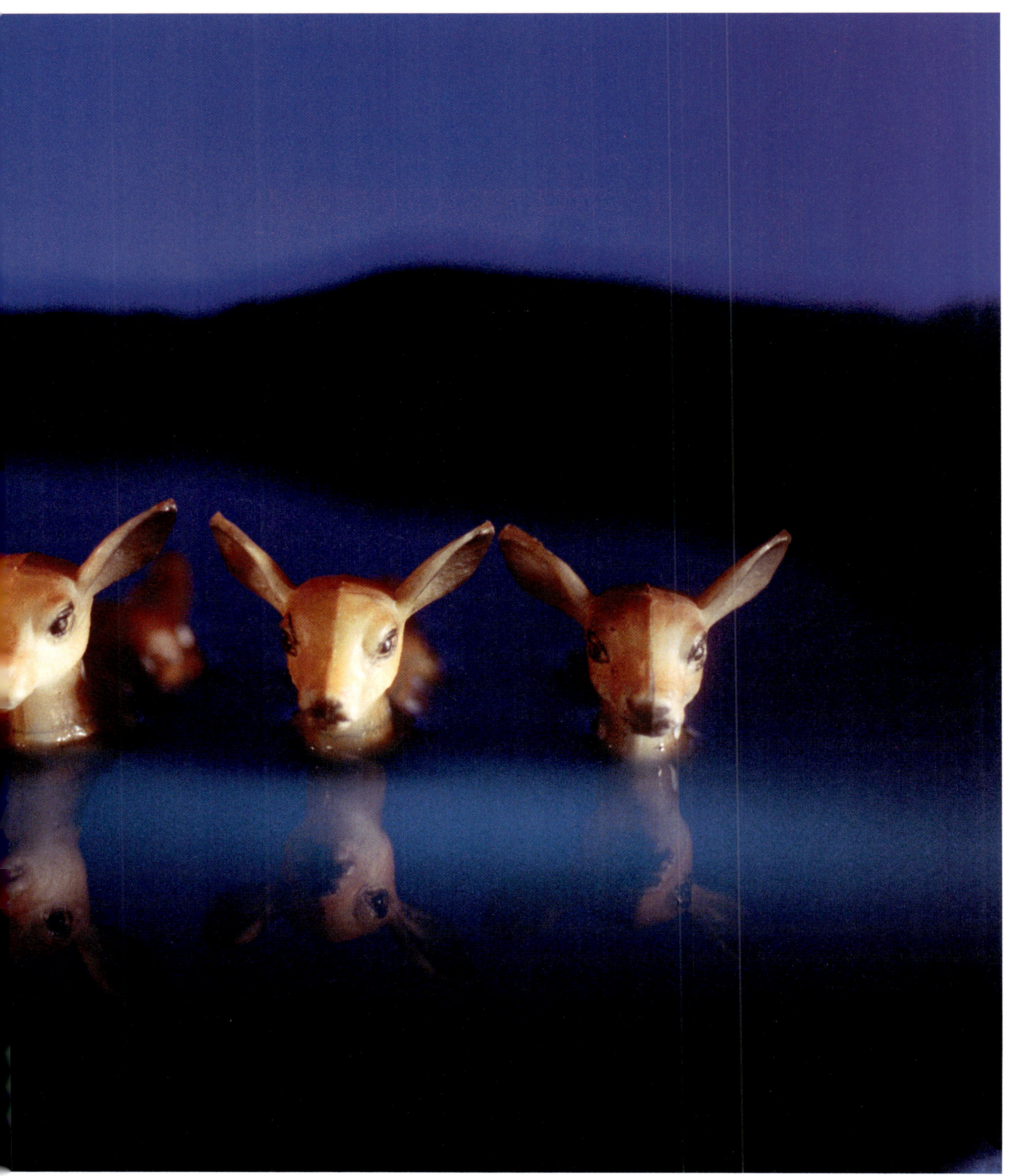

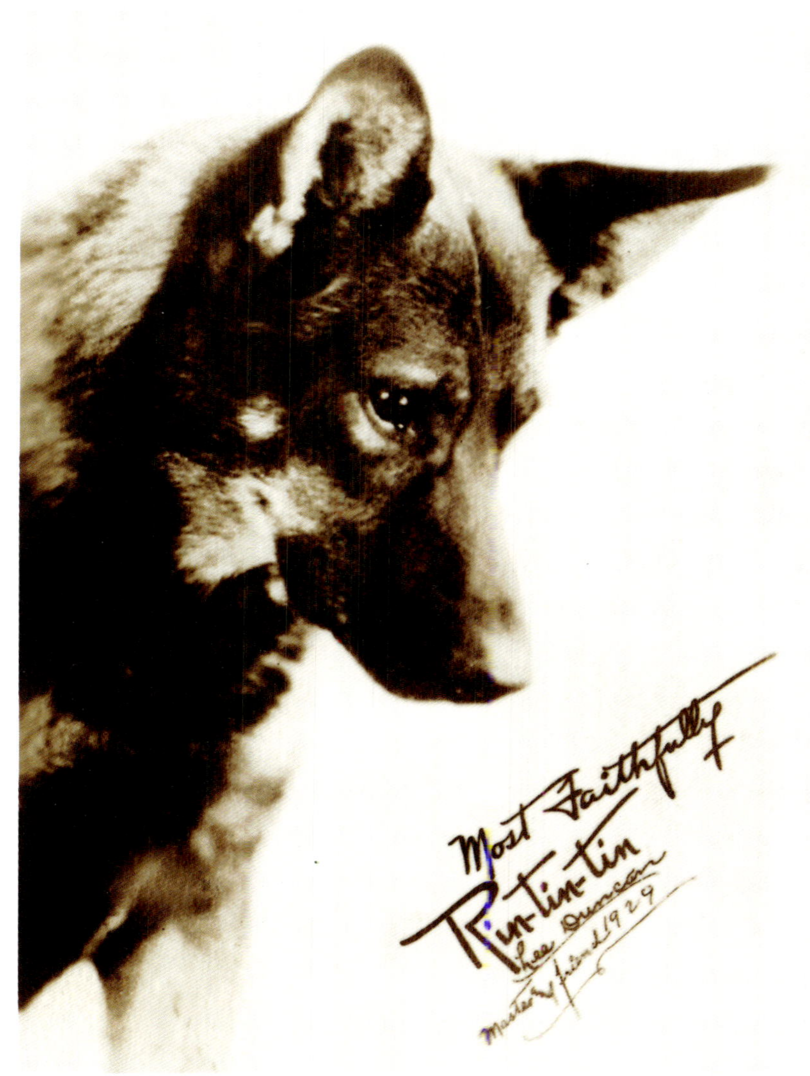

Anonym

Rin Tin Tin, 1929

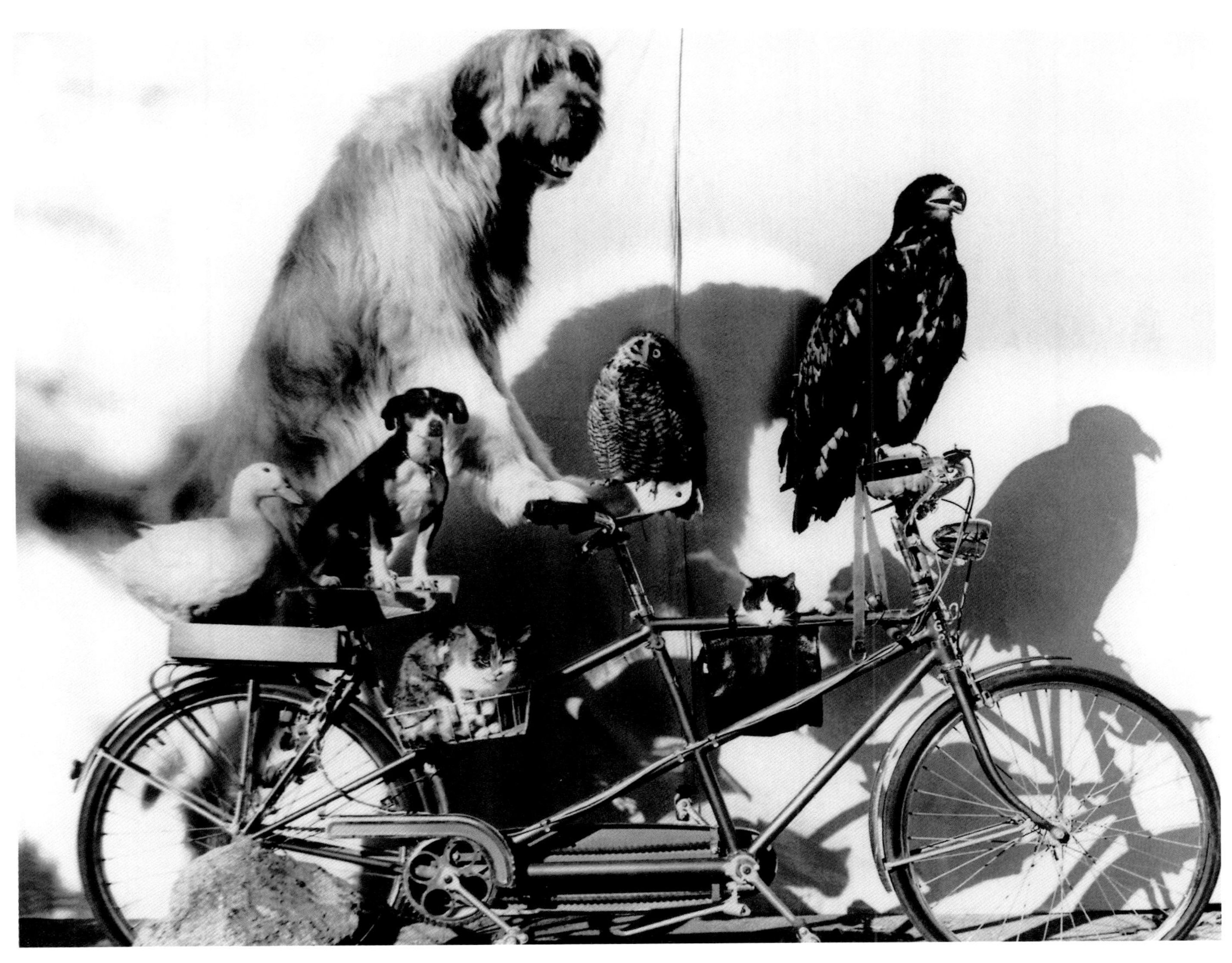

Anonym
Tierschauspieler /
Animal actors, 1950er

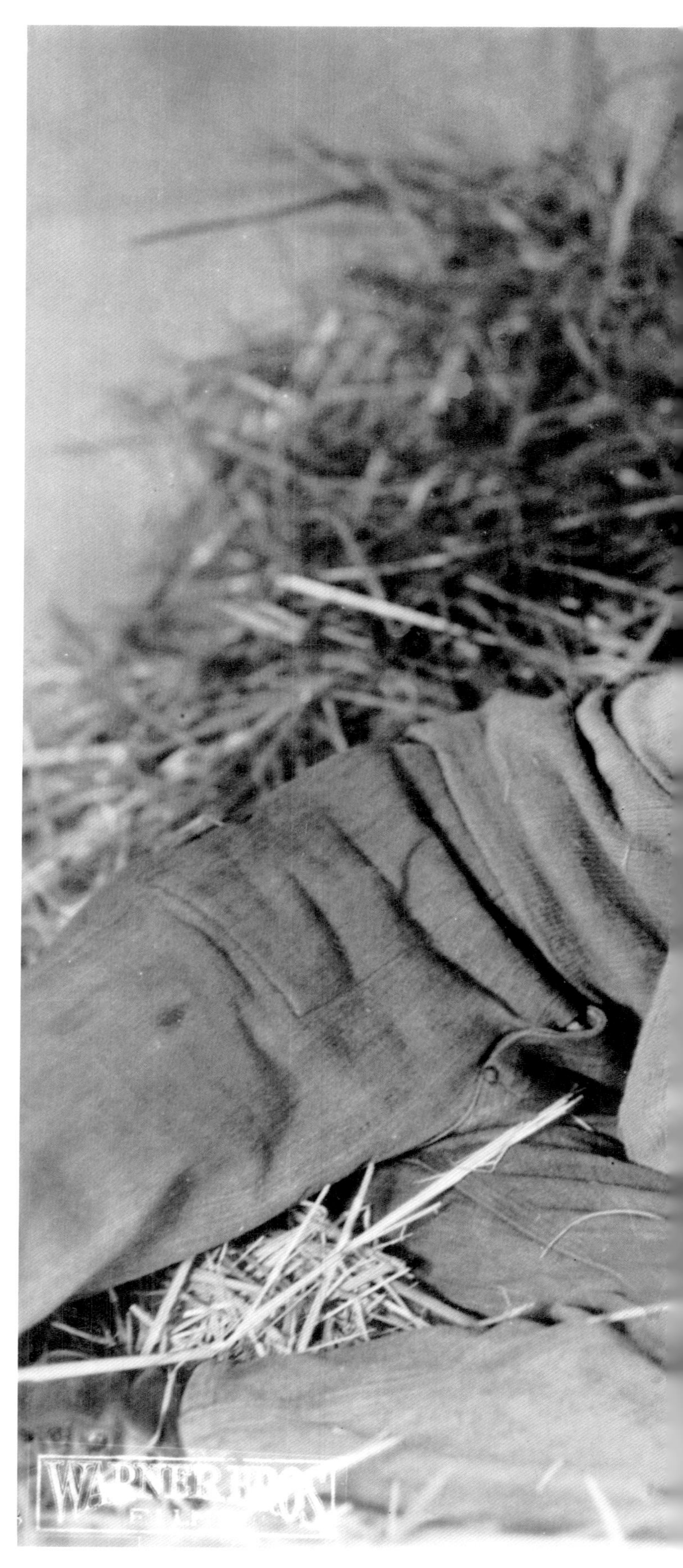

Anonym
Rintintins schwerster Sieg,
A Race for Life, USA, 1928

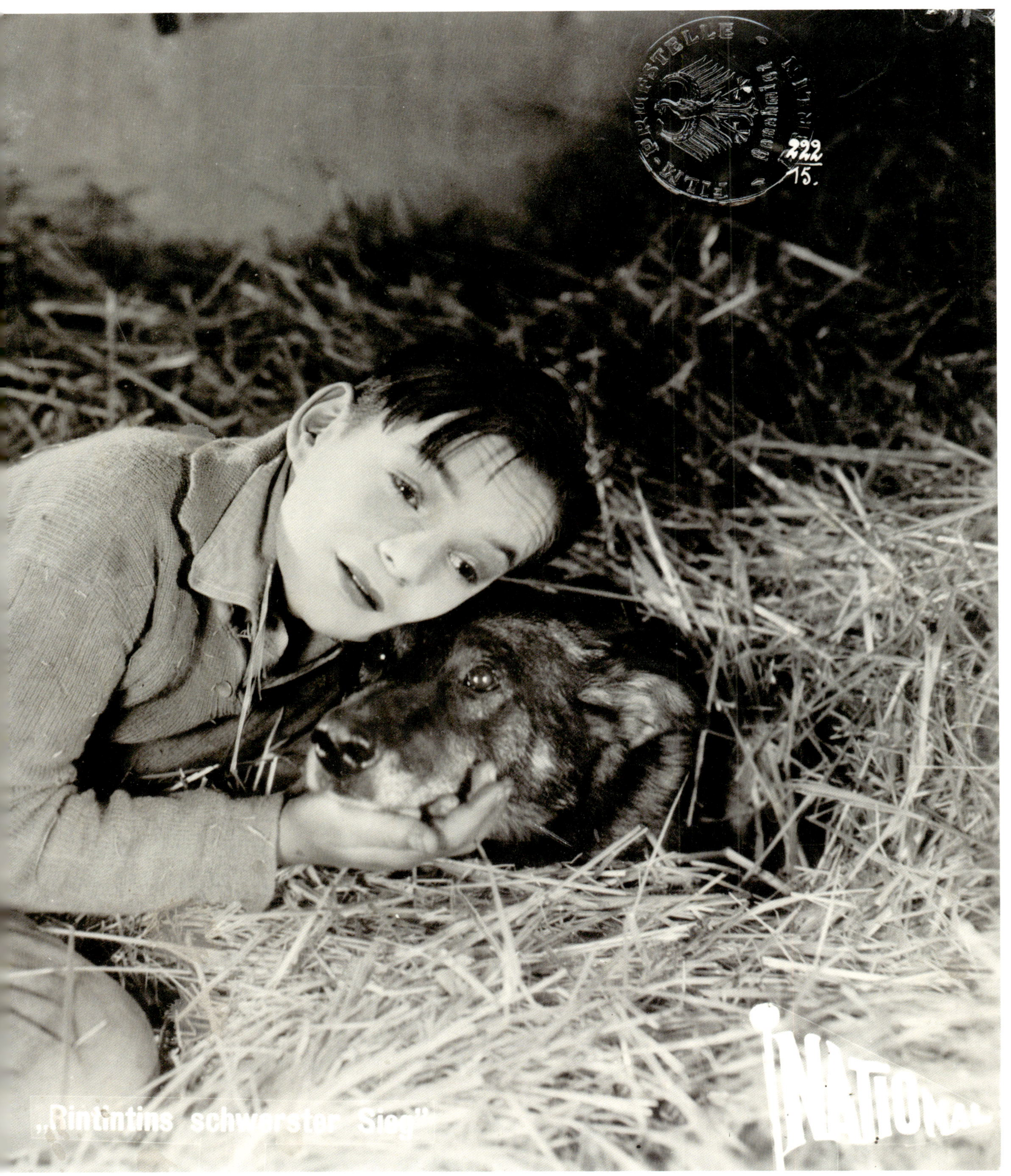
„Rintintins schwerster Sieg"
NATIONAL

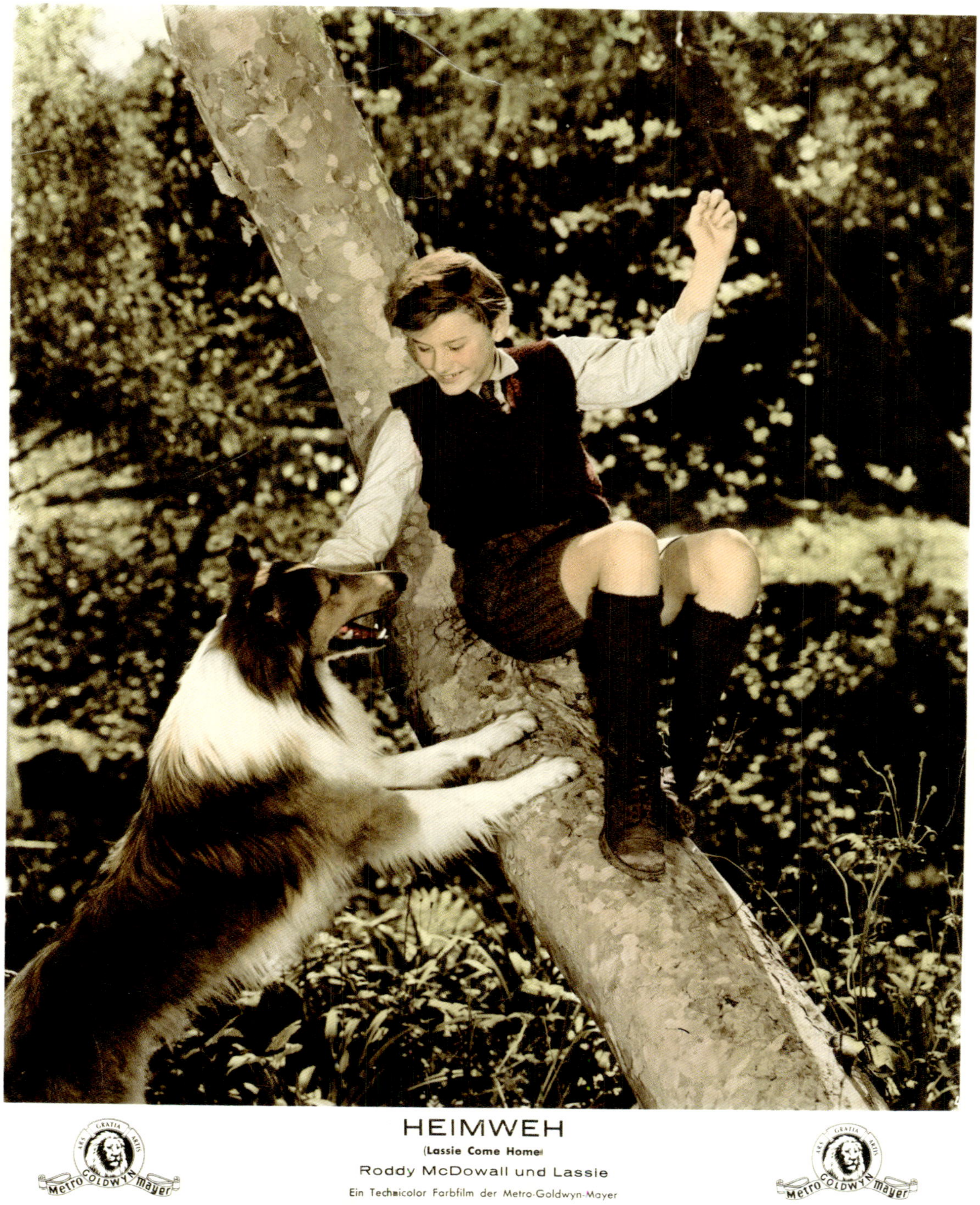

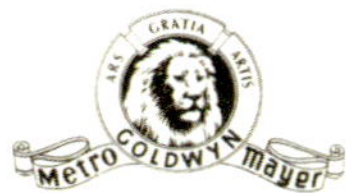

HEIMWEH

(Lassie Come Home)

Roddy McDowall und Lassie

Ein Technicolor Farbfilm der Metro-Goldwyn-Mayer

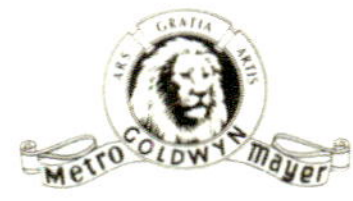

Anonym

Heimweh /

Lassie come home, USA 1943

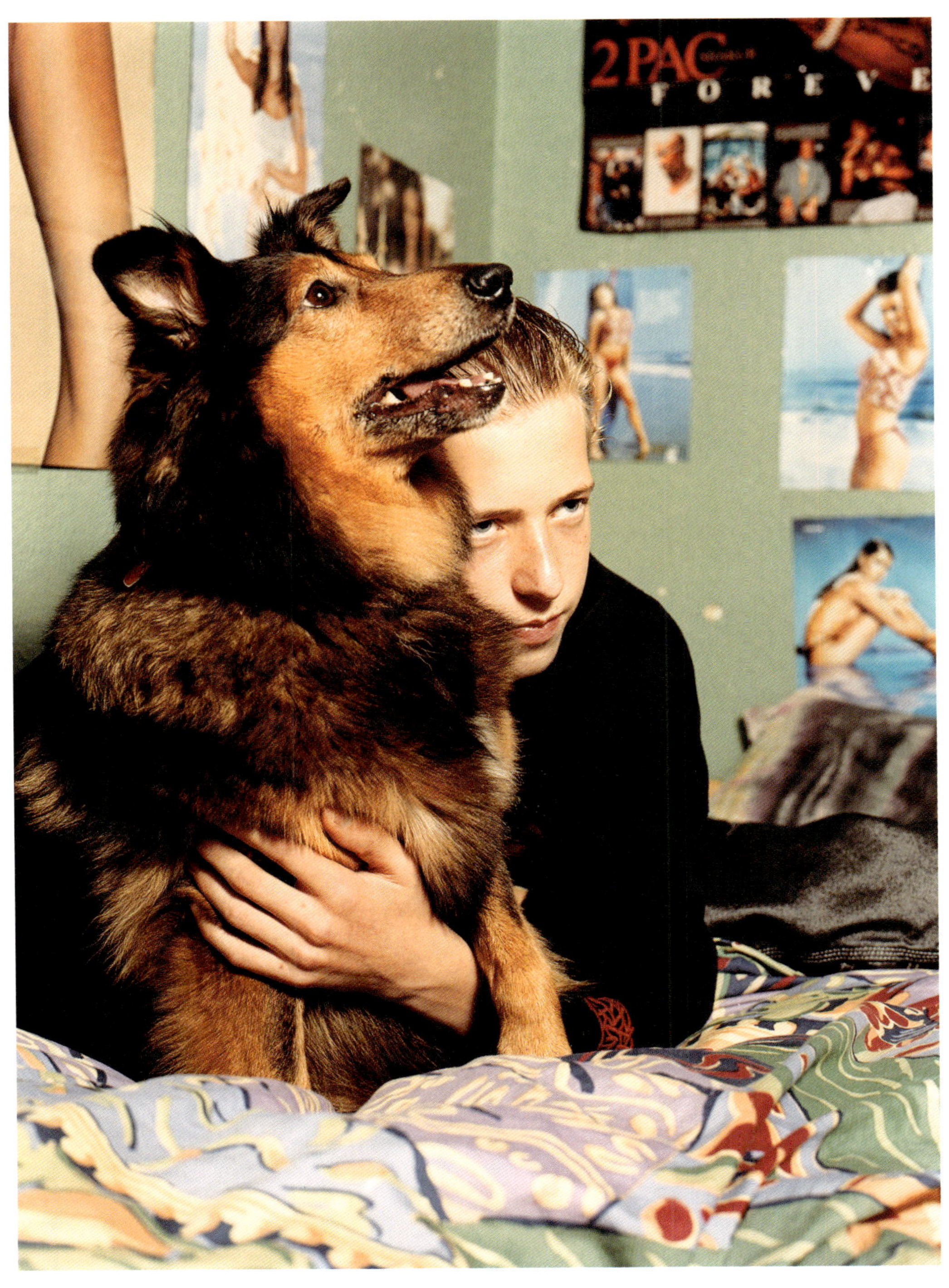

Isadora Tast

a. d. Serie: *Schmerzlich-süße Zeit*, 2001/02

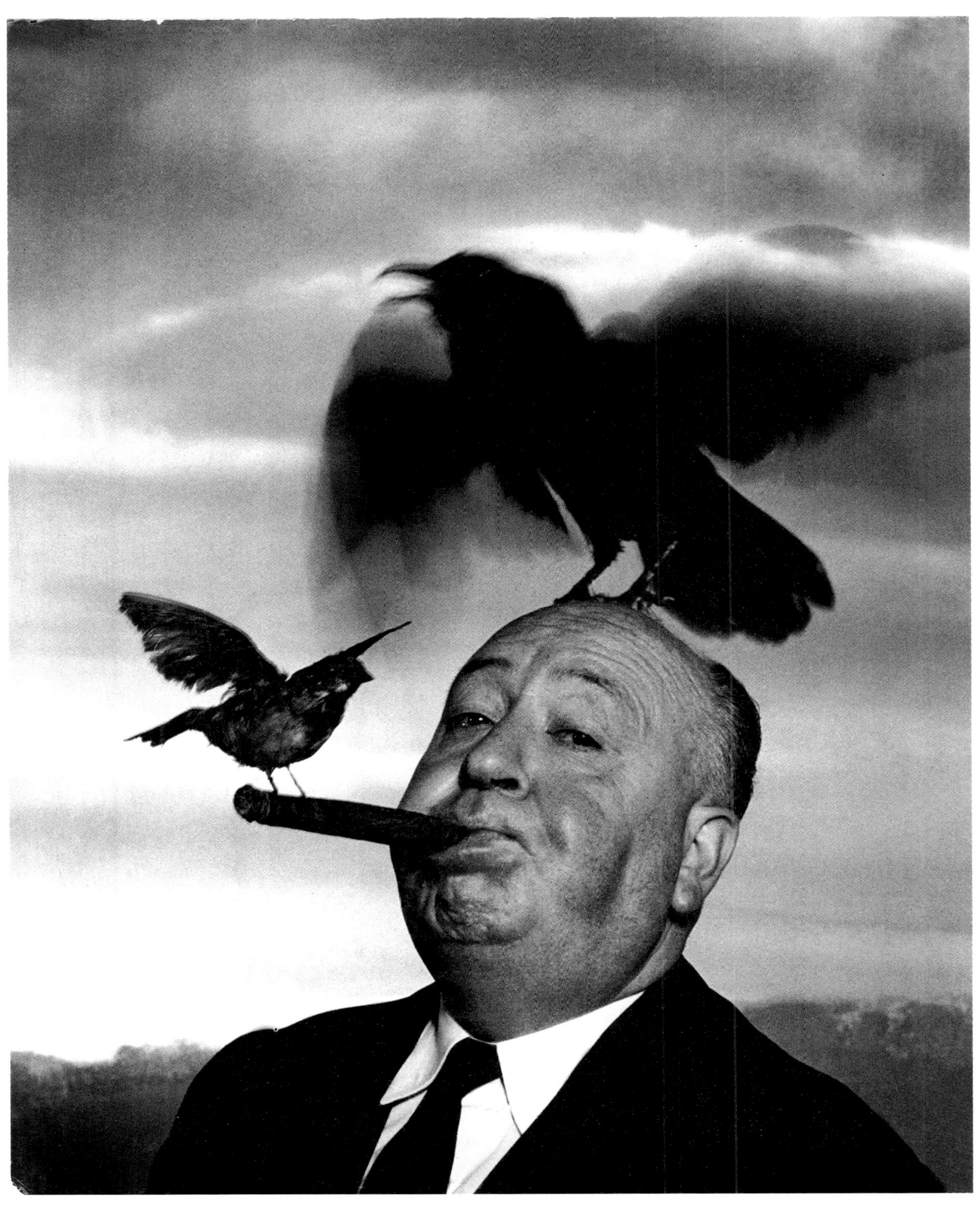

Philippe Halsman
Alfred Hitchcock, 1963

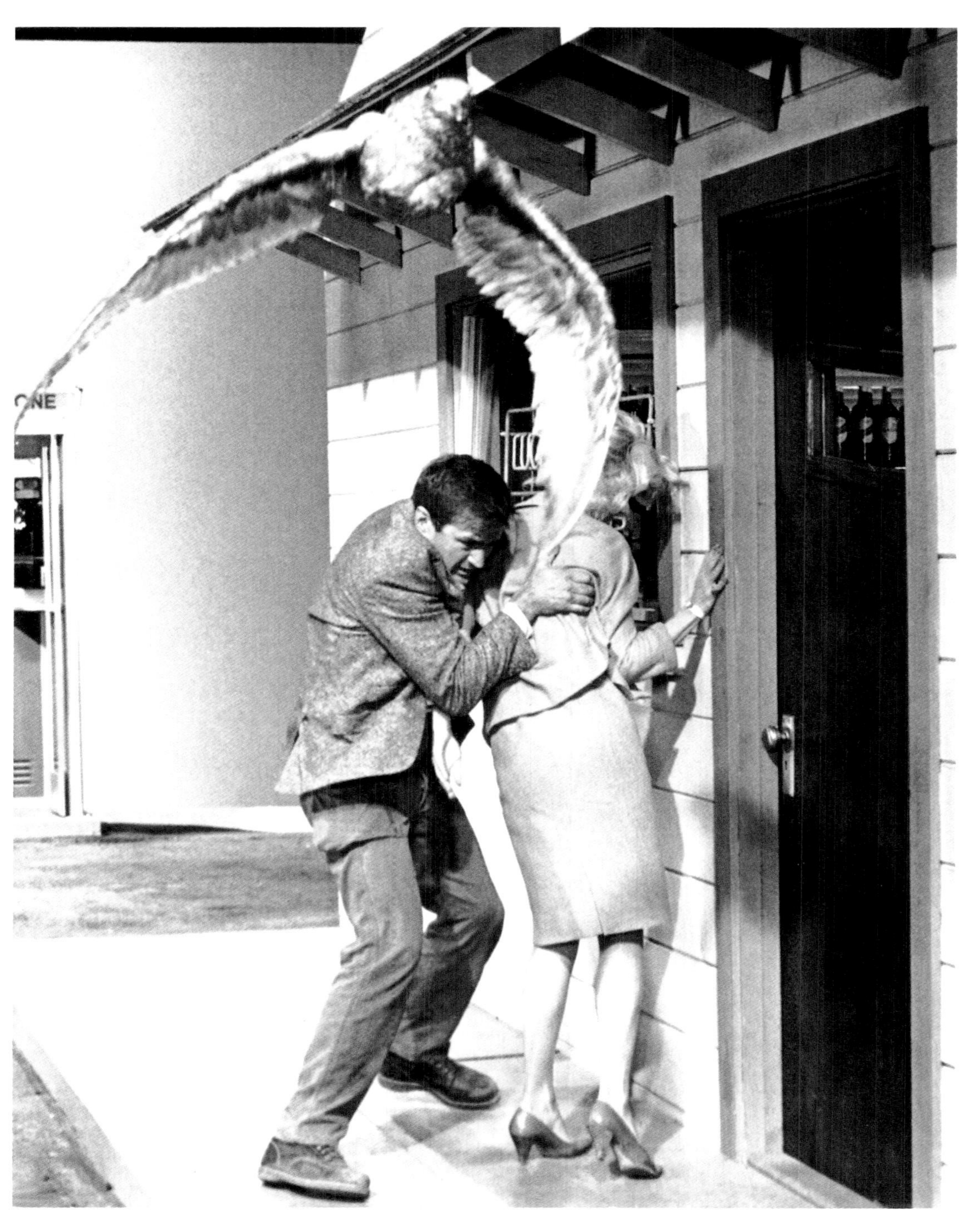

Anonym (Fotografische Montage IB Iwerks)
Film Stills aus/from: Alfred Hitchcock, *The Birds*, 1963

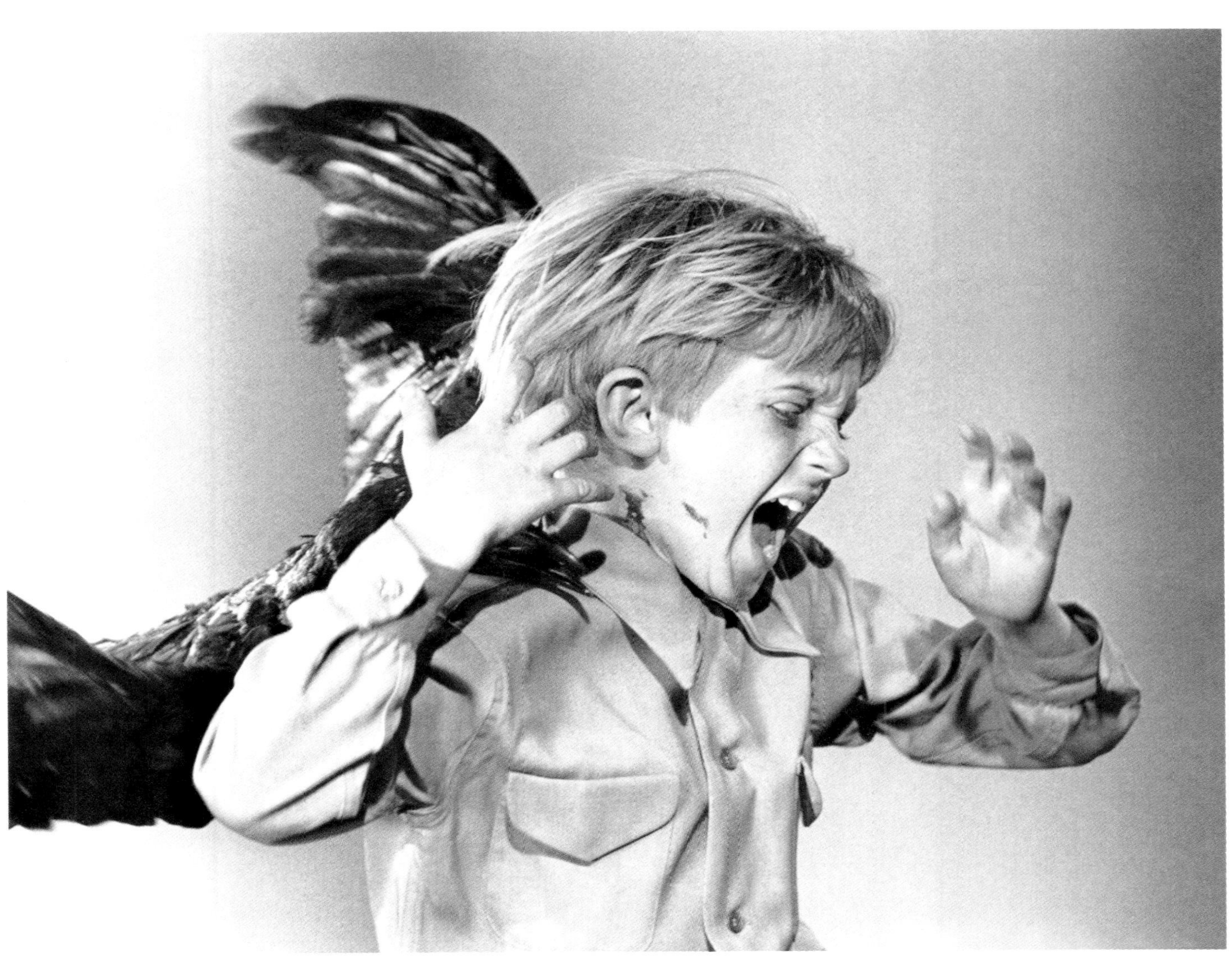

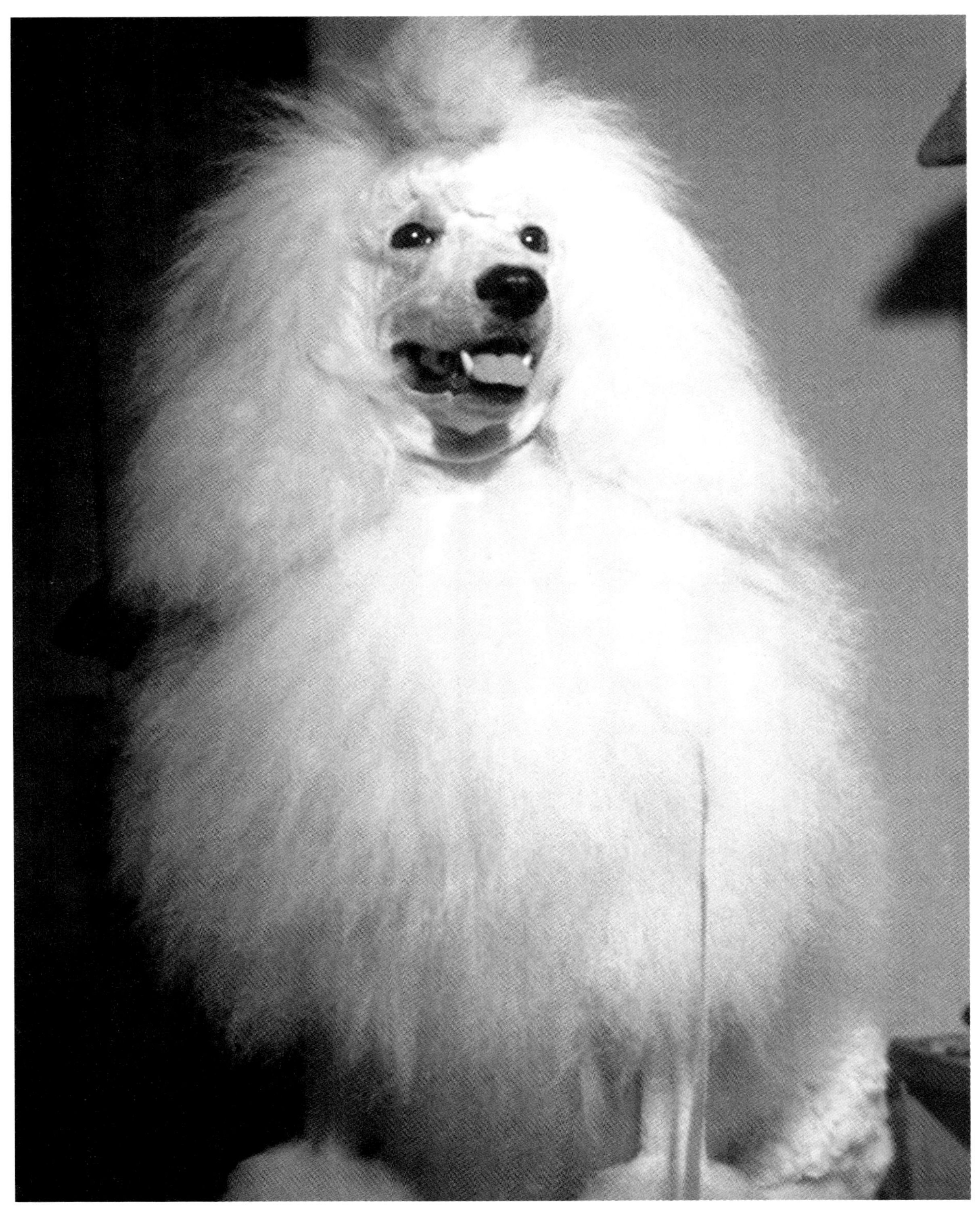

Lisette Model

Dog Show, Westminster Kanal Club, New York, 1946

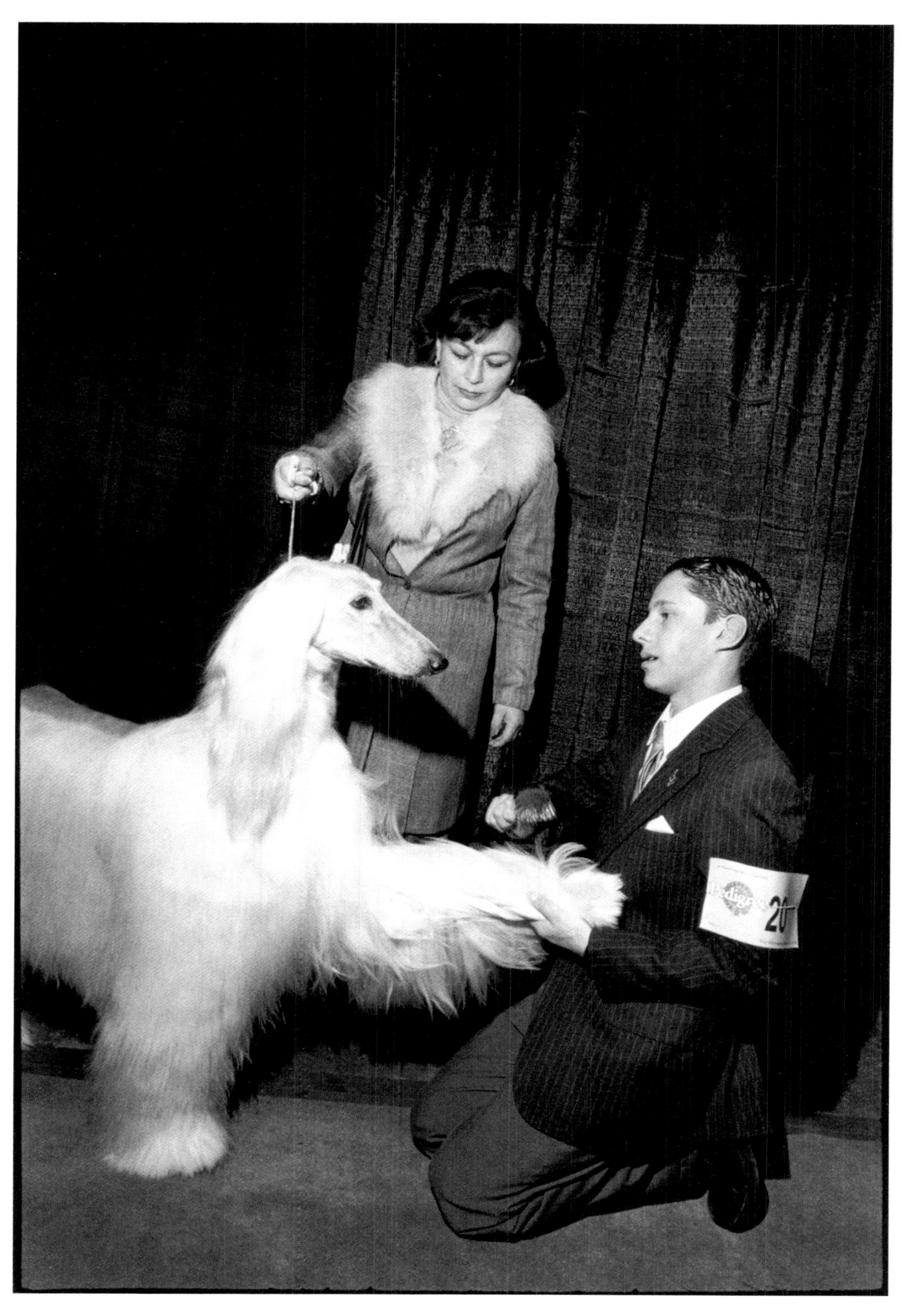

Bruce Gilden

NYC Dog Show. A junior handler from Mexico with his mother and Afghan hound, New York City, 2003

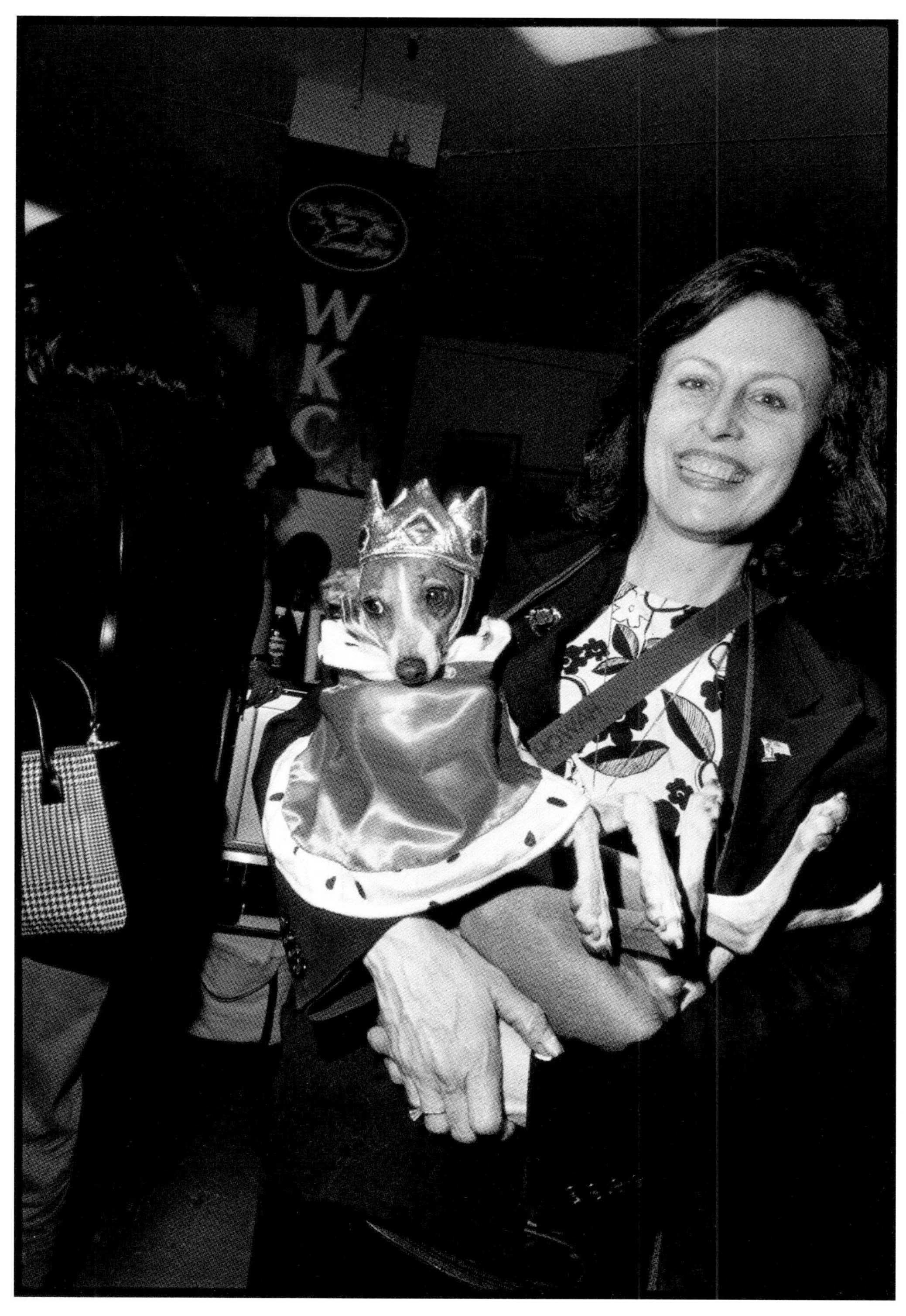

Bruce Gilden

NYC Dog Show. Owner with her crowned dog,

New York City, 2003

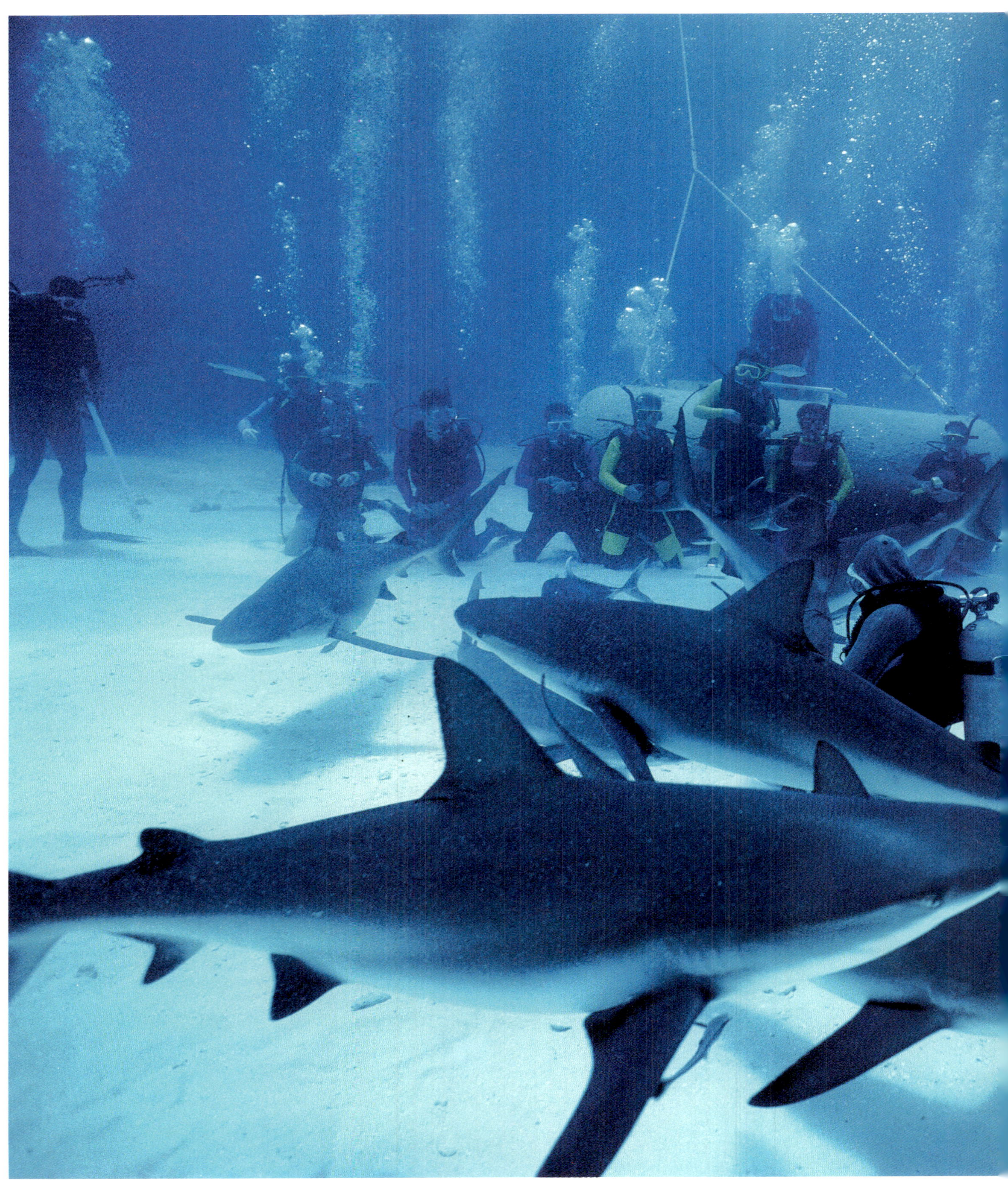

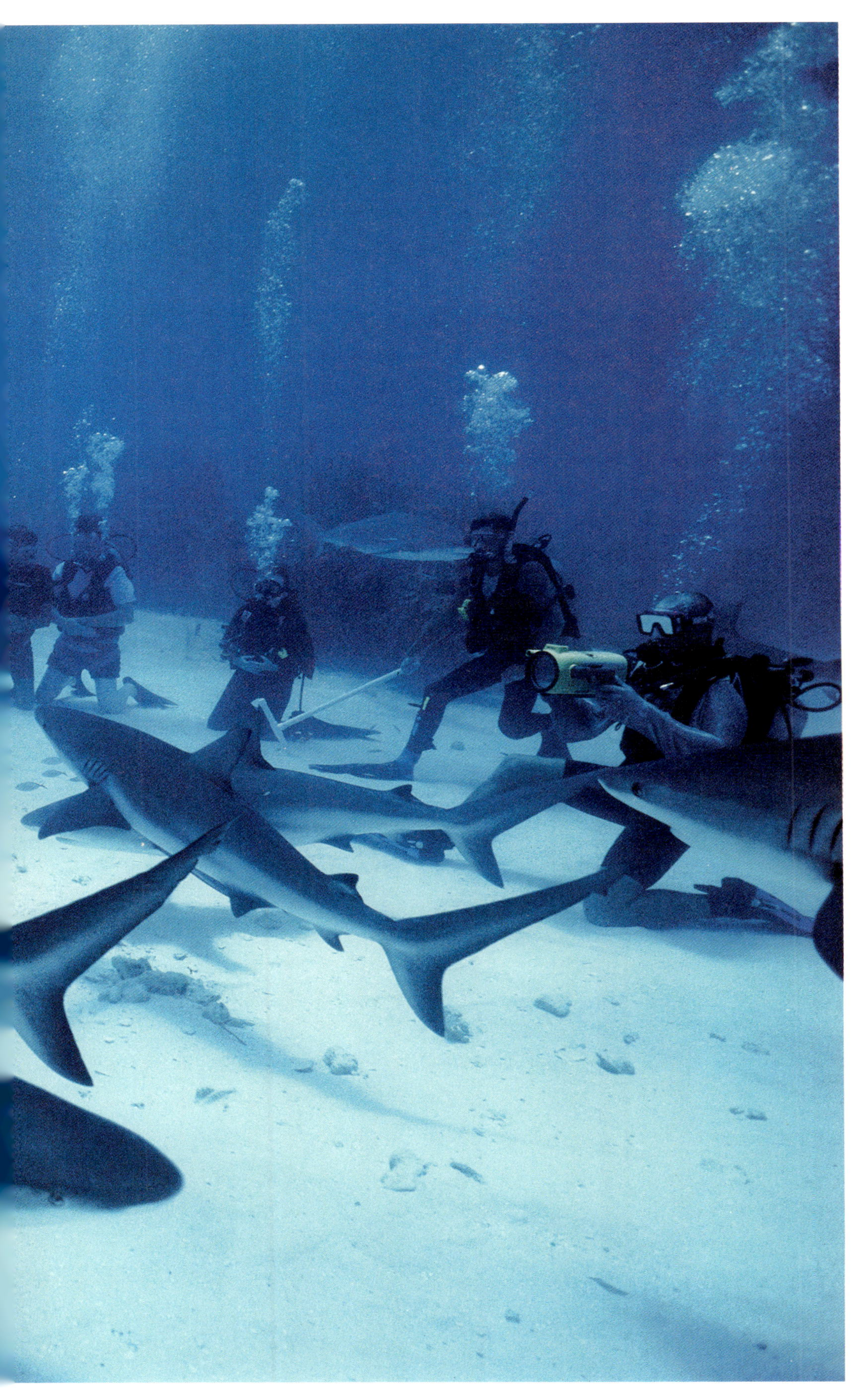

Jeffrey L. Rotman
Caribbean Reef Shark, 1997

„Die Kunst des Tierfotografen, so scheint es, liegt im ökonomischen Umfang mit der kostbaren Aufmerksamkeit des Tieres, und vielleicht ist dies nur die pragmatische Kehrseite von der idealistischen Konzeption des einfühlsamen Porträtisten.“

“The art of an ‘animal photographer,’ it seems, lies in the economical way of dealing with the valuable attention of an animal, and perhaps that is only the pragmatic downside of the idealistic conception of a sensitive portraitist.”

Florian Ebner

Bildmodelle Picture models

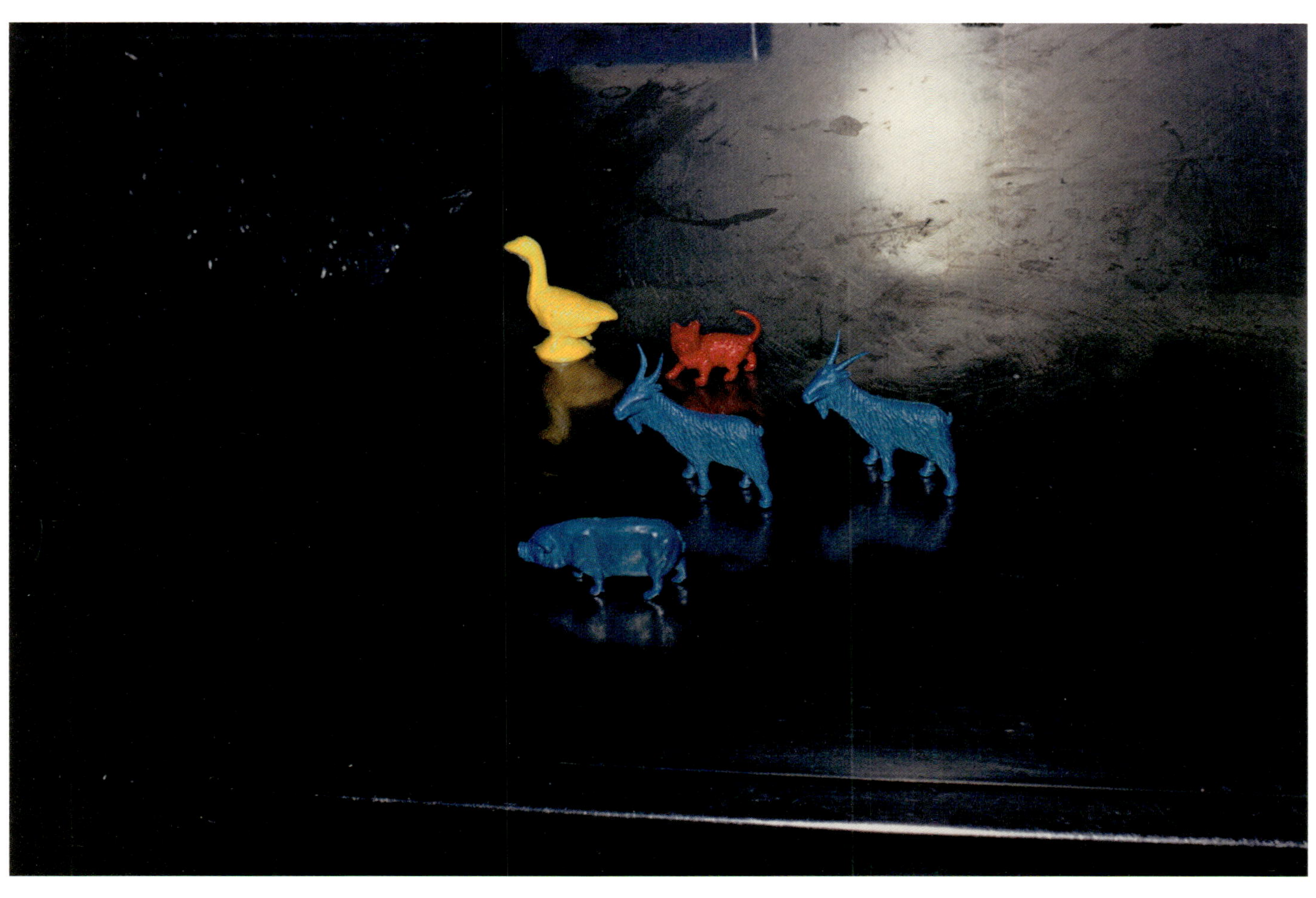

William Eggleston
Memphis, 1971

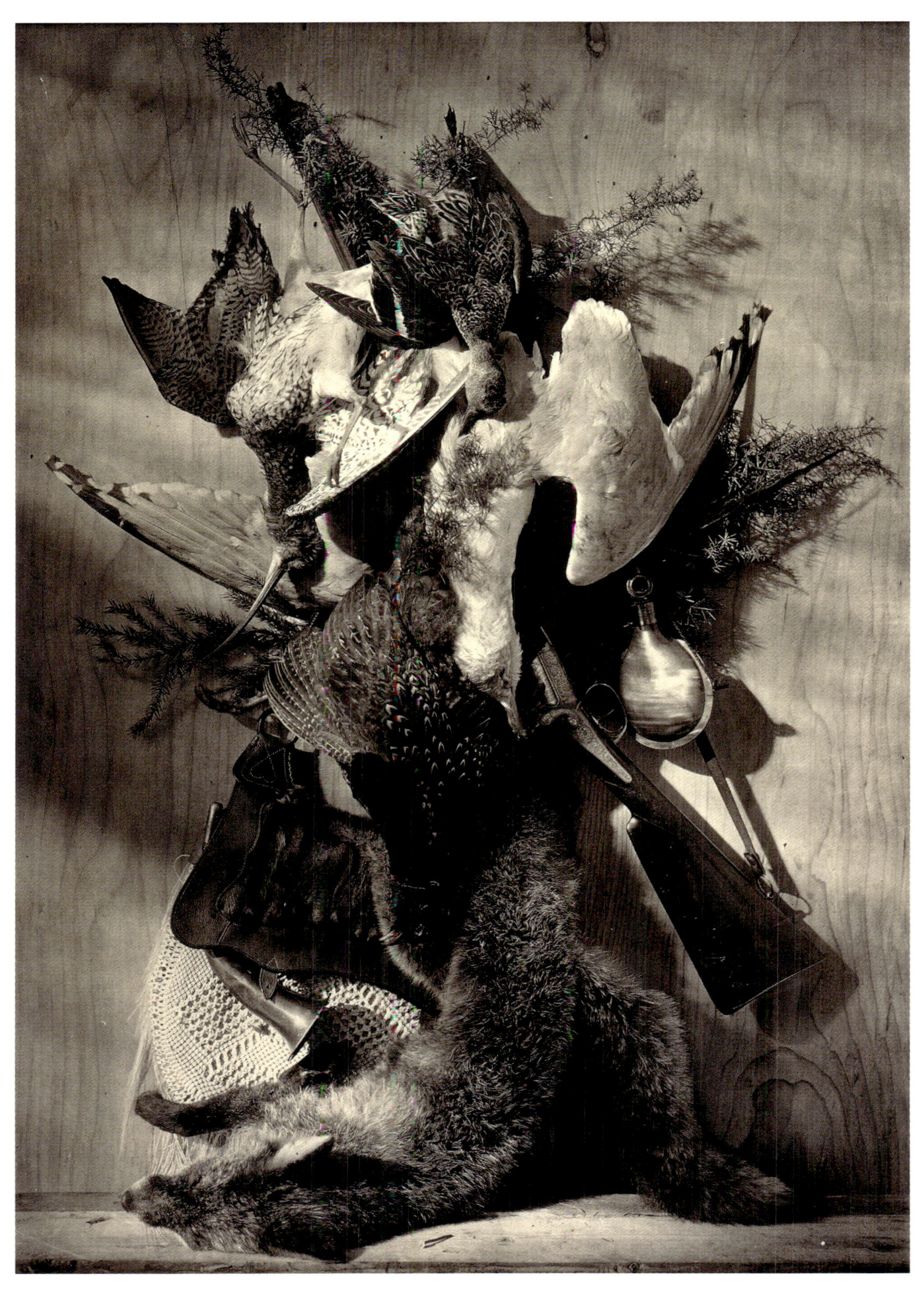

Adolphe Braun

Trophée de chasse au renard, 1867

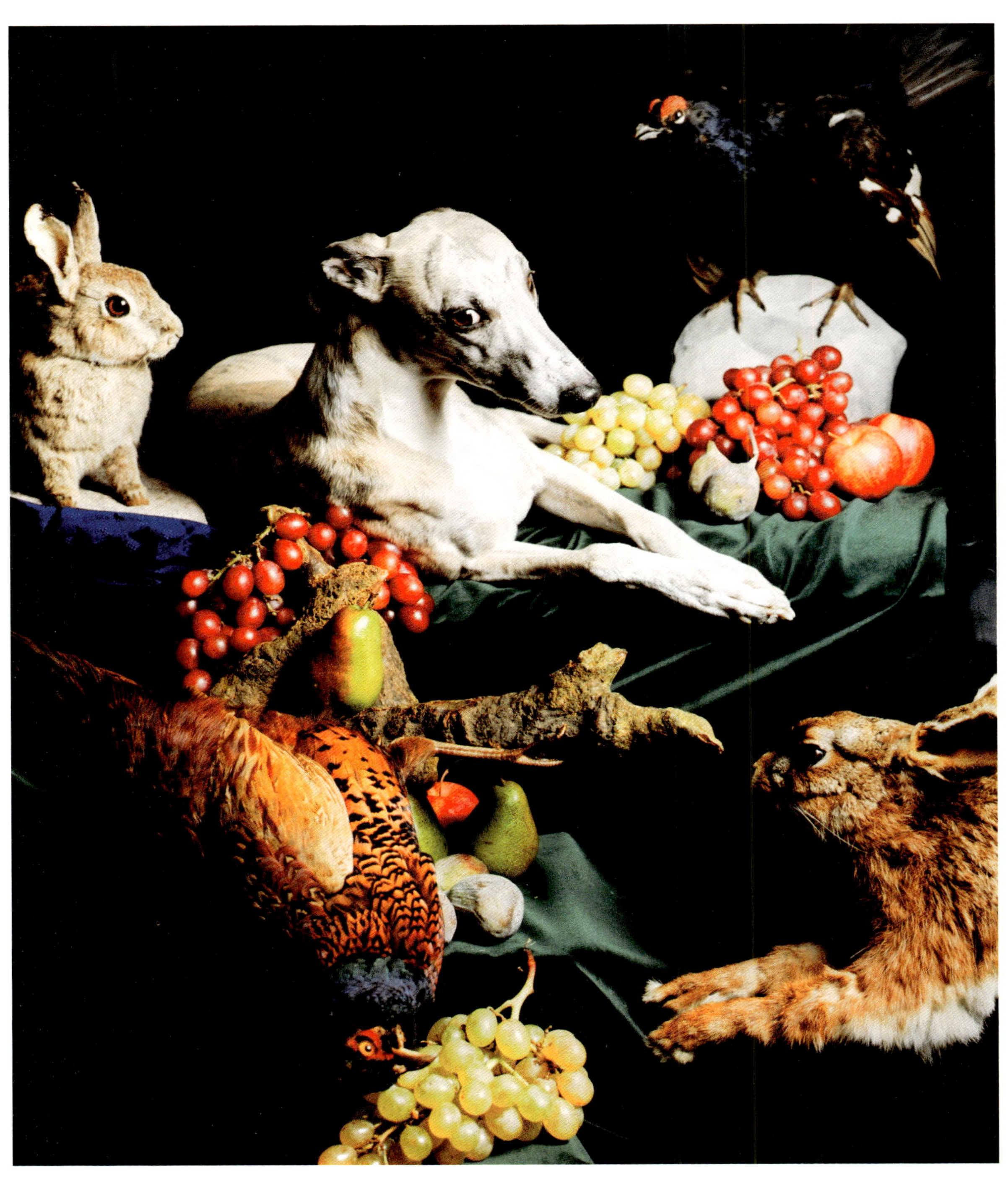

Nadin Maria Rüfenacht
Nature Morte, a. d. Serie: *Helden*, 2005

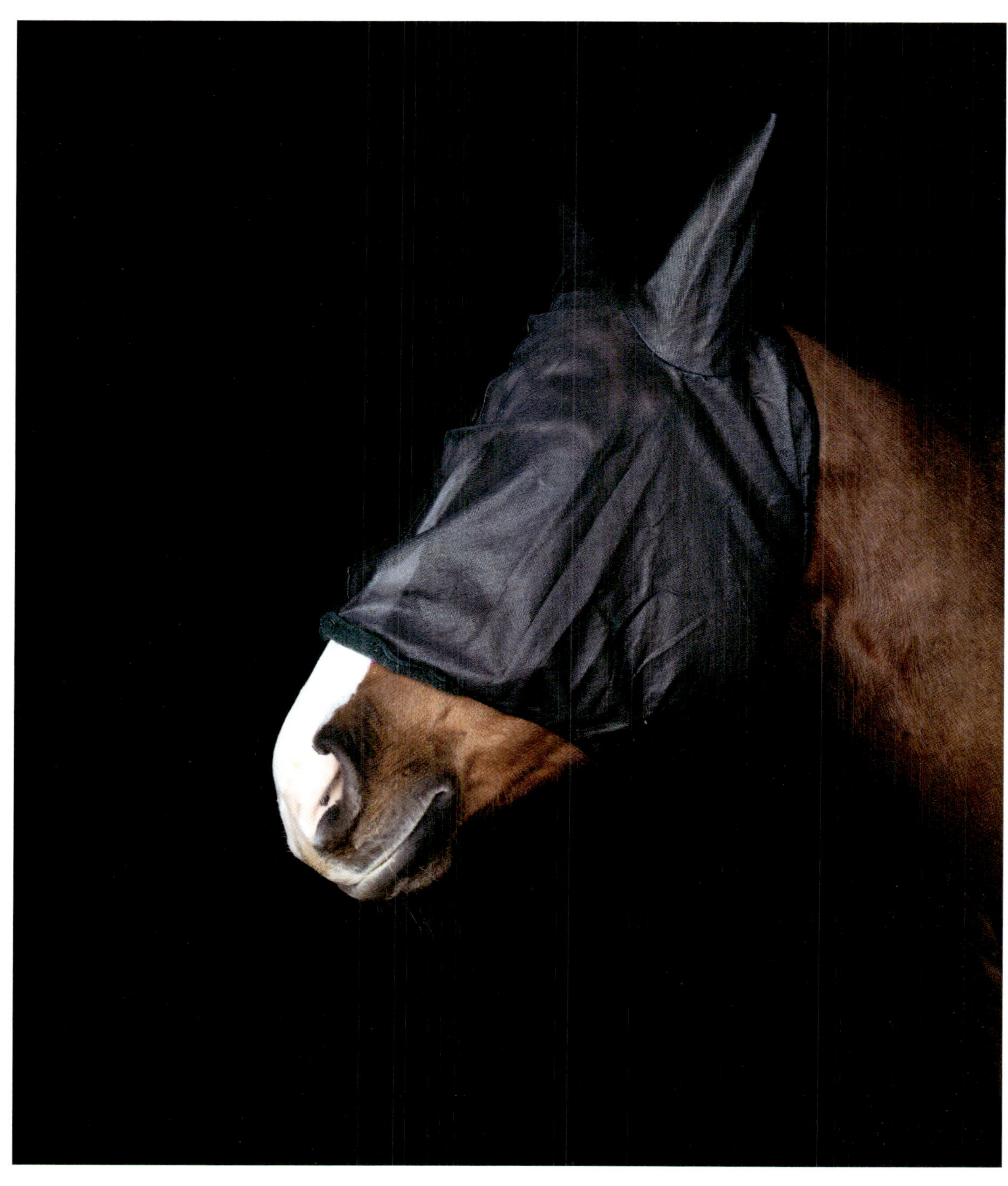

Geissler/ Sann

Bright Indian Dream, 2002

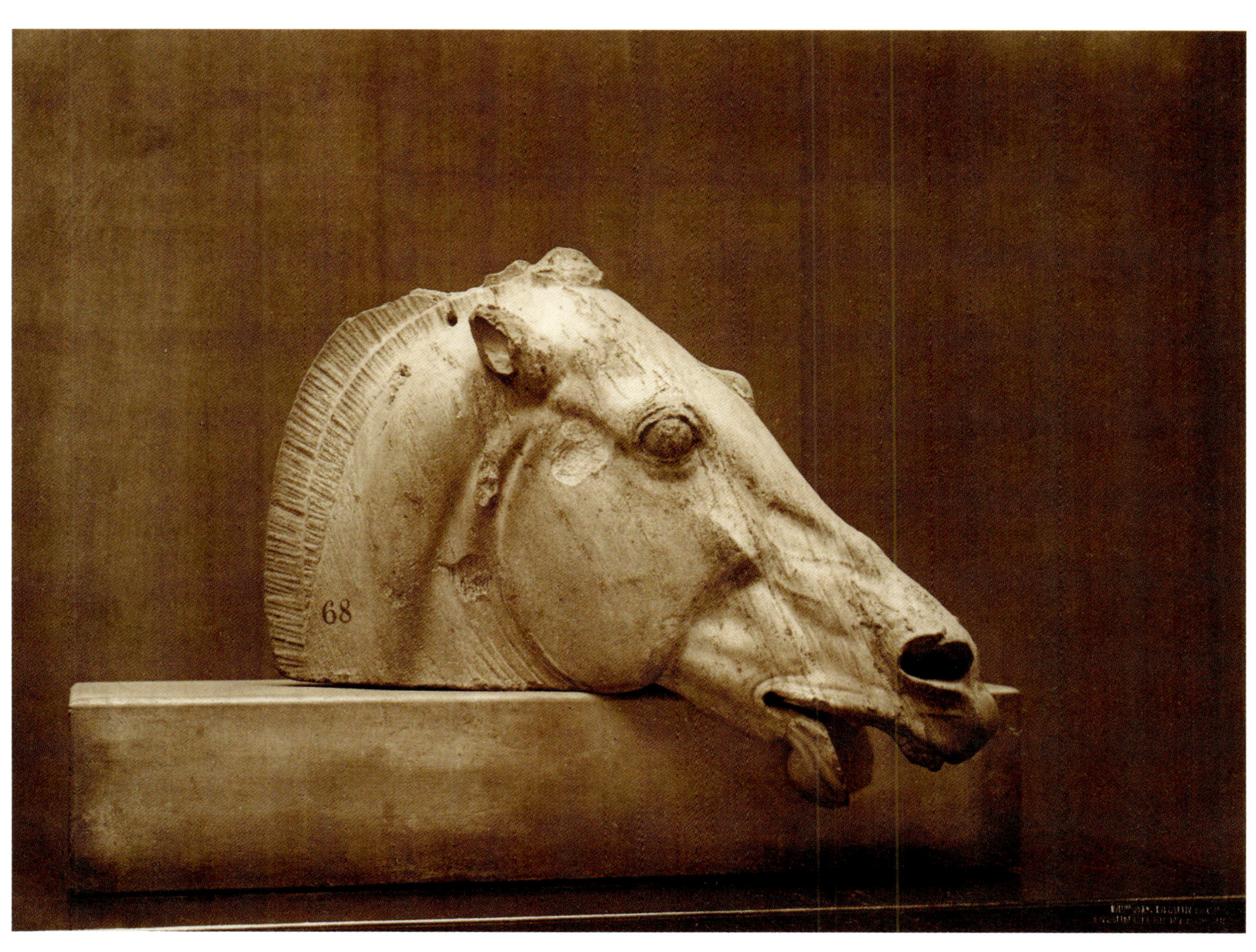

Adolphe Braun

Pferdekopf vom Giebeldreieck des Parthenons, British Museum /

Head of a Horse from the Pediment of the Parthenon, British Museum, ca. 1865

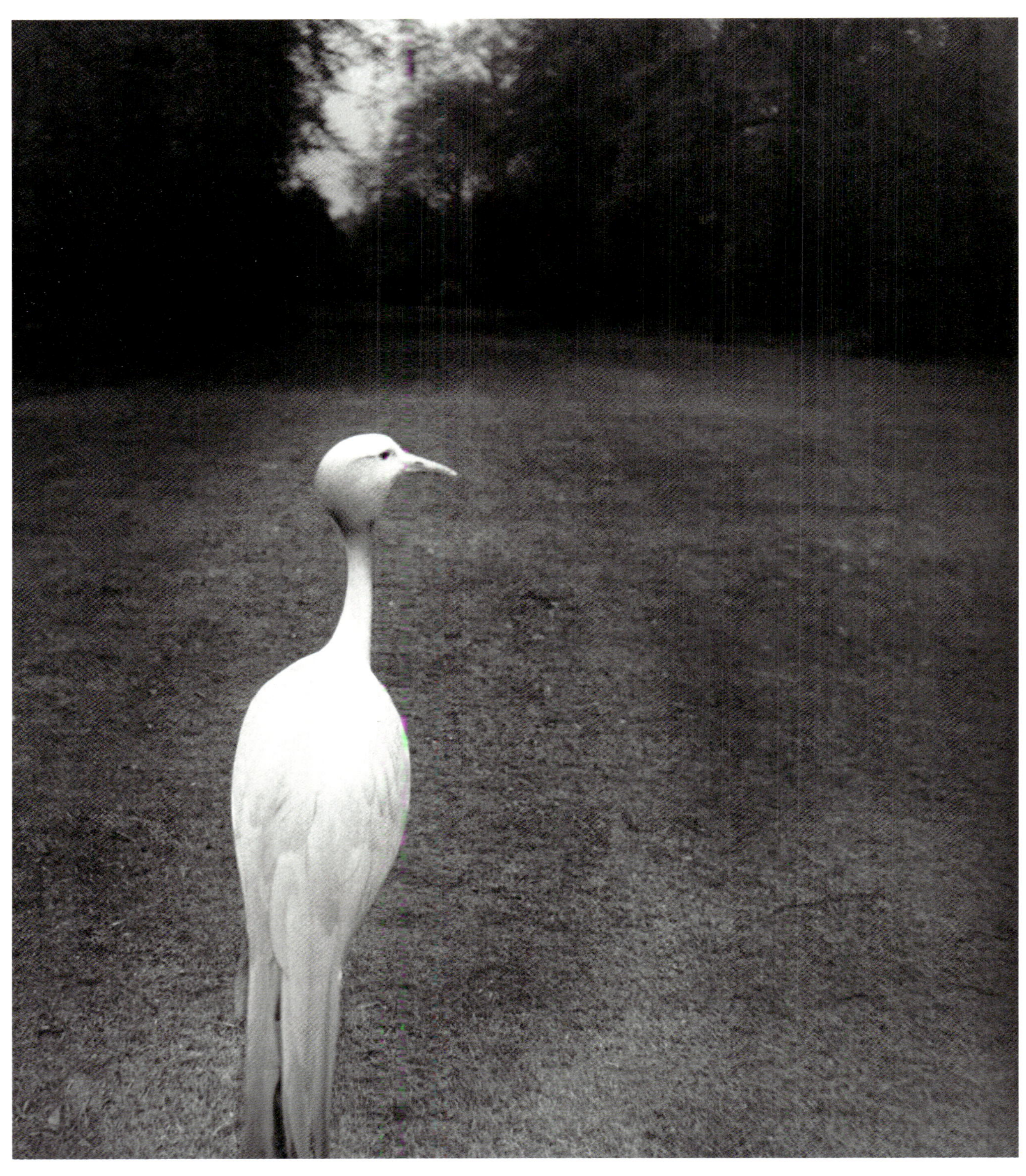

Bill Brandt

Evening in Kew Gardens, 1932

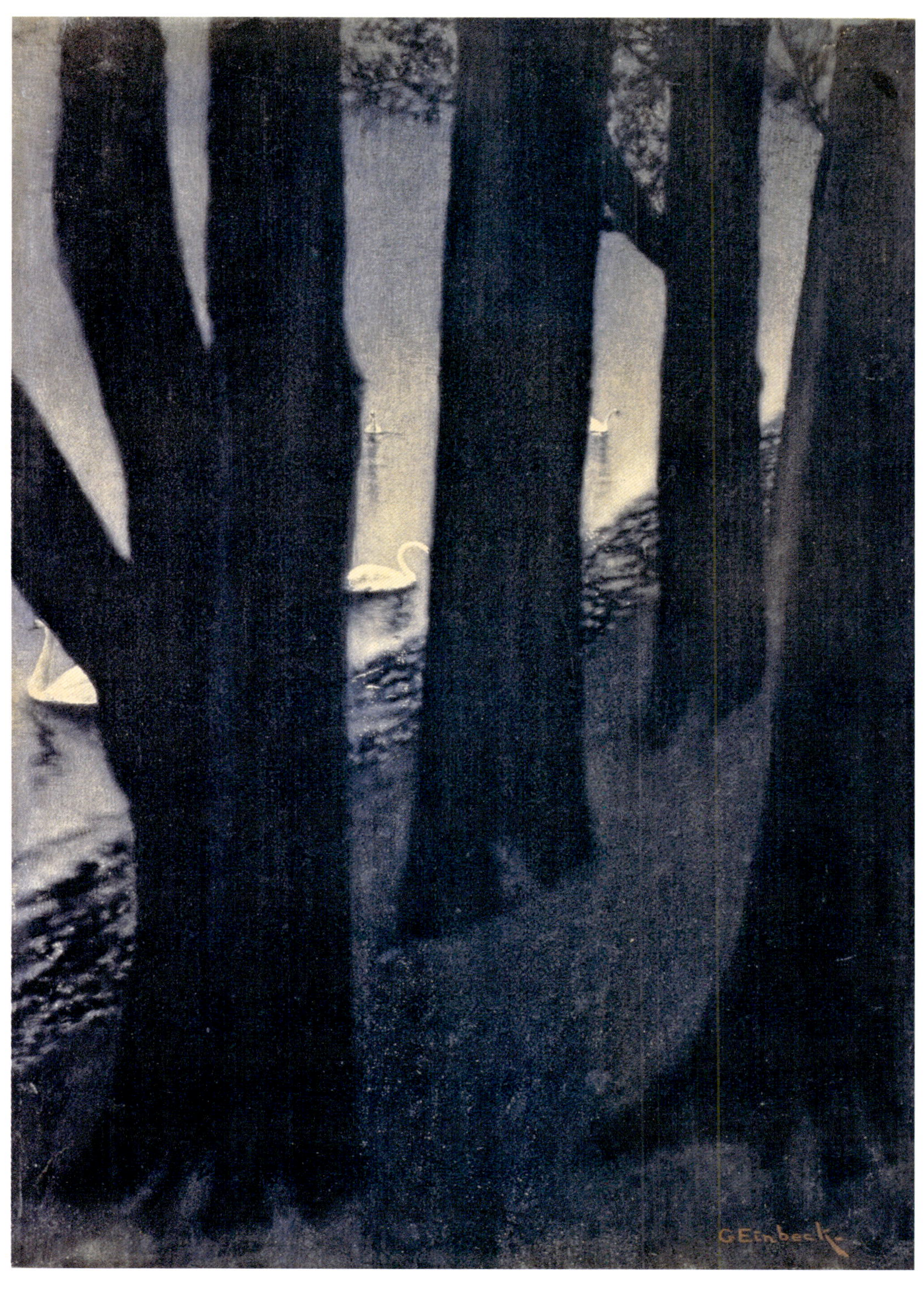

Georg Einbeck

Das Schweigen, 1898

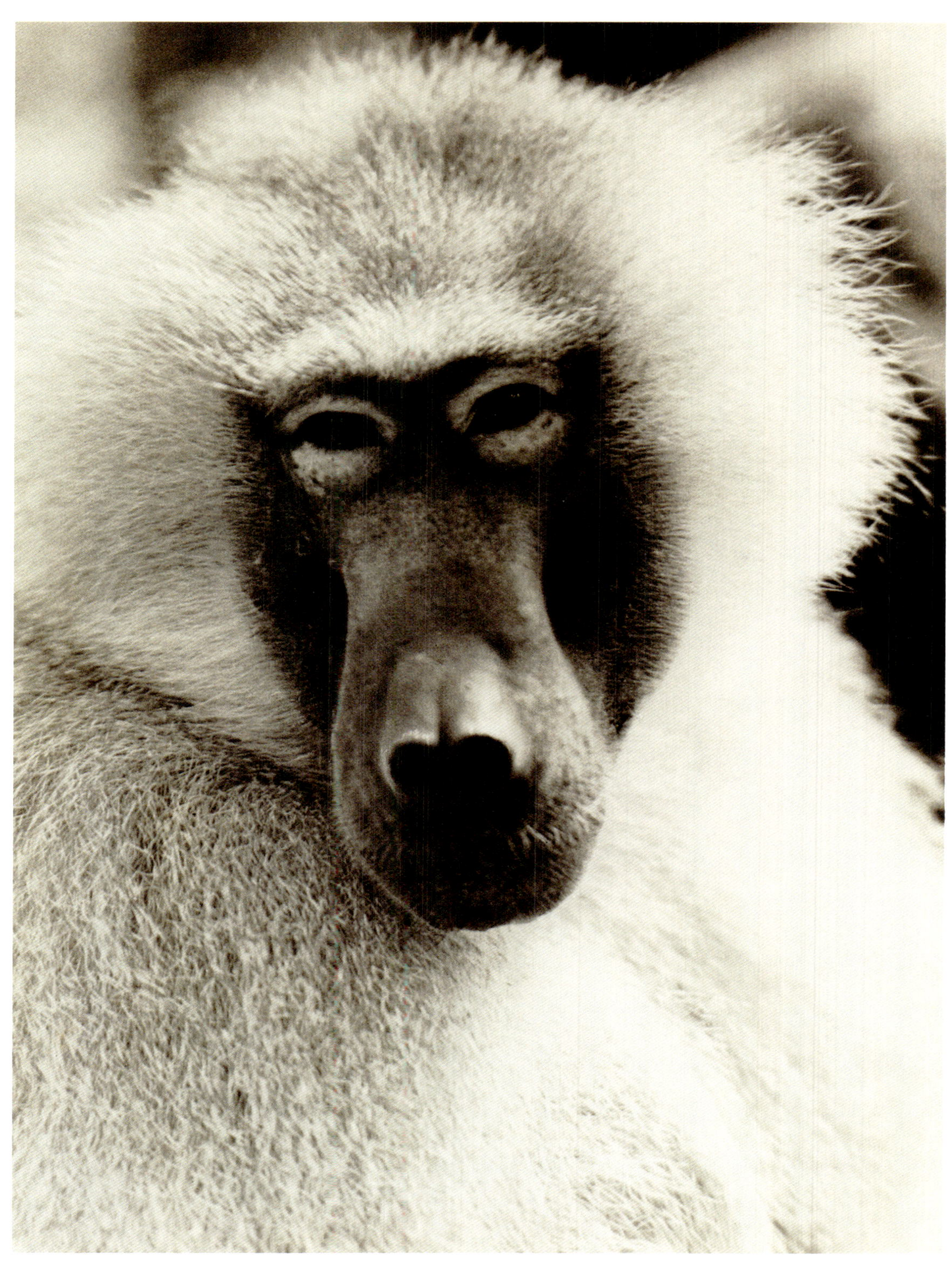

Albert Renger-Patzsch
Mantelpavian /
Sacred baboon, 1930

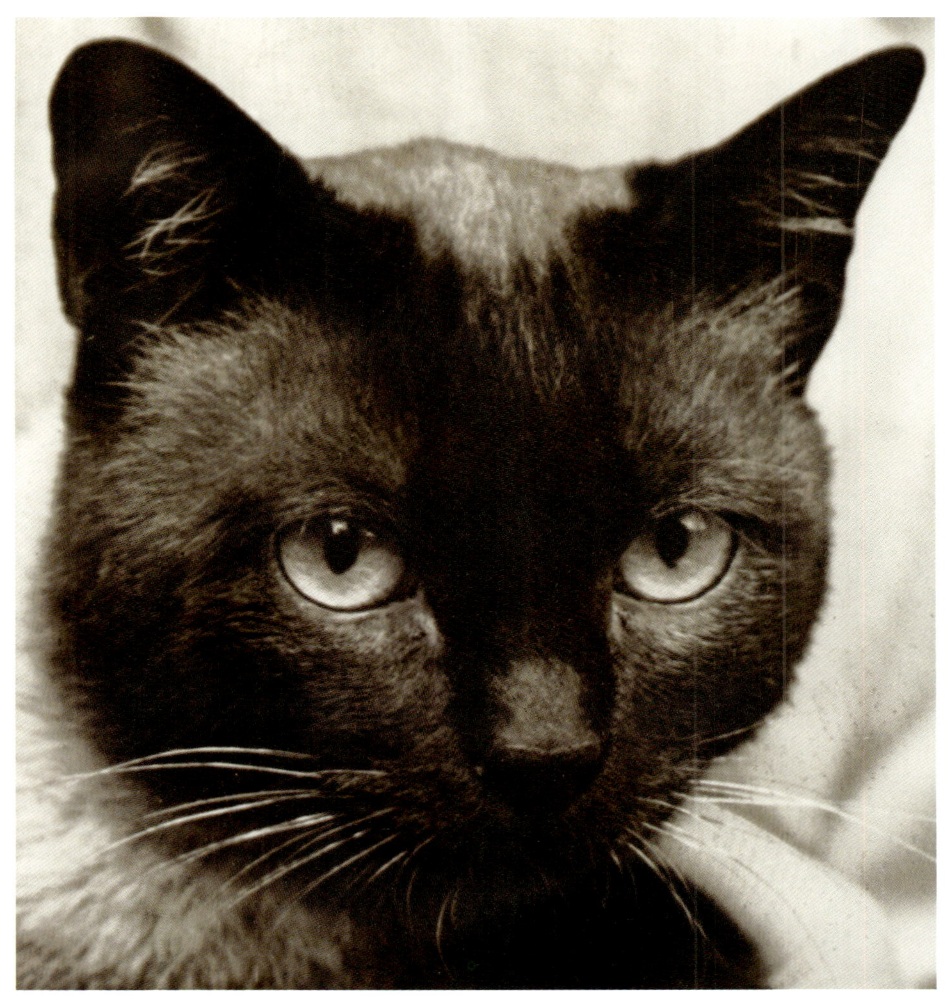

André Kertész
Siamese Cat, Paris, 1928

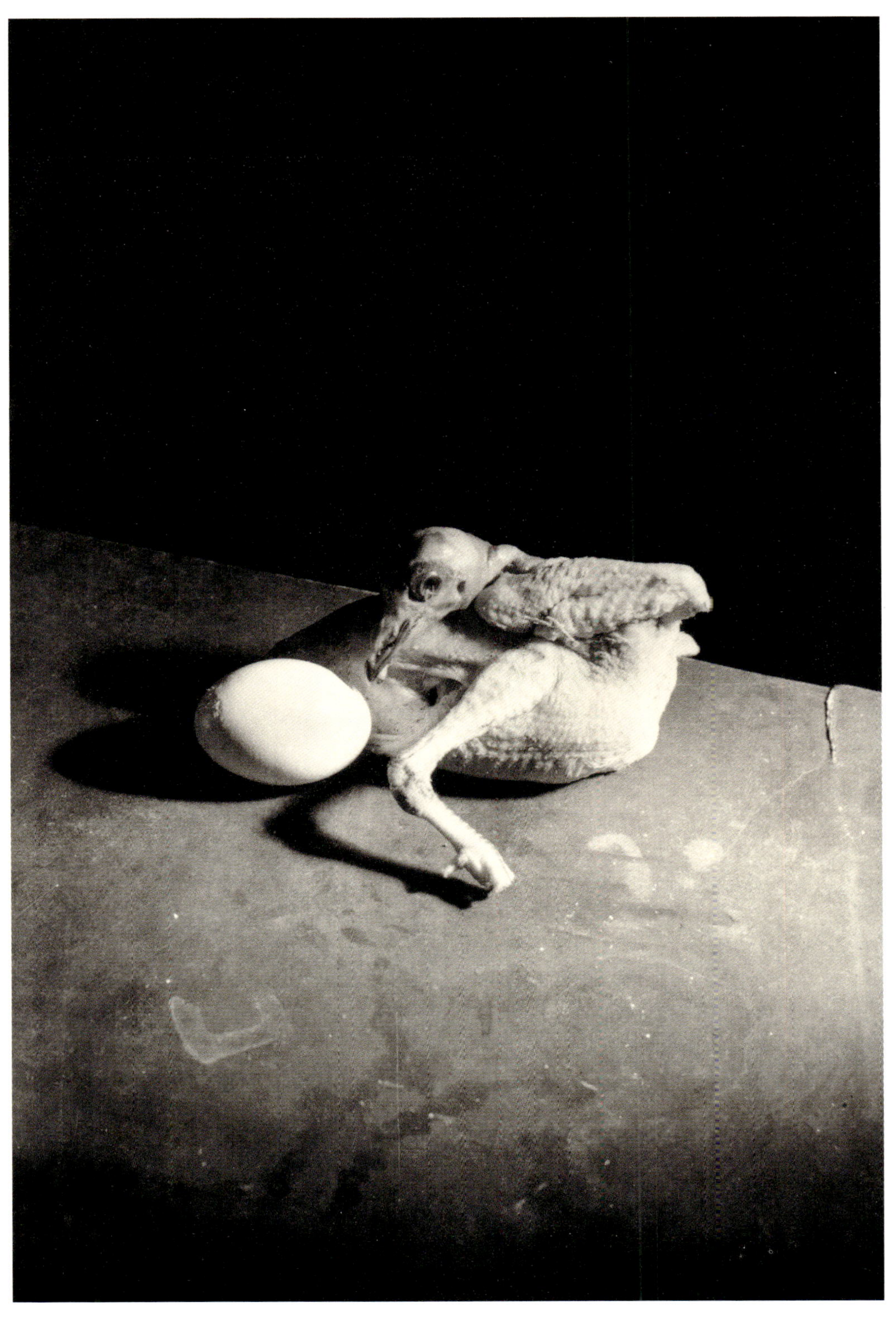

WOLS
ohne Titel /
Untitled 1938/39

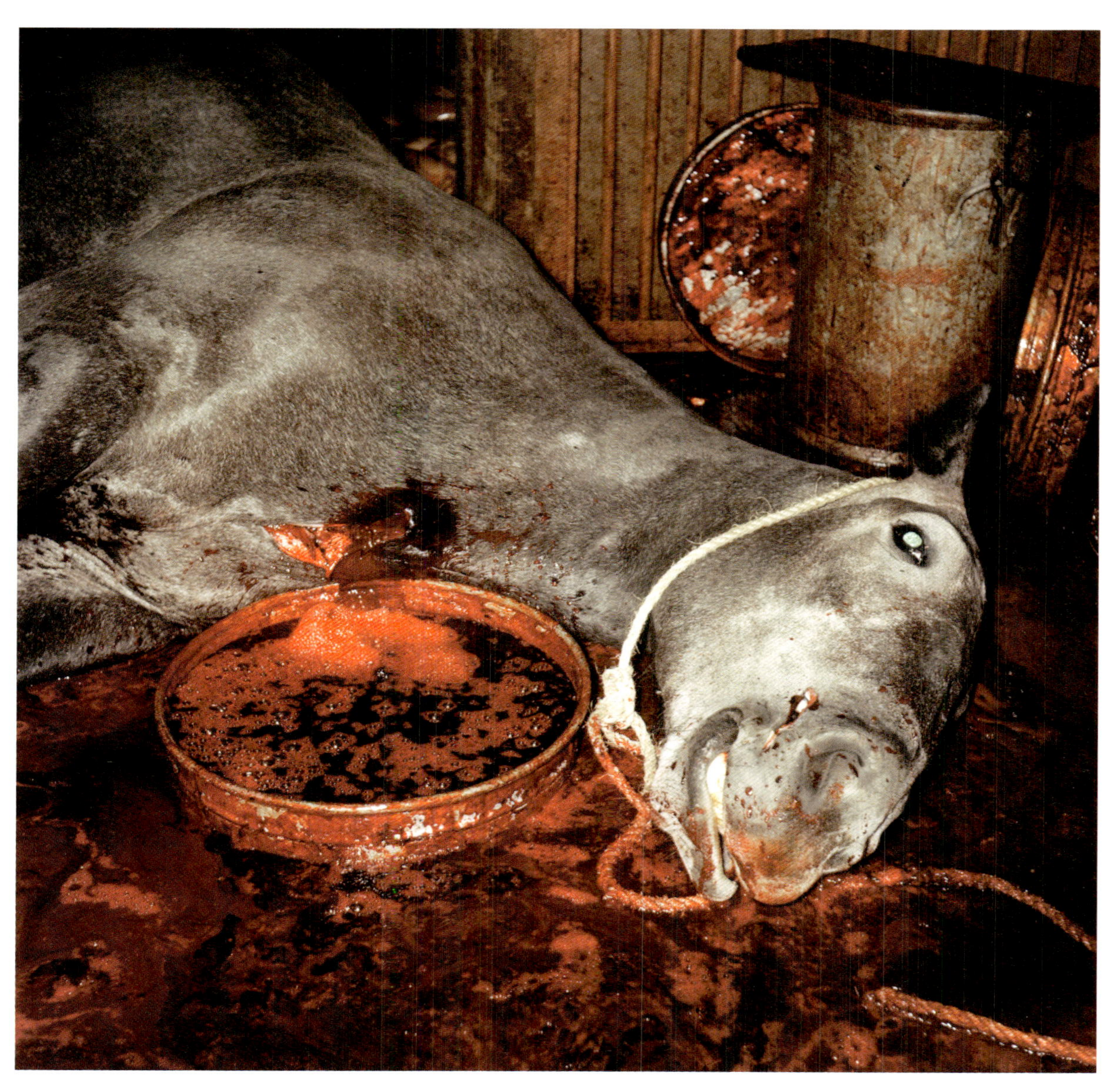

Madame d'Ora

Schlachthofpferd, in geronnenem Blut liegend,

a. d. Serie: *Schlachthof*, vor 1958

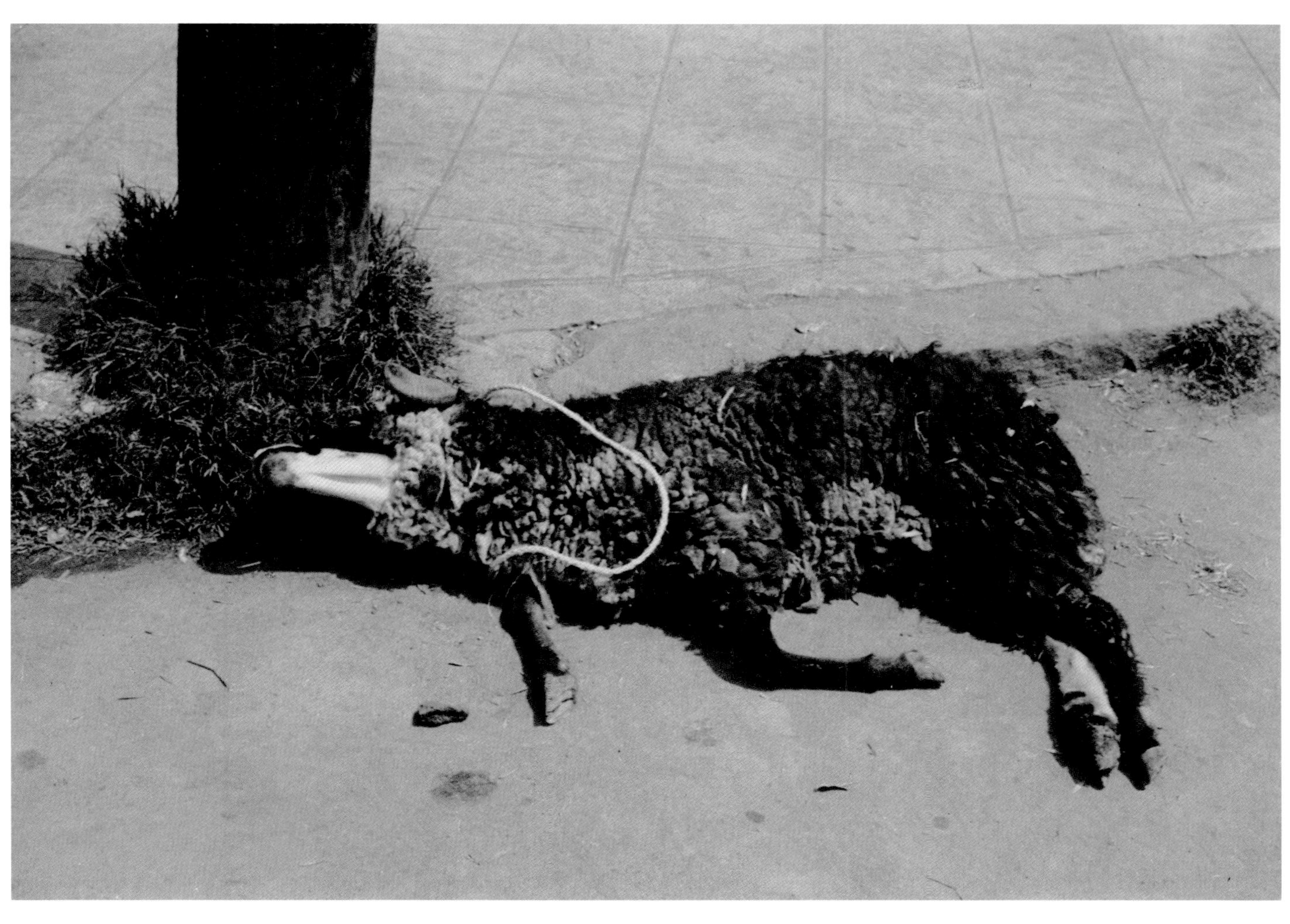

Manuel Alvarez Bravo
For the Sheep's Wool, 1932

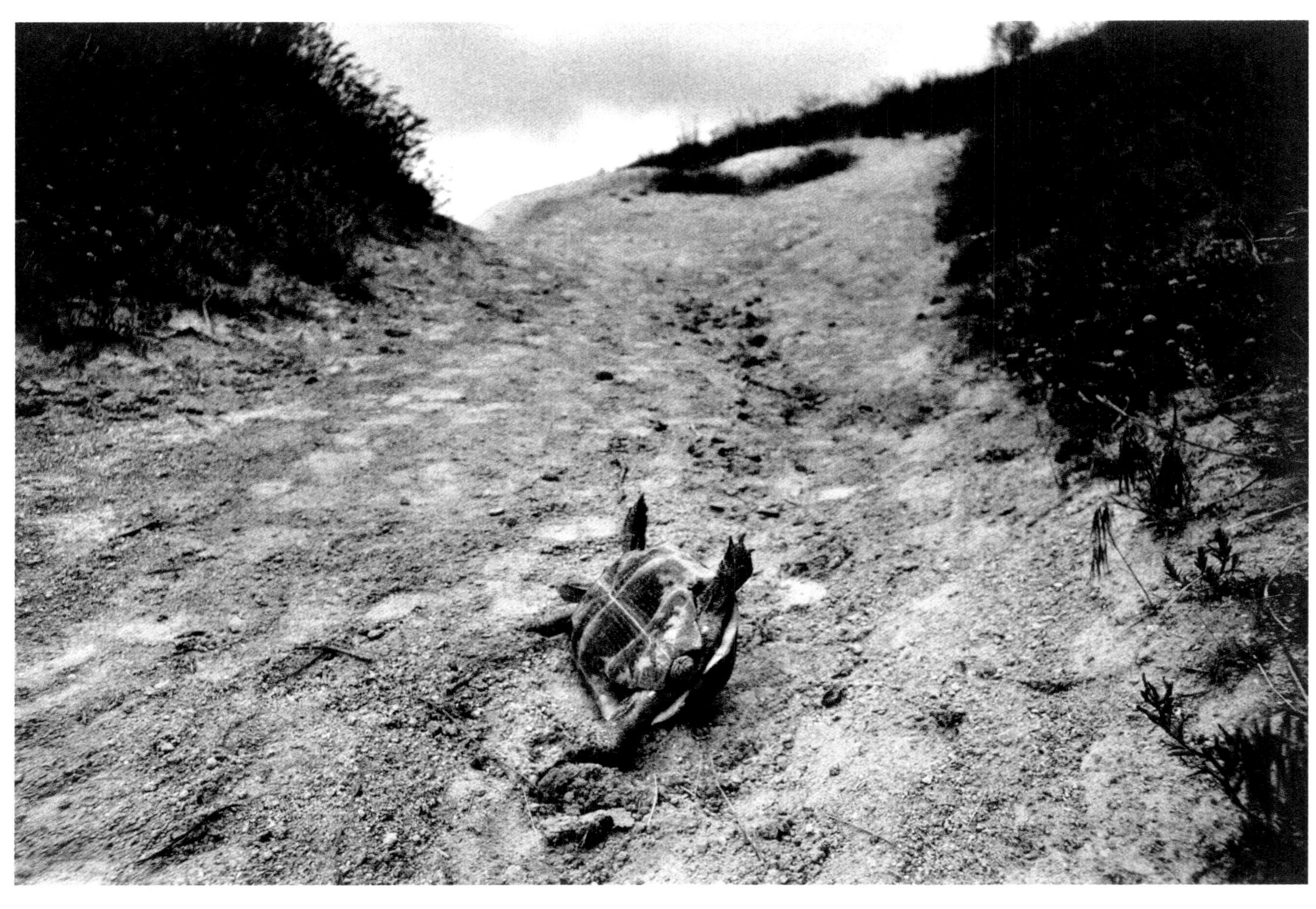

Josef Koudelka

Türkei, 1984

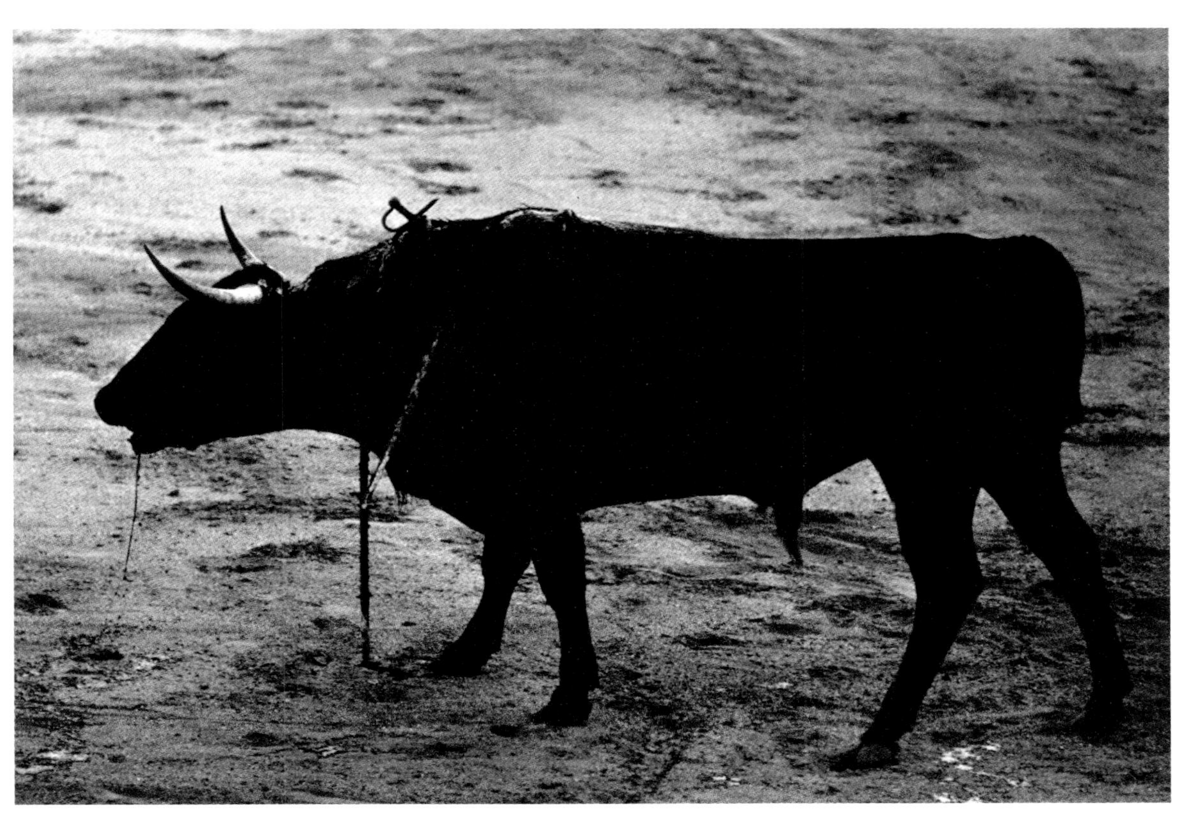

Christer Strömholm
Spanien, 1959

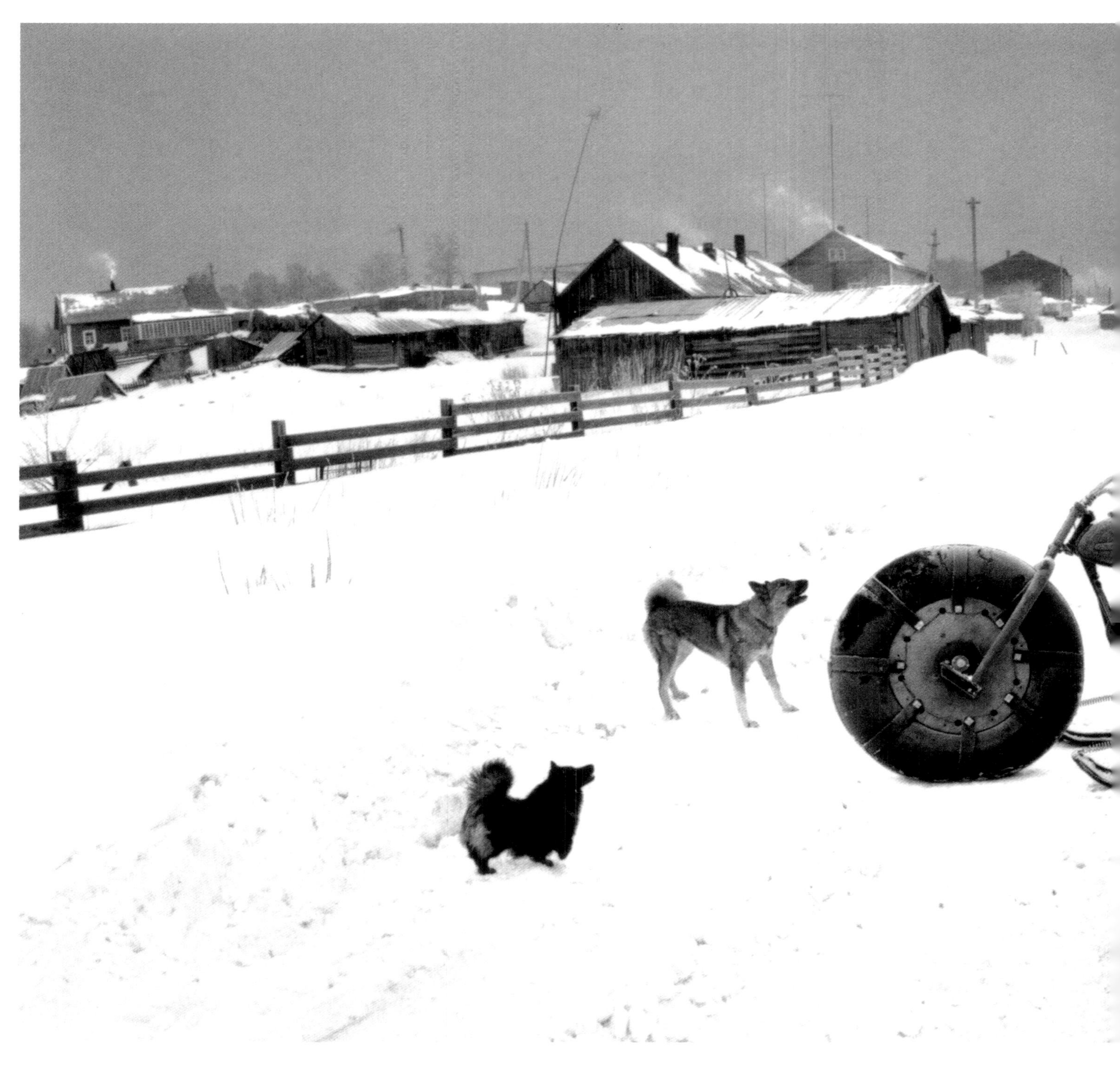

Pentti Sammallahti
Solovki, White Sea, Russland, 1992

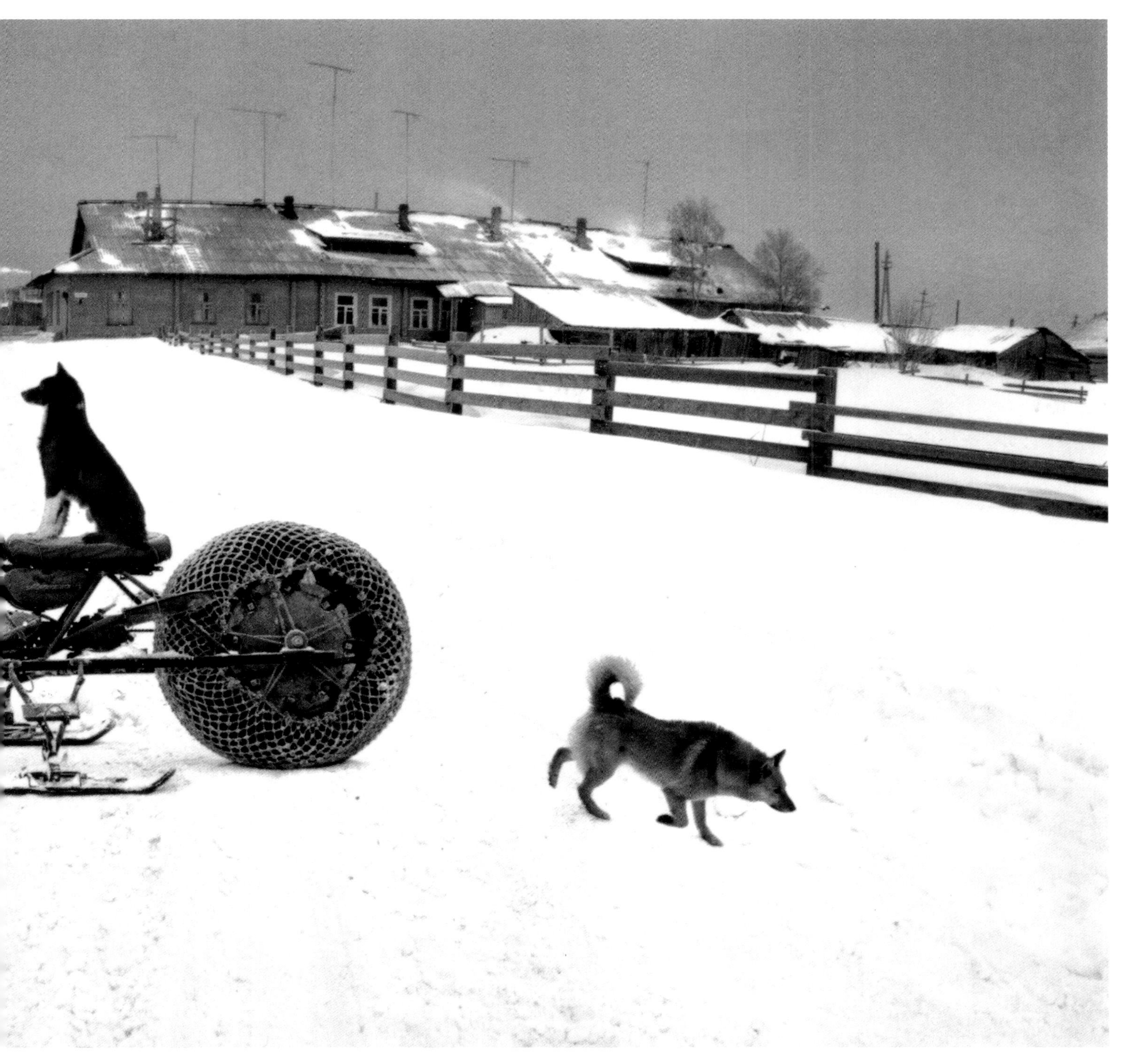

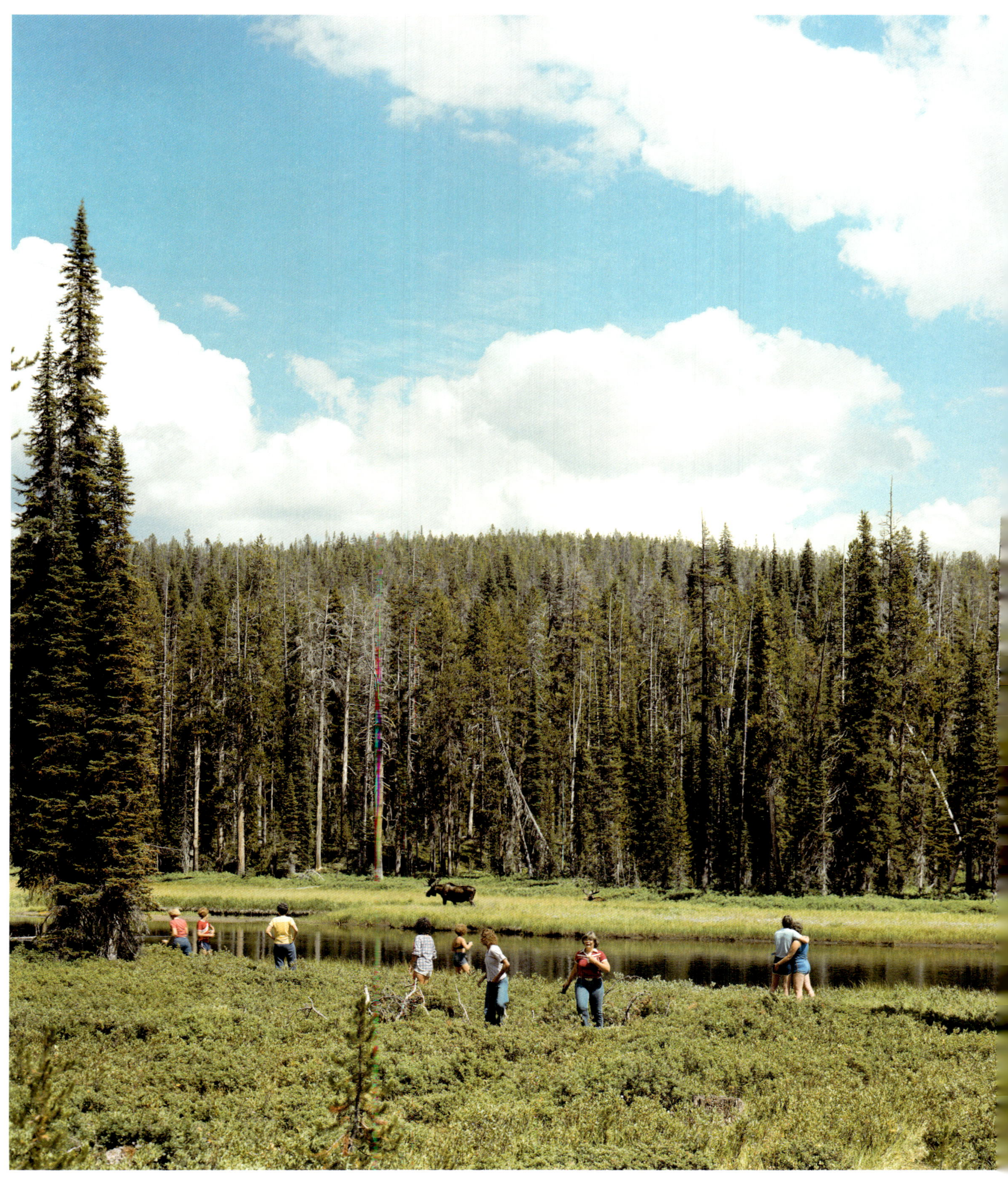

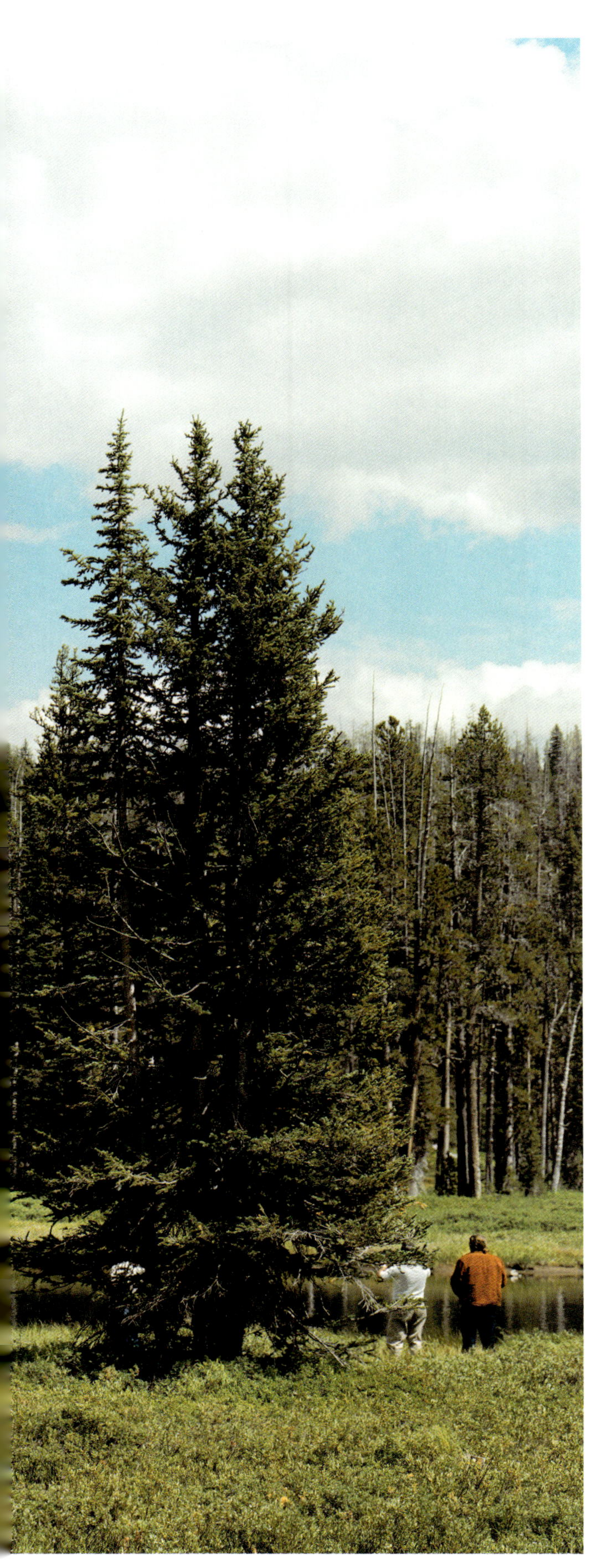

Joel Sternfeld

Yellowstone National Park, 1979

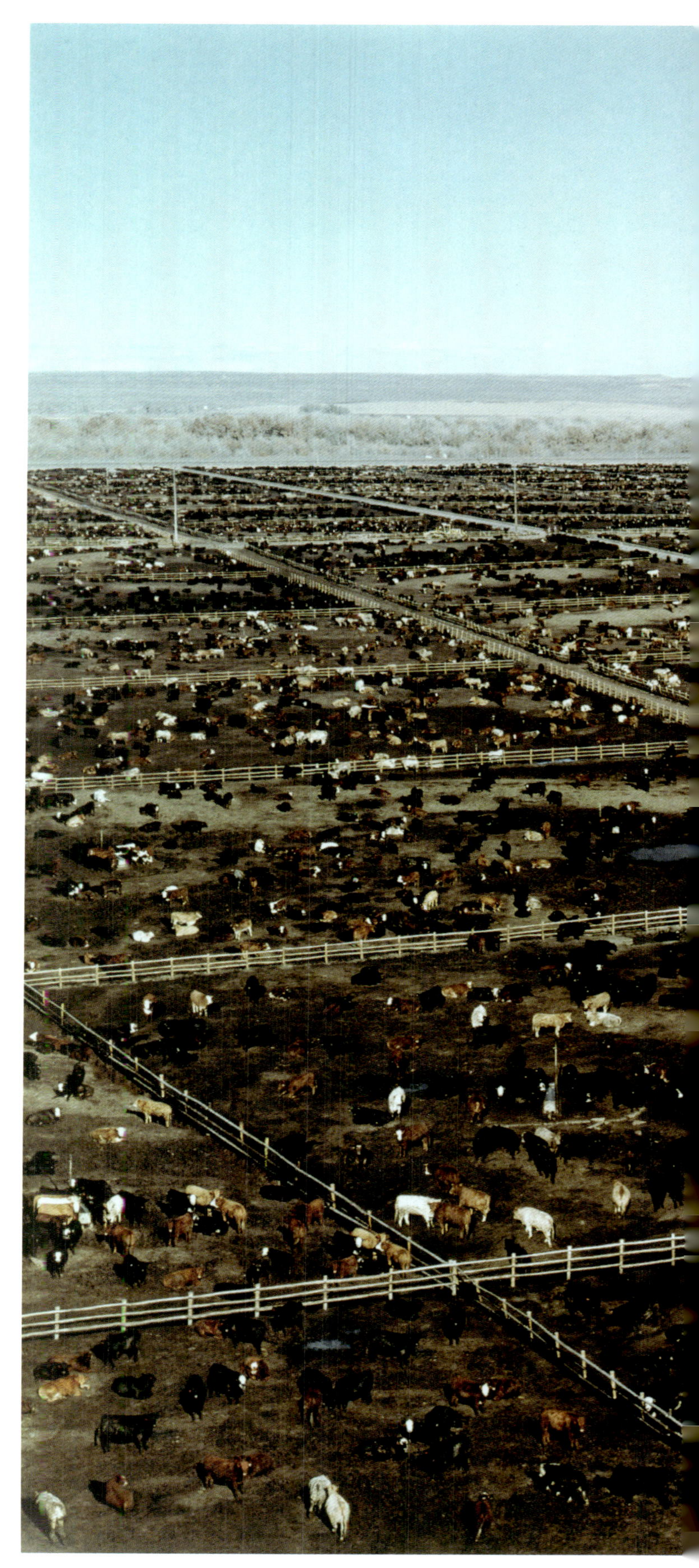

Andreas Gursky

Greeley, 2002

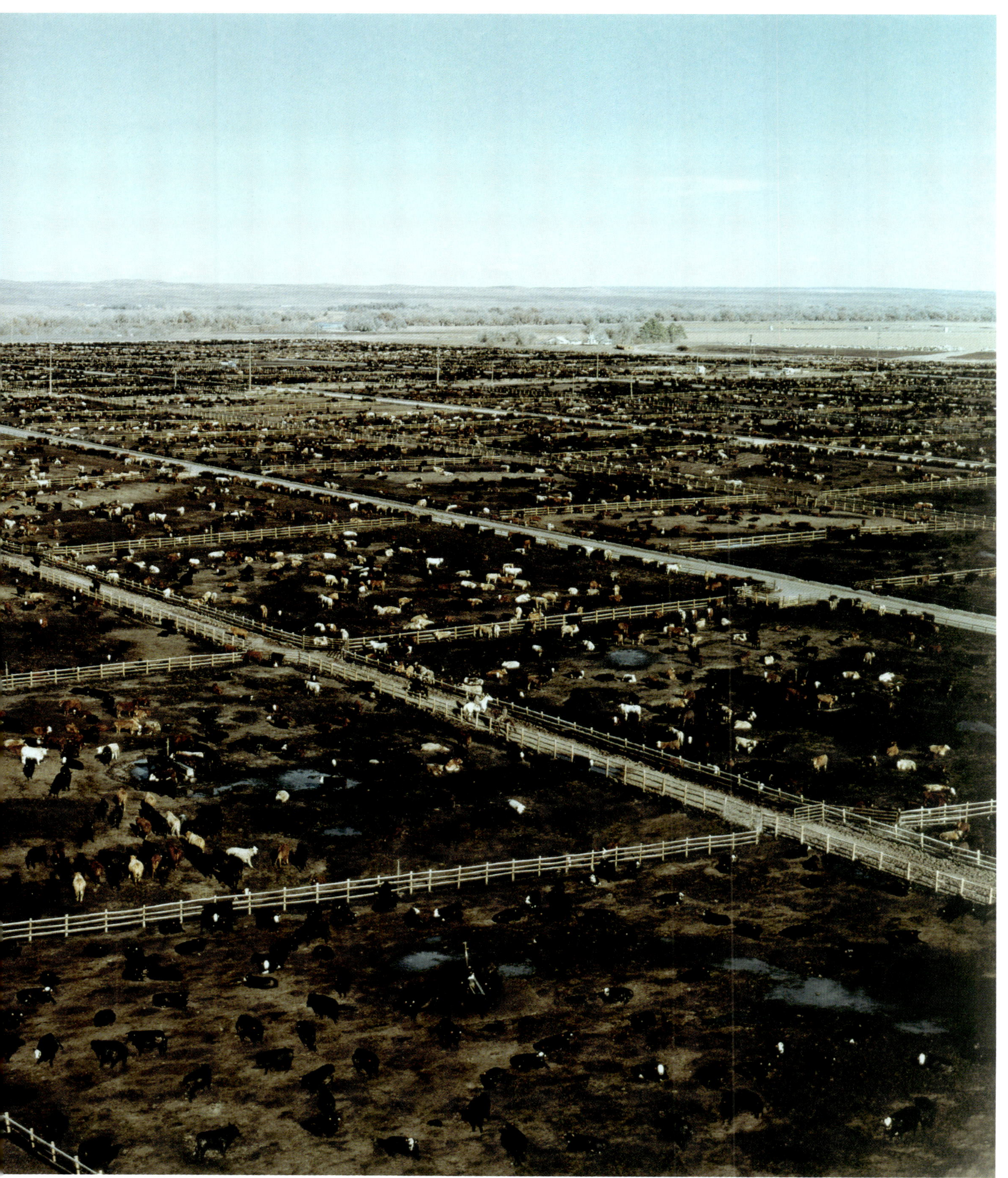

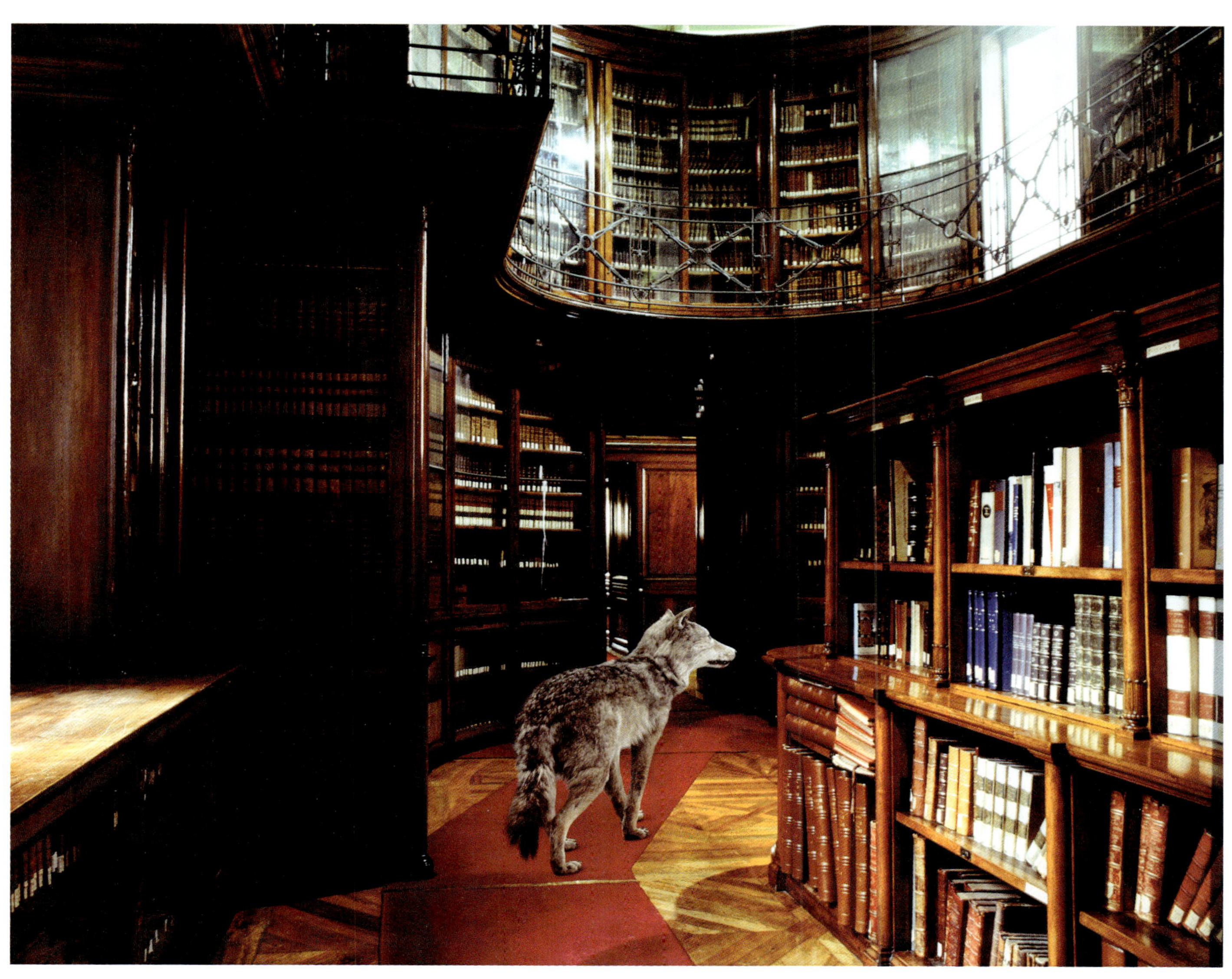

Karen Knorr

The peripatetic philosopher, 1998

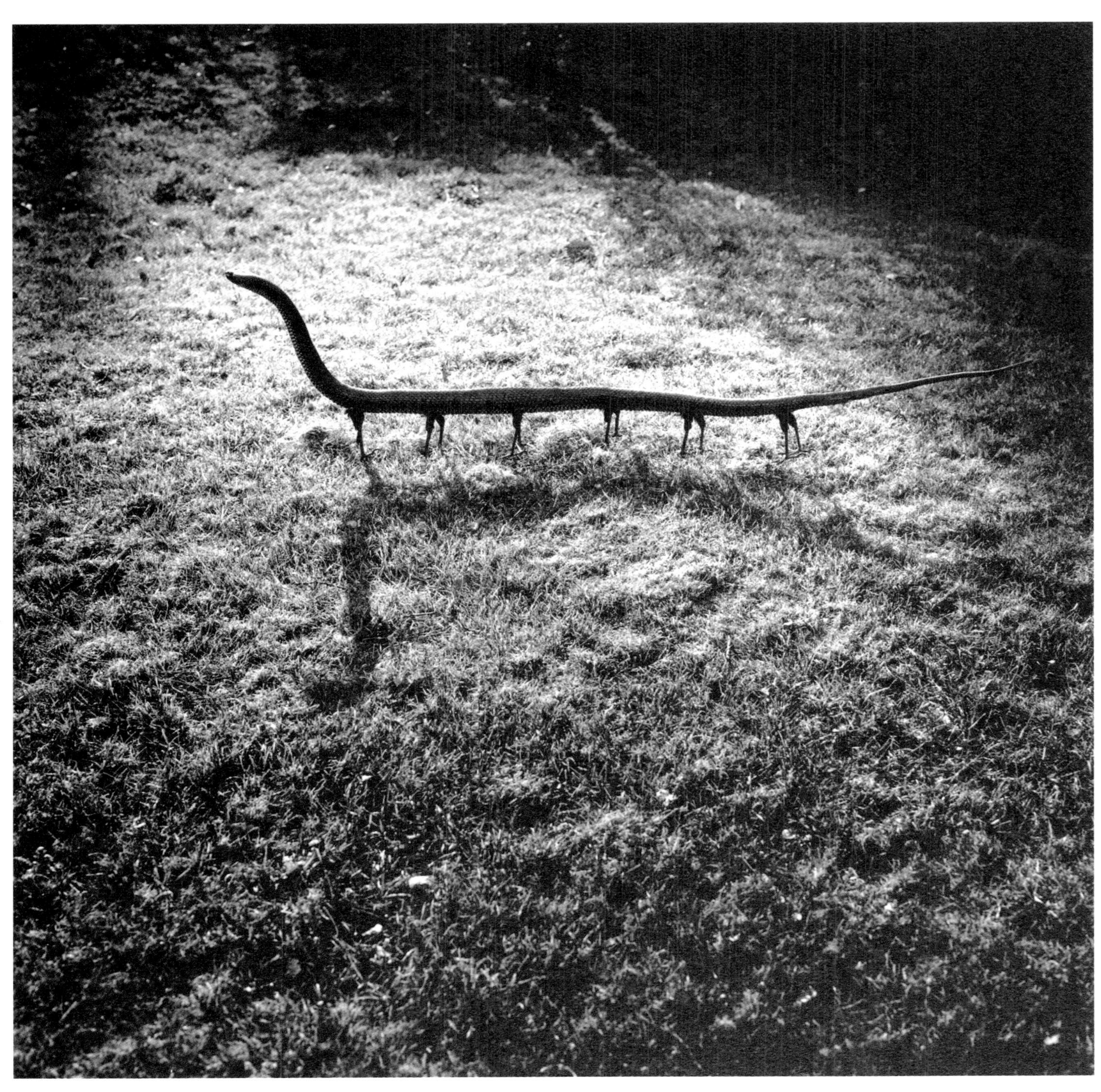

Joan Fontcuberta / Pere Formiguera

Solenoglypha Polipodida, 1986

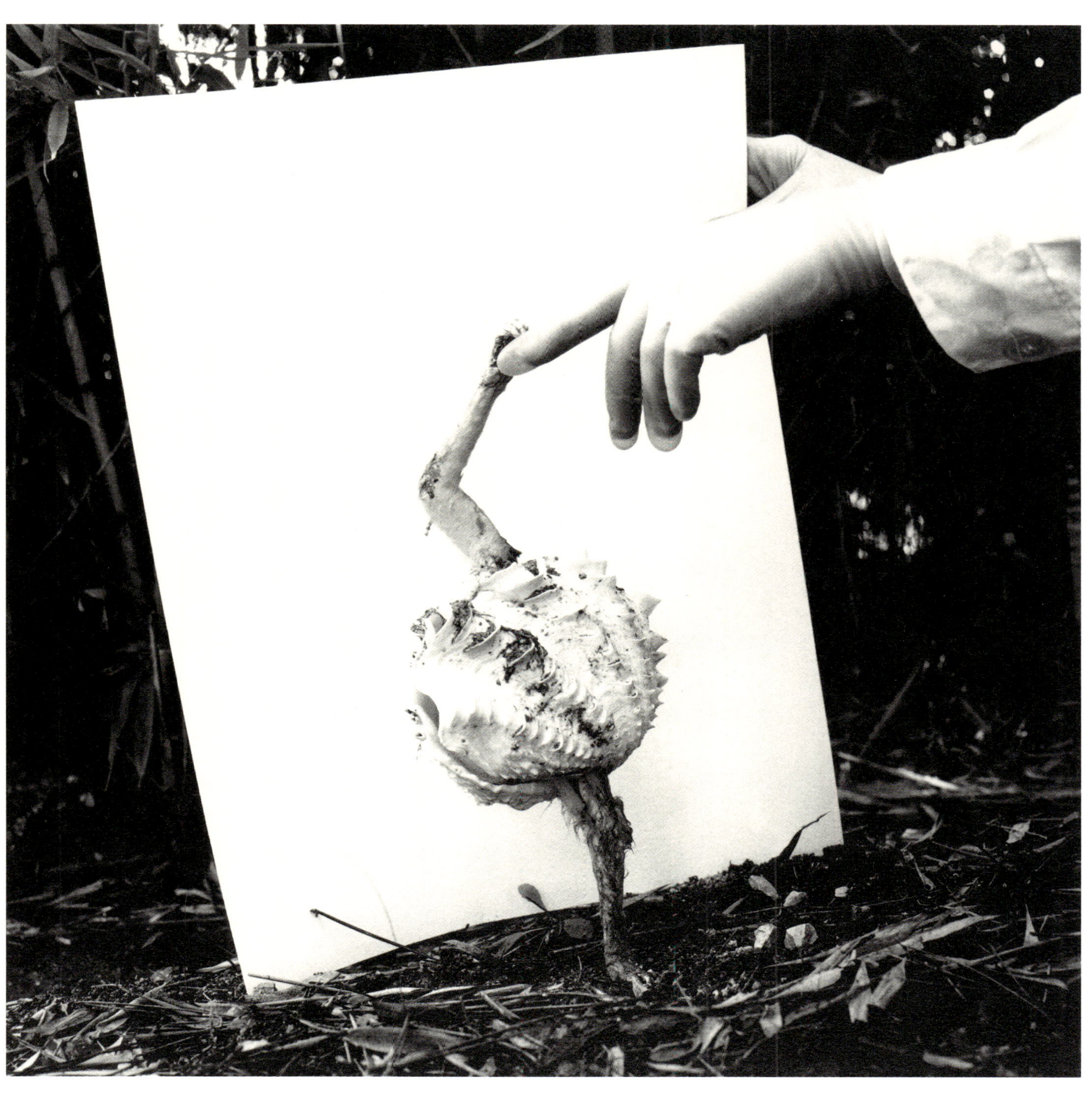

Joan Fontcuberta / Pere Formiguera

Micostrium Vulgaris, 1986

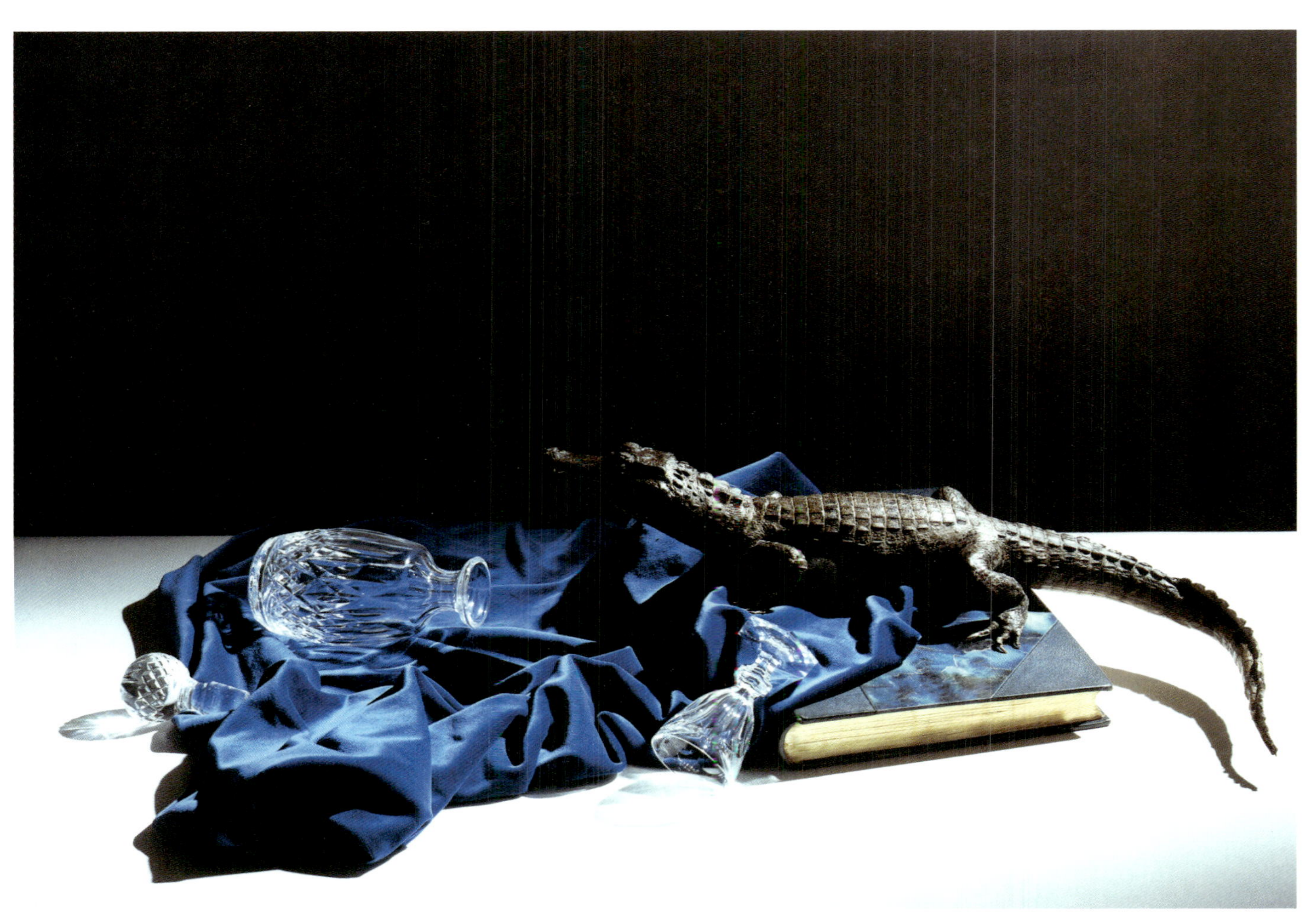

Olivier Richon
The Passion for Mourning, 1985

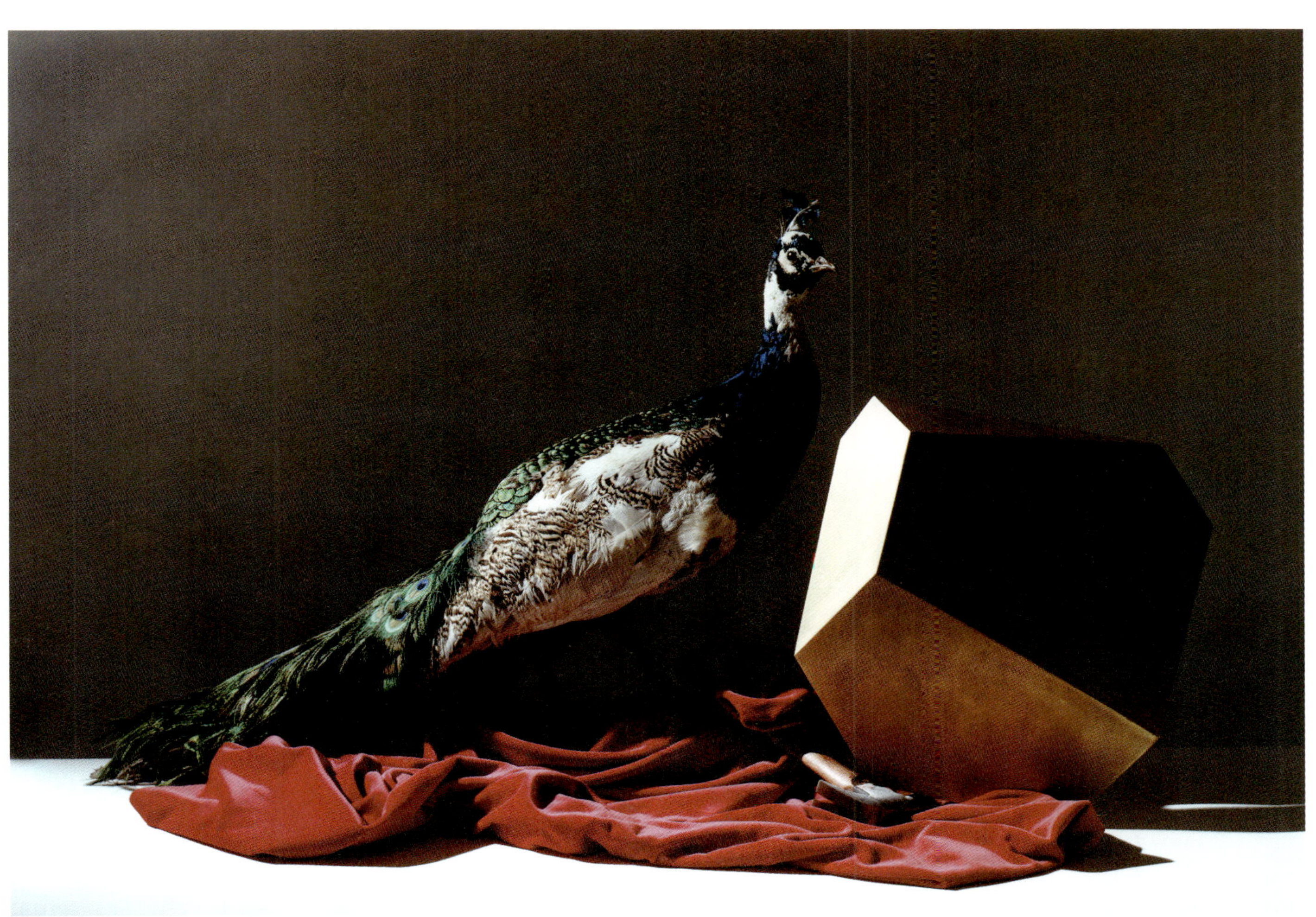

Olivier Richon

The Anatomy of Melancholia, 1985

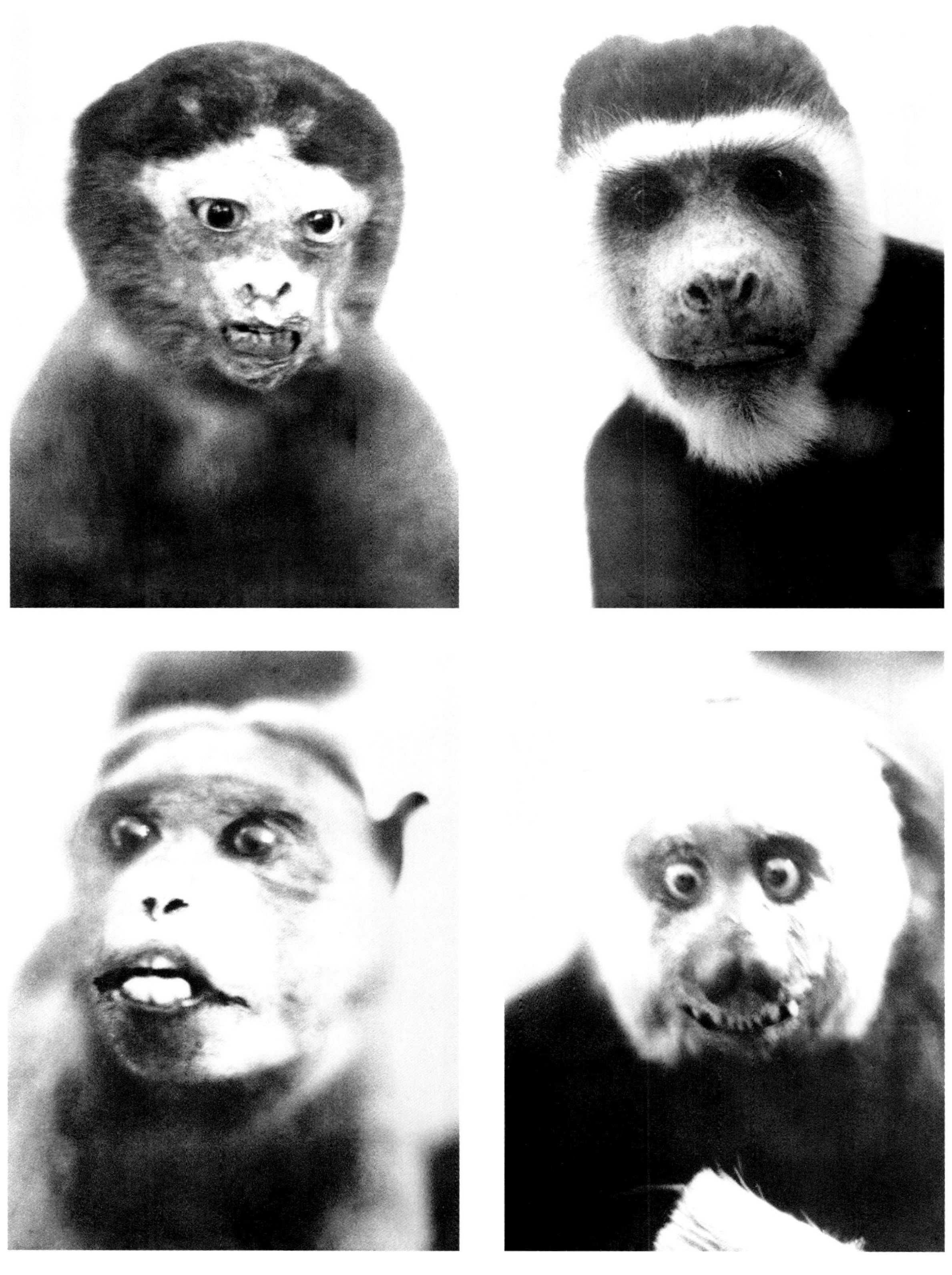

Jochen Lempert
Ohne Titel, 1997

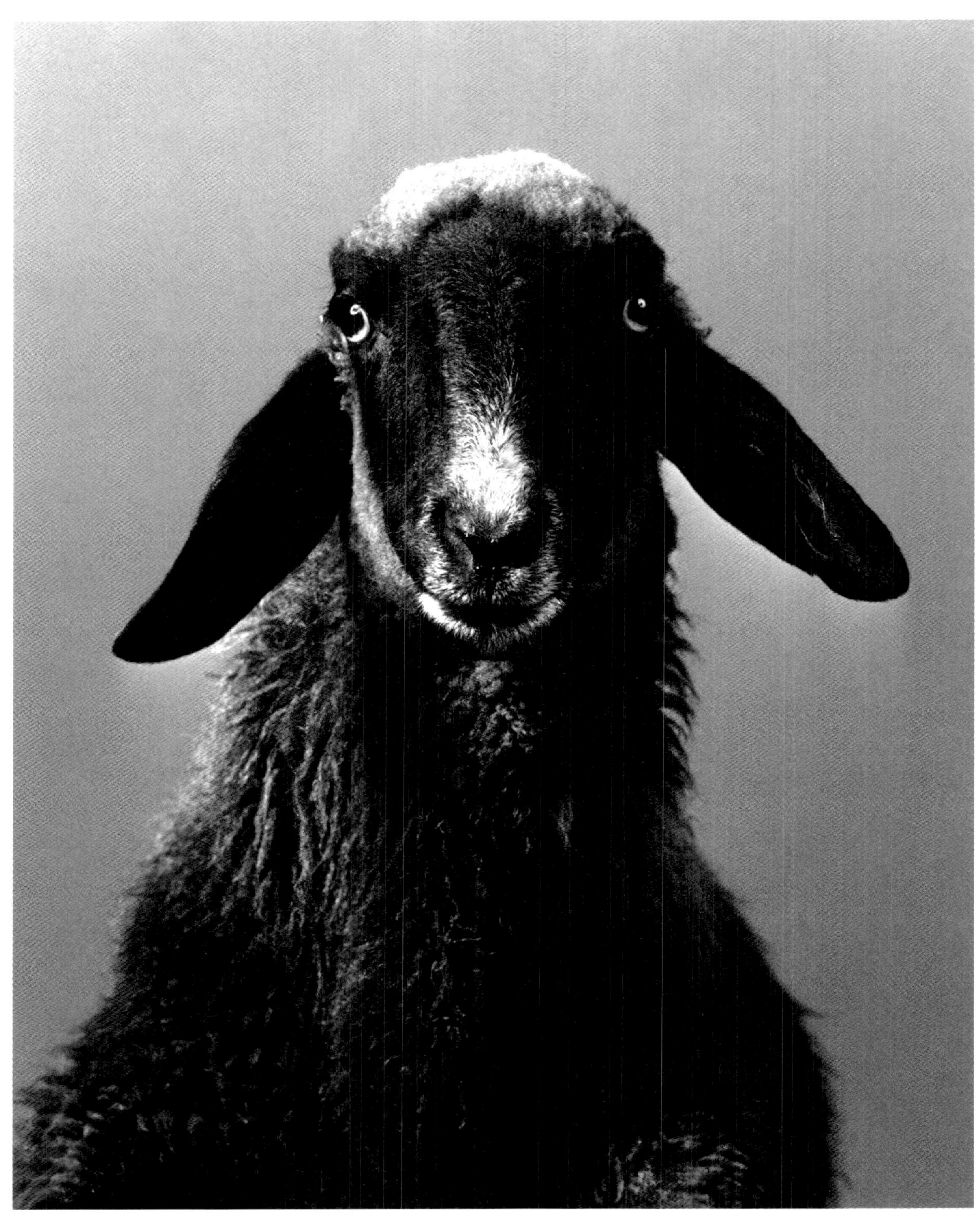

Walter Schels

Schwarzes Schaf, 1984

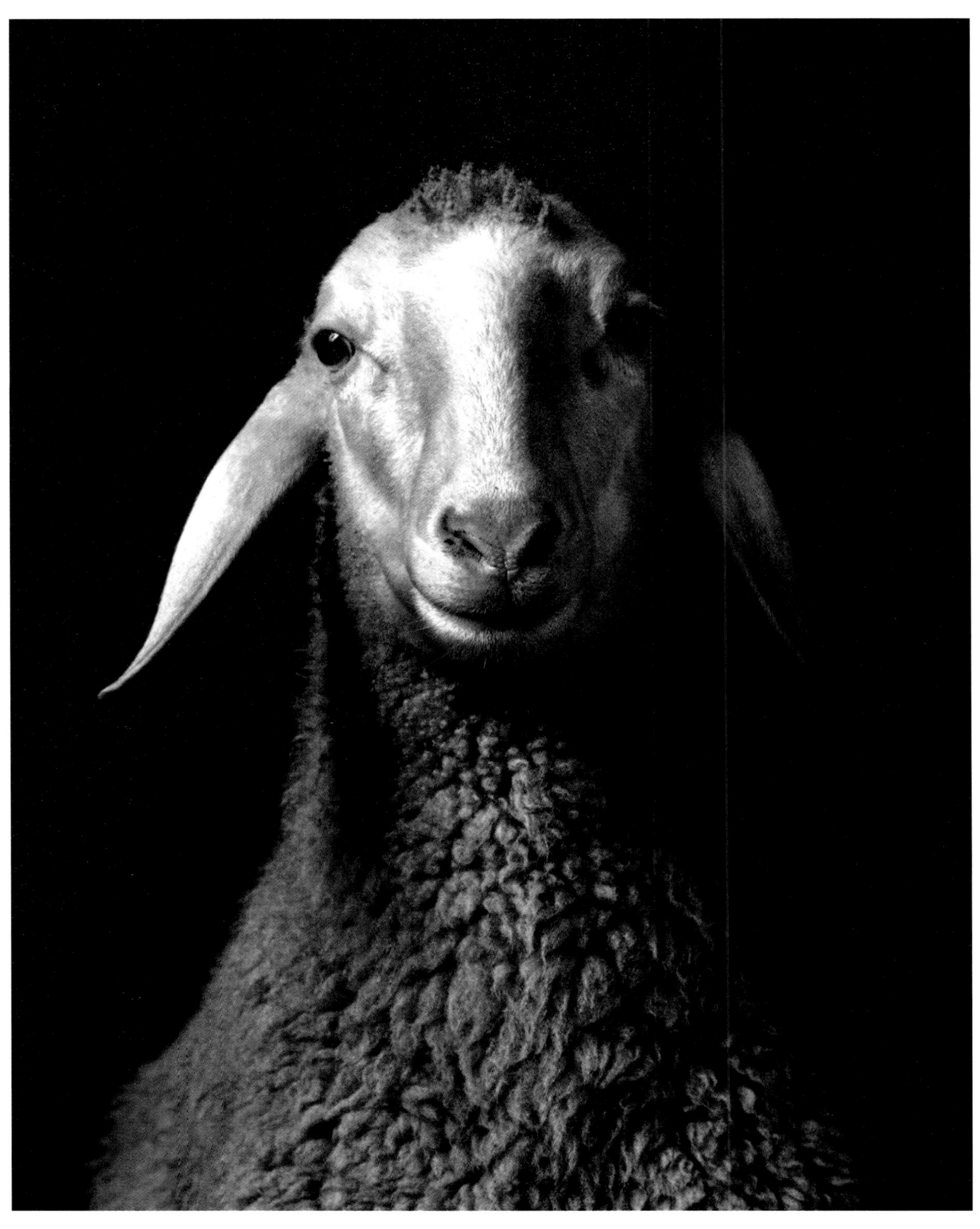

Walter Schels
Schaf, 1984

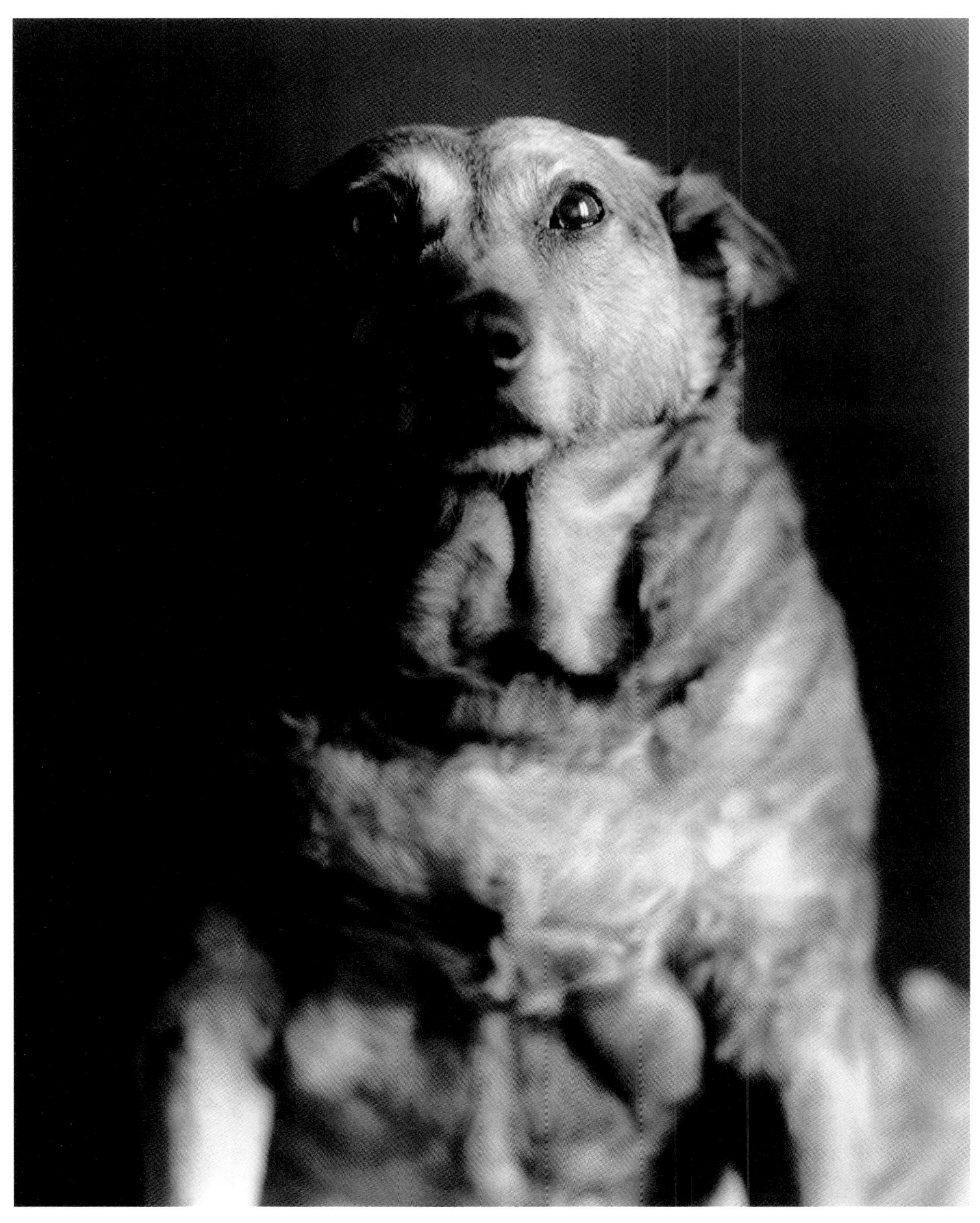

Humberto Rivas
Tomasa, 1988

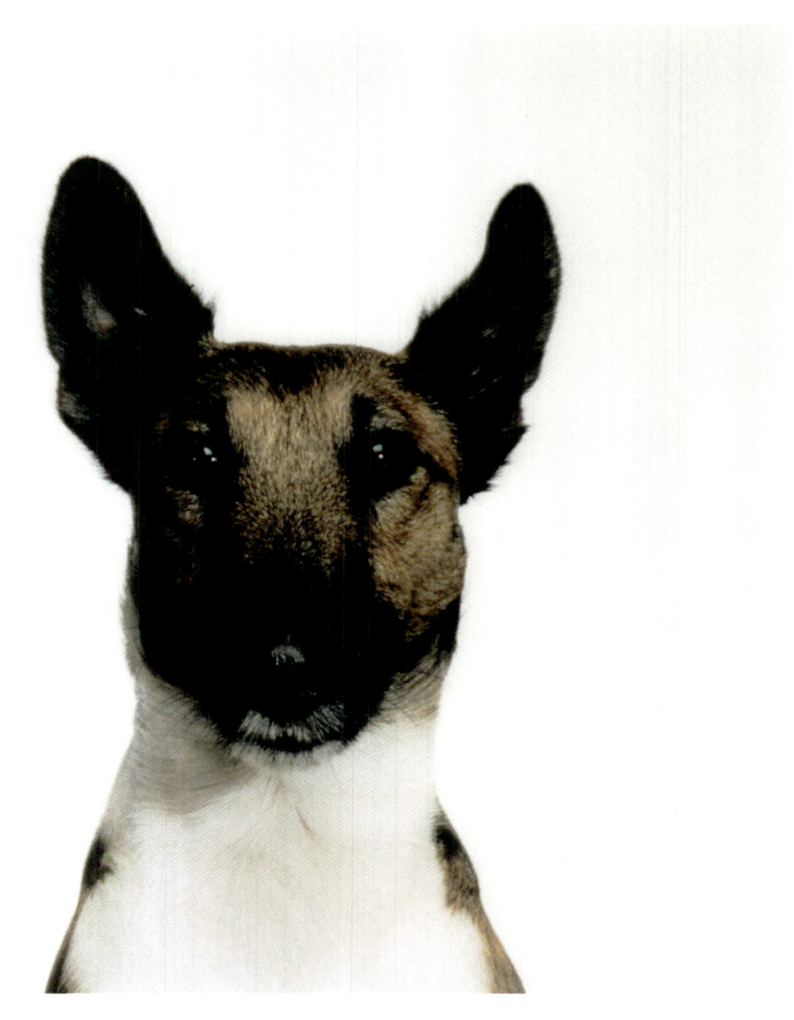

Rosemarie Trockel
Hannah I, 1993

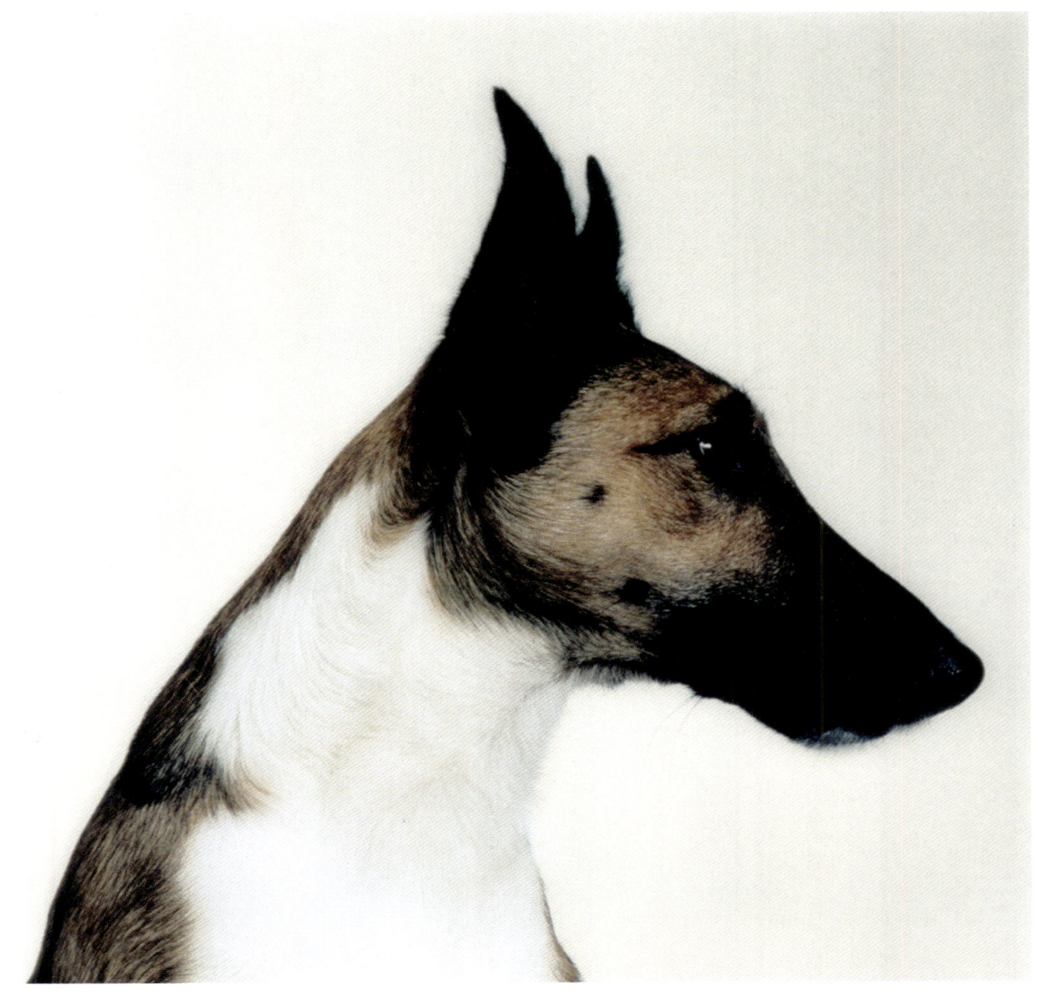

Rosemarie Trockel
Hannah II, 1993

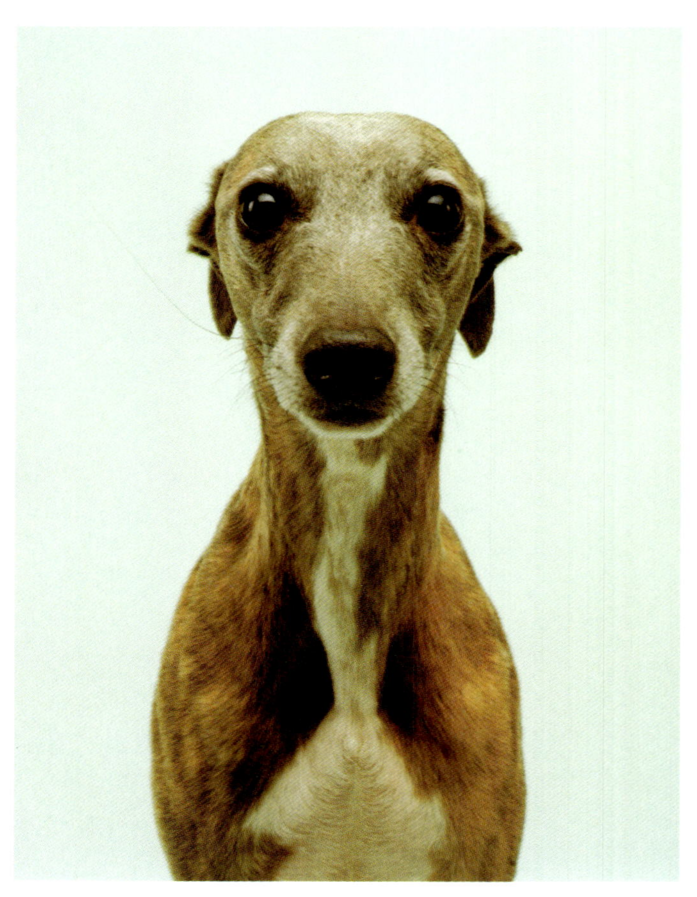

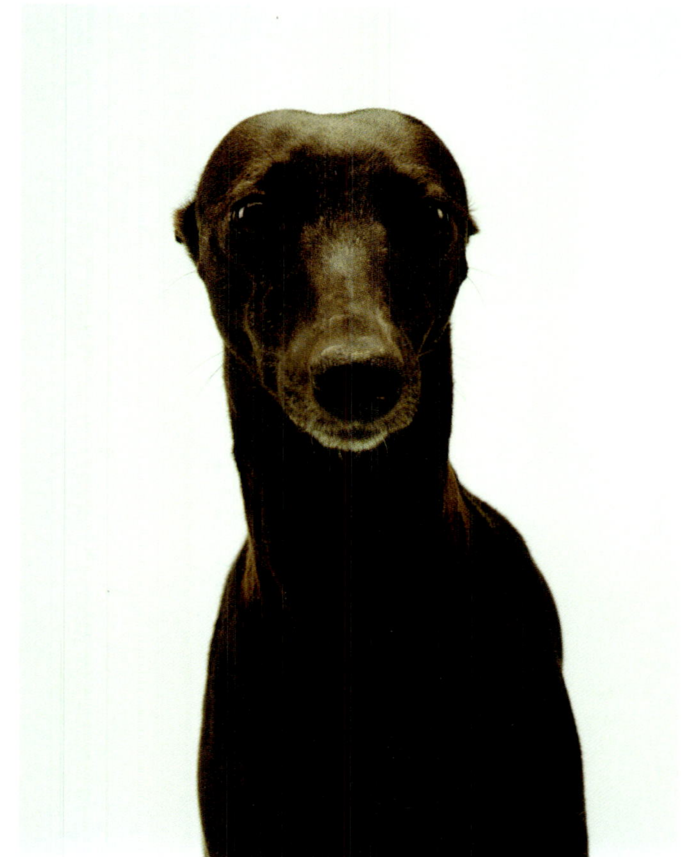

Jo Longhurst
a. d. Serie: *I know what you're thinking*, 2003

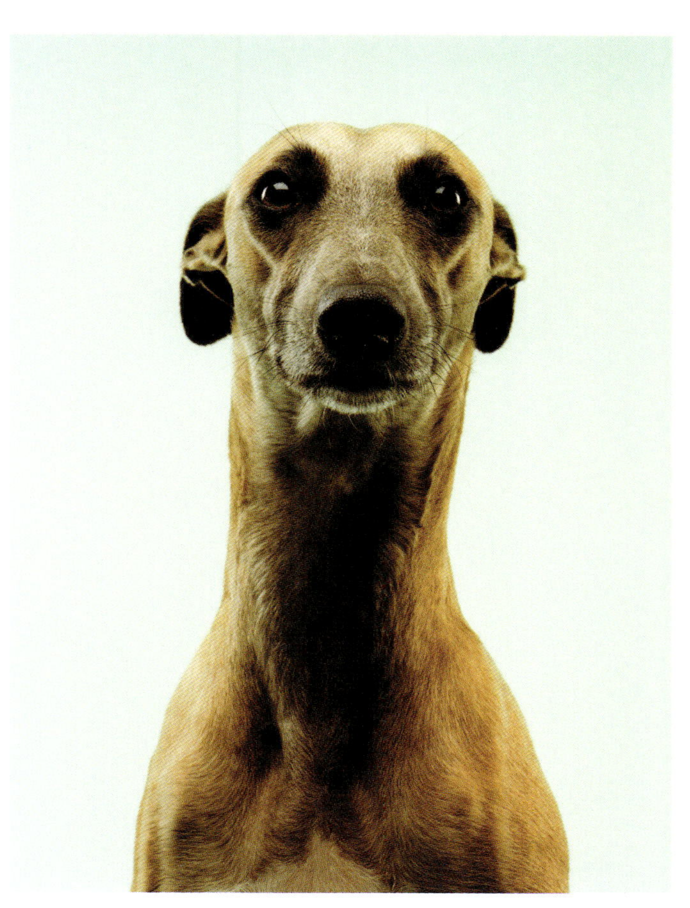

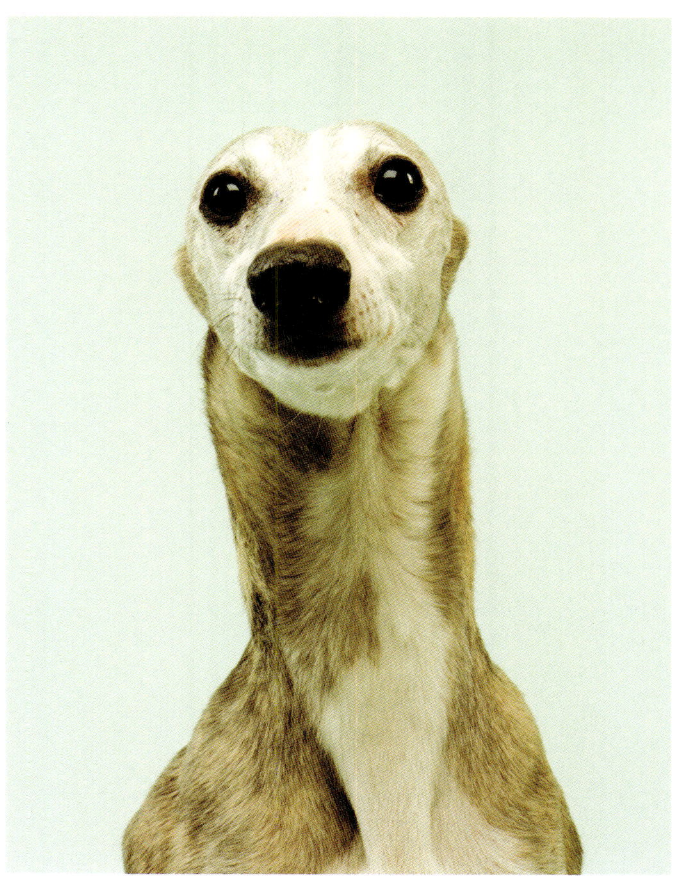

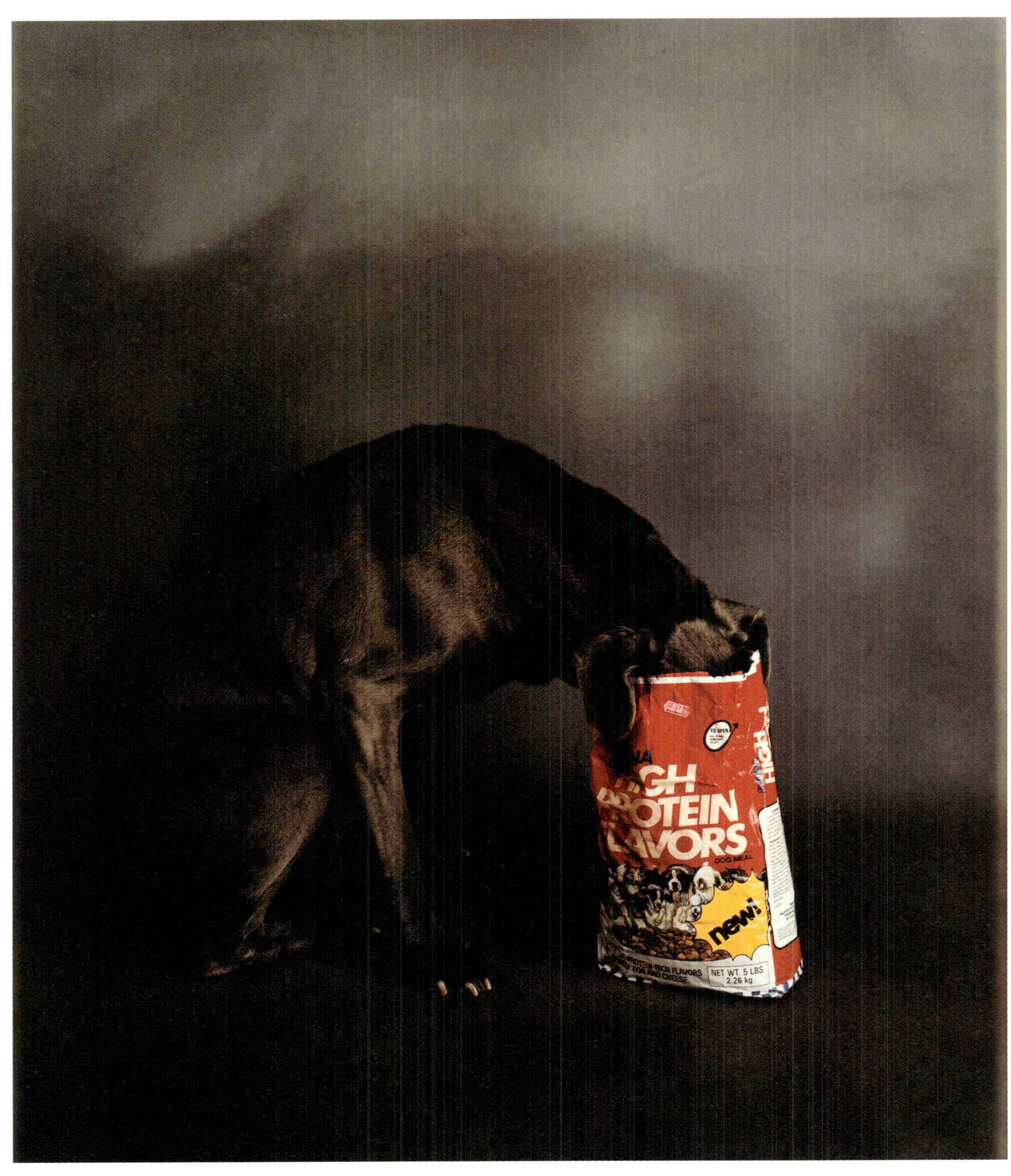

William Wegman

Purina Red, 1981

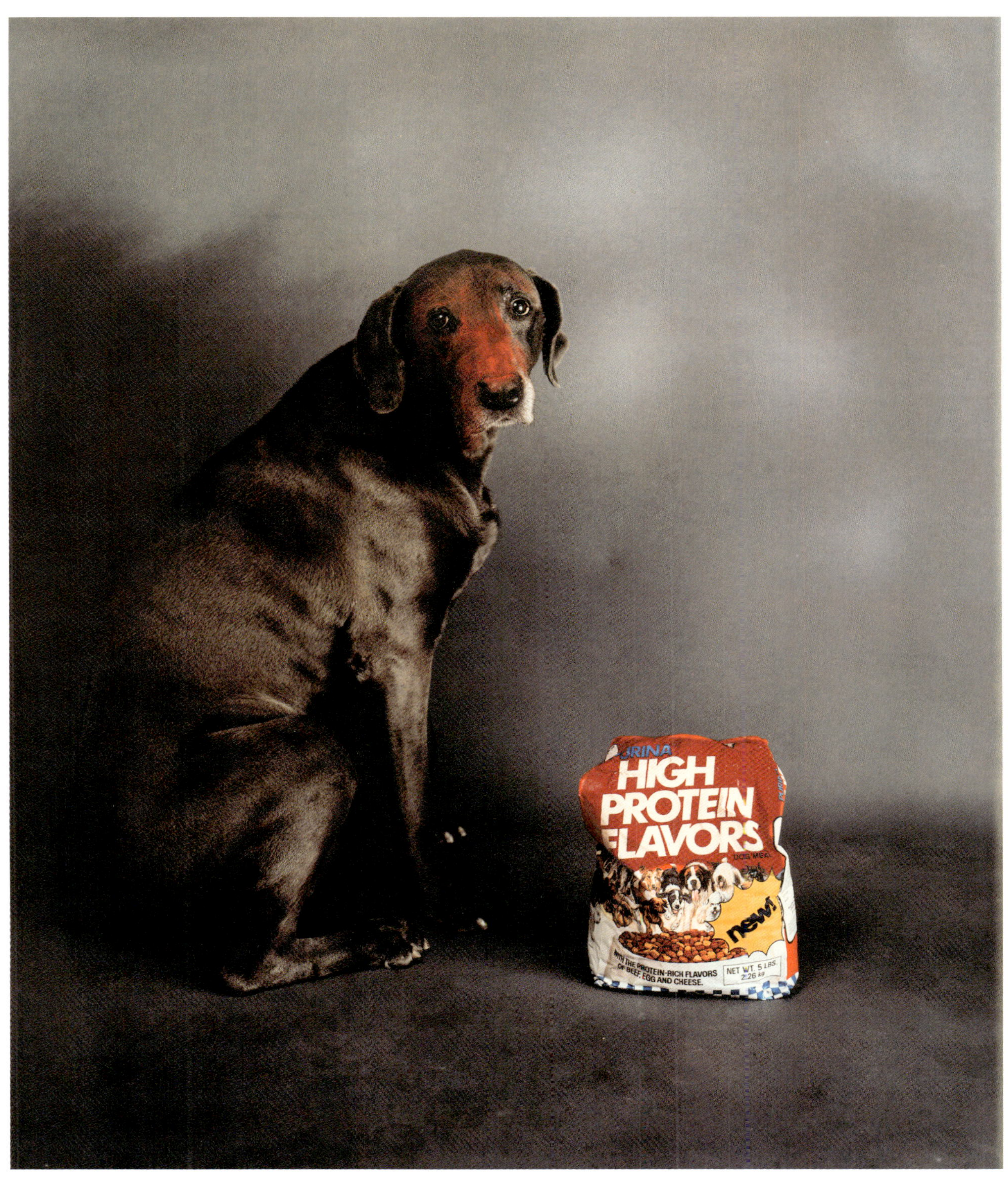
URINA
HIGH
PROTEIN
FLAVORS
DOG MEAL
new!
WITH THE PROTEIN-RICH FLAVORS
OF BEEF, EGG AND CHEESE.
NET WT. 5 LBS.
2.26 kg

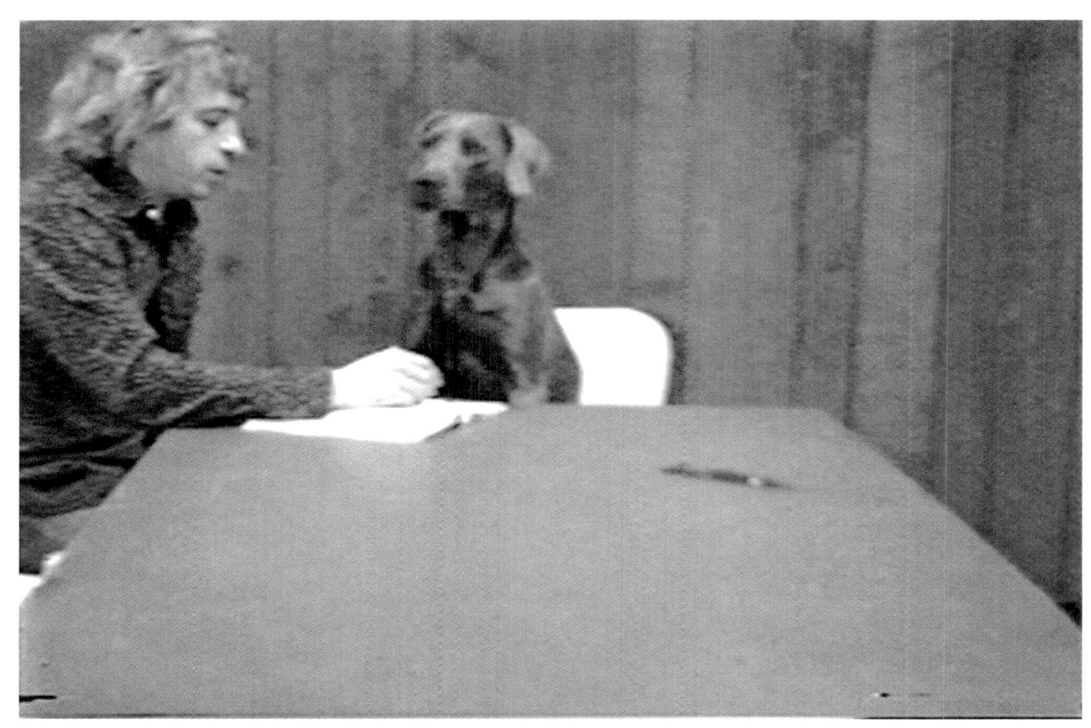

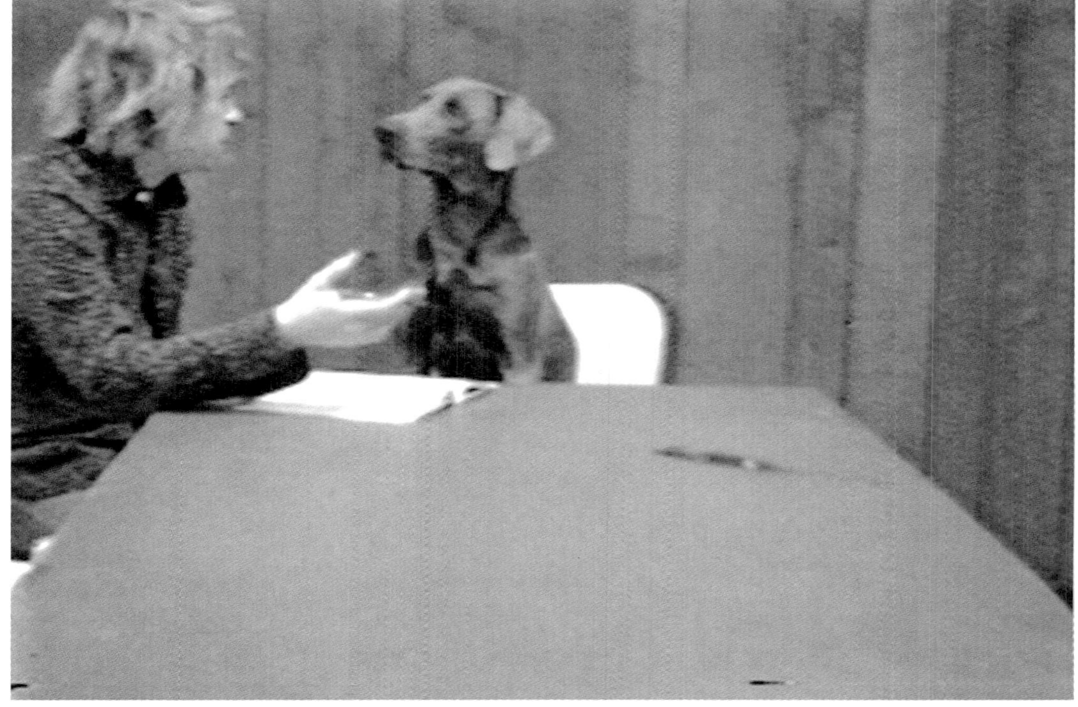

William Wegman

Video Stills aus/from *Spelling Lessons*, 1973/74

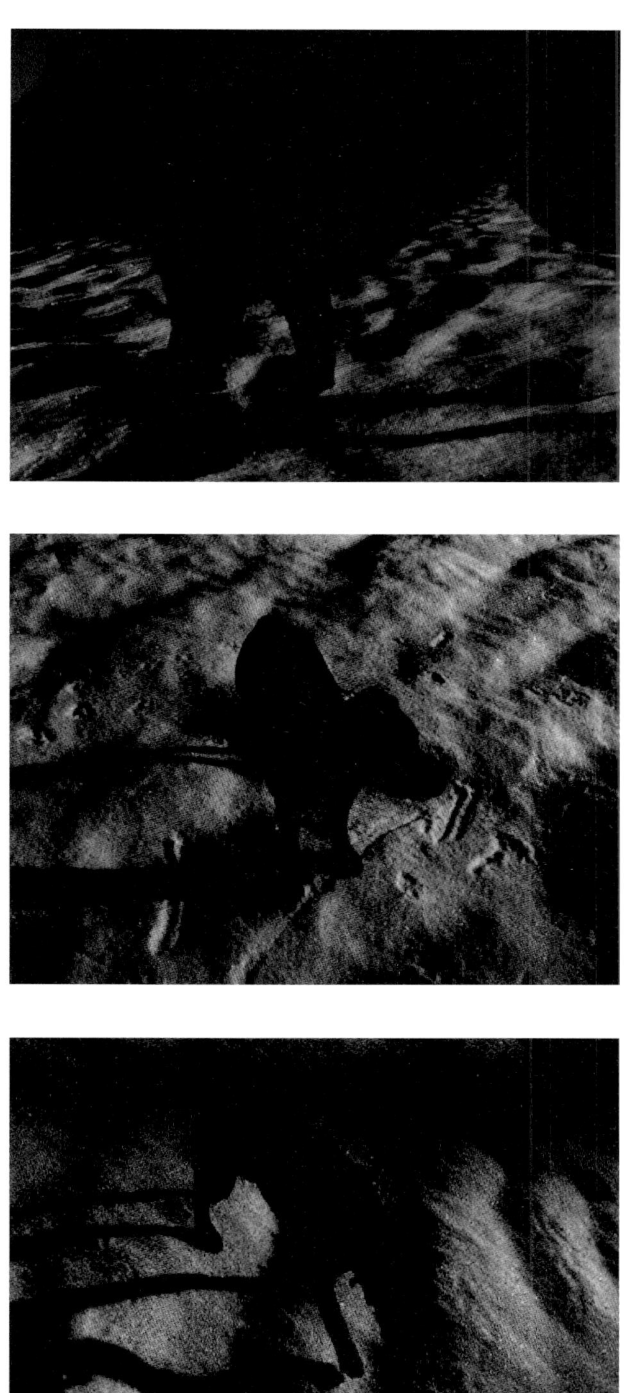

Per Maning

Video Stills aus/from: *Now you see me, now you don't*, 2002

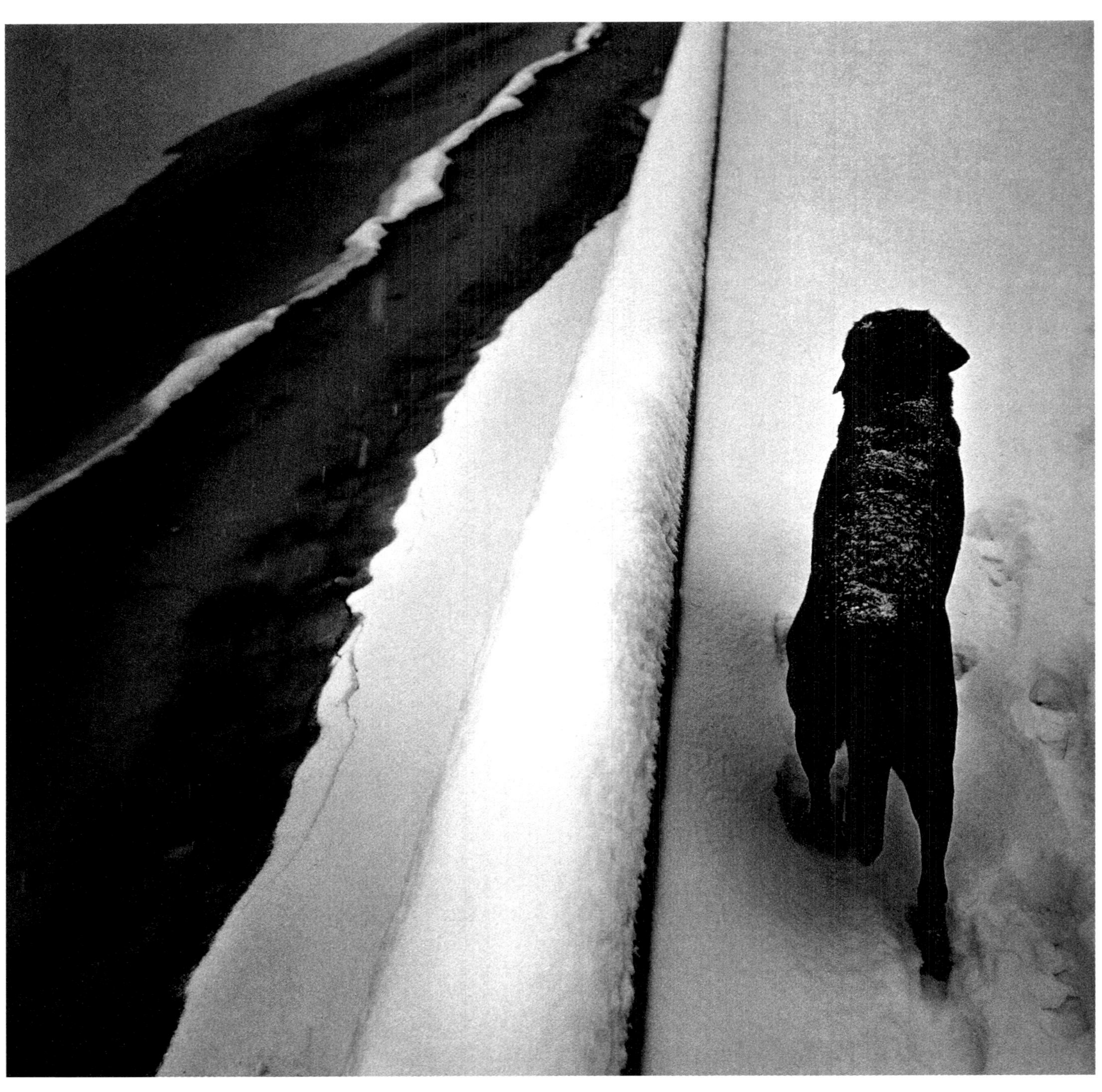

Per Maning
Leo, 1986/87

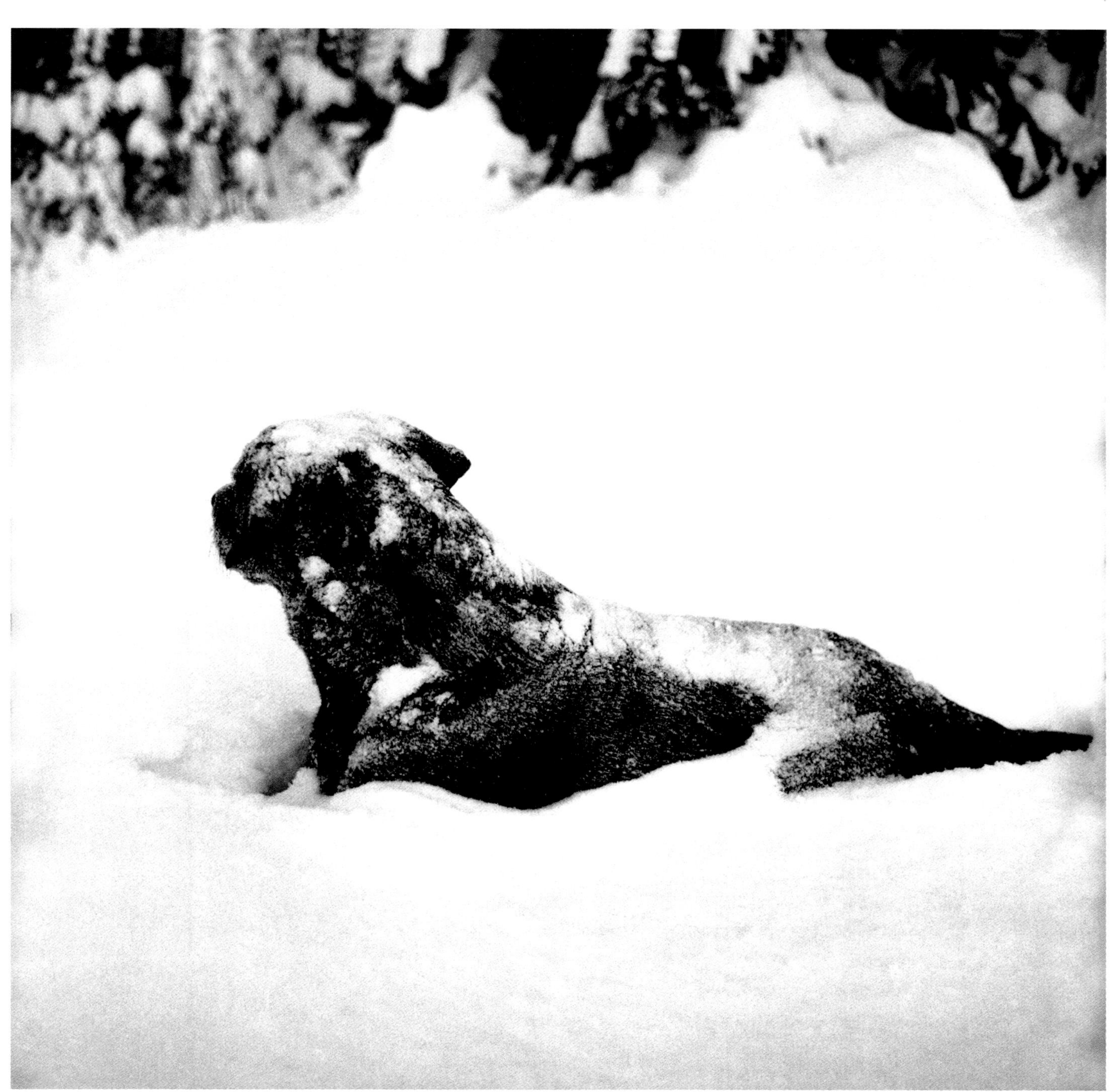

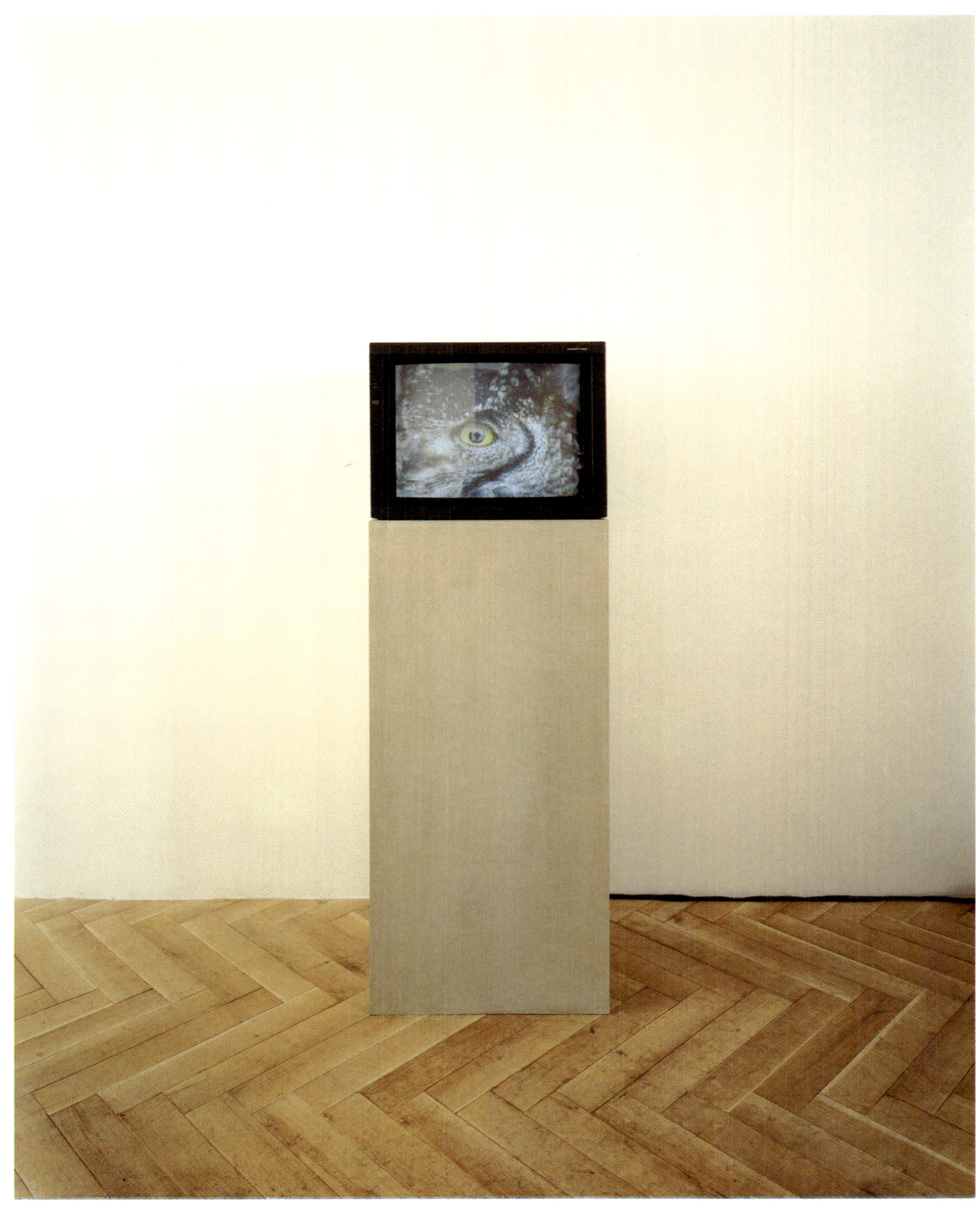

Marie José Burki

Video installation *Hibou*, 1994

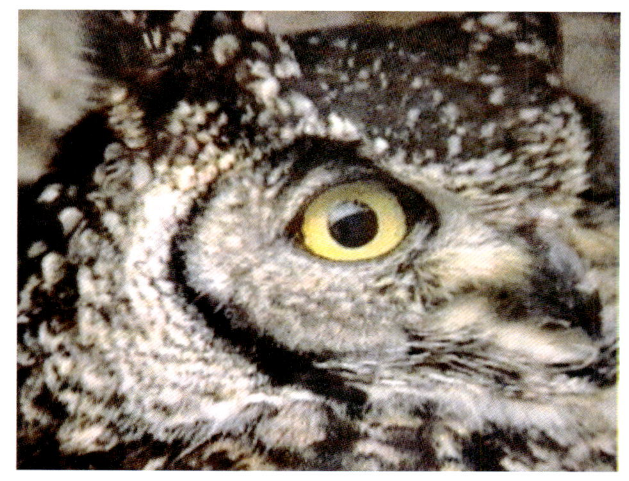

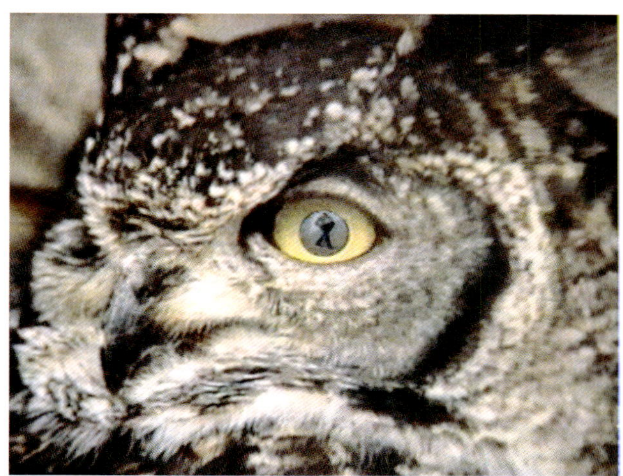

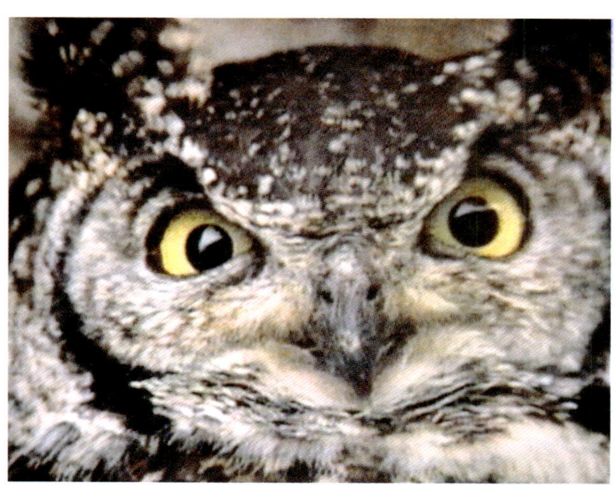

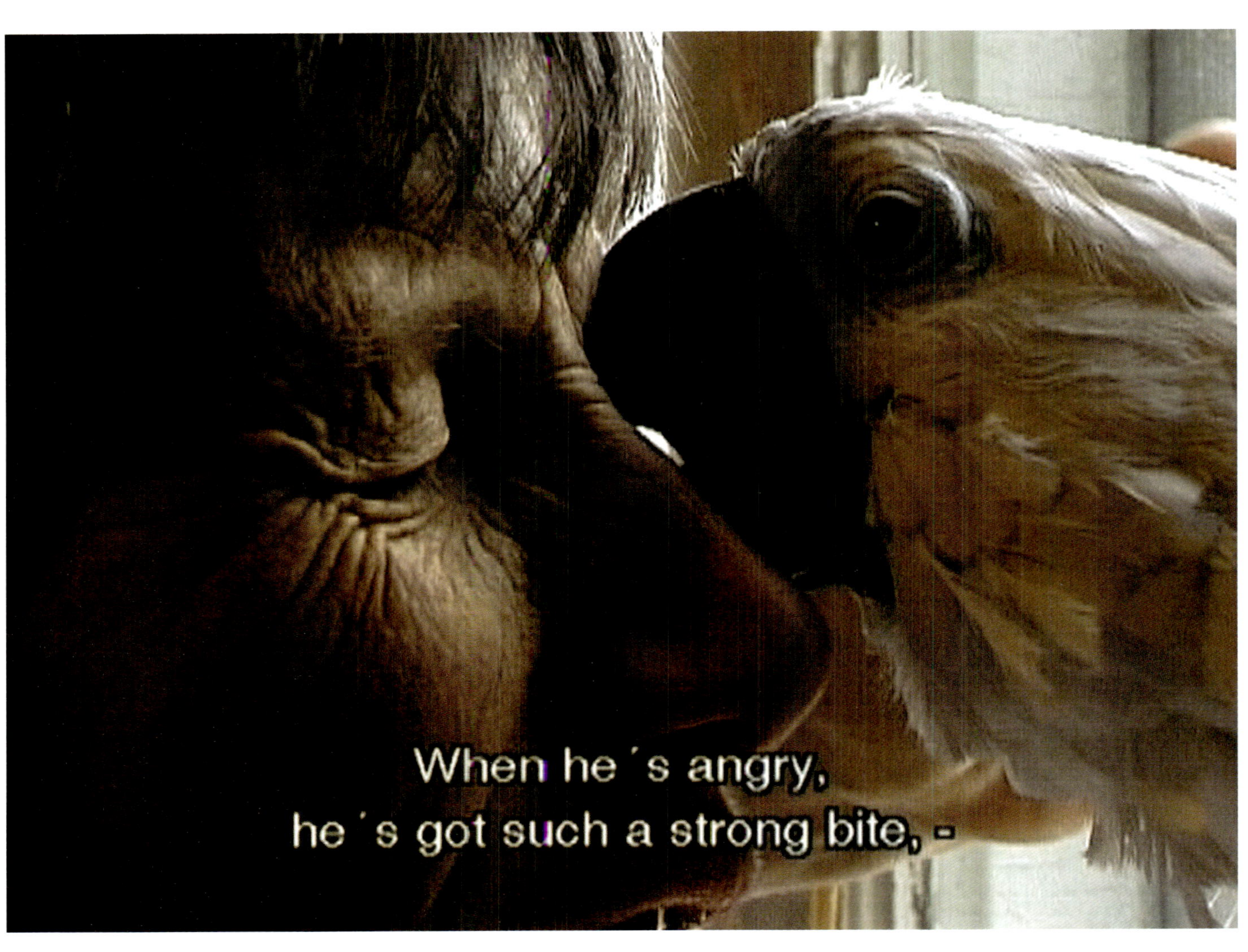

Anne Lise Stenseth
Video Stills aus/from *Birdess*, 2001

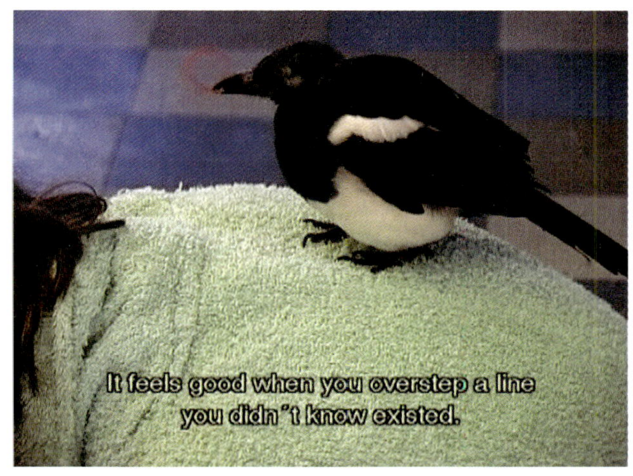
It feels good when you overstep a line
you didn´t know existed.

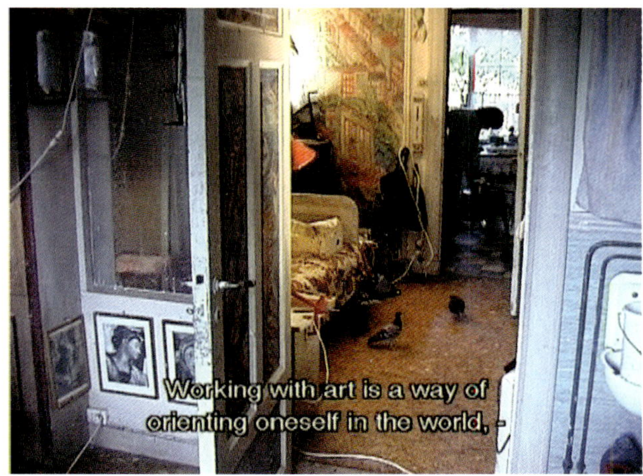
Working with art is a way of
orienting oneself in the world, -

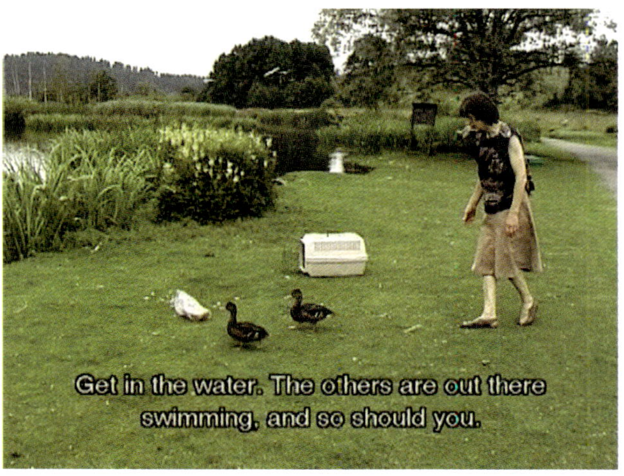
Get in the water. The others are out there
swimming, and so should you.

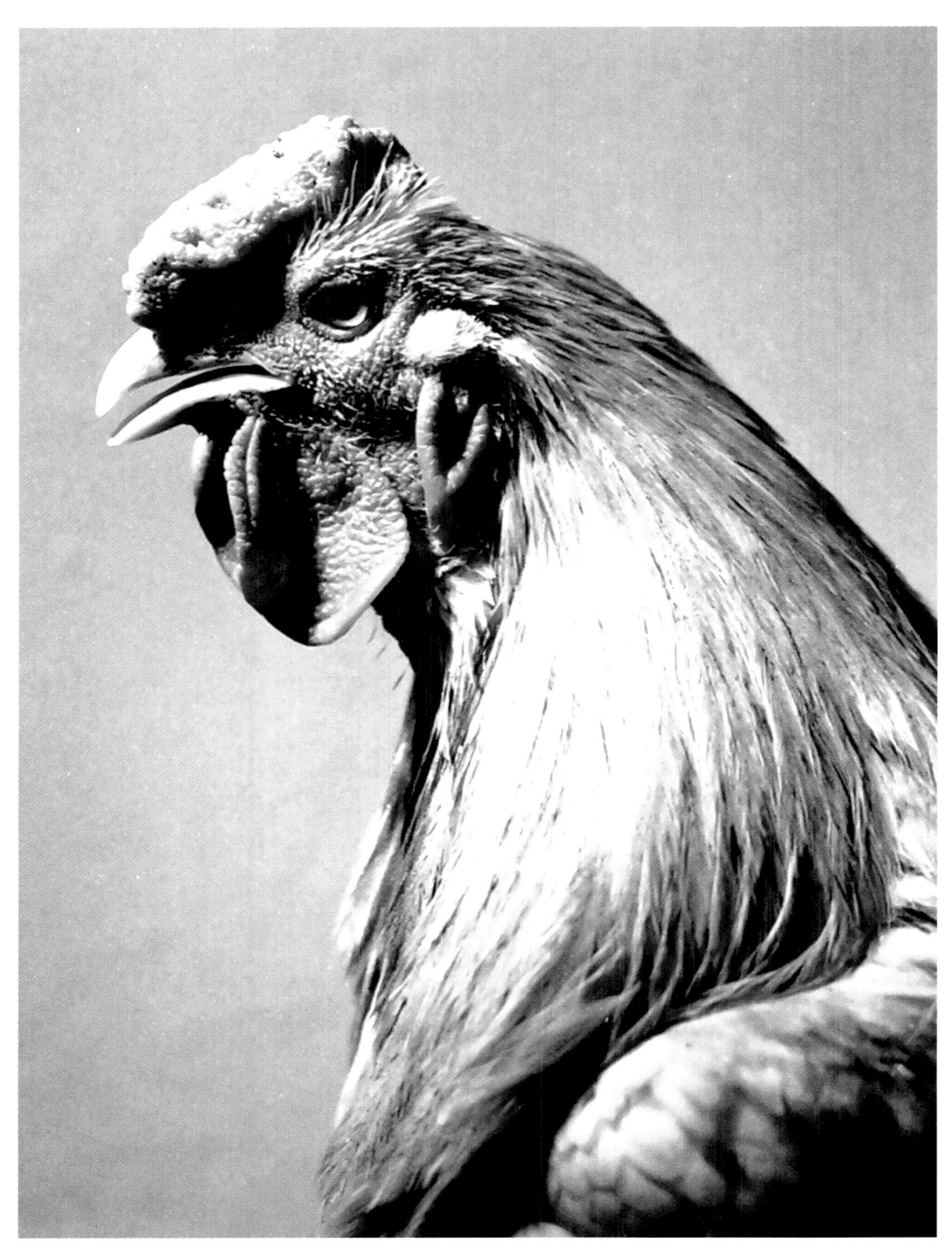

Sabine Emmerich
Hühnerportraits, 2001

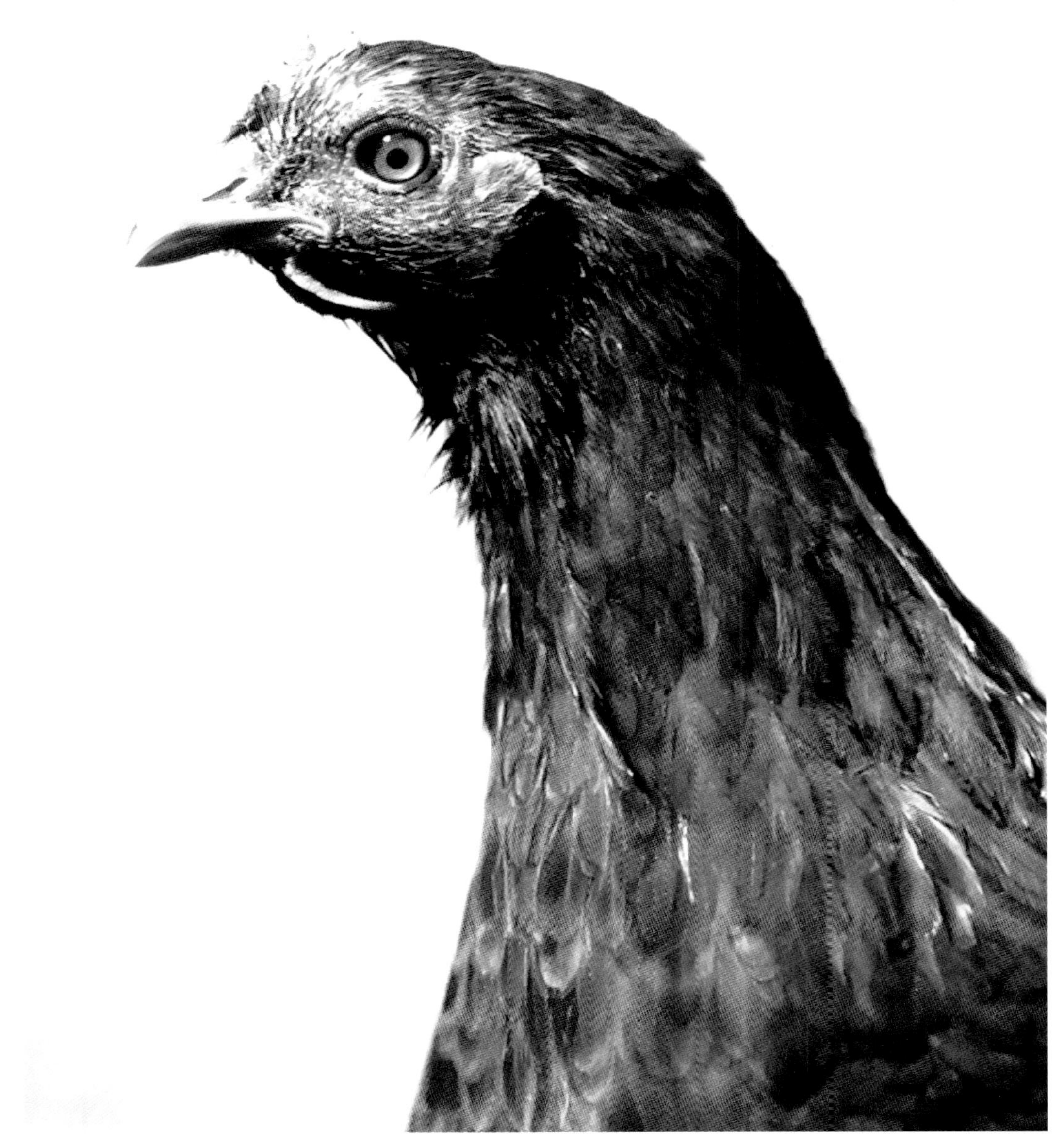

„Wenn man die Umwelt erhalten will, was ich versuche, braucht man eine riesige Leserschaft. Ich fände es nicht richtig, die Dinge, die ich fotografiere, für nur 200.000 Leute zu fotografieren.“

“If you try to do conservation, what I am trying to do, I need a huge audience. It wouldn’t be right for me to photograph something like I do for just 200 thousand people.”

Michael Nichols

Bücher Books

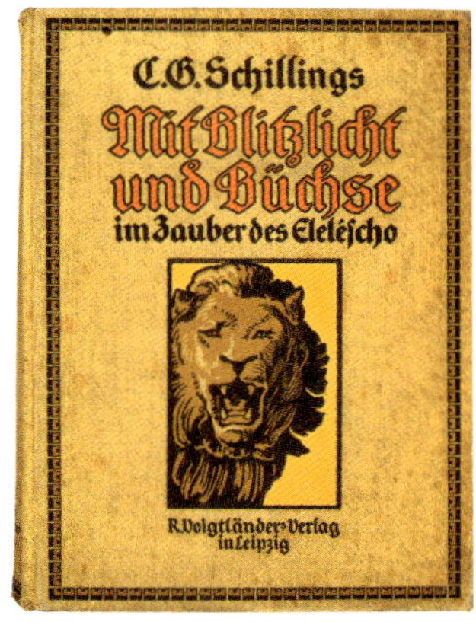

1

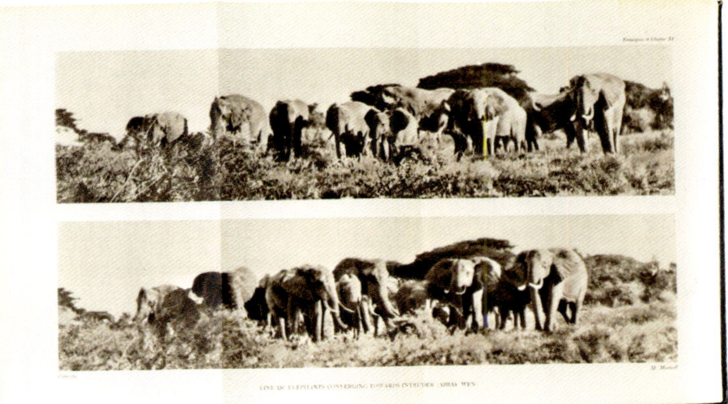

2

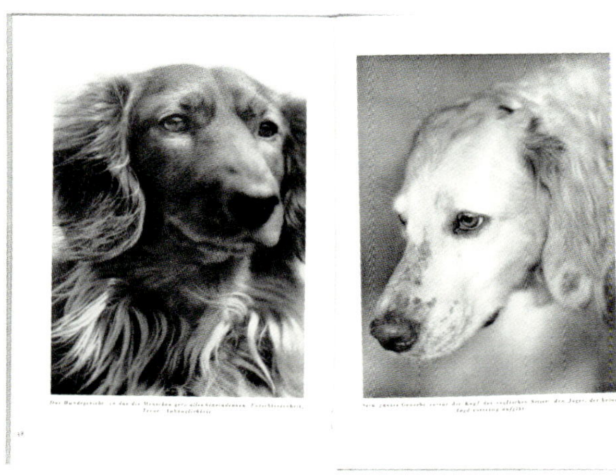

3

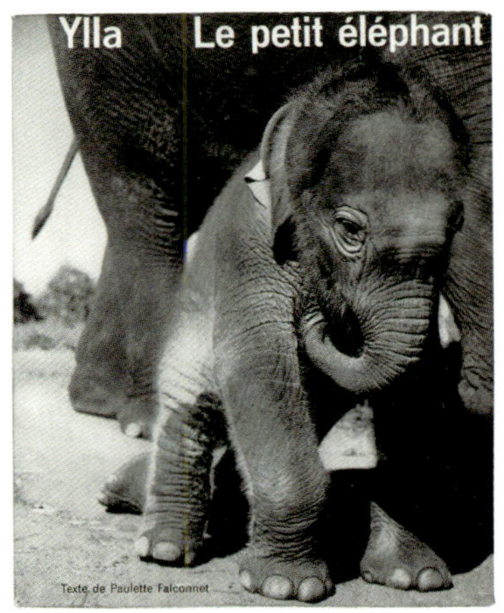

4

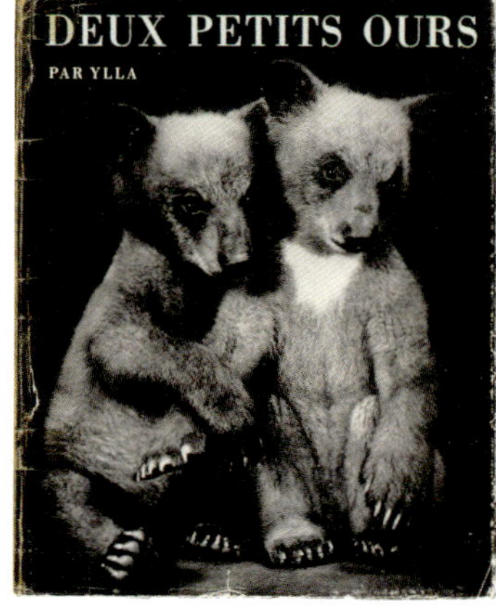

5

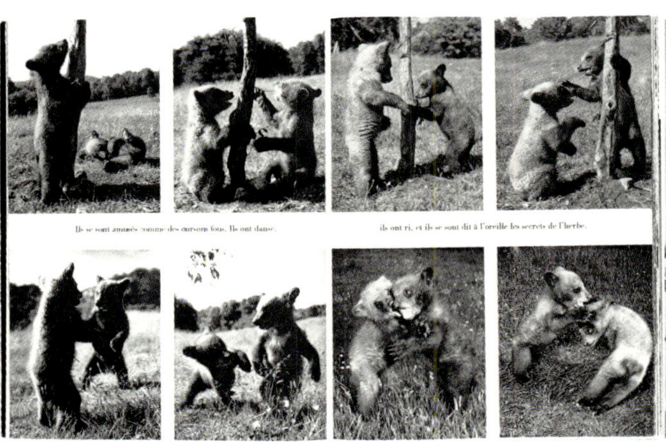

6

1 Carl Georg Schillings: *Mit Blitzlicht und Büchse. Im Zauber des Eléscho*, Leipzig 1920
2 Marius Maxwell: *Stalking big game with a camera in Equatorial Africa*, London 1925
3 Hedda Walther: *Mein Hundebuch*, 48 Bildnisstudien, Berlin 1931
4 Ylla: *Le petit éléphant*, Lausanne 1955
5 + 6 Ylla: *Deux petits ours*, Lausanne 1954

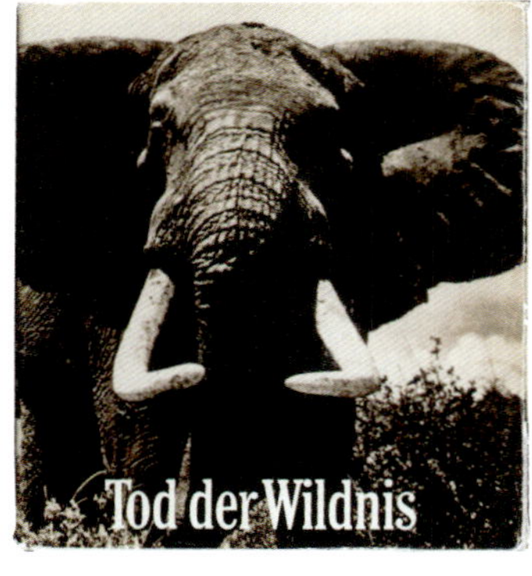

7

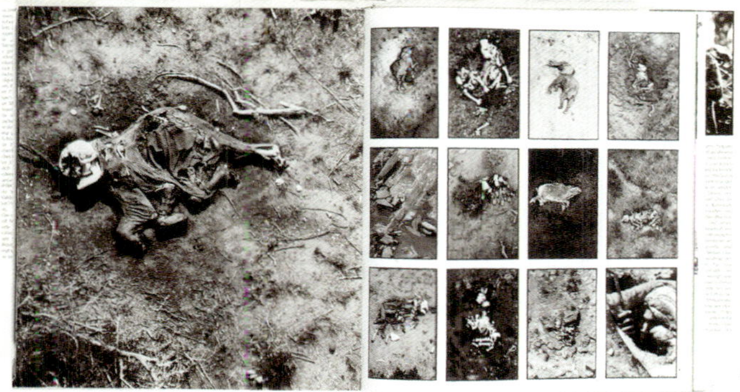

8

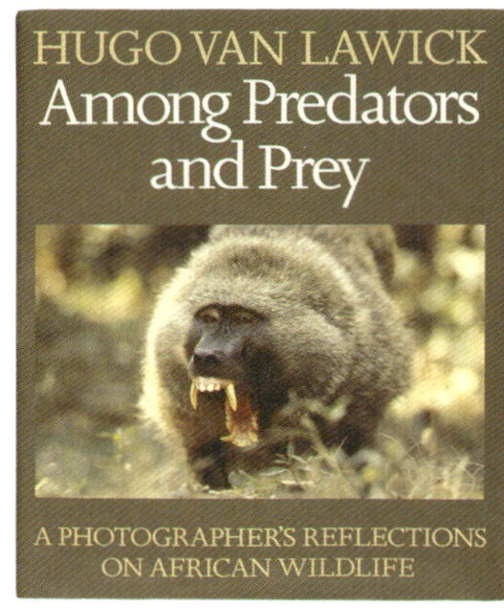

9

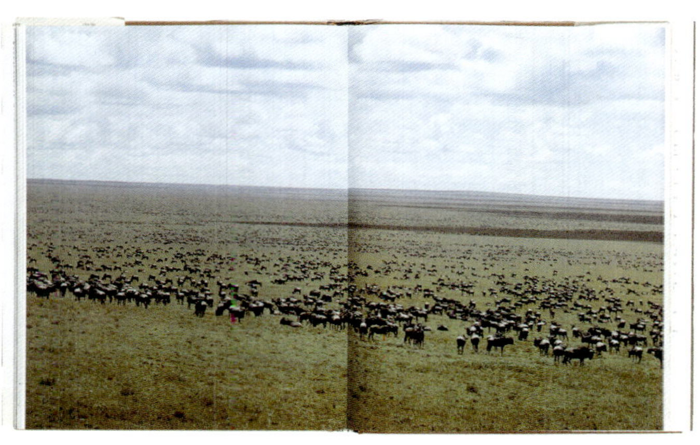

10

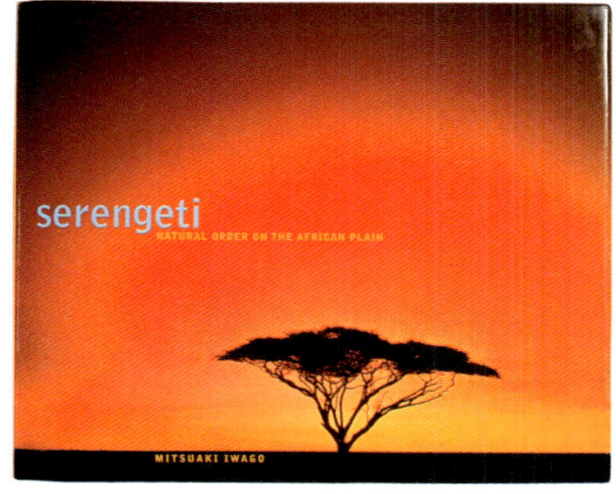

11

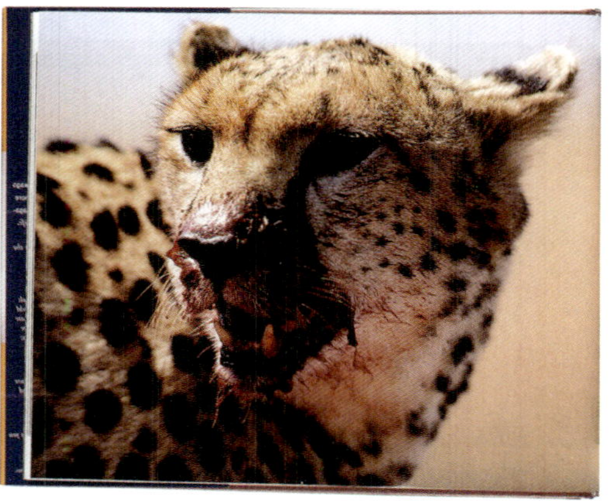

12

7 + 8 Peter H. Beard: *Tod der Wildnis*, München 1978

9 + 10 Hugo van Lawick: *Among Predators and Prey*, London 1986

11 + 12 Mitsuaki Iwago: *Serengeti. Natural Order on the African Plain*, London 1987

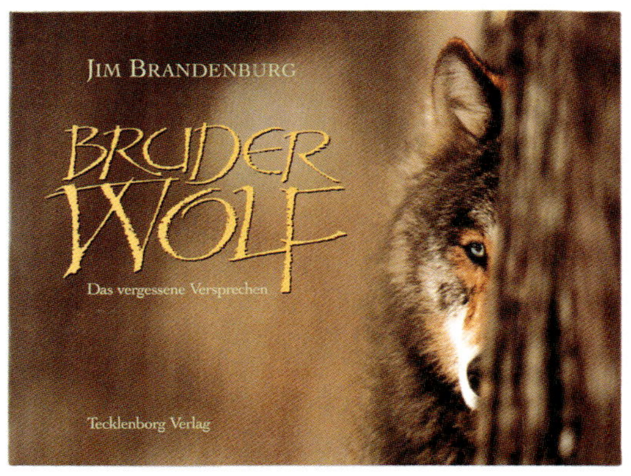

13

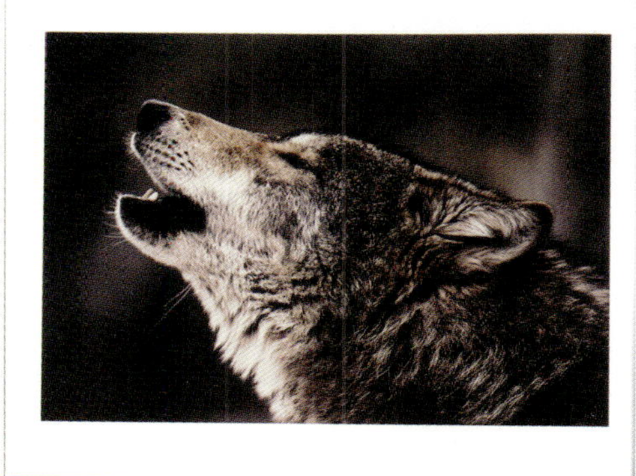

14

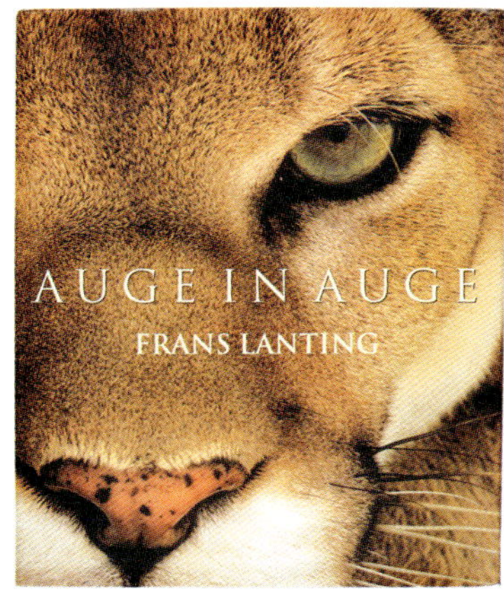

15

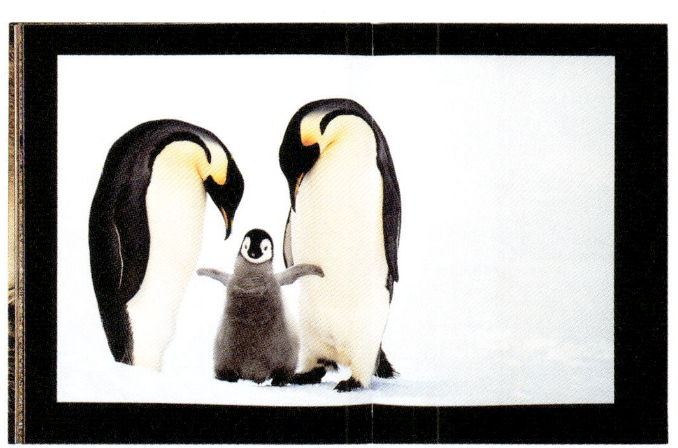

16

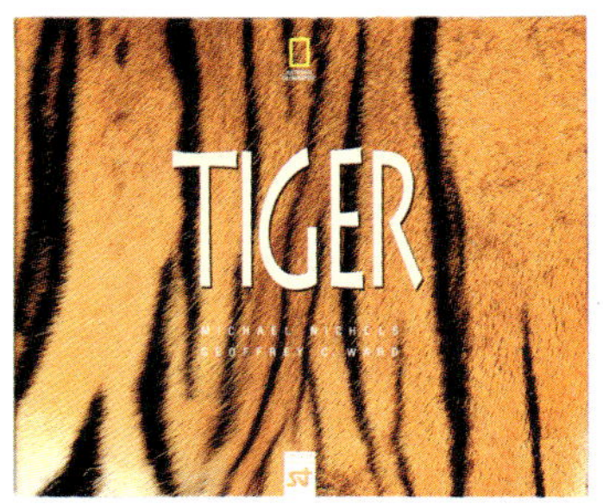

17

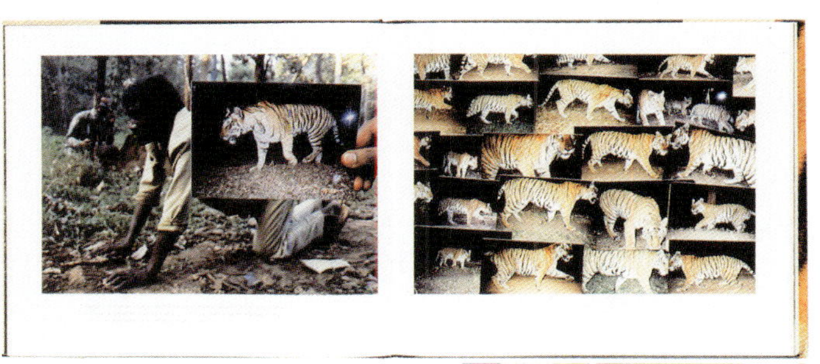

18

13 + 14 Jim Brandenburg: *Bruder Wolf. Das vergessene Versprechen*, Steinfurt 1996

15 + 16 Frans Lanting: *Auge in Auge. Begegnungen in der Welt der Tiere*, hg. von Christine Eckstrom, Köln 1997

17 + 18 Michael Nichols and Geoffrey C. Ward: *Tiger*, Washington 1998

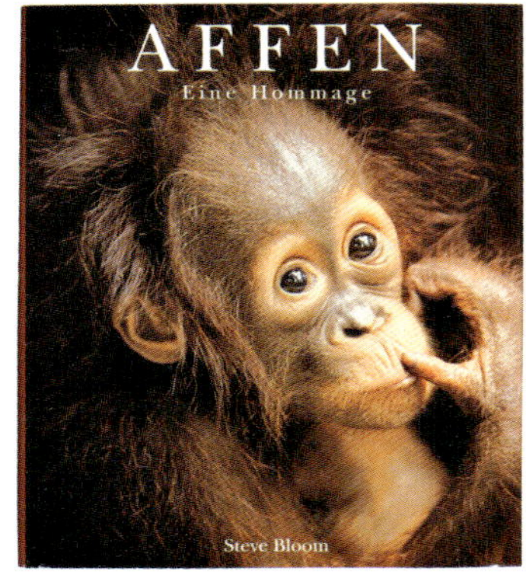

19

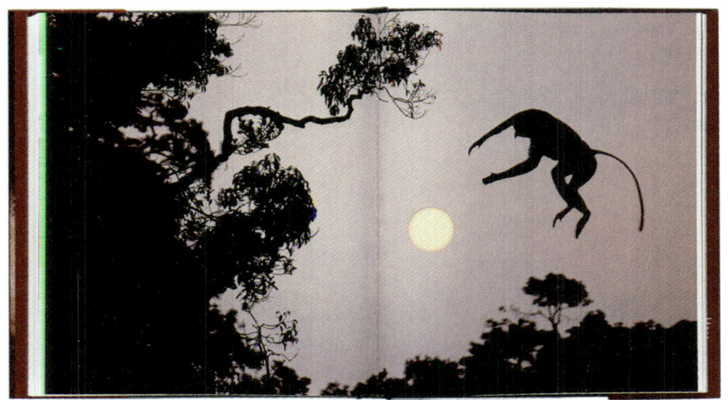

20

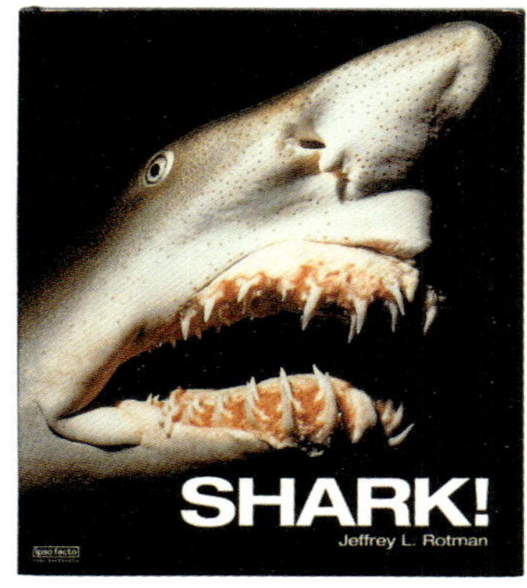

21

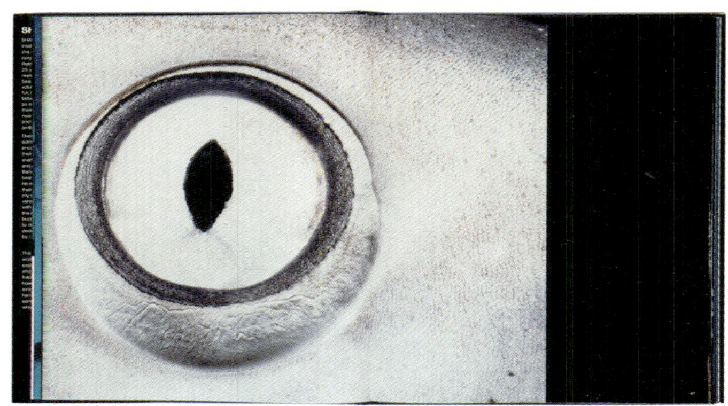

22

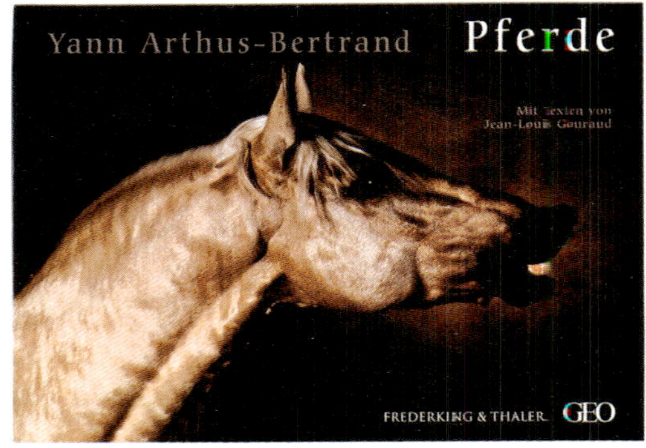

23

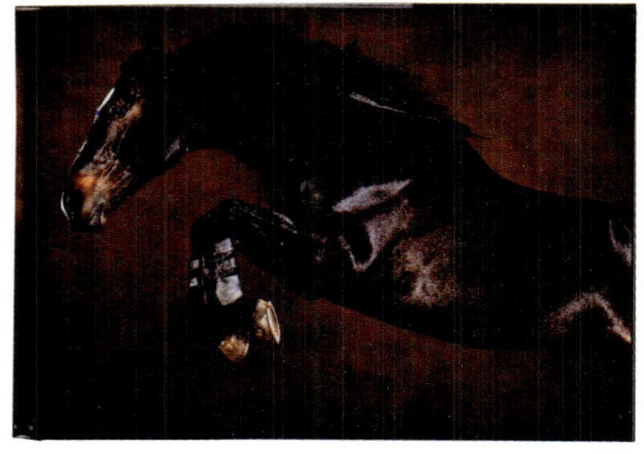

24

19 + 20 Steve Bloom: *Affen. Eine Hommage*, Köln 1999

21 + 22 Jeffrey L. Rotman: *Shark!*, New York 1999

23 + 24 Yann Arthus-Bertrand: *Pferde*, München 2005

Angaben zu den Abbildungen Notes to Illustrations

Originaltitel sind kursiv gesetzt. Beschreibende Titel und fotografische Verfahren sind ins Englische übersetzt. Sofern nicht anders angegeben, handelt es sich um Vintageabzüge. Bei späteren Abzügen ist das Jahr nach dem fotografischen Prozess/Verfahren vermerkt. Die Maße sind Höhe vor Breite angegeben und bezeichnen das Bildmaß in cm. Bei aufgezogenen Objekten ist das Kartonmaß in Klammern gesetzt.

Original titles are printed in italics. Descriptive titles and photographic processes are translated into English. If not otherwise mentioned, the prints are vintage prints. Later prints show the year after the photographic process. Measurements are given in height before width and indicate the size of the picture in cm. In case of mounted objects, the cardboard measurement is given in brackets.

Abkürzungen:
BS: Bromsilbergelatine
a. d. A.: aus dem Album
a. d. P.: aus dem Portfolio
a. d. S.: aus der Serie
a. d. R.: aus der Reportage

Abbreviations:
BS: Bromide silver gelatine
a. d. A.: from the album
a. d. P.: from the portfolio
a. d. S.: from the series
a. d. R.: from the reportage

JAMES ABBE
Anna Pavlova, 1927
BS, 25,2 x 20,4
Sammlung Kothenschulte, Köln
Abb. S. 217

AGENTUR SCHERL
Oberpräparator Keller, Zoologisches Museum / Senior taxidermist Keller, Zoological Museum, Berlin 1941
BS, 17,5 x 23,4
Ullstein Bild, Berlin
Abb. S. 74

COMTE OLYMPE AGUADO
Chien assis devant une porte, 1857
Albumin/Albumen, 22,7 x 17,9
Société Française de Photographie, Paris
Abb. S. 127

COMTE OLYMPE AGUADO
Deux ânes, 1857
Albumin/Albumen, 16,8 x 22,2
Société Française de Photographie, Paris
Abb. S. 89

MANUEL ALVAREZ BRAVO
For the Sheep's Wool, 1932
BS, 16,2 x 21,1
The J. Paul Getty Museum, Los Angeles, Cal.
Abb. S. 261

CLAUDIA ANGELMAIER
Hase, 2004
C-Print, 200 x 110
Sammlung Hans Hansen, Hamburg
Abb. S. 17

LUDWIG ANGERER
Portrait, ca. 1860
Albumin/Albumen, 9 x 5,5 (10 x 6)
Albertina, Wien. Dauerleihgabe der Höheren Graphischen Bundes-Lehr- und Versuchsanstalt, Wien
Abb. S. 128

ANONYM
A Member of a Maiden Lady's Family, ca. 1865
Albumin, stereoskopische Aufnahme/ Albumen, Stereoscopic Photograph (8,5 x 17,5)
The J. Paul Getty Museum, Los Angeles, Cal.
Abb. S. 130

ANONYM
Afrikanisches Kaninchen, ca. 1895
Albumin/Albumen, 9,7 x 13,2 (11 x 16,8)
Gewöhnlicher Stallhase, ca. 1895
Albumin/Albumen, 9,2 x 12,5 (11 x 16,8)
Sammlung Herzog, Basel
Abb. S. 18

ANONYM
Frau mit kleiner Katze, März 1954 / Woman with little cat, March 1954
BS, 8,1 x 10,2 und 8,1 x 5,2 (9,4 x 17,5)
Deutsches Literaturarchiv, Marbach
Abb. S. 134

ANONYM
Käuzchen und Hund, 1920er / Screech owl and dog, 1920s
BS, 3 x ca. 6,2 x 9,4
Privatsammlung, Essen
Abb. S. 135

ANONYM
Bell & Bell, Kopenhagen 1949
BS, Fotomontage, Postkarte, 11,2 x 15,3
Circus- und Varieté-Archiv Reinhard Tetzlaff, Hamburg
Abb. S. 183

ANONYM
Junge mit Spielzeugpferd / Boy with toy horse, 1880er
Albumin/Albumen, Carte de Visite

Museum Folkwang Essen, 8/2004
Abb. S. 25

ANONYM
Hund mit Pfeife / Dog with pipe, ca. 1910
Hund in Matrosenanzug/ Dog in sailor suit, ca. 1906
BS, Postkarte
Sammlung Weiss, Hamburg
Abb. S. 216

ANONYM
Tierschauspieler / Animal actors, 1950er
BS, 18,2 x 23
Academy of Motion Picture Arts and Sciences, Beverly Hills
Abb. S. 233

ANONYM
Rin Tin Tin, 1929
BS, Repro, gedruckte Autogrammkarte, 15 x 11,4
Academy of Motion Picture Arts and Sciences, Beverly Hills
Abb. S. 232

ANONYM
Rintintins schwerster Sieg/A Race for Life, USA 1928
BS, Aushangfoto, 23,8 x 30,4
Deutsches Filmmuseum, Frankfurt
Abb. S. 234/235

ANONYM
Heimweh / Lassie come home, USA 1943
BS, Aushangfoto, 26,2 x 21,9
Deutsches Filmmuseum, Frankfurt
Abb. S. 236

ANONYM
Kanonier Sauerbier bei der 4. Batterie, 2. Kurhessisches Feld-Artillerie-Regiment, Nr. 47, Fulda, 1909/11 / Gunner Sauerbier at the 4th battery, 2nd Kurhesse field-artillery-regiment, No 47, Fulda, 1909/11
Albumin/Albumen, Collage, 45,8 x 57
Museum Folkwang, Essen, 1244/83
Abb. S. 30

ANONYM
Hirsch von 12 Enden, 470 pf. schwer, welcher am 18.9.1861 im Leonberger Stadtwald (Württemberg) durch einen Blattschuss erlegt und nach der Natur photographiert wurde / Stag of twelve points, 470 pounds, shot through the shoulder to the heart on September 18, 1861 in the Leonberg municipal forest (Württemberg), photograph taken after nature
Albumin/Albumen, 18,3 x 26,2 (32 x 43,6)
Sammlung Herzog, Basel
Abb. S. 44

ANONYM
Lord Charles Beresford, a. d. A.: *Nepaul*, 1883
Albumin/Albumen, 19,9 x 24,3 (33 x 38,1)
The J. Paul Getty Museum Los Angeles, Cal.
Abb. S. 52/53

ANONYM
Dozent A. F. Verhaar mit Studenten während einer Präparationsübung zur Anatomie des Pferdes an der Veterinärschule in Utrecht / Lecturer A. F. Verhaar with students during a dissection lesson on the anatomy of the horse at the School of Veterinary Medicine in Utrecht, 1879
BS, Repro, 14,5 x 22,3
Collection University Museum Utrecht, department of Veterinary Medicine
Abb. S. 66

ANONYM
Zoologisches Präparat, Pferd / Zoological preparation, horse, ca. 1890
Albumin, stereoskopische Aufnahme/ Albumen, Stereoscopic Photograph, 10,8 x 15,8 (11,9 x 16,6)
Museum Folkwang, Essen, 25/2003
Abb. S. 58

ANONYM
Schaf / Sheep, 1910-1920
BS, 68,5 x 96 (78,5 x 106)
Sammlung Herzog, Basel
Abb. S. 81

ANONYM
Männer mit einem Bullen / Men posing with a Bull, ca. 1850
Daguerreotypie/-type, 5,6 x 6,7
The J. Paul Getty Museum, Los Angeles, Cal.
Abb. S. 91

ANONYM
Flämische Milchkarrenhunde / Flemish milk cart dogs, ca. 1905
Albumin/Albumen, 17,3 x 22
Museum Folkwang, Essen, 21/2003
Abb. S. 95

ANONYM
Flämische Milchkarrenhunde / Flemish milk cart dogs, ca. 1905
Albumin/Albumen, 18 x 24
Galerie Baudoin Lebon, Paris
Abb. S. 95

ANONYM
Lord and Lady Curzon on an Elephant, 1903
Platindruck/Platinotype, 28,8 x 23,1
National Museum of Photography, Film & Television, Bradford
Abb. S. 96

ANONYM
Rapportierhund überbringt einen Bericht an die vorderste Stellung / Report dog brings a report to the frontline, 1916-1917
BS, 17 x 23,5
Stiftung Museum Schloss Moyland, Sammlung van der Grinten, Bedburg-Hau
Abb. S. 102/103

ANONYM (Action Press)
Verbrennung BSE erkrankter Huftiere, Great Walley Farm, Großbritannien / Burning of BSE infected hoofed animals, Great Walley Farm, Great Britain, 27.2.2001
C-Print, 26,2 x 40
action press, Hamburg
Abb. S. 116

ANONYM (Neue Photographische Gesellschaft)
Verdauung des Hundes, a. d. B.: Heinrich Ernst Albers-Schönberg: *Fortschritte auf dem Gebiet der Röntgenstrahlung*, Bd. XIX, 1912/13, Tafel II
BS, Röntgenfotografie/X-Ray Radiograph, 28,9 x 19,3
Deutsches Röntgen-Museum, Remscheid
Abb. S. 71

ANONYM (Fotografische Montage Ub Iwerks)

Film Stills aus/from: Alfred Hitchcock, *The Birds*, 1963
BS 2005, 19,5 x 24,8 und 24,9 x 19,4
Academy of Motion Picture Arts and Sciences, Beverly Hills
Abb. S. 240/241

ANONYM (Schering AG Berlin)
Hormonforschung, Kammbildung / Hormone research, crest forming 1971
C-Print, je 24,2 x 18,1
Ullstein Bild, Berlin
Abb. S. 115

ANONYM (Verlag AL)
Hund mit Fliege / Dog with bow tie, 1908
BS, Postkarte
Sammlung Weiss, Hamburg
Abb. S. 216

ANONYM (Verlag DLG)
Hund mit Haube / Dog with cap, 1908
BS, Postkarte
Sammlung Weiss, Hamburg
Abb. S. 216

OTTOMAR ANSCHÜTZ
Affen / Apes, 1886
Albumin/Albumen, 4 x ca. 20 x 14,5 (je 30 x 23)
Universität der Künste Berlin, Universitätsarchiv
Abb. S. 194

EUGÈNE ATGET
Marchande de poissons, rue Mouffetard, 1898
Albumin/Albumen, 23,1 x 17,3
Musée Carnavalet – Histoire de Paris
Abb. S. 109

JOSÉ AZEL
Confiscated illegal Rocky Mountain Bighorn Sheep, 1996
C-Print, 34,6 x 50
Aurora Photos, Portland
Abb. S. 119

GEORGE BARKER
Success – Dressing the Big Buck, 1893
Albumin, stereoskopische Aufnahme/Albumen, Stereoscopic Photograph, (9 x 17,8)
The J. Paul Getty Museum, Los Angeles, Cal.
Abb. S. 43

CECIL BEATON
Katharine Hepburn, 1935
BS, 25,2 x 20,2
Sammlung Kothenschulte, Köln
Abb. S. 219

ALBIN BIBLOM
Mechkar, bulgaria's last dancing bears and their owner, 2004
C-Print, Kopiermontage, 100 x 100
Albin Biblom, Berlin
Abb. S. 190

LOUIS-AUGUSTE BISSON
Reptiles – Famille des Varaniens – Genre Varan. Merrem, 1853
Fotogravüre/Heliogravure, 27,6 x 21,6
Société Française de Photographie, Paris
Abb. S. 70

LOUIS-AUGUSTE BISSON
Taureau, Aurillac, 1850
Daguerreotypie/-type, 17 x 21
Sammlung Gérard Lévy, Paris
Abb. S. 79

LOUIS-AUGUSTE BISSON
Concours de Nismes, espèce ovine race du Larzac, ca. 1845-1850
Daguerreotypie/-type
Sammlung Gérard Lévy, Paris
Abb. S. 90

BISSON FRÈRES
Das Pferd "Mouton" / The horse "Mouton", 1844-1848
Daguerreotypie/-type, 8 x 10,5
Musée d'Orsay, Paris
Abb. S. 23

STEVE BLOOM
Snow monkeys (Japanese macaques) bathing in hot springs, Jigokudani National Park, Japan, January 1998
C-Print, 29,5 x 44,9
Steve Bloom / stevebloom.com
Abb. S. 206

STEVE BLOOM
Chacma Baboon yawning, Kruger National Park, South Africa, August 1993
C-Print, 29,8 x 42,6
Steve Bloom / stevebloom.com
Abb. S. 207

BILL BRANDT
Evening in Kew Gardens, 1932
BS, 31,4 x 26,9
Museum Folkwang, Essen, 542/79
Abb. S. 254

ADOLPHE BRAUN
Trophée de chasse au renard, 1867
Pigmentdruck/Carbon print, 73,5 x 51
Musée d'Orsay, Paris
Abb. S. 250

ADOLPHE BRAUN
Pferdekopf vom Giebeldreieck des Parthenons, British Museum / Head of a Horse from the Pediment of the Parthenon, British Museum, ca. 1865
Albumin/Albumen, 20,5 x 27,1
The J. Paul Getty Museum, Los Angeles, Cal.
Abb. S. 253

BALTHASAR BURKHARD
Friesisches Pferd, 1995
BS, 230 x 288
Museé national d'art moderne, Centre Georges Pompidou, Paris
Abb. S. 38 /39

MARIE JOSÉ BURKI
Installation: *Hibou*, 1993
Coll. Manor, dépôt Mamco, Genève
Abb. S. 292

MARIE JOSÉ BURKI
Video Stills aus/from: *Hibou*, 1993
DVD
Coll. Manor, dépôt Mamco, Genève
Abb. S. 293

LEWIS CARROLL (Charles Lutwidge Dodgson)
Reginald Southey with Skeletons, 1857
Albumin/Albumen, 13 x 16,8 (15,5 x 21,8)
Wilson Center for Photography, London
Abb. S. 61

HENRI CARTIER-BRESSON
Boulevard Richard Lenoir, 1952
BS, 41 x 30,4
Musée Carnavalet – Histoire de Paris
Abb. S. 187

CHIEN-CHI CHANG
Motala receives intensive care after her operation, a. d. S.: *Elephant Hospital, Thailand, Lampang* 1999
BS, 25 x 38
Magnum Photos, Paris/Agentur Focus, Hamburg
Abb. S. 104/105

JUAN CARLOS MARIA ISIDOR DE BORBON COMTE DE MONTIZON
Giraffe, London Zoo, 1852
Salzpapier/Salted paper, 12,7 x 11,3
Royal Photograph Collection, Windsor
Abb. S. 155

JUAN CARLOS MARIA ISIDOR DE BORBON COMTE DE MONTIZON
Hippopotamus (without spectators), London Zoo, 1852
Salzpapier/Salted paper, 8,2 x 9
Royal Photograph Collection, Windsor
Abb. S. 156

F. D. CONARD
The Train Hold-Up, 1938
BS, Postkarte, 13,5 x 8,5
Sammlung Weiss, Hamburg
Abb. S. 214

OTTO CROY
Haselnußfüßler, 1930er
BS, 22,2 x 17,2
Museum Folkwang, Essen, 349/91
Abb. S. 73

LOUIS-ADOLPHE-HUMBERT DE MOLARD (De Molard)
Chasseur assis, 1840er
Daguerreotypie/-type, 13,5 x 10,5
Musée Gatien-Bonnet, Lagny-sur-Marne
Abb. S. 41

HENRY DIXON
Löwe / Lion, 1879-1884
Pigmentdruck/Carbon print, 24,1 x 33,3 (33,2 x 44,7)
Universität der Künste, Berlin
Abb. S. 158

THOMAS JAMES DIXON
Löwe im Zoo / Lion at Zoo, 1879
Albumin/Albumen, 25,6 x 34,6
The J. Paul Getty Museum, Los Angeles, Cal.
Abb. S. 159

THOMAS JAMES DIXON
Löwe im Zoo / Lion at Zoo, London, 1879-1884
Pigmentdruck/Carbon print, 21,6 x 27,5 (29,3 x 38,5)
Museum Folkwang, Essen, 4/A/2004
Titelbild hinten

JOHN DOMINIS
Leopard chasing a baboon up a tree, 6. Januar 1967
C-Print 2005, 40,1 x 27
Abb. S. 56

Leopard chasing a baboon up a tree, 6. Januar 1967
C-Print 2005, 42,5 x 26,5
Abb. S. 56

Leopard chasing terrified baboon across the sands of the kalahari desert, 6. Januar 1967
C-Print 2005, 27 x 40
Abb. S. 56

Leopard killing a baboon, Botswana, 6. Januar 1967
C-Print 2005, 30 x 40
Abb. S. 57
Getty Images, München

MADAME D'ORA
(Dora Philippine Kallmus)
Schlachthofpferd, in geronnenem Blut liegend, a. d. S.: *Schlachthof*, vor 1958
C-Print 2005, 30,5 x 27,7 (39,8 x 29,8)
Museum für Kunst und Gewerbe Hamburg
Abb. S. 260

PIERRE DUBREUIL
Petite place de province, 1908
BS, 28,2 x 22,2
Museum Folkwang, Essen, 205/2
Abb. S. 103

J. ADÉODAT DUMONT
Mädchen mit Spielzeugpferd / Girl with toy horse, ca. 1880
Albumin/Albumen, Carte de Visite
Museum Folkwang, Essen, 13/2004
Abb. S. 25

THOMAS EAKINS
Boyce, Portrait of a setter dog, 1880-1890
Albumin/Albumen, 6,2 x 9,5
The J. Paul Getty Museum, Los Angeles, Cal.
Abb. S. 133

FLORIAN EBNER
Etna, 1997, a. d. S.: *Nomades*
C-Print, 75 x 75
Museum Folkwang, Essen, 69/2002
Abb. S. 153

WILLIAM EGGLESTON
Memphis, 1971
Dye Transfer, 32,9 x 47,9
The J. Paul Getty Museum, Los Angeles, Cal.
Abb. S. 249

GEORG EINBECK
Das Schweigen, 1898
Gummidruck/Gum-Print, 45,5 x 33 (Repro 2005: Christoph Irrgang/Karin Plessing, Hamburg)
Museum für Kunst und Gewerbe Hamburg
Abb. S. 255

SABINE EMMERICH
Hühnerportraits, 2001
BS, 22,5 x 17
Sabine Emmerich, Vorwerk
Abb. S. 296/297

LOTTE ERRELL
Nardine Yuan, China, 1931
BS, 21,2 x 17,7
Museum Folkwang, Essen, 1/80/92
Abb. S. 144

ERRELL (Richard Levy)
Dunlop-Werbung, vor 1930
BS, 45,8 x 31,2
Museum Folkwang, Essen, 1033/82
Abb. S. 220

ELLIOTT ERWITT
USA, *Alaska, The Fairbanks Family*, 1964
BS, 30,5 x 46

Magnum Photos, Paris/Agentur Focus, Hamburg
Abb. S. 148 /149

FRANK EUGENE (Frank Eugene Smith)
The Horse, 1898
in: Camera Work, April 1910
Fotogravüre/Heliogravure, 11,5 x 9
Museum für Kunst und Gewerbe Hamburg
Abb. S. 33

WALKER EVANS
Beschädigtes Ringling Brothers-Plakat / Torn Ringling Brothers Poster, 1941
BS, 16,6 x 20,5 (18 x 22,1)
The J. Paul Getty Museum, Los Angeles, Cal.
Abb. S. 185

CONSTANT ALEXANDRE FAMIN
Pastorale, ca. 1870
Albumin/Albumen, 12,4 x 16,4
Museum Folkwang, Essen, 2868/88
Abb. S. 92

PAUL FAULSTICH
Brillenträger am Seehundgehege / Person wearing glasses standing at the seal compound, 1927
BS, 16,7 x 22,5
Zoo Leipzig
Abb. S. 165

GEORG FISCHER
National Institute of Animal Industry, 1980
C-Print 2005, 40,3 x 50,5
Georg Fischer, Hamburg
Abb. S. 85

JOAN FONTCUBERTA / PERE FORMIGUERA
Solenoglypha Polipodida, 1986
BS, 35,2 x 35,1
Museum Folkwang, Essen, 160/88
Abb. S. 272

JOAN FONTCUBERTA / PERE FORMIGUERA
Micostrium Vulgaris, 1986
BS, 49,6 x 39,8
Museum Folkwang, Essen, 153/88
Abb. S. 273

ROBERT FRANK
Paris, 1949
BS, 34 x 18,5
Museum Folkwang, Essen, 1385/87
Abb. S. 36

GEISSLER / SANN (Beate Geissler & Oliver Sann)
Bright Indian Dream, 2002
C-Print, 95 x 80
Geissler/Sann, Köln
Abb. S. 252

PAUL GÉNIAUX
Le marché aux chevaux, boulevard de l'Hôpital, ca. 1900
Kollodium/Collodion, 8,6 x 11,7
Musée Carnavalet – Histoire de Paris
Abb. S. 34

ARNOLD GENTHE
Mrs Patrick Campbell, 1902
BS, 25,5 x 33,9
The J. Paul Getty Museum, Los Angeles, Cal.
Abb. S. 129

KARL GERSTNER
Geweih von Capreolus capreolus, L., erlegt von Fabrikant Robert Senner, jun., 6. Juni 1907, Revier Scheibenhardt Karlsruhe (Baden) / Antlers of Capreolus capreolus, L., shot by industrialist Robert Senner, jun., 6 June 1907, hunting-ground Scheibenhardt, Karlsruhe (Baden)
Chlorsilbergelatine/Chlorid silver gelatin, 17 x 12 (18 x 13)

Geweih von Capreolus capreolus, L., Rehbock, erlegt in Auental auf Markusweg Gaechingen bei Urach, 8. Juli 1915, von Dr. Ing. Robert Bosch / Antlers of Capreolus capreolus, L., roebuck, shot in Auental on Markusweg Gaechingen near Urach, 8 July 1915, by Dr. Ing. Robert Bosch
Chlorsilbergelatine/Chlorid silver gelatin, 17 x 11,4 (18 x 13)

Geweih von Capreolus capreolus, L., Rehbock, erlegt Gross-Sachenheim von Oberleutnant v.L. Ungerer, 24.Juli 1915 / Antlers of Capreolus capreolus, L., roebuck, shot Gross-Sachenheim by Lieutenant v. L. Ungerer, 24 July 1915
Chlorsilbergelatine/Chlorid silver gelatin, 17 x 10,8 (18 x 13)

Geweih von Capreolus capreolus, L., Rehbock, erlegt Hagelschiess (Württemberg), 1869 / Antlers of Capreolus capreolus, L., roebuck, shot in Hagelschiess (Württemberg), 1869
Chlorsilbergelatine/Chlorid silver gelatin, 17 x 10,8 (18 x 13)
Staatliches Museum für Naturkunde Stuttgart
Abb. S. 47

MARIO GIACOMELLI
Via Mastai 6 – Senigallia (Ancona), Italia, 1957/58
BS, 27,6 x 38,2
Museum Folkwang, Essen, 625/79
Abb. S. 101

BRUCE GILDEN
NYC Dog Show. A junior handler from Mexico with his mother and Afghan hound, New York City, 2003
BS, 38,2 x 25,9
Magnum Photos, Paris/Agentur Focus, Hamburg
Abb. S. 245

BRUCE GILDEN
NYC Dog Show. Owner with her crowned dog, New York City, 2003
BS, 38 x 25,8
Magnum Photos, Paris/Agentur Focus, Hamburg
Abb. S. 244

GREENPEACE
Puten-Fabrik, 2001, a. d. R.: *Masttierhaltung*
C-Print, 42 x 61
Greenpeace, Hamburg
Abb. S. 117

LUDWIG GRILLICH
Schausäle Naturhistorisches Hof-Museum Wien, Säugetiervitrinen / Naturhistorisches Hof-Museum Exhibition area, display cases for mammals, ca. 1890
Kollodium, stereoskopische

Aufnahme/Collodion, Stereoscopic Photograph, 18 x 9
Archiv und Wissenschaftsgeschichte, Naturhistorisches Museum Wien
Abb. S. 69

ANDREAS GURSKY
Greeley, 2002
C-Print, 206 x 264
Courtesy Monika Sprüth/Philomene Magers, Köln
Abb. S. 268/269

EUGENE S. M. HAINES
"The Bar. – Where Justice is dispensed with", from Hurst's Stereoscopic Studies of Natural History, 1870
Albumin, stereoskopische Aufnahme/ Albumen, Stereoscopic Photograph, 7,62 x 15,24 (8,89 x 17,78)
Wm. B. Becker Collection/American Museum of Photography, Huntington Woods
Abb. S. 196

PHILIPPE HALSMAN
Alfred Hitchcock, 1963
BS, 33,5 x 26,7
Howard Greenberg Gallery, New York
Abb. S. 239

ELISABETH HASE
Leopard hinter Gittern / Leopard behind bars, 1932
BS, 22 x 18
Nani Simonis, München
Abb. S. 163

DR. HERMANN HEID
Viehauktion in Wien, ca. 1881
Albumin/Albumen, 19,5 x 26,7 (32,6 x 45,9)
Albertina, Wien. Dauerleihgabe der Höheren Graphischen Bundes-Lehr- und Versuchsanstalt, Wien
Abb. S. 82

HIRO (Yasuhiro Wakabayashi)
Harry Winston Necklace, New York City, 1963
C-Print, 63,5 x 48,3 (76,2 x 50,8)
Courtesy of Pace/MacGill, New York
Abb. S. 229

CANDIDA HÖFER
Zoologischer Garten Washington DC II 1992
C-Print, 26 x 50
Candida Höfer, Köln
Abb. S. 174

CANDIDA HÖFER
Zoologischer Garten London III 1992
C-Print, 26 x 44
Candida Höfer, Köln
Abb. S. 175

CANDIDA HÖFER
Naturkunde-Museum Rotterdam II 1999
C-Print, 85 x 85
Candida Höfer, Köln
Abb. S. 77

FREDERICK HOLLYER
Schafschur, 1868
Platindruck/Platinotype, 16,4 x 12 (35 x 25,7)
Museum für Kunst und Gewerbe Hamburg
Abb. S. 93

WILLOUGHBY WALLACE HOOPER
Tiger Hunt. Marked Down!, ca. 1872, a. d. S.: *The Tiger Hunt*
Albumin/Albumen, 17,8 x 23,3
National Museum of Photography, Film & Television, Bradford
Abb. S. 48

WILLOUGHBY WALLACE HOOPER
Tiger Hunt, Dead!, ca. 1872, a. d. S.: *The Tiger Hunt*
Albumin/Albumen, 18,7 x 22,5
National Museum of Photography, Film & Television, Bradford
Abb. S. 49

GEFREITER INGENBRAND
Album *Pferd zwischen den Fronten* / Horse between the front lines, 1940/45
BS, 39 x 39
Tierärztliche Hochschule Hannover, Veterinärmedizinhistorisches Museum
Abb. S. 96

HENRY IRVING
Walross / Walrus, ca. 1904
BS, 18,7 x 23,4
Natural History Museum, London
Abb. S. 164

STEFFEN JUNGHANS
6, a. d. S.: *Einrichten*, 2000
C-Print, 78,5 x 115 (100 x 129)
Museum Folkwang, Essen, 7/2002
Abb. S. 75

ANDRÉ KERTÉSZ
a. d. S.: Hund und Katze / Dog and Cat Series, no. 1, 5, 6, 7, 8, 1934
BS, ca. 23,7 x 17,8
The J. Paul Getty Museum, Los Angeles, Cal.
Abb. S. 136/137

ANDRÉ KERTÉSZ
New York, 1936
BS, 21 x 16
The J. Paul Getty Museum, Los Angeles, Cal.
Abb. S. 180

ANDRÉ KERTÉSZ
Siamese Cat, Paris, 1928
BS, 17,5 x 15,9
The J. Paul Getty Museum, Los Angeles, Cal.
Abb. S. 257

PHILIPP KESTER
Zahmes Damwild im Nymphenburger Hirschgarten, München, 1909
BS 1991, 12,8 x 17,8
Fotomuseum im Münchner Stadtmuseum, München
Abb. S. 215

AART KLEIN
Acrobat, 1954
BS, 40,1 x 30,5
Museum Folkwang, Essen, 753/79
Abb. S. 189

KAREN KNORR
The peripatetic philosopher, 1998
C-Print, 101 x 124
Museum Folkwang, Essen, 245/2001
Abb. S. 271

WILMAR KOENIG
Hase auf dem Feld, 1992, a. d. S.: *Le Bestiaire*

C-Print, 120 x 145
Wilmar Koenig, Berlin
Abb. S. 21

ATELIER KÖLLA
Schlachthof (Auftrag der Firma Presswerk Esser) / Slaughterhouse (Commission by Presswerk Esser), ca. 1910
BS, retuschiert, 16,7 x 11,7 (30 x 24)
Sammlung Herzog, Basel
Abb. S. 113

JAN KORNSTAEDT
Junger Beagle im Käfig, Hamburg, 2003
C-Print, 50 x 50
Jan Kornstaedt, Buxtehude
Abb. S. 123

JOSEF KOUDELKA
Spanien, 1978
BS, 36,2 x 54
Museum Folkwang, Essen, 266/89
Abb. S. 205

JOSEF KOUDELKA
Türkei, 1984
BS, 36 x 54,1
Museum Folkwang, Essen, 267/89
Abb. S. 262

HEINRICH KÜHN
Schäferhund im Interieur / Alsatian dog inside, ca. 1900
Fotogravüre/Heliogravure, 22,5 x 16
Museum Folkwang, Essen, 100/2-110
Abb. S. 132

ADOLF KULL
Java-Tiger, Oktober 1886
Albumin/Albumen, 9,5 x 13,5 (16,5 x 10,8)
Staatliches Museum für Naturkunde, Stuttgart
Abb. S. 162

JACQUES-HENRI LARTIGUE
Dick, 1963
BS 2005, 27,7 x 20,1
Museum Folkwang, Essen, 36/2005
Abb. S. 125

FRANZ LAZI
Königspinguine mit Auto, Persiflage, 1989
C-Print, Fotomontage, 60 x 50
Museum Folkwang, Essen, 46/2005
Abb. S. 221

FRANZ LAZI
ohne Titel, 1960
C-Print, 60 x 50
Museum Folkwang, Essen, Titelbild

HENRI LE LIEURE
Junge mit Spielzeugpferden / Boy with toy horses, ca. 1875
Albumin/Albumen, Carte de Visite
Museum Folkwang, Essen, 11/2004
Abb. S. 25

ROBERT LEBECK
Willy Brandt in Fuerteventura, 1972
BS 1986, 25,1 x 37
Museum Folkwang, Essen, 334/86
Abb. S. 139

JOCHEN LEMPERT
Ohne Titel, Affen / Apes, 1997
BS, 4 x ca. 73 x 54
Museum Folkwang, Essen, 115–118/97
Abb. S. 277

JO LONGHURST
a. d. S.: *I know what you're thinking*, 2003
C-Print, 4 x je 76 x 101,6
Jo Longhurst, London
Abb. S. 284/285

ALEKSANDRAS MACIJAUSKAS
a. d. S.: *In the Veterinary Clinic in Kaunas, No 52*, 1978
BS, 39,4 x 30
Aleksandras Macijauskas, Kaunas
Abb. S. 87

EDWARD MALINDINE (Daily Herald Archive)
Bertram Mills Touring Circus beim Training in Ascot. Miss Priscilla Kayes übt mit ihren 6 Löwen / *Bertram Mills Touring Circus in training at Ascot. Miss Priscilla Kayes rehearsing her 6 lions*, 1.4.1936
BS, 8,6 x 11,3
National Museum of Photography, Film & Television, Bradford
Abb. S. 179

PER MANING
Leo, 1986/87
BS, 2 x je 42,8 x 42,8
Museum Folkwang, Essen, 5/90, 2/90
Abb. S. 290/291

PER MANING
Video Stills aus/from: *Now you see me, now you don't*, 2002
DVD
Nasjonalmuseet for Kunst, Arkitektur og Design, Oslo
Abb. S. 289

ETIENNE-JULES MAREY
Horse's Hooves, ca. 1892
BS, Reprint, 51 x 27,7
National Museum of Photography, Film & Television, Bradford
Abb. S. 29

W. H. MARTIN
When we go after anything we get it, 1910
BS, Postkarte
Sammlung Weiss, Hamburg
Abb. S. 19

MAYER & PIERSON (Léopold Ernest Mayer & Pierre Louis Pierson)
Le dompteur Hermann à l'hippodrome de Paris, garanti d'après nature, 1863
Albumin/Albumen, Carte de Visite
Bibliothèque nationale de France, département des estampes et de la photographie, Paris
Abb. S. 178

Ölverschmutzter Seevogel, Benetton-Werbung, Konzept Olivier Toscani, Foto Steve McCurry / Sea bird, badly soiled by oil, Benetton advertising, concept Olivier Toscani, photo Steve McCurry, September 1992
Offset Druck/print, 29,5 x 42
Deutsches Plakatmuseum, Essen
Abb. S. 118

LISETTE MODEL
Promenade des Anglais, Nice, ca. 1934
BS, 28,9 x 23,2 (30,8 x 25,2)
The J. Paul Getty Museum, Los Angeles, Cal.
Abb. S. 145

LISETTE MODEL
Elefanten im Zoo von Vincennes / Elephants, Vincennes Zoo Paris, 1933-1938
BS, 22,7 x 28,2 (25 x 30)
Galerie Baudoin Lebon, Paris
Abb. S. 171

LISETTE MODEL
Rhinoceros im Zoo von Vincennes / Rhinoceros, Vincennes Zoo Paris, 1933-1938
BS, 28,7 x 22,2
The J. Paul Getty Museum, Los Angeles, Cal.
Abb. S. 170

LISETTE MODEL
Dog Show, Westminster Kanal Club, New York, 1946
BS, 34,5 x 27
Museum Folkwang, Essen, 1/2002
Abb. S. 243

MARTIN MUNKACSI
Balancierender Hund, ca. 1930
BS Späterer Abzug/Modern Print, 33,7 x 26,9
The Estate of Martin Munkacsi, Woodstock
Abb. S. 186

EADWEARD MUYBRIDGE
Eagle walking, free, Plate 576, aus: *Animal Locomotion*, 1887
Lichtdruck/Collotype, 32,4 x 49
Universität der Künste Berlin, Universitätsarchiv
Abb. S. 26 /27

ARTHUR B. R. MYERS
a. d. B.: *Life with the Hamran Arabs*, London 1876
Woodburytypie/-type, Repro, 22 x 14,5
Rijksmuseum Amsterdam
Abb. S. 50

MICHAEL NICHOLS
Mr. Jiggs, 1990
C-Print, 32,5 x 48,8
Agentur Focus, Hamburg
Abb. S. 147

MICHAEL NICHOLS
Babuínos de Gelada, Etiopia, 2002
C-Print, 40 x 50
National Geographic Image Collection, Washington D.C.
Abb. S. 193

MICHAEL NICHOLS
Jane with Gremlin, Gombe, Tanzania, 1995
C-Print, 32,6 x 48,7
Agentur Focus, Hamburg
Abb. S. 208

JOHAN NÖHRING
Troglodytes Gorilla, femina et juvenis, Ex Museo natur. Lubecensi, 1880er
Albumin/Albumen, 23,2 x 28,2 (24 x 31.8)
Museum für Naturkunde, Berlin
Abb. S. 63

CAS OORTHUYS
TNO Research Institute, 1960er
BS, 6 x 6 Kontaktabzüge
Nederlands Fotomuseum, Rotterdam
Abb. S. 201

CAS OORTHUYS
Faculty of Veterinary science, University Utrecht, 1962
BS, 30 x 24
Nederlands Fotomuseum, Rotterdam
Abb. S. 67

CAS OORTHUYS
Faculty of Veterinary science, University Utrecht, 1962
BS, 30 x 24
Nederlands Fotomuseum, Rotterdam
Abb. S. 84

HILMAR PABEL
Dämonen unter Wasser, Zoo Berlin, 1930er
BS, 5 x ca. 24,5 x 18
Deutsches Literaturarchiv, Marbach
Abb. S. 172/173

HILMAR PABEL
a. d. R.: *Bobby*, 20. Juli 1935
BS, 5 x ca. 24,3 x 18
Deutsches Literaturarchiv, Marbach
Abb. S. 198/199

MARTIN PARR
Thailand, 1998, a. d. S.: *Common Sense*
C-Print, 49,5 x 75
Museum Folkwang, Essen, 25/99
Abb. S. 152

IRVING PENN
Cracking a Lobster Claw, New York 1999
C-Print, 60,5 x 76
Museum Folkwang, Essen, 43/2002
Abb. S. 224

IRVING PENN
Turducken, New York, 1999
C-Print, 76 x 60,5
Museum Folkwang, Essen, 46/2002
Abb. S. 225

PHOTOGRAPHISCHES ATELIER der Gussstahlfabrik von Friedrich Krupp, Essen
Rohr-Tragethier, Munitions-Tragethier, 1883, a. d. A.: *Artillerie-Material I. Essen*, 1892
Fotogravüre/Heliogravure, 14,6 x 20,9
Historisches Archiv Krupp, Essen
Abb. S. 98

PIERRE LOUIS PIERSON
Napoleon III and the Prince Imperial, ca. 1859
Albumin/Albumen, 21 x 16
The J. Paul Getty Museum, Los Angeles, Cal.
Abb. S. 24

ERIC POITEVIN
Ohne Titel (No 8), 2000
C-Print, 216 x 172
Sammlung Schöller, Brüssel
Abb. S. 37

HERBERT GEORGE PONTING
„Vida", one of the best of the dogs used by Capt. Smith on his South Pole Expedition (1910-13), ca. 1912
BS, 35,9 x 30
The J. Paul Getty Museum, Los Angeles, Cal.
Abb. S. 94

ALBERT RENGER-PATZSCH
Mantelpavian / Sacred baboon, 1930
BS, 17 x 22,9

Museum Folkwang, Girardet Archiv, Essen
Abb. S. 256

OLIVIER RICHON
The Passion for Mourning, 1985
C-Print, 70 x 150
Olivier Richon, London
Abb. S. 274

OLIVIER RICHON
The Anatomy of Melancholia, 1985
C-Print, 70 x 150
Olivier Richon, London
Abb. S. 275

MARTIN RICHTER
a. d. S.: *Moderne Ställe #5*, ca. 2001
C-Print, Diasec, 80 x 100
Martin Richter, Hamburg
Abb. S. 122

HEINRICH RIEBESEHL
Dompteur mit Ziege / Trainer with goat, 1974
BS, 14,5 x 21,7
Privatsammlung, Essen
Abb. S. 191

HUMBERTO RIVAS
Tomasa, 1988
BS, 47,5 x 37,3
Museum Folkwang, Essen, 263/2001
Abb. S. 281

HENRY PEACH ROBINSON
Little Red Riding Hood, 1858
Albumin/Albumen, 24,1 x 19,1
National Museum of Photography, Film & Television, Bradford
Abb. S. 65

ALEXANDER RODTSCHENKO
Horse race / Pferderennen, 1935
BS, 29,7 x 43,2
The J. Paul Getty Museum, Los Angeles, Cal.
Abb. S. 212/213

HORATIO ROSS
Italienischer Orgelmann und Affe / Italian organ man and monkey, 1858
Salzpapier/Salted paper, 19,7 x 15,9
The J. Paul Getty Museum, Los Angeles, Cal.
Abb. S. 204

HORATIO ROSS
The Four Graces, ca. 1858
Albumin/Albumen, 21 x 34 (36 x 45)
Janet Lehr, New York
Abb. S. 45

JEFFREY L. ROTMAN
Caribbean Reef Shark, 1997
C-Print, 40 x 60
Jeffrey Rotman, Lawrenceville
Abb. S. 246/247

NADIN MARIA RÜFENACHT
a. d. S.: *Vieh*, 2003
C-Print, Diasec, 75 x 50
N. M. Rüfenacht, Leipzig
Abb. S. 111

NADIN MARIA RÜFENACHT
Nature Morte, a. d. S.: *Helden*, 2005
C-Print, 125 x 100
N. M. Rüfenacht, Leipzig
Abb. S. 251

PENTTI SAMMALLAHTI
Solovki, White Sea, Russland, 1992
BS, 16,4 x 35
Museum Folkwang, Essen, 237/2001
Abb. S. 264/265

AUGUST SANDER
Der Notar Dr. Quinke, Köln-Lindenthal, 1924
BS 1979, 29,8 x 21,3
Museum Folkwang, Essen, 43/2/81
Abb. S. 140

AUGUST SANDER
Försterkind aus dem Westerwald, ca. 1925
BS 1982, 31 x 23,6
Museum Folkwang, Essen, 23/8/81
Abb. S. 141

WALTER SCHELS
Schwarzes Schaf, 1984
BS, 40 x 50
Walter Schels, Hamburg
Abb. S. 278

WALTER SCHELS
Schaf, 1984
BS, 40 x 50
Walter Schels, Hamburg
Abb. S. 279

CARL GEORG SCHILLINGS
Album *Specialausstellung von Jagdtrophäen, ausgestellt gelegentlich der Deutschen Geweihausstellung 1889. Ost und Aequatorialafrika, erlegt 1896–97 von C. G. Schillings Weiherhof Gürzenich* / Special exhibition of hunting trophies, shown on the occasion of the German Antler Exhibition 1889, East- and Equatorial Africa, shot 1896-97 by C.G. Schillings Weiherhof Gürzenich
BS
Stadt- und Kreisarchiv Düren
Abb. S. 112

CARL GEORG SCHILLINGS
Löwin in einer Falle / lioness in a trap, ca. 1900
BS, 18 x 24
Stadt- und Kreisarchiv Düren
Abb. S. 54

CARL GEORG SCHILLINGS (?)
Trophäen-Pyramide, ca. 1900
BS, 7,5 x 10,4
Stadt- und Kreisarchiv Düren
Abb. S. 76

JULIUS EDUARD SCHINDLER
Graues Wasserhuhn – Taligula atra, 1867-1868
Albumin/Albumen, 13,8 x 9,8 (42,8 x 60,5)
Albertina, Wien. Dauerleihgabe der Höheren Graphischen Bundes-Lehr- und Versuchsanstalt, Wien
Abb. S. 46

WALTER SCHMITZ
a. d. S.: *Tiere als Therapeuten*, 2001
C-Print, 34 x 50
Bilderberg, Hamburg
Abb. S. 106

WALTER SCHMITZ
Hunting, shot deers, 1992
C-Print 2005, 26,6 x 40
Bilderberg, Hamburg
Abb. S. 58

ROBIN SCHWARTZ
Peedee and Missy, Hoboken, New Jersey,

1987
BS, 47,3 x 31,6
Robin Schwartz, Hoboken
Abb. S. 146

FERDINAND ALBERT SCHWARTZ
Sau "Melodie" und *Eber "Prachtkerl"*, a. d. A.: *Deutsche Landwirtschaftsgesellschaft, Wanderausstellung Köln 6.-10. Juni 1895 / Sow „Melodie"* and *boar „Prachtkerl", German agricultural show, touring exhibition, Cologne 6-10 June 1895*
Albumin/Albumen, 2 x je 16 x 20 (24,5 x 33)
Sammlung Dietmar Siegert, München
Abb. S. 80

EBERHARD SEELIGER
Hirnforschung – Prof. Delgado, USA, April 1973
BS, 21,9 x 29,9
Museum Folkwang, Essen, 145/95
Abb. S. 120

FRIEDRICH SEIDENSTÜCKER
Hundegrab, Berlin Stahnsdorf, 1920er
BS, 18,1 x 13,1
Bildarchiv Preußischer Kulturbesitz, Berlin
Abb. S. 143

FRIEDRICH SEIDENSTÜCKER
Eisbär, vor 1933
BS, 18 x 13
Bildarchiv Preußischer Kulturbesitz, Berlin
Abb. S. 161

FRIEDRICH SEIDENSTÜCKER
Strauß rupft die Hecke ab / Ostrich picking at a hedge, ca. 1930
BS, 17,6 x 13
Galerie Berinson, Berlin
Abb. S. 167

FRIEDRICH SEIDENSTÜCKER
Eingeschneites Pferd vor einer Kutsche am Kaiserplatz, 1930er / Horse Carriage at Kaiserplatz, 1930s
BS, 13,1 x 17,2
Bildarchiv Preußischer Kulturbesitz, Berlin
Abb. S. 32

FRIEDRICH SEIDENSTÜCKER
Gefleckte Dogge, 1930er
BS, 11,3 x 17,3
Bildarchiv Preußischer Kulturbesitz, Berlin
Abb. S. 142

ANATOLIJ SKURICHIN / WLADIMIR GRÜNTAL
Hühnerkombinat, a. d. P.: *Lebensmittelindustrie*, 1936 (Gestaltung El Lissitzky)
Druck/Print, 37,1 x 21,3
Museum Folkwang, Essen, 67/55/96
Abb. S. 114

FREDERICK SOMMER
Jack Rabbit, 1939
BS, 18,7 x 23,8
The J. Paul Getty Museum, Los Angeles, Cal.
Abb. S. 20

DAVID STEETS
Urnen für Haustiere / Urns for pets, 2001/02
C-Print, 12 x je 18 x 18
David Steets, München
Abb. S. 151

CARL FERDINAND STELZNER
"Ulla", der Hund im Hause Stelzner, o. D.
Daguerreotypie/-type, 7,3 x 6,1 (13,9 x 11,1)
Museum für Kunst und Gewerbe Hamburg
Abb. S. 126

ANNE LISE STENSETH
Video-Stills aus/from: *Birdess*, 2001
23 min.
Anne Lise Stenseth, Oslo
Abb. S. 294/295

WARWARA STEPANOWA
Ergebnisse des 1. Fünfjahresplans, 1933
BS, Fotocollage, 29 x 40,2
Galerie Alex Lachmann, Köln
Abb. S. 31

JOEL STERNFELD
Yellowstone National Park, 1979
C-Print, 121,92 x 148,59
Courtesy of the artist and Luhring Augustine Gallery, New York
Abb. S. 266/267

ALEX STÖCKER
Joko hält still, ca. 1926
BS, 23,8 x 18,1
Ullstein Bild, Berlin
Abb. S. 200

SASHA STONE
Circus Hagenbeck, Tierdressur, 1930
BS, 3 x je 17,5 x 23,5
Archiv Hagenbeck, Hamburg
Abb. S. 181

WILLIAM STRODE
a. d. R.: *Charlys treuer Killer*, 1979
C-Print 2005, 33,4 x 50
Agentur Focus, Hamburg
Abb. S. 211

CHRISTER STRÖMHOLM
Spanien, 1959
BS, 21 x 30
Museum Folkwang, Essen, 63/2005
Abb. S. 263

PETER STRONG
The Laughing Monkey, 2002
C-Print, 37,6 x 50
Peter Strong, London
Abb. S. 209

STRUMPER & CO.
aus dem Geschäfts-Album der Firma Heinrich AD. Meyer, ca. 1905
BS, ca. 17,2 x 23,5
Stadtarchiv Düren
Abb. S. 51

STRUMPER & CO.
Fürst Bismarck in Friedrichsruh am 6. Juli, 1891
Chlorsilbergelatine/Chlorid silver gelatin, 15 x 21 (31 x 37,7)
Historisches Archiv Krupp, Essen
Abb. S. 138

JUHA SUONPÄÄ
Suomussalami, Finnland, 1991
C-Print, 60 x 40
Juha Suonpää, Tampere
Abb. S. 59

HENK TAS
Dreambrothers, 2000
C-Print, 123 x 180
Henk Tas, Rotterdam
Abb. S. 230/231

ISADORA TAST
a. d. S.: *Schmerzlich-süße Zeit*, 2001/02
C-Print, 59,8 x 44,5
Isadora Tast, Hamburg
Abb. S. 237

RICHARD TEPE
Cavias, ca. 1930
BS, 16,3 x 22,5
Rijksmuseum, Amsterdam
Abb. S. 131

WARREN T. THOMPSON
Selbstporträt als Jäger mit Hasen / Self-portrait as hunter holding a hare, ca. 1855
Daguerreotypie, stereoskopische Aufnahme, handcoloriert/Daguerreotype, Stereoscopic Photograph, hand-colored, 6,7 x 5,8 (8,5 x 17,1)
The J. Paul Getty Museum, Los Angeles, Cal.
Abb. S. 42

WARREN T. THOMPSON
A Macaque in Aggressive Pose, 1853-1959
Daguerreotypie, stereoskopische Aufnahme, handcoloriert/Daguerreotype, Stereoscopic Photograph, hand-colored, 7,62 x 15,24 (8,9 x 17,8)
Wm. B. Becker Collection/American Museum of Photography, Huntington Woods
Abb. S. 62

WALDEMAR TITZENTHALER
Städtischer Schlachthof, Hammelschlachthaus, Friedrichshain, 1897
Kollodium/Collodion, 16,5 x 22,3 (24 x 31,5)
Ullstein Bild, Berlin
Abb. S. 110

ADRIEN ALBAN TOURNACHON
(Nadar Jeune)
Programmnummern aus dem Zirkus von Napoléon III und der Kaiserin / Programme numbers from the circus of Napoléon III and the empress, 1861
Salzpapier/Salted paper, 8 Cartes de Visite
Bibliothèque nationale de France, département des estampes et de la photographie, Paris
Abb. S. 177

ADRIEN ALBAN TOURNACHON
(Nadar Jeune)
Catharina, a. d. A.: *Race Chevaline. Concours de 1860*
Salzpapier/Salted paper, 16,7 x 23
The J. Paul Getty Museum, Los Angeles, Cal.
Abb. S. 83

ROSEMARIE TROCKEL
Hannah I, 1993
C-Print, 100 x 100
Courtesy Monika Sprüth/Philomene Magers, Köln
Abb. S. 282

ROSEMARIE TROCKEL
Hannah II, 1993
C-Print, 100 x 100
Courtesy Monika Sprüth/Philomene Magers, Köln
Abb. S. 283

VIVOT
Junge mit Spielzeugpferd / Boy with toy horse, 1876
Albumin/Albumen, Carte de Visite
Museum Folkwang, Essen, 14/2004
Abb. S. 25

A. VON ZHILINSKY
Goliath in seiner Transportkiste beim Eintreffen im Tierpark, 1920er
BS, 11,6 x 17
Deutsches Literaturarchiv, Marbach
Abb. S. 157

VW KAMPAGNE
In 6,6 Sekunden von 0 auf 100 km/h, 2002
Foto von Bob Elsdale und Denis Felix
Offset Druck, Fotomontage, Zeitschriftenseite/Offset Print, photomontage, page of a magazine
Volkswagen AG, Wolfsburg
Abb. S. 222/223

WALMSLEY BROTHERS
A Lonely Valley, ca. 1900
Platindruck/Platinotype, 28,7 x 37,5
The J. Paul Getty Museum, Los Angeles, Cal.
Abb. S. 35

HEDDA WALTHER
Hahn / Rooster, 1927
BS, 15,5 x 11,5
Deutsches Literaturarchiv, Marbach
Abb. S. 169

HEDDA WALTHER
Sperbergeier, vor 1931 / Sparrow hawk, before 1931
BS, 17 x 12,3
Deutsches Literaturarchiv, Marbach
Abb. S. 169

HEDDA WALTHER
Junger Schimpanse, 1920er / Young chimp, 1920s
BS, 22,9 x 17,6 (24 x 18,1)
Deutsches Literaturarchiv, Marbach
Abb. S. 195

WOLFGANG WEBER
a. d. R.: *Ein Nashorn greift mein Auto an*, 1934
BS, je 15,4 x 20,4
Ullstein Bild, Berlin
Abb. S. 55

WILLIAM WEGMAN
Purina Red, 1981
Polaroid Print, 73 x 55,9
Courtesy of Pace/MacGill, New York
Abb. S. 286/287

WILLIAM WEGMAN
Video Stills aus/from: *Spelling Lessons*, 1998
Polaroid Print, 155 x 50,8
Courtesy of Pace/MacGill, New York
Abb. S. 288

MANFRED WILLMANN
Pferd, 1982, a. d. S.: *Die Welt ist schön*, 1981–83
Cibachrome, 50,6 x 51,2
Museum Folkwang, Essen, 218/89
Abb. S. 107

GARRY WINOGRAND
Park Avenue, New York, 1959
BS, 34 x 22,1
The Museum of Modern Art, New York
Abb. S. 197

GARRY WINOGRAND
Texas State Fair, Dallas, 1964
BS, 21,7 x 32,6
The Museum of Modern Art, New York
Abb. S. 86

MICHAEL WOLF
Pinker Pudel in Hongkong, 2004
Light Jet, 40 x 50 (45 x 55)
Michael Wolf, Hongkong
Abb. S. 150

WOLS (Alfred Otto Wolfgang Schultze)
ohne Titel (Chicken and Egg), 1938/39
BS, 22,2 x 14,8
The J. Paul Getty Museum, Los Angeles, Cal.
Abb. S. 259

YLLA (Kamilla Koffler)
Nellie and Judie, ca. 1950
BS, 20,1 x 24,3
Center for Creative Photography, University of Arizona: Ylla Archive, Tucson
Abb. S. 182

YLLA (Kamilla Koffler)
Circus Chimpanzee, ca. 1950
BS, 24,5 x 20
Center for Creative Photography, University of Arizona: Ylla Archive, Tucson
Abb. S. 203

ATELIER ADELPHI UND CONSTANTINE ZANGAKI
Gemüsehändler, Aegypten, ca. 1880
Albumin/Albumen, 21,9 x 27,6 (27 x 35,7)
Völkerkundemuseum der Universität Zürich
Abb. S. 100

FRITZ ZIELESCH
Tierversuche, Versuchsanordnung mit Frosch / Animal experiments, experiment with frog, 1930
BS, 8,5 x 11,1 (23,5 x 16,8)
Ullstein Bild, Berlin
Abb. S. 121

BÜCHER

YANN ARTHUS-BERTRAND
Pferde, München 2005
Abb. S. 302

PETER BEARD
Tod der Wildnis, München 1978
Abb. S. 300

STEVE BLOOM
Affen. Eine Hommage, Köln 1999
Abb. S. 302

JIM BRANDENBURG
Bruder Wolf, Steinfurt 1996
Abb. S. 301

MITSUAKI IWAGO
Serengeti. Natural Order on the African Plain, London, 1987
Abb. S. 300

FRANS LANTING
Auge in Auge. Begegnungen in der Welt der Tiere, hg. von Christine Eckstrom, Davenport, Köln 1997
Abb. S. 301

MARIUS MAXWELL
Stalking big game with a camera in Equatorial Africa, London 1925
Abb. S. 299

MICHAEL NICHOLS AND GEOFFREY C. WARD
The year of the tiger, Washington 1998
Abb. S. 301

JEFFREY L. ROTMAN
Shark!, New York 1999
Abb. S. 302

CARL GEORG SCHILLINGS
Mit Blitzlicht und Büchse im Zauber des Eleléscho, Leipzig 1920
Abb. S. 299

HUGO VAN LAWICK
Among Predators and Prey, London 1986
Abb. S. 300

HEDDA WALTHER
Mein Hundebuch, 48 Bildnisstudien, Berlin 1931, S. 38/39
Abb. S. 299

YLLA
Deux petits ours, Lausanne 1954
Abb. S. 299

YLLA
Le petit éléphant, Lausanne 1955
Abb. S. 299

James Abbe
(1883 Alfred/Maine – 1973 San Francisco)
Starfotograf der Stummfilmära und einer der ersten amerikanischen Vertreter des Fotojournalismus.
Star photographer of the silent film era and one of the first American photojournalists.

Comte Olympe Aguado
(1827 Paris – 1894 Compiègne)
Der spanische Bankierssohn war Schüler von Gustave Le Gray, Vicomte Vigier und Edouard Delessert. Sein Werk besteht größtenteils aus Tier- und Landschaftsfotografien, die er Mitte des 19. Jahrhunderts in Fontainebleau und im Bois de Boulogne gemacht hat.
The Spanish son of a banker was a student of Gustave Le Gray, Vicomte Vigier and Edouard Delessert. His work consists mainly of animal and landscape photographs, which he produced in the mid 19th century in Fontainebleau and Bois de Boulogne.

Manuel Alvarez Bravo
(1902 Mexico City – 2002 Mexico City)
Alvarez studierte Literatur, Musik und Malerei und begann 1922 mit der Fotografie. Seit den 1930er Jahren gehört er zu den Vertretern der straight photography in Mexiko.
Alvarez studied literature, music and painting. Took up photography in 1922. Since the 1930s one of the representatives of straight photography in Mexico.

Claudia Angelmaier
(1972 Göppingen)
Angelmaier studierte Geographie, Anglistik und Kunstgeschichte, bevor sie 2001 an die Hochschule für Grafik und Buchkunst Leipzig wechselte. In ihren großformatigen Farbfotografien eignet sie sich Werke der bildenden Kunst an.
Studied geography, English language and literature, and arts before she changed to the Hochschule für Grafik und Buchkunst Leipzig in 2001. In her large-format colour photographies she refers to works of fine arts.

Ludwig Angerer
(1827 Malaczka/Ungarn – 1879 Wien)
Angerer arbeitete als Pharmazeut beim Militär und betätigte sich während dieser Zeit als Amateurfotograf. 1858 eröffnete er ein Atelier in Wien und erhielt 1860 den Titel des Hoffotografen. Er war vorrangig Porträtfotograf, fertigte aber auch Stadtansichten an, Kunstreproduktionen und Studien von präparierten Tieren.
Whilst a pharmacist in the army, he also worked as amateur photographer. 1858 he opened a studio in Vienna and in 1860 he received the title of court photographer. Mainly portraiture, but also town views, art reproductions, and studies of preserved animals.

Ottomar Anschütz
(1846 Lissa/Posen – 1907 Berlin)
Sein Name ist untrennbar mit der Entwicklung der Momentaufnahme und der Reihenfotografie verbunden. Er nutzte die Fotografie zur Sichtbarmachung schneller Bewegungen.
His name is synonymous with the development of the photograph and serial photography. He used photography to make quick movements visible.

Eugène Atget
(1857 Libourne – 1927 Paris)
Sein Ziel war es, die Stadt Paris so umfassend wie möglich fotografisch zu erfassen. Über drei Jahrzehnte spürte er bildwürdige Details im Stadtbild und Szenerien auf. Er gilt heute als Vorbild für viele Dokumentaristen.
His aim was to produce a photographic documentation of the town of Paris. For more than three decades he photographed urban details and Parisian scenery. Today he is considered an example for many documentarists.

José Azel
(1953 Havanna)
Azel ist freischaffender Fotojournalist. Seine Laufbahn begann 1978 beim *Miami Herald*. Er arbeitet u.a. für *National Geographic* und *Geo*. Er sucht mit seiner Fotografie Themen, die zwischen Natur und Abenteuer angesiedelt sind.
Azel works as a freelance photojournalist. He started his career in 1978 with the Miami Herald. Also works for National Geographic and Geo. Is attracted by subjects situated between nature and adventure.

George Barker
(1844 – 1894)
Amerikaner, Biografie unbekannt.
American, biography unknown.

Cecil Beaton
(1904 London – 1980 Broadchalke)
Beaton ist einer der Hauptvertreter der britischen Mode- und Gesellschaftsfotografie. Neben dieser Arbeit war er auch schriftstellerisch tätig und entwarf Bühnenbilder.
Beaton is one of the main representatives of British fashion and society photography. He also worked as writer and set-designer.

Albin Biblom
(1975 Västervik/Schweden)
Der Fotograf und Filmemacher Biblom studierte am International Center of

Photography New York und an der Gerrit Rietveld Academie Amsterdam. Er setzt sich fotografisch mit Zoos und naturhistorischen Museen auseinander. Aktuell arbeitet er an einem Projekt über die letzten Tanzbären in Bulgarien.
Photographer and film-maker. Studied at the International Center of Photography, New York, and the Gerrit Rietveld Academie, Amsterdam. His photographic subjects are zoos and natural history museums. At the moment he is working on a project about the last dancing bears in Bulgaria.

Louis-Auguste Bisson
(1814 Paris – 1876 Paris)
Louis-Auguste Bisson eröffnete unmittelbar nach der Veröffentlichung des fotografischen Verfahrens in Paris ein eigenes Fotoatelier. Erfolgreicher wurde es allerdings erst, als sein Bruder Auguste-Rosalie (1826 Paris – 1900 Paris) mit in das Geschäft einstieg. Das Atelier der Bisson-frères wurde zum Treffpunkt der künstlerischen Zirkel.
Shortly after the photographic process had become known, Louis-Auguste Bisson opened his own photographic studio in Paris. It became, however, more successful when his brother, Auguste-Rosalie (1826 Paris – 1900 Paris), joined the business. The studio of Bisson-frères became a meeting-place for artistic circles.

Steve Bloom
(1953 Südafrika)
Bloom ist freier Fotograf, dessen fotografische Arbeit mit der Dokumentation der 1970er Jahre in Südafrika begann. Seine 'Wildlife'-Fotografie versteht sich nicht als Dokumentation, sondern er möchte ein Gefühl für die bedrohte Tierwelt schaffen.
Independent photographer, whose photographic work started off with a documentation of the 1970s in South Africa. Considers his 'Wildlife' photography not as documentation, but as a means of creating a feeling for endangered species.

Bill Brandt
(1904 Hamburg – 1983 London)
Die fotografische Laufbahn Brandts beginnt mit einem dreimonatigen Praktikum im Atelier von Man Ray 1929. 1969 hatte er im Museum of Modern Art New York eine Einzelausstellung und gilt heute als einer der bedeutendsten britischen Fotografen im 20. Jahrhundert.
Bill Brandt's photographic career started in 1929 with three months of practical training in the studio of Man Ray. In 1969 he had a solo exhibition in New York's Museum of Modern Art. Is now considered one of the most important British photographers of the 20th century.

Adolphe Braun
(1812 Besançon – 1877 Dornach)
Seinen größten wirtschaftlichen Erfolg hatte Braun mit fotografischen Reproduktionen von Kunstwerken. Er war ursprünglich Stoffdesigner und hatte ab 1850 ein Atelier in Paris. Er stellte Vorlagenbücher mit Blumen und Tiermotiven für Dekorationsmaler und Stoffgestalter her.
He was most successful with photographic reproductions of art works. Above all a textile designer, he opened a studio in Paris in 1850. He produced model books for decoration painters and textile designers with floral and animal motives.

Balthasar Burkhard
(1944 Bern)
Nach einer Fotolehre bei Kurt Blum arbeitet Burkhard seit 1965 als freischaffender Fotograf. Von 1974 bis 1980 lebte er in Chicago und wurde hier in einer ersten Einzelausstellung gezeigt. Seine erste Retrospektive fand 1997 im Musée Rath bei Genf statt.
After a photographic training by Karl Blum, has been working as freelance photographer since 1965. From 1974 until 1980 he lived in Chicago and had his first solo exhibition there. His first retrospective exhibition was shown in Musée Rath near Geneva in 1997.

Marie José Burki
(1961 Biel)
Die schweizer Videokünstlerin lebt und arbeitet in Brüssel. Ihre erste Einzelausstellung fand 1986 im Centre Culturel in Paris statt. Seitdem hatte sie zahlreiche Präsentationen unter anderem *A dog in my mind*, 1998 in der Kunsthalle Bern, *What could Saint Francis have been saying to the birds?*, 2003 im Musée des Arts Contemporains, Le Grand Hornu, Belgien.
Swiss video artist. Lives and works in Brussels. First solo exhibition 1986 in the Centre Culturel in Paris. Since then numerous presentations, e.g. *A dog in my mind*, 1998 in Kunsthalle Bern, *What could Saint Francis have been saying to the birds*, 2003 in Musée des Arts Contemporains, Le Grand Hornu, Belgium.

Lewis Carroll
(1832 Daresbury – 1889 Guildford)
Der Engländer, der mit bürgerlichem Namen Charles Lutwidge Dodgson hieß, studierte Mathematik. Weltruhm erlangte er durch sein 1865 erschienenes Buch *Alice's Adventures in Wonderland*. Seine ersten Fotografien, vorwiegend Mädchenporträts und Aktbildnisse, entstanden 1856. Steichen integrierte 1955 seine Fotos in die Ausstellung *Family of Man*.
Carroll, Englishman, originally named Charles Lutwidge Dodgson, studied mathematics. World famous by his book *Alice's Adventures in Wonderland*, published in 1865. His first photographs, mainly girls portraits and portraits of nudes, were produced in 1856. Steichen included his photos in his exhibition *Family of Man*.

Henri Cartier-Bresson
(1908 Canteloup – 2004 Paris)
Cartier-Bressons künstlerische Laufbahn begann mit einem Malereistudium in Paris. 1931 begann er mit Fotografie und seit 1947 war er Gründungsmitglied der Agentur *Magnum*. Zu seinem 95. Geburtstag 2003 wurde er mit einer Retrospektive in der Bibliothèque nationale de France in Paris geehrt.

Cartier-Bresson's artistic career started with a study of painting in Paris. 1931 he took up photography. In 1947 he was one of the founders of Magnum. On the occasion of his 95th birthday, 2003, he was honoured with a retrospective exhibition in the Bibliothèque nationale de France in Paris.

Chien-Chi Chang

(1961 Taichung/Taiwan)

Chien-Chi Chang ist Mitglied der Fotoagentur *Magnum*. Er lebt und arbeitet in Taipei und New York. Seine Fotos werden unter anderem in *Geo* veröffentlicht.

Member of the photo agency *Magnum*. Lives and works in Taipei and New York. Publishes in *Geo* and other magazines.

Juan Carlos María Isidor de Borbón Comte de Montizon

(1822 – 1887)

Der im englischen Exil lebende spanische Baron war Amateurfotograf und einer der ersten, der sich an die Darstellung von exotischen Tieren begab. Seine Aufnahme eines Nilpferdes im Zoo des Regent Parks ist berühmt und wurde in *The Photographic Album for the year* 1855 veröffentlicht.

Comte de Montizon, Spanish baron living in exile in England, was an amateur photographer and one of the first who tried the representation of exotic animals. His photograph of a hippopotamus in the zoo of Regent Park is famous and was published in *The Photographic Album for the year* 1855.

F. D. Conard

Conard montierte in den 1930er Jahren Postkartenmotive. Die so genannten Giant-Postcards wurden seit der Jahrhundertwende als ironische Reaktionen auf Katastrophen in der Landwirtschaft entwickelt. Conard kommentierte die Heuschreckenplage in Kansas 1935.

Mounted postcard subjects in the 1930s. The so-called giant-postcards were developed since the turn of the centruy as ironic reactions to disasters in agriculture. Conard commented on the grasshoppers' plague in Kansas in 1935.

Otto Croy

(1902 Prag – 1977 München)

Der promovierte Chemiker Croy war nach seiner Tätigkeit an der Karls-Universität in Prag am fotochemischen Institut der Technischen Hochschule in Berlin tätig. Nebenher arbeitete er als freier Bildjournalist und Redakteur der *Photo-Rundschau*. 1950 übernahm er die Chefredaktion des *Photo-Magazins* und veröffentlichte seine Arbeiten in Büchern.

PhD in chemistry. After Karls-Universität in Prague he worked at the Photochemical Institute of the Technische Hochschule, Berlin. At the same time worked as independent photojournalist and journalist of *Photo-Rundschau*, Berlin. In 1950 became chief-editor of *Photo-Magazin* and published his works in books.

D'Ora, Madame

(Dora Kallmus)

(1881 Wien – 1963 Frohnleiten)

Die Österreicherin Dora Philippine Kallmus eröffnete 1907 zusammen mit Arthur Benda in Wien ein Fotoatelier mit dem Namen D'Ora. Er wurde zum Pseudonym für die Fotografin, die vor allem durch ihre Porträts, Mode- und Glamourbilder berühmt wurde. 1925 eröffnete sie ein zweites Studio in Paris. Nachdem sie während des Krieges in der Ardèche lebte, kehrte sie 1947 nach Paris zurück. Ihre Schlachthofserie, die hier in den 1950er Jahren entstand, bildet einen bizarren Kontrast zu ihrem Frühwerk.

The Austrian Dora Philippine Kallmus, together with Arthur Benda, opened a photo studio in Vienna in 1907 and called it D'Ora. The name became the photographer's pseudonym. Famous especially for her portraits, fashion and glamour photographs. 1925 she opened a second studio in Paris. Having lived in the Ardèche during World War II, she returned to Paris in 1947. Her slaughterhouse series in the 1950s forms a bizarre contrast to her early works.

Louis-Adolphe-Humbert de Molard

(1830 Paris – 1874 Paris)

Baron de Molard beschäftigte sich mit den frühen fotografischen Techniken und entwickelte eigenständige Verfahren mit Albumin-Glasnegativen. Sein Metier war die Darstellung des alltäglichen Landlebens. Die ersten Aufnahmen dieser Genredarstellungen entstanden ab 1848. Er war Gründungsmitglied der Société Française de Photographie.

Baron de Molard occupied himself with early photographic techniques and developed his own processes with albumen glass negatives. Devoted himself to the representation of the ordinary country life. First photographs of this genre in 1848. Founding member of the Société Française de Photographie.

Thomas James Dixon

(1857 London – 1943 London)

Sohn des Londoner Fotografen Henry Dixon (1820–1893), mit dem er zusammenarbeitete. Sie lebten in direkter Nähe des Londoner Zoos und spezialisierten sich, neben der Dokumentation alter Londoner Gebäude, auf die Tierfotografie. Von 1878 an ist T. J. Dixon Mitglied der Photographic Society of Great Britain.

Son of the London photographer Henry Dixon (1820–1893), with whom he collaborated. They lived close to the London zoo, and, apart from the documentation of old town buildings, they specialized in animal photography. Member of the Photographic Society of Great Britain in 1878.

John Dominis

(1921 Los Angeles)

Dominis ist freischaffender Bildberichterstatter. Er studierte Fotografie und Film und arbeitet für *Life* und andere Magazine. 1951 nahm er an der Ausstellung *Memorable Life Photographs* im Museum of Modern

Art New York teil. Er reist und fotografiert in Amerika, Asien und Afrika.
Freelance photo journalist. Studies photography and film. Works for *Life* and other magazines. 1951 member of the exhibition *Memorable Life Photographs* in Museum of Modern Art New York. Travels and photographs in North America, Asia and Africa.

Pierre Dubreuil
(1872 Lille – 1946 Brüssel)
Der gelernte Kaufmann Dubreuil ist wie viele Fotografen seiner Generation Autodidakt. Dubreuil war Mitglied der fotografischen Gesellschaft in Lille. 1912 hatte er die erste Einzelausstellung, 1935 eine Retrospektive in der Royal Photographic Society in London.
With qualifications in business, Pierre Dubreuil was – like many of his contemporaries – a self-educated photographer. Member of the photographic society in Lille. First solo exhibition in 1912. 1935 retrospective exhibition in the Royal Photographic Society in London.

J. Adéodat Dumont
Dumont fertigte Fotografien im Carte de visite-Format in den 1880er Jahren an.
In the 1880s he produced photographs in the format of carte de visite.

Thomas Eakins
(1844 Philadelphia – 1916 Dakota)
Eakins ist vorrangig Maler. Er studierte an der Pennsylvania Academy of Fine Arts und der École des Beaux Arts in Paris. Seine ersten Fotografien sind als Vorstudien zu seinen malerischen Arbeiten zu sehen. Er war mit Eadweard Muybridge befreundet, mit dem er 1884–1885 zusammenarbeitete. Zu seinem fotografischen Werk gehören neben Porträts auch Landschafts- und Naturbilder.
Primarily a painter. Studied at the Pennsylvania Academy of Fine Arts and the École des Beaux Arts Paris. His first photographs were drafts for his paintings. Friend of Eadweard Muybridge, with whom he collaborated 1884–1885. His photographic works include portraits, landscape- and nature photographs.

Florian Ebner
(1970 Regensburg)
Studium der Fotografie an der École Nationale de la Photographie in Arles sowie der Kunstgeschichte und Geschichte an der Ruhruniversität Bochum. Veröffentlichungen zur Fotografie, u.a. *Metamorphosen des Gesichts. Die Verwandlungen durch Licht von Helmar Lerski*. Arbeitet als Assistent für Fotografie an der Hochschule für Grafik und Buchkunst, Leipzig.
Studied photography at the École Nationale de la Photographie in Arles, and art history and history at the Ruhruniversität Bochum. Publications on photography, e.g *Metamorphosis of the face. The "Verwandlungen durch Licht" by Helmar Lerski.* Assistant professor of photography at the Hochschule für Grafik und Buchkunst, Leipzig.

William Eggleston
(1939 Memphis)
Eggleston ist Pionier der künstlerischen Farbfotografie. Seine Bildthemen kommen aus der amerikanischen Alltagswelt, er macht Stadt- und Naturstudien. 1976 zeigt das Museum of Modern Art New York seine Werkschau mit dem Titel *William Eggleston's Guide.*
Pioneer of artistic colour photography. His subjects are taken from the American everyday life; town and nature scenes. 1976 Museum of Modern Art New York presented his works under the title *William Eggleston's Guide.*

Georg Einbeck
(1871 Gollnschütz/Westpreußen – 1951 Paris)
1896 ging Einbeck nach Hamburg und arbeitete als Kaufmann und Kunstmaler. Zwischen 1897 und 1903 war er Mitglied der Gesellschaft zur Förderung der Amateurphotographie in Hamburg.
In 1896 Einbeck moved to Hamburg, where he worked as businessman and painter. Between 1897 and 1903 he was a member of the Gesellschaft zur Förderung der Amateurphotographie in Hamburg.

Sabine Emmerich
(1964 Marburg)
Die in Hamburg lebende Fotografin studierte Freie Kunst an der Hochschule für Bildende Künste Lerchenfeld. Ihre Arbeiten wurden seitdem mehrfach ausgestellt.
Photographer, living in Hamburg. Studied free arts at the Hochschule für Bildende Künste Lerchenfeld. Several exhibitions.

Lotte Errell
(1903 Münster – 1991 München)
Errell ist vor allem als Reisefotografin der 1930er Jahre bekannt. Sie war Autodidaktin und fing Mitte der 1920er Jahre als Mitarbeiterin im Werbeatelier Richard Levy Errells in Berlin an zu fotografieren, mit dem sie 1924–1933 verheiratet war. Ihre Reise- und Expeditionsfotos aus Ghana, der Mongolei, China, Kurdistan und dem Irak wurden zahlreich veröffentlicht.
Especially known as travelling photographer in the 1930s. Self-taught. Started photographing in the mid 1920s working in Richard Levy Errells advertising agency in Berlin. Married with Errell from 1924–1933. Her travel- and expedition photos from Ghana, Mongolia, China, Kurdistan and Iraq were frequently published.

Richard Levy Errell
(1899 Krefeld – 1992 Locarno)
Das Betätigungsfeld Errells war nicht ausschließlich die Fotografie, sondern er war ebenso Grafiker und Redakteur. 1937 emigrierte er nach Palästina und wurde 1948 grafischer Berater der israelischen Regierung. 1961 zog er in die Schweiz.
Photographer, graphic designer and editor. Emigrated to Palestine in 1937. 1948 became graphic consultant for the Israeli government. Moved to Switzerland in 1961.

Elliott Erwitt
(1928 Paris)
Der Sohn russischer Emigranten ging 1939 in die USA und studierte Fotografie und Film in Los Angeles. Neben seinen Bildessays ist er berühmt durch seine interpretativen und tragikomischen Hundefotos.
Son of Russian emigrants. Went to the United States in 1939 and studied film and photography in Los Angeles. Famous for his photo essays and his interpretative and tragicomic dog photos.

Frank Eugene
(1865 New York – 1936 München)
Eugene studierte in der Zeit von 1886 bis 1894 an der Königlichen Akademie der Künste in München Zeichnung und Malerei. Er war Mitbegründer der *Photo-Secession.*
Studied drawing and painting at the Königliche Akademie der Künste in Munich from 1886-1894. Co-founder of the *Photo-Secession.*

Walker Evans
(1903 Saint Louis – 1975 New Haven)
Evans' fotografische Laufbahn begann als Autodidakt 1928 mit einer kleinen Rollfilmkamera. Seine Bilder und Reportagen vom alltäglichen Leben in Amerika sind in der Tradition der straight photography zu sehen.
His photographic career started in 1928 with a small roll film camera. His pictures and documentations of American ordinary life are in the tradition of straight photography.

Constant Alexandre Famin
(1827 – 1888)
Famin, dessen Vorname teilweise als Charles überliefert wurde, war sowohl Maler als auch Fotograf. 1858 eröffnete er ein Atelier in Paris. Später arbeitete er in Orléans. Neben seiner Tierfotografie befasste er sich mit Landschaftsfotografie und ländlichen Genrebildern.
In the written records his first name is sometimes given as Charles. Painter and photographer. 1858 opened a studio in Paris. Later worked in Orléans. In addition to his animal photography he photographed landscapes and rural genre pictures.

Paul Faulstich
Faulstich führte in den 1920er Jahren das Atelier Helionovum in Leipzig.
In the 1920s Faulstich owned a studio in Leipzig called Atelier Helionovum.

Georg Fischer
(1947 Bonn)
Nach einer industriellen Ausbildung studierte Fischer bei Otto Steinert an der Folkwang Hochschule in Essen. Er ist von dieser Zeit an als freier Fotojournalist tätig und arbeitete in den Anfangsjahren vor allem in Kriegsgebieten und Entwicklungsländern. Ab den 1980er Jahren stehen bei ihm Themen aus den Bereichen Wissenschaft, Technik und Werbung im Vordergrund.
After a practical training in industry, Fischer studied at the Folkwang Hochschule in Essen and had lessons with Otto Steinert. Freelance photojournalist, in his first years mainly in war areas and developing countries. From the 1980s on has been concentrating on science, technique and advertising.

Joan Fontcuberta
(1955 Barcelona)
Der Spanier Fontcuberta gilt als der Erfinder von phantastischen Tier- und Pflanzenwelten. Er studierte Journalismus und arbeitete in der Werbebranche. Anfang der 1970er Jahre begann er mit der Fotografie.
Spanish, Fontcuberta is regarded as inventor of fantastic animal- and plant worlds. He studied journalism and worked in the field of advertising. Began to work with photography beginning of the 1970s.

Pere Formiguera
(1952 Barcelona)
Formiguera ist Schriftsteller und Fotograf. Er ist Mitbegründer des Centre de Creació Fotografica in Barcelona.
Formiguera is writer and photographer. He is co-founder of the Centre de Creació Fotografica in Barcelona.

Robert Frank
(1924 Zürich)
Frank ist sowohl Fotograf als auch Filmemacher. Er fotografiert den amerikanischen Lebensstil und ist Wegbereiter einer neuen dokumentarischen Bildsprache.
Photographer and filmmaker. Photographed the American style of life. Is regarded as path breaking innovator for a new documentary photography.

Geissler & Sann
Die Videokünstler Beate Geissler (1970 Neuendettelsau) und Oliver Sann (1968 Düsseldorf) arbeiten seit 1993 als Team zusammen. Sie nehmen an zahlreichen Ausstellungen teil und waren 2002 Sonderpreisträger beim Videokunstpreis in Marl.
Videoartists Beate Geissler (1970 Neuendettelsau) and Oliver Sann (1968 Düsseldorf) have been working together since 1993. Participants in numerous exhibitions and 2002 special prize winners at the video art prize in Marl.

Paul Géniaux
(1873 – ?)
Die fotografische Tätigkeit Géniaux ist bis 1930 belegt. Um den Jahrhundertwechsel befasste er sich fotografisch mit dem täglichen Leben in Paris und der Bretagne. Seine Fotos sind an den Realismus von Atget angelehnt.
Géniaux's photographic activities can be traced up to 1930. Around the turn of the century he documented the daily life of Paris and the Bretagne. His photographs can be seen in the tradition of Atget's realism.

Arnold Genthe
(1869 Berlin – 1942 New Milford/Connecticut)
Genthe war einer der frühen Reportagefo-

tografen, aber auch Porträtist. 1897 eröffnete er sein Studio in San Francisco. 1911 ging er nach New York und widmete sich hier vor allem der Fotografie von Schauspielern und Tänzern.
One of the early reportage photographers, but also portraitist. Opened a studio in San Francisco in 1897. Moved to New York in 1911, where he concentrated on photographing actors and dancers.

Karl Gerstner
Gerstner betrieb ein Fotoatelier in Stuttgart und spezialisierte sich auf Jagddarstellungen.
Ran a photo studio in Stuttgart, specialized in hunting scenes.

Mario Giacomelli
(1925 Senigallia – 2000 Ancona)
Das Werk des italienischen Neorealisten besteht sowohl aus journalistischen als auch aus fototechnisch-experimentellen Arbeiten. Ursprünglich war Giacomelli Typograf. Seine fotografische Tätigkeit begann 1952 als Autodidakt, seit dieser Zeit war er freischaffend und machte neben Reisereportagen auch Porträts und Naturaufnahmen.
Italian neorealist. Journalistic as well as phototechnical-experimental works. Educated in typography, his photographic activities started in 1952 by self-education. Since that time freelance photographer. Travel reports, portraits and nature photography.

Bruce Gilden
(1946 New York)
Gilden besuchte Kurse an der School of Visual Arts in New York und ist bei seiner street photography von William Klein und Diane Arbus beeinflusst. Seine Szenerien zeigen das Leben in der Metropole.
Courses at the School of Visual Arts in New York. His street photography was influenced by William Klein and Diane Arbus. His sceneries document life in a metropolis.

Ludwig Grillich
(1856 – 1926 Wien)
Grillich eröffnete sein erstes Atelier in Wien 1885, ein weiteres 1890. Er war vor allem als Porträtfotograf tätig und engagierte sich in verschiedenen fotografischen Vereinigungen, wie der Photographischen Gesellschaft in Wien und dem Österreichischen Photographenverein. Daneben trug er ab 1888 den Titel des schwedischen Hoffotografen und ab 1890 auch den russischen Hoftitel.
Opened his first studio in Vienna in 1885, another in 1890. Mainly active as portrait photographer. Member of different photographic circles, e.g. the Photographische Gesellschaft in Vienna and Österreichischer Photographenverein. 1888 received the title of Swedish Court photographer, 1890 the title of Russian Court photographer

Andreas Gursky
(1955 Leipzig)
Nach einem Studium 1978–1981 an der Essener Folkwang Schule wechselte Gursky an die Kunstakademie in Düsseldorf, wo er Meisterschüler bei Bernd Becher wurde. 2001 hatte er eine Einzelausstellung im Museum of Modern Art New York.
After his studies at the Folkwang Schule in Essen 1978–1981, changed to Kunstakademie Düsseldorf, where he became master student of Bernd Becher. 2001 he had a solo exhibition at the Museum of Modern Art New York.

Eugene S. M. Haines
Haines war in den 1870er Jahren in Albany, New York tätig.
Worked in Albany, New York, in the 1870s.

Philippe Halsman
(1906 Riga – 1979 New York)
Halsman studierte 1924–1928 Elektrotechnik in Dresden. Er war Autodidakt und begann parallel zu seinem Studium als Fotograf für den Ullstein Verlag zu arbeiten. 1928 zog er nach Paris, wo er sich mit Mode- und Porträtfotografie selbstständig machte. 1941 floh er in die USA, wo er in New York fortan als Fotojournalist und Modefotograf tätig war.
Halsman studied electrical engineering in Dresden from 1924–1928. He was self-educated and, parallel to his studies as photographer, began working for Ullstein Verlag. Moved to Paris in 1928, where he set up his own business with fashion and portrait photography. 1941 he fled from Germany to the United States, where he worked as photo journalist and fashion photographer.

Elisabeth Hase
(1905 Döhlen – 1991 Frankfurt)
Vor ihrer Fotolehre im Atelier von Dr. Paul Wolff studierte Hase an der Kunstgewerbeschule, der späteren Städelschule, in Frankfurt/Main Werbegrafik und Buchgestaltung. 1932 machte sie sich selbstständig als Presse- und Werbefotografin.
Before her practical photographic training in the studio of Dr. Paul Wolff, Hase studied at the Kunstgewerbeschule, the later Städelschule in Frankfurt/Main, commercial design and book design. In 1932 set up her own business as press and commercial photographer.

Hermann Heid
(1834 Darmstadt – 1891 Wien)
Der promovierte Chemiker machte im Anschluss an sein Studium eine Fotolehre bei Julius Schnauß in Jena. Er wechselte von hier aus nach Wien, wo er ab 1868 ein eigenes Atelier leitete. Sein Werk umfasst Porträts, Architekturansichten sowie Tier- und Körperstudien. Diese wurden als Serien in Paris publiziert und dienten als Vorlagen für Künstler und Kunsthandwerker. Er war auf den Weltausstellungen 1873 in Wien und fünf Jahre später in Paris mit seinen Fotovorlagen vertreten.
Doctorate in chemistry, followed by a practical training in the studio of Julius Schnauß in Jena. Went to Vienna, where he opened his own studio in 1868. Photographed portraits, architectural views,

animal- and body studies. These were published in serial in Paris and used as drafts for artists and artistic craftsmen. His photographic models were exhibited 1873 at the world fair in Vienna and five years later in Paris.

HIRO
(1930 Shanghai)
Der als Yasuhiro Wakabayashi geborene Fotograf studierte nach seiner Emigration in die USA an der New Yorker School for Social Research bei Alexey Brodovitch. Gleichzeitig wurde er Assistent bei Richard Avedon. 1958 eröffnete er sein eigenes Studio.
Photographer, born as Yasuhiro Wakabayashi. After his emigration to the United States he studied at the New York School for Social Research with Alexey Brodovitch. At the same time he was assistant of Richard Avedon. Opened his own studio in 1958.

Candida Höfer
(1944 Eberswalde)
Die Becher-Schülerin setzt sich seit den 1970er Jahren konzeptionell mit öffentlichen Interieurs auseinander. Vor ihrem Düsseldorfer Studium absolvierte sie ein Volontariat im Kölner Studio Schmölz-Huth und studierte dort an der Werkschule.
Since the 1970s this Becher student has been conceptually working on public interieurs. Before her studies in Düsseldorf she was trainee in the Schmölz-Huth studio in Cologne, where she also attended the Werkschule.

Frederick Hollyer
(1837 London – 1933 London)
Hollyer spezialisierte sich auf die Reproduktion von Gemälden und zählt hiermit zu den bedeutendsten seiner Zeit in England. Um 1860 begann er mit der Fotografie. Die Vervielfältigung von Kunstwerken blieb auch hier seine Hauptbeschäftigung, neben Künstler- und Schriftstellerporträts. Darüber hinaus machte er eine Anzahl von Tierstudien, Stillleben und Seestücken. 1913 setzte er sich zur Ruhe und überließ das Geschäft seinem Sohn.
Specialized in the reproduction of paintings, for which he was most famous at the time in England. Took up photography around 1860, but here too, the reproduction of art works remained his chief occupation, aside from portraits of artists and writers. Also produced a number of animal studies, still life and sea views. In 1913 he retired and gave the business to his son.

Willoughby Wallace Hooper
(1837 Kennington – 1912 Klimington)
Der Engländer gilt als der Pionier der ethnographischen Fotografie. Als Kavallerie-Leutnant ging er 1858 nach Indien, hier begann er mit der Fotografie des britischen Lebens in der Kolonie, der indischen Einwohner und deren kultureller Tradition.
Regarded as the pioneer of ethnographic photography. As lieutenant of the cavalry went to India in 1858, where he began to take photographs of British life in the colony, the Indian people and their cultural traditions.

Henry Irving
Irving machte um die Jahrhundertwende Fotoserien zu Verhaltensweisen von Zootieren.
Around the turn of the last century Irving produced photo series about the behaviour of zoo animals.

Steffen Junghans
(1963 Leipzig)
Der gelernte Werkzeugmacher begann 1992 als freier Bildreporter, bevor er 1994 ein Fotostudium an der Hochschule für Grafik und Buchkunst in Leipzig begann. Er ist seit 2001 freischaffend.
Originally trained as toolmaker, Junghans started his career as freelance photojournalist in 1992, followed by studies in photography at the Hochschule für Grafik und Buchkunst in Leipzig in 1994. Since 2001 freelance.

André Kertész
(1894 Budapest – 1985 New York)
Kertész begann autodidaktisch mit der Fotografie. 1925 zog er nach Paris und machte unter anderem die Bekanntschaft von Man Ray und André Breton. Seine erste Einzelausstellung fand hier 1927 statt. Zu dieser Zeit begann seine Tätigkeit für zahlreiche Zeitschriften, die er nach seiner Emigration nach New York 1936 fortführte.
Kertész was a self-educated photographer. In 1925 he moved to Paris, where he met Man Ray and André Breton. Had his first solo exhibition in Paris in 1927. At this time he started working for numerous magazines, which he continued after his emigration to New York in 1936.

Philipp Kester
(1873 Kirchenlaibach/Oberfranken – 1958 München)
Der Schriftsteller und Pressefotograf Kester belieferte seit den 1890er Jahren illustrierte Wochenzeitschriften in Deutschland und Nordamerika. Er zählt zu den herausragenden Figuren der frühen Pressefotografie und gründete 1910 den Verband deutscher Illustrations-Fotografen mit.
Kester, writer and press photographer, worked for illustrated magazines in Germany and North America from the 1890s. He ranks as one of the leading figures of early press photography and in 1910 co-founded the Verband deutscher Illustrations-Fotografen.

Aart Klein
(1909 Amsterdam – 2001 Amsterdam)
Klein ist vor allem als Presse- und Dokumentarfotograf bekannt. Er war Autodidakt und arbeitete in den 1930er Jahren für die Agentur Polygoon. Während des Zweiten Weltkriegs wurde er nach Deutschland deportiert und als Porträtfotograf eingesetzt. Neben Architektur und Thea-

teraufnahmen ist vor allem die Landschaft sein späteres Thema. 1954 nahm er an der Ausstellung *Subjektive Fotografie II* in Saarbrücken teil.
Mainly known as press- and documentary photographer. He was self-educated and worked for the agency Polygoon in the 1930s. During World War II he was deported to Germany to work as portrait photographer. Apart from architecture and theatre photography he later concentrated on landscapes. In 1954 he took part in the exhibition Subjektive Fotografie II in Saarbrücken.

Karen Knorr
(1954 Frankfurt)
Knorr stellte erstmalig im Zusammenhang der Ausstellung *Punks & Teds* in der Photographers' Gallery in London 1978 aus. Sie studierte Fotografie am Polytechnic of Central London und arbeitet heute als freie Fotografin.
First exhibitions as member of the exhibition *Punks & Teds* in the Photographers' Gallery in London 1978. Studied photography at the Polytechnic of Central London. Freelance photographer.

Wilmar Koenig
(1952 Berlin)
Neben seinem Architekturstudium 1972 bis 1982 widmete sich Koenig der Architekturfotografie und engagierte sich bei freien Fotoprojekten. 1984 verbrachte er einen Studienaufenthalt bei William Eggleston, was ihn in seiner dokumentarischen Arbeitsweise prägte.
Parallel to his studies in architecture 1972–1982 Koenig photographed architecture and engaged in independent photo projects. In 1984 he spent some time training at William Eggleston's which influenced his documentary style.

Jan Kornstaedt
(1969 Berlin)
Kornstaedt studierte in Essen und arbeitet heute als freier Fotograf für verschiedene Magazine und Werbeaufträge.
Studied in Essen. Freelance photographer for different magazines and advertising companies.

Josef Koudelka
(1938 Boskovice/Tschechoslowakei)
Die ersten Fotografien Koudelkas entstanden 1952. Er ist seit 1974 Mitglied bei *Magnum* und hatte im darauffolgenden Jahr eine Einzelausstellung im Museum of Modern Art New York.
First photographs in 1952. Since 1974 member of *Magnum*. 1975 solo exhibition at the Museum of Modern Art New York.

Heinrich Kühn
(1866 Dresden – 1944 Birgitz)
Der Kunstfotograf Kühn studierte Botanik und Medizin. 1888 begann er mit seinen fotografischen Experimenten im Bereich der Edeldruckverfahren. Seine großformatigen Gummidrucke von Stillleben und Landschaften wurden in *Camera Work* publiziert. 1914 eröffnete er in Innsbruck eine Schule für Fotografie.
The pictorial photographer Kühn studied botany and medicine. In 1888 he started with his photographic experiments in the field of high-quality print processing. His large-size rubber prints of still life and landscapes were published in *Camera Work*. In 1914 he opened a school for photography in Innsbruck.

Adolf Kull
Kull betrieb im ausgehenden 19. Jahrhundert ein Fotoatelier in Stuttgart. Die Fotografie und die Darstellung von Tieren entsprach seiner Familientradition. Sein Vater arbeitete als Porträtist und Lithograf nach fotografischen Vorlagen, sein Bruder Albert spezialisierte sich auf Tierillustrationen für naturkundliche Bücher und Zeitschriften.
In the 1890s Kull ran a photo studio in Stuttgart. Photography and the portrayal of animals were a family tradition. His father worked as portraitist and lithographer after photographic models. His brother Albert was specialized on animal illustrations for natural history books and magazines.

Jacques-Henri Lartigue
(1894 Courbevoie – 1986 Nizza)
Lartigue war Fotoamateur, der das Medium nutzte, um seine unmittelbare bürgerliche Lebenswelt bildnerisch zu erfassen. 1963 wurde er im Museum of Modern Art New York in einer Einzelausstellung gezeigt.
Lartigue was a photo amateur who used the medium to document the bourgeois lifestyle. 1963 he had a solo exhibition in the Museum of Modern Art New York.

Franz Lazi
(1922 Freudenstadt – 1998 Stuttgart)
Nach einer Fotolehre bei seinem Vater Adolf Lazi arbeitet er ab 1949 selbstständig und war Mitbegründer des Bunds Freischaffender Fotodesigner. Er war Produzent von Experimental- und Werbefilmen und unternahm Expeditionen, unter anderem zum Südpol, wo er sowohl filmte als auch fotografierte.
After a practical training in the studio of his father, Adolf Lazi, he worked independently after 1949 and was co-founder of the Bund Freischaffender Fotodesigner. Produced experimental- and advertising films and went on expeditions, inter alia to the South Pole, where he filmed and photographed.

Henri Le Lieure
(1831 Nantes – 1914 Rom)
Le Lieure begann 1861 in Turin zu fotografieren. Er betrieb ein Porträtatelier und fertigte Stereoaufnahmen an. Ab 1870 lebte und arbeitete er in Rom.
Took up photography in Turin in 1861. Ran a portrait studio and produced stereo prints. From 1870 on he lived and worked in Rome.

Robert Lebeck
(1929 Berlin)
Im Zusammenhang seines Studiums 1949–1951 an der Columbia University, New York,

kam Lebeck in Kontakt mit der amerikanischen illustrierten Presse, deren Fotografie und Grafik. Nach seiner Rückkehr 1952 nach Deutschland arbeitete er erst als freier Fotojournalist, dann für den *Stern* und *Geo*.
During his studies at the Columbia University, New York, in 1949-51 Lebeck came into contact with American illustrated press, photography and design. After his return to Germany in 1952 he was first a freelance photojournalist, then worked for *Stern* and *Geo*.

Jochen Lempert
(1958 Hamburg)
Der Biologe Lempert beschäftigte sich anfänglich mit experimentellen Filmen, bevor er Ende der 1980er Jahre mit der Fotografie begann. Er verbindet seine naturwissenschaftlichen Interessen mit dem Medium und geht den verschiedenen Spielarten von Natur- und Tiernachahmungen nach. Seine Arbeiten *365 Tafeln zur Naturgeschichte* wurden 1997 in Bonn ausgestellt.
Biologist by profession, Lempert first tried experimental filming before he took up photography at the end of the 1980s. Combined his scientific interest with the medium and explored the various kinds of nature- and animal imitation. His works *365 Tafeln zur Naturgeschichte* were exhibited in Bonn in 1997.

Jo Longhurst
(1976 Chelmsford/Essex)
Seit mehreren Jahren beschäftigt sich die Künstlerin Longhurst mit der Darstellung von Hunden und erkundet die Ideen von Konformität und Differenzierung, Zucht und Eugenik – die Suche nach Perfektion.
For many years artist, Longhurst has been working on the presentation of dogs, exploring the notions of conformity and distinction, breed and eugenics – the search for perfection.

Aleksandras Macijauskas
(1938 Kaunas/Litauen)
Macijauskas arbeitet als Fotojournalist. Im Mittelpunkt seiner Arbeit steht der Mensch, den er ungeschönt und in über Jahre angelegten Reportagen in Szene setzt. Seit 1980 ist er Präsident der Photography Society of Lithuania.
Photojournalist, focussing on the unvarnished man, staging him in series that last over years. Since 1980 president of Photography Society of Lithuania.

Edward Malindine
Britischer Pressefotograf. Er arbeitete für den *Daily Herald Newspaper* in den 1930er Jahren.
Press photographer, worked for the Daily Herald Newspaper in the 1930s.

Per Oddvar Maning
(1943 Oslo)
Maning, der an der dänischen Akademiet for Fri og Markantil Kunst in Kopenhagen studierte, sagte über seine Tierfotografie: Die Ähnlichkeit zwischen Mensch und Tier liegt im Tier. Die Suche nach dem Anderen ist die Motivation seiner Arbeit. Seine erste Einzelausstellung hatte er 1988 in Oslo. Er gestaltet Fotobücher und arbeitet ebenfalls als Videokünstler.
Studied arts at Akademiet for Fri og Markantil Kunst in Kopenhavn. Said about his animal photography: Resemblance between man and animal lies in the animal. His work is motivated by the search for the other. Had his first solo show in Oslo in 1988. Designed photo books and works as video artist.

Etienne-Jules Marey
(1830 Beaune – 1904 Paris)
Marey war Physiologe und Fotograf und einer der wichtigsten Vertreter der Chronofotografie. Er studierte 1849–1859 Medizin in Paris, ehe er 1868 fotografisch die Bewegungsabläufe von Vögeln untersuchte. Ab 1882 experimentierte er zusammen mit Muybridge.
Physiologist and photographer. One of the most important representatives of chronophotography. Studied medicine in Paris from 1849–1859. 1868 first photographic studies about the sequence of movements of birds. From 1882 on he experimented together with Muybridge.

W. H. Martin
(1865 – 1940)
Der Amerikaner Martin montierte um 1910 ironische Postkarten mit Motiven des ländlichen Lebens im Mittelwesten.
American. Around 1910 he developed mounted, ironical postcards with subjects from the rural life in the Midwest.

Mayer & Pierson
Léopold Ernest Mayer (1817 – 1865)
Pierre Louis Pierson (1822 – 1913)
Pierson eröffnete 1844 ein Daguerreotypiestudio in Paris. Später arbeitete er mit Léopold Ernest und Louis Frederic Mayer zusammen und obwohl sie weiterhin in getrennten Studios arbeiteten, vertrieben sie ihre Fotografien unter dem gemeinsamen Titel „Mayer et Pierson". Sie wurden die führenden Gesellschaftsfotografen in Paris. Mayer setzte sich 1878 zur Ruhe und Pierson führt die Geschäfte mit seinem Schwiegersohn Gaston Braun fort.
In 1844 Pierson opened a daguerreotype studio in Paris. Later he collaborated with Léopold Ernest and Louis Frederic Mayer. Although working in different studios, they sold their photographs under the common title "Mayer et Pierson". Became the leading society photographers in Paris. In 1878 Mayer retired and Pierson continued the business with his son in law, Gaston Braun.

Lisette Model
(Elise Amelie Felicie Stern) (1901 Wien – 1983 New York)
Models erste Fotografien entstanden 1934. Sie entwickelte eine radikale, neue fotografische Sichtweise und war in den 1950er und 1960er Jahren die einflussreichste Lehrerin in New York u.a. für Diane Arbus.
First photographs in 1934. Developed a new, radical photographic view and in the

1950s and 1960s had great influence as teacher for artists like, for example, Diane Arbus.

Martin Munkacsi
(1896 Kolozsvar – 1963 New York)
Der gebürtige Ungar begann seine Laufbahn als Sportfotograf 1921, ab 1927 arbeitete er für den Ullstein Verlag. Nach seiner Emigration in die USA arbeitete er vorrangig als Modefotograf.
Born in Hungary, Munkacsi began his carreer as sports photographer in 1921. From 1927 on he worked for Ullstein Verlag, Berlin. After his emigration into the United States worked mainly as fashion photographer.

Eadweard Muybridge
(1830 Kingston-on-the-Thames – 1904 Kingston-on-the-Thames)
Herausragender Vertreter der Fotogeschichte mit bahnbrechenden Bewegungsstudien. 1872 wurde Muybridge vom Gouverneur von Kalifornien berufen, das Traben eines Pferdes fotografisch zu untersuchen. 1880 veröffentlichte er die Ergebnisse seiner Forschung in *Attitudes of Animals in Motion.*
Outstanding representative of photographic history with pioneering studies of motion. 1872 Muybridge was commissioned by the Governor of California to examine photographically the trot of a horse. In 1880 he published the results of his research in *Attitudes of Animals in Motion.*

Michael Nichols
(1952 Muscle Shoals/Alabama)
Seine fotografische Tätigkeit bei der US-Army war für Nichols der Einstieg in eine professionelle Fotografenlaufbahn. Nach dem Militärdienst studierte er an der University of North Alabama. Seit 1996 ist er Mitarbeiter bei *National Geographic.*
His photographic work in the US-Army was the starting point for a professional career as a photographer. After his military service he studied at the University of North Alabama. Since 1996 works for *National Geographic.*

Johan Nöhring
Der Lübecker Fotograf arbeitete im ausgehenden 19. Jahrhundert. Seine Sujets sind neben der Tierfotografie topografische Aufnahmen.
Photographer in Lübeck in the late 19th century His subjects were animal photography and topographical photographs.

Cas Oorthuys
(1908 Leiden – 1975 Amsterdam)
Oorthuys ist einer der bedeutenden Vertreter der politisch motivierten Bildreportage, daneben entstehen Dokumentationen und Reisefotografien. Menschen und ihr Verhältnis untereinander standen bei ihm im Mittelpunkt.
One of the most important representatives of politically motivated reportages. Also documentations and travel photography. Focussed on people and interactive processes.

Hilmar Pabel
(1910 Rawitsch/Schlesien – 2000 Xanten)
Pabel besuchte 1929 die Agfa Fotoschule in Berlin. Er wurde Kriegskorrespondent bei der Deutschen Wehrmacht. Nach dem Krieg fotografierte er für das Rote Kreuz Kriegswaisen für die Kindersuchaktion, die er 1945 mitbegründete. Als Bildreporter war er für *Quick* und *Stern* tätig.
Attended the Agfa Fotoschule Berlin in 1929. War reporter with the German Wehrmacht. After the war photographed for the Red Cross and for the Children's Search Operation of which he was a cofounder. As photojournalist he worked for *Quick* and *Stern* magazines.

Martin Parr
(1952 London)
Parr ist Mitglied bei *Magnum* und vor allem bekannt durch seine satirischen Gesellschaftsdokumentationen. Neben der Sammlung von Kitschpostkarten beschäftigt sich Parr auch mit der Geschichte des Fotobuches.
Member of *Magnum* and especially known for his satirical society documentations. Apart form collecting kitsch postcards, has been working on the history of the photo book.

Irving Penn
(1917 Plainfield/New Jersey)
Penn ist Mode- und Porträtfotograf und Autor bemerkenswerter Pflanzenstudien und Stillleben. 2001 fand unter dem Titel *Irving Penn. Objects for the Printed Page* eine Ausstellung im Museum Folkwang statt.
Fashion- and portrait photographer and author of remarkable floral studies and still life. 2001 the Museum Folkwang organised an exhibition under the title *Irving Penn. Objects for the Printed Page.*

Eric Poitevin
(1961 Longuyon)
Der Franzose Poitevin ist freier Bildautor. Seine erste Einzelausstellung hatte er 1991 bei den Rencontres Internationales de la Photographie in Arles.
French, independent photographer. First solo exhibition in 1991 at the Recontres Internationales de la Photographie in Arles.

Herbert George Ponting
(1870 – 1935)
Der Engländer Ponting war gelernter Bankier, übte diesen Beruf aber nur wenige Jahre aus. Bekannt ist er durch seine Reise- und Expeditionsfotografie, die er auf seinen Weltreisen oft als Stereoaufnahmen anfertigte und auch publizierte. 1910 begleitete er Robert Scott bei seiner zweiten Antarktis-Expedition. Sein fotografischer Reisebericht *The great white south* erschien 1921.
English, trained as a banker, but only a few years of practical work. Known for his travel- and expedition photography, which he produced and published on his world travels often as stereo photographs. In 1910

he accompanied Robert Scott on his second expedition to the Antarctic.
His photographic travel report *The Great White South* was published in 1921.

Albert Renger-Patzsch
(1897 Würzburg – 1966 Wamel)
Der führende Vertreter der Neuen Sachlichkeit in Deutschland. 1922 entstanden seine ersten Tier- und Pflanzenaufnahmen, die 1924 publiziert wurden.
Leading representative of Neue Sachlichkeit in Germany. In 1922 he produced his first animal and plant studies, which were published in 1924.

Olivier Richon
(1956 Lausanne)
Richon studierte Film und Fotografie. Seine Ausstellungstätigkeit begann 1981. Er untersucht das Verhältnis von Symbol und Allegorie in Bezug auf das Bild und die Sprache. Darüber hinaus beschäftigt er sich mit Fragen, wie das Tier als kulturelles Zeichen verstanden werden kann. Seit 1997 ist er am Royal College of Art in London und leitet die Abteilung Fotografie.
Studied film and photography. First exhibition in 1981. Explores the relationship of symbol and allegory with regard to picture and language. Moreover, has been working on the question of how the animal can be understood as cultural sign. Since 1997 at the Royal College of Art in London, director of the department of photography.

Martin Richter
(1974 Offenbach)
Richter studierte an der Bielefelder Fachhochschule Fotodesign. 2002 wurde er für sein Projekt *Moderne Ställe* ausgezeichnet. Er arbeitet als Pressefotograf für verschiedene Magazine u.a. für *Geo*.
Studied photo design at the Bielefelder Fachhochschule. In 2002 was honoured for his project *Moderne Ställe*. Press photographer for different magazines, notably for *Geo*.

Heinrich Riebesehl
(1938 Lathen)
Riebesehl studierte Mitte der 1960er Jahre an der Folkwang Schule bei Otto Steinert. Er arbeitet als Bildjournalist und lehrte bis 1997 an der Fachhochschule in Hannover. Er befasst sich mit der künstlerischen Dokumentation norddeutscher Kulturlandschaften.
In the mid 1960s studied at the Folkwang Schule under Otto Steinert. Photojournalist. Until 1997 lecturer at the Fachhochschule in Hannover. His subject is the artistic documentation of North-German culture landscapes.

Humberto Rivas
(1937 Buenos Aires)
Rivas beschäftigte sich zuerst mit Malerei und Grafik, bevor er 1957 mit der Fotografie begann. 1977 eröffnete er in Barcelona sein eigenes Studio. 1999 zeigte das Centro Galego de Arte Contemporánea in Santiago de Compostela eine Retrospektive.
Occupied himself with painting and design before he took up photography in 1957. In 1977 opened his own studio in Barcelona. 1999 the Centro Galego de Arte Contemporánea in Santiago de Compostela showed a retrospective.

Henry Peach Robinson
(1830 Ludlow – 1901 Tunbridge Wells)
Der ausgebildete Maler und Radierer Robinson begann 1852 mit der Fotografie. Er eröffnete 1857 ein Porträtstudio in Leamington, wobei er aber auch Genrebilder anfertigte. Von Oscar Gustave Rejlander erlernte er die Negativmontage, die er in seinen fotografischen Bilderzählungen anwendete. 1900 wurde er zum Ehrenmitglied der Royal Photographic Society.
Training in painting and etching. Took up photography in 1852. Opened a portrait studio in Leamington in 1857, but also made genre pictures. Oscar Gustave Rejlander taught him the negative montage, which he used in his photo stories. In 1900 he became honorary member of the Royal Photographic Society.

Alexander Michailowitsch Rodtschenko
(1891 Sankt Petersburg – 1956 Moskau)
Rodtschenko, der nicht nur Fotograf, sondern auch Maler, Bildhauer, Architekt und Typograf war, ist ein Wegbereiter des 'Neuen Sehens'. Das Museum of Modern Art New York zeigte 1998 das umfassende Werk Rodtschenkos.
Photographer, painter, sculptor, architect and typographer. Pioneer of 'Neues Sehen'. Rodtschenkos comprehensive work was shown in 1998 in the Museum of Modern Art New York.

Horatio Ross
(1801 – 1886)
Der schottische Amateurfotograf Ross fertigte Daguerreotypien und Kalotypien. Die technischen Fähigkeiten erlernte er bei James Ross in Edinburgh, mit dem er nicht verwandt war. 1856 war er Mitbegründer und Vizepräsident der Photographic Society of Scotland. Ross machte Daguerreotypien von Landschaften und Fischerszenen.
Scottish. Amateur photographer, produced daguerreotypes and calotypes. Technical training at James Ross' in Edinburgh, with whom he was not related. In 1856 cofounder and vice president of the Photographic Society of Scotland. Produced daguerreotypes of landscapes and fishing scenes.

Jeffrey L. Rotman
(1949 Boston)
Der freie Fotograf Rotman ist berühmt für seine Unterwasserfotografien, die in zahlreichen Büchern veröffentlicht sind. Seine Artikel und Fotos erscheinen regelmäßig in Magazinen wie *Live* und *Geo*.
Independent photographer, famous for his underwater photography, published in numerous books. His articles and photographs are regularly published in magazines like *Geo* and *Life*.

Nadin Maria Rüfenacht
(1980 Burgdorf)
Die Schweizerin ist freie Fotografin und hat an der Hochschule für Grafik und Buchkunst Leipzig Fotografie studiert. Sie beschäftigt sich explizit mit der Darstellung von Tieren.
Swiss, independent photographer. Studied photography at the Hochschule für Grafik und Buchkunst in Leipzig. Focusses on animal portraiture.

Pentti Sammallahti
(1950 Helsinki)
Das Hauptarbeitsfeld des finnischen Fotografen sind die nordische Landschaft und Porträts. Die ersten Fotos machte Sammallahti 1961. Mitte der 1970er Jahre begann er seine Lehrtätigkeit an der University of Art and Design in Helsinki. Ab Mitte der 1990er Jahre wird er auch international ausgestellt. Die Vereinbarkeit von Natur und Kultur bleiben stets seine Themen.
Main subject of the Finnish photographer is the nordic landscape as well as portraits. First photos in 1961. By the mid 1970s he began teaching at the University of Art and Design, Helsinki. From the mid 1990s international exhibitions. His subject is the compatibility of nature and culture.

August Sander
(1876 Herdorf – 1964 Köln)
Das Lebenswerk Sanders war der Versuch, die deutschen Gesellschaftsschichten fotografisch darzustellen und damit das *Antlitz der Zeit* zu dokumentieren.
Sander's lifework was the attempt to produce a photographical documentation of German society, the *Antlitz der Zeit*.

Walter Schels
(1936 Landshut)
Schels arbeitete anfänglich als Dekorateur und ging 1965 nach New York, wo er mit der Fotografie begann. Er ist freiberuflicher Fotograf und entwickelt neben Werbefotografien insbesondere Porträts und Tierbildnisse.
Interior designer. Went to New York in 1965, where he took up photography. Freelance photographer, advertisement photography, portraits and animal portraiture.

Carl Georg Schillings
(1865 Gürzenich – 1921 Berlin)
Prof. Schillings machte auf vier Expeditionsreisen in Ostafrika zoologische Forschungen und Fotografien wild lebender Tiere. Der passionierte Jäger zeigte seine Ergebnisse in den umfangreichen Publikationen *Mit Büchse und Blitzlicht* und *Im Zauber des Eleléscho*. Seine nächtlichen Blitzlichtaufnahmen erregten 1907 bei der Veröffentlichung großes Aufsehen. Für Schillings waren diese Fotografien 'Naturkunden'.
Professor, four expeditions to East Africa, where he did zoological research and photographed wild animals. The passionate hunter published his results in thick books, for example, *Mit Büchse und Blitzlicht* and *Im Zauber des Eleléscho*. When published in 1907 his flash photos taken at night caused a sensation. Schillings regarded these photographs as "nature documents".

Julius Eduard Schindler
(? – 1873 Wien)
Der Atelierfotograf arbeitete ab 1865 in Wien und spezialisierte sich auf die Landschaftsfotografie, Stillleben und Tierstudien.
Studio photographer, since 1865 in Vienna. His subjects were landscape photography, still life and animal studies.

Walter Schmitz
(1946 Bayreuth)
Schmitz ist freischaffender Fotograf und hat sich vor allem auf Sportfotografie spezialisiert. Seit 1974 veröffentlicht er seine Reportagen in Magazinen.
Freelance photographer, specialized on sports photography. Since 1974 has published his reportages in magazines.

Robin Schwartz
(1957 Passaic/New Jersey)
Die Tierfotografien der amerikanischen Fotografin Schwartz sind vielfach publiziert und ausgestellt. 1993 erschien ihr Fotobuch *Like us: Primate Portraits*, 1995 *Dog Watching*. Sie ist Professorin für Fotografie an der William Paterson University, New Jersey.
American photographer. Her animal photographs have been widely published and exhibited. In 1993 she published her photo book *Like us: Primate Portraits*, 1995 *Dog Watching*. Professor for photography at William Paterson University, New Jersey.

Ferdinand Albert Schwartz
(1836 Berlin – 1906 Berlin)
Schwartz machte eine Fotografenausbildung bei seinem Onkel und eröffnete um 1860 sein erstes Atelier auf der Friedrichstraße. Er arbeitete anfangs im Auftrag verschiedener Firmen. Als so genannter Stadtfotograf dokumentierte er ab 1880 den Wandel der Metropole.
Was trained as a photographer at his uncle's. Opened his first studio in Berlin, Friedrichstrasse in 1860. At first worked for different companies. From 1880 on he documented, as a so-called town photographer, the changing city of Berlin.

Eberhard Seeliger
(1914 Berlin – 1982 Bad Pyrmont)
Der ausgebildete Architekt arbeitete nach dem Krieg 1947 für eine Jugendzeitschrift als Redakteur und Fotograf. Das Blatt wurde durch Henri Nannen übernommen und Seeliger wechselte in das Redaktionsteam des *Stern*. Bis 1953 entwarf er hierfür das Layout und arbeitete bis 1981 als Bildreporter für die Illustrierte.
Trained as architect. After the war, in 1947, journalist and photographer for a youth magazine. When Henri Nannen, editor of the magazine *Stern*, took over the youth press, Seeliger changed to the journalistic team of *Stern*. Until 1953 he was responsible for the layout and until 1981 worked as photojournalist for the magazine.

Friedrich Seidenstücker
(1882 Unna – 1966 Berlin)
Seidenstücker studierte Maschinenbau. Seine erste Kamera baute er selbst. 1904 begann seine fotografische Laufbahn als Amateur in Berlin. Die erste große Fotoserie machte er im Berliner Zoo und entwickelte sich zum Chronisten des alltäglichen Großstadtlebens. Er arbeitete für die *Berliner Illustrirte* und den Ullstein Verlag.
Studied mechanical engineering. His first camera was self-constructed. Started his photographic career in 1904 as amateur photographer in Berlin. Made his first big photo series in the Berlin zoo and became a chronicler of the everyday life in a big city. Worked for *Berliner Illustrirte* and Ullstein Verlag.

Anatolij Skurichin
(1900 Kirow – 1989 Moskau)
Wladimir Grüntal
(1889 – 1966 Moskau)
Skurichin war seit Anfang der 1930er Jahre als Fotojournalist tätig. Grüntal begann seine Laufbahn als Regieassistent, bevor er als Fotograf für verschiedene Zeitschriften arbeitete.
Skurichin worked as a photojournalist since the early 1930s. Grüntal started his carreer as assistant producer before he worked as photographer for different magazines.

Frederick Sommer
(1905 Angri – 1999 Prescott)
Sommer studierte Kunst und Architektur. 1936 machte er seine ersten Fotografien und hatte 1941 die erste Fotoausstellung mit Landschaftsaufnahmen. 1974 erhielt er das Stipendium für Fotografie der Guggenheim Foundation und stellte ein Jahr später im Museum of Modern Art New York aus.
Studied art and architecture. Took his first photographs in 1936. 1941 first photo exhibition with landscape photographs. In 1974 he received the Guggenheim Foundation grant for photography and one year later had his show in the Museum of Modern Art New York.

David Steets
(1973 Offenbach)
Steets schloss sein Studium an der Staatlichen Fachakademie für Fotodesign in München mit der Arbeit *Tschernobyl – Leben mit dem Unfall* 1997 ab, für die er mit dem Bayerischen Fotopreis der Danner-Stiftung ausgezeichnet wurde. Er ist selbstständiger Fotograf und arbeitet für verschiedene Magazine wie *Geo*, *Stern* und *Die Zeit*.
Finished his studies at the national Fachakademie für Fotodesign in Munich with the project *Tschernobyl – Leben mit dem Unfall* in 1997, for which he was awarded the Bavarian Photo prize of the Danner-Stiftung. Freelance photographer. Works for different magazines, e.g. *Geo*, *Stern* and *Die Zeit*.

Carl Ferdinand Stelzner
(1805 Gömnitz – 1894 Hamburg)
Stelzner arbeitete, nachdem er in Paris studiert hatte, von 1837 an als Porträtmaler in Hamburg. Zwei Jahre später kehrte er nach Paris zurück und lernte bei Daguerre. 1842 eröffnete er ein Atelier für Daguerreotypien in Hamburg. In der Folgezeit arbeitete er auch mit Papierabzügen. Durch den Umgang mit den fotografischen Chemikalien erblindete er. Sein Fotoatelier blieb noch bis 1864 bestehen, wurde aber von angestellten Fotografen betrieben.
After studies in Paris, from 1837 on Stelzner worked as portrait painter in Hamburg. Two years later returned to Paris and was trained by Daguerre. In 1842 opened a studio for daguerreotypes in Hamburg. Later he also worked with paper prints. Because of the work with photographic chemicals he went blind. His photo studio existed until 1864, but was run by employed photographers.

Anne Lise Stenseth
(1959 Floro)
Die Videokünstlerin Stenseth studierte 1989–1993 an der Akademie in Oslo, wo sie auch heute lebt. Seit dieser Zeit ist sie an zahlreichen Ausstellungen beteiligt.
Video artist. Studied at the Academy in Oslo from 1989–1993. Lives in Oslo. Has been shown in numerous exhibitions.

Warwara Stepanowa
(1894 – 1958)
Ab 1920 war Stepanowa zusammen mit ihrem Mann Alexander Rodtschenko an der theoretischen Entwicklung des Konstruktivismus maßgeblich beteiligt. In dieser Zeit schuf sie ihren Zyklus *Figuren*. Sie analysierte Bewegungsabläufe, die sie in flache geometrische Formen übertrug. 2000 wurden ihre Arbeiten im Zusammenhang der Ausstellung *Amazons of the Avant-Garde* im New Yorker Guggenheim Museum gezeigt.
From 1920, together with her husband, Alexander Rodtschenko, Stepanowa played an important role in the development of constructivism. During these years she created the cycle *Figuren*. She analysed sequences of movement which she translated into flat geometrical forms. In 2000 her works were shown in the exhibition *Amazons of the Avant-Garde* in the New York Guggenheim Museum.

Joel Sternfeld
(1944 New York)
Sternfeld ist als Fotograf Autodidakt. Seit 1970 macht er Farbfotografien, die 1976 in der Pennsylvania Academy of Fine Arts in einer Einzelausstellung zu sehen waren. Ein Jahr später nahm er an der Schau *La deuxième génération de la photographie en couleurs* in Arles teil. Er reiste durch die USA und entwickelte großformatige Landschaftsbilder in einer kühlen und distanzierten Bildsprache. 1978 und 1982 erhielt er das Guggenheim Stipendium sowie ein Stipendium des New Yorker Art Councils.
Self-taught photographer. From 1970 colour photographs which were shown in 1976 in a solo exhibition in the Pennsylvania Academy of Fine Arts. One year

later he took part in the show *La deuxième génération de la photographie en couleurs* in Arles. Travelled the United States and developed large-size landscape photographs in a rather cool and distanced visual language. In 1978 and 1982 he received the Guggenheim Fellowship and a grant from the New York Art Council.

Alex Stöcker

Stöcker war in den 1930er Jahren als Pressefotograf in Berlin tätig und hatte einen eigenen Illustrationsverlag in Friedenau.
In the 1930s press photographer in Berlin. Owned a publishing company for illustrations in Friedenau.

Sasha Stone

(1895 Sankt Petersburg – 1940 Perpignan)
Aleksander Serge Steinsapir machte eine Ausbildung als Elektroingenieur 1911–1913 in Warschau, danach emigrierte er in die USA. 1922 ging er nach Berlin. 1924 gründete er zusammen mit Cami Stone das *Atelier Stone* und arbeitete als Bildjournalist unter anderem für *Uhu* und *Die Dame*.
Aleksander Serge Steinsapir was trained as electrical engineer in Warsaw from 1911–1913. After that he emigrated into the United States. 1922 went to Berlin. In 1924, together with Cami Stone, founded the *Atelier Stone* and worked as photojournalist, amongst others for *Uhu* and *Die Dame*.

William Strode

Strode ist amerikanischer Pressefotograf und zweimaliger Gewinner des Pulitzer Prize für Fotografie.
American press photographer who twice won the Pulitzer Prize for Photography.

Christer Strömholm

(1918 Stockholm – 2002 Stockholm)
Strömholm studierte in Dresden und Paris Malerei, bevor er 1946 anfing zu fotografieren. In den frühen 1950er Jahren war er Mitglied der Gruppe *fotoform*.
Studied painting in Dresden and Paris, before he took up photography in 1946. In the early 1950s he belonged to the group of *fotoform*.

Peter Strong

(1963)
Der englische Amateurfotograf Strong verbindet seine Interessen fürs Reisen, Tauchen und die Natur mit seiner Fotografie. Bildthemen sind bei ihm u.a. die Darstellung von Primatenaffen und Haien.
English amateur photographer. Combines his interest in travelling, diving and nature with photography. Amongst his subjects are primates and sharks.

Strumper & Co.

Das Metier des Ateliers Strumper & Co. war ab den 1870er Jahren die Dokumentation der Hafensituation in Hamburg.
In the 1870s the studio Strumper & Co. documented the situation of the port of Hamburg.

Juha Suonpää

(1963)
Suonpää ist freier Fotograf, Filmproduzent und Dozent. Er studierte in Tampere und Helsinki Fotografie und Kunstgeschichte. Die Darstellung der finnischen Landschaft und Tierwelt steht im Mittelpunkt seiner Arbeit.
Finnish freelance photographer, film producer and teacher. Studied photography and art history in Tampere and Helsinki. Central to his work is the depiction of the Finnish landscape and fauna.

Henk Tas

(1949 Rotterdam)
Der freischaffende Fotograf und Kurator Tas studierte an der Rotterdamer Akademie voor Beeldende Kunsten. Anfangs verwendete er die Fotografie nur als Reproduktionsmittel im Stil der Pop Art. Seit Mitte der 1970er Jahre inszenierte er Motive für großformatige Farbfotografien.
Freelance photographer and curator, Tas studied at the Rotterdam Akademie voor Beeldende Kunsten. In the beginning he used photography only as a means of reproduction in the style of Pop Art. Since the mid 1970s he staged themes for large-sized colour photographs.

Isadora Tast

(1973 Hildesheim)
Tast studierte 1995–2002 Fotografie und Film an der Fachhochschule Bielefeld. Bereits während ihres Studiums nahm sie an Ausstellungen teil. Ihre Diplomarbeit *Schmerzlich-süße Zeit* wurde mit dem Kodak Nachwuchs Förderpreis 2001 und dem BFF-Förderpreis ausgezeichnet. Sie arbeitet freischaffend für Magazine und Werbeaufträge.
Studied photography and film at the Fachhochschule Bielefeld from 1955–2002. During that time she already took part in different exhibitions. Her graduate work *Schmerzlich-süße Zeit* was honoured with the Kodak Nachwuchs Förderpreis 2001 and the BFF-Förderpreis. Now freelance photographer for magazines and advertising commissions.

Richard Tepe

(1864 Amsterdam – 1952 Apeldoorn)
Tepe ist einer der ersten Naturfotografen der Niederlande. Sein Hauptinteresse galt der Vogelkunde und dem in der Zeit um 1900 aufkommenden Naturschutz. 1909 erschien sein Werk *De Jacht met de Camera*. Neben den Fotografien von Vögeln und Nestern entstanden ab 1915 neu-sachliche Aufnahmen von Haustieren, Landschafts- und Genreaufnahmen.
One of the first Dutch nature photographers. His main interest was ornithology and nature protection arising around 1900. In 1909 his work *De Jacht met de Camera* was published. Apart from photographs of birds and nests after 1915 he created 'new-functional' photographs of pets, landscape and genre photos.

Warren T. Thompson

Thompson ist einer der frühen amerikanischen Daguerreotypisten in Philadelphia.

In der Zeit nach 1846 zog er nach Paris, wo er bis 1860 ein Atelier betrieb. Hier entstanden auch stereoskopische Daguerreotypien. Er fotografierte unter anderem Stillleben, Objektstudien und inszenierte Jagdaufnahmen.
One of the early American daguerreotypists in Philadelphia. After 1846 moved to Paris, where he ran a studio until 1860. Here he produced stereoscopic daguerreotypes. Photographed still life, studies of objects and staged hunting scenes.

Waldemar Titzenthaler
(1869 Laibach – 1937 Berlin)
Titzenthaler kommt aus einer Fotografenfamilie. 1896 ging er nach Berlin, um sich dort selbstständig zu machen. Ab 1897 machte er Fotoserien für den Ullstein Verlag. Er arbeitete in den Bereichen Architektur, Landschaft und Reportage.
Born into a family of photographers. 1896 moved to Berlin in order to make himself independent. From 1897 on made photo series for Ullstein Verlag. Worked in the fields of architecture, landscape and reportage.

Adrien Alban Tournachon
(1825 Paris – 1903 Paris)
Der kleine Bruder Nadars eröffnete 1854 sein eigenes Atelier, nachdem er Unterricht bei Gustave Le Gray genommen hatte. 1856 fotografierte er Tiere auf der Landwirtschaftsmesse, die in der Société Française de Photographie gezeigt wurden. 1861 fotografierte er im Zirkus Akrobaten und Zirkustiere.
Nadar's younger brother opened his first studio in 1854, after he had taken training with Gustave Le Gray. 1856 he photographed animals at an agricultural fair, which were shown in the Société Française de la Photographie. In 1861 he photographed acrobats and animals in the circus.

Rosemarie Trockel
(1952 Schwerte)
Die Künstlerin studierte 1974–1978 an der Kölner Werkkunstschule. Sie hat kein einheitliches künstlerisches Programm, sondern arbeitet bildhauerisch, zeichnet, malt und fotografiert.
From 1974–1978 studied at the Werkkunstschule in Cologne. The artist has no defined artistic scheme, but sculpts, draws, paints and takes photographs.

Vivot
Französisches Atelier in Amiens, Mitte des 19. Jahrhunderts.
French studio in Amiens in the mid 19th century.

Walmsley Brothers
Die britischen Fotografen arbeiteten in den 1890er Jahren.
British photographers in the 1890s.

Hedda Walther
(1894 Berlin – 1979 Berlin)
Ihre fotografische Ausbildung machte Walther an der Berliner Lette-Schule und eröffnete 1925 ein Atelier für Kinderbildnisse. Sie publizierte ihre Bilder in verschiedenen Zeitschriften. 1928 wurde sie durch die Veröffentlichung *Tiere sehen dich an* von Paul Eipper international als Tierfotografin bekannt. Nach dem Krieg arbeitete sie vornehmlich als Modefotografin. Die professionelle Arbeit gab sie 1960 auf.
Received her photographic training at the Lette-Schule Berlin. Opened a studio for children's portraiture in 1925. Her photos were published in different magazines. In 1928 she became internationally known as animal photographer when she published Paul Eippers *Tiere sehen dich an*. After 1945 she worked mainly as fashion photographer. In 1960 she retired from professional work.

Wolfgang Weber
(1902 Leipzig – 1985 Köln)
Weber studierte in München Ethnologie und Musikwissenschaften und begann im Zusammenhang einer Forschungsreise mit der Fotografie. Von 1925 an war er als freiberuflicher Fotojournalist tätig, in der Zeit des Zweiten Weltkriegs für den Ullstein Verlag und die *Berliner Illustrirte Zeitung*. Nach dem Krieg arbeitete er weiter journalistisch, auch für das Deutsche Fernsehen.
Studied ethnology and musicology in Munich and took up photography on the occasion of an expedition. From 1925 worked as freelance photo journalist, during World War II for Ullstein Verlag and *Berliner Illustrirte Zeitung*, Berlin. After the war he continued as a journalist, also for German television.

William Wegman
(1943 Holyoke)
Wegman, der vor allem durch seine Hundefotografie bekannt ist, studierte Malerei. Anfang der 1970er Jahre begann er mit seinem Hund *Man Ray* zu arbeiten, den er verkleidete und in inszenierten Situationen fotografierte.
Wegman, especially known for his photography of dogs, originally studied painting. In the beginning of the 1970s he started working with his dog *Man Ray*, whom he put into fancy dresses and photographed in staged settings.

Garry Winogrand
(1928 New York – 1984 Mexiko)
Winogrand ist einer der bedeutendsten Vertreter der amerikanischen street photography. 1969 zeigte das Museum of Modern Art New York seine Arbeiten in einer Einzelausstellung, 1988 in einer großen Retrospektive.
One of the most important representatives of the American street photography. 1969 the MoMA showed his work in a solo exhibition, 1988 in a big retrospective.

Michael Wolf
(1954 München)
Wolf ist freier Fotojournalist und für Zeitschriften, Magazine und Industriefirmen tätig. In den letzten Jahren arbeitete er vielfach in Hongkong und China. Seine

Reportage *China – Fabrikhalle der Welt* wurde 2005 beim World Press Photo Award ausgezeichnet.
Freelance photojournalist working for magazines and industrial companies. During the last years he has worked a lot in Hong Kong and China. His reportage *China – Fabrikhalle der Welt* was honoured as part of World Press Photo Award 2005.

WOLS
(1913 Berlin – 1951 Paris)
Der gebürtige Alfred Otto Wolfgang Schulze war 1931 als Assistent im Studio von Genja Jones in Dresden tätig. 1932 zog er nach Paris und feierte hier seine ersten Erfolge als offizieller Fotograf auf der Weltausstellung 1937. Von dieser Zeit an legte er sich das Pseudonym WOLS zu. 1947 gab er die Fotografie zugunsten der Malerei auf.
Born as Alfred Otto Wolfgang Schulze. In 1931 he assisted in the studio of Genja Jones in Dresden. 1932 he moved to Paris and had his first success as official photographer at the world exhibition in 1937. From this time on he worked under the pseudonym of WOLS. 1947 he gave up photography for painting.

Ylla
(1911 Wien – 1955 Bharatpur)
Die Tierfotografin Ylla, die mit bürgerlichem Namen Kamilla Koffler hieß, widmete sich zuerst der Bildhauerei. Durch die Bekanntschaft mit Ergy Landau in Paris kam sie in Kontakt mit der Fotografie und machte hier 1932 eine Fotolehre. Ab 1933 entstanden die ersten eigenständigen Fotos mit dem Schwerpunkt Tiere in Haus und Zoo. 1940 emigrierte sie in die USA, wo sie als Zoofotografin erfolgreich war.
Animal photographer Ylla, whose civil name was Kamilla Koffler, was above all a sculptor. Through Ergy Landau in Paris she came into contact with photography and underwent a photographic training in 1932. From 1933 on she produced her first independent photographs, focussing on pets and zoo animals. In 1940 she emigrated into the United States where she became a successful zoo photographer.

Atelier Zangaki
Die griechischen Brüder Adelphi und Constantine Zangaki waren von 1860 bis 1880 als Fotografen aktiv. Sie fotografierten im gesamten Nahen Osten, vor allem in Algier, Palästina und Ägypten.
The Greek brothers Adelphi and Constantine Zangaki were active photographers from 1860 – 1880. They photographed everywhere in the Middle East, especially in Algiers, Palestine and Egypt.

Fritz Zielesch
Zielesch war Schriftsteller und Fotograf. Ende der 1920er Jahre arbeitete er in Berlin als Bildjournalist zusammen mit Umbo für *UHU*.
Writer and photographer. End of the 1920s he worked, together with Umbo, as photojournalist for *UHU* in Berlin.

A. von Zhilinsky
Fotografierte in den 1920er Jahren in Hamburg.
Photographer in Hamburg in the 1920s.

Nachweis der Zitate References of the Quotations

Die Zitate wurden dem nur in deutscher Sprache erhältlichen Textband zur Ausstellung entnommen, der gleichzeitig mit diesem Bildband erschienen ist.

All quotations have been excerpted from the text book (in German only) being published simultaneously with this Picture Book, which both accompany the exhibition *Useful, Cute and Collected. The Photographed Animal* in the Museum Folkwang, October 22, 2005 – January 15, 2006.

S. 16 Jürgen Müller
Die Fotografie als Instrument der Popularisierung.
Der Hase von Albrecht Dürer

S. 22 André Gunthert
Der weite Ritt.
Das Pferd im Zeitalter seiner technischen Reproduzierbarkeit

S. 40 Bernhard Gissibl
Exotische „Natururkunden".
Tierfotografie im Kontext des deutschen Kolonialismus

S. 60 Hans-Jürgen Lechtreck
Fotografie und Tierpräparation komplementär.
Anmerkungen zur gemeinsamen Geschichte
zweier zoologischer Aufzeichnungsmedien des 19. Jahrhunderts

S. 78 Cristina Grasseni
Tierdarstellung, agrarischer Fortschritt und
die Ökologie des Blicks für die agrarische Landschaft

S. 108 Rainer E. Wiedenmann
Spiegel und Fenster.
Zur Semantik der Blicke in Tierfotografien

S. 124 Bernhard Kathan
„Creda" – Meine kleine Seele!
Das Tierbild in der Amateurfotografie

S. 154 Eckhardt Köhn
„Rätsel der Tiernatur".
Aspekte der Zoo- und Zirkusfotografie in der Weimarer Republik

S. 176 Jo Longhurst
Anmerkungen zum fehlenden Haustier

S. 192 Jane Goodall im Gespräch mit Lisa Marei Schmidt
„Es gab bis dahin keine Fotos von wild lebenden Schimpansen,
daher war ich durch nichts beeinflusst."

S. 210 Hermann Sturm
Zugtiere für Werbekampagnen

S. 248 Florian Ebner
Affe wie Eule. Neue Gesichter für ein altes Genre

S. 298 Michael Nichols im Gespräch mit Lisa Marei Schmidt
„Die Welt brauchte keinen weiteren Fotojournalisten, sie brauchte
einen Fotojournalisten, der etwas über die Umwelt erzählen konnte."

Dank Acknowledgments

Für die finanzielle Unterstützung von Ausstellung und Publikation danken wir den folgenden Institutionen und Stiftungen / The exhibition and its accompanying publication were supported by:

The J. Paul Getty Museum, Los Angeles
Erna och Viktor Hasselblads Stiftelse, Göteborg
Kunststiftung NRW, Düsseldorf
Stiftung Presse-Haus NRZ, Essen
Wüstenrot Stiftung, Ludwigsburg
Folkwang Museumsverein, Essen

Besonderer Dank gilt den Leihgebern / We express our thanks to the lenders:

Claudia Angelmaier, Yann Arthus-Bertrand, José Azel, Roger Ballen, Albin Biblom, Steve Bloom, Marie José Burki, Chien-Chi Chang, Sabine Emmerich, Elliott Erwitt, Georg Fischer, Joan Fontcuberta, Pere Formiguera, Beate Geissler und Oliver Sann, Bruce Gilden, Andreas Gursky, HIRO, Candida Höfer, Wilmar Koenig, Jan Kornstaedt, Jochen Lempert, Jo Longhurst, Aleksandras Macijauskas, Per Maning, James Mollison, Michael Nichols, Eric Poitevin, Olivier Richon, Martin Richter, Humberto Rivas, Jeffrey Rotman, Nadin Maria Rüfenacht, Pentti Sammallahti, Walter Schels, Walter Schmitz, Robin Schwartz, David Steets, Joel Sternfeld, Anne Lise Stenseth, William Strode, Peter Strong, Juha Suonpää, Henk Tas, Isodora Tast, Rosemarie Trockel, William Wegman, Michael Wolf

Academy of Motion Picture Arts and Sciences, Beverly Hills
Robert Cushman, Janet Lorenz

Action Press, Hamburg

Albertina, Wien
Monika Faber, Maren Gröning

American Museum of Photography, Wm. B. Becker Collection, Huntington Woods
Bill Becker

Archiv Circus Busch, Berlin
Martin Schaaf

Archiv Hagenbeck, Hamburg
Klaus Gille

Archiv- und Museumsstiftung Wuppertal
Julia Besten

Aurora Photos, Portland
Jess Hesslen

Benetton Group S.p.A., Ponzano, Treviso

Berliner Trabrennverein e.V., Berlin

Bibliothèque centrale du Muséum national d'Histoire naturelle, Paris
Françoise Serre, Véronique van de Ponseele

Bibliothèque nationale de France, département des estampes et de la photographie, Paris
Sylvie Aubenas, Thierry Grillet

Bildarchiv Preußischer Kulturbesitz, Berlin
Hanns-Peter Frentz, Elke Schwichtenberg

Bilderberg, Hamburg
Silvia Schwack-Schmitz

Center for Creative Photography, Tucson
Douglas Nickel, Andrew Wallace

Circus- und Varieté-Archiv Reinhard Tetzlaff, Hamburg

Deutsches Filmmuseum, Frankfurt
Beate Dannhorn, Julia Welter

Deutsches Jagd- und Fischereimuseum, München
Bernd E. Ergert

Deutsches Literaturarchiv Marbach
Michael Davidis

Deutsches Museum, München
Cornelia Kemp

Deutsches Plakatmuseum, Essen
René Grohnert

Deutsches Röntgen-Museum, Remscheid
Christina Falkenberg

Galerie Ulrich Fiedler, Köln

Focus, Hamburg
Margot Klingsporn

Fotomuseum im Münchner Stadtmuseum, München
Ulrich Pohlmann

Galerie Berinson, Berlin

Galerie Alex Lachmann, Köln

Galerie Baudoin Lebon, Paris

Galerie Ockhardt, Essen

Gebrüder Knie, Schweizer Nationalzirkus AG, Rapperswil

Getty Images, München

Greenpeace, Hamburg
Sonja Umhang, Conny Boettger

Howard Greenberg Gallery, New York
Karen Marks

Historisches Archiv Krupp, Alfried Krupp von Bohlen und Halbach-Stiftung, Essen
Mark Stagge

Imperial War Museum, London

Werner Kourist, Linz a. Rhein

Lydia Lazi, Stuttgart

Janet Lehr, New York

Leopold-Hoesch-Museum, Schillings-Archiv, Düren
Dorothea Eimert

Gérard Lévy, Paris

Luhring Augustine Gallery, New York
Natalia Mager

Magnum Photos, Paris
Andréa Holzherr

Her Majesty Queen Elizabeth II

Musée d'art moderne et contemporain, Genf
Françoise Ninghetto

Musée national d'art moderne, Centre Georges Pompidou, Paris
Alfred Pacquement, Alain Sayag

Musée Carnavalet, Paris
Françoise Reynaud, Jean-Marc Léri

Musée d'art moderne et contemporain, Genf
Françoise Ninghetto

Musée d'Orsay, Paris
Françoise Heilbrun, Serge Lemoine

Musée Gatien Bonnet, Lagny-sur-Marne
Françoise Copeland

Museum Diergeneeskunde, Universiteit Utrecht
Willemijn van Helbergen

Museum für Kunst und Gewerbe, Hamburg
Gabriele Betancourt Nuñez

Museum für Naturkunde der Humboldt-Universität zu Berlin, Historische Bild- und Schriftensammlung, Berlin
Sabine Hackethal

Museum Ludwig, Photographische Sammlungen, Köln
Bodo von Dewitz

Nasjonalmuseet for Kunst, Arkitektur og Design, Oslo

National Geographic Image Collection, Washington D.C.

National Museum of Photography, Film & Television, Bradford
Russel Roberts, Toni Booth, Brian Liddy

Natural History Museum, London and The Walter Rothschild Zoological Museum, Tring
Christopher Mills, Annabel Curteis

Naturhistorisches Museum, Archiv und Wissenschaftsgeschichte, Wien
Christa Riedl-Dorn

Nederlands Fotomuseum, Rotterdam
Flip Bool, Loes van Harrevelt

Pace/MacGill Gallery, New York
Peter MacGill, Kimberly Jones

Rijksmuseum, Amsterdam
Mattie Boom, Ronald de Leeuw, J. P. Sigmond

Ruhrlandmuseum, Essen
Sigrid Schneider

Sammlung Hans Hansen, Hamburg

Sammlung Herzog, Basel

Sammlung Kothenschulte, Köln

Sammlung Schöller, Brüssel

Sammlung Dietmar Siegert, München

Sammlung Weiss, Hamburg

Schweizerisches Landesmuseum, Zürich
Andres Furger, Ricabeth Steiger

Nani Simonis, München

Société Française de Photographie, Paris
Michel Poivert, Katia Busch

Monika Sprüth/Philomene Magers, Köln
Franziska von Hasselbach, Jutta Küper

Staatliches Museum für Naturkunde, Stuttgart
Rotraud Harling

Stadt- und Kreisarchiv Düren
Helmut Krebs

Stadtbibliothek Essen

Stiftung F. C. Gundlach, Hamburg

Stiftung Museum Schloss Moyland, Sammlung van der Grinten, Bedburg-Hau
Reggy Havekes-van Creij, Barbara Strieder

The Estate of Martin Munkacsi, Woodstock
Joan Munkacsi

The J. Paul Getty Museum, Photography Department, Los Angeles
Weston Naef, Anne Lyden

The Museum of Modern Art, New York
Linda May Wacker, Susan Kismaric

The Wilson Center for Photography, London
Violet Hamilton

Tierärztliche Hochschule, Veterinärmedizinhistorisches Museum, Hannover
Johann Schäffer

Übersee-Museum, Bremen
Silke Seybold

Ullstein Bild, Berlin
Frank Frischmuth, Karin Buch

Universität der Künste, Universitätsarchiv, Berlin
Dietmar Schenk

Völkerkundemuseum der Universität Zürich
Michael Oppitz, Philippe Dallais, Johannes Herold

Volkswagen AG, Wolfsburg
Manfred Grieger, Claudia Nieke

Zoo Leipzig
Manfred Haude

Zoological Society of London
Ann Sylph

Copyright der abgebildeten Fotografien:

Copyright:

José Azel, Claudia Angelmaier, Albin Biblom, Steve Bloom, Marie José Burki, Florian Ebner, Sabine Emmerich, Georg Fischer, Steffen Junghans, Karin Knorr, Wilmar Koenig, Jan Kornstaedt, Robert Lebeck, Jochen Lempert, Jo Longhurst, Aleksandras Macijauskas, Per Maning, Martin Parr, Olivier Richon, Martin Richter, Heinrich Riebesehl, Jeffrey Rotman, Nadin Maria Rüfenacht, Pentti Sammallahti, Walter Schels, Walter Schmitz, Robin Schwartz, David Steets, Peter Strong, Juha Suonpää, Henk Tas, Isadora Tast, Manfred Willmann, Michael Wolf

James Abbe: Tilly Abbe/ The Estate of Abbe
Manuel Alvarez Bravo: The Estate of Manuel Alvarez Bravo
Anonym: Rintintin a race for life: Warner Bros. Entertainment
Anonym: Lassie come home: Warner Bros. Entertainment
Anonym: Verbrennung BSE: action press, Hamburg
Anonym: Film Stills Alfred Hitchcock, The Birds: NBC Universal Studios, Los Angeles
Cecil Beaton: Cecil Beaton Archive, London
Benetton-Werbung: Benetton Group S.p.A., Treviso
Bill Brandt: Bill Brandt Archive Ltd., London
Balthasar Burkhard: Balthasar Burkhard/ Courtesy Galerie Sfeir-Semler, Hamburg
Henri Cartier-Bresson: Cartier-Bresson/ Magnum Photos
Chien-Chi Chang: Chang/ Magnum Photos
Corbis Kampagne: Corbis Corporation, Düsseldorf
John Dominis: Getty Images
Pierre Dubreuil: VG Bild-Kunst, Bonn 2005
William Eggleston: Eggleston Artistic Trust/ Courtesy Cheim & Read, New York
Georg Einbeck: Museum für Kunst und Gewerbe, Hamburg
Lotte Errell: Museum Folkwang, Essen
Errell (Richard Levy): Museum Folkwang, Essen
Elliott Erwitt: Erwitt/ Magnum Photos
Frank Eugene: Fotomuseum im Münchner Stadtmuseum, München
Walker Evans: Walker Evans Archive, The Metropolitan Museum of Art, New York
Joan Fontcuberta: VG Bild-Kunst, Bonn 2005
Pere Formiguera: VG Bild-Kunst, Bonn 2005
Robert Frank: Robert Frank/ Courtesy of Pace/MacGill Gallery, New York
Beate Geissler & Oliver Sann: VG Bild-Kunst, Bonn 2005
Arnold Genthe: The J. Paul Getty Museum, Los Angeles
Mario Giacomelli: Estate of Mario Giacomelli Senigallia/ Courtesy Photogolgy, Milano
Bruce Gilden: Gilden/ Magnum Photos
Greenpeace: Greenpeace, Hamburg
Andreas Gursky: Courtesy Monika Sprüth Galerie, Köln / VG Bild-Kunst, Bonn 2005
Philippe Halsman: Philippe Halsman Estate/ Courtesy Howard Greenberg Gallery, New York
Elisabeth Hase: Nani Simonis, München, New York
HIRO: Courtesy of Pace/MacGill Gallery New York
Candida Höfer: VG Bild-Kunst, Bonn 2005
André Kertész: Ministère de la Culture et de la Communication, France
Philipp Kester: Fotomuseum im Münchner Stadtmuseum, München
Aart Klein: Aart Klein/ Nederlands Fotomuseum, Rotterdam
Joseph Koudelka: Koudelka/ Magnum Photos
Heinrich Kühn: Dr. Diether Schönitzer, Innsbruck
Jacques-Henri Lartigue: Ministère de la Culture et de la Communication, France
Franz Lazi: Lydia Lazi, Stuttgart
Edward Malindine: Daily Herald Archive, National Museum of Photography, Film & Television, Bradford
Lisette Model: Estate of Lisette Model, Courtesy Baudoin Lebon/ Keitelman
Martin Munkacsi: Estate Munkacsi, Woodstock
Arthur B. R. Myers: Rijksprentenkabinet/ Rijksmuseum, Amsterdam
Michael Nichols: Michael Nichols/ National Geographic Image Collection
Cas Oorthuys: Cas Oorthuys/ Nederlands Fotomuseum, Rotterdam
Hilmar Pabel: Bildarchiv Preußischer Kulturbesitz, Berlin
Irving Penn: Condé Nast Publications Inc., New York
Eric Poitevin: VG Bild-Kunst, Bonn 2005
Albert Renger-Patzsch: Albert Renger-Patzsch Archiv/ Ann und Jürgen Wilde/ VG Bild-Kunst, Bonn 2005
Humberto Rivas: VG Bild-Kunst, Bonn 2005
Alexander Rodtschenko: Estate of Alexander Rodtschenko/ RAO, Moscow/ VAGA, New York/ VG Bild-Kunst, Bonn 2005
August Sander: Photographische Sammlung/ SK Stiftung Kultur - August Sander Archiv, Köln/ VG Bild-Kunst, Bonn 2005
Friedrich Seidenstücker: Bildarchiv Preußischer Kulturbesitz, Berlin
Frederick Sommer: Frederick & Frances Sommer Foundation, Prescott
Anne Lise Stenseth: VG Bild-Kunst, Bonn 2005
Warwara Stepanowa: VG Bild-Kunst, Bonn 2005
Joel Sternfeld: Joel Sternfeld/ Courtesy of Luhring Augustine Gallery, New York
Sasha Stone: Serge Stone, Blaricum
William Strode: Strode/ Agentur Focus, Hamburg
Christer Strömholm: Joakim Strömholm, Stockholm
Richard Tepe: Rijksprentenkabinet/ Rijksmuseum, Amsterdam
Waldemar Titzenthaler: Bildarchiv Preußischer Kulturbesitz, Berlin
Rosemarie Trockel: VG Bild-Kunst, Bonn 2005
Wolfgang Weber: Museum Folkwang, Essen
William Wegman: William Wegman/ Courtesy of Pace/MacGill Gallery, New York
Garry Winogrand: Eileen Hale/ The Estate of Garry Winogrand
VW Kampagne: Volkswagen AG, Wolfsburg
Hedda Walther: Bildarchiv Preußischer Kulturbesitz, Berlin
WOLS: VG Bild-Kunst, Bonn 2005
Ylla: Pryor Dodge, New York

Dieses Buch erscheint anlässlich der Ausstellung
nützlich, süß und museal. Das fotografierte Tier
Museum Folkwang, Essen, 22. Oktober 2005 bis 15. Januar 2006.
Es wird von einem Textband begleitet.

This Book is published on the occasion of the exhibition
Useful, Cute and Collected. The Photographed Animal
Museum Folkwang, Essen, October 22, 2005 – January 15 2006.
It will be accompanied by a textbook (only in German language).

Herausgegeben von / edited by Ute Eskildsen

Konzeption / Concept: Ute Eskildsen
in Zusammenarbeit mit / in collaboration with Hans-Jürgen Lechtreck
Assistenz / Assistance: Lisa Marei Schmidt
Mitarbeit / Contribution: Christiane Kuhlmann, Petra Steinhardt,
Christina Buschmann, Robert Knodt, Kathrin Kohle
Sekretariat / Office: Anne Küppers
Übersetzungen / Translations: Christel Liesenfeld-Steinberg, Louisa Schaefer
Reproduktionen / Reproductions: Jens Nober

Erste Auflage / first edition 2005

Buchgestaltung / book design: Steidl Design, Claas Möller
Scans: Steidl's digital darkroom
Gesamtherstellung / printing and production: Steidl, Göttingen

Steidl
Düstere Str. 4 / D-37073 Göttingen
Phone +49 551 49 60 60 / Fax +49 551 49 60 649
E-mail: mail@steidl.de
www.steidl.de / www.steidlville.com

ISBN 3-86521-237-9
Printed in Germany